A Limited Edi...
of

THE LIFE OF HERBERT HOOVER
Master of Emergencies, 1917–1918

Presented by the Herbert Hoover
Presidential Library Association, Inc.

To:

Copy Number ______ of 2,000

THE LIFE OF HERBERT HOOVER

Master of Emergencies

1917–1918

ALSO BY GEORGE H. NASH

The Life of Herbert Hoover: The Engineer, 1874–1914
The Life of Herbert Hoover: The Humanitarian, 1914–1917
The Conservative Intellectual Movement in America Since 1945
Herbert Hoover and Stanford University

THE LIFE OF HERBERT HOOVER

Master of Emergencies

1917–1918

GEORGE H. NASH

W. W. NORTON & COMPANY
New York London

Printed in the United States of America
First Edition

The text of this book is composed in Janson
with the display set in Trump. Composition and manufacturing by The Maple-Vail Book Manufacturing Group.

Library of Congress Catalog Card Number: 82-14521

ISBN 0-393-03841-6

W. W. Norton & Company, Inc., 500 Fifth Avenue, New York, N.Y. 10110
http://web.wwnorton.com

W. W. Norton & Company Ltd., 10 Coptic Street, London WC1A 1PU

1 2 3 4 5 6 7 8 9 0

T O

Jeremiah Milbank, Jr.
and William F. Buckley, Jr.

Contents

Preface

ON April 6, 1917 the United States of America entered the First World War as a belligerent against the imperial government of Germany. Never before had the American people, by an act of Congress, sent their sons into combat in the Old World. For the citizens of the once-isolated nation, the twentieth century—a century of war and revolution—had begun.

For the subject of the pages that follow, the spring of 1917 was also a time of upheaval. Just three years earlier, Herbert Hoover had been a highly successful but relatively unknown American mining engineer living in London. Then, in August 1914, the month of his fortieth birthday, war—the Great War—had come, and with it an opportunity to ascend to the public stage. In the autumn of that year, Hoover founded and became chairman of a unique institution known as the Commission for Relief in Belgium, which provided desperately needed food supplies to more than 9,000,000 Belgian and French citizens trapped between the German army of occupation and the British naval blockade. His emergency relief undertaking quickly evolved into the greatest humanitarian enterprise in world history. By 1917 Hoover was an international hero, the embodiment of a new force in global politics: American benevolence. When his native country solemnly declared war, he returned home and entered the administration of President Woodrow Wilson.

Hoover's contribution to America's war effort is the focus of the book before you. In 1917 and 1918, he served his nation as head of the United States Food Administration, a specially created wartime agency of the federal government. As U.S. Food Administrator, and as a member of the President's War Cabinet, he endeavored to stimulate food conservation and food production, to control surging inflation of food prices, and to create surpluses of exportable foodstuffs for America's allies, who faced privation and even starvation if the necessary supplies were not delivered to them through the German submarine blockade. In the titanic conflict of 1917–18, food joined ships and soldiers as a critical component of victory over the enemy. "Food Will Win the War" was Hoover's slogan. The architect of America's food policies was one of the most important war leaders.

As readers will shortly discover, meeting these multiple challenges proved anything but routine for the humanitarian-turned-public servant. At home Hoover encountered a drumfire of contentious opposition, both in Congress and in parts of rural America. In dealing with the Allies, he engaged in a perpetual and precarious balancing act of "coordination": of providing them enough food to live on, but not too much, lest his own people incur shortages and runaway prices. Acutely anxious to restrain inflation and its perceived threat to national "efficiency" and urban tranquillity, Hoover collided with wheat farmers and others who resented his attempts to "stabilize" the free market. All of this made for tense navigation of the political rapids.

For the U.S. government as well as Hoover, 1917–18 was not a placid time. Like the war abroad, mobilization at home was a constant struggle. In this, the first *world* war and the first *total* war, everything—even food—mattered. Time and again on the food front, emergencies arose. One way or another, Hoover overcame them. Hence this book's title, which is adapted from the title of a documentary film about him that was made during the presidential campaign of 1928.

Hoover's wartime service has significance for another reason. Historians have long recognized that 1917–18 was a time of profound transition for the United States. This was the moment when the emerging colossus of the New World indisputably became a great power. It was the moment when a traditionally decentralized and libertarian society made a staggering leap toward a centrally managed economy. Never before had the federal government regulated the lives of its citizens, even unto their eating habits, as it proceeded to do after April 1917. Never before had the government instituted price controls and other forms of social constraint as extensively as it did in the months the United States waged war. Of this convulsive wave of interventionism, Hoover was both an agent and a catalyst.

The ascendancy of the state over society in World War I was neither total nor unchallenged. Moreover, it was limited—and to some degree palliated—by a vigorous philosophy of voluntarism, which Hoover particularly espoused. Still, the Great War was a watershed. In the years after 1918, the United States never quite returned to the institutional and ideological patterns of prewar days. Hoover's relationship to this great transformation forms a significant part of a consequential story.

There is another other reason for examining Hoover's experience in the First World War in detail; it is biographical. The man who became our thirty-first President was not an easy person to understand. Both friends and adversaries were often puzzled by him. *Who's Hoover?* was the title of a book written about him in the 1920s. But if his personality was not what the world as a rule deems colorful, he was nevertheless a man of amazing drive and achievement. One way better to understand him is to observe him in action—in battle, as it were—as he sought to do what he most liked to do in life: build institutions and accomplish things. Hoover the builder, the bureaucrat, a man of tremendous force and ability, a dedicated and comparatively youthful war administrator: this is the Hoover you will meet in *Master of Emergencies*.

At this point, a contextual word is in order. The book at hand is the third volume of a comprehensive biography of one of the most extraordinary and elusive figures in American history. My first volume is entitled *The Life of Herbert Hoover: The Engineer, 1874–1914*. The second bears the title *The Life of Herbert Hoover: The Humanitarian, 1914–1917*. In the installment before you, I turn to the next phase in his remarkable succession of careers.

As readers of my previous volumes will know, in 1975 I was invited to undertake this project by the Herbert Hoover Presidential Library Association, a nonprofit, educational foundation in Iowa. Under the terms of my contract with the Association, all decisions concerning the contents of the biography—including fact and interpretation, proportions and emphasis, inclusions and exclusions—have been mine alone. Like its two predecessors, the volume before you is a work of free and independent scholarship.

As I complete my third book under the Association's sponsorship, it is a pleasure to acknowledge those who have made my path smoother. At the Herbert Hoover Presidential Library in West Branch, Iowa, Jim Detlefsen, Mary Evans, Mildred Mather, Dale Mayer, Dwight Miller, Scott Nolen, Cora Pedersen, Wade Slinde, Richard Norton Smith, Shirley Sondergard, Timothy Walch, Patrick Wildenberg, and Cindy Worrell were always helpful. Their interest and responsiveness to my inquiries made the library's reading room a very congenial place. Indeed, the entire staff of the library has set a high standard of professionalism and good cheer, as numerous other scholars will attest. Up the hill, at the offices of the Herbert Hoover Presidential Library Association, Patricia Forsythe, Kathleen Grace, Patricia Hand, Corinne James, and the late Emma Wright were unfailingly courteous and supportive. Farther west, at the Hoover Institution on War, Revolution and Peace at Stanford University, Sondra Bierre, Ronald Bulatoff, Elena Danielson, Keith Eiler, Thomas Henriksen, Carol Leadenham, Charles Palm, John Raisian, Anne Van Camp, and their colleagues helped to make my research there an exhilarating experience. At the Claremont Colleges,

David Kuhner was an enthusiastic pathfinder through the William L. Honnold Papers. In Washington, D.C., my forays into the bulky holdings of the National Archives were facilitated by John Fawcett, Sharon Fawcett, Lane Moore, David Pfeiffer, and many others. At the Library of Congress, David Wigdor and John E. Haynes of the Manuscript Division gladly shared their expertise, while Barbara Natanson of the Prints and Photographs Division was an invaluable guide to its treasures. In my hometown of South Hadley, Massachusetts, where portions of this volume were written, the library of Mount Holyoke College at times became my "branch office." In Iowa City, Iowa (at the time my place of residence), the University of Iowa Library served the same agreeable function. I am grateful to the librarians at both of these institutions for graciously and knowledgeably answering my sometimes complicated questions.

It is not possible to name all of the librarians and archivists at other repositories in the United States and abroad who in some way facilitated my research. If any of them read these words, I hope that they will recognize themselves among those to whom I now say: thank you.

Not all of those who have assisted me work professionally in libraries or archives. I think of Herbert Hoover's son Allan Hoover (1907–1993). Always supportive of the biography project, he willingly shared his insights about his father, and from these I benefited. In Washington, D.C., Senator Mark Hatfield of Oregon—a Hoover scholar in his own right—was unstinting in his enthusiasm and words of encouragement. It is a pleasure also again to acknowledge two of my former mentors at Harvard University, Donald Fleming and the late Frank Freidel, whose scholarship and thoughtful counsel continue to inspire me.

In preparing this volume I have benefited from excellent technical assistance. Marlene Neville cheerfully and efficiently typed the entire first draft of my manuscript, as well as its revisions: a large task capably performed. In proofreading the galleys, I was ably assisted by Sharon Dash, Andrea Gralenski, Judith Lidberg, Jean Nash, and Nancy Nash. At W. W. Norton & Company, my editor, Donald Lamm, and his assistant, Cecil G. Lyon, along with their colleagues, expertly facilitated the transition from manuscript to book. It is a pleasure also to thank Ann Adelman for her proficient copyediting.

I am grateful to the following institutions and individuals for permission to quote from various documents cited in my footnotes: the Bancroft Library, University of California, Berkeley; Special Collections, Clemson University Libraries; Columbia University Oral History Research Office; Rare Book and Manuscript Library, Columbia University; Herbert Hoover Foundation; Herbert Hoover Presidential Library Association; Minnesota Historical Society; Missouri Historical Society; University of Notre Dame Archives; Western History Collections, University Libraries, University of Oklahoma; Princeton University Libraries; Stanford University Libraries; State Historical Society of Wisconsin; and Yale University Library. Quotations from the Walter Hines Page Papers and William Phillips diary appear by permission of the Houghton Library, Harvard University. Quotations from letters by Henry A. Wallace and Henry C. Wallace appear by permission of the University of Iowa Libraries (Iowa City). For permission to quote from the diary of H. A. L. Fisher, I thank Mrs. Mary Bennett (Fisher's daughter) and the Bodleian Library at Oxford University. I also have occasion to draw upon the David Lloyd George Papers in the custody of the House of Lords Record Office in London; quotations are reproduced by permission of the Clerk of the Records on behalf of the Beaverbrook Foundation Trustees. Crown copyright material in the Public Record Office in Great Britain is reproduced by permission of the Controller of Her Majesty's Stationery Office.

One of the rewarding aspects of preparing this volume has been the task of selecting illustrative material from the holdings of several fine repositories. Illustrations no. 15 (photo no. 4-G-1-21) and no. 22 (photo no. 4-G-27-6) come from the National Archives. Illustrations 2, 3, and 4 are reproduced from the collections of the Library of Congress. Illustrations 1, 14, 16, 19, 20, 21, 23, 24, 25, and 26 were supplied from the Herbert Hoover Presidential Library-Museum in West Branch, Iowa. Illustrations 5, 11, 13, and 18 were obtained from the U.S. Food Administration Collection, Hoover Institution Archives, Stanford University. Illustrations 6, 7, 8, 9, 10, 12, and 17 come from the Poster Collection at the Hoover Institution Archives. I am grateful to each of these repositories for permission to reproduce the listed items.

And now, once again, I am pleased to thank the Herbert Hoover Presidential Library Association for its support during the preparation of my biography. I am particularly grateful to those members and trustees who have personally offered their encouragement along the way.

It is impossible to mention here each of the individuals whose interest has sustained me during far-flung research and writing. But I must say a word about two whose names appear before this preface. Both were "present at the creation" of the Herbert Hoover biography project—and more than merely present. To these friends of Herbert Hoover—and of mine—this book is dedicated.

And finally, I thank my family, my first and best "network": ever faithful, and still going strong.

THE LIFE OF HERBERT HOOVER

Master of Emergencies

1917–1918

1

The Return of "Hoover of Belgium"

I

EARLY on the morning of May 3, 1917 the S.S. *Philadelphia* made its way through a spring fog into New York Harbor. Eight days before, bedecked with newly installed anti-submarine guns, the vessel had sailed from the British port of Liverpool on a lonely journey across the Atlantic. Less than a month had passed since the United States of America had declared war upon the imperial government of Germany, thereby at last entering World War I. In the cold, unfriendly ocean that separated the New World from the Old, wolf packs of German U-boats were at work, sending Allied and neutral shipping to a watery grave.

The *Philadelphia*'s voyage had not been a placid one. Only six hours out, the liner averted two deadly floating mines by less than fifty feet. During its first day at sea the crew's radio picked up distress calls every half hour from ships that had been torpedoed and were going down. The *Philadelphia* could not respond, lest it give its own position away. Taking a course nearly as far north as the Arctic Circle, the vessel encountered bad weather, adding physical discomfort to the psychic strain. It was with unalloyed joy, relief, and tears that the passengers on May 3 espied the Statue of Liberty through the morning mist.[1]

Among those who reached New York on the *Philadelphia* was a forty-two-year-old American mining engineer returning home to embark upon a new career. For most of the past twenty years Herbert Hoover had lived abroad, pursuing his profession in some of the remotest regions on earth. From his base in London, the world capital of mining finance, he had amassed a respectable fortune as an engineer, entrepreneur, and financier. By 1914 his business interests girdled much of the globe.

Preeminent in his profession, Hoover in his late thirties had become increasingly restless. He wished, he said, to do more with his life than accumulate wealth. He told friends that he wanted to return to America and enter the "big game" of public service. But how, and in what capacity? Of that he was uncertain. Then, in August 1914, the very month of his fortieth birthday, war—the Great War—broke out in Europe and redirected his yearnings.

The terrible conflict that overwhelmed the Old World gave Hoover his long-sought entrance into public life. In the autumn of 1914, with the consent of the affected belligerent powers, he founded in London an organization known as the Commission for Relief in Belgium, or CRB. Its purpose was to procure and provide food for the desperate civilian population of Belgium, invaded and largely conquered by Germany in the first weeks of the war. Dependent upon imports for much of its sustenance, Belgium found itself trapped between a hostile army of occupation and a British naval blockade. As the little nation's domestic food stocks dwindled, a catastrophe of horrific proportions drew near. Between Belgium and mass starvation stood Hoover and the CRB.

For the next two and a half years Hoover's London-based organization, in collaboration with the Belgians' own Comité National, acquired, transported, and distributed over 2,500,000 tons of foodstuffs to more than 9,000,000 helpless people in Belgium and German-occupied northern France. An emergency relief effort directed by an American engineer evolved into a gigantic humanitarian undertaking without precedent in history.[2]

The superlative achievement of the CRB earned Hoover international acclaim, including the admiration of the President of the United States. Not surprisingly, then, among those who greeted him at dockside in New York City on May 3, 1917 were the Belgian minister to the United States and an emissary of President Woodrow Wilson's confidant, Colonel Edward M. House.[3] Disappointingly, Hoover's family was not there. Back in January, his wife Lou and their two sons had preceded him from London. Now they were in Palo Alto, California, which Hoover and his wife, both Stanford University graduates, considered home. The older boy, Herbert, Jr., was nearly fourteen. Allan, the younger, was almost ten. Because of what she called "health conditions," Lou did not think it advisable to take them east to greet their father at this time.[4]

But if Hoover's family was not present, a horde of newspaper reporters was, and with good reason. On April 6 the United States had formally gone to war against Germany. The very next day the Council of National

Defense—charged by law with making plans for mobilizing America's resources for the war effort—asked Hoover by cable to chair its new committee on "food supply and prices." There was plenty of logic in the council's choice. Certainly no American knew more than Hoover about European experience in this vital dimension of modern warfare. From Europe, the CRB chairman cabled his acceptance of the council's invitation and immediately started to collect data on the Allies' food control policies and requirements. It was not difficult to do. He was already well acquainted with the senior political leaders of several belligerent powers and had traveled extensively on both sides of the lines.[5]

The council's summons was welcome news to the engineer-turned-humanitarian. For several months he had been energetically campaigning for a position of influence in the Wilson administration should the United States be drawn into the conflict. On a trip to Washington, D.C., in February, he had proposed both to the council and to Colonel House that in the event of war with Germany the U.S. government should appoint "a man of Cabinet rank" to serve in Europe as supreme coordinator of the American war effort overseas. It took little discernment to identify Hoover's candidate, and House promptly recommended Hoover to President Wilson for the job, if it were created.[6] The subsequent offer of April 7 from the Council of National Defense was a far cry from the prestigious office that Hoover craved. But at least it gave him an entrée into the government and a chance to parlay his post into one of greater power.

The information that Hoover now brought with him was bleak. By the spring of 1917 five million soldiers had died on the battlefields of Europe.[7] Millions more faced each other in a labyrinth of trenches—25,000 miles of them—stretching in parallel from the English Channel, across Belgium and France, to the Swiss frontier.[8] In a daring bid to break the ghastly deadlock, Germany in early 1917 resumed unrestricted submarine warfare around the British Isles. The German high command calculated that by sinking or frightening off all shipping it could starve the western Allies into surrender in a few months. By April, the gamble appeared to be succeeding. That month the Allies lost more than 866,000 tons of shipping; one vessel out of every four that ventured from a British port never returned.[9]

As food-bearing ships from afar failed to penetrate the war zone, the specter of mass privation increasingly loomed. In France and Italy, Hoover learned in April, scarcely eight weeks' supply of breadstuffs remained.[10] One French official told him that before the United States entered the war the French had concluded that they could not hold out unaided beyond October.[11] In England also, grain reserves were plummeting. Taking into account the time needed to distribute existing stocks throughout the country, "only one month's real reserve," said Hoover, was left.[12] On April 25 the British Ministry of Food announced that without economy in domestic bread consumption there might not be enough food to last until the next harvest.[13]

Nor was grain the only food source in jeopardy. By the end of April less than ten days' supply of sugar remained in Great Britain.[14]

Before boarding the *Philadelphia*, Hoover publicly warned the American people about the Allies' peril.[15] He notified Secretary of State Robert Lansing by cable that the Allies' "food situation" was "most critical," and that the United States and Canada must export 100,000,000 bushels of grain to Europe in the coming months. Otherwise "public tranquility" in the Allied nations would be at risk.[16] Upon arriving in New York, Hoover bluntly informed the press that the U-boat menace was "far greater than any one in the United States realizes."[17] Because of it, he said, the situation in Europe was "extremely grave."[18]

Hoover had not come home, however, simply to be a bearer of bad tidings. While in London in April, he had not confined himself to investigating food conditions in the Allied countries. Instead, he had begun to develop a "comprehensive plan" for an American food control policy.[19] Alarmed by what he called an "impending world food shortage" and by a "tide of rising prices" caused in part by Allied buyers' bidding against one another in foreign markets, Hoover proposed to create an inter-Allied food board which would control and consolidate such purchases. Such an organ, he believed, could eliminate competition among the associated governments and thereby do much to stabilize food prices.[20] On April 18 he persuaded the War Cabinet of Prime Minister Lloyd George to approve his scheme in principle.[21] A few days later Great Britain's food controller, Lord Devonport, publicly endorsed it.[22] Anxious to move ahead (and probably to forestall any opposition in the United States), Hoover attempted to have the Wilson administration approve his plan immediately, even before he returned home.[23]

The Yankee food expert also lobbied in London for new solutions to the worsening shipping crisis. The United States, he declared, should create a committee "at once" to "undertake all chartering" of Allied and neutral tonnage and should prohibit "absolutely" the unauthorized hiring of neutral ships by private interests. The U.S. government should also form a committee to license the purchasing of bunker coal. Such an entity, acting in concert with the Allies, would "control practically all bunker coal in the world." By exploiting this monopoly, said Hoover, America and the Allies could compel the ships of *neutral* countries to carry food and other goods to the Allies, "at the peril of being" deprived of fuel for their ships.[24] Such a policy would win no friends among the neutrals, but Hoover showed no signs of caring about that.

Where, though, would Hoover himself fit into his contemplated apparatus of absolute power? Just before leaving England, he told Ambassador Walter Hines Page that America's own food control effort should take the form of a new governmental department to be established for the duration of the war—a department that would handle shipping as well.[25] Although he did not explicitly say so, there was little doubt that he hankered to lead it.

Indeed, while still in London Hoover apparently believed—or wanted others to believe—that an executive post for himself in the Wilson administration was a fait accompli. On April 18 he personally informed the British War Cabinet that he was returning forthwith to the United States "to take up the Chairmanship of a Food Board there."[26] The next day he told the American ambassador to Russia that he, Hoover, had been "asked to take over a job as Food Controller in the United States, and will be stationed in Washington."[27]

As the celebrated humanitarian reached New York on May 3, however, his future role was not nearly so certain. The Council of National Defense, after all, had only appointed him chairman of an advisory committee.[28] From the White House itself, he had heard nothing.[29] To be sure, when the council's invitation—and his acceptance—became public, many in the press immediately depicted him as the head of the nation's "food board" and even as America's prospective "Food Controller."[30] But was this what the council itself had in mind? From the reports emanating from Washington, Hoover could not be sure.[31] Moreover, the member of the council most affected by the food issue—Secretary of Agriculture David Houston—was more than a little concerned that Hoover's work would encroach upon the Agriculture Department's functions.[32]

On April 21, in fact, while Hoover was still abroad, Houston prevailed upon the Council of National Defense to issue a press release minimizing Hoover's status. The statement announced that Hoover had become the council's "adviser" on "food problems and prices" and would soon return "to assume that capacity." The council then expressed its desire that Hoover "report" to it on European experience respecting food, that he make various "suggestions and recommendations," and that, "cooperating with the Department of Agriculture," he "assist" states and cities in the "study, distribution, and conservation of food supplies."[33]

Report. Suggest. Recommend. Cooperate. Assist. These were not the words of authority that a dynamic, aspiring war manager wanted to hear.

If Secretary Houston believed that the council's "clarification" settled the matter, he did not reckon with the resourcefulness of his rival. Upon reaching New York, Herbert Hoover made a beeline for Colonel House.[34] For two years, as chairman of the CRB, Hoover had cultivated, and been cultivated by, the man who was Woodrow Wilson's closest adviser.[35] More than once House had commended Hoover to the President for a high assignment if war should come,[36] and he did not fail his anxious caller now. Soon after their interview the colonel dispatched a letter to the White House.

> Hoover, as you know, is just back. . . .
>
> I trust Houston will give him full powers as to food control. He knows it better than anyone in the world and would inspire confidence both in Europe and here. Unless Houston does give him full control I am afraid

> he will be unwilling to undertake the job, for he is the kind of man that has to have complete control in order to do the thing well.[37]

The battle for an appropriate niche in the war effort, however, would not be decided in a New York apartment. After a day of consultation with House and the CRB's local office staff, and an evening of patriotic entertainment at Madison Square Garden, Hoover took the midnight train down to Washington.[38]

II

As Hoover's train rolled into Union Station in the nation's capital on the morning of May 4, the government of the United States was laboring to give meaning to its belligerency. At the moment that Congress declared war, the U.S. Army consisted of fewer than 200,000 men. Its General Staff comprised but nineteen officers.[39] Returning from a Europe grim, taut, and regimented, with at least 40,000,000 soldiers already under arms,[40] Hoover was not reassured by the contrast.[41]

His discouragement would have been deeper still had he observed the political partisanship of the past month. Four weeks into the state of war, Congress had yet to enact legislation enlarging the army. To the consternation of many throughout the country, the Wilson administration had called for conscription—a draft of 2,000,000 men. This departure from the American tradition of voluntary military service evoked outrage on Capitol Hill. The Speaker of the House likened conscripts to prison convicts, while one senator predicted that the streets of America would flow with blood on the day that the draft was implemented. Complicating the issue was Colonel Theodore Roosevelt's boisterous campaign to create a division of American volunteers and lead them personally into battle in France. Rebuffed by Woodrow Wilson's War Department, the fifty-eight-year-old former President turned to Congress for support, in the form of an amendment to the conscription bill that would force the War Department to let him raise and command 100,000 volunteers. The administration and its allies strongly resisted; for weeks the issue—and with it the entire draft legislation—embroiled Congress in angry polemics and deadlock.

If Roosevelt's quest appeared to his enemies to be egomaniacal, the performance of Woodrow Wilson seemed, to his critics, no better. Inflaming an already combustible environment on the Hill, the President requested authority from Congress to censor all publications, including newspapers, in the United States for the rest of the war—and to punish severely any who violated his rules. The chief executive's proposal ignited a firestorm of opposition from the press, as well as from Republicans and anti-administration Democrats who found in it further proof of his dictatorial proclivities. In the end Congress sanctioned the military draft (but not the censorship plan), and Wilson was able to thwart his arch rival Roosevelt's bid for glory on the battlefield. But the price in rancor and contentiousness dispelled any illusion that the fruit of war would be instant national unity.[42]

While Congress and the White House struggled to create a military machine from almost nothing, they began to come to grips with a far less conventional challenge. Since the eruption of gunfire across Europe in 1914, the Allied governments of Great Britain, France, and Italy had turned increasingly to the United States for munitions and foodstuffs, notably wheat, without which they could not prosecute the war. By 1917 their dependence upon the North American breadbasket was acute. At first the Allies' food purchases had not been disruptive, thanks largely to a record billion-bushel American wheat harvest in 1915. But in 1916 American wheat production fell to fewer than 640,000,000 bushels, barely enough to cover domestic consumption. Fortunately, the surplus from the preceding year permitted America to export more than 200,000,000 bushels to the Allies—a figure roughly double its immediate prewar average. Still, the balance between supply and demand had begun dangerously to tilt in the direction of scarcity.[43]

The combination of shrinking American food reserves and ever-increasing Allied purchases soon had an inevitable consequence. From July 1916 to April 1917 the price of food in the United States increased by more than 40 percent.[44] In the key milling center of Minneapolis, a barrel of flour that had averaged $5.09 in 1914 reached $11.62 in the month America entered the war.[45] A month later it leaped to $14.88.[46] The wholesale food price index, which stood at a baseline of 100 in 1913, climbed to 150 in January 1917, and to 182 just three months later.[47]

The exploding cost of living quickly unleashed a political tempest. In late 1916 and early 1917 angry consumer groups clamored for an embargo on food exports, farmers and exporters stoutly resisted, and the Wilson administration—blaming middlemen and "food gamblers"—groped for an alternative.[48] Then, in February and March, something almost unthinkable in America happened: food riots in working-class and immigrant neighborhoods in New York, Philadelphia, and Boston. Furious at spiraling prices and the prospect of privation for their families, mobs of housewives attacked peddlers, looted grocery stores, fought with police, and staged stormy protest rallies and marches. Shocked by these manifestations of discontent, and aware after mid-March of similar unrest in Russia that led to the overthrow of the Czar, a determined group of American Progressives began to agitate for drastic remedial measures, including a government guarantee of wheat prices as an incentive to farmers to augment wheat production. Unless more crops were planted, these Progressives feared further shortages, further disturbances, and new demands for a total embargo on food exports to the desperate Allies.[49]

In the first weeks following America's decision for war, the Wilson administration at last took the initiative. On April 20, 1917, after consulting with various farm leaders, Secretary of Agriculture Houston announced that the federal government would seek unprecedented regulatory authority over the nation's food supply. Houston's plan called for vesting enormous new powers in his own department and in the Council of National Defense.[50]

Learning of this development from the British press, Hoover turned anxiously to his friend and ally in relief work, Ambassador Page. "I am afraid" the Wilson administration "wont get off on the right foot," Hoover complained. He asked the ambassador to cable Hoover's alternative plan (for a separate governmental food agency) to Washington.[51] The hero of Belgian relief had his own ideas for organizing the economic side of the war, and they did not include the Department of Agriculture. America needed new "social machinery," he believed—machinery administered by its "best brains," which were to be found in private industry. "The first difficulty of democracy at war," he told a friend, was to "transfer the direction" of it from an inherently mediocre "bureaucracy" to the nation's preeminent "industrial brains."[52] It now appeared that the Department of Agriculture had other intentions.

By the time the *Philadelphia* touched America's shores, the Wilson administration's preparations for wartime food control were well under way. On April 25 the Department of Agriculture announced plans for a conference to mobilize the nation's housewives for food conservation.[53] A few days later, while Hoover was in the North Atlantic, two members of Congress introduced an administration-backed bill to give Secretary Houston part of the power he sought. Included in the proposal was authority for the secretary to license any business in the United States engaged in the manufacture, storage, or distribution of foods, and to compel such licensees to charge "fair" prices as well as refrain from monopolistic and "discriminatory" trade practices.[54]

Then, on May 3, as Hoover set foot in Manhattan, the Wilson administration unveiled an even more draconian proposal. It would empower the President of the United States to fix the maximum and minimum prices of food, clothing, fuel, and other "necessaries" of life throughout the country whenever, in his opinion, the war emergency required it. It would permit him to prescribe regulations for the production of these commodities and to requisition factories and mines. It would authorize him to compel the railroads to give priority to the transit of "necessaries." It would allow him to impose import duties in order to prevent excessive "dumping" of foreign goods. The bill also proposed to grant broad licensing powers to the Secretary of Agriculture. The next day the administration's request was front-page news across the land. With little exaggeration the *New York Tribune*'s headline read: "President Asks for Unlimited Economic Power."[55]

In neither bill was there provision for Herbert Hoover.

III

INTO this maelstrom of political uncertainty and intrigue a perturbed Hoover stepped on the morning of May 4. Not a man to waste time on social pleasantries when there was work to be done, within an hour or two of his arrival he was conferring over breakfast with officials at the Department of Agriculture.[56] During that first day he briefed another of his political patrons from CRB days, Secretary of the Interior Franklin K. Lane.[57] That evening, on less than an hour's notice, Senator James Phelan of Hoover's adopted state of California hosted a private dinner for the returning humanitarian. Five U.S. senators, two Cabinet secretaries, and several other government officials came.[58] No doubt they were curious to meet the engineer who had been acclaimed for more than two years as the saviour of Belgium. For all his heroic status in Europe, he was known to but a handful of men in power in his native land.

Hoover did not disappoint the assembled guests. At his best as an expositor in such small-group settings, for several riveting hours he shared his knowledge and apprehensions of the Allies' deepening plight.[59] Hoover's mood was pessimistic.[60] The next day his closest friend, President Ray Lyman Wilbur of Stanford University, who had journeyed east to meet him at the dock, told an assemblage in Washington that Hoover was "exceedingly discouraged and disheartened at the whole situation, both on the sea and abroad, after what he sees when he gets here."[61]

One source of Hoover's dejectedness had nothing to do with U-boats. On his first day in Washington he had not seen the person he most wanted to see: the man in the Oval Office. Before departing from New York, Hoover told a journalist that he would report to President Wilson the next morning on conditions in Europe.[62] The next morning came and went with no such meeting and no explanation from the White House. Finally, on May 5, Hoover received word that he could see the President—four days later.[63] This was not the kind of reception he was expecting.

Hoover had several reasons for wanting to confer with the President as quickly as possible. For one thing, he was carrying an urgent message from the U.S. Navy's liaison officer in London, Admiral William Sims. Tell the President, Sims had said, to demand that the Allies adopt a convoy system for their imperiled merchant ships crossing the Atlantic.[64] For another, Hoover was more convinced than ever that effective conduct of the war made governmental reorganization imperative. It was surely no coincidence that on May 5 his friend Wilbur publicly urged President Wilson to create a "war council" containing three emergency positions: one for munitions, one for ships—and one for food.[65] In all likelihood, Hoover hoped to make this plea directly to the one man in Washington who could do something about it. Above all, Hoover undoubtedly wanted to ascertain from the country's commander in chief just what role he would have in the war effort. Was he or was he not going to take over the nation's food control?

With Secretary Houston plainly hostile and Woodrow Wilson for the moment inaccessible, Hoover was obliged to tread warily. "I've just come home to 'do my bit,' " he declared cautiously upon arrival in New York. "It is premature to talk about my new duties, as they are very indefinite as yet."[66] To the Washington press corps the next day, he stated that Secretary Houston would control the nation's food supplies under the proposed legislation and that "I will assist him and the Council of [National] Defense by supplying information gathered in relief work abroad." "I do not know what the Government will require of me," Hoover added. "I am acting in an unofficial capacity, and no plans have been made."[67]

The returning relief expert carefully denied that he was, or aspired to be, America's "food dictator."[68] Privately, however, he was more unrestrained. There *must* be a food dictator, he told Secretary of the Navy Josephus Daniels on May 7. Afterwards Daniels wrote in his diary that Hoover himself wished to be just that. Moreover, Daniels recorded, Hoover "[t]hinks it should not be under Agriculture. People fear beaurocrocy [sic] & would wish dictatorship ended when war closes."[69]

While Hoover waited for the White House door to open, he began to plead his case on Capitol Hill. On the morning of May 7 he appeared before a confidential session of the House of Representatives' committee on agriculture, chaired by Asbury F. Lever of South Carolina. To the assembled legislators he painted a somber portrait of food conditions in Western Europe. England, France, and Italy, with a combined population of 120,000,000, had only eight to ten weeks' worth of breadstuffs in hand. Every circumstance seemed to be combining against them. Prewar food suppliers like Russia and Romania were cut off by enemy lines. Argentina had suffered a crop failure and declared an embargo. Australia had food to export but was prohibitively distant; the Allies could not afford to tie up scarce tonnage on voyages that took three times as long as those from the east coast of North America. In France itself, a severe frost had just destroyed at least half of the winter wheat harvest. On the home fronts, said Hoover, women cultivating the fields had been "totally unable to make up for the depletion of the men," while soldiers in the trenches and workers in the munitions industries were necessarily consuming more food than heretofore. As a result of these factors, Hoover estimated that the Allies would need to import at least 800,000,000 bushels of grain of all kinds in the coming year and that the bulk of it—more than ever before—must come from Canada and the United States.[70]

Hoover also informed the committee of the plan he had devised in Europe to consolidate the western Allies' food purchasing in a single body. Competitive bidding among the Allies, he argued, had been a prime source of the "extraordinarily high prices" now prevailing in America. Before we in the

United States can "move one step . . . to remedy price conditions" and protect consumers from "extravagant prices and speculation," he asserted, we must persuade the Allies to concentrate their buying "into one hand in order that we may have one hand to deal with." Such a foreign combination, he acknowledged, could be "a dangerous implement for our own country unless we participate in its control." This was one reason why the United States itself needed "some organization for food control."[71]

Hoover did not stop here. Boldly and candidly, he took issue with the Wilson administration's food bills now before the committee. He particularly objected to provisions for presidential fixing of minimum and maximum prices of commodities. The setting of a minimum price might stimulate the producer, he noted, but it would not protect the consumer. On the other hand, a maximum price was "intended to protect the consumer only." According to Hoover, except where governments had been able directly to control "a large portion of the commodity in question," maximum price-fixing had proven "a universal failure in Europe." Legal prohibitions and punishments had failed. Enterprising producers and consumers had simply created "channels of contact" outside the controlled market, and consumers engaged in this illicit trade had then hoarded what they had obtained. The result had been increased shortages except for the favored few.[72]

Instead of trying to control inflation from the bottom up by enforcing maximum prices at the retail level, Hoover proposed that the government intervene at the top by setting and underwriting "an absolutely fixed price" on as many as ten key crops. Consider wheat, for instance. Here the government, in consultation with "all sides," could determine a price based on the prewar average plus an agreed-upon markup sufficient to cover current costs, stimulate production, and provide wheat farmers a "right profit." Having thus stipulated the price, the government would then request grain elevators (which handled over 90 percent of the nation's grain) to pay farmers this price for their wheat. After buying the grain from farmers at this figure, the elevator operators could then resell it at a higher price (also fixed) to the millers, who in turn would sell their flour at another predetermined price to their customers. In effect, the elevator owners and millers would become "agents of the Government working on a commission from the Government." The ultimate result, said Hoover, would be "a fixed price of bread" and the complete elimination of pernicious speculation. If at the end of a crop year the elevator men had been unable to sell all the wheat in their bins, the government itself would buy it from them.[73]

Breaking openly with the Department of Agriculture, Hoover told the committee that "an independent executive organ operating directly under the President" should administer the pricing mechanism that he sketched. After three years of "turmoil" and "blundering," every European government, he asserted, had evolved in this direction. The Europeans, he claimed, had found it necessary to create separate "administrative bodies of equal importance with the other administrative bodies of the Government," both for the sake of "prestige" in dealing with commercial interests and foreign governments and for creating "in the minds of people a certain imaginative alarm" resulting in food conservation.

Hoover did not rest his case exclusively on the subtleties of "prestige." He declared forcefully that the task ahead was a "commercial job," requiring "the maximum of initiative and willingness to assume responsibility." It must therefore be undertaken by "commercial men, and not by minds that are instinctively of the Government character." In "the soul of a bureaucracy," he testified, "there is an instinctive avoidance of responsibility or initiative; to avoid error is the essence of successful promotion." These were not the traits required for successful food control. Without being too explicit or offensive, Hoover intimated that his "organism" would perform far more effectively if it were not an adjunct of a stodgy government department—like the Department of Agriculture.[74]

There was one other argument that Hoover invoked for seeking independence from the permanent agencies of government. Eager as he was to enter the political arena and assume powers never before wielded by an American, he nevertheless worried that he might be creating a monster. Temperamentally a power seeker, and convinced that total war required dictatorship,[75] he remained, philosophically, an individualist, concerned that the necessary expansion of wartime restraints and regulation might result in "the total eclipse of individual initiative."[76] He therefore told the House committee that a *separate* and *temporary* agency could best avert the collectivist danger:

> My feeling is that the whole basis of democracy lies in the free and rightful play of individual effort, and here [food regulation] is the most tremendous restraint which can be put upon the free play of individualism in the country, and it is a most serious restraint to undertake. That restraint is only justified by the exigency of a very great emergency, and it should carry within itself the seeds of its own destruction. To set it up as a part of the existing organism of the Government means its continuance after the war, but if it is set up boldly and frankly as an emergency measure, dying absolutely with the coming of peace, you will save the possibility of facing an enormous difficulty in the end.[77]

Furthermore, he asserted, the staffing of his food control agency with "commercial minds" would provide insurance against statism. As businessmen, they "would be jealous in their desire" for the agency's "ultimate suppression" and would "insist" on its prompt dismantlement after the war.[78]

Hoover therefore urged the committee to revise drastically the food legislation before it. Everything pertaining to the Department of Agriculture should be put in one bill, he said, while a second bill should unequivocally establish a new "department of food control."[79]

Hoover's appearance before the House agriculture committee was a triumph. Many congressmen were impressed with the desirability of placing management of food prices and distribution in a presidentially appointed board of businessmen rather than in existing government departments.[80] The next day the press reported that Hoover would probably administer the price-fixing of food if the bills were passed.[81] The *New York Herald* went further. In a banner headline it reported: "Mr. Hoover May Become Food Dictator of the World."[82]

On May 8 and 9 the chairman of the CRB took his case to the Senate committee on agriculture and forestry.[83] He told it that the food crisis in Europe was now more critical than questions of munitions and manpower for the armies. Why? Because food "strikes at the root of public tranquility—the people have got to be fed." America, too, was in danger: "If we allow the normal course of commerce to run loose," said Hoover, the people of Europe "in clamorous desire for food will buy this market mad" and send American prices skyward. From the standpoint of maintaining America's own "public tranquility," it was now as important that we "see that those people do not suck too much food out of our country . . . as it is that we provide them" with food. We must "protect ourselves from our allies" as well as assist them.[84]

To the listening senators Hoover explained his scheme for first establishing the price of wheat and then—by determining the allowable margins for middlemen—stabilizing prices. Again eschewing maximum and minimum prices, he argued that a year-long, government-supported, "fixed price" was "the only practicable solution." This, he said, was what he had done with the farmers of Belgium.[85]

While Hoover expected the vast majority of grain elevators and other wheat distributors to cooperate voluntarily with the government, he was not so naive as to expect universal assent. He therefore contended that the government must have power to coerce compliance from a small minority of "stinkers" who would otherwise "destroy the equity of the whole arrangement." At the same time, he shied away from the even more coercive idea of food rationing—a "hopeless suggestion." If his experience in Belgium was any guide, rationing the widely dispersed American populace would require at least 1,750,000 bureaucrats to administer.

Instead, Hoover preferred to rely upon what he called "engines of indirection," including propaganda for decreased food consumption. War has "very few even partial compensations," he testified, but one of them was "the stirring up in the heart of a people of the spirit of self-sacrifice." Propaganda for food conservation would be "absolutely necessary"; one target, he disclosed, would be the American home. By a "sufficiently intensive organization" of women throughout the country, said Hoover, "we might introduce into every household a feeling of sacrifice in the interests of the country in this war." We "ought to be able to teach the women of this country the rudiments of dietetics," he added. This kind of activity—the "voluntary side"—could have "the most lasting importance," long after the instruments of coercion had been abolished.[86]

All of this, however, required power, and Hoover did not neglect the bottom line. In order to "compel the imagination of this country as to the possibilities of saving and self-denial," to "command prestige" among the nation's "large commercial bodies," and to "erect a temporary organism here which will appeal to the people as a temporary organism," the contemplated food control agency, he declared, must be endowed with the rank and power of a Cabinet department. "To set it up as a bureau in the Department of Agriculture is hopeless."[87]

Watching his rival's well-publicized progress on Capitol Hill, David Houston grew increasingly perturbed. As Secretary of Agriculture since 1913, Houston held that all governmental functions relating to food properly belonged within the purview of his department. The creation of an independent food agency, he felt, could only reflect adversely on his own agency's efficiency. "How would you like it," he complained to his Cabinet colleague, Josephus Daniels, "if the President were to put the destroyers in a separate bureau and deny you control of an important arm of the Navy?" Daniels disagreed. "The Food Commissioner," he replied, "must do a work that will not appeal to people, for they will not wish to deny themselves wheat and sugar. If you or any other member of the Cabinet should ask people to give up food to which they are accustomed, they would resent it. But if the Almoner of starving Belgium, crowned with world praise, makes the request, the people will respond."[88] Houston was unconvinced. In meetings of the Council of National Defense he continued to resist the appointment of an independent food controller.[89]

The resolution of this impasse obviously rested with Woodrow Wilson. On the afternoon of May 9, Hoover entered the White House for one of the pivotal conversations of his life.[90] According to the *New York Times* the next day, he reported to the President on food conditions in Europe and Allied requirements for the coming year.[91] In all likelihood the two men discussed much more.

Years later, in his *Memoirs* and other writings, Hoover recalled what transpired. According to Hoover, the President was reluctant to establish a single-headed agency with comprehensive authority over food. Anxious to "avoid anything that smacked of the building of dictatorial powers," aware of intensifying Congressional hostility to presidential aggrandizement, and fearful of conflict with the Department of Agriculture, Wilson instead proposed the simple creation of a food commission, with Hoover as its chairman. The body would include representatives of agriculture, industry, and labor.

To Hoover, the President's offer was completely uncongenial. Wilson, he thought, was "headed for the old rock of divided responsibility" that (in Hoover's view) had wrecked so many Allied efforts early in the war. He told the

President that European boards and commissions had been beset with failure, "inescapable frictions, indecisions, and delays." The "whole genius" of American business and government, he argued, "prescribed a single responsible executive, with boards only in an advisory, legislative, or judicial capacity." Furthermore, an individual food controller "could induce a wealth of voluntary action which no impersonal board could command." In such voluntarism lay America's defense against "Prussianizing" itself. To allay Wilson's fears about creating—or appearing to create—a "food dictator," Hoover suggested that the controller be called an "administrator," a reassuring title that would connote "co-ordination and executive leadership." It proved to be a clever semantic stroke. Although Hoover's later accounts of the meeting do not mention it, he probably advanced also the argument that he had just made to the Congress: the proposed agency should consist of businessmen, not bureaucrats, and should be extinguished after the war.[92]

Hoover's hour-long interview with the President ended inconclusively.[93] But the would-be food administrator's arguments apparently had some effect. The next day, May 10, President Wilson conferred with Secretary Houston and two leading congressmen and urged the immediate passage of the administration's two food bills. Since one of these would empower him to regulate food prices and distribution through a government agency of his choosing, this would enable him to establish an emergency food control agency on Hoover's lines if he wished. On May 11 the press reported the probability that Wilson would do precisely that—and the "increasing likelihood" that he would select Herbert Hoover for the new mission.[94]

Press speculation, however, was one thing, a firm presidential decision quite another. Despite his meeting with Wilson on May 9, Hoover's place in the war effort was not yet assured. Hoover telegraphed his wife on May 11:

> Matters are very uncertain here as to organization and unless it is put on footing that gives some promise of success I certainly do not intend [to] become connected with it. It may be some time before situation becomes definite. . . .[95]

For the moment he must take care not to offend presidential sensibilities or appear overweeningly ambitious. Emerging from the White House on May 9, he was asked by the press whether he would accept appointment as "food dictator" if one were established. "I don't want to be food dictator for the American people," he answered. "The man who accepts such a position will die on the barbed wire of the first line entrenchments."[96]

Meanwhile Hoover began to disengage himself from the now unwanted embrace of the Council of National Defense. On May 13 he submitted to the council a nineteen-page memorandum explaining the international food crisis and his recommendations for America's response. It was a lucid synthesis of his recent testimony before Congress. What it boiled down to, he wrote in a cover letter, was this: "the necessity of an immediate, powerful and independent administrative organ of Food Control."[97] Lest anyone miss the point, he declared that he understood his services to the council to be limited to his presentation of "this information and recommendations, and I trust that I have acquitted myself of my duty upon furnishing this memorandum."[98] A few days later the council agreed that "the further pursuit of the question must await determination by Congress of the distribution of power."[99]

As the second week of May progressed, Hoover endeavored to make certain that the "distribution" would be as he desired. On May 8 and 16 two of his associates in the Commission for Relief in Belgium followed him to the Congressional witness table, each echoing his themes and assertions.[100] On the tenth, Hoover himself issued a dramatic press release warning the American people that without food control the price of flour might reach $20.00 a barrel (nearly 50 percent above its current level) by the end of the year. Without control, the continuing "unrestrained drain on our wheat abroad" could leave America "bare of breadstuffs" in "the last three months of next year." With control, however, the present price of flour could be reduced by 40 to 50 percent while simultaneously treating wheat producers "in a liberal manner." To protect our nation's consumers yet increase exports without jeopardizing our necessities, said Hoover, the government must have vast and "absolutely immediate" powers—not for use against "the legitimate interests of trade and production" but against the "small minority of skunks" who were besmirching the reputation of "our great producing and distributing classes."[101]

Hoover was now convinced, or so he informed the press, that "special interests" were opposing the President's food proposals and that hoarding and speculation were "rife."[102] He was also convinced, he told a gathering of women in New York on May 10, that America could not "go on with the unlimited rise of prices" of the past five months and expect the "consuming classes" not to "rebel" against this burden.[103] If the twin specters of runaway inflation and social upheaval were the stick, the ideology of voluntarism provided Hoover the carrot. Again and again he abjured any desire to impose repressive rationing.[104] Yet repression of consumption must occur, and Hoover asserted that "if democracy is a faith worth defending, our people will do this service voluntarily and willingly."[105] He therefore urged the women he met in New York to "set this city in order":

> Every block requires a small committee well instructed in all the principles we need to enforce. Every household needs regular instruction, sympathy, support, direction and help. Public opinion needs to be created which sets its face against public entertainment, suppers, waste in public places, extravagance in every form.

All this, said Hoover, should be done with spontaneous assent: ". . . if we cannot produce in the American people voluntarily and willingly that sacrifice which our position now calls for, democracy will have gone a long way to prove its inability as a basis of civilization."[106]

As the "Almoner of starving Belgium" attempted to shock his fellow Americans into accepting government management of the food supply, powerful organs of liberal opinion rallied to his support. "Mr. Hoover enjoys the confidence of his countrymen upon the food question," the *New York Times* editorialized on May 12. "He does not propose to interfere with the ordinary course of trade. He only proposes to put a governor on the machine and not allow it to run away."[107] There was only one man in America, asserted the *Times* two days later, to be "the world's Joffre against hunger"; it was Hoover.[108] Similarly, the *New Republic*, an ardent booster of Hoover's relief work in Belgium, declared that the "whole world" recognized him as "preeminently fitted" for the emergency control of food consumption and distribution.[109]

Yet even as he worked the levers of "imaginative alarm" and sought powers "such as this democracy has never hitherto granted,"[110] Hoover continued to disclaim all ambition. In his press release of May 10 he denied that he had returned to America "to take the position of Food Dictator or Food Controller." Rather, he had come home "at the request of the Government" to "advise" on food control organization, and had now done so. As to his future, he affected unconcern:

> Legislation has already been introduced into Congress looking toward the creation of food control. . . . No one would be willing to take the position as head of such a department for food control if it is based absolutely upon restriction and control of diverse interests and is subject to a daily harvest of opposition. I do not want the position and I feel there are many others who could handle its concrete problems better than I, and I will have done my service in advice better than in execution. I feel that there must be dozens of men in this country better fitted than I for such office. No one who knows me will assert that I have any natural disposition to hold public office. Such positions as I have held have been forced upon me as a public duty. My only desire is to see the proper instrumentality set up to meet this, one of our greatest emergencies, and a man of courage, resource and experience at its head who is willing to sacrifice himself on the altar of the inarticulate masses whom he must protect. Such a man can be sure that I will place my advice at his disposal.[111]

Hoover's words were remarkably modest. They were also remarkably disingenuous and gave no hint of the struggle for power occurring behind the scenes.

While Hoover lobbied in the press and on Capitol Hill, events elsewhere provided new ammunition for his cause. On May 8 the Department of Agriculture issued its official wheat crop estimates. They disclosed that the nation's recent harvest of winter wheat was the smallest in thirteen years and that existing reserves were at record low levels and falling. Even if the coming spring wheat crop should be above average, the department predicted that the total supply available for the coming year would be barely sufficient to meet domestic needs. Unless Americans substantially reduced their wheat consumption, they would have none whatever to export to the hardpressed Allies.[112]

For the already nervous grain exchanges of the United States, the Agriculture Department's forecast was stunning. A year before, the price of wheat had averaged about a dollar a bushel.[113] As recently as April 2, contracts for the delivery of wheat in May had sold for $1.29 per bushel in Chicago. Since then the price had advanced relentlessly.[114] Then, on May 8, as word of the Department of Agriculture's bombshell circulated, May wheat futures rose to an unbelievable $3.00 a bushel—the highest price ever recorded.[115]

For the next several days pandemonium reigned in the grain markets, as frantic agents of European governments bid against American millers and one another for whatever remaining wheat that they could find. By May 11 the Chicago price of May futures had risen to $3.25. Desperate to stop the panic, the directors of the Chicago Board of Trade ordered the discontinuance of further trading in May futures and the settling of all May futures contracts at $3.18. Three days later the board suspended purchases of wheat altogether for forty-eight hours, except to liquidate existing contracts. Both actions were utterly without precedent.[116]

Thoroughly alarmed, the Illinois state council of defense—whose members included J. Ogden Armour and other business titans—beseeched Congress on May 12 to intervene. The council urged Congress to enact immediately a law placing control of the nation's foodstuffs in a presidentially appointed commission. The very "safety and preservation of our nation" depended on it.[117]

The tumult in the grain exchanges and the clamor for intervention that it generated probably helped to turn the political tide in Washington. Within days signs multiplied that the Wilson administration and its Congressional supporters were about to accept Hoover's approach. On May 14 Senator Thomas P. Gore of Oklahoma introduced a resolution approved by the committee on agriculture that he chaired. The proposed resolution would empower the President to appoint, subject to Senate confirmation, a Controller General of Supplies at a salary equal to that of a Cabinet member. The press reported that Hoover was the person most likely to receive such an appointment.[118]

Meanwhile, on Sunday evening, May 13, Hoover called upon President Wilson at the White House.[119] Whatever the commander in chief said that night must have been highly encouraging, for two days later Hoover telegraphed his wife in California that he would remain in Washington all summer and was looking for a house to live in.[120] On May 15 also his close associate Edgar Rickard told Mrs. Hoover that "Bert is very hopeful" of complete victory, despite his "extremely hard time fighting against the departmental heads and other old-timers in Washington who are desirous of holding their jobs."[121]

On the evening of May 15 Hoover achieved a definitive breakthrough. At a White House conference with Secretary Houston and members of the House and Senate committees on agriculture, President Wilson expressed himself emphatically: Food control legislation was needed, and needed at once. He asked the committees to agree upon a single bill that could be speedily enacted.[122] The President's pep talk was efficacious. Shortly afterward the press reported that the second of the administration's pending bills in Congress would be redrafted to vest its regulatory powers exclusively in the President (and not the Department of Agriculture) and to authorize creation of an emergency food agency. In all likelihood, said the *New York Times*, Herbert Hoover would be selected for this position.[123] The *Philadelphia Inquirer* went further. On the morning of May 16 it announced unequivocally that Hoover would be "the food dictator of the United States" and that President Wilson had ordered him "to immediately place in operation his plans for food control."[124]

With the press now reporting that Wilson had either selected or all but selected Hoover,[125] the outmaneuvered Secretary of Agriculture made a volte-face. The day after the May 15 conference at the White House, David Houston publicly denied a newspaper report that he was against Hoover's appointment as chairman of the proposed food control board. "There has not been the slightest difference between Mr. Hoover and me," Houston claimed. "We are entirely in accord on the matter of food control, that is, we believe the special powers we have asked Congress to grant should be exercised by an emergency agency, and not by the Department of Agriculture."[126] Hoover, too, now endeavored to create a veneer of public harmony. He professed to be as displeased as Houston at the published accounts of their differences. According to one newspaper, the two men had enjoyed "the most cordial relations" since Hoover's return.[127]

More and more, the would-be manager of the nation's food supplies was behaving as though he would prevail. On May 17 he conferred with the vice chairman of Great Britain's Royal Commission on Wheat Supplies and with many of America's principal grain dealers.[128] He sent Representative Lever letters outlining his rationale for a regulatory bill, and containing his suggestions for revisions. Among other things, Hoover urged that the measure be called the "food administration bill." This, he suggested, "would be helpful in forming public opinion." We "do not want to give the complexion of food dictator or controller," he said, "as this creates opposition at once." Still, the new bill should have teeth, including the power to establish "a fixed price at which goods must be bought and sold either between traders or by the Government." A "fixed price," he insisted, was "the only positive, absolute method of eliminating speculation."[129] Here was a man who knew what he wanted.

To a caller at his hotel on May 16, he was even more outspoken. "If it falls to my lot to control the food supply of the United States," said Hoover, "I shall begin at once to cut off every official and every theorist. There must be, above all, no professors on this job." The "only people in the country," he went on, who knew anything practical about food were the "commercial interests." It was "to them [that] I shall look exclusively for aid in helping me to solve the big and complex problems which are involved in this work." Hoover made it plain that he would not be pushed around:

> I will not be shackled by anybody in the Department of Agriculture and will not allow a single job hunter or profit monger to help me.
>
> Patriotic and unselfish men, every one of them working without pay or compensation of any kind, will be my assistants.

Impatient to get to work, he declared that his job would be to "drop the outrageous price of flour" (currently about $14.00 a barrel) to $6.60. "I know of no more diabolic or wicked thing in all this hellish business than the crime against humanity by the damned robbers, for that is exactly what they are, who have shot up the price of flour to its present level."[130]

Nevertheless, nothing official had yet emanated from the White House, and even as much of the press reported the virtually definite appointment of Hoover as food "dictator," a backlash suddenly flared on Capitol Hill. On May 16, in an extraordinary secret session of the Senate, a number of senators led by Henry Cabot Lodge accused the Wilson administration of egregious usurpation of power, failure to inform the Congress about its war policies, and dilatory prosecution of the conflict. For three and a half hours the critics held sway, and in their barrage of censure Herbert Hoover became a target. One senator described him as a "man who had emerged from obscurity only a short time ago, and whom the Administration now wants to make a food dictator." Where, one legislator wondered, did the administration get the notion that Hoover (in the words of the subsequent press report) was "the only man on earth capable of handling the food problem"?[131]

The next day the anti-Hoover rebellion intensified, with a number of senators openly belittling his qualifications. They claimed that Hoover had insufficient experience to be "food dictator" and that anyone could have succeeded in the Belgian relief with the support from the American government that he had enjoyed. It would be far better, they contended, to appoint as food administrator someone of "large business experience" who had already proven that he could tackle a challenge of this magnitude. The anti-administration forces warned that if President Wilson insisted on placing food control in Hoover's hands, there would be an even greater revolt in the Senate.[132]

Clearly not everyone in the nation's capital had been awed by the returning hero of the CRB. Years later George Creel, whom the President had appointed head of the Committee on Public Information, recalled that Hoover, when he came to Washington, had greeted its officialdom coldly, speaking "only in chill monosyllables."[133] Josephus Daniels, too, had been "disillusioned" in his first meeting with Hoover on May 7. The Secretary of the Navy had expected to encounter a man of warmth and sentiment. Instead, Daniels wrote, "He told of the big work in Belgium as coldly as if he were giving statistics of production. From his words and his manner he seemed to regard human beings as so many numbers. Not once did he show the slightest feeling or convey to me a picture of the tragedies that went on while he was relieving the necessities."[134] Daniels did not see that day the hidden, passionate side of Herbert Hoover. He did not see the Hoover who could cry at the sight of Belgian breadlines or suffering children. He saw rather the impersonal manner of an engineer with a mission, a man in a hurry who had no time to waste on emotions.

But if a few who met Hoover had misgivings,[135] his personality was not at this point the source of the Senate's qualms.[136] For many senators, the Wilson administration was proposing to leap into uncharted territory at the behest of a man, however estimable, whom they hardly knew. One senator opined that the "Emperor of Germany, even in his palmiest days, never exercised a greater power nor wielded a more dangerous authority" than Woodrow Wilson would possess, if the food and other emergency measures were enacted.[137] War or no war, the Senate was not about to grant such power automatically.

If the anti-administration senators thought that they could stop Hoover's selection, they erred. At his conference with the congressional agriculture committees on May 15, President Wilson had been urged to issue a statement clarifying the maximum price provision in the pending legislation.[138] Four days later he did just that and more. On May 19 he publicly announced at last that he had invited Hoover to be his commissioner of food administration.

In a press release drawn up with Hoover's assistance,[139] the President revealed his plans. The Department of Agriculture would administer "normal activities" relating to food production, conservation, and marketing. The new commissioner, appointed by and reporting directly to the President, would handle "emergency activities" affecting distribution, consumption, exports, imports, and prices.

> I have asked Mr. Hoover to undertake this all-important task of food administration. He has expressed his willingness to do so on condition that he is to receive no payment for his services and that the whole of the force under him, exclusive of clerical assistance, shall be employed so far as possible upon the same volunteer basis. He has expressed his confidence

> that this difficult matter of food administration can be successfully accomplished through the voluntary cooperation and direction of legitimate distributors of foodstuffs and with the help of the women of the country.

In his statement the President tried to allay Congressional uneasiness about this total break with American precedent. Yes, he admitted, the bill would confer "very great powers," but no greater than what other belligerent governments had already found necessary. Moreover, the "object" of these powers would be "stimulation and conservation, not arbitrary restraint or injurious interference with the normal processes of production." Yes, he was seeking authority to "establish prices"—not, however, to curb the profits of farmers but to "guarantee to them when necessary a minimum which will insure to them a profit where they are asked to attempt new crops. . . ." Another purpose of price-fixing, he said, would be "to secure the consumer against extortion." How? By "breaking up corners and attempts at speculation . . . by fixing temporarily a reasonable price at which middlemen must sell."

The President expressed confidence that the exercise of these powers would only be necessary in a few instances "where some small and selfish minority" was "unwilling to put the Nation's interests above personal advantage." He promised that the "ordinary economic machinery" of America would be "left substantially undisturbed," that the food administration would disappear as soon as the war ended, and that because it would be largely composed of volunteers no "permanent bureaucracy" would result. Adopting Hoover's equation of democracy with voluntarism, Wilson declared:

> The successful conduct of the projected food administration by such means will be the finest possible demonstration of the willingness, the ability, and the efficiency of democracy, and of its justified reliance upon the freedom of individual initiative. The last thing that any American could contemplate with equanimity would be the introduction of anything resembling Prussian autocracy into the food control of this country.[140]

The President's message was designed to be reassuring. So, too, was Hoover's formal response, which appeared in the nation's press alongside it. Hoover announced that his acceptance of Wilson's invitation was "entirely upon the assumption" that Congress would grant the President "broad powers" for a "competent" food administration. Implementation of food policy, he stated, would be governed by five "principles." First, the food problem was one of "wise administration," expressed not by the words "dictator" or "controller" but by "food administrator." Second, this administration would largely operate through existing channels of production and distribution. Third, communities should be organized for voluntary conservation of food.

Fourth, "all important positions," so far as possible, should be staffed by volunteers. Fifth, the food administration would be independent and accountable directly to the President but would cooperate with "the great and admirable organization" of the Department of Agriculture and other relevant agencies. Hoover averred that he had "no instinct to be a food dictator." His goal was "to see my own people solve their own problem." After outlining his plan of organization, he made a nonthreatening appeal which the press quickly proclaimed as the nation's motto: "Eat plenty, wisely, without waste."[141]

Fifteen days after reaching the Union Station, he had argued, lobbied, and maneuvered his way to the senior echelons of national leadership.

IV

WHY had Hoover prevailed? Fundamentally, because his conception of proper management of the food crisis appealed to the one man who had authority to confer power upon him. Woodrow Wilson shared Hoover's aversion to bureaucracy and statism. Yet, like Hoover, he believed that success in the war required an unprecedented state-directed mobilization of the American economy. Hoover's solution persuaded the man in the Oval Office: vast, "unquestionable," absolute power—but exercised by "administrators," not "dictators." Absolute power on paper—yet so intimidating that it would rarely be invoked or need to be, if the people could be awakened, exhorted, and mustered into action without coercion.[142] Absolute power but also temporary power, safeguarded from abuse by the altruism and impermanence of volunteers. Voluntarism was the linchpin, the path to "planning without bureaucracy,"[143] the way to mediate successfully between a libertarian political system and the collectivist demands of a world war. The well-to-do Hoover, who had directed the Belgian relief for two and a half years without accepting a salary or expenses, articulated the code of voluntarism masterfully. The President of the United States was convinced.

Hoover was also aided by the character of his principal opponent. Neither popular with his agrarian constituency nor (it seems) particularly influential with the President,[144] David Houston could not long block Hoover's path. Scholarly by temperament and devoid of rhetorical skills, he lacked "the energy and driving force" which Colonel House and so many others noticed in Hoover.[145] The CRB chairman's displacement of Houston as the government's principal arbiter of food policy set a pattern that soon affected much of Wilson's Cabinet: new men—able, energetic, and ambitious—creating novel, ad hoc agencies and shunting traditional government departments aside.[146]

Above all, Hoover succeeded because of his reputation as the man who had "held dying Belgium in his arms."[147] The *New York Times* was correct:

Hoover enjoyed the confidence of his compatriots on food issues, and no one else had his "prestige."[148] No man anywhere, said the *New Republic*, equaled him in "experience in international food administration."[149] Enwrapped in two and a half years of international approbation, he could not but be, for the American public, a satisfactory choice. Wrote one newspaper on the day of Wilson's announcement: " 'Hoover of Belgium' is a title as significant of a great work well done as 'Kitchener of Khartoum.' "[150]

So Hoover had won his jurisdictional battle with Houston and with it the chance for an unfettered entrance upon the American stage. Now he must persuade Congress to furnish the requisite power to go with his title. The enabling legislation was not yet written; the independent agency he was promised did not exist. And as he was about to discover, the "big game" of political high hurdles could be a marathon.

2

A Man in a Hurry

I

ON Sunday, May 20, 1917, as news of Hoover's selection as "food administrator" appeared in the nation's press, the challenge he confronted was stark. The United States, under his direction, must supply more food to the Allies or risk their collapse and defeat. And he, as the President's chosen agent, must somehow stop rampant inflation of food prices at home or risk "social disruption" and perhaps fatal impairment of the war effort.[1]

Hoover was confident that both objectives could be achieved, and without resorting to what he called "the power of Prussianism." Speaking on May 20 at Brown University, where he received his first honorary degree, he declared: "I believe our faith is right. I believe democracy cannot only defend itself, but it can prepare in time. I believe that the spirit of self-sacrifice and idealism runs higher among our people than in any other land."[2] He now had his opportunity to test this proposition.

Since arriving in Washington, Hoover had been working out of a suite at the New Willard Hotel. On May 22 his embryonic Food Administration took up offices in the Department of the Interior Building, courtesy of Franklin K. Lane. From here the new agency planned to operate, pending Congressional enactment of the President's food legislation.[3]

Meanwhile, from all over the country, offers of assistance were pouring in by the hundreds—a gratifying testimonial to Hoover's faith in American altruism.[4] Characteristically, however, he turned first not to strangers but to friends of proven competence, friends drawn from the three great, intersecting networks that he knew best: the Commission for Relief in Belgium; the mining engineering profession; and Stanford University, his beloved alma mater.

One such recruit—selected by Hoover even before he left England—was Ben S. Allen, a Stanford-educated journalist employed by the Associated Press in London. For nearly three years, from this strategic position, Allen had effectively publicized the CRB's cause. Then, in April 1917, Hoover invited him to accompany him home as, in effect, his press secretary. Now, back in the States, Allen took charge of the infant agency's public relations.[5]

From the CRB itself came Vernon Kellogg, a Stanford University biologist who had headed the commission's offices in Brussels and northern France. Numerous other CRB men, not a few of them mining engineers, also came on board.[6] One of these, Edgar Rickard, had long been a Hoover intimate. Soon he would be the Food Administration's office manager as well as overseer of Hoover's private financial affairs.

From California came friends willing to drop everything and enlist at once in Hoover's crusade. In most instances, it seemed, a single summons by telegraph or cable was enough. Hence Ray Lyman Wilbur temporarily forsook his duties at Stanford, met Hoover at the dock in New York, and speedily plunged into plans to enlist the women of America in food conservation.[7] Hence Mark Requa, a California oilman and acquaintance of Hoover from before the war, arrived in Washington in early June, and immediately became a senior assistant.[8] In June, too, the eminent San Francisco mining attorney Curtis H. Lindley journeyed east at Hoover's request. I just want you to "sit around and advise" for a month or two, Hoover told him.[9] Instead, Lindley (whom Hoover had known since the 1890s) became the agency's chief counsel and remained so until ill health compelled him to resign some months later.[10]

Despite Hoover's well-publicized warning that there would be "no professors on this job," he did make a few notable exceptions. One was Kellogg; another was Alonzo Englebert Taylor, a nationally recognized authority on nutrition. Taylor had met Hoover in Europe in 1916 and had come away tremendously impressed. A few months after his return to the United States, the professor published a newspaper article in the *Philadelphia Inquirer* extolling Hoover as a man superbly qualified to assume control of American food supplies if the United States should enter the conflict. According to Taylor, Hoover was regarded in Europe as "one of the unique creations of the war." He predicted that Hoover, a man who "does not know the word fail," would be found "large enough for the largest tasks."[11] Just two months later the admiring professor became a charter member of the Food Administrator's inner circle.[12]

Among Hoover's initial staff of lieutenants, then, the bonds of devotion were exceptionally strong. All could be counted upon to be loyal to the man some of them already called "the Chief."

Not all of the growing fraternity of "Hoover men" were at the Food Administration. With the skill of a master administrator, the "food czar" had begun to colonize other critical centers of power. Before leaving England he asked W. A. M. Goode, a Canadian-born journalist with whom he had worked closely in Belgian relief, to keep British officials stationed in Washington apprised of Great Britain's food needs. Like Professor Taylor and so many others, Goode was an unabashed eulogist of Herbert Hoover. He is "a remarkable man in every way," Goode told a friend in April 1917—"in fact, so remarkable that I think if he really makes his mind up, he will become President of the United States."[13] By early May, Goode was strategically ensconced at the British Ministry of Food and was ready for effective liaison with his American patron.[14]

Hoover attempted a similar coup at the American State Department, where his friend Hugh Gibson was then assigned. For the past two years Hoover and the young career diplomat had collaborated intimately in the Belgian relief. Each held the other in highest esteem. In late May Hoover asked the Secretary of State to designate Gibson as the department's representative to the Food Administration.[15] In this instance Hoover did not succeed, nor did he ever, despite persistent efforts, manage to detach Gibson from the State Department during the war. But Gibson, right where he was, could and did serve ably in Hoover's expanding network of influence.

Another rare rebuff occurred when Henry L. Stimson, a member of the CRB's New York advisory committee, turned down Hoover's telegraphed plea to join the Food Administration. Having strenuously advocated American preparedness and intervention in the Great War, Stimson felt called to volunteer for military service. Unaccustomed to taking no for an answer, Hoover telegraphed a second time. Again Stimson declined.[16] This time Hoover replied with a blunt letter:

> I am a good deal grieved by your attitude as I believe that we are going to win or lose this war on the basis of mobilizing our civilians rather than our soldiers, and that the mobilization of the civilians is going to depend on our getting a proper start with this new executive organization, with every bit of prestige and help that we can bring to bear. Even if you should want to leave us later you might have helped us get over the rough end of the trail by taking on the job for three or four months!![17]

Stimson was grieved and sought an immediate retraction.[18] Whether Hoover gave it is unknown. Evidently the rift healed, for twelve years later—such are the twists and turns of life—President-elect Hoover appointed Stimson his Secretary of State.

If Hoover was highly assertive in his search for executive talent, he could also on occasion be impulsive. A few days before the Food Administrator moved to the Interior Department Building, a twenty-one-year-old shoe salesman from Richmond, Virginia, appeared at the New Willard Hotel. Having read about Hoover's noble deeds and plans in the newspaper, Lewis L. Strauss was filled with a desire to join the great man's staff as an unpaid volunteer. Upon reaching Hoover's suite, Strauss found his access blocked by the Chief's private secretary, a young Englishman named Leslie Havergyle Bradshaw. Hoover was busy, Bradshaw declared—so busy that he might be unavailable all day. Refusing to accept this brush-off, Strauss sat down and waited.

A few minutes later Hoover emerged from an adjoining hotel room. Seizing his chance, Strauss jumped up, introduced himself, and breathlessly announced that he wanted to work for Hoover without a salary for the next two months. The busy "food dictator" stopped. Perhaps there flashed through Hoover's mind the day in early 1896 when, not yet twenty-two years old, he had similarly won an office job with a noted mining engineer in San Francisco. It had been a turning point in his life.[19] Perhaps he now saw himself in the countenance of the hopeful youth standing before him.

Such thoughts could only have absorbed an instant. Without bothering to learn his visitor's credentials, Hoover asked, "When do you want to start?" "Right now," Strauss replied. "Take off your coat," Hoover said—and walked out the door to an appointment.[20]

For the next few weeks Strauss worked as an assistant to Bradshaw, all the while having virtually no direct contact with the Chief. Then one day Hoover called the young Virginian into his office. Bradshaw is going to leave, the Food Administrator announced. "Would you like the job?" "I certainly would," Strauss replied. Whereupon Hoover asked, "What's your name?"[21]

Thus began one of the deepest friendships of Hoover's life. For the next forty-seven years he would be like a second father to Strauss, and Strauss like another Hoover son. In all those years not a month went by without some contact between the older man and his protégé.[22] Once again Hoover had displayed his uncanny ability to select men of exceptional talent and turn them into loyalists for life.

As the Food Administrator assembled his senior staff, he began to reach out to the constituencies that his apparatus would touch. As early as May 6, he worked out a tentative mechanism of wheat and flour control with William C. Edgar, editor of the influential *Northwestern Miller*, and James F. Bell, a leading grain miller.[23] On May 17 and 18 he conferred with Julius Barnes of Duluth, one of the country's principal grain exporters, and invited him to head the government's anticipated wheat control agency, to be known tentatively as the Grain Executive.[24] To the nation's governors Hoover telegraphed an appeal to set up state food administrations to cooperate with the federal one. From more than half the governors came back quick pledges of support.[25] To Samuel Gompers, president of the American Federation of Labor, who had asked him to confer with the trade unions, Hoover promptly promised a meeting as well as unspecified measures to ameliorate the prices of the "great staples."[26]

Throughout the hectic days of late May and early June a ceaseless flow of correspondents and visitors clamored for Hoover's attention: members of the British government's Balfour Mission, members of Congress, representatives of meat-packing houses and grain exchanges, wholesale grocerymen, and many more. "We are going along—or better around—like whirling dervishes," Vernon Kellogg remarked. "Hoover . . . is booked up with interviews like a barber's chair on Saturday night. . . ."[27] "Who's Hoover?" people had wondered when the little-known engineer had founded the CRB in 1914. Now business leaders, bankers, politicians, and housewives across America were asking, "What does he want us to do?"

In conferences, interviews, and letters, the Food Administrator divulged and refined his intentions, always keeping in mind his twin objectives of feeding the Allies and preventing "excessive" domestic prices.[28] One obvious way to augment food supplies for export was for Americans to curb their own consumption and waste. It was a subject about which Hoover spoke with almost puritanical zeal. "One of the greatest wastes in America today is the entertainment on a lavish scale both in public places and in homes," he told one group of women.[29] To a Congressional committee he was even blunter:

> . . . it is so much worse from the social standpoint that 15 per cent of our people duplicate the feeding facilities of the country by eating in public places. A man has a home where he has the machinery of feeding, and then he goes to a public place and duplicates the whole economic machinery. And in public places he eats and destroys twice as much as he does in his home. Then there is the question of the fourth meal in the day, the supper, which is one of the worst pieces of extravagance that we have in this country.

Hoover did not advocate "sumptuary legislation"—"I think it is one of the most hideous of things." But he did assert that "if we get at this with sufficient intensity we ought to be able to establish a public opinion against" such practices that "will in large degree eliminate them."[30]

On May 27 Hoover unveiled his first plan to "establish" this public opinion. He announced that, if Congress passed the pending food legislation, every woman in America who presided over a household would be asked to enroll as a member of the Food Administration and pledge to carry out its directives. Many "careless customs," he declared, must be repressed or altered. The "gospel of the clean plate . . . must become universal." It might even be, he added, that if the food bills on Capitol Hill were enacted the women of America would "play a deciding part in the great war."[31]

Hoover told the President that the work of the Food Administration's conservation division would be an "educational proposition," dependent upon systematic propaganda.[32] For both practical and philosophical reasons Hoover continued to reject European-style rationing. Aside from the "stupendous" bureaucracy and financial outlays that implementation of such a plan would entail, he was convinced that it would yield "no consequential savings" of food among the 40 percent of the American populace living on or near a farm. There was no practical way, he said, to confine rural Americans to what a ration card would permit. Hence the burden of belt-tightening would fall exclusively upon the cities and towns. Most importantly of all, Hoover knew that imposition of such unfamiliar and highly intrusive coercion would grate upon the libertarian psyche of his countrymen. Americans, he later wrote, "can be led to make great sacrifices, [but] they do not like to be driven."[33] Rationing would surely be unpopular, and Hoover had no desire to be that.

Propaganda, then—propaganda to the uttermost—would become an indispensable weapon in Hoover's food arsenal. Fortunately for the campaign ahead, he was superbly fitted for the task. At the CRB he had become adept at idealistic exhortation and at wielding what he called "the club of public opinion."

A second method of creating a surplus for the Allies was to enlarge American production of exportable crops. Although this task lay nominally within the province of the Department of Agriculture, Hoover was convinced that extraordinary stimulative measures—such as a guaranteed minimum price for certain staples—might be required to induce farmers to increase their planting.[34] On May 28 he promised a delegation of farmers that a commission including farmers' representatives would be established to determine a minimum price for grain.[35] As he explained to President Wilson a few days later, it would be necessary to "assemble the best thought of the country" to ascertain "desirable" price levels for various crops.[36]

Expanding the domestic food supply and reducing domestic food demand could not, however, in Hoover's judgment stabilize the soaring retail price of food. To Hoover, the cataclysm of world war had temporarily destroyed the self-regulating mechanisms of the free market.[37] Some other economic balance wheel must therefore be found. By late May this goal had taken priority in his mind. Food prices in the United States were too high, he announced. The very first task of the Food Administration would be to steady them and bring them down.[38]

Earlier in May, in testimony before Congress, Hoover had summarily dismissed one seductive panacea: arbitrary governmental fixing of maximum prices by law. This had been tried in Europe, he warned, and it had failed. All it had done was to cause hoarding and black markets.[39] He repeated his strictures on May 25.[40] Instead, four days later he announced a plan to create a series of governmental "executive bodies" that themselves would engage in market operations for grain, sugar, and other commodities in coordination with the purchasing agents of the Allies.[41] These "commodity executives," he told President Wilson, would stabilize prices not by "legal enactment" but by "a series of commercial operations" that would "greatly diminish the growing margin between producer and consumer due to war conditions and speculation." By buying and selling in bulk, and by determining just how much to send abroad, these new entities could dominate and hence "stabilize" the market.[42] They could also curb the Allies' disastrously inflationary competitive bidding against one another.[43] By concentrating all government purchasing into a single hand, said Hoover, and by reducing the number of buying agencies, the Food Administration could stabilize the maximum price of key commodities and break the current speculative fever.[44] In the case of wheat and flour, he contended that his method of control could shrink the price margin between producer and consumer by approximately 60 percent.[45]

Hoover's scheme was breathtaking in scope, and it may have been his most creative contribution to winning the war. Instead of abolishing the free market entirely, he proposed that the government itself *enter* the market and operate within it as its biggest—hence dominant—player. Instead of imposing price controls and rationing at the retail level, he would attempt to *manage* prices at the producer-distributor level—a nexus more easily monitored and regulated.[46] Moreover, the "bodies" he intended to create would be staffed not by inexperienced bureaucrats but by seasoned businessmen drawn from the world of commerce. What Hoover was proposing (although he did not yet use the term) was the creation of government-owned and government-administered corporations, an innovation for which there was very little precedent.[47]

The Food Administrator fully realized that he was advocating a spectacular injection of the federal government into the nation's economy. Nothing like this had ever been done before in the United States. To the president of the Erie Railroad he even conceded that his undertaking amounted in some respects to "a sort of socialization of industry."[48]

Again and again, therefore, Hoover attempted to reassure the business community that he did not wish to disturb the country's "existing economic machinery" any more than "absolutely necessary."[49] His "whole plan," he insisted, was not "food dictatorship" but an effort to "remedy . . . the abnormal conditions imposed by the war . . . by cooperation with the great trades and distributive agencies throughout the country. . . ."[50] He stressed that his agency would be filled with the most capable and representative business executives, and he emphasized his commitment to business/government collaboration.[51] He proclaimed his opposition to "bureaucracy" and held up the principle of "free service" as an antidote to it. He wanted "the best men in the country," he wrote, but he wanted them to be "entirely free of Government pay and therefore more independent in mind as a guarantee of the complete extinction of the organization at the end of the war."[52] In essence, Hoover was arguing that the national emergency made socialism necessary but that he could mitigate its ill effects by relying upon presumably anti-socialist businessmen who, along with his agency, would vanish when the war was won.

For all his efforts to minimize the radical character of his plan and to cloak it in the comforting language of voluntarism and public-private partnership, Hoover was truly envisaging a mighty leap. How much money, he asked Julius Barnes, would be needed to buy, sell, store, and efficiently allocate the nation's food grain crops between domestic and Allied customers? One hundred million dollars plus commercial borrowings by banks, Barnes replied.[53] One hundred million dollars! Why, the entire outlay of the federal government in fiscal year 1916 had only been $712,967,000.[54]

By the end of May, barely ten days after his designation as Food Administrator, Hoover had formulated the key components of his food strategy: an elaborate national campaign of conservation and elimination of waste; incentive prices for producers of a few essential staples; and a network of powerful commodity boards which would control distribution, coordinate with the Allies, and squeeze out speculative excess in the distribution chain.

One thing only he now needed: authority from the Congress of the United States.

II

As Hoover prepared to launch his food crusade, the Wilson administration was struggling to devise a legislative framework for it. By mid-May the President and his Congressional allies had settled upon a strategy calling for enactment of not one but two food-related bills. The first would mandate a national census of the nation's food resources and would stimulate agricultural production, notably through direct federal provision of seeds to farmers. These responsibilities would devolve upon the Department of Agriculture.[55] The second would grant the President (and through him his chosen surrogate, Hoover) a panoply of regulatory powers over the nation's food manufacturing and distribution.

Representative Lever had introduced such a measure on May 3.[56] But because of Hoover's and President Wilson's objections to certain of its provisions, the bill's sponsor had been obliged to rewrite it.[57] On May 22 Lever brought forth his revised version, conferring upon the President what one newspaper called "absolute power" to control foodstuffs and other necessities of life. Herbert Hoover immediately endorsed this measure.[58]

The South Carolina Democrat's bill now went to committee, while both houses of Congress turned their attention to the less controversial food survey proposal.[59] On May 28 it overwhelmingly passed the House of Representatives. The Senate adopted its version without dissent a few days later.[60]

The lopsided approval of the food survey bill proved deceiving. In both houses of Congress it elicited a storm of ridicule. Some members questioned whether a food census would accomplish anything significant. Others wondered whether it would merely create seven thousand census-taking jobs, all for Democrats.[61] What most dismayed the critics, however, was not the survey bill itself but its preview of things to come. As the sheer enormity of the Wilson administration's request for regulatory power sank in, spasms of uneasiness erupted on Capitol Hill. Why should the farmer be singled out? Representative Joseph G. Cannon of Illinois asked, "If you are going to have a dictator for one-third of the people, why not have dictators for the other two-thirds?"[62] The Lever bill was "vicious," said Senator Hoke Smith of Georgia, for it placed "control of the whole food problem into the hands of a dictator. We don't want dictators."[63]

As the debate proceeded, Hoover himself came in for criticism. In the Senate, James C. Reed accused him of contributing to the recent surge in wheat prices by predicting that uncontrolled flour might soon reach $20.00 a barrel. "Hoover has thus far been worth millions to the bulls," the Missouri Democrat charged. We are bound to suffer high prices, he added, as long as government officials "announce to the people of the world that they are about to starve to death."[64] In the House, Hoover's much-publicized announcement that he and his assistants would receive no governmental salary prompted one representative to wonder whether "we might have a dictator unsupported by any power of Congress, but by voluntary contributions."[65] In the eyes of some suspicious solons, Hoover's self-sacrificing gesture looked like a way of circumventing Congress's power of the purse.

Not content with a few verbal volleys, the Senate proceeded to tinker with the President's request. Before approving the innocuous food survey measure, the Senate adopted an amendment making it a felony for anyone to hoard food. It also authorized the President to abolish dealings in grain futures if such transactions "unreasonably" raised wheat or other cereal prices to the detriment of the American people. In effect the Senate transformed the administration's food census bill into a substitute for its more stringent food regulation bill. For some senators this was just fine; in their view the new provisions against hoarding and grain gambling were all that were really necessary under the circumstances.[66]

With the Senate's food survey bill now divergent from that of the House, a reconciliation of the two in conference committee became necessary. Meanwhile, on both sides of the Capitol, spokesmen for the nation's wheat farmers were becoming apprehensive. Should one man, they wondered, be given the power to set the price that wheat growers would receive for their product?[67] In the House agriculture committee, Representative James Young of Texas thought not. Hoover "knows nothing about farming," Young exclaimed. He did not know what farmers were up against. Give Hoover "the autocratic power of fixing the prices," and whose viewpoint would he adopt: the producers' or the more numerous consumers'? Young was convinced that the Lever bill had but one purpose: "to hold down the price of farm products." "[I]t is wheat that [Hoover] is after," Young charged. If farmers produced too much of it, they would lose. But if they produced too little, Hoover would intervene and "hold down" the price, "because the consuming world needs the stuff." Young felt it would be better for Congress itself to pass a law controlling the "intervening agencies" between producer and consumer, and then "stand on the law of supply and demand," than to vest price-fixing power in Herbert Hoover.[68]

By June 1 the agrarian outcry was having an impact in the corridors of Congress. That day Senator Henry Hollis of New Hampshire, an ardent Wilsonian, privately warned the President that his food control legislation was in trouble. It could not pass the Senate without the "most strenuous efforts" by the administration, he reported, and very few Democratic senators at present were "well enough disposed" to Wilson to help.[69]

Compounding the difficulty was public sentiment of a different sort. For more than a decade the American people had been taught by muckrakers and reformers to distrust and restrain big business. The air had been filled with denunciations of "trusts" and "malefactors of great wealth." Now, suddenly, successful business leaders were in demand in wartime Washington, and Hoover, for one, was preparing to welcome them en masse. Would they be as unselfish as he believed? Could they be trusted to regulate themselves and behave in the public interest? Americans of an anti-corporate bent were not sure.[70] To the concerns of constitutional conservatives and wheat farmers were now added the apprehensions of some Progressives.

As the winds of doubt gained velocity, Hoover found himself in an anomalous position. Absorbed in developing his plans and "machinery," he had no formal power to implement them. Nor did he have a sure source of funds outside his own savings, into which he was obliged to dip substantially.[71] Finally, on May 29, he asked President Wilson for $10,000 from a discretionary fund that Congress had recently granted the chief executive for national defense purposes. This money, Hoover said, was needed for "necessary expenses" in his "preparatory work." Wilson at once complied; the anomaly deepened.[72] Now Hoover was spending government money on an agency with no legal standing.

Publicly Hoover said little about his mounting predicament other than to unveil some of his plans in general terms and exhort his fellow Americans to eliminate waste.[73] Behind the scenes, however, he pulled every lever he could think of. He asked a biographer of Abraham Lincoln for quotations from "our greatest national leader" on the need for "increased centralization of authority in the Federal Government" during an emergency.[74] He cabled W. A. M. Goode at the British Ministry of Food for "more anxiety"—that is, more statements of British concern about the American food situation. Goode quickly solicited remarks from British officials pleading for prompt enactment of the Lever bill.[75] Duly reported in the press, these supposedly spontaneous "anxiety expressions" circulated in the United States as part of Hoover's lobbying effort in Congress.

The fledgling food controller also tried to downplay the revolutionary character of his program. In publicly explaining his plan for "commodity executives," for instance, he dismissed as mere rumor the report that he was preparing to create "big corporations" to control the distribution of certain commodities.[76] Several days later he admitted that his food administration *might* buy and sell a few commodities—but only, he said, if it were absolutely necessary to order to break up illegal "corners" and protect the general welfare.[77] In fact, he had already informed President Wilson and others that the exercise of broad buying and selling power—including complete control of the wheat supply by a Grain Executive—would be integral to his price stabilization plans.[78]

With the regulatory bill still languishing in committee, an impatient President urged key senators on June 6 to expedite its passage. The measure—including formal provision for a food administrator—was needed quickly, Wilson contended. Without it the country's condition would be grave.[79] Hoover, too, was growing impatient. Conferring with a delegation of labor leaders on June 8, he warned: "Throughout the last three years two words have been written on the pages of English history: 'too late.' Unless the Lever bill is passed immediately, before the grain is harvested, 'too late' will be written in our history."[80] Persuaded by Hoover's analysis, and convinced of his fitness to lead, a group of trade unionists led by Samuel Gompers visited the White House on June 11. They told the President bluntly that his food legislation must be passed immediately. Otherwise there would be "discontent . . . of the greatest injury" among working-class Americans battered by the high cost of living.[81]

Even as the labor representatives converged on the White House, a breakthrough was occurring at the other end of Pennsylvania Avenue. On June 11 the House committee on agriculture adopted a third version of the Lever bill.[82] Nearly three weeks had elapsed since the second version (redrawn to Hoover's liking) had come before it. Now, at last, full Congressional deliberation could proceed.

That same afternoon Herbert Hoover visited President Wilson for nearly an hour.[83] Despite Representative Lever's prediction that the House would pass the revised bill with less than two weeks' debate,[84] Hoover was (or professed to be) increasingly agitated. The next day he sent the President a memorandum encapsulating his fears.

When it came to voicing "imaginative alarm," Hoover was not given to understatement. He informed Wilson that the nation was "rapidly drifting toward an acute crisis" brought on by "discussion and uncertainty" about the Food Administration's powers and goals. Already, he noted, the 1917 harvest had begun. Yet middlemen were unable to obtain credits until the government's policy was officially announced, and leading millers were curtailing their operations. The Allies were withholding purchases at Hoover's request but were anxious to line up wheat shipments for the autumn. Indeed, claimed Hoover, if "all the forces now desirous" of wheat should "enter today into a general scramble to secure it," the price of flour would rocket to $19.00 a barrel in a month.

Nor was this all. According to Hoover, neutral governments were competing in the American market and disturbing the price structure. Speculative activity was spreading to rice and potatoes. The cost of living was "steadily increasing," threatening "an early reorganization of the wage scale" and "consequent social disorganization, to the loss of national efficiency." If the necessary food control laws were not passed by July 1—barely two and a half weeks away—much of the value of the Food Administration would be rendered "nugatory."[85]

It is impossible to know whether Hoover truly believed his nearly apocalyptic message to the White House. Perhaps he had convinced himself that potential disaster lay just ahead. Perhaps he merely wished to convince the President. More likely he—with the President's blessing—had contrived a *specter* of calamity that Wilson could now use to frighten an obstinate Congress into action. Certainly the shocking vision of flour (and hence bread) advancing 50 percent in price *in one month* would send chills down almost any politician's spine.

In separate memoranda Hoover sketched his plans for commodity controls and an ambitious campaign for voluntary food conservation in households and public eating places.[86] Action at once on the latter front was imperative, he argued, in order to persuade Americans to eat more vegetables and spare the staples so much needed in Europe. Such an effort, he thought, would also curtail "national food expenditure" and instill a necessary spirit of wartime self-sacrifice in every home.[87]

Hoover now resorted to a technique that he would employ repeatedly and successfully with Woodrow Wilson. Instead of waiting passively for the President to respond, Hoover ghost-wrote a letter addressed to himself for the harried chief executive to sign. He then sent it on to the White House. As it happened, Wilson needed no coaxing. He signed the proffered letter as written.

In this communication, dated June 12, Wilson gave his Food Administrator "full authority" to implement his "national mobilization of the great voluntary forces of the country" to save food and eliminate waste. "While it would in many ways be desirable to await complete legislation establishing the Food Administration," the President acknowledged, "it appears to me that so far as voluntary effort can be assembled, we should not wait any longer, and therefore I would be very glad if you would proceed in these directions at once."[88]

Apparently anxious to lay the groundwork for this coup de main with Congressional leaders, Wilson did not release his letter immediately.[89] Meanwhile, in Washington and across the country, the battle lines over food legislation were tightening. On June 14, haunted by fear that outright hunger would soon afflict many families suffering from high food prices, organized labor launched a national campaign for passage of the Lever bill by July 1.[90] Across the political barricades the *Commercial and Financial Chronicle* reacted in horror to the amplitude of the Lever proposal. "The President is not commanded to do anything, but is empowered to do nearly everything," the *Chronicle* observed. "He is to decide when the emergency requires action, and also what is 'reasonable' in methods, practices or rates." In the opinion of the *Chronicle* the Lever bill envisaged nothing less than "an unlimited and un-American dictatorship."[91]

The conservative business journal's rhetoric was pallid compared to that already emanating from Capitol Hill. Rising in the Senate chamber on June 14, James C. Reed of Missouri unleashed a vehement attack on the revised Lever bill. He found it reeking with grants of "despotic and unconstitutional powers"—powers that no man, not even Hoover, should be permitted to exercise in a republic. Section 3, for instance, would establish "a governmental control of necessaries," including food—a sweeping power that in Reed's opinion would include "the right to say what the people shall eat and how much they shall eat."

> That, sir, is the power of life and death. That power of life and death it is proposed to confer upon the nameless agents whom the President may hereafter select. I repeat, the power to regulate the consumption of food and fuel is the power of life and death. The emissaries and agents of the food dictator can enter every home in this land, tell the housewife how much bread she may set before her children, the quality of flour she shall use; they can tell the head of the family how much coal he shall consume and the kind of coal he shall use; they can, under these powers, dictate to the American people what they shall eat, what they shall wear, how they shall manufacture it, how they shall produce it, how they shall ship it, and whether they shall have it at all or not.
>
> The power demanded is greater than has ever been exercised by any king or potentate of earth; it is broader than that which is exercised by the Kaiser of the Germans. It is a power such as no Caesar ever employed over a conquered province in the bloodiest days of Rome's bloody despotism.

Nor was this all. Look at section 5, Reed said. It would empower the President to license and regulate all businesses in the country dealing in "necessaries" and would forbid any businesses covered by a presidential decree to operate without obtaining a license. "In a word," said Reed, "and put into plain, brutal English, the right of the American citizen to engage in his ordinary occupation, to buy and sell, to trade and to traffic, to ship abroad or purchase from abroad, is made dependent upon the will of some one man."

> . . . George III never dared assert or ask for rights such as are here demanded. When did George III of England say that no man should do business without his license, making it broad, and applying it to everybody? . . .
>
> Everybody is going to be required to keep his books now according to Hoover or somebody else; and then everybody is going to swear to them in the manner and form set forth by Hoover or somebody else; and in this land of the free and home of the brave, where law doth rule and Liberty holds aloft her bright and glorious countenance, we will all form in procession and march forward to make our sworn accounts of our businesses as licensees graciously permitted by Hoover or somebody else to live!

Reed insisted that he was casting no aspersions on Hoover's intelligence or integrity. Nevertheless, Hoover—"a man of whom this country knows but little"—had voluntarily "sought his fortune in other lands," had lived abroad for "a number of years," and had "practically made his home in foreign countries." For these reasons, said Reed, Hoover was less qualified "to deal with questions affecting the American people" than someone who had been living in the United States.

For three electric hours Reed held the floor. The next day his furious assault was front-page news in the nation's press.[92]

The acerbic orator from Missouri was not alone. From Democrats and Republicans alike came expressions of concern at the Lever bill's breadth and at its vesting in the President of what Senator Henry Cabot Lodge called "despotic power."[93]

The rising political storm seemed only to deepen the President's ire. On June 15 he sternly warned the Senate's majority leader that if Congress did not stop dawdling on the Lever bill and other vital war legislation he, Woodrow Wilson, would "take the fight in his own hands."[94] The chief executive also let it be known that if the food control measure were to accomplish any good this season, it must be on the books before harvesting began in July.[95]

The President's intervention had its desired effect. The very next day the Senate committee on agriculture reported the embattled Lever bill to the floor.[96] Three days earlier, the House of Representatives had agreed to take up the same measure the following week.[97] By Saturday, June 16, Congressional consideration of the food regulatory proposal was imminent.

Wilson now selected this moment to release the ghost-written letter of June 12 instructing Hoover to initiate his campaign of voluntary food conservation. The presidential directive appeared in the newspapers on Sunday, June 17, twenty-four hours before the House of Representatives was scheduled to begin debate on the Lever bill.[98] This timing was no coincidence. According to the *New York Times*, the President wanted Hoover to be "in full swing" even while the Congressional debate was taking place. In this way, the *Times* reported, Hoover's work could serve as an "object lesson" to the Congress and the country and prove the need for "immediate action." It would also demonstrate Wilson's determination "not to be balked" in a policy he deemed crucial to the national welfare.[99]

The President's partial launching of the Food Administration, even before it was legally authorized or funded, strongly resembled a favorite Hooverian gambit: the fait accompli. But if he and Hoover thought that they could thereby outflank Congress, they had underestimated the resistance now erupting on Capitol Hill.

III

SECURE in his backing by the President, Hoover promptly issued an appeal to the women of the United States. "We must enter a period of sacrifice for our country and for our democracy," he declared. "We have the major burden of feeding the whole world." Since "food will decide the war," every American woman could perform "a real national service" by "protecting" the nation's food supply. "Ninety per cent of American food consumption passes through the hands of our women," he said. "In no other field do small things, when multiplied by our 100,000,000 people, count for so much."

Hoover thereupon announced a drive to register "every woman in the country" as a member of the United States Food Administration. Every housewife would be asked to sign a pledge to carry out his directions and advice as much as her circumstances permitted. In return for her promise, she would receive instructions and a "household tag" to be hung in the window. The tag would display the Food Administration's insignia: the shield of the United States surrounded by heads of wheat.

Hoover also announced several "general principles of instruction" for his prospective army of volunteers. We must "save the wheat" by eating at least one wheatless meal a day. We must "save the meat" by buying less of it, serving smaller portions, and allowing no waste. We must "save the fats" by such means as no longer using butter in cooking. We must increase our consumption of vegetables, corn, and other foods in ample supply. We must consume more products of local origin. We must preach "the gospel of the clean plate."[100]

Hoover did not confine himself to this generalized summons to action. On June 18 he authorized the National Association of the Motion Picture Industry and the Associated Motion Picture Advertisers to prepare Food Administration propaganda for use among American women.[101] That same day the Women's Committee of the Council of National Defense ordered each of its state divisions to "Get Behind Hoover."[102] Twenty-four hours later, leaders of the 150 major women's organizations in the country converged on Washington and promised Hoover their support. The women of America, he told them, were just as much a part of the national army as the men fighting at the front.[103] Perhaps to underscore his point, the Food Administration announced that every participating woman would be asked to wear a uniform apron in her kitchen and wear the Food Administration's shield on her sleeve.[104]

Simultaneously Hoover mobilized the clergy. In mid-June he sent out 200,000 letters, one to "every minister of the gospel in the country," asking them to preach on the subject of conservation of food on Sunday, July 1—the date he intended to inaugurate his women's registration drive.[105] Leaving nothing to chance, he prevailed upon the American Telephone and Telegraph Company to have its district managers telephone every pastor in their districts and repeat Hoover's request.[106] Hoover urged the ministers to involve the women of their congregations in the observance of what he hoped would become known as Food Saving Day. "Without food conservation," he wrote, "we cannot win the war." The very outcome of the conflict, he warned, was "in the hands of the women no less than in the hands of the men."[107] Overlooking no constituency, he called upon the nation's most influential Roman Catholic prelate, James Cardinal Gibbons of Baltimore, and persuaded him to promulgate an appeal throughout his diocese for economy in food consumption.[108]

All the while, the Food Administrator kept up a drumfire of exhortation aimed at the custodians of the home front. "The women of America have a unique and wonderful part to play in the work of war," he proclaimed. The task of saving food was "America's first and most important duty in this war."[109] He urged employees of the federal government to sign a food economy pledge, promising among other things to eat more vegetables and less sugar for the rest of the war.[110] He asked the 6,500 restaurants of New York City to organize as the first step in a national mobilization of all food purveyors.[111] He dispatched 21,000 letters to newspaper editors asking them to urge the public to make an individual effort to save food.[112] He even told a group of women's representatives that abolishing cabarets would permit the feeding of millions.[113]

On July 1—"Conservation Sunday"[114]—the Food Administration's canvas of women officially began. For the next two weeks nearly 100,000 Camp Fire Girls and other volunteers under the supervision of the Women's Committee of the Council of National Defense conducted the solicitation from coast to coast.[115] Hoover asked the Boy Scouts of America to assist them.[116] Each enrollee received not only an emblem for window display but a card containing such admonitions as these: use stale bread for cooking and toast; eat less cake and pastry; consume less cream and candy; serve smaller portions; don't eat a fourth meal; don't waste soap.[117]

The Food Administration's use of quasi-military insignia and paraphernalia was no doubt intended to create a sense of meaningful involvement in the war effort among the women who "enlisted." It also served as a subtle reproach upon nonparticipants—a function of which Hoover seemed aware. He told a Congressional committee that a woman receiving a Food Administration "tag" could display it outside her door in order to "free herself from the persistent inquiry which we hope to install through the Boy Scouts and other associations in the country."[118] A few weeks before, Hoover had exhorted the women of New York City to form block committees. Now, through uniformed Scouts and other volunteers, he hoped to bring the power of patriotism to bear upon every household in the land.

For Hoover the drive for conservation transcended the immediate exigencies of the war. The United States "has been given to extravagance," he told a group of state food administrators in July. Thirty percent of its people were the main culprits, with a resultant rise in "class feeling." "If we can persuade the 30 per cent to simple living," he declared, "we shall have accomplished a great objective in the moral consolidation of our people." Furthermore, *after* the war the world would enter "a new economic era," for which the nations of Europe, "disciplined . . . in simple living," would be prepared. It would be "an era of intense competition," and "unless our people have adopted a similar discipline we shall be outrun in this race for economic life."[119] Hoover did not base his public campaign on these considerations, but he clearly perceived the crusade as a valuable piece of social engineering.

First to take the pledge was Mrs. Woodrow Wilson, who promptly hung her red-white-and-blue card on a window in the White House dining room.[120] Another enthusiastic registrant was Eleanor Roosevelt, wife of the Assistant Secretary of the Navy, who reported that each of her ten servants had signed a pledge card and that she conferred with them daily. The Roosevelt home had stopped using bacon and was serving meat just once a day, she said; already these and other economy measures had proven to be "highly profitable." Impressed by her food-saving program, the Food Administration selected it as a model for large households.[121]

In a few quarters Hoover's campaign evoked parody and derision. The wife of an anti-Wilson congressman scoffed at Hoover's tips to housewives for saving food. Do not eat a fourth meal—"as if any American west or south of the afternoon tea belt ever did take a fourth meal!" Hoover, she exclaimed, had come to America "as the conqueror comes. We all stood on tiptoe waiting for Congress to give him authority to announce his system for food conservation. . . . At last Mr. Hoover's sense of duty overcame him. He would not wait for authority; he would divulge his system at once, and lo! the mountain brought forth a mouse."[122]

In the Senate, Reed of Missouri ridiculed Hoover's rules for food economy, to the merriment of fellow senators and the galleries. "Cut the loaf on the table only as required," said the Food Administration's card of instructions. "How," retorted Reed, "have we gotten along all of these years without that knowledge? How does it occur that in the flight of time and the mutation of life the human race has blundered on and on without some Hoover to tell them to cut their bread on the table and only as required?" To the sarcastic senator, these and other admonitions bespoke Hoover's "lack of knowledge of the commonest affairs of American life."[123]

Such dissonant notes, however, were rare. As the women's conservation drive wound down in late July, Hoover had reason to be gratified. More than 2,000,000 housewives had signed pledge cards, a creditable figure in light of the Food Administration's lack of funds and grass-roots organization.[124]

Hoover was delighted by the initial response to his war upon overconsumption. In the four months since America took up arms against Germany (he declared in late July), "the greatest spontaneous volunteer effort ever made in history" had augmented our food production and done much to eliminate waste. All this, he said, had happened "without compulsion of the law, but by spontaneous effort and self-denial of the people." "No autocratic government could accomplish this," Hoover asserted triumphantly. This vast and intricate "organization of Democracy" was a vindication of the American people and their political faith.[125]

Yet all was not well on the Potomac.

3

"From the Soil to the Stomach"

I

ON June 18, 1917 the Congress of the United States took up the food regulatory bill.[1] In the House, Representative Asbury F. Lever appealed for swift action. Yes, he acknowledged, the bill was "unprecedented and remarkable." But America was engaged in an "unprecedented war"—a struggle against "the most powerful autocracy the world ever saw." In this contest organization was "the only weapon with which organization can be overcome." Lever argued that virtually unlimited presidential control of "necessaries" was imperative to stop the "chaos and confusion and waste and lost motion and manipulation and sky-rocketing prices of the past few months." He predicted that his bill would drive the "market manipulator" and "gambler" from the "established agencies of distribution."[2]

In a much-publicized letter the same day to a congressman from Missouri, President Wilson directly entered the fray. The objective of the Lever measure, he claimed, was "not to control the food of the country but to release it from the control of speculators and other persons who will seek to make inordinate profits out of it, and to protect the people against the extortions which would result." Pleading again for passage of the legislation by July 1, the President none too subtly warned its opponents that they might be making themselves responsible for the "oppressive price of food" in the country.[3]

If Hoover and his allies feared unchecked inflation, the bill's critics feared even more the power that it would confer upon the President and his chosen deputy. This proposal "has no parallel in the history of any other country in the world," one representative charged. You "have got to forget that you have a Constitution if you vote for everything that there is in this bill."[4] In the Senate, Thomas P. Gore of Oklahoma declared that if the power that the measure vested in a food controller were ever exercised, it would precipitate an economic crash.[5] So sweeping were the bill's provisions, he said, that "no farmer could mortgage a mule if this universal overseer [Hoover] should forbid it."[6]

Gripping many of the bill's opponents was another worry: that the true target of the legislation was not the iniquitous "speculator" but the American farmer.[7] Representative Gilbert Haugen of Iowa asserted flatly that "the purpose of this bill is to reduce the price of farm products"—above all, wheat and sugar.[8] According to Senator Reed, the bill would effectively "fix one price for all the American farmer produces." How? By granting the U.S. government complete power over farm exports and Allied purchases. "Give me control of the foreign market for wheat," he declared, "and I will fix the price of wheat to every American consumer." Under this bill, he prophesied, one man would acquire "a power that will control the price of everything the farmer has—of his entire surplus—and whoever controls that surplus will control the profits and the destiny of the farmer."[9]

To farm state solons, the Lever bill seemed not only dangerous but discriminatory. Why, Haugen asked, should the farmer be singled out and "made the goat"? "If food control is a good thing for the consumer, why not a shoe control?"[10] In the Senate, Sherman of Illinois wondered: "Why regulate and fix the price of everything the farmer produces and leave him to shift for himself on everything he has to buy?"[11]

As the debate commenced, there was little doubt that the House of Representatives would enact the Lever bill.[12] Prodded by a clamorous phalanx of urban newspapers, middle-class journals of opinion, organized labor, and a general public aroused to what one legislator called "hysteria," most lawmakers in the chamber seemed anxious to do something quickly to arrest the rising cost of living.[13]

In the Senate, however, it was a different story. There, so adamant were the bill's opponents, and so uncertain were many others of its implications, that Hoover himself was asked to testify anew before the committee on agriculture.[14] On June 19, therefore, the Food Administrator appeared again on Capitol Hill. At least twenty-two senators—and perhaps as many as fifty—crowded into the hearing room.[15]

The portrait that Hoover painted that day was grim. Unless America increased its food shipments to the Allies, it would face the armies of Germany alone. Events in Russia provided a case in point. The revolution that had just toppled the Czar had been a "food riot" in which "the violences of starving thousands" had been "seized upon . . . by the radical and pacifist element." If, Hoover warned, Americans "through any failure of ours" should precipitate a similar catastrophe "among our western allies or among our own people," the United States would bear "the responsibility for a failure of civilization and government larger than has ever rested upon a nation."

At home, too, the situation was somber. Thanks to "unchecked suction from the food vacuum of Europe," America was beset with "unprecedented prices" and "rampant" speculation all along the chain of food distribution. Hoover predicted "an entire rearrangement of the wage level" and attendant "social disturbances" unless the high cost of living was ameliorated. He claimed that bread in the United States now cost 30–40 percent more than in England, France, and occupied Belgium—proof, to him, of the desirability of food control. Even more sensationally, he asserted that "some one" was obtaining an excess profit of $5.00 per barrel on every barrel of flour now sold in the United States, at a total cost thus far to consumers of over $250,000,000.

The Food Administrator denied that the Lever bill was aimed at food producers. Rather, it sought to exclude "speculative profits from the handling of our foodstuffs." He also denied that the bill contained any provision for price-fixing. A few weeks earlier, of course, he had advocated just such authority.[16] A fixed price, he had told Lever, was "the only positive, absolute method of eliminating speculation."[17] Now, however, sensitive to the fierce opposition of farmers to restraints upon producer prices, he retreated. He wanted only to "stabilize" prices, he testified. He wanted only to "regulate the profits and speculation out of handling commodities." Like Woodrow Wilson, he insisted that his real target was the middleman.

Hoover asserted that the Lever bill would not create a "food dictatorship." The apparatus that he proposed to build was based, he said, upon "an entirely different conception from that of Europe." In Europe, governments had swallowed up the functions of middlemen and had imposed "iron-clad" rationing. In the United States, by contrast, he proposed to "assemble the voluntary effort of the people" and to regulate (not destroy) "the distributing machinery of the country." The hallmark of his effort would be "cooperation" and voluntarism. Of course, he added, in every population there was "some residue" who would "refuse to cooperate and would thereby nullify every endeavor of the majority." For this reason, he told the senators, he would require "considerable powers for the regulation of trade" in order to compel the recalcitrant minority to collaborate.[18]

Hoover's opening statement may have reassured some of his listeners, but it did not satisfy Senators Gore and Reed. For the next three and a half hours the two men subjected Hoover to a barrage of hostile questioning. Repeatedly the senators zeroed in on the unsettling potentialities of the bill. Repeatedly the Food Administrator disclaimed any intent to administer it in a dictatorial fashion. Thus section 9 would empower the President to force a farmer to sell to him any wheat that the farmer did not require for home consumption. Pressured by his senatorial antagonists, Hoover testified that he would not "attempt to execute that provision." In fact, he volunteered, he would like to exempt farmers entirely from the bill's provisions.[19] Hoover also denied that he would possess any power under the bill to dictate what his fellow citizens could eat at their tables. "We have no desire to ration the American people," he announced, "except so far as they voluntarily fall in with our scheme."[20]

On one point, though, Hoover appeared to give ground. If the government had an agency (such as Hoover proposed) that could buy surplus grain, hold it, and dispose of it at will on the market (or to the Allies), might it not—Reed wondered—be able to prevent the price of grain from falling very low?

> *Mr. Hoover.* Yes.
>
> *Senator Reed.* And the Government could also, by the very same power of selling, I assume, keep the price from going very high, so that the consumer would not be robbed at the other end?
>
> *Mr. Hoover.* That is the idea.
>
> *Senator Reed.* In other words, the exercise of that power amounts probably to the ability to fix prices, does it not, within reasonable limits?
>
> *Mr. Hoover.* Yes; it all depends upon how far one would exercise that. . . .
>
> *Senator Reed.* . . . Haven't you just now admitted that you have in this bill the power to fix maximum prices?
>
> *Mr. Hoover.* Only in those commodities where we buy and sell a sufficient quantity.

Despite Hoover's insistence, then, that he lacked *specific* power to fix prices, it was evident from his testimony that he planned to engage in commercial practices that would substantially do just that.[21]

You "have undertaken to take over the right to fix the price to the producer," Reed charged; "I want the American farmer to know just where he is getting off under this bill." And you, Hoover retorted, ought to add that everyone who considers agricultural production from "a war point of view" realizes that "we must maintain a very high level of prices in this country to induce the production; that the price the farmer receives must be an extraordinary price."[22] In effect, Hoover was promising to use his powers fairly and wisely. Reed was aghast that Hoover would hold such powers at all.

In his colloquy with the senators, Hoover did not disclose that only four days before, with the President's approval, he had asked President Harry A. Garfield of Williams College to chair a committee dealing with "price questions on agricultural products." This committee was to be set up after the Lever bill was passed. Hoover told Garfield that it would have "the most far-reaching responsibility in the whole Food Administration": it would make "the actual determination of prices" that the government would pay farmers for their produce.[23] Technically, this body would not *fix* the price of food commodities. Rather, as a board of experts it would recommend a price that the Food Administration could then implement in its market operations. But the Senate agriculture committee, had it known on June 19 the specifics of Hoover's plan, might well have wondered whether this was not price-fixing in all but name.

The next day the sympathetic *New York Times* reported that Hoover had comported himself with "perfect sang froid" and had "routed his antagonists."[24] In the House of Representatives, meanwhile, debate was approaching a climax. On June 22 the House defeated an attempt to eliminate the Lever bill's licensing section, after Lever announced that both the President and Hoover deemed it "vital."[25] A day later the House approved an amended version of the bill by a vote of 365 to 5.[26]

Not, however, without taking a last-minute lurch that threw the entire course of the legislation into disarray. In 1917 national sentiment against the manufacture and consumption of alcoholic beverages was reaching a fever pitch. Seizing the opportunity provided by the Lever food bill, Prohibition forces in the House carried a sweeping amendment sponsored by Representative Alben Barkley of Kentucky outlawing the manufacture of intoxicating liquors during the war. Passage of the "bone dry" amendment occurred only after a bitter debate that nearly turned violent, and it presaged further rancor and delay in the Senate.[27]

The upper house hardly needed Prohibition to add to the political stew. Day after day a small band of opponents led by Reed was subjecting the Lever bill to scathing analysis. Reed denied that wicked speculators had forced up the price of flour, to the injury of farmers and consumers. On the contrary, he claimed,

> it was only when Mr. Hoover and men of his ilk in the United States began to say that this country was going to starve to death, and it was only when the allies had cornered something like 100,000,000 bushels of wheat on the Chicago market and forced up the price that the price of wheat went kiting and the price of flour followed it.
>
> That is a very different thing from a statement to the effect that the farmer was bilked out of his wheat for a few cents and then that the consumer during the entire year was robbed on $17 flour.[28]

According to Reed, the American consumer had not been swindled out of $250,000,000 (as Hoover alleged) but had enjoyed "flour at reasonable prices until the allies cornered the wheat in the American market."[29]

The senator from Missouri also took aim at the "fairness" issue. If the government is going to control the markets in which the farmer sells, he argued, then it should also control the products that he buys.[30] By late June his fulminations appeared to be succeeding, as a movement arose in the Senate to extend the bill's coverage to commodities other than food.[31]

On June 25 the Senate officially received the version of the Lever bill just adopted by the House. Instead of offering it at once on the Senate floor as a substitute for the unamended version already being debated, Senator George Chamberlain of Oregon, the bill's manager, agreed to send the House version to the Senate agriculture committee for redrafting.[32] Many senators evidently hoped thereby to effect a compromise, particularly on the sticky issue of Prohibition. The Senate now suspended floor debate while its agriculture committee tramped into the briar patch.[33]

The effect of this decision was further confusion and delay. Only a few days before, supporters of the food control bill in the Senate had been confident of its passage within a week. Now, thanks to the victory of "bone dry" Prohibitionists in the House, the Senate faced a bitter battle and the prospect of no final action for at least a fortnight.[34] For Hoover and Woodrow Wilson, who had predicted the direst consequences unless the bill were passed by July 1, it was not an auspicious development.

On June 27 the Senate agriculture committee voted 9–7 for an amendment to the Lever bill that would outlaw the manufacture of all alcoholic beverages except wine for the duration of the war. The stage was now set for a fractious debate and perhaps even a filibuster in the full Senate.[35] But the committee did not stop there. Instead, in an apparent attempt to make the bill obnoxious to everyone (and thus kill it), the committee adopted an amendment extending government control beyond food, feeds, and fuel to include iron, steel, copper, lead, farm implements and machinery, fertilizer, and binding twine. The committee also voted to authorize the government to seize and operate factories, packing houses, oil wells, and mines. As a result of all this, the Lever bill was more radical than ever.

But then—having expanded the scope of the bill to previously unimagined proportions—the committee acted to strangle its most critical clause. Hoover, as Food Administrator, could not hope to regulate businesses effectively unless he could license them and force them out of business (by revoking their license) if they failed to comply with his regulations. The Senate committee on agriculture now voted to restrict the application of the licensing clause to distributors of products delivered *in interstate commerce.*[36]

Late in the afternoon of June 27 this newest version of the Lever bill was reported to the Senate floor.[37] The next day the Senate substituted it for the version it had been discussing.[38]

Hoover was appalled by this unexpected turn of events. He immediately notified President Wilson that some of the Senate committee's amendments would render the bill "nugatory for food administration." Above all, if his agency were confined to regulating interstate commerce, it would be "impossible for us to control any commodity unless it had some time in its career passed a state line." The result would be to make "the whole operation hopeless and worthless to undertake."[39]

This was not the only matter vexing Hoover. For attentive readers of his

Congressional testimony and other public statements, it must have been obvious that he intended to institute a comprehensive control of the nation's wheat. On June 19, for instance, he told the Senate agriculture committee that he proposed to establish a "wheat commission" that by "judicious use" of its purchasing power might be able to "stabilize" the price.[40]

Then, on June 28, after a two-day conference with Hoover and Julius Barnes, President J. P. Griffin of the Chicago Board of Trade announced that the U.S. Food Administration had settled upon a plan for wheat control. "Naturally," he told the press, Hoover and his colleagues were "withholding the announcement" of this until Congress enacted the food control bill. Nor would he, Griffin, divulge the details given to him in confidence. Nevertheless, the trade official went on to reveal the thrust of Hoover's scheme. The Food Administration would "completely dominate distribution of wheat" at home and for export. It would purchase wheat for the U.S. government, the Allies, and the neutrals. It would also control the nation's grain millers.[41]

Griffin's revelation may have been innocent. Or perhaps—since he soon became a severe critic of the Food Administration's grain control—it may have been a deliberate attempt at sabotage. In either case, Hoover was greatly disturbed. Instead of admitting that the leak was in substance true, he immediately issued a press release regretting that Griffin had made a statement about subjects examined in "preliminary conferences." According to Hoover, it was "obvious" that no plan could be "settled" by the Food Administration "at present." Furthermore, "all discussions" thus far had been "entirely tentative" and constantly subject to "radical change," involving measures which "might or might not" be implemented "if and when" Congress took action. As for the "method" of dealing with speculation and other problems, this, said Hoover, could not be determined until Congress established the Food Administration and until every facet of the issue had been analyzed. Such words carried a reassuring sound. Nevertheless, for all his insistence that nothing had been irrevocably decided, he did not deny that Griffin had described his intentions precisely.[42]

Hoover had good reason to worry. The day after Griffin's disclosure, the nation's newspapers carried headlines like "Government to Take Control of Nation's Wheat."[43] It was the kind of publicity that could only cause trouble in the Senate.

Griffin's indiscretion was not the only reason for Hoover to tread warily. Under the terms of the Lever bill, the federal government would be granted $150,000,000 in working capital for the purchase and sale of foodstuffs. But how would the executive branch allocate this money? For reasons of commercial efficiency Hoover wished to set up a government corporation, but he was not certain that the bill, as presently written, would permit it. He therefore asked President Wilson whether he deemed the bill satisfactory on this point or whether Hoover should seek an amendment specifically authorizing the President to create such corporations. The problem with the latter approach, said Hoover, was that it would "inject a new and probably bitter discussion into the bill" (presumably from senators who distrusted corporations and big business).[44]

Hoover's uneasiness was well founded. Government corporations were not only almost without precedent. In every instance where the federal government had created one, the law had expressly authorized it.[45] The present language of the food bill, however, merely permitted the President "to create and employ any agencies" he desired. Could such nonspecific language be stretched to sanction Hoover's plan?

Wilson replied that the present language of the bill would suffice.[46] Taking his cue, the Food Administrator dropped the subject and thus avoided a controversy he did not need. Once again he put his plans as much as possible under a veil.

The issue of alcohol posed another test of his political agility. Whatever Hoover's private opinion of the merits of Prohibition,[47] upon his return to the United States in 1917 he was convinced that drastic restraints upon the manufacture of intoxicants were necessary, as a measure to help win the war.[48] If we were to produce the maximum amount of food for the Allies, he told a Congressional committee in early May, we would need legislation "looking toward the abolition of brewing and distilling."[49] In fact, if brewing were suspended entirely, he confidently predicted that America could save at least 50,000,000 bushels of grain per year.[50] Carefully sidestepping the ethics of temperance, Hoover said that he advocated such constraints solely as a wartime expedient to save food.[51]

As the days passed, Hoover's self-assurance on this subject—or perhaps his willingness to address it—seemed to wane. On May 26 he declared publicly that if he had to consider the question of banning brewing and distilling under the Lever bill, he would ask the President to appoint an impartial committee to determine just how much cereal grain could be saved. After that, said Hoover, the President would have to weigh the benefits against the costs. The President, be it noted—not Hoover. The Food Administrator now contended that what was needed was "facts." He hastened to add that "it would be impossible to collect such fundamental data" until *after* the Lever bill was passed.[52]

Having thus neatly passed the political buck, the Food Administrator clammed up and said no more. For him the Prohibition issue was a diversion from his immediate objective: passage of the bill that would give him power. Meeting with members of the Senate agriculture committee to discuss amendments to the bill on July 1, Hoover was silent when the issue of Prohibition arose. "He is said to feel," the *New York Times* reported the next day, "that war prohibition is solely a question of foodstuff conservation."[53]

Diversion or not, the Prohibition question now roared onto the floor of the Senate. Alarmed by this threat to speedy passage of legislation he deemed "vital" to national defense, President Wilson publicly asked leaders of the "dry" lobby to abandon their attempt to impose complete Prohibition on the nation via the Lever bill.[54] The dry leaders acquiesced but warned that they would attempt to secure their objective by other legislation as soon as possible.[55] Despite (or perhaps because of) this tactical retreat by the "drys," the President felt compelled to endorse a new amendment to the Lever bill that would prohibit the manufacture of distilled spirits (such as whiskey) for the rest of the war.[56]

For the next several days conditions in the Senate were "chaotic."[57] While the faction-ridden agriculture committee attempted to draft new compromise language on liquor,[58] the chamber as a whole inflated the bill to elephantine dimensions. No longer, it seemed, would the measure be concerned solely with food, feed, and fuels. Instead, on July 2, the Senate voted overwhelmingly to impose government control on petroleum, steel, iron, copper, aluminum, cotton, wool, lumber, fertilizer, farm machinery, and several other products as well.[59] You are "destroying this bill," one senator cried; "you are making Congress appear absurd and ridiculous. . . . God have mercy on you if you continue the course of delay that has been followed here during the last two weeks."[60] But the avalanche of amendments continued, apparently abetted by opponents of Prohibition and others hoping to scuttle the measure entirely.[61]

On July 3 a new threat to the bill—and to Hoover—emerged from an unexpected direction. Senator Kenneth McKellar proposed that instead of creating a single food controller the bill should establish a food *board*—appointed by the President, subject to confirmation by the Senate, and paid a government salary. This, said the Tennessee Democrat, was the correct, constitutional way to carry out "the most important law that has ever been enacted in this country." McKellar offered no objection to Hoover personally or to his service on such a board. But the senator criticized a system of administration under which wealthy volunteers would work in government without compensation and simultaneously draw their income from the private sector. This, he claimed, was "an open door to graft." "Let us have paid agents," he said, "and give them salaries worthy of their ability, and have them responsible alone to the Government that pays them." Once more—and from a senator professedly friendly—came a challenge to Hoover's request for unchecked power.[62]

As the Senate plodded on through the quagmire of Prohibition, Hoover grew increasingly restless. On the Fourth of July he conferred with Colonel House at the latter's summer home in Massachusetts. For seven hours the Food Administrator surveyed the international food crisis and poured out his pent-up frustration. Why, he wondered, didn't President Wilson act to resolve the growing mess in Washington? In the past two weeks, Hoover disclosed, he had seen the President but once for a mere twenty minutes.[63]

House and Hoover thereupon crafted a bold proposal to reorganize the nation's war machinery—a proposal that Hoover submitted to the President on July 5. It called for the establishment of separate war agencies or "administrations" for food, raw materials, and munitions, with a "Priority Administration" determining allocation of resources, and with the Federal Trade Commission ascertaining appropriate price and profit levels.[64] Alas for Hoover and House, the President did not heed their advice.

On one matter, though, Hoover did succeed. The Espionage Act, approved on June 15, empowered the President to take control of the nation's exports. Within days Woodrow Wilson announced his intention to do so through a system of licensing.[65] Hoover was pleased; such a mechanism would enable the U.S. government to restrict exports to European neutrals that were in turn trading with the Germans. Hoover, in fact, planned to charge these neutrals an artificially high price for the flour they bought in America and to use the profits to reduce the price paid by Americans.[66]

By early July Hoover had more than regulation in mind. On July 7 he sent the President an anxious letter alleging that European neutrals were draining the country of fodder—and at soaring prices that were forcing American dairymen to slaughter their herds because they could not afford to feed them. The only remedy for these and other grain shortages, said Hoover, was "immediate embargo."[67] That same day, he visited the President and urged immediate action; in this he had the support of the Secretaries of Agriculture and Commerce.[68] The very next day Wilson announced a comprehensive embargo on the export of grains and other goods to a long list of foreign nations, particularly neutral states that had been reshipping American foodstuffs into Germany. Beginning July 15, none of the enumerated commodities could leave the United States except under a license granted by the recently created Exports Council, of which Hoover was a member.[69] A crucial part of Hoover's apparatus of control was finally in place.

Meanwhile, at the other end of Pennsylvania Avenue, the Senate was at last emerging from its morass. On July 7 the upper house of Congress adopted an amendment to the Lever bill forbidding the use of food or feeds in the production of distilled beverages during the war. By avoiding any reference to beer or wine the Senate in effect voted to permit the manufacture of these products to continue. The "bone dry" proposal was defeated.[70]

With the Prohibition issue disposed of for the time being, the food control bill now came under fresh attack. After the Senate voted on July 2 to put cotton on the list of government-controlled "necessaries," the price of cotton suddenly plummeted, shocking southern senators, who threatened to obstruct the bill as it now stood. It also awakened new fears about the possible consequences of the legislation. After all, if the "mere threat" of government control caused such havoc in the market, what might the future bring?[71]

On July 10 Henry Cabot Lodge of Massachusetts articulated this new wave of apprehension. The bill before the Senate, he asserted, was "an attempt to set aside and disregard economic laws." Such meddling always resulted in "disaster." The senior senator from the Bay State was aghast at placing "gigantic powers"

> into the hands of men of whom we know very little, to distribute them among hundreds of agents of whom we know nothing, to give these agents the power under the licensing clause to put out of business any concern, partnership, individual, or corporation which is engaged in foreign or interstate commerce. . . . I say that is a power which should not be intrusted to any human being.

If we are to set the price of wheat and establish minimum prices, said Lodge, we in the Congress—"where the farmers are represented"—should do this price-fixing ourselves. We should "not have it done by a man who is thinking neither of the shareholder nor of the business man nor of the farmer, but simply how he can buy most cheaply for the allies." Instead of giving "blank checks" to Hoover and his "nameless agents," Lodge proposed that Congress and the President jointly establish a commission to administer the law.[72]

Later in the day Reed of Missouri added his own indefatigable voice to the growing clamor for a commission of experts to control food prices. Becoming more vehement and personal in his attacks, Reed now berated Hoover as "the greatest calamity howler who has appeared upon this earth since Jeremiah went about crying out 'Woe! Woe! Woe!' to all the earth."[73]

While Lodge and Reed engaged in verbal pyrotechnics, a few blocks away Hoover doggedly tried to douse the flames. "It is not the intention of the Food Administration to fix the price of wheat," he announced in a press release, "nor is it expected that it will have any such powers. If the food bill passes Congress, however, we certainly will not stand for speculative buying of wheat." Hoover affirmed that the export price of wheat must be maintained at a figure that would stimulate wheat production as much as possible. His words were meant to assure nervous producers that the current high price of their crop was not about to tumble. It is doubtful, however, that his statement made much difference on Capitol Hill.[74]

In the Senate, in fact, the parliamentary tussle now took another unexpected turn. On July 9, unable to obtain unanimous consent to close debate and bring the measure to a vote, Senator Chamberlain filed a petition to invoke the cloture rule for the first time in the history of the Senate.[75] In the face of a storm of opposition, he withdrew his motion the next day. After further negotiations Chamberlain obtained his colleagues' assent to a final vote on the measure.[76] But the price he paid was high. The vote would not take place for eleven days. Even worse, he and other Democratic leaders had to agree to an opposition demand that the entire measure first be rewritten and stripped of some of its most drastic provisions.[77]

At this point Senator Gore—irreconcilable enemy of the Lever bill—came forth with a complete substitute of his own. It would confine the scope of the legislation to food, feed, and fuels. But instead of a single food controller, there would be a paid food administration board, consisting of the Secretary of Agriculture and two persons nominated by the President and confirmed by the Senate. Furthermore, the bill would guarantee farmers a minimum price for their wheat—specifically, $1.50 per bushel—lest Hoover, left to his own discretion, set the price too low.[78] On July 11 the committee on agriculture decided almost unanimously to support Gore's alternative after voting to expand the food board to five.[79] It was the most dangerous menace yet to Herbert Hoover.

The embattled Food Administrator was incensed by the Gore substitute. It "extracts absolutely the whole of the teeth from the bill," he informed the President. It "renders it impossible for us to control speculation," impossible "to control wasteful practices in distribution and manufacture," and "impossible to control extortion in profits and charges." It would "destroy the whole question of the imaginative side of leadership of yourself and sense of volunteer service in the interest of the nation"—a sense "absolutely critical in order to amass the devotion of the people."

> I simply cannot hope to secure this sort of administration if it is to be controlled by a meticulous "board" with its impossible mixture of irresponsible executive and advisory functions. Moreover, at your wish the Food Administration was launched upon this basis and it becomes merely a drive at yourself personally and to a lesser degree at me.[80]

Hoover's indignation was undoubtedly genuine. It was also expressed in language likely to arouse the President's fighting instincts. As it happened, Woodrow Wilson needed little persuasion. After studying the text of the Gore substitute, the President emphatically informed the Senate majority leader that "it would be fatal to pass it." In "practically every important particular," Wilson charged, it "emasculates the original measure." The occupant of the White House was in no mood for compromise. The country "expected" and even "demanded" food control legislation along the lines of the unamended Lever bill, he declared. He wanted it enacted without further delay.[81]

If Woodrow Wilson was increasingly impatient at the senatorial impasse, his Food Administrator seemed almost beside himself. On July 10, just hours after the Senate agreed on its timetable for the final vote, Hoover, with Wilson's approval, published a letter to the President about the wheat situation. According to Hoover, both consumers and producers were imperiled as never before. On one front the price margin between producer and consumer had increased to an "unbearable" degree, and it was "vitally necessary" to take steps that would "absolutely eliminate all possibility of speculation, cure extortionate profits, and effect proper distribution and restriction of exports to a point within our protection." This could not be done by punishment of "evil-doers," said Hoover, but only by "proper and anticipatory organization and regulation all along the distribution chain." On another front—thanks to Allied consolidation of buying and a shortage of oceanic shipping—American wheat farmers faced an impending glut at interior terminals and a consequent slump in wheat prices unless the U.S. government took "strong and efficient action." Without such intervention, the Allies would dictate the American export price, and "speculators" would control the glut.

Three things, said Hoover, were clear: American wheat farmers needed price protection; "large masses of people" in urban centers were now suffering undernourishment because of "the exorbitant cost of living"; and speculators ("legitimate or vicious") had grabbed "a large part of the money now being paid by the consumer." Having exposed the dangerous flaws in the status quo, Hoover declared himself "practically helpless to safeguard either the farmer or the consumer until the pending legislation is passed."[82]

In one respect Hoover's rationale for governmental intervention was a curious one. To consumers he raised the fear that, if nothing were done, "speculation" would continue unchecked and prices would rise. To farmers he raised the fear that, if nothing were done, *their* prices would fall. He appeared to see no inconsistency. Apparently he had come to believe that producer prices could plummet and consumer prices soar, *simultaneously*, because of the demands of everyone in between for protective profit margins.

In another respect also Hoover's letter was curious. On June 12, in a private memorandum to President Wilson, he had warned that the price of wheat could conceivably jump to $3.00 a bushel in a month.[83] Now, one month later, he predicted that the price of wheat was about to collapse—unless, of course, the food bill were enacted. Were Hoover's fears that the Allies would sharply depress wheat prices really justified? After all, President Wilson had just announced a system of export controls, applicable to the Allies and neutrals alike. From now on not a grain of wheat could be shipped abroad unless the U.S. government first granted a license, a mechanism that could surely be used to regulate price.[84] Moreover, the Allies were increasingly dependent on U.S. government loans for money with which to purchase American goods. Under the circumstances they were hardly in a position to turn the screws on American farmers.

Was Hoover as fearful of the Allied buying cartel as he publicly professed to be? Or was he deliberately conjuring up a bogey to scare farmers (and balky U.S. senators) into the Food Administration's embrace? And was he as frightened as he frequently claimed to be about the imminence of runaway inflation? Or was this, too, a useful apparition?

Whatever Hoover's inner convictions, his letter to the President—which leading newspapers printed on their front pages—was obviously aimed squarely at the Senate. Its timing and manner of release left no doubt.[85] Frantic to break the Congressional logjam, Hoover now intensified his lobbying efforts. Day after day the Food Administration's department of public information, managed by his deputy Ben S. Allen, churned out press releases asserting the need for, and public support for, the food control bill.[86] Allen himself was working up to eighteen hours a day in the campaign.[87] On July 13 Hoover conferred with Senator Chamberlain and pleaded for speedy authorization to take control of the nation's food. The Gore substitute, Hoover declared, was unsatisfactory. The next day, accounts of his meeting appeared in the press.[88]

All this was characteristic of a man who had long ago learned how to generate and marshal publicity. Repeatedly, during his Belgian relief years, Hoover had mobilized public opinion to put pressure on European governments. Now he was employing similar techniques against his own.

Privately he was pessimistic and disgusted. "We are having a terrible time here," he wrote a Belgian relief colleague on July 11, "and I am becoming discouraged as to getting enough legislation to make it worth while to go on with the Food Administration. . . . We have been working night and day . . . and it does not seem to have amounted to much."[89] At one point he even told an associate that he would give up the whole business.[90] But he could, perhaps, take wry comfort from the advice that his friend Ambassador Walter Hines Page gave him about Congress: "The only way to manage that beast is, after cajoling and explaining, to go ahead and to show you care not a tinker's dam for it. Then it acts."[91]

Hoover was also acutely embarrassed by the endless delay. Time and again in late June and early July the press had predicted imminent passage of the Lever bill. Confident that the measure would be adopted by July 11, Hoover invited to Washington more than a dozen men whom he intended to appoint as food administrators of their respective states. All had been cleared by the White House. On July 10 his designees convened in the nation's capital, only to find the food bill stalled and Hoover without authority to appoint them. After two anticlimactic days of conferences they departed, still in limbo.[92]

By now some of Hoover's associates were convinced that more than constitutional scruples about the Lever bill were holding up its passage. According to one assistant, "big speculators" were "fighting the bill here for all they are worth."[93] According to another, farmers and commission merchants were increasingly antagonistic to the legislation, and the U.S. Department of Agriculture was egging them on.[94] The fact that the Food Administration was steadily taking shape as the politicians fussed was also unsettling. One Hoover lieutenant observed that Congress was "surprised at the idea of an organization going ahead and doing such things without any legal sanction. . . ."[95]

Hoover's political inexperience did not help. At the beginning of July he brought to Washington John Francis Neylan, a prominent California Democrat. To Neylan's practiced eye, Hoover was "about as far away from the mechanics of American political life as the Gaekwar of Baroda"—a fact that had led him to commit some nearly fatal blunders. In selecting his prospective state food administrators, for instance, he had innocently sought the advice of state governors but had neglected to consult each state's senators and representatives in Washington. This astonishing oversight at once aroused suspicion on Capitol Hill that Hoover was aligning himself with gubernatorial political machines. To compound the error, when a certain member of Congress sent Hoover a letter suggesting a constituent for a job in the Food Administration, Hoover or one of his colleagues mailed him a brusque rebuff, which quickly circulated to Hoover's detriment in Congress.[96]

These and other incidents helped to feed an undercurrent of doubt in the Senate about this newest political meteor streaking across the sky. Who was Hoover, anyway? What did he want? Hoover, of course, disclaimed political ambition. In an autobiographical statement released to the press on July 2, he even asserted about himself, quite inaccurately: "Never sought public office in any shape or form."[97] John Francis Neylan was not so sure. Observing the Food Administration's personnel in mid-July, the California lawyer concluded that Hoover was surrounded by men whose "dominating thought" was to make their leader President of the United States. In Neylan's judgment, Hoover himself was concentrating at present on the job at hand—"a Herculean task which he is tackling for the love of the game"—"but of course he knows if he wins it will make him the great American figure."[98] Whether or not Neylan was correct, his perception was certainly not unique. Mistrust of Hoover's tactics and personal agenda undoubtedly increased the desire of some senators to put a brake on this unorthodox man in a hurry.

Senator James C. Reed—fast emerging as Hoover's nemesis—was determined to do more. On the afternoon of July 16 he launched his most vitriolic assault yet in the Senate chamber. Hoover "actively seeks" to be Food Administrator, the Missouri Democrat charged.

> He actively solicits the creation of the position. His efforts to influence congressional action have been bold, open, and notorious. J. Rufus Wallingford [a fictional financial swindler] never walked into a community a stranger and within 24 hours startled it with elaborate schemes and within the next 24 hours further astonished it by an enormous organized working force as completely as has Mr. Hoover the American people.

Reading aloud Hoover's entry in *Who's Who*, Reed asserted that the Food Administrator had lived outside the United States "practically all the time" for the past twenty years. His business connections had been British; in fact, practically all his engagements as a mining engineer had occurred outside his native land. At one point referring sarcastically to "Sir Herbert Hoover," Reed asked his colleagues whether they were ready to turn "45,000,000

American farmers and all the vast American consuming public over to the control of a gentleman, however good he may be, who has been a nonresident of our country, whose home is in the city of London, and whose interests are in London and China and Australia and Russia, and perhaps elsewhere." All this, in the senator's eyes, rendered Hoover unfit to assume control of America's food supplies.

Reed did not stop here. Before his election to the Senate he had been a formidably successful prosecuting attorney in Kansas City. Now, on the floor of the Senate, he proceeded to prosecute once more. He cited as evidence a recent eulogistic article about Hoover in the *Saturday Evening Post*. The article revealed that in purchasing supplies for the Commission for Relief in Belgium between 1914 and 1917, Hoover and his associates had repeatedly bought, sold, rebought, and resold goods on the open market in such a way as to hammer down prices and buy at the lowest possible figure. To Reed this disclosure was nothing less than an admission that Hoover himself had "engaged in gambling operations and 'rigging' the market to an extent never before known to the American people." Herbert Hoover, he thundered, was "the chief gambler of the food and wheat pits of America."

> I do not claim that he took a single penny of profit to himself, but I deny, sir, that it is right to "rig" the market of 104,000,000 people and put provender at a starvation point in order to make gambling profits to feed the people of some other land.

By manipulating the international market in grain, Reed contended, Hoover himself had been "one of the chief instruments in bringing about that very deplorable condition which is now offered as the excuse for this legislation."[99]

Reed's sensational accusation shocked the Senate. As he spoke, his colleague James C. Phelan telephoned Hoover for a response. Hoover denied that he had speculated for the CRB. He had gone into the market and bought goods, and if he had subsequently sold goods he had done so in order to make better purchases.[100] Hoover made no further public rejoinder. But that night his Belgian relief colleague John Beaver White issued a statement flatly denying that Hoover or the CRB's American purchasing division had speculated in any commodity for the relief. White then quoted Hoover as having said at the founding of the CRB in 1914: "I do not want myself to handle any of these hundreds of millions of dollars, for some day some swine will turn up in this country and say I have stolen it."[101] It did not take much guesswork to name the "swine" White and Hoover were now thinking of.

Reed's immoderate onslaught provoked a new row in the Senate. Phelan of California extolled Hoover as a modest, accomplished, thoroughgoing American, born in Iowa and educated in California: a "pioneer American . . . both in the world development of resources and in the practical expression of humane sentiments." As for the charge of engaging in speculation, Phelan saw no need to apologize for Hoover's attempting "to force down the mounting prices which heartless speculation had sought to impose even upon a charity fund."[102] Henry L. Myers of Montana averred that there was no man in the country who had more experience in food control than Herbert Hoover.[103] John Sharp Williams of Mississippi declared that he himself would like to designate Hoover food controller right in the bill, "especially because of the absolutely uncalled for, unprovoked, and unjustified attacks that have been made upon him."

> If America appoints Hoover, she will appoint a great American for this position, one of the greatest in this country. . . . Mr. Hoover is head and shoulders above the average man. His Americanism cannot be challenged. . . . Mr. Hoover is as honest as God makes men. He has not merited a particle of the abuse which has been showered upon his head merely because he has answered a call to duty by the President of the United States.[104]

Not content with rallying to Hoover's defense, several senators angrily expressed their repugnance at Reed's tactics in language seldom heard on the Senate floor. Henry Hollis of New Hampshire accused Reed of "mercilessly" cross-examining Hoover at the Senate agriculture committee hearing on June 19 as if Hoover "had been up before a police court for stealing chickens in Kansas City." Reed was outraged, but Hollis refused to recant.[105] When Reed introduced an amendment that would disqualify Hoover from serving on the proposed food board because of his long absence abroad, Senator Henry F. Ashurst of Arizona described it as "a dirk in the belt ready to be thrust at Mr. Hoover in some way, any way, to prevent Hoover from being appointed on this board." The senator from Missouri, said Ashurst, "is willing now to transcend the bounds of the Constitution, which he has invoked so many times in this debate, in order to do what? To do a disservice to his country."[106] Reed's amendment was swiftly voted down.[107]

It was apparently at this juncture that a group of young Hoover loyalists in the Food Administration conceived a plot to kidnap Reed and keep him in hiding for the rest of the war. Fortunately for the national equilibrium (and Hoover's career), his secretary, Lewis Strauss, managed to dissuade them.[108]

Hoover, meanwhile, had more than Reed to worry about. On July 17 the *Washington Post* printed a story on its front page:

> Hoover Makes Threat
> to Expose the Foes
> of Food Control Bill
>
> "If I were not convinced I can beat down the price of flour to $9 a barrel and bread to 5 cents a loaf, I'd—

"Nobody knows what I am up against here. Nobody knows the forces I have to fight. I have done everything in my power, still the food bill is held up. If it isn't passed soon I'll go to the country and tell the people the truth. They shall know the men who are holding me back, and when the people know heaven help these men."—Hoover in statement to Miss Helena Todd, who arranged for him to hear a delegation of New York women.[109]

Hoover's reputed threat ignited yet another squall at the Capitol. Senator Chamberlain himself admitted that his initial reaction to the statement had been disgust. Senator Gore pointed out that he and his colleagues had already bound themselves to vote on the food bill in just four days. Any further speeches or debates in the meantime would not delay the decision at all. "Possibly," he added sarcastically, "Mr. Hoover has been too busy revising upward the dining-car menus to have his attention called to this order of the Senate."[110]

Hoover immediately denied that he had uttered the statement, and Miss Todd eventually corroborated him.[111] When Gore tried to revive the Senate's lobby committee in order to investigate Hoover's supposed charges, his resolution for that purpose was blocked.[112] The crisis passed with little further comment.[113]

But if Hoover survived the Todd incident, he could not but view with foreboding other news emanating from the Senate's corridors. At this point no fewer than three competing versions of the food control legislation were before the Senate: (1) the House-passed Lever bill, acceptable to the Wilson administration except for the "bone dry" amendment; (2) the Senate agriculture committee's alternative version, now amended to cover seemingly every commodity but the kitchen sink; and (3) the Gore substitute, upon which Wilson had just pronounced his anathema.[114] For several days a bipartisan committee of senators had been struggling to fashion a compromise, as Democratic leaders had promised to do in return for an end to the de facto filibuster.[115] On July 16 the committee finally reached an agreement, whose terms were reported in the press the next day. The proposed compromise would return the bill's focus to food by eliminating extraneous commodities (like cotton and steel) from the control list. This was the good news for Hoover. The bad news was everything else. The all-important licensing clause would be restricted to businesses engaged in interstate commerce. The measure would fix a minimum price for wheat of $1.75 a bushel. Worst of all for Hoover, the compromise would abolish the office of Food Administrator and create in its place a paid, three-member board of food administration.[116]

For Herbert Hoover, July 17, 1917 must have been a day of agony. The *Washington Post* was claiming that he had threatened to expose the nefarious enemies of the food bill. The press of the country was reporting Senator

Reed's accusation that he was a food gambler. And now a group of senators including Wilsonian stalwarts had just rewritten the food legislation in a way that would deny him the leadership role for which he yearned.

For Hoover's associates, too, the news that day seems to have been unsettling. In the papers of Harry A. Garfield, then assembling a wheat price advisory commission, there survives an unsigned, unsent letter, dated July 17, 1917, addressed to Hoover from his Food Administration staff. The letter asserted that "quite independently and entirely without conference," the staff had arrived at "a unanimity of thought":

> In the event of the passage of the proposed Senate food bill and the creation of a commission to administer the bill, it is our conviction that our usefulness will be at an end and that it would be no longer desirable that we should serve as volunteers in a new food administration.

The staff declared that "the highest development of modern business administration" was that governed by "the delegation of ample administrative authority to one centralized controlling head."

> We have to request, therefore, that the passage of the food bill in commission form be taken as automatically terminating our connection with the Food Administration and that immediately thereafter we may be permitted to return to our several homes.[117]

Attached to this unsent letter was a second unsigned document, evidently a preliminary draft. In this version, the Food Administration staff declared that a commission form of governance "strikes absolutely at the vitals of efficiency in administration" and that "divided headship" was "entirely contrary to the instincts of our people." Success on the food front, it said, could only come under "imaginative leadership of a volunteer leader," not from a "nebular board." The attempt to establish a food commission, the document alleged, arose from a desire in certain quarters to "humiliate" the President and Hoover for having organized "the volunteer sentiment of the country" without waiting for action to control speculation. After reciting these and other arguments, the draft concluded that a commission form of administration was doomed to fail. "Therefore," it announced, "we are in complete agreement that we cannot continue to serve in event of legislation taking that form."[118]

The unsent letter from Hoover's volunteers was a remarkable document, if indeed it was as spontaneous as it purported to be. Even more remarkable was the attached preliminary draft, which contained extensive revisions *in Hoover's own handwriting*. In fact, the vocabulary and the syntax of this attachment compellingly suggest that Herbert Hoover was its author.[119] In all likelihood, the father of the plan to have the Food Administration staff threaten a mass resignation was none other than the Food Administrator himself.

The undelivered letter of July 17 was clearly more than a notice of intent. It was a weapon. If shown to Woodrow Wilson or key senators at a strategic moment, it might yet turn the tide. But what if the gamble should fail and the obnoxious food board should be established anyway? Surely Hoover knew that if his team of volunteers then departed in a bloc, it would throw his food control apparatus into chaos and jeopardize all the preparatory work of the past two months. Perhaps in his heart Hoover was bluffing. Perhaps he planned to reject his staff's "request" for termination of their services if the food commission plan went through. Still, there is no better measure of his desperation that bleak July day than his willingness to risk dismantlement of the U.S. Food Administration unless he alone could lead it.

The letter of July 17 was not sent; instead it was held in reserve.[120] But Hoover was hardly inactive. The next day he complained to the President that the bipartisan Senate committee's handiwork was being misrepresented as a Wilson administration measure. The compromise did *not* conform to the administration's desires, he insisted. It contained "many vicious provisions" and "deficiencies."[121] Wilson hastened to reassure his agitated food controller that while the bill might be unsatisfactory when it passed the Senate, the joint House-Senate conference committee that would then reconcile the different versions would come to the rescue.[122] Wilson's secretary, Joseph Tumulty, also endeavored to cheer Hoover up: "Kipling's lines are a tonic in these days of slander and vituperation. We are all with you heart and soul."[123]

Hoover was grateful for the White House's confidence, as he quickly indicated to Tumulty. He then added:

> If there was ever a time when decent men should hold up the President's hands it is right now. If I had any ambition other than that our country under the great leadership of the President should carry this war with distinction and thereafter for the opportunity to return to my neglected lead mine, I should get more annoyed. On the other hand there is a time when stock needs to be taken by every man in service to determine the moment when he becomes a liability to the President and not an assett. The moment this occurs—and it must occur in war conditions to every man in [an] important administrative post—then he should efface himself. My anxiety therefore is only to determine the moment.[124]

Despite this hint that he might shortly resign, it is highly unlikely that Hoover was contemplating such an act. In the heat of battle he sometimes *talked* about resigning, but he was too combative—and too eager to be in the "big game"—to do anything that might end his public service. More revealing was his cable to W. A. M. Goode that same day. "Any developments in legislation?" Goode had inquired. "Reported here [London] it may be hung up indefinitely and radically altered."[125] Hoover's reply was terse but confident: "You know have never lost a fight yet."[126]

Each day, however, seemed to bring him new embarrassments. On July 20 Senator Reed pounced upon a document that the Food Administration's food conservation section had issued to the newspapers a week before:

> Post-office clerks rubbed their eyes to-day when they found in an incoming mail sack a letter bearing no other address than "Mr. Miracle-Man Hoover, Washington." On a guess as for whom it was intended the letter was carried to Herbert Hoover, United States Food Administrator. The guess proved correct. The writer tells of the pressing need for conservation, and adds "God bless you in your service to our country."

To his fellow senators Reed cited the "Miracle-Man" press release as evidence that Hoover was trying to "glorify himself"—and presumably at government expense besides.[127]

Attempting to control the damage, Hoover at once ordered his food conservation department to submit all future publicity material to his trusted assistant, Edgar Rickard, for "censorship." Hoover also reminded the staff that it was "extremely undesirable to personalize this work into the name Hoover. Every effort must be made to eliminate the use of such terms as 'Hoover's Pledge' and to use 'Food Administration' instead."[128]

Reed's nettlesome outbursts, however, were now a sideshow. As the Senate's deadline for a final vote approached, the bipartisan redrafting committee presented its compromise. On July 19 the Senate overwhelmingly adopted key elements of the committee's plan, including the provision for a three-member board of food administration appointed by the President. When Senator John F. Shafroth of Colorado offered an amendment providing for a single Food Administrator, it was defeated by a vote of 63 to 10. As a result of the Senate's action, President Wilson would be free to appoint Hoover, but only as one commissioner out of three.[129]

Working with unwonted rapidity, the Senate disposed of other issues, in most cases staying close to the committee's desires. But even now the upper house of Congress could not refrain—at least in Hoover's view—from making matters worse. Instead of guaranteeing the price of a bushel of wheat at $1.75—a figure that the committee had chosen, Hoover charged, without any "adequate consideration" of its propriety[130]—the Senate decided to set the minimum higher still, at $2.00 a bushel.[131] Heeding its worried constituents in the wheat belt, the body explicitly rejected a proposal to let the President fix the price. And in the final hours of debate it adopted a controversial rider, known as the Owens-Weeks amendment, which would create a joint Congressional committee to monitor the Wilson administration's expenditures in its conduct of the war.[132]

On July 21, after five weeks of some of the bitterest wrangling in the history of Congress, the Senate adopted its version of the food control bill by a vote of 81 to 6.[133] For Hoover, the bill was laden with obnoxious features. With some justification Senator Gore asserted that most of his substitute bill had been "transferred into the pending bill upon the installment plan."[134]

Yet even now the contest was not over. Before the legislation could become law, the widely divergent Senate and House versions must be reconciled, and each body must then accept the result. The issue must therefore now go to a conference committee, where deadlock and still more delay seemed likely. To complicate things even further, the chairman of the Senate's conferees would be—of all people—Senator Gore.[135]

And so, nearly four months after the United States entered the war, the shape of the nation's food policy remained in doubt. It would be up to the House and Senate negotiators to settle the contours of the bill and the political fate of Herbert Hoover.

II

By the last week in July, the Washington staff of the United States Food Administration had grown to 104 volunteers and 313 paid clerks and other employees of similar rank. The agency was spending $25,000 a week and had exhausted the $80,000 already received from the President's special national security fund.[136] The Food Administrator and his colleagues were preparing to leave their crowded quarters at the Interior Department for a new temporary home in the Hotel Gordon at Sixteenth and I Streets.[137]

Among those making the move was a recent appointee to the Food Administration's legal staff named Robert Taft, son of Woodrow Wilson's predecessor in the White House.[138] Like Lewis Strauss, the youthful Taft became a virtual protégé of the Chief.

As his food control apparatus prepared to spring fully into action, Hoover was enjoying a crescendo of national acclaim. In the *Saturday Evening Post*, his friend Will Irwin eulogized him as "The Autocrat of the Dinner Table."[139] In the New York *Evening Post Magazine*, David Lawrence, a friend of Hoover's press secretary, described the Food Administrator as "a genius in executive organization" and "a commission in himself."[140] In *The Century Magazine* and *World's Work* appeared encomiums by his relief colleagues Vernon Kellogg and Hugh Gibson.[141] The Washington correspondent of an important business journal called him "masterful."[142] Justice Louis D. Brandeis, who had made his acquaintance some months before, told a friend that Hoover "seems to me the biggest figure injected into Washington life by the war. . . . Indeed he is the strongest argument of recent years for the needlessness of law."[143]

It was not his rapidly expanding bureaucracy, however, or the applause (some of it inspired) in the press that mattered most to Hoover now. It was thwarting the odious Senate bill that could shrivel his role in the war effort. Swiftly he marshaled his arguments for the White House. The form of administration provided in the Senate's version was "totally impracticable and inadequate," he wrote the President.[144] It would mean a "three-headed administration"—a guarantee of "friction" and the eventual "total disintegration" of staff morale. Such a format was "a direct violation of our national instinct of organization," as shown by the office of the presidency itself as well as the Cabinet and corporations. The thought of receiving remuneration also offended the Food Administrator. He claimed that he had been able to obtain men "of the first importance" for his agency "upon no other footing" than that they serve without pay. The "very essence of democracy," he asserted, was self-sacrifice in a national emergency. To offer money for such "patriotic service" was an insult. He predicted flatly that "unless the administration can be put in the main upon a volunteer basis, dominated by a spirit of sacrifice and cooperation of all classes, it will fail."[145]

Loftily if implausibly, Hoover declared that he had "no concern for being the head of the Food Administration." He had repeatedly expressed his willingness, he said, to offer his "experience and advice" to whomever the President might select for the job, provided that the agency were set up on a "basis of administrative authority" that permitted success.[146] This self-renunciatory gesture was in all likelihood only that: a gesture, an act of political etiquette. On the same day that he forwarded this letter to the White House, Hoover privately told an official in the State Department that he thought he could get away with administering food control without any legislation at all! This, he said, would be infinitely better than a three-member federal food commission.[147]

Still, Hoover did not mind creating the impression—both in Congress and possibly the White House—that he might yet walk away from his ordeal. Many times, during his direction of the Belgian relief, he had threatened or "offered" to resign in order to get his way. Now, without directly or irrevocably committing himself, he wielded the weapon of his indispensability. On July 26 a member of his staff prepared a memorandum asserting that while Hoover had "no particular concern" about whether or not he would head the Food Administration, nevertheless it was "quite certain that no man with any good red American blood in his veins would accept a membership on a board of three (3) for carrying on this work."[148] This memorandum was probably meant for the press. In any event, two days later the *New York Times* reported a consensus in Washington that if the food board amendment were not quashed in the House-Senate conference committee, Hoover would refuse to serve in the Food Administration.[149]

As it happened, he did not have to worry about the White House. Supportive of Hoover to the hilt, President Wilson told a correspondent that "if I can help it 'there ain't going to be no Food Control *Board*.' . . . It makes the bill practically unworkable."[150] Even more obnoxious to Wilson was the Owen-Weeks amendment. To Wilson, a Congressional committee's supervision of his war expenditures would be an act of usurpation and "daily espionage." It reminded him of a similar committee that bedeviled President Lincoln during the Civil War.[151] In a letter to Representative Lever, Wilson all but promised a veto if the Owen-Weeks rider were retained. It would "render my task of conducting the war practically impossible," he stated, and he "could only interpret" its final adoption "as arising from a lack of confidence in myself."[152]

Even before Wilson's letter to Lever became public on July 24, speculation was afoot in Washington that the President, if necessary, would veto the bill for a second reason: if it mandated a food control board.[153] Hoover, meanwhile, was turning his artillery on still another upsetting feature of the Senate bill: its fixing of a guaranteed price of wheat at $2.00 a bushel. On July 24 and 25 he reported to Representative Lever that this provision was already causing havoc in the wheat belt. Wheat was "ceasing to come into the markets," the mills were "short of supplies," and the price of wheat was soaring. According to Hoover, wheat farmers—confident that they would receive a minimum of $2.00 a bushel—were withholding their crop from the market in the hope that the price would rise to $3.00 by the end of the year.

> The result of the situation will be $3.00 wheat within a month, and if we have $3.00 wheat we will have a further rise of 25% in the price of bread.
>
> I am absolutely satisfied that we cannot maintain public tranquility if we have to face this situation. . . .

Hoover did not object (he said) to $2.00 a bushel as a "fair price" (not a minimum price) for the current (1917) crop, although he wished that an independent commission of experts could determine the precise figure. He did, however, strenuously object to $2.00 as a guaranteed minimum for *next* year's crop. In his judgment, the guaranteed price for the 1918 crop should be only $1.35 to $1.50. He urged that the legislation be rewritten along these lines.[154] In a separate letter to another member of the House he predicted that unless Congress gave him authority soon to "extend the steadying hand to every facility between producer and consumer," the result would be "chaos."[155]

Hoover or chaos. The bill without the Owen-Weeks amendment or no bill at all. The bill without the food board amendment or no Hoover. The battle of Capitol Hill was reaching its climax.

Once again Hoover felt obliged to pursue a strategy of concealment. He informed Ralph Pulitzer of the New York *World* that "the critical period in publicity" would not arrive until the Food Administration had acquired "official powers" and could finally explain its objectives to the nation.

> We have been unable to do this hitherto because of the currents which any statement of that kind would start running in the country and the opposition which they would create from some quarter or other. Obviously, the need of Food Administration in many directions is of a repressive order, and any kind of repression starts opposition here. Therefore, our most critical period will be the seven days following the signing of the Food Administration bill. . . .

He hoped that Pulitzer would cooperate when the time for full disclosure arrived.[156]

But would the Food Administrator get that far? When the House of Representatives received the Senate's version of the food measure on July 24, the Republican minority leader, James Mann, precipitated pandemonium by refusing to grant unanimous consent to send the legislation to conference unless the House agreed to vote separately on whether it wished to accept the Owen-Weeks amendment loathed by Woodrow Wilson.[157] Mann hoped to put the House on record in favor of the amendment and thus of retaining it in conference. Infuriated at this parliamentary maneuver, pro-administration Democrats the next day rammed through a special rule sending the food bill to conference at once, without instructions—in effect giving House negotiators, led by Lever, a free hand. Sobered by a perception of rising public disgust at Congressional bickering, a majority of the House clearly favored the Lever bill, unadorned.[158]

On July 26, amidst a reservoir of rancor that was now poisoning both chambers of Congress, fourteen conferees—seven from each house—began their work.[159] For the next four days they struggled, gradually achieving agreement on every issue but two: Owen-Weeks, and the food board vs. Hoover.[160] By Sunday evening, the twenty-ninth, the conference appeared deadlocked over these points. In desperation the lawmakers turned to Woodrow Wilson for his views.[161]

On Monday morning, July 30, Representative Lever and Senator Chamberlain conferred with the President. The commander in chief was totally uncompromising. Without explicitly threatening a veto, he informed his callers that under no circumstances would he accept Owen-Weeks or a food board.[162]

Lever and Chamberlain raced back to the Capitol. In order to dissolve the impasse, a majority of each negotiating team must agree, and until then a majority of the Senate's conferees had held firm. But now, in the face of Woodrow Wilson's intransigence, at least one senator switched. By a vote of

4–3 the Senate conferees agreed to "recede" from their position and abandon their insistence on a food board. By a margin of one vote Herbert Hoover was saved.[163]

The next day, by the same margin, the Senate conferees abandoned Owen-Weeks, although apparently only after reaching a tacit understanding that the amendment would be considered by the full Senate as a separate resolution later on.[164] The conference committee's handiwork, which now looked far more like the House's version than the Senate's, was returned to each chamber for final action.

In the House, Representative Jeff McLemore of Texas inveighed at Hoover and his "Hooveristas." A man who had not been a resident of the United States for more than twenty years was being granted "autocratic powers greater than those ever exercised by kaiser, emperor, or czar." A "mining expert . . . brought over from England" was going to take control of American farm prices in the interest of "the country where he made his home" and maintained his "business interests."[165] The Texas Democrat's oratory was in vain. The vast majority of his colleagues—whether from conviction, fear of public indignation, or simple weariness with the whole business—were ready to accept the amended food bill and move on. By a vote of 360–0, with McLemore and one other merely voting "present," the House accepted the conference committee's compromise on August 3.[166] Then, almost as an afterthought, the body adopted an amended version of the food survey bill—the *first* food bill—that had been languishing half-forgotten for weeks.[167]

The two measures now moved to the Senate, where Reed and other bitter-enders lay in wait. The Missouri senator was enraged at the House's choosing this moment to act upon and release the food survey bill.

> Why was that bill, that had been driven through under whip and spur, held up in the House? I answer, because a Cabinet officer telephoned to a man on the House committee the instructions to hold it up, and to hold it up because if the food survey bill were passed there would not then be any pressing necessity for passing the food-control bill. . . . And so the food survey bill remained held back, throttled, smothered, sat upon, until this food-dictator bill could be forced through.[168]

Taking this final opportunity to derail the food control bill he so despised, Reed accused Hoover of being a "voluntary expatriate" tainted by his years of residence in Great Britain. He termed Hoover a "promoter," who was now engaged in the "largest promotion scheme" of his life—one that would control American markets for the benefit of the British. He accused the "Hoover organization" of having "seized the reins of power before the powers have been legally created." He predicted that the country was about to be subjected to an "infamous dictatorship" at the hands of a man "who so loves publicity that when he started in the Belgian relief work he employed the English representative of the Associated Press [Ben S. Allen] as his press agent and has him here now in Washington." "How did we get along before Mr. Hoover came?" the former Kansas City prosecutor demanded. "What will we do when he returns to his English home?" Hour after hour, day after day, Reed railed, a desperate lawyer before an increasingly unconvinced jury.[169]

At times the tempers of the senators knew few bounds. Irate at his fellow conferees for capitulating, Gore suggested that they should have tattooed on their heads the word "recede"—"I will not say a sort of mark of Cain." Senator Chamberlain shot back that Gore's forehead and that of some others should be stamped with the word "obstruct." When Gore denied that he had been an obstructionist, Chamberlain retorted that there were two ways to obstruct: by bludgeon and by stiletto.[170]

Hoover, for his part, was disgusted at the "damn lies that have been perpetuated during the last ten days."[171] It was "nauseating," he wrote a friend, "to have personal and irrelevant matters discussed when the whole Country is urgently crying for action."[172] Hoover had made no reply to Reed or other antagonists, he told the President's secretary. Hardly anything they said contained "an element of truth," except for "some foolish stuff sent to the press as a result of a hurried volunteer organization" (the "Miracle-Man" press release) and the "overzealousness" of "some ladies who were anxious to get their stories in the papers" (the Todd affair).[173] While the Senate harangued and debated, Hoover worked out a modus vivendi with the Department of Agriculture demarcating their respective responsibilities under the pending legislation.[174] This, in fact, was a contrast that appealed to Hoover and his admirers: while politicians prated and postured, the determined and masterful Chief got things done.[175]

On August 8, 1917 the "Hundred Days' War" on Capitol Hill came to an end.[176] By a vote of 66 to 7 the Senate accepted the conference committee's version of the food control bill.[177] The chamber then adopted the food survey bill by a voice vote.[178] After political trench warfare of a kind Congress had seldom seen for decades, Woodrow Wilson and his beleaguered appointee had prevailed.

III

ON August 10—Hoover's forty-third birthday—the President signed the food control bill into law.[179] Moments later, by executive order, he formally created the United States Food Administration and appointed Hoover its administrator.[180] Under the terms of the new law, popularly known as the Lever Act, Wilson did not have to submit Hoover's name to the Senate for confirmation.

Hoover immediately issued a press release. The Food Administration, he disclosed, had three goals: (1) to "guide the trade in the fundamental food commodities" in such a way as to "stabilize prices" and "eliminate vicious speculation, extortion, and wasteful practices"; (2) to "guard our exports" in order to "retain sufficient supplies" for ourselves as well as "prevent inflation of prices" in cooperation with the Allies; and (3) to stimulate food conservation in order to increase our exports to the Allies. Hoover stressed that his agency wished to "stabilize" conditions, not "disturb" them, and that he intended to rely on "coordination" with the trades and "constructive regulations," not "punitive measures." He did not think he would need to employ "drastic force" to "maintain economic distribution and sane use of supplies by the great majority of the American people." He had developed, he said, "a deep and abiding faith in the intelligence of the average American business man." Nevertheless, he candidly announced that if anyone sought to "exploit this hour of sacrifice," he, Herbert Hoover, would not hesitate to apply to the utmost the "drastic, coercive" powers that Congress had just granted.[181]

Certainly the Lever Act was a formidable piece of legislation.[182] It outlawed the hoarding or monopolization of food and other specified "necessaries" as well as the willful destruction of these for the purpose of increasing their price. It outlawed "discriminatory," "unfair," "deceptive," and "wasteful" practices in handling "necessaries" as well as "unjust and unreasonable" rates and charges. It authorized the President to compel businesses engaged in the production and distribution of "necessaries" to obtain a license as a condition of doing business. It authorized the President to prescribe regulations for the issuance of these licenses. It empowered him to order licensees to discontinue any commission, profit, or practice that he deemed "unjust, or unreasonable, or discriminatory and unfair, or wasteful." If any person refused to obey the President's orders or tried to operate without a compulsory license, he could be fined or sent to prison for up to two years.

The Lever Act also authorized the President to buy, store, and sell wheat, flour, meal, beans, and potatoes. It gave him the power to seize and operate any factory, packing house, or other plant engaged in the production of "necessaries." It empowered him to regulate commodity exchanges and boards of trade in order to prevent "injurious speculation" and other "evil practices." In pursuance of these and other provisions of the Act, the President was authorized to "create and use any agency or agencies" he wished.

The law was not entirely without limits. In deference to the fears and political clout of the nation's farmers, the Lever Act specifically exempted them from its licensing and hoarding provisions. It also exempted retailers with gross sales of less than $100,000 per year from licensing. In other words, Hoover would have no direct power over farmers and small businesses. It remained to be seen whether these exclusions would effectively constrain him.

Nor was this the only rebuff that he was obliged to accept. At the insistence of the Senate, the Lever Act established a government-guaranteed minimum price of $2.00 per bushel, at the principal interior primary markets, for No. 1 Northern Spring wheat harvested in 1918. Other grades of wheat would be priced in accordance with this norm. Confused by, and distrustful of, the Food Administrator's intentions, the Senate successfully demanded the guaranteed price as protection against Hoover.[183]

In addition, the Act outlawed the wartime manufacture of distilled beverages and authorized the President to restrict or even prohibit outright the production of beer and wines, if he deemed it necessary for national security reasons or to ensure "an adequate and continuous supply of food."[184] The entanglement of Prohibition would not disappear.

And thus came into being a law described at the time as "the most revolutionary measure ever enacted by an American Congress."[185] In the course of nearly two months of debate, it had encountered the bitterest and most protracted resistance of any legislation passed during America's belligerency in World War I.[186] Many factors contributed to the ferocity of the Congressional opposition: hostility to the man in the White House and his seemingly imperious ways; farm state apprehension about wheat prices and the pricing of commodities by bureaucrats; the divisive distraction of Prohibition; the unorthodox expedient of setting up a government agency with presidential discretionary funds before Congress itself had authorized it; fear of the exercise of power by big business volunteers; unfamiliarity with the man President Wilson selected to administer food control; and Hoover's own lack of political finesse and of what Colonel House called "personal charm"[187]—the skills and ingratiating manners likely to pacify professional politicians.

Above all, the sheer audacity of the Lever Act staggered many members of Congress, including some who believed that the war emergency necessitated its adoption. For more than a century the federal government had impinged very little on the daily lives of its citizens. Now, in one unprecedented stroke, it was about to affect the eating and drinking habits of 103,000,000 people. Coming before the Congress on the heels of a stunning new draft law and a presidential demand for press censorship, the Lever measure—so alien to American traditions and peacetime mores—could hardly fail to evoke unease. In effect the United States in the spring and summer of 1917 was attempting to accomplish in one hurtling leap what it had taken another largely libertarian society, Great Britain, three years to do.

For many apprehensive members of Congress and their constituents, the Lever Act was nothing less than the beginning of what one newspaper called a "national socialistic experiment."[188] Not without justification did a leading magazine call it "the longest step toward state socialism ever taken by the national Government."[189] Under the unfamiliar pressures of modern, total warfare, the United States was making at least a temporary transition from a market-based to a centrally managed economy. The Food Administration law was the most spectacular manifestation of this development, and Herbert

Hoover, willy-nilly, became one of its paramount symbols.

For the newly ensconced Wilsonian war manager, it had been a painful initiation. He had returned in May a hero, and for most of his fellow citizens he so remained: Hoover of Belgium, the humanitarian, the "American pioneer." But as a result of the Congressional debate, Senator Reed—now his bitter arch enemy—had defined a negative political image that critics would exploit for many years: Hoover of London, "Sir Herbert," the expatriate who was not truly American; Hoover the seeker of publicity and of power without constraint. The debate in the Senate left a residue of suspicion that would not entirely vanish for a generation.

But that was a worry for another day. In the spring of 1917 Hoover had sought authority to regulate food "from the soil to the stomach."[190] He had gotten nearly all that he desired. Through President Wilson he now possessed vast powers—"the greatest ever held by any man in the history of the world."[191]

Across the water in London, Ambassador Walter Hines Page, who had helped to launch Hoover's relief career in 1914, sent congratulations to the man he thought of as his discovery. "It's an awful job you have," Page wrote, "but you are a man made for awful jobs, so that it's a mere process of nature that you and such a job should come together."[192]

1. *Herbert Hoover in 1917*. Herbert Hoover Presidential Library-Museum.

2. *Representative Asbury F. Lever*. Library of Congress.

3. *Senator James A. Reed*. Library of Congress.

4. *Senator Thomas P. Gore*. Library of Congress

5. *Cartoon in New York* Evening World, *August 11, 1917 (the day after the food bill empowering Hoover became law).* U.S. Food Administration Collection, Hoover Institution Archives.

4

The Visible Hand

I

HOOVER'S formal appointment as U.S. Food Administrator brought no discernible change in his lifestyle. Each weekday morning at 7:00 A.M. his senior colleagues arrived at his temporary home on Sixteenth Street for a conference over breakfast. An hour and a half later they departed together for the Food Administration's offices, there to remain until six o'clock at least. Work without stint was their regimen. Even noon hours were conscripted for the cause. As in his days at the Commission for Relief in Belgium, Hoover converted staff lunches into sessions at which he and his principal aides assailed their problems.

The waning of the afternoon sun brought him no surcease. Evening after evening he dined at home with fellow government officials and discussed their wartime perplexities still further. Usually it was midnight—sometimes even 1:00 A.M.—before Hoover finally took to his bed.[1] Throughout it all, his appetite for work was insatiable. He appeared "tireless," one awed assistant observed.[2] Others told of the day in which the Chief held separate conferences with seventy-four people.[3]

The harried Food Administrator had ample reason for his pace. The inflationary fever of early 1917 was not yet tamed. Of all the commodities whose market value was rocketing upward, wheat and its derivatives flour and bread were the most critical. Although the price of a bushel of wheat had receded from its peak of $3.45 in mid-May, across much of the country it continued to hover around $3.00. Farmers expected it to shoot even higher. For angry, middle-class consumers and the urban poor, it was a frightening prospect.[4]

Although the air had been rife for months with bitter complaints about "vicious" speculation and "food gambling," no angry oratory could negate a fundamental fact: for the second consecutive year the American wheat harvest was less than 640,000,000 bushels, barely enough to cover the nation's needs.[5] Nor, unlike the year before, was there a surplus to fall back on. As of July 1, 1917, at the start of the new harvest season, the carryover from the preceding year's crop was only 48,000,000 bushels, or less than one month's supply.[6] At least on paper, the United States had little wheat to export.

For the hard-pressed western Allies it made no difference. Facing economic strangulation from German submarines, and unable to divert precious shipping to far-off wheat suppliers like Australia, the purchasing agents for England, France, and Italy continued to clamor for wheat and flour from North America. With other critically needed food sources, the essential pattern was the same: the combined domestic and Allied demand was impinging upon a deficient supply.

Ordinarily, when demand for a product exceeds supply, the temporary result is higher prices, which thereupon stimulate increased production and decreased consumption until a new equilibrium is reached. Such is the way free markets work in times of peace. But peace was not at hand in the summer of 1917, and Hoover had long since concluded that he dare not wait for the distorted world market to readjust. The price of such passivity, he feared, could be massive social misery and *dis*equilibrium, leading even to loss of the war.

Time and again, therefore, in his early weeks as Food Administrator, Hoover asserted that the law of supply and demand for vital foods had "broken down" and that corrective governmental intervention was obligatory.[7] Because of the Allied shipping shortage, and the consequent "isolation" of distant wheat-producing nations, "the normal determination of the price of wheat by the ebb and flow of commerce" was "totally destroyed."[8] "The large question of the hour is price fixing," he declared in September. The "suspension" of supply and demand "as an equitable, economic law" was "forcing our hand in every direction."[9]

For Hoover, decisive governmental action was not only an economic necessity but a military one. Food was assuming an ever larger role in the strategy of the belligerents, he declared, so much so that he was now convinced that "food will win this war—starvation or sufficiency will in the end mark the victor." Every government in the conflict was confronted with "reduction of consumption, stimulation of production, control of prices, and readjustment of wages. The winning of the war is largely a problem of who can organize this weapon."[10]

For those who remained skeptical, the Food Administrator invoked the specter of "rising Radicalism" if present economic trends went unchecked. He warned the U.S. Chamber of Commerce that a "looming shadow of this war" was "its drift toward socialism," and that America would surely hit "that rocky coast" unless "our commercial institutions" cooperated in "public service."[11] He told his state food administrators that if speculators in sugar continued to "run loose," its price would double within three months and provoke a "radical" protest leading to probable socialization of the industry.[12] He attributed the March revolution in Russia to a lack of the kind of food regulation that he was now introducing in the United States.[13] As a result, he said, of "speculation, profiteering, and failure in commerce to serve public interest, the condition of the industrial classes [in the Czar's empire] became so intolerable as to steam the hotbed of revolution."[14] To Hoover, the "moderate and equitable measures of control" that he was implementing were "the best and only guarantee" that "the red fire of social rebellion" would find no fuel to feed upon in the United States.[15]

If Hoover's rhetoric at times seemed hyperbolic, it was not without a perturbing foundation. Across the United States, the flames of labor unrest were on the rise. Despite all the pressures for national unity unleashed by the declaration of war, in 1917 the nation experienced 4,450 strikes, a number without precedent in its history.[16] To Hoover the fundamental cause of this eruption was the high and increasing price of the "necessities of life." It was obvious that a "brake" on prices must be applied.[17] For if the government did nothing, wages would rise unequally, and the door would be open to "strikes, disorder, to riots, and defeat of our national efficiency." Under the circumstances, the imposition of "price control" was "the lesser evil."[18]

Hoover did his best to make his medicine palatable. As he had argued to President Wilson and the Congress since spring, so now he reiterated to business leaders whose expertise and cooperation he would need: The Food Administration wished to achieve its objectives through volunteer service, without resorting to autocratic organization of industry along German lines. Autocracy—the mobilization of people "from the top down"—"breeds bureaucracy," said Hoover. It "stifles initiative, thus democracy, at its birth." In marshaling our "national energy" to defeat the Germans, he wished to organize America "from the bottom up."[19]

Nevertheless, the Food Administrator's initial problem was daunting. For the next twelve months, until a new and perhaps more bountiful harvest became available, he must contend with an ineluctable scarcity in the nation's wheat. He must control—or as he preferred to put it, "guide"—the nation's food trades in order "to stabilize prices in the essential staples."[20] And all this in a nation unaccustomed to such guidance.

But how, precisely, did he intend to proceed? As soon as the Lever Act was safely passed, Hoover began to deploy the weapons that until then had lain enshrouded in benevolent vagueness. As he entered his campaign "to provide some substitute for the law of supply and demand,"[21] he was driven both by faith and by fear. Faith, as he told a gathering of state food administrators, that "there is no problem of economic or national character that a body of intelligent and devoted men if they apply themselves, cannot solve."[22] And fear of the social and military consequences of failure. Inflation had put Hoover in power. The conquest of inflation was his first and most importunate priority.

II

WHEAT was to be the centerpiece of Hoover's interventionism—the initial target of his war against rising prices.

Throughout the spring and early summer of 1917, Hoover had not been alone in perceiving a need to regulate wheat and flour. Week after week, from the commercial centers of America, worried delegations of grain dealers, flour millers, and other wheat-related interest groups descended on his Washington office with pleas for draconian government action, including price-fixing. One result of these contacts was an early decision by Hoover to create a governmental "grain executive."[23] Another was his appointment in June of an unofficial committee of grain millers known as the United States Milling Committee, which set to work to develop a stabilization policy for the flour milling trade.[24]

Despite these steps and preparations, conditions in the milling industry rapidly worsened. By early July, uncertainty about the government's impending food control, and plummeting wheat deliveries from farmers, had caused flour mills across the country to cut production. Fearful of a total shutdown followed by a national shortage of flour, Hoover authorized his Milling Committee to implement an emergency plan under which the five thousand flour mills of the country would apportion business among themselves and limit their profits. This desperate scheme of self-regulation almost certainly violated the Sherman Anti-Trust Act. Hoover, who had no authority to sanction such a thing, was uneasy. Nevertheless, his acquiescence bought time; the prospect of stability allayed the millers' fears. Although flour production in July and August dropped to less than half of normal, the shaken industry managed to avert complete collapse.[25]

By midsummer, Hoover's consultation with the flour and grain interests had yielded a plan of "efficient Government action" to supplant the "broken-down," "price-making machinery" of the free market.[26] When the Lever Act took effect on August 10, he was ready to take the public into his confidence.

Two days later the Food Administrator officially announced to the nation an elaborate program for controlling wheat and flour. In order to "eliminate speculation," all wheat elevators and flour mills with a daily capacity of more than one hundred barrels would have to obtain a license. In order to keep it, each elevator would be obliged to make only "reasonable and necessary charges" and to store no wheat for more than thirty days without government permission. In this way Hoover and his colleagues could affect the flow of wheat to market and prevent hoarding for speculative purposes. The Food Administrator simultaneously asked the country's grain exchanges to suspend all trading in wheat futures. He wanted no repetition of the panicky bidding wars of the previous May.

Hoover warned that he would prosecute "with vigor" anyone who held wheat or flour contracts in excess of the quantities needed "for the ordinary course of their business." He declared that his organization would establish government "agencies" for the purchase of wheat at all major terminals and would resell this wheat to foreign buyers and domestic grain millers. In effect the United States government was about to become a gigantic grain buyer and seller, injecting itself into the distribution chain between producer and consumer. Indeed, Hoover announced that his administration was "prepared to take the whole [wheat] harvest if necessary in order to maintain a fair price."

By what criteria would this new and mighty customer be guided in its forthcoming wheat purchases and sales? Hoover made it plain that he had no intention of submitting to the vicissitudes of the free market. Instead, he disclosed on August 12 that his agency would pay a single, undeviating "fair price" for the entire 1917 harvest year—in other words, until the 1918 crop became available. To determine what this "fair price" would be, he now revealed that President Wilson had approved creation of a committee chaired by Harry Garfield, son of the nation's twentieth President. This body would be charged with ascertaining a price that would simultaneously provide a "fair return" to the farmer and "a proper reduction of the cost of flour to the consumer." By all these measures, Hoover declared confidently, he expected to "stabilize" the price of wheat throughout the coming year—and "stabilize" the price of flour and bread as well.[27]

The Food Administrator now moved swiftly to implement his policies. On August 14 President Wilson formally authorized him to establish his long-planned "Grain Executive," to be known as the Food Administration Grain Corporation.[28] It was the first government-owned corporation ever created by executive order.[29] With a capital of $50,000,000 taken from the Lever Act's appropriation of $150,000,000, the Grain Corporation intended to buy, sell, and store wheat and flour on a massive scale, starting on September 1.[30] Hoover himself became the corporation's chairman and Julius H. Barnes its president.[31] The next day the Food Administration announced the composition of the committee to determine the "fair basic price" for government purchases of wheat; each member had been selected by Hoover and Garfield and approved by President Wilson.[32] Meanwhile, from the Middle West came word that in obedience to Hoover's wishes the Chicago Board of Trade had decided to halt all trading in wheat futures after August 25.[33] The Food Administrator was off to a flying start.

Within days, however, signs of trouble appeared. The Lever Act, under which Hoover now operated, explicitly guaranteed the wheat farmers of America a minimum price (based upon $2.00 per bushel for the best grade) for all wheat grown in 1918. About the *current* crop, however—that is, the 1917 harvest now at hand—the law was completely silent.[34]

Behind this strange lacuna lay the long summer's political struggle and—for the farmers and their Congressional allies—a fateful miscalculation. Upon returning from Europe in the spring, Hoover (as we have seen) initially favored setting a fixed price for certain key commodities, only to retreat in the face of hostility on Capitol Hill. By June 19 he was publicly asserting that the Lever bill contained no provision for price-fixing whatsoever.[35] Such denials failed to convince farm state senators, who suspected that if Hoover were given unlimited discretion in this matter he would fix the price of wheat at $1.50 per bushel, or less.[36] While Hoover carefully avoided being pinned down to a precise figure, some of his early statements appeared to imply that he considered $1.50 a reasonable price.[37] Although Hoover by late July was prepared to accept $2.00 a bushel as a "fair price" for the crop now being harvested, he did not approve $2.00 if it were a *minimum* price. Nor did he think that anything like $2.00 was needed for profitable wheat growing next year.[38] It was one more signal that in his judgment the price of wheat was too high.

The growers of wheat and their allies disagreed. Anxious to protect wheat producers from Hoover's "steadying hand," the Senate on July 21 voted to place a minimum price of $2.00 per bushel on *all* wheat, present and future.[39] Hoover, aghast, lobbied furiously for a revision.[40] In the end the Lever Act retained the two-dollar-per-bushel minimum guarantee for the wheat crop of 1918. About the 1917 harvest it said nothing.[41]

The farmers' advocates in the Senate appeared satisfied by this compromise. Not only had they forced Hoover to accept a higher minimum guarantee than he had wanted for *next* year's wheat production; they also evidently believed that until then the price of wheat would be unregulated. For the next twelve months, in other words, wheat farmers would be free to receive whatever price the market would bear.[42]

Fighting for passage of the Lever bill, Hoover seemed to encourage this misperception. When a rumor swept the wheat belt in July that his Food Administration would soon fix an arbitrary price of less than $2.00 a bushel on the 1917 crop, Hoover promptly and emphatically denied it. The Food Administration did not intend to fix the price of wheat, he asserted, nor did it expect to have any such power.[43] Neither then nor at any time before the passage of the Lever Act did he publicly disclose that he was already assembling his "fair price" committee.

It is no wonder, then, that Hoover's announcement of August 12 surprised so many. At first glance his press release appeared to contain nothing controversial. Since the government of the United States was about to become the nation's principal grain buyer and seller, it would obviously soon be in a position to influence the market price. Under these circumstances Hoover proposed to set this price equitably by creating a representative commission of producers and consumers. What could be fairer and more sensible than that?

But to those who read his press release with care, it was evident that Hoover was planning much more. If the wary senators from the farm states thought that they had effectively shackled his power over wheat prices, they had failed to reckon with his boldness and ingenuity. On August 12 the Food Administration announced that as soon as the "fair price" for 1917 wheat was determined, the Administration would "use every authority" under the Lever Act, as well as "the control of exports," to "effect the universality of this fair basis throughout the whole of the 1917 harvest year without change or fluctuation." It planned, that is, not only to establish the price that the government would pay for wheat but, if possible, to make this the price that *everyone* would pay.[44]

Nothing in the Lever Act authorized the President of the United States or his agents to fix the price of wheat sold in private transactions, as Julius Barnes, for one, later admitted.[45] Nevertheless, Hoover and Barnes had concluded that stability in the nation's wheat market required no less. The government not only had to "establish a fair buying basis" for its own purchases but also had to "induce other buyers to pay the same price."[46] Thus, although Hoover's Food Administration lacked formal price-fixing authority, it now embarked upon a policy that approximated price-fixing in all but name.

This was not the only feature of the August 12 press release that must have startled attentive readers on the farm. Largely in response to agrarian fears of the unprecedented regulatory powers contained in the Lever bill, the final Act exempted the nation's farmers from key provisions, including licensing.[47] Nevertheless, the Food Administration proceeded to warn wheat farmers that they would find no advantage in withholding their grain from the market "in anticipation of further advance." If they did, it said, they would only incur additional costs of storage and interest.[48]

Even more revealing of the agency's consumerist orientation was the August 12 press release's final sentence, which Hoover himself probably composed: "It must be evident to all thinking persons that unless the price of wheat, flour and bread can be materially reduced, we cannot expect to maintain the present wage scale of the country and that we must in this social readjustment, lose efficiency at a time when we can afford no such sacrifice."[49] The allusion to reducing the price of flour and bread was not new; Hoover had been promising such relief for some time. What was new was his unequivocal declaration that the price of *wheat* must come down. For Hoover, the maintenance of urban and industrial tranquility required that farmers sacrifice the prospect of windfall profits—something he had not hitherto dared publicly to say.

Aware of the unpalatability of his message, Hoover at once tried to sweeten the pill by denying that it was a pill at all. Instead, in his very same announcement on August 12, the Food Administrator asserted that he was intervening in the wheat market, not to prevent or roll back high prices, but to protect wheat and flour producers from *low* prices if (for example) the war should end suddenly and the bottled-up wheat in the southern hemisphere should flood the markets of Europe. As in his letter of July 10 to President Wilson,[50] so now on August 12 and for years to come, Hoover contended that his wheat control policy was designed to save farmers from a disastrous *slump* in their prices at the hands of the Allies' buying cartel. If the export price of American wheat and flour is not controlled, he warned, it "will be subject to almost a single will" of a foreign purchasing agency.[51]

In raising the possibility of the Allies' driving the price of wheat to unwelcome depths, Hoover did not mention that by the summer of 1917 the western Allies were heavily in debt to the United States and reliant on American loans for the purchase of their food.[52] It was a condition of weakness that Hoover himself shortly exploited. And as he soon discovered, his country's farmers were not about to accept his protestations of solicitude.

Hoover's pronouncement of August 12 did not expressly contradict his reassuring statement to the country's wheat farmers on July 9. What he had said then was still technically true: the Food Administration did not intend to fix the price of wheat. It intended to "stabilize" the price, at a level decreed not by itself but by the President after hearing from Garfield's fair price committee. Still, such literalism could not conceal the reversal in public posture embodied in the Food Administrator's announcement of August 12. It was only a matter of time before wheat farmers and their spokesmen caught on.

Less than twenty-four hours later the first premonitory squall hit Capitol Hill. Rising to address the Senate, James A. Reed launched a bitter blast at Hoover. The Food Administrator's "decree" of the day before, Reed charged, marked the first time in history that a "single man" had "undertaken to control the markets of a free people." By placing the "destiny and fortunes" of 45,000,000 American farmers and their families in the hands of one individual, Congress had "committed a crime against liberty." Accusing Hoover of creating and abetting the very disruptions in "market machinery" that he now proposed to repair, Reed relentlessly analyzed the proffered remedies:

> . . . if Mr. Hoover can license every mill in the country and can control the foreign market he can easily choke the farmers' elevators into submission, because he will control the only market its owners have for their

> wheat. The plain truth must be faced that Mr. Hoover is absolute and sole dictator over the farmers, so far as his wheat is concerned.

The American consumer was also "at Mr. Hoover's mercy," Reed cried. "The only wheat he can get he must get from Mr. Hoover and upon Mr. Hoover's terms." If Hoover saw fit, he could compel the entire American population to eat substitutes for wheat and could compel licensed millers to "make nothing but adulterated flour."[53]

Reed did not content himself with a single sortie. In the following days he distributed his printed remarks to the agricultural press of the country, along with a letter warning that the American farmer was in Hoover's clutches. The Missouri Democrat asked all farm newspapers to publicize this threat to agrarian interests.[54]

To an outraged Hoover, Reed's appeal bordered on sedition. The Missourian's letter was nothing less than "an attempt to create opposition to war measures necessary to the defense of the country," he fumed, and he requested his legal counsel to "see if it cannot be brought to book."[55] Nor was Reed the sole offender. At least two members of North Dakota's Congressional delegation, Hoover discovered, were encouraging their state's farmers to withhold wheat from the market. His anger mingling with foreboding, Hoover informed President Wilson that if Reed and the North Dakotans succeeded in inciting "the agricultural sections of the country against our efforts to secure an equitable position between the producer and the consumer," the "whole question of food administration" would "absolutely break down." And if that happened, he predicted, the "whole problem" of supplying food to the Allies and protecting the American people during the coming winter would be imperiled.[56]

The President immediately tried to soothe Hoover's anxiety. Reed's letter was "perfectly outrageous," Wilson admitted, but the senator had so "tarred" himself as to have "negligible" political influence.[57] Thus mollified, Hoover evidently abandoned his intention to retaliate.

In any case, he had far more than Reed's slings and arrows to think about. On August 17 the Food Administration's fair price committee convened in Harry Garfield's office.[58] Hoover had done his best to assemble a balanced and (he hoped) responsible body. Of the eleven committee members who finally served,[59] four were leaders of farm organizations and two were presidents of agricultural colleges in the wheat belt. Hence Hoover could claim—and later did—that the agrarian interest was in the majority. But the committee also contained two representatives of organized labor, one self-identified capitalist, and two presumably independent-minded academics.[60] For such a group to arrive at a recommendation for the President, it would have to reconcile some very divergent perspectives.

As the committee began its work, a sense of deepening emergency stalked its chambers. Across much of the nation, wheat shipments and milling of flour had virtually ceased as farmers, traders, and businessmen awaited the government's decisions.[61] In New York City and at major interior wheat terminals, Julius Barnes's Grain Corporation was preparing to enter the market at the beginning of September. Convinced that quick action was imperative, Garfield and his colleagues gave themselves just two weeks to complete their task.[62]

Except for an oral report to the committee about the world wheat situation on August 20, Hoover kept away from the body's early deliberations.[63] Keenly sensitive to the charge that he was a food despot, he refrained from making any formal recommendations about prices. No doubt he realized that it would be politically advantageous to have an independent committee rather than himself take the heat for such a decision. Behind the scenes, however, he apparently endeavored to steer the committee toward a middle ground. When one of the labor union representatives suggested that the committee consider recommending that the government subsidize bread prices by purchasing wheat from farmers at a "fair price" and then selling it to consumers for less, the Food Administration's counsel, Curtis H. Lindley, quickly ruled that Hoover had no such power under the Lever Act. The law authorized the government to buy and sell wheat at "reasonable prices," said Lindley, and selling wheat below cost would not be "reasonable." Moreover, it would put the government in competition with private business, something that Lindley deemed "not a proper Governmental function." Likening the proposed subsidy to the discredited ancient practice of "bread and circuses," Lindley declared it to be a policy question which only Congress—not the committee—could resolve. In all probability his legal opinion had the prior approval of Herbert Hoover.[64]

The principal threat that Hoover faced, however, did not emanate from those who would peg the price artificially low. As the eleven committeemen collected data and pondered their options, a political cyclone began to whip through the halls of Congress. To senators like Thomas Gore of Oklahoma and Asle Gronna of North Dakota, Hoover's creation of a price-fixing committee was nothing less than a brazen usurpation of power.[65] Again and again senators from wheat-growing states charged that the Lever Act had conferred no authority on anyone to fix the price of the 1917 harvest. The Lever Act said nothing at all about 1917 wheat, they argued, and was silent precisely because Congress intended to let the 1917 wheat crop alone, subject solely to the market forces of supply and demand.[66] Now, in disregard of this Congressional understanding, Hoover was preparing to fix the price anyway.

For farmers who had believed that the Lever Act set only a *minimum* price for wheat (and not until 1918), Hoover's action caused a terrific shock.[67] Out on the Great Plains and the prairies, astonishment turned rapidly to rebellion. On August 20 Representative George M. Young of North Dakota advised a meeting of his constituents in Fargo to bombard Harry Garfield with telegrams:

> If Hoover can influence the committee, the price of wheat will be $1.65 a bushel. Tell Garfield without mincing words that the Government can grab this year's crop but cannot compel the farmers to grow wheat in 1918. . . . Anything we get above $1.65 a bushel will be on account of clenched fists shaken in the faces of Garfield and Hoover.[68]

From the Dakotas and other wheat-growing areas around the country, angry protests poured into Washington.[69]

Furious at Young's "misrepresentations,"[70] Hoover swiftly issued a denial:

> I have not only never proposed $1.65 per bushel for wheat, but no other price either, above or below, nor have I given any advice or suggestions as to price for the committee appointed by President Wilson to determine a fair price. . . .
>
> My duty is simply to see that the farmer realizes this fair price, whatever it may be, and to see that the consumer obtains his bread without the speculative profits in between the farmer and the consumer, which were maintained over the first half of this present year.[71]

Nevertheless, the price-fixing committee as well as Congressional offices continued to be barraged with mail from indignant wheat growers requesting a high price for their crop.[72] *Wallaces' Farmer*, the preeminent agrarian journal in the Middle West, exhorted the farmers' representatives on the committee to insist on $2.50.[73] Angry farmers in North Dakota and Minnesota even dispatched a delegation to Garfield's committee. Barred from presenting their case in person, the protestors submitted a brief calling for a price of at least $3.00 a bushel.[74]

Meanwhile, amidst the sultry heat of a Washington August, Garfield and his colleagues continued to labor without result. Hoover was increasingly agitated. He informed the committee on the twenty-third that while he had no desire to "hurry" its work, the body should bear in mind that grain trading throughout the country was "almost at a standstill" and that flour mills were finding it difficult to get supplies.[75] Five days later he warned the committee in a memorandum that the world actually had a wheat surplus, counting currently inaccessible stocks in Australia, India, and Argentina. It was obvious from his figures that if the war suddenly ended or if the German U-boat menace were overcome, the United States would be unable to sustain a high price for its wheat.[76] It was a subtle warning against setting the price too high. Without committing himself to a specific figure, Hoover was evidently hoping for a much lower price than the current market commanded.

From the outset Garfield's committee was split between those who wanted to keep the price of wheat low (thus benefiting urban consumers) and those who wished to set it high as a stimulus to production. By August 28 the gap between the factions was deep indeed. In the committee's first formal ballot taken that evening, the two labor leaders voted to set a price of $1.84 per bushel, four of the farm leaders voted for $2.50, and the other committeemen opted for various figures in between. The body immediately took a second formal vote. Not one of the eleven members budged.[77]

The next day, as rumors of a deadlock swept Washington, Garfield and his colleagues called in Hoover to answer questions. Just what they asked him and what he said was not recorded.[78] A few blocks away, a delegation of farm state senators descended on the White House and asked President Wilson to fix the price of wheat at its present market value (well above $2.00). After presenting their plea, they asked the President to intercede with Garfield and Hoover. The President promised only to consider the senators' views and to give "fair play to all."[79]

But Wilson, too, was becoming impatient. He let it be known that he intended to have the price of wheat fixed before another day had passed.[80] In the meantime, the Garfield committee took six more inconclusive ballots; its principal factions appeared as intransigent as ever.[81]

Facing reports of a virtual ultimatum from the White House, the price-fixing committee gathered again on August 30. By midafternoon it had taken several more ballots to no avail.[82] Suddenly James Sullivan, representing the American Federation of Labor, told his colleagues that unless they acceded to the price of wheat he was holding out for, he would leave the chamber and issue a call for a nationwide strike. The committee was stunned; for a moment no one moved or spoke. Then Eugene Funk of the agrarian bloc responded that if Sullivan did so, Funk would leave the room with him and telegraph the nation's farmers to store food in their cellars and withhold all their produce from shipment until the strike was abandoned.[83]

Having peered into the abyss, the committee at last had had enough. Within an hour it unanimously agreed to recommend that the government purchase 1917 wheat on the basis of $2.20 per bushel for No. 1 Northern Spring wheat sold in Chicago.[84]

Early that evening the committee, joined by Hoover, presented its report to President Wilson at the White House.[85] In a statement that Hoover himself probably ghost-wrote, Wilson at once announced that the Food Administration would "rigidly" adhere to the stated price. After expressing his hope that this action would immediately stabilize and "keep within moderate bounds" the prices of wheat, flour, and bread, the President declared: "Mr. Hoover, at his express wish, has taken no part in the deliberations of the committee on whose recommendation I determine the Government's fair price, nor has he in any way intimated an opinion regarding that price."[86] Once again Hoover was doing all he could to protect his flanks.

The decision announced on August 30 embraced more than the price for the highest grade of wheat sold at the most important interior market. While the Garfield committee had been laboring to determine this benchmark figure, Julius Barnes and his colleagues in the Grain Corporation had been devising a schedule of differentials that would establish the price of lesser grades of wheat as well as wheat sold in other domestic outlets. Barnes had persuaded a somewhat reluctant committee to leave this task to him, and he urged Hoover to make certain that the committee not tinker with his handiwork.[87] In the end, after making a few adjustments, the Garfield committee acquiesced. As a result, the price that the government would pay for 1917 wheat would vary significantly from market to market.[88]

If the creation of the fair price committee had made farmers angry, the price that it settled upon made them furious. Throughout the grain-growing regions of the country that August, a bushel of wheat had been selling for $2.50 to $3.00 (and even higher).[89] Now the Food Administration was about to reduce this figure by as much as one third. One agrarian spokesman later accused Hoover of staging "a Nation-wide bear raid upon the price of wheat."[90] In September the radical Nonpartisan League's newspaper asserted that price-fixing at $2.20 was tantamount to "commandeering the crop."[91] In their rage and disillusionment farmers seemed not to consider that the price of wheat had doubled in less than a year. What impressed them more was that a prospective bonanza had gone aglimmering.

The Food Administration's schedule of price differentials only aggravated agrarian discontent. In the key terminal of Minneapolis, the government price for No. 1 Northern Spring wheat would be only $2.17; in Kansas City and Omaha, even less.[92] By the time farmers in places like Montana paid their shipping costs and other charges, their net receipt per bushel would be under $2.00—far from the $3.00 (and higher) of which they had dreamed.[93] Once again, the bird in the hand seemed less alluring than the gilded bird in the bush that had been yanked away.

Before long the wheat belt quivered with bitter accusations that Hoover personally had engineered this turn of events.[94] The Food Administrator, of course, had a ready answer: that he was not a member of the price committee and had deliberately refrained from participating in its decisions. In this claim Harry Garfield later sustained him.[95] But while Hoover himself did not stipulate the *precise* 1917 wheat price, he was undoubtedly in accord with its downward thrust. Indeed, this was the reason he had created the Garfield committee in the first place: to find a below-market price at which the government could secure a critical crop. There would have been no need for the committee if Hoover had been willing to let supply and demand operate freely. Having made the political judgment that flour and bread prices were intolerably high, he decided upon and initiated a program of price restraint. The first step was to set a "just price" at the point of production.

The controversy over the 1917 wheat price was Hoover's first crisis as Food Administrator, and its echoes would haunt him politically for a decade. At first he contented himself with denying responsibility for the Garfield committee's recommendation and with stressing that the committee had had an agrarian majority.[96] But as the issue surfaced and resurfaced in the years ahead, he developed an audacious counterclaim: that in August 1917 he and the much-maligned price committee had actually saved wheat farmers from *lower* wheat prices—lower by far than what they got.[97] According to Hoover, that summer the powerful Allied wheat-purchasing commission wanted to pay American wheat farmers a mere $1.50 per bushel and was prepared to enforce its request.[98] In fact, he later alleged, "the price was already falling rapidly toward that level."[99] But Hoover (as he himself eventually put it) "refused to allow this injustice to the American farmer" and instead arranged for the creation of the fair price committee.[100] Without his intervention, he asserted, the price of wheat would have plummeted to $1.50.[101] Without the Garfield committee's "courageous action," American farmers "would have realized far less" for their wheat then they eventually did.[102]

Thus, instead of admitting that he had deliberately acted in the national interest to thwart runaway profits for farmers, Hoover portrayed himself as the man who had saved the farmers from a financial catastrophe. He had done what he had done, he insisted, "to protect the American farmer." Furthermore, the farmer's "own views as to prices" had been "accepted."[103]

Hoover's later claims were implausible. His own files contained no evidence either that the Allies demanded a price of $1.50 per bushel in the summer of 1917 or that they threatened to send their ships to the southern hemisphere if they did not get it. In 1924, when he was searching for such evidence ("I am strong on heaving some of this situation on the Allies," he told Barnes),[104] He located no document in support of his contention. He concluded that the Allies must have demanded the low price in an oral conversation.[105] Yet even if Allied agents did desire a low price for American wheat in mid-1917, there is no evidence that they could have imposed their will successfully on American producers. Desperate for foodstuffs and financing from the United States, and even then negotiating in Washington for massive American loans, they were scarcely in a position to shatter the American market or divert their scarce shipping elsewhere.

Nor is there much evidence for Hoover's assertion that the price of wheat was falling rapidly in the summer of 1917. To be sure, just after the Lever bill was enacted, the price in Chicago dropped considerably from $2.90—not, however, because of foreign pressure but apparently because of domestic anticipation that Washington would soon impose a lower price.[106] Still, throughout the wheat belt that August, the price per bushel continued to range generally from $2.50 to $3.00, and farmers expected it to go higher still. *Wallaces' Farmer* expressed the sentiments not only of its constituency but also of many later observers when it editorialized on September 7, 1917:

> If the government had not fixed a price, but had allowed the law of supply and demand to operate, the price very likely would have been considerably above $2.50, even if there had been no unwarranted speculation. The official fixing of the price will unquestionably prevent the farmer from

receiving the profit that would have been his under normal conditions of trade.[107]

It is very doubtful that many wheat farmers were persuaded by Hoover's later apologia, expounded primarily in the 1920s when he was a presidential prospect. Actually, Hoover had a good case for restraining wheat prices in 1917, and one wonders why he did not make it forthrightly to farmers in the first place. Why did he not frankly say to them, "Yes, you could have had $5.00 wheat, but it would have been ruinous to the rest of the nation"? Only once, in April 1918, did he publicly venture such an argument (although not to an audience of farmers).[108] Julius Barnes's Grain Corporation made the same point in 1920.[109] To be convincing, however (as distinct from being true), this argument would have obliged farmers to subordinate their material self-interest to the common good. One suspects that Hoover doubted they would do it.

In any case, during the 1920s, with agrarian enemies attacking him harshly and with his eye almost certainly on the White House, Hoover daringly shifted his defense. Instead of telling wheat farmers that they had had to sacrifice enormous prospective profits for the nation's sake during the war, he resorted to the unconvincing assertion that he had protected them from imminent disaster. Having devised his rationale, he and his friends reiterated it tirelessly.[110]

If political considerations dictated Hoover's counteroffensive, his temperament influenced it as well. While supervising the preparation of an elaborate report in 1925 defending his wheat price policies during the war, he remarked to an associate that it was a fundamental mistake to admit an attack.[111] Combative by temperament, Hoover rarely acknowledged the validity of a public criticism. Hence it came about that his wheat price policymaking in the summer of 1917 was much more defensible than his own later defenses of it.

All this, however, lay well in the future. With the "fair price" for the government's wheat purchases now determined, the Food Administration Grain Corporation could proceed. On September 4, 1917 it commenced operations at grain terminals throughout the United States.[112]

Meanwhile Hoover had been taking steps to bring the entire chain of wheat distribution under his control. Despite the powers that President Wilson had conferred upon him, the Food Administrator faced a significant hurdle. For all the public uproar about price-fixing, the only price that had now been set was that at which the U.S. government would purchase wheat. Nothing in the new law forbade farmers from selling wheat to other buyers for a higher figure. Nevertheless, Hoover was determined, as he put it, to "universalize" the government's price. Achieving this was essential to his ultimate goal of steadying and reducing the cost of bread. And so he took aim, not directly at the wheat farmers who were legally beyond his reach, but at the grain elevator operators and flour millers who bought and handled the farmers' crop. If he could compel these middlemen to buy from farmers at the *government's* price, he could make his "fair price" supreme.

At first Hoover apparently believed that he could attain his goal simply by licensing the mills and elevators and then ordering them to pay his designated price. But in late summer his plans hit a snag when his staff attorneys informed him that he could not legally prescribe by regulation the exact price at which private businesses traded their commodities. The Lever Act could not be stretched that far.[113] If Hoover hoped to bend the grain industry to his purpose, he would have to find another way to do so.

His solution was quick and ingenious. The Lever Act authorized the government to "enter into any voluntary arrangements or agreements" in pursuance of the purposes of the law.[114] On August 28, 1917 Hoover invited all flour millers in the United States to enter into *voluntary* agreements with his Food Administration and Grain Corporation—contracts whose terms would give him the power that he desired. Appealing for "patriotic co-operation," he declared that "stabilizing" wheat prices was "an imperative war service."[115] Appealing simultaneously to the millers' pocketbooks, his Grain Corporation promised to guarantee "agreement" mills against loss if their stocks of unsold wheat and flour ever fell in value below the "fair price."[116] In return for this and other inducements, the Food Administration required contracting mills to pledge that in purchasing wheat they would adhere to the government's regulations. Among these, two were vital to Hoover's scheme: the mills must not buy wheat from anyone at more than the government's "fair price," and they must refer all orders for export flour to the Food Administration.[117]

In mid-September Hoover offered a parallel agreement to the owners of the nation's 21,600 country grain elevators. As with the flour mills, the Food Administration promised to make up the difference if the market value of the elevators' wheat sank below the government's fixed price. For their part the elevator proprietors must agree to pay only the official "fair price" in their private wheat purchases. In the case of the "country" elevators—the first, critical link in the distribution chain—Hoover requested much more: the right to order the retention and control the distribution of all wheat stored in their bins. In this way the government could regulate both the rate of outflow and the precise destination of the vast majority of the country's wheat supplies. In return for this indispensable economic lever, the Grain Corporation pledged to pay the elevator proprietors an attractive storage fee for any wheat held in the bins at its demand. Since Hoover had already forbidden the proprietors to store wheat on their own account for more than thirty days, his offer was a strong incentive to sign up.[118]

But would the grain industry comply? Would the lure of stability and security overcome the traditional incentives of market freedom? Despite Hoover's plea on August 29 for speedy execution of the agreements,[119] the response, in numerical terms, was not impressive. By mid-November, only 2,500 of the nation's 9,000 millers had signed; eventually the number slightly exceeded 3,100.[120] The elevator proprietors proved somewhat more receptive; more than two thirds of them entered into the desired contracts by the end of the crop year.[121] But here, too, several thousand businesses refused to enter the fold. Hoover's regulatory system was consequently porous. In the months to come, the so-called nonagreement mills often—and quite legally—paid wheat farmers more than the government's "fair price," to Hoover's unending vexation.[122]

Fortunately for the Food Administrator, the economic significance of this anomaly was slight. The flour mills that accepted his terms accounted for 95 percent of the milling capacity of the country—enough for him and his colleagues to eliminate "speculation" (that is, higher prices).[123] The adherence of these mills to his "fair price" schedule was absolutely critical to the success of his stabilization policy. "If it had not been for this agreement," he confessed to Barnes in October, "our whole plan would have broken down."[124]

In its complicated involvement with the grain trade, then, Hoover's organization never dealt with wheat farmers directly.[125] But by the novel device of voluntary agreements between the government and middlemen, it effectively boxed wheat farmers in and largely determined their price. Moreover, once the crop left the producers' hands, Hoover and his colleagues were able to manage both its storage and its distribution. It was their strongest weapon against spot shortages and sudden inflation.[126] All this and more they accomplished, as a Grain Corporation booklet later proudly put it, "without legal power to establish and fix any prices which should govern the public."[127]

It was not enough, however, for Hoover simply to "universalize" the price of wheat. He now had to make certain that the middlemen who dealt in wheat "reflected" this price in their own products and services. Otherwise the consumer would not benefit. To attain this goal, Hoover turned not only to voluntary agreements but to coercion.[128] If he could not directly stipulate prices under the Lever Act, he could legally compel businesses to make only "fair" and "reasonable" *profits*. In mid-August, therefore, at his request, Woodrow Wilson ordered that all wheat elevators and flour mills in the United States with a daily capacity exceeding one hundred barrels must obtain a license from the Food Administration by September 1. Within hours Hoover issued a set of regulations governing the licensees' businesses, including a prohibition of "unjust or unreasonable" profits. After consulting with the affected industries, Hoover decreed that their maximum reasonable profits would be 25 cents per barrel on flour and 50 cents per ton on feed. In order to keep within these prescribed bounds, the millers would have to pass along their savings on wheat to consumers.[129] This, at least, was the theory; how well it would work in practice remained to be seen.

By early September, then—less than a month after he took his oath of office—Hoover (in the later words of Senator Reed) had "completely cornered" the domestic market in wheat and flour.[130] But the fledgling Food Administrator now discovered that his bold assertion of power would not necessarily generate compliance. Already aware that farmers in the West were turning against him, he gloomily predicted to a journalist that there would be "storms ahead."[131] He was even more prescient than he realized.

For in the first weeks of September, from the Mississippi to the Pacific, agrarian wrath at the Food Administration crystalized into revolt. In North Dakota and Oklahoma, mass meetings of farmers vehemently demanded that the government revise upward its "fair price."[132] In Kansas, wheat growers joined in the agitation.[133] In New Mexico, farmers protested upon learning that they would receive the Kansas City price for wheat ($2.15) *minus* the cost of freight to ship it there—or as much as 70 cents a bushel less than they had anticipated.[134] Meanwhile, throughout the wheat belt, the average farm price of wheat that autumn fell to $2.01 per bushel, well under the price set at interior terminals.[135]

Particularly incensed were the wheat growers of the Pacific Northwest, who discovered that Julius Barnes's price schedule would bring them only $1.90 a bushel for No. 1 Northern Spring wheat sold in Portland. Barnes argued vigorously that the established price was fair. It would, he claimed, yield them just as much profit as they would gain from shipping their wheat by rail to Chicago. Nevertheless, the farmers of Washington and Oregon demanded more, and they did not hesitate to use their crop as a weapon. While their Congressional delegation importuned Hoover in his office, word reached him from Portland that the region's flour mills were paralyzed for lack of wheat. The angry farmers of the Northwest were withholding their crop from the market. They would "sell nothing," Hoover was told, until they knew whether President Wilson would grant their petition.[136]

Farmers were not the only ones besieging the Food Administration with grievances. The president of the Chicago Board of Trade complained that the Grain Corporation's price differentials unjustly discriminated against his city.[137] In Minnesota and other states, local business interests demanded that the corporation place an additional wheat-buying agent in their territory.[138] On another front, the dilatory response of flour millers to Hoover's voluntary agreement suggested that they, like many farmers, remained suspicious of his pleas for "co-ordination."

Back on the east coast, Frank Cobb—editor of the influential New York *World*—counseled Hoover not to be afraid. Farmers were always complaining, he said, and nobody paid them much attention, particularly when their demands were excessive.[139] Nevertheless, Hoover was alarmed by increasing indications that wheat farmers were refusing to market their crop in the hope of forcing him to raise its price. He told Woodrow Wilson's secretary that the mass meetings in North Dakota had "apparently" been marked by "a good deal of anti-war sentiment"—an undisguised hint that some of his agrarian critics were disloyal.[140] Framing the issue for the President, he remarked with manifest acerbity:

> The whole question is whether or not the consumer is to pay another $5.00 or $6.00 per barrel for flour in order to please a lot of malcontents, and if they are to pay this higher price, the problem will arise at once whether we can maintain tranquillity in the large industrial centers during this winter.[141]

By September 14 the backlash against Hoover's policies had reached such intensity that he began to waver. We must "pacify" the Chicago Board of Trade by granting it a hearing, he informed Julius Barnes that day.[142] Worried by the "row" in North Dakota, where the Nonpartisan League was flourishing, the Food Administrator suggested that Barnes undercut it by creating an agency in St. Paul, Minnesota, that would buy wheat from the militant, farmer-owned marketing organization known as the Equity Cooperative Exchange. The exchange was hated by the organized grain trade of Minnesota, in which Julius Barnes himself was a leading figure. Even so, Hoover felt the need to defuse the radicals' discontent. "We must bend at some points if we are to weather this rising storm," he declared, "and if it can possibly be done [I] should like to conciliate everywhere we can. The ultimate issue is to break the whole administration if we cannot silence some of the opposition."[143]

Disturbed by these signs of vacillation, Barnes counseled his chief to stand firm. You must make no concessions to the Nonpartisan League whatsoever, Barnes argued; it is a movement that "savors of sedition."[144] Barnes was equally hostile to the Equity movement in St. Paul, whose "unpatriotic and disloyal efforts" were fueling the trouble in North Dakota. The Equity Society men, he said, "should forfeit every consideration until they return to Sanity and public spirit." The Grain Corporation president assured his boss that conditions in the country were not as desperate as they seemed. He added: "You are in the heighth [sic] of all the suggestions for government aid in every direction that can be devised by needy or selfish men. We have a sound plan sit tight and let it work."[145]

In the end Hoover had to bend very little.[146] But in one case the political pressure was too great. On September 20 Senator George Chamberlain of Oregon led a delegation of northwestern wheat growers' representatives to the White House, where they pleaded directly with the President for an increase in the government price for their crop. Evidently relying upon a memorandum that Hoover had supplied him beforehand, Wilson raised the now familiar bogeyman: If wheat farmers of the Northwest withheld their crops from the market, Allied buyers would simply go to Argentina and Australia. Eventually the price of wheat would collapse and the American wheat surplus would "go begging."[147] Like Hoover, the President hoped to frighten the farmers into cooperating by invoking the menace of a glut, and disastrously lower prices, if they did not.

In this case the argument evidently did not persuade; it was Hoover who had to retreat. Just two days after the White House meeting, he instituted an increase of 15 cents a bushel for wheat received at several terminals on the Pacific coast.[148]

As summer yielded to autumn, the trend of the previous weeks persisted: to an unprecedented and unforeseen degree, the nation's farmers were failing to market their wheat.[149] By September 13 the great flour-milling industry of Minneapolis was threatened with paralysis because of a lack of wheat to grind. According to a leading newspaper, the Minneapolis mills faced closure within forty-eight hours.[150] In Chicago, grain elevators held only 174,000 bushels of wheat on September 1, compared to 5,077,000 bushels a year before. By mid-month, many of Chicago's flour mills had suspended operations.[151]

The effect of this constriction was soon apparent on the east coast. By mid-September the supply of flour in New York City was only enough to last three days. Desperate to relieve the growing shortage, Hoover and his colleagues arranged to acquire several thousand tons of flour in New York that was bound for Norway. Initially the Norwegian owners were reluctant to release their precious stock. But they finally agreed to do so, if the Food Administration would promise to replace it in November and guarantee an export license for it. Hoover promised, and the deal went through.[152]

Confronted by increasing public suspicion—especially in New York—that something was seriously amiss, Hoover and his lieutenants flooded the press with reassuring denials. On September 14, the Food Administrator asserted that except "in very limited areas where anti-war and pro-German propaganda is being carried on," there was "no disposition to withhold the wheat from the Government and the Allies."[153] That same day the head of his milling division joined Julius Barnes in announcing that the current slow movement of wheat to the terminals was not abnormal at all. The farmers were merely taking advantage of a stable price and good weather to do other work, they said. Both men insisted that dissatisfaction with the "fair price" was an inconsequential source of the delays in marketing. According to Barnes, the "vast majority" of the wheat growers considered the government's price "not only fair but generous."[154] The next day Barnes told the *New York Times* that the "primary marketing of wheat" was "increasing steadily," albeit somewhat later than usual.[155] On September 19 he went further still: "There is no flour famine nor will there be one."[156]

Behind this facade of nonchalance lay a number of disquieting realities. On September 17, even as the Food Administration was proclaiming that all was well, Barnes telegraphed an extraordinary request to Hoover: "Ask Chambers [the head of the Food Administration's transportation division] if

[he] cant force [railroad] cars to be used for Wheat only for a week." Barnes reported that many grain elevators were "letting wheat rest" and were transporting more profitable grains in its place.[157] If this kept up, there would soon be flour and bread shortages in the cities. No wonder, then, that the president of the Grain Corporation wanted Hoover to resort to coercion. If the Food Administrator could deprive grain dealers of railway transport for everything *except* wheat, he might be able to force the crop into the distribution pipeline.

Certainly the Food Administration's own statistics suggested the need. On September 21 Hoover's agency released data showing that the flour mills of Minneapolis were operating at less than three quarters of capacity, and those in Buffalo at barely half.[158] A few days later a press report from the Midwest disclosed that farmers in Oklahoma were still holding 60 percent of their 1917 wheat crop and were now feeding some of it to their hogs, partly in protest at the government's pricing policies.[159] In New Mexico, dissatisfied farmers were reportedly giving wheat to their cattle and horses rather than import other, apparently more expensive, feeds. The low price of New Mexico wheat (based on the Kansas City differential) was said to be the reason for this anomaly.[160]

Faced with these multiplying challenges and complications, Hoover intensified his efforts at self-defense. Privately he accused farmers—and the American people generally—of being greedy. Our "plans of price control" have stirred "a mighty resentment amongst all of our producers," he wrote to a friend in September.

> I regret to say that there is an enormous patriotism for the other fellow in the United States, and our people generally have had such a fine go at profiteering and enjoying the luxuries of war production without any of its penalties that we have a double job to get them down even to a normal basis of profits and conduct.[161]

Publicly his posture was different. Donning the mantle of the farmer's saviour, he told a member of Congress from Kansas that the Food Administration was actually "standing under the wheat situation" to the farmer's "entire protection," and that "if it were not for the Government's purchases" the price of wheat would fall below $2.00. He warned the congressman that farmers would be "well-advised" to sell their wheat now at the government's price "while we can still secure a market at this figure from the Allies." He asserted that he was "acting as an intermediary" between wheat farmers and the Allies in order to hold the price up to levels that would "properly stimulate production."[162]

Repeatedly Hoover pointed out that farmers had held a majority on the Garfield committee.[163] At one point he even alleged that this was "the first occasion in history where the grower himself has practically named his own price"—a claim that ignored the bitter committee battle that had yielded a compromise far below farmers' wishes.[164] In a bid to rally support for himself in the cities, he contended in September that his policies had already achieved a savings of $3.00 per barrel of flour to consumers, even as farmers were receiving an average of 60 cents per bushel *more* for their wheat than last year.[165] Never before, he declared, had there been "so narrow a margin as there is on flour and wheat today."[166]

Hoover, of course, could expostulate with his critics and claim credit until he was blue in the face, but he would fail as Food Administrator unless unhappy farmers cooperated. By the end of September his own statistics told the story. During the entire month, he admitted privately, "we moved 57,000,000 bushels of wheat," in contrast to a normal figure of 150,000,000.[167]

And now, in early October, a new cloud of accusations swirled out of the heartland: that flour millers and other middlemen were failing to reduce the prices of their products to conform with the decreased price that they had to pay for farmers' wheat.[168] Already aggrieved at having to curb their own profits, wheat growers were infuriated when grain millers instituted a price increase on mill feed that they sold to farmers.[169] The millers retorted that the farmers' withholding action had hampered mill production and had thereby forced up milling costs.[170]

Hoover, more than ever, was on the spot. On September 29 he had publicly predicted a large impending reduction in the cost of flour to consumers. It did not materialize. Just two weeks later he conceded to his state food administrator in Kansas that flour dealers and millers were not "interpreting the price of wheat all over the country" and that flour retailers especially were "not giving the public the benefit of it."[171] The middlemen, in short, were not behaving as intended.

On October 12 the Food Administration ordered all flour mills in Minneapolis to reduce their production to 40 percent of capacity, in order to "relieve the scarcity of wheat" at mills in the East.[172] Hoover tried to put the best face possible on the crisis. He asserted that farmers were marketing slowly because they knew that "the market is safe" and that they could therefore do other things for the moment than ship wheat.[173] It was a comforting interpretation that some of his defenders later repeated.[174] Still, the wheat did not come. Toward the end of October he confessed that he was "a good deal worried" and that shipments were running 1,000,000 bushels a day below normal.[175] According to *Wallaces' Farmer*, wheat growers who were dissatisfied with the price ceiling had "no objection to making the government 'sweat.' "[176] In a spontaneous, unorganized, yet grimly effective manner, a significant number of the nation's farmers had gone on strike.

Alarmed at the incessant "misrepresentation" that was sapping "the failing foundations of the whole Food Administration," Hoover floated a proposal to Julius Barnes:

> The great tendency of all our people like yourself is to believe that a great, stable and well founded enterprise in the interest of the people will gain the confidence of the people themselves. You can take it from me that this is not true. The thing that gains the confidence of the people is the thing that is represented to them.

"There is nothing so delicate and so difficult to maintain as public confidence," Hoover continued, "and it can only be obtained by the constant reiteration of the work and its objectives." He therefore urged the embattled Grain Corporation to hire a public speaker who could "go on the road" defending it at farmers' gatherings in the West.[177]

The same day that he wrote to Barnes, Hoover himself attempted to rally public confidence. He announced that, "subject to co-operation" from farmers and food retailers, "the corner has now been turned in high prices" and that most "essential commodities" should become cheaper. "Hoover Predicts Drop in Prices," headlined the *New York Times* the next morning.[178] But his fate was in the hands of those he did not yet control.

In mid-October, at last, there came a serendipitous break. For some weeks the financially straitened British government had been seeking a gigantic loan from the United States that would enable the western Allies to buy the Canadian wheat surplus. A draft of this agreement came to Hoover's attention on October 11.[179] Seizing his opportunity, he quickly asked the American and British negotiators to insert a clause permitting the Food Administration to acquire Canadian wheat "in excess of Allied shipments."[180] After a flurry of negotiations the British agreed, as a condition of the loan, to hand over to the Food Administration whatever Canadian wheat it required "from time to time," in return for the American release of equivalent quantities of flour to the Allies "without delay."[181]

The Allied loan arrangement was a godsend to Herbert Hoover. By importing as much wheat from Canada as he desired, he could undermine the American farmers' withholding action, "put the big milling centers running full blast," and "flood the American market with flour made from Canadian wheat."[182] In other words, until the stubborn wheat farmers of the United States finally surrendered their crop, Hoover could use Canadian imports to keep American mills employed and avert disastrous shortages of flour in eastern cities. He might even be able to drive down the price of bread for urban consumers.

The Grain Corporation promptly swung into action. Even before the British loan was formally signed, Barnes obtained 200,000 bushels of wheat grown in Manitoba and diverted it to the hardpressed mills of Buffalo, New York.[183] On October 25 the Food Administration officially lifted its restrictions on the flour mills of Minneapolis and announced that "large supplies of Canadian wheat" would be shipped via the Great Lakes to eastern mills, enabling these to resume full operation.[184]

The prospect of wheat from the north also provided Hoover a weapon against the "uncontrolled miller," with whom he was becoming increasingly annoyed.[185] Publicly, as always, he exuded confidence. On October 18 he even told the press that the "intermediate trades" were "co-operating finely" with his regulations and that the "millers especially are playing the game well all over the country."[186] Privately, however, he spoke and acted otherwise. In mid-October he developed a scheme whereby he would sell his imported Canadian wheat to "big millers" only—and only upon condition that they sell the flour they made from it at a price that would earn them less than the allowable 25 cents-a-barrel profit. In this way Hoover proposed to force the major mills to undercut their small competitors and thereby "force the smaller millers into a better attitude of mind."[187]

Two weeks later he tried another maneuver, aimed at the country elevators outside his system. He asked the head of his transportation division to persuade the railroads to give "absolute priority" to wheat bound for the Grain Corporation and the "agreement" mills, and "to put wheat shipped for other people behind all the other grains." By manipulating transportation to the advantage of his agency and cooperating middlemen, he hoped to prod recalcitrant grain elevator owners into joining his apparatus of control.[188]

Apparently neither of these initiatives came to fruition. Instead, as the days passed, Hoover relied increasingly upon his powers of regulation. By late October he was issuing milling regulations with the expressed hope that they would "drive more millers into [signing] the voluntary agreement" with the Grain Corporation.[189] Perhaps with this objective in mind, on October 30 he ordered all American flour mills, however small, to obtain a license as a condition of doing business and to make weekly reports to the government on their transactions. With this extension of coverage, Hoover's supervision of the country's flour producers was complete.[190]

All these edicts and stratagems, and Hoover's manifest willingness to resort to them, stood in growing contrast to his public advocacy of voluntarism. In his own mind he possibly saw no contradiction. From the start he had consistently argued that he must have broad powers of enforcement in order to control unethical "skunks" and "stinkers" who would take advantage of the patriotic majority. But the thousands of "non-agreement" millers and elevator men were not cheaters. They had simply declined to sign the voluntary contract that Hoover had offered them. Nevertheless, if his stabilization policy were to succeed, he was convinced that he must control them regardless. It was a testament of his certitude and frustration that his methods seemed ever more coercive.

With the aid of imported wheat from Canada, Hoover was able to win his tug-of-war with the farmers. As the weeks went by and the government refused to modify its fixed price, more and more wheat growers evidently saw the futility of resistance. In a report to Congress in November, Hoover asserted that wheat deliveries were up substantially and that a "normal" proportion of the 1917 crop was now leaving the farm.[191] By the end of December wheat marketings were satisfactory.[192]

But if the farmers' rebellion finally subsided, the resentment that ignited it did not. As the reconvening of Congress shortly revealed, Hoover had won a truce, not a peace. As for the grain millers and their profiteering, the time was coming when they, too, would feel the weight of the government's "steadying hand."

In the meantime Hoover's war against inflation had reached another link in the food chain. The Food Administrator realized that his curbs on wheat and flour prices would mean little unless he could cap the price of a loaf of bread. This was the decisive test of his policies, the standard by which his service would be judged. It would not suffice to bridle farmers and middlemen. Somehow he must elicit the cooperation of the nation's bakers, who were responsible for 40 percent of the bread baked in the United States.[193]

But how? Hoover knew well that his agency had no power to fix the price of consumers' bread.[194] Undeterred, he resorted to a blend of consultation, coordination, and coercion. He conferred at length with representatives of the baking industry and other experts.[195] He announced that it might be possible to reduce the price of a one-pound loaf of bread by 20 percent if a "standardized loaf" were created and if the industry eliminated certain "wasteful practices" that had "grown up out of competitive conditions."[196] He revealed that the Food Administration was conducting experiments on the feasibility of certain weights and formulas.[197] He asked the Federal Trade Commission to investigate the baking industry's commercial practices.[198]

On November 3 the commission reported that bakers' costs could indeed be cut substantially by the standardization of loaf sizes and other reforms.[199] Buttressed by its findings, Hoover proceeded to intervene. Just four days later, at his request, President Wilson invoked the Lever Act and ordered all bakers in the country whose monthly usage of flour and meal exceeded ten barrels to obtain a license from the Food Administration or face the legal penalty.[200] Approximately 26,000 baking establishments duly applied.[201]

Hoover immediately promulgated a series of regulations that the licensed bakers must henceforth obey, at the risk of being closed down for noncompliance. They must manufacture bread only in multiples of a pound and not in the thirty-seven different sizes hitherto prevailing (a practice Hoover and others had condemned). They must no longer accept returns from their retail distributors—thus ending a custom that had led to the wastage of day-old bread.[202] The licensees must not destroy any bakery products, "wilfully permit preventable deterioration," or "knowingly commit waste."[203]

Hoover hoped that his rules would "reduce the cost of public baking and distribution" as well as the misuse of flour. None of his regulations, of course, actually compelled bakers to reduce prices to their customers. For this he had no legal warrant. But by imposing standardized loaf sizes on the industry, he wished, he told the President, to "focus competition on the question of price."[204]

And having done so, Hoover was quick to proclaim victory. On November 26, more than two weeks before his baking regulations took legal effect, the Food Administration announced triumphantly that its policies were working. According to its statistics, the price of flour had declined steeply since August. The stabilization of wheat prices, and the consequent steadying of flour prices at the mills, had permitted "the stabilization of the wholesale business in flour" throughout the country. Already, said the Food Administration, "the result has been reflected in the price of bread." Thanks to this success, and to the "total elimination of hoarding and speculation" in the industry, wheat farmers were now receiving twice as much, relative to the price of a loaf of bread, as they had in 1916.[205]

Every sector of society, then, was benefiting from his massive intervention in the wheat and flour trade: this was the reassuring message that Hoover issued to the nation less than four months into his tenure. By the most sensitive criterion of all—the price of bread in the big cities—he was, he believed, on track.

III

IF wheat price restraint was Hoover's first priority in his early weeks as Food Administrator, controlling the nation's sugar supply was his second. In one respect the challenge that he faced here was different. While self-sufficient in the production of wheat, the United States grew less than 25 percent of the sugar it consumed and thus relied upon imports for the rest.[206] But in other respects conditions affecting sugar in 1917 were depressingly familiar. Because of the vicissitudes of the war in Europe, America's western Allies had lost a large proportion of their prewar sources of sugar. Already reduced to a consumption level less than half that of Americans, they dared not restrict their sugar intake much further. Nor did they dare divert their shipping to the sugar-rich but remote East Indies.

Only one source remained readily available: Cuba, hitherto an American preserve and the supplier of half of America's needs. As Allied buyers entered the Cuban market in competition with American refiners, the price of the coveted commodity surged to unparalleled heights. Then, in mid-1917, in a period of less than ten weeks, the price of Cuban raw sugar delivered in New York rose nearly 28 percent. Although certain transitory factors accounted for the spurt, the underlying inflationary pressures seemed unappeased. For Hoover it was all too reminiscent of the eruption of wheat prices during the spring.[207]

Even before the spiral in sugar prices reached its climax, Hoover had become convinced that the free market could not cope with it—not amidst such wartime dislocations. The world is "very much undersupplied with sugar," he told a Congressional committee on May 7. Unless we approach the question "with a strong hand" and "secure our position," the American people would be "starving for sugar within six or eight months."[208] Pessimistic, almost apocalyptic, in his analysis, he informed another hearing two days later that there would probably be no sugar left in the United States by mid-October.[209]

The prospective food controller was equally emphatic about the solution. We must cease competing with the Allies, he said to a committee of senators on May 9. We must take over "all the stocks" of sugar in the country in order to limit their sale and avert future shortages.[210] To Representative Lever in early June, he proposed the creation at once of an "executive body" that would "join with the Allies" in purchasing sugar abroad and then resell it to Allied and American refineries. This kind of intervention in the market, he declared, would "reduce the price of raw sugar very considerably and stabilize prices throughout the year."[211] Later that month, in testimony before the Senate agriculture committee, he advocated establishment of a "sugar commission" that in cooperation with the Allies would "take over the Cuban crop" at a "fixed price," thereby steadying sugar prices for an entire crop year.[212]

Hoover's candor soon got him into trouble. When reports circulated in June that he had predicted to Congress that the sugar supply would soon be exhausted and that exorbitant prices lay ahead, he replied evasively that he had never made any statement on sugar "for publication." Apparently fearful of touching off a buying panic among housewives, he now declared that there "will be no famine in sugar," and that incomplete accounts of his privately expressed views were causing "wholly unnecessary alarm" to consumers.[213]

Urban housewives were not the only people disturbed by Hoover's opinions. At least a few members of Congress suspected him of deliberate scaremongering. When the Lever Act was finally passed, it contained no authority for Hoover to control the price of sugar or even to purchase it. To the Food Administrator's lasting annoyance, the Senate deliberately excluded sugar from the list of commodities that the government was empowered to buy or sell.[214] But if Hoover's Congressional enemies thought they had thereby checkmated him, they were mistaken. As with the price determination for wheat, they had failed to gauge his cleverness and his will.

Hoover's first initiatives on the sugar front were well within the limits of his statutory authority. On August 15, for instance, he asked the New York Coffee and Sugar Exchange to suspend all futures trading in sugar in order to quell the "speculation" that the current "undersupply" must engender. The exchange at once acceded to his request.[215] Later in the month, on his advice, the recently created Exports Administrative Board embargoed all exports of sugar from the United States.[216] In mid-September he had President Wilson issue a proclamation requiring all manufacturers, importers, and refiners of sugar to obtain a license from the Food Administration by October 1.[217]

Yet all this, for Hoover, was insufficient. Licensing would give him power over "exorbitant profits" and "wasteful practices" but not the direct control of prices that he wanted.[218] Lacking the legal authority to buy or sell sugar, he could neither establish a "fair price" à la Garfield or create the equivalent of a Grain Corporation to enforce it. To steer the sugar trade into channels that would bring relief to consumers, he would have to depend almost totally on a single weapon: voluntary agreements between himself and the private sector.

From the outset Hoover knew exactly what he wanted. It was nothing less (he told President Wilson on August 22) than creation by the Food Administration of "a combination in restraint of trade to reduce prices." Hoover was convinced that merely limiting the profits of sugar manufacturers and refiners would never benefit individual consumers. He therefore proposed that his agency and the nation's sugar processors jointly agree upon a single, nationwide price. Once this was done, the government would permit the processors to pool their production as well as their costs of distribution. In a word, he proposed to sanction and supervise an enormous and unprecedented cartel for the purpose not of raising prices but of lowering them.[219]

Hoover's plan was remarkably audacious. But was it legal? Would the Sherman Anti-Trust Act countenance such massive interference with free markets? With Wilson's sympathetic permission, he asked Attorney General Thomas Gregory for a legal opinion.[220] The next day the Attorney General ruled that Hoover's scheme was indeed admissible. The Sherman Act, he held, pertained to private restraints of trade, not governmental ones. Agreements "made with producers or traders *by the Government itself*" when "natural laws of trade break down" were not what the Sherman Act prohibited.[221]

Having cleared away the legal underbrush in his path, Hoover now concentrated on inducing the nation's sugar interests to cooperate. Early in the summer he had asked the general manager of a prominent west coast sugar-refining company, George M. Rolph, to join the Food Administration. Rolph refused, citing the extraordinary demands of his business, and suggested other names as alternatives. But Hoover was not one to take no for an answer and refused to accept Rolph's rejection of his offer. Finally the Food Administrator said, "Mr. Rolph, if you will say to me that your personal interests and the interests of your company are paramount to your duties as an American citizen, I will release you." Unable to make such a claim, Rolph relented and became chief of the Food Administration's sugar division in mid-August.[222]

Having secured Rolph, Hoover invited representatives of the domestic beet sugar industry to Washington for a conference in late August. On August 26 the Food Administration announced that the assembled producers, representing 80 percent of their trade, had "patriotically agreed" to limit the price of their product to a figure well below its current market value—a value inflated by the "exorbitant" demands of holders of what remained of the 1917 Cuban crop. According to the Food Administration, the beet sugar manufacturers' exemplary action would save American consumers $30,000,000 during the next four months. It would also help to hold down the price of imported sugar in the year ahead. In other words, it would depress the market price artificially until a new crop in Cuba became available in December.[223]

The mood of patriotic sacrifice soon dissipated. When Hoover put the verbal understandings of August into the form of a contract, the much-flattered beet sugar manufacturers angrily balked. This was not what they had agreed to at all, they charged. Hoover was asking them "to promise everything, while he promises them nothing."[224] By September 13 nearly every beet sugar manufacturer east of the Mississippi had refused to sign the proposed agreement.[225] The sugar men, like the wheat farmers, were in revolt.

Four days later, beet sugar processors and brokers from across the continent converged on Washington, ostensibly to work out plans for implementing the August decisions. Hoover was ready for a showdown. When some of the refiners protested that they could not accept his price ceiling because they had already contracted to pay sugar beet farmers more than this amount for their crop, the Food Administration countered that "practically all" the farmers would be willing to accept a lower price "as a patriotic duty."[226] This claim may or may not have been accurate;[227] holed up in the capital, the beet sugar processors could not be sure. One thing, however, they did know: on the eve of their arrival in Washington, President Wilson had placed them all under license.

Hoover himself appealed to the conferees' patriotism and sense of self-esteem. In an address to the gathering, he preached the importance of "voluntary service" by business in the war emergency. In the great contest between autocracy and democracy, he contended, America's economic problems should be regulated "from below"—by businessmen cooperating with the government—and not arbitrarily "from above."[228]

Whether it was Hoover's pep talk, the prospect of generous profits under his maximum price agreement,[229] the intimidating reality of licensing, or perhaps some other factor that turned the tide, the rebellious beet sugar manufacturers quickly capitulated. On September 20 the Food Administration announced that the beet sugar men at the conference had unanimously signed Hoover's contract.[230]

Under its terms, the producers agreed to sell their product during the coming year for no more than $7.25 per hundred pounds[231] and to market it in strict obedience to the orders of a Sugar Distributing Committee appointed by Hoover. This committee, composed of industry representatives, would thus control and direct the "equitable distribution" of all beet sugar produced in the United States.[232] If any beet sugar producer violated this contract, he would be subject to revocation of his license.[233]

Once again Hoover had adroitly circumvented the intent of Congress. Since the Lever Act did not authorize price-fixing, his licensing authority could hardly be used as a means to that end. Nevertheless, here he was, invoking the licensing power to enforce his bargain with the beet sugar manufacturers. But he was doing so as part of a *voluntary agreement.* If anyone contested his action, he could reply that the Lever Act permitted him to make such agreements and that he and the contracting businesses were free to formulate any terms they liked. So far as is known, no one ever challenged him on this point. And thus in a circuitous but brilliantly efficacious manner he converted the licensing clause of a law aimed at profiteering into the ultimate sanction for a plan of price-*fixing* beyond the wildest imaginings of Congress.

While all this was going on with the beet sugar producers, Hoover was simultaneously addressing another component of the sugar industry: the refiners of cane sugar imported from Cuba. At the end of August he proposed to his British counterpart that the Allied and American governments form a single buying agency in New York to purchase the coming Cuban sugar crop and then apportion it equitably among themselves.[234] The British readily agreed.[235] By pooling the strength of the buyers, Hoover hoped to forge a powerful united front against the sellers and thus contain the unending pressure toward higher prices.

The success of this strategy obviously depended upon eliminating independent competitors for Cuban sugar. The British promised to take care of the Canadians, who had been dealing with the Cubans on their own.[236] For his part, Hoover offered to "arrange for all American buyers" of Cuban sugar to acquire it solely through the prospective intergovernmental buyer.[237] Accordingly, in the first days of September, representatives of virtually every sugar refinery in the United States journeyed to Washington, D.C., for a conference at his invitation. It did not take them long to accept his proposal. On September 5 the Food Administration announced that the refiners had voluntarily and enthusiastically agreed to import their foreign sugar exclusively through the body that Hoover would appoint. The refiners' action, said the Food Administration, was "taken as a patriotic duty."[238]

On September 20 the Food Administration duly announced the formation of the International Sugar Committee, containing three American and two Allied members.[239] Except for the power to buy and sell (which it technically lacked), it was the functional equivalent of the Grain Corporation—a governmental body interposing itself between farmers (in this case Cubans) and middlemen. As the committee prepared to negotiate the purchase and allotment of the Cuban harvest, Hoover moved to codify his verbal agreements with the refiners. In contracts with the Food Administrator on October 1, the refiners pledged to acquire their imported sugar solely from the International Sugar Committee and to abide by its distribution arrangements. The refiners further agreed to sell their product for not more than $1.30 per hundred pounds wholesale above the price of imported raw sugar. Hoover acknowledged in the contract that he lacked "any statutory power" to fix the price of sugar. Nevertheless, he promised to endeavor to keep the refiners from suffering any loss on their purchases. And just as in his parallel agreements with the beet sugar interests, so now with the refiners of cane: if they violated any terms of their contract, they could lose their license to do business.[240]

Once more the resourceful Food Administrator had outsmarted Congress. Although his agency had neither the explicit authority nor the funds to buy raw sugar, nothing apparently prevented him from creating a committee to "arrange for" such purchases.[241] Since the Allies and domestic cane sugar processors would be the legal buyers, the Lever Act technically would not be violated, even if Hoover's committee dictated both the price and the distribution. Furthermore, the committee's expenses would be met by a fee levied on the refiners; no taxpayers' money would be involved. Thus no one could accuse Hoover of using federal funds for a purpose not authorized by law.

As for the cane sugar processors, whether from patriotism, fear, or calculations of commercial self-interest, they seemed content. True, they had surrendered their right to bid independently for Cuban sugar and to sell it freely in refined form at home. But in return, they had received a guarantee of raw sugar in proportion to their share of the domestic market. And the margin over cost allowed to them was high enough to live on. Like the grain elevator men in the wheat belt, in exchange for the loss of market freedom they gained a profitable stability.

Hoover was delighted by this outcome. The demise of "competitive buying," the Food Administration announced in late September, should save American consumers "many millions of dollars" and "prevent the rapid fluctuation in prices" that had rattled the markets since 1914. The cane sugar refiners' voluntary restraints on their own profits, it said, would help substantially to stabilize prices and conquer the evil of speculation. The Food Administration also praised the beet sugar producers, whose timely pledge to charge no more than $7.25 per hundred had broken a dangerous speculative bubble in imported sugar. According to the Food Administration, the Hawaiian cane sugar industry had also now acceded to Hoover's terms. His control of domestic wholesale prices and profit margins was nearly complete.[242]

Meanwhile, in the plantations of Cuba, the sugar crop of 1917 was maturing. It now remained for the buyers' cartel known as the International Sugar Committee to acquire it in toto from its owners.[243] Despite initial professions of cordiality from the Cuban government, the negotiations over a purchase price soon stalled. Hoover recommended $4.50 for each one hundred pounds of raw sugar obtained at Cuban ports—a figure that would work out to $4.80 per hundred pounds (counting shipping costs) in New York.[244] It was evidently on this basis that he had reached his various agreements with American refiners. If the Cubans did not go along, it could throw his elaborate structure of price control into a heap.

The Cuban planters, however, had their own ideas about price. Insisting that $4.50 per hundred was insufficient to cover their costs, they called upon their government to protect them. On October 26 the Cuban minister to Washington wrote to the State Department in support of a price of $4.75 to $5.00 per hundred in Cuba—which would translate into $5.05 or even $5.25 in New York.[245]

Hoover was not amused by the Cuban government's intervention. At his request the State Department pointedly informed the Cubans that the price should be fixed by the buyers and sellers, not by the government of the United States. Having thus washed its hands of what it chose to regard as a purely commercial dispute, the department then went on to give the Cubans reasons why they should not hold out for too high a price![246] When the Cuban minister persisted in lobbying the State Department for a $4.75 minimum,[247] an irritated Hoover complained directly to President Wilson. Not only were the Cubans' demands excessive, he charged; the president of Cuba was attempting to inject "governmental pressure" into "simply a commercial transaction."[248] Wilson agreed and instructed the State Department to act accordingly.[249]

Hoover did not get his way completely, however. Fearful that the Cuban countryside would erupt in revolution unless the government in Havana secured an agreeable price, the State Department asked Hoover to raise his offer to $4.60.[250] The Food Administrator took its advice. When the Cuban negotiators returned to the bargaining table in late November, they and their American counterparts quickly compromised at this very figure.[251] A few weeks later a contract formally ratified the bargain, and more than 2,500,000 tons of Cuban sugar began to move—one third, by agreement, to the European Allies, and two thirds to the United States.[252]

With this achievement Hoover's second great pillar of commodity control was finally, fully, in place. Step by step—by exhortation and cajolery, appeals to pride and patriotism, the lure of guaranteed profits and the cudgel of regulatory power—he had persuaded a great American industry to replace free competition with a remarkable experiment in price repression. How well it would function the months ahead would disclose.

IV

MEANWHILE Hoover's regulatory dominion was expanding on a multitude of fronts. By the first week of October, he and his lieutenants had held two hundred separate conferences in Washington with representatives of food-related interests—all, as a press release put it, for the purpose of devising "regulations and constructive methods of control."[253] Hoover was anxious to win the "cooperation of all patriotic men in the various trades" in drafting and implementing these mechanisms. The great goal, he announced, was to abolish "speculation, hoarding, unreasonable profits, [and] wasteful practices" from the food distribution system of the nation.[254] He wished, as he later phrased it, to limit "the margin between the producer and the consumer to the least possible figure compatible with the normal and proper functioning of business."[255]

But if Hoover desired the "patriotic cooperation"[256] of affected industries, he had no intention of simply hoping for their assent. His handling of wheat and sugar demonstrated that. While the Food Administrator professed to believe that the overwhelming majority of businessmen were honest and eager to work harmoniously with their government, he also insisted that he must protect them from "slackers."[257] The system of industrial governance that he was building would not, therefore, be elective or self-administered. It would contain a coercive element for all to see.

And so on October 10, 1917, at Hoover's request, President Wilson ordered all persons and businesses in the United States engaged in the manufacture, storage, importation, or distribution of more than twenty basic foodstuffs to obtain a license by November 1 from the Food Administration. In scope as well as intent, this was perhaps the most extraordinary regulatory act ever taken by the federal government. Meat packers, canners, millers, grain dealers, cold-storage warehousemen, wholesale distributors, and major retailers: all were required to secure a permit from the government to do business. Wheat, corn, oats, barley, rice, beef, pork, milk, butter, cheese, poultry, eggs, fish, sugar, fresh fruits, and fresh vegetables: these foods and more came under federal control. While farmers, small retailers, and certain others were exempted from the proclamation's writ, everyone else who handled the listed commodities was subject to license and to the rules to be promulgated thereunder.[258] Without a license, businesses could not trade in these goods.[259] By November 1 more than 40,000 applications had flooded into Washington.[260] Eventually the Food Administration issued nearly 300,000 licenses of all kinds.[261]

On November 3 Hoover unveiled the rules with which all licensed businesses must comply.[262] They must keep appropriate records and send reports to the Food Administration as required. They must open their records and facilities to inspection upon its request. They must refrain from taking any "unjust, exorbitant, unreasonable, discriminatory or unfair commission, profit, or storage charge." They must resell no goods to competitors without "reasonable justification." As a deterrent to hoarding (and its destabilizing effects on prices), they must hold in stock no more food products than they would normally require during a period of sixty days.[263] The Food

Administration was determined that no one should acquire "speculative profits from a rising market."[264] And it warned that any violation of its rules would be cause for revocation of a license as well as the criminal penalties prescribed in the law.[265]

To give teeth to his prohibition of "speculative profits," Hoover ordered wholesalers in various nonperishable goods to sell their produce at no more than a "reasonable advance" over what they paid for it. But what if a commodity had shot upward in value in the meantime? For Hoover it did not matter. The wholesaler must base his resale price and profit margin on his own actual cost, not on the items' current market value.[266] Such was the "cost basis" rule that Hoover imposed to prevent price-gouging and profiteering. According to one of his associates, it saved consumers at least half a billion dollars on nonperishable food grown in 1917 alone.[267]

What, however, constituted a "reasonable advance" or a "normal" profit? What profits were "unjust" and "unfair"? In late November, upon Hoover's recommendation, President Wilson issued a definition by executive order. A "just, reasonable, and fair profit" under the Lever Act would be "the normal average profit which persons engaged in the same business and place obtained prior to July 1, 1914, under free competitive conditions." Wilson authorized Hoover to determine just what margins above cost would yield such a rate of profit and to prohibit any profit taking above this limit.[268]

By establishing a prewar baseline, Hoover refused to accept as normative the boom years of 1914–17 with their "very large profits earned from war conditions." These had created "a fictitious basis of commerce," he argued. At first many businessmen complained bitterly, but Hoover, undeterred, insisted that "no one has a right to take an extra profit from America at war."[269] In the months ahead he steadily converted the President's broad criterion into detailed restraints upon the profits of numerous food industries.[270]

And now only one link in the food distribution chain still eluded his ever-widening net: the small businesses that sold food directly to consumers. The Lever Act, of course, explicitly exempted from licensing all retailers whose gross sales amounted to less than $100,000 a year—in effect, 95 percent of the more than 350,000 retail food dealers in the United States.[271] For Hoover this was a potentially fatal flaw. His regulators might fix prices "at the production point" (as he later put it) and then control profit differentials at every step of distribution.[272] Every step, that is, but the last. What if the unlicensed small retailers—the corner grocery stores and similar outlets where most Americans actually bought their food—failed to pass along the savings imposed from above? What if the retailers cheerfully profiteered?

Whatever the intent of Congress in drafting this provision in the Lever Act, Hoover and his colleagues could not abide it. Threatened with the complete subversion of his anti-inflation program, in the late summer and autumn of 1917 he groped for ways to bring wayward retailers into line. He tried persuasion—what a later generation would call jawboning—with at least an initial appearance of success: in mid-October a representative assembly of retail food distributors meeting in Washington unanimously pledged "whether licensed or not" to cooperate in enforcing his rules.[273] The pledge was disseminated to businesses throughout the country; more than 3,000,000 copies were requested.[274]

The Food Administration also tried bluff by intimating to the press in September that if retailers failed to cooperate, the President would compel them to seek a license.[275] Hoover and his lieutenants tried legal interpretation by arguing that even if small retailers were exempted from licensing, they were still subject to other provisions of the Lever Act, including section 4, which forbade unreasonable charges, hoarding, and waste.[276] The Food Administration tried "the club of public opinion." On October 18 Hoover disclosed that his agency would issue weekly statements listing the prices that food wholesalers charged their retailers in various cities *and* the prices at which retailers sold the same goods to consumers. In this way the retailers' profits would be exposed. Hoover clearly hoped that his floodlight of publicity would shame retailers into holding down their prices—or inspire consumers into pressuring retailers to do so.[277]

None of these tactics, however, was immediately effectual. The Food Administrator and his associates could huff and puff, but what could they really do? While small retailers were arguably subject to section 4 of the Lever Act, the section provided no penalty for its violation. But Hoover's men were nothing if not resourceful, and it was his senior adviser Mark Requa who found a solution to their quandary. At one of Hoover's 7:00 A.M. breakfast conferences, Requa suggested that the Food Administration simply forbid its licensed *wholesalers* from selling goods to unlicensed *retailers* who failed to obey the Food Administration's rules.[278] Thus deprived of their source of supplies, the offending retailers would either have to submit or go out of business.

And so in November, among its general requirements for licensees, the Food Administration included the following rule: No wholesaler, manufacturer, or other food handler under Food Administration license would be permitted to sell any food commodity to any business (whether licensed or not) which, in violation of the Lever Act, made "unreasonable" rates and charges, or which bought products in excess of its "reasonable" needs.[279] The determination of violations would be made solely by the Food Administration. By this single, daring regulatory act, Hoover and his colleagues invented a penalty that did not exist in the law and closed the last avenue of escape from their authority. In a nation at war, apparently no one challenged them.

By late autumn 1917, then—barely 120 days after its official inception—Hoover's crusading consumer protection agency had established an elaborate framework of authority over the nation's food staples, from the soil almost literally to the stomach. He had promised that he would "guide the trade" in the interest of defeating inflation, and this he was doing, with a zeal, ingenuity, and persistence that few in Washington had ever seen. He had promised "constructive regulations" that would make "gambling," "extortion," and waste "impossible" in America's food sector.[280] From his agency, rules and directives were pouring forth to accomplish these ends.

Yet even as his machinery of control began to hum with Hooverian efficiency, he was turning to other battlegrounds in his war. Not all his targets were domestic. He faced plenty of impediments abroad.

5

America First

I

As Hoover responded to impending food scarcity in the summer of 1917, he knew that his war on inflation had more than a single front. Abolishing "speculation," setting "fair" prices and profits, "reflecting" these to consumers, regulating and even suspending free competition: all these measures would prove inadequate unless he could also repress demand, both foreign and domestic. With a finite and inelastic supply of key crops for months to come, he must somehow direct their allocation or face the kind of stampede that had ravaged the wheat market in the spring. Unbridled, competitive buying, particularly by agents of foreign countries: this, in Hoover's judgment, was the fundamental cause of runaway prices.[1] Unfettered, competitive buying must therefore cease.

This meant controlling—or, more politely, "coordinating"—the food requirements and purchasing practices of America's western Allies. He had testified to Congress in June and had thoroughly meant what he said: England, Italy, and France must not be permitted to "vacuum" America's food reserves to the point of leaving the United States with a food shortage next spring.[2] We must "guard our exports," he announced on August 10, both to "retain sufficient supplies" for ourselves and to "prevent inflation of prices."[3] The stringent stewardship of America's food exports was the second part of his grand design.

Yet by midsummer, more than three months after his return from Europe, Hoover's system of control was incomplete. His proposal in April to consolidate Allied food purchasing under a single intergovernmental food board had yet to materialize. Italy and France, it seemed, were reluctant to surrender their freedom of action to a body on which Great Britain would have more influence than they, while Britain was loathe to yield its preeminence to a board that would inevitably be dominated by the United States.[4]

For Hoover, such considerations were no doubt trivial. Far more worrisome was the Allies' continuing failure (except for wheat) to pool their orders in the American market. As a result of their "furious competition" for meats and fats, he charged, the price of domestic beef and pork was soaring and would cost American consumers hundreds of millions of dollars per year.[5] Repeatedly that summer he urged the Allies to consolidate their purchases of meat products in the hands of a single agent in New York.[6] When his pleas went unanswered, he hinted to a British official that the United States might be driven to use its controls over exports to "induce" the Allies to act.[7] On August 16 he became more explicit. If the Allies refused to join a unified buying entity, he told a British visitor, the United States would stop granting export licenses for its food.[8]

By August 23 no definitive response to his entreaties had come from across the Atlantic,[9] and Hoover's slim stock of patience had vanished. Convinced that a crisis was at hand, and that a total embargo of fat exports must be considered "unless we can get a proper organization in this matter," the Food Administrator invoked another weapon. Great Britain, Italy, and France were now receiving enormous loans from the U.S. government. Hoover therefore asked Secretary of the Treasury William McAdoo, who was administering these disbursements, to notify the Allies that, unless they immediately set up a coordinated purchasing mechanism for American meat and fats, McAdoo would simply withhold all further advances.[10]

Never content with one form of pressure when two or more were available, Hoover aimed his next salvo at London. The day after his letter to McAdoo, he dispatched a cable to the Surveyor-General of Supply at the British government's War Office, a man with whom he had had business ties before the war:

> It is probable that unless Allies have adopted a common buying policy in all fats that we shall embargo all exports until it is done. We simply cannot have our whole consuming population demoralized and hate started against the Allies by this mad competition between themselves.[11]

Twenty-four hours later, in a conversation in Washington with the head of the British War Mission (Lord Northcliffe), Hoover bitterly denounced the Allies' indiscriminate buying of American meat products and demanded that it be controlled at once. He also reminded Northcliffe that one of his primary goals as Food Administrator was "to prevent a runaway market" for foodstuffs in the United States.[12]

Hoover's cabled warning to London may have been a bluff. Neither it nor his letter to McAdoo appear to have been authorized by the White House, and it is doubtful that President Wilson would have sanctioned such drastic steps. But Hoover had learned as Belgian relief director that threats, if credible, could concentrate the minds of his adversaries in a hurry. Once again his tough tactics paid off. Within days of his thinly disguised ultimatum, the governments of Great Britain, France, and Italy agreed to establish an Inter-Allied Meat and Fats Executive headquartered in London.[13] Several weeks later the Executive's newly formed New York buying organization, known as APEC, began to function.[14] Eventually nearly all Allied food purchases in the United States other than cereals and sugar became APEC's responsibility alone, in cooperation with the U.S. Food Administration.

Hoover's success on the meat front was quickly followed by another, when the European Allies agreed to his creation of an International Sugar Committee to bargain for and apportion the world's harvests. It did not escape their notice, however, that this new committee had an American majority. Before long, the British suspected that Hoover's representatives were attempting "to secure for America an undue share of the easily accessible supplies."[15] Such tensions probably disturbed Hoover very little. What mattered more was that he had gained his fundamental objective: elimination of independent bidding for a scarce commodity.

In the case of wheat, his task was easier still. Here America's wartime associates had already reached an enviable level of efficiency. In late 1916 the western European Allies had created a body known as the Wheat Executive for the purchase, transport, and allocation of cereals from abroad. Shortly thereafter, the Wheat Executive had assigned many of its functions to the British government's Royal Commission on Wheat Supplies, which in turn employed a purchasing agent called the Wheat Export Company in the United States.[16] Impressed by the efficiency of this system, Hoover tried to have the Wheat Export Company take over meat transactions as well. When the British declined to do this,[17] the eventual result was the formation of APEC as a separate but analogous organization. While Hoover would have preferred one commodity executive instead of two, at least with wheat he did not have to force the Allies' hand. Instead, he could concentrate on meshing their existing machinery with his own.

Meanwhile the Food Administrator worked to perfect domestic mechanisms that would collaborate with—and dominate—their Allied counterparts. Hoover was not the only American official thinking in these terms. For some time Secretary of the Treasury McAdoo had also been worried by the economic and political consequences of the Allies' scramble for war materiel in the United States. How could he go on dispensing ever-increasing credits to the Allies unless they could justify their expenditures? During the summer he pressed the Allies to establish procedures for determining their priorities and coordinating their purchases of American supplies. Unless they did so, he warned, he would refuse to grant them further loans. On August 24 the European governments accepted his terms. From now on they must make their purchases in America solely through, or with the approval of, a specially created American board called the Allied Purchasing Commission.[18] The new system was codified in formal contracts between the Treasury and the European debtors.[19] Once more the administration of Woodrow Wilson had interposed itself between its wartime associates and the American economy.

The President apparently intended the new commission to delegate its power over Allied food purchases to Hoover.[20] Certainly Hoover expected and desired this authority; he declared that his task of food control would be "hopeless" without "immediate direction" of Allied buying.[21] Late in September, after he appealed (perhaps unnecessarily) to the White House, the commission formally authorized his agency to "purchase, and direct the purchase" of all food that the Allies might require within the United States under their arrangements with McAdoo.[22] While the commission continued to approve or disapprove the Allies' estimates of need in this area, effective control now passed to Hoover. Henceforth the Europeans could acquire no food products in America without the Food Administration's knowledge and sanction.

Hoover assigned the management of Allied cereal purchases to his Grain Corporation, which worked with the Wheat Export Company.[23] For all other commodities except sugar, he created a branch of the Food Administration called the Division of Coordination of Purchase, which collaborated and negotiated with APEC.[24] By late autumn the symmetry was complete: for each intergovernmental Allied food-buying organization (one of which he himself had forced into being) there was a parallel American governmental entity, determining both outflow and price. The symmetry, however, was artificial, as both Hoover and the Allies knew. Thanks to the Allies' deepening dependence on American loans and resources, it was the seller, not the buyer, who was in command.

In no case was this reversal more obvious than with wheat. During the summer the Wilson administration had created an Exports Administrative Board to develop and enforce its trade policy. On August 28 Hoover boldly asked the board to grant export licenses for wheat only upon condition that the prospective shipment be purchased from his Grain Corporation.[25] The board responded by giving him power to quash any wheat export licenses that it granted.[26] In this way Hoover gained a monopoly over the wheat export trade and was able to prevent foreign buyers from causing what he called "speculation"—meaning higher prices—on the American market.[27] By the time the Wilsonian trade regulations were fully elaborated a few months later, no food products of any kind could receive clearance for Europe until the Food Administration approved the exporter's application for a license.[28]

Hoover's expanding control of the wheat supply soon led to difficulties from an unusual direction: America's wartime ally to the north. Like the United States, the Dominion of Canada was a major wheat producer, whose 1917 harvest was awaited anxiously in Europe. Like America also, Canada had experienced chaotic market conditions and soaring grain prices in the spring. In response, the Dominion government on June 11 had created a "Board of Grain Supervisors for Canada," with power to fix the price of Canadian wheat.[29]

Anxious to treat the North American harvest as a single unit, Hoover conferred in July with a delegation from the Canadian board.[30] It soon developed that on two critical issues the two sides disagreed. The Canadians—reflecting, perhaps, the political clout of their farm interests—wanted to set the price of wheat much higher than did Hoover.[31] The Canadians also wanted the price at terminals to increase until the following May in order to cover storage charges. After all, their chairman later pointed out, this had always been standard commercial procedure. Wheat held over the winter in an elevator *should* cost more than wheat sold early in the fall.[32]

For Hoover and Julius Barnes—committed to an unchanging price for wheat for an entire year—the Canadian position, however plausible, was wrong. To Hoover, a single, unvarying price was a political necessity, vital to the psychology of stability that he was trying to foster among nervous consumers. To Barnes, it was an economic incentive to farmers to market their crop at once rather than hold it back in storage at their own expense.[33] The sooner the farmers sold their wheat, the sooner Barnes could stabilize flour and bread prices.

The Canadians, however, seemed unmoved by these arguments. On August 17, just as Hoover's fair price committee began its deliberations, the Board of Grain Supervisors temporarily fixed the price of No. 1 Northern wheat at $2.40 per bushel.[34] The Food Administrator now faced a disconcerting prospect: If the Canadians established a higher price for wheat than the Americans, or if the Canadians permitted the same initial price to rise each month while the American price was held steady, the resulting divergence would produce a political thunderclap in the American heartland.[35] When Yankee wheat growers discovered that the same crop sold for more money north of the border, they would vent their wrath on Hoover and Julius Barnes.

In late summer, then, Barnes and his chief attempted to bring the balky Canadians into line. Barnes pleaded with the head of the Canadian grain board, Robert A. Magill, to accept a stabilized price. Let the European Allies absorb the accumulating storage charges, Barnes argued; the Allies "could well afford to assume this obligation and expense."[36] Unknown to Magill, Barnes also approached H. T. Robson, vice president of the Allies' Wheat

Export Company in New York. "It is absolutely necessary" that the American and Canadian wheat prices be "uniform," said Barnes; "widespread political disturbance" was the alternative. We cannot let American farmers sell wheat for less than their Canadian counterparts, Barnes declared, nor can we let the Canadians jeopardize "fair protection" for American consumers. He therefore urged Robson to have his superiors in London order him to "disregard" Canadian wheat "offerings" if Magill and his colleagues acted "unreasonably." Such action, Barnes predicted, would force the Canadian price to come down.[37]

As it happened, the British government hardly needed this suggestion. By August 1917 the United Kingdom was on the brink of financial catastrophe. Critically short of currency exchange and fearful for the stability of the pound sterling, the British government was obliged to stop all purchases of meat in Canada on August 23.[38] That same day a British representative in Washington asked the U.S. Treasury for permission to use a portion of its recent loan to purchase the new Canadian wheat crop.[39] Such a step would violate the U.S. government's rigid requirement that all its advances to the Allies must be spent within the borders of the United States. When the Americans proved reluctant to grant an exception, the British government was forced into a desperate act: in the last days of August the Wheat Export Company suspended its purchases of Canadian wheat.[40]

The British government's embargo caused consternation in Canada. When the Canadian food controller notified Hoover of the Wheat Export Company's action, the Food Administrator seized the weapon thrust into his hands. At Barnes's suggestion, Hoover informed the Canadians that he understood the Wheat Export Company to be "abstaining from [the] market in order to be sure Canadian prices" were not fixed above the American price. The implication was unmistakable that the British would again buy Canadian wheat when the Canadians lowered their price to the American level.[41]

Hoover's response was almost certainly based on a misconception. There is no evidence that Barnes (whose advice he followed) was right in his assessment of the Wheat Export Company's motives. It was Great Britain's financial weakness, not its anger at the Canadian wheat price, that had forced the suspension of purchases.[42] Nevertheless, Hoover's reply to Ottawa appeared to be efficacious. In any case, the Board of Grain Supervisors for Canada soon retreated.[43] On September 12 it announced that the price of No. 1 Manitoba Northern wheat in the dominion would be $2.21—only a penny above the comparable American price—and that it would remain uniform for nearly a year.[44] On both issues in dispute, Hoover had emerged victorious.[45]

The Food Administrator's involvement with the Canadians, however, had not ended. A few weeks later, after tortuous negotiations in Washington, the Department of the Treasury abandoned its policy that U.S. government credits must be spent on purchases inside the country. It now consented to loan Great Britain $200,000,000 with which to buy the 1917 wheat surplus of Canada.[46] The purchasing agent would be the Wheat Export Company.

Hoover was anxious that a substantial portion of the Canadian harvest be diverted to American mills for conversion to flour prior to export.[47] This proposal did not endear him to the Canadian milling industry, which preferred to keep such business for itself. Nevertheless, at his request the British, Canadian, and American governments agreed to let him obtain whatever Canadian wheat he required from the Wheat Export Company's purchased stocks, provided that he promptly supply equivalent amounts of flour for export.[48]

Unknown to the Allies, Hoover was contemplating more than an occasional, limited tapping of the Canadian supply. He told a Treasury official in October that he would want to acquire at least twenty to twenty-five million bushels from this source.[49] Yet if Hoover was eager to funnel Canadian wheat into American grain mills, he emphatically did not want to import Canadian *flour*. Early in October, in apparent violation of an understanding with the Food Administration, the Canadian food controller authorized a number of Canadian businesses to export flour to the United States.[50] This action (which Hoover as yet had no legal power to stop) quickly antagonized American flour millers, who feared that their Canadian competitors would undercut them. On October 12 James F. Bell—head of Hoover's milling division and himself a leader in the American trade—urged his chief not to accept Canadian wheat to relieve American mills if this meant allowing Canadian flour to come in also. Such a step, he asserted, would reduce American output and ultimately raise the price to American consumers.[51]

Three days later Hoover fired off a telegram to Ottawa. Asserting forcefully that Canadian flour imports were "entirely disrupting our flour control and price levels," he asked his Canadian counterpart to prohibit all shipments exceeding fifty barrels.[52] The Canadian food controller apparently complied.[53] At the same time James F. Bell went north to reach a modus vivendi with the Canadians. On October 19 the two countries agreed to trade no flour across their border for the rest of the war.[54] Once again the imperatives of regulatory stability had taken precedence over free competition. A few days later, the Canadian pledge to cease flour exports to the United States was included in the terms of the $200,000,000 loan to Great Britain.[55] Hoover had plugged another hole in the dike.

By the end of October, with the approval of the British government, Hoover's Grain Corporation was siphoning off 200,000 bushels of Canadian wheat per day at the Great Lakes port of Buffalo.[56] Then, without warning, a dangerous challenge to his entire structure of wheat control erupted on the plains of Manitoba. Early in September the Board of Grain Supervisors for Canada had apparently agreed with Julius Barnes that all Canadian wheat exports would go exclusively to the Wheat Export Company. If the United States wanted any of this stock, it would have to obtain it by negotiating with the company.[57] A few weeks later this understanding was incorporated in the $200,000,000 loan agreement by which the United States financed the British purchase of the Canadian crop. So, at least, Barnes and Hoover later insisted.[58]

It soon transpired that the government in Ottawa had evidently neither consulted its grain board in Winnipeg during the loan negotiations nor subsequently informed it about the terms.[59] Angered at being left out of the action, and professing ignorance even of the existence of the loan contract, Chairman Magill of the Canadian board announced at the beginning of November that his agency would shortly issue permits for the private export of Canadian wheat to the United States. He did not want the Wheat Export Company to have a monopoly on Canadian wheat, he said. Besides, he asserted, the understandings of September were only temporary.[60]

For Hoover this act of defiance could not stand. If private Canadian exporters were allowed to ship wheat across the border, they could threaten the American price scale and upset his delicate system of wheat allocation to the mills.[61] Magill must be put in his place. Hoover therefore authorized Barnes to tell Magill that if the Canadian grain board violated its "agreement," Hoover would ask the U.S. Treasury to cancel the whole $200,000,000 loan![62] In the next few days a series of pointed cables from Barnes, high-ranking British officials, and even the visiting Canadian food controller speedily forced the mutinous Magill to back down.[63] There would be no disturbing, uncontrolled competition from Canadian wheat exporters. Hoover had gotten his way.

This brush with chaos only deepened Barnes's conviction that the United States must immediately prohibit imports of foreign wheat. Repeatedly in November he lobbied Hoover on this point.[64] Hoover agreed. Later that month, in response in part to his urgings, the War Trade Board recommended that the importation of wheat and certain other foodstuffs be controlled by a system of licenses. President Wilson duly issued the proclamation.[65] As with food exports, so now with food imports: the War Trade Board henceforth granted licenses only upon the advice—in effect the approval—of the Food Administration.[66]

With this act Hoover's diligent erection of barriers to independent Allied commercial transactions was complete. The food arsenal of America was now a fortress, the keys to which rested securely in his hands. Creation of regulatory machinery and of export-import controls, however, was only the first step in his plan to restrain America's wartime associates. The second was to implement a policy. How much should the Allies be permitted to ship from America's shores before next summer? How much could he dare to spare?

II

MEETING with Harry Garfield's "fair price" committee on August 20, Hoover asserted that the United States had just escaped a "grave crisis." Because America had sent more wheat abroad than it prudently should have in the 1916–17 crop year, the nation's reserves in early summer had dipped to virtually the lowest ever recorded, and prices had raced to "abnormally high" levels. Hoover was determined that this "over-export situation" must never recur. For the coming year, he announced, the government would limit exports "to an amount which will protect our consumption."[67]

The fledgling Food Administrator, then, faced two contradictory challenges. On the one hand he must send the western Allies as much food as possible; if he failed, the war could be lost. On the other hand, he must send them as little as possible, lest his own people suffer hardship and want. Publicly, officially, he was committed to feeding the Allies and to the proposition that "simple duty to humanity" obliged his country to succor a suffering world.[68] But behind the scenes, away from formal displays of lofty rhetoric, two other considerations loomed as large: he must quench the fires of inflation, and he must protect America first.

It soon became evident that Hoover had more in mind than eliminating uncontrolled Allied buying of American wheat and flour. He wanted—though he could hardly say so openly—to *reduce* the amount of wheat that the Allies were taking from America's granaries. During the spring and summer, before the Food Administration was fully organized, Allied agents had bought heavily in the American market. The ever present threat of starvation-by-submarine had egged them on. Back in March, when wheat stocks in Great Britain dipped to nearly the vanishing point, a frightened British Cabinet had ordered the Royal Commission on Wheat Supplies to build up a thirteen-week reserve of breadstuffs. By August the commission had succeeded—by drawing voraciously upon the North American source of supply.[69] For the desperate Allies it was an insurance policy against catastrophe if future supplies were ever cut off. For Hoover it posed unacceptable risks of another sort.

Accordingly, in September 1917 American wheat and flour shipments to England began to decline—a trend that continued throughout the autumn. The Food Administration blamed the initial slump on a shortage of wheat occasioned by the farmers' "strike" against the newly announced fixed price. Later, Hoover asserted that early frosts had reduced the exportable surplus. But whatever the reason (or excuse), the first effect of the mediocre American wheat crop of 1917 could not have been more contrary to Allied expectations.[70]

Meanwhile the British, French, and Italian governments were preparing their estimates of future need. On October 6 they made their first submission: in the next four months they would require an "absolute minimum" of 5,000,000 tons of cereals from the United States and Canada, including 1,400,000 tons of American wheat and flour.[71] Studying this request, Hoover was seized by a nightmare. If the Allies were permitted to raid the North American market without letup, the United States would be denuded of wheat altogether by the coming May or June—well before the harvest of 1918 was ready. Then would come famine, rationing, hyperinflation, and the social unrest he continuously feared. Hoover was determined to avoid this peril at all costs. His resolve was probably strengthened when he heard from his London agent in mid-October that the British had already accumulated sufficient wheat and flour to sustain themselves for at least five months.[72]

The Food Administrator was now convinced that the Allies must be brought firmly to heel. In late October the means to do so became available. Colonel Edward M. House, confidant of the President and patron of Hoover's career, was assembling a mission to Europe to coordinate America's economic and military resources with those of its wartime partners.[73] In preparation for the inter-Allied conference ahead, House invited Professor Alonzo Taylor, the nutritionist who was also a staunch Hoover loyalist, to represent the Food Administration on the mission. For Hoover the opportunity for decisive action had come. On October 27, the day before the mission's departure, he laid a stunning memorandum in the colonel's hands.

In it the Food Administrator asserted that the relative proximity of North American food to Allied ships, and "American prodigality" in loaning money for Allied purchases, were creating an intolerable danger. There was no way that Canada and the United States alone could supply all that the Allies needed to eat. Yet if the British and their cohorts were allowed to draw upon this convenient food source without stint, they would "exhaust our entire surplus long before the next harvest," and would then be driven to more distant markets. For Hoover, such a course was "the negation of good statesmanship." The American "food hoard," he declared, "should be held on to until the last" as a reserve against unexpected losses of Allied shipping.

In fact, Hoover now contended, America ideally should carry over a huge surplus *even beyond* the next harvest ("as the last resort of a degenerating world's food supply") and should let the rest of the world feed the Allies in the meantime. Such a policy, he hinted, would help to control domestic inflation as well as relieve pressure on the nation's railways. It would also (though he did not say this) give the United States tremendous leverage against the Allies after the war. In a recommendation at startling variance with his public posture as the Allies' saviour, Hoover urged that the coming inter-Allied conference in Europe use "every possible engine . . . to increase the transport from markets furthest afield," in order to reserve "as large a stock of food in the United States as may be possible." In short, the Food Administrator was boldly proposing that America send its European associates as little sustenance, not as much, as it could.[74]

By now—or so he later indicated—Hoover was even more pessimistic than his recommendation to Colonel House let on. In a memorandum that he later said he gave to Professor Taylor before he departed for Europe, Hoover disclosed that the exportable surplus of American wheat had been exhausted. Until the American people reduced their consumption of the 1917 crop now being harvested, there would be no wheat available for shipment to the Allies. Hoover therefore ordered Taylor to tell them that they had better look elsewhere in the interim.[75]

Hoover's instructions to Taylor were decidedly odd. On October 13 the U.S. Department of Agriculture had publicly announced that the 1917 wheat crop would yield a surplus of nearly 78,000,000 bushels, or about 11.8 percent of the total harvest.[76] Moreover, in a speech in late September, Hoover himself had estimated that the United States would have an exportable surplus of 80,000,000 bushels from the new harvest. He had even published this speech as a Food Administration document on October 25.[77] Now, just a day or two later, he apparently concluded that the surplus had disappeared.

What had happened? Obviously some of the surplus had already been shipped to the Allies.[78] But more importantly, in projecting an 11.8 percent margin over domestic needs, the Department of Agriculture assumed that the nation's per capita annual consumption of wheat in 1917–18 would be 10 percent less than normal.[79] In their consultations on or around October 27, however, Hoover evidently convinced Taylor—or vice versa—to make no such optimistic assumption. Using the normal per capita consumption of 5.3 bushels per year as a basis for calculation, Hoover concluded that he had no wheat left to export, unless he shipped what he had at hand and risked disaster in the spring.[80]

Having briefed Taylor with this lugubrious news, Hoover dispatched him to Europe without consulting or notifying Julius Barnes, who, as head of the Grain Corporation in New York, was more conversant with the wheat business than either of them.[81] Thus it came about that at the beginning of November, while Taylor was somewhere in the North Atlantic, Barnes sent an unsolicited letter to his chief. Unaware of Hoover's sudden gloom about the wheat supply, Barnes reported that the United States would be in a position to export only about 30,000,000 bushels of wheat after the rest of the 1917 crop was used for seed or milled into flour. But on the basis of data showing markedly declining flour consumption in New York City since 1916, Barnes was convinced that the American people as a whole would not consume all the flour manufactured by the mills. In fact, he informed Hoover, the United States would likely end up with an exportable surplus of 40,000,000 barrels, far more than ever before.[82] In Barnes's eyes, at least, the outlook was distinctly encouraging.

Now occurred yet another odd development in Washington. Ignoring Barnes's optimistic projections about flour, Hoover notified his representative in London on November 8 that the "exportable balance" of *wheat* from the United States was only 33,000,000 bushels ("disregarding conservation"). With the Allies in need of 40,000,000 bushels per month, and with the Canadian surplus insufficient to fill the gap for long, Hoover deemed it "absolutely imperative" that the Allies go to Argentina for their wheat as soon as possible.[83] A week later he cabled London again and more emphatically: the wheat situation was even "more serious" than previously thought; America's domestic requirements had been underestimated. According to Hoover, there was "no alternative" to the Allies' turning to India and Australia for imports prior to the ripening of the Argentine harvest. In fact, the Allies should henceforth import their wheat from "all . . . quarters" *except* the United States and should rely upon America for corn and oats instead.[84]

Hoover therefore demanded that his representative on the House mission, Alonzo Taylor, obtain "relief from Allied pressure" as soon as possible.[85] In the meantime he strove to enlist the support of the White House for his initiative. On November 15 he informed President Wilson that, based on average domestic consumption since 1914, the nation now had no wheat whatever to spare. The Food Administrator acknowledged that Americans might by "forced measures" in the months ahead cut their intake by as many as 100,000,000 bushels, which could then be exported. But this, he warned, was "a speculation" on conservation—a "gamble" that he clearly did not care to take. For Hoover, the imperatives were bleak. The United States government, he told Wilson, must "put the country on a mild war bread" containing wheat substitutes; it must cease exporting wheat to neutral nations; and it must order the Allies to buy their wheat somewhere else. If the United States exported any more wheat abroad at all, these shipments must be replaced from Canada or Argentina. Hoover warned the President that if the nation fell 10 percent short in its "prime food," the urban and industrial classes would suffer and the nation's "tranquility" would be imperiled. The battle to control prices would also be "hopeless."[86]

Hoover was depressed, dreading the day (he told a friend) when the country would run out of wheat, which it surely would unless Americans began to conserve as never before.[87] Clearly he had no faith in spontaneous belt-tightening or switching to other foods. Woodrow Wilson, too, was disturbed. Without questioning Hoover's statistics, he at once ordered Colonel House in Europe to insist on the "imperative necessity" of the Allies' obtaining their wheat first from Australia, then from Argentina, and only lastly from the United States.[88] The Allies, Wilson remarked, must be compelled to do this.[89] The Hoover-orchestrated campaign of high-pressure diplomacy was in full swing.

Meanwhile, in London, Alonzo Taylor had detonated Hoover's bombshell, to the consternation of Allied officials.[90] The Allies had been listening to their Wheat Export Company, which in turn had been relying on data from Julius Barnes.[91] On this basis, the Wheat Executive had confidently planned upon importing nearly 260,000,000 bushels of wheat from Canada and the United States in the 1917–18 crop year. Now, according to Hoover and Taylor, the combined exportable surplus from the two countries amounted to fewer than 133,000,000 bushels. In one radical stroke Hoover had cut the Allies' projected North American import program nearly in half.[92]

As the Allied authorities recovered from their shock, Taylor sternly lectured them on the need to repress their cereal consumption. According to Taylor, his European counterparts were loath to do so—and particularly to ration bread lest they incite the anger of their restive working classes. If the Allies had gotten their way at the conference, Taylor reported afterwards, they would have kept their people on normal consumption, would have scooped up wheat in North America at the rate originally planned, and would have forced the United States to impose "great public control" over its own population. Taylor bluntly refused to permit this shifting of the burden; in this he had the complete backing of Hoover.[93]

Staggered by the dismal statistics emanating from Washington, the Allied governments on November 16 accepted Hoover's claim: the combined exportable wheat surplus from Canada and the United States would be only 132,000,000 bushels from the 1917 crop.[94] Upon receiving this news from Taylor, Hoover tightened the screws even further. On November 8 he had informed Europe that the remaining American wheat surplus was 33,000,000 bushels and the Canadian 100,000,000. Now, just nine days later, and less than a day after the Allies capitulated, he put the Canadian surplus at 120,000,000 bushels and the American at zero. What this meant, he told Taylor, was that the Allies must henceforth obtain *all* their wheat from Canada and other sources. Since Canadian wheat could not be transported across the frozen Great Lakes during the winter, and since Argentine wheat was not yet fully available, the United States might have to export wheat to Europe temporarily. But if so, Hoover declared, such provisions should be considered a loan, repayable from Canadian stocks later on.[95]

Hoping to salvage something from the wreck, Taylor's European associates asked for delivery of most of the North American wheat surplus in the next three months, in order to tide them over pending shipments from Argentina.[96] According to Taylor, the Allies preferred to obtain all of their reduced allotment that quickly if they could.[97] Hoover did not immediately commit himself. On November 19 he notified London that he could supply the 132,000,000 bushels, but he did not say exactly when. He did add that he might be able to increase the weekly flow of wheat and flour from North America by 33 percent if the Allies furnished the ships. At that rate it would take about four months (not three) to funnel the surplus to the Allies.[98]

The Allied governments were far from happy with the regimen that Hoover had just imposed on them. On November 24 the British food controller, Lord Rhondda, warned Hoover bluntly that unless the Allies could count on more wheat from North America than 133,000,000 bushels, the Allies would face "a situation of extreme gravity." He urged Hoover to dilute the wheat content of American bread or take other measures to increase his meager exportable surplus.[99] A couple of weeks later the head of the Wheat Export Company made a similar plea to Julius Barnes.[100]

For Rhondda and his colleagues it was a time of nervewracking apprehension. By early December, British imports of wheat from abroad were averaging only half those of the same period a year before. The British wheat reserve was falling because of the need to divert cargoes to the more desperate Italians and French. Only on December 12 did Rhondda win assurance from his War Cabinet of enough money to purchase wheat from Argentina, and only on the thirteenth did the Cabinet grant him absolute priority for the necessary shipping.[101] Everywhere that dark December, catastrophe seemed to stalk him like a beast of prey.

In his cable of November 24 Rhondda did not disclose that his wheat reserve, though declining, was presently enough to feed the British population for twenty weeks.[102] In other words, the British were not nearly so hard-pressed, at the moment, as they had been back in the spring. Perhaps Hoover knew this already. Perhaps it explained his obduracy as well as Taylor's stiffness toward the Europeans. In any case, the American Food Administrator refused to budge a single inch. The Allies must turn to Australia, Argentina, and India, he replied to Rhondda. If the United States assisted now, it must recover an equivalent amount of wheat from Argentina at a later time.[103] As late as December 8, the Food Administrator insisted through Taylor that "we cannot export wheat we hope to save by conservation until after we have saved it in other words not until just before the next harvest. . . ."[104] If the Allies were testy, so was Hoover. "They seemed to believe," he wrote long afterward, "that we could produce miracles out of a statistical vacuum and ignored our need to keep some wheat for our own use during the period until harvest."[105]

But was there a "statistical vacuum" at all? What about the 40,000,000 barrels of flour that Julius Barnes expected American consumers to save by mid-1918, over and above the 30,000,000 bushels of surplus American wheat that Barnes anticipated from the 1917 harvest? Whatever the validity of Barnes's projections, one thing seemed clear: Hoover was unwilling to count on food conservation until it actually happened.

The immediate issue, however, was not how much more wheat Hoover might be able to save and ship but how soon he would deliver the 132,000,000 bushels of North American wheat already available and now committed to Europe. At the beginning of December the Allies brought the matter to a head: they asked the American Food Administrator to send them 1,100,000 tons of cereals per month from Canada and the United States during December, January, and February.[106] As usual, Hoover was cautious, even wary. While awaiting details from an Allied representative, he told Barnes that he wished "to push Canadian [sic] to the limit." He also wanted it understood that if the United States supplied Europe with "deficiencies" of wheat that Canada could not deliver during the "closed season," he would obtain "corresponding amounts" from the Canadians later on.[107]

In support of their request, the Allies furnished Hoover a schedule of projected cereals imports for 1917–18 that the Wheat Executive had prepared prior to meeting Alonzo Taylor. Among other things, the chart called for the United States alone to deliver 2,400,000 tons of wheat and flour to the Allies between December 1917 and the summer of 1918, at the rate of 300,000 metric tons (or more than 11,000,000 bushels) per month.[108] Hoover, of course, through his mouthpiece Taylor, had just scuttled this program by announcing that America had no such wheat reserves to send. But now, on December 11, Hoover partially relented and agreed to fulfill the specified quota through February 1918.[109] With respect to wheat, this meant that the United States would indeed supply 33,000,000 of the surplus 132,000,000 bushels calculated to exist on the North American continent. To this extent Hoover backed off from his assertion on November 17 that America had no surplus wheat at all.

It is not clear that the Allies or the Canadians understood Hoover's intent to reclaim from Canada any wheat that the United States shipped during the next three months in excess of its 33,000,000 bushel quota. But to Barnes, at least, he made his policy plain—as well as his commitment to the Allies' import program only until the end of February. "After that," he warned, "it is another story, and I am certain that they can make other arrangements."[110] More trouble with the Allies lay ahead.

Meanwhile, on the home front, Hoover's pessimism about domestic wheat supplies nearly landed him in a swamp of controversy. After a meeting with the Chief in Washington in November, the state food administrator of Illinois told at least two leading newspapers that America was in danger of running entirely out of wheat flour a full sixty days before the next harvest. This startling disclosure—which accurately reflected Hoover's views—immediately raised the danger that the public would panic and start hoarding flour, thereby destroying Hoover's war on inflation.[111] When Julius Barnes brought the newspaper story to Hoover's attention, the Food Administrator could only agree that the leak was "very unfortunate." "I have tried to deny it," he said.[112]

Hoover was walking a tightrope. Fortunately, the inopportune newspaper report did not provoke a stampede by nervous consumers. Nor did it detract from the victory that he had just won over the Allies. In the face of their wails of protest, he had protected America's uncertain wheat reserves, restricted its exports to a level far below Allied expectations, and transferred the principal task of supply to the Canadians, who, with their small population and large crop, had far more wheat to offer for export.[113]

As it happened, Hoover was not quite done with his northern neighbors. During the autumn the Allies' Wheat Export Company had been shipping much of the Canadian wheat surplus across the Great Lakes to Buffalo and thence, eventually, to British ports. On November 27 Julius Barnes proposed to Hoover that the Americans take over at Buffalo "the entire Canadian wheat movement between now and the close of navigation" in December—or as much of it as needed to add up to fifteen to twenty million bushels. This would be enough, Barnes calculated, to keep America's eastern flour mills operating through the winter.[114] Hoover approved, and Barnes took the matter to the Allies.[115]

For the Allied food authorities, still staggering from Hoover's halving of their anticipated wheat imports from North America, Barnes's request was a further painful surprise. The Wheat Export Company had been planning to ship 75,000,000 bushels of Canadian wheat by February. Now Hoover wished to siphon off at least one fifth of it.[116] The Allies evidently feared that Hoover, looking out as always for American interests, might refuse to surrender an equivalent amount of flour when the Europeans needed it, as he had solemnly pledged to do back in October.[117] In London, the chairman of the Royal Commission on Wheat Supplies was so angry that he wondered whose side Hoover was on in this war:

> Hoover now demands ten million bushels more of our Canadian wheat to keep the Buffalo mills going till the spring. Where do the interests of the Allies come in? We are now feeding America as well as France and Italy—and nobody exploits and blackmails us with greater zest than Hoover. He could not act in a more unfriendly way towards us. Is the man straight? I feel that he is doing us more injury than some of our avowed enemies.[118]

To further complicate matters, Barnes discovered that certain Canadian grain officials were jealous of Hoover and had never expected that such enormous quantities of their wheat would be used to maintain employment in American flour mills.[119] Hoover was winning his policy disputes, but he was not winning friends in the process.

The Allies acquiesced in Barnes's plan after he promised to replace diverted wheat with American flour whenever they required it.[120] As it turned out, severe weather forced an early closing of transportation on the Great Lakes. Still, the amount of Canadian wheat that Barnes secured was enough, he believed, to keep the Buffalo mills running almost until the reopening of navigation in the spring.[121] Once more America's priorities had prevailed.

If the head of the Grain Corporation was eager to accommodate his country's key flour mills, his chief had more long-range concerns upon his mind. At the end of December, Hoover instructed Barnes to consider creating a reserve of 50,000,000 bushels of wheat to be held in various terminals until the following May or June. In this way, if the precious grain ran short, the Food Administration could rush food to the all-important "industrial centers" and let the "agricultural districts" take the squeeze. Hoover was certain that American farmers had been hoarding, just as he believed from his Belgian relief experience that European peasants always took care to stash away enough food for themselves. Besides, he told Barnes, if the crunch came, American farmers would not only have food reserves of their own to fall back on but could also "substitute corn more easily."[122]

Whatever might happen, then, in Europe or upon the high seas, the civilian population of America—above all, those in the cities—would be provided for: this was Hoover's unwavering objective. By the end of 1917 he was well on his way to attaining it.

The Food Administrator, however, paid a price for his relentlessness in frayed tempers and recriminations from his European associates.[123] Even worse, he came dangerously close to alienating Julius Barnes. In a long and remarkably outspoken letter on January 4, 1918, Barnes challenged directly the entire rationale for Hoover's recent conduct toward the Allies. Barnes was dismayed that Hoover had dispatched Alonzo Taylor to Europe with a wheat program without even discussing it with Barnes or the "experienced grain men" at the Grain Corporation. Barnes was even more upset by the "purely academic" calculations upon which Taylor had announced that the United States no longer had a surplus of wheat for export. In reaching this alarming and (to Barnes) unjustified conclusion, Taylor had assumed that American wheat consumption in the current crop year would be normal, that is, 5.3 bushels per capita—a figure Barnes found ridiculous. Not only did it ignore the fact that Americans had consumed much less than this in the past year. It also overlooked completely the probable effects of conservation efforts and increasing availability of substitute crops, notably potatoes.

Barnes was also angered by Taylor's behavior toward the Europeans. Instead of promising them "generous cooperation," the professor had presented a wheat plan that was "startlingly the reverse," and in a manner that was "thoroughly unsympathetic." Above all, by unveiling such a "radical alteration in the American estimates" without warning—to the "total surprise" of the Allies and Barnes himself—Taylor had discredited Barnes's own estimates, had cruelly discredited the Wheat Export Company's officers, and had jeopardized the rapport that should exist between the Wheat Export Company and the Grain Corporation.[124]

Although Barnes aimed his fire solely at Taylor, he must have realized that behind the professor stood the Chief. The Grain Corporation president's letter therefore raised many questions. Why had Hoover failed to inform or consult Barnes before Taylor dropped his bombshell in London? Had it been an oversight in an atmosphere of haste? Or did Hoover suspect that Barnes was too optimistic and perhaps too cozy with the Allies' agents in New York?

Moreover, why did Hoover and Taylor rest their entire case on the 5.3 bushel statistic when there was reason to expect that per capita consumption of wheat in the coming year would decline? Was Hoover just being cautious? Had he, the temperamental pessimist, leaped prematurely to an unnecessarily somber conclusion? Or had he—as some later historians suspected—deliberately manufactured an emergency, the better to cushion his wheat reserves and enhance his reputation as a "miracle man"?[125]

Hoover immediately came to Taylor's defense. In a lengthy letter of rebuttal, the Food Administrator told Barnes that he thought they *had* discussed Taylor's instructions before the latter departed for Europe. More importantly, Hoover insisted that by December 1, 1917 America *had* exported its "theoretical surplus of wheat" (a point he thought "no one will deny") and that any future American exports must be "entirely the reciprocal of savings made"—an amount "impossible to determine" ahead of time. What it all boiled down to, he said, was that Barnes believed that conservation had achieved substantial results by December 1, while Taylor assumed that "any such savings could only be properly interpreted when they had been demonstrably realized" later in the season. This was not quite an accurate statement of Barnes's position. Barnes believed that much wheat would be saved by mid-1918 and that America could therefore safely export some of its existing stocks. Hoover, on the other hand, was unwilling to export any wheat until it *had* been saved (unless, of course, he could be certain of replacement, if need be, from Canada).

As for the Allies, Hoover—like Taylor—was decidedly unsympathetic. Our European associates have adopted no "conservation measures of any importance whatever," he asserted, except "the mixing of other cereals in bread." All the Allies, especially the French and the Italians, consumed far more bread than Americans did. The Allies, moreover, had had "the foolish idea that we had an unlimited bank upon which they could draw." Under the circumstances, said Hoover, Taylor had been obliged to "show great firmness" in forcing them drastically to curb their unrealistic demands.[126]

It is hard to know how much of Hoover's reply represented genuine conviction and how much of it may have been a bluff. As one who believed that the best defense against criticism was a good offense, the Food Administrator was not given to admitting miscalculations. He admitted none here. In any case, his letter apparently mollified Julius Barnes, who remained as head of the Grain Corporation. Never again, so far as is known, did Barnes contest Hoover's position on the wheat surplus.

Whatever Hoover's inner convictions or motives, it was evident now that he would not build his wheat export policy on hope. Having drawn and imposed his statistical conclusions, he resolutely if a bit defensively stuck to his guns. And, from his perspective, why shouldn't he? For all its panicky alarums and entreaties, Great Britain, at least, had a considerable reserve of wheat: four times, in fact, what it had been at its nadir in the spring. To him the insatiable demands of the Allies for still more wheat constituted a threat as serious as that from the German army. In a battle between present Allied needs (as they defined them) and the possible future needs of the United States, the latter, for Hoover, took priority. His tough, unyielding handling of the wheat export issue was the best demonstration yet of the supremacy in his mind of the principle: America first.

III

AND yet the Allies still had to be fed. For all Hoover's efforts to persuade them to take less of those foodstuffs that were in short supply, conflicting pressures kept arising to confound him.

By late summer 1917 Hoover's earlier warnings of an impending scarcity of sugar in the United States were coming true. On August 28 he predicted confidentially that the nation would be short by 100,000–200,000 tons until the next Cuban harvest became available.[127] Publicly, while urging conservation, he tried to minimize the threat lest he touch off a wave of panic buying in American grocery stores.[128] But even as he did so, Hoover knew that a season of turbulence lay ahead.

Then, in mid-September, an unforeseen message from Paris turned a difficulty into an emergency: the government of France, its stocks of sugar exhausted, appealed to America for 100,000 tons during the next month.[129] Hoover could hardly refuse. Reeling from military losses and army mutinies earlier in the year, and teetering on the brink of collapse, the French population was already enduring a sugar ration of under one ounce per person per day—less than one quarter of America's rate of consumption.[130]

Asserting now that America had "just sufficient sugar to maintain our normal consumption" until the next harvest, Hoover called upon his countrymen to reduce their sugar and candy intake by one third. If they did, he announced, the "French situation" could be saved.[131]

Meanwhile he began to search for existing stocks to ship abroad. It was not easy. In Cuba, where the next crop was still growing in the fields, only 25,000 tons of the old harvest were left.[132] To Hoover's chagrin, Canadian refiners had scooped up the rest of what had been available on the island despite British promises weeks before to make them desist.[133] It was another bitter case of *sauve qui peut*.

Fortunately for the Food Administrator, one other source held some promise. Late in August, at his insistence, the U.S. government had imposed an embargo on all exports of sugar from America to other than Allied destinations.[134] The effect of this measure was to strand on the U.S. mainland considerable quantities of sugar already purchased by representatives of neutral nations. If Hoover could get control of these cargoes, he could send them to France.

The Food Administrator's search had barely begun when an even more alarming crisis overtook him: in early October, as supplies from Cuba and elsewhere dwindled, his long-feared sugar famine became a reality in the urban Northeast.[135] By the middle of the month supplies of the commodity were so scarce that most refineries had been forced to shut down.[136] "We will be entirely out of sugar at least one month," Hoover's chief assistant gloomily predicted on the eleventh.[137] A few days later Hoover himself informed the American people in a dramatic press release that all of the country north of Savannah and east of Pittsburgh would be short of sugar for the next six weeks. It would be that long before any new sugar became available.[138]

Hoover blamed the scarcity on "the failure of the American public outside many loyal homes" to heed his pleas to conserve, and on the "unusual exports made to France" to maintain its ration. If the American people had curbed their intake of candy and soft drinks by one third, he declared with ill-concealed irritation, the eastern states would not be in their present predicament. The Food Administrator again exhorted the public to eat less candy, ice cream, and sweetened beverages. He asked the people of the West especially to sacrifice in order to free up Hawaiian cane and western beet sugar for shipment to the hard-hit Atlantic seaboard.[139]

In the waning days of October Hoover tried frantically to contain the deepening emergency. On October 19 he again admonished the American people to reduce their sugar consumption so that France and the other Allies could be supplied.[140] His words boomeranged. Hearing of impending shortages, panicky housewives in New York City rushed to neighborhood grocery stores and snatched up nearly all the sugar on the shelves.[141] On October 20 Hoover's Sugar Distributing Committee ordered every sugar-producing factory in the country to divert its shipments to the east coast states and leave the West and Middle West "only the scantiest minimum."[142] That same day Hoover himself disclosed that he had ordered all manufacturers and distributors of sugar in the United States to sell no more sugar whatsoever to makers of confections, syrups, gum, and ice cream until the Cuban sugar crop came on the market in January 1918.[143] Five days later, protests from the affected industry compelled Hoover to modify his decree: the makers of these nonessential sweets would only be required to reduce their use of sugar by half.[144]

Meanwhile, from neutral stocks and other sources, Hoover managed to assemble a substantial cache of sugar in New York City for the French.[145] When added to a previous French purchase, it reached a total of 26,500 tons.[146] Now, with America's greatest metropolis itself facing possible privation, Hoover asked the French to release these stocks to him.[147] Unable to find trans-Atlantic shipping for the precious cargo, the French agreed to surrender it, on condition that Hoover (as he had offered) replace it with a substitute shipment in December.[148]

With the aid of this borrowed supply, and of 16,500 further tons that had been destined for Russia, Hoover was able to "tide over" the emergency in New York until replenishments arrived later in the autumn.[149] Before long the great sugar famine of 1917—and his response to it—would be the subject of a Congressional investigation. But for the moment he could take satisfaction that the nation's largest city had eked by without distress or social disorder, thanks to the sacrificial acquiescence of a desperate ally.

Hoover had little time to contemplate the irony. Early in October news of even grimmer portent came from France. In a cable to Washington on October 7, Premier Paul Painlevé revealed that because of poor harvests and greatly diminished imports his country now confronted a grave deficit in its cereal supplies. Raising the specter of mass starvation in French cities as well as insufficient food for his army, the premier beseeched the United States to give priority to wheat shipments and to assign its own vessels to the task.[150]

Many years later Hoover recorded that he was convinced that the "emotional" Painlevé was exaggerating.[151] Nevertheless, as soon as the cable arrived, the Food Administrator responded with the single-minded purposiveness for which he had grown famous in Belgian relief. Searching for exportable flour in American ports, Hoover's agents discovered substantial stocks in New York and Baltimore—all purchased by and destined for the government of Finland, an autonomous grand duchy in the Russian empire.[152] The next step was drastic and swift. Acting under newly granted authority from President Wilson to requisition foodstuffs, Hoover commandeered the Finnish flour.[153] By late autumn his agency had seized at least 40,000 tons of it for quick dispatch to Italy and France.[154] It was a measure of Hoover's unorthodoxy that much of the flour he requisitioned was not even American in origin but was Canadian flour that happened to be in transit to American seaports when he took it.[155]

Needless to say, the Finns were not happy to lose their purchased cargo. Soon they attempted strenuously to get it back.[156] For Hoover, striving with even greater strenuosity to aid the French, his sweeping acts of requisition were fully justified. If the Finns were offended, so be it. There was no alternative, he told the State Department. He had only twenty days' supply of wheat products left for the western Allies.[157]

The Finnish Senate now appealed to the U.S. government's War Trade Board for the right to import American flour—and pointedly mentioned Hoover's seizure of the Canadian consignment.[158] The Finns won the support of Secretary of State Robert Lansing, who on December 6 asked the War Trade Board to permit the export to Finland of sufficient flour to replace what Hoover had seized.[159] Six days later the board agreed.[160]

Hoover, meanwhile, had come forward with an apparent alternative: instead of flour he would let the Finns obtain some corn at ports in the Gulf of Mexico. The Food Administrator frankly confessed his "greatest reluctance" to give the Finns anything. "I do not find any great inspiration in it," he told the State Department, "for it simply means that somebody else will have to go short." So far as wheat was concerned, the Finns—if they found shipping—should "go to Australia."

But Hoover, this time, had to bend a little. On December 6 the government of Finland declared its independence of Russia, where Lenin and the Bolsheviks had just seized power. The United States now had overriding political as well as humanitarian reasons for assisting the regime in Helsinki. Under strong pressure from the State Department, Hoover on December 12 granted the Finns permission to take 40,000 tons of corn and oats in compensation for their commandeered flour.[161]

The Finns therefore never recovered their flour. Instead, in late December the War Trade Board ratified Hoover's arrangement and issued the requisite export licenses.[162] Once more, by one means or another, he had accomplished his objective.

IV

THE French government's plea for American ships to transport wheat—and to do so ahead of all other cargo—brought Hoover face to face with a constraint that was to tax even his tenacity. By the autumn of 1917 the cumulative effect of the Germans' submarine warfare was staggering. In the first ten months of the year the three western Allies lost more shipping tonnage than in the previous thirty months of the war.[163] Between January and October more than 3,000,000 tons of British merchant shipping alone went down—far more than they or anyone else could quickly replace.[164] Although the United States had launched a gigantic shipbuilding program in the spring, the existing American merchant fleet at the end of the year remained small—barely one quarter that of Great Britain.[165] The ineluctable consequence was clear: If the Allies wanted to procure American food, they must not only borrow money from the U.S. government to pay for it. They must carry it back from American ports by themselves.

Hoover was well aware of the burgeoning shortage of ocean shipping and its distorting effect on the worldwide movement of food. Still, during the month of September he appeared to believe that sufficient vessels could be found to meet the Allies' necessities. In a private address in Philadelphia he declared:

> . . . if we can produce such economies in consumption and such stimulation of production [of wheat] in the United States and Canada as will enable us to feed the Allies absolutely from this continent, and thus enable them in the final analysis to live without sending a ship further afield than our Atlantic seaboard, we can resist the submarine indefinitely.

"The question of who wins this war," he added, "is the question of who can endure the longest, and the problem of endurance, in a large degree, is a problem of food and ships to carry it in."[166] As for the Germans, they were running dangerously short of fats—he told his state food administrators—and were "in a position where they cannot endure forever." If, on the other hand, the American people "can endure long enough and keep our Allies fed long enough we have practically nothing to do but keep the supplies moving to the Allies."[167]

Hoover's strategy, then, for winning the war was simple: Feed the Allies, maintain the blockade, and starve the German enemy into surrender. This approach was based on the assumption that the great armies in Europe had reached a "military deadlock"—a viewpoint Hoover explicitly enunciated in September.[168] It also assumed that his responsibility—food—would have first claim on the storage space of vessels bound for Europe. But as President Painlevé's frantic cable of October 7 made plain, the assignment of shipping priorities was by no means settled in Hoover's favor. The Food Administrator's concept of a war fought not with guns but with butter—of a passive war that food alone could win—collided in October with the mounting demands of the U.S. Army.

The conflict had its roots in events of the previous spring and summer. In June 1917 General John J. Pershing arrived in France with the first elements of the American Expeditionary Force (AEF). It did not take him long to determine that more than a token American army would be required to tip the scales toward victory. On July 6 he cabled the War Department: "Plans should contemplate sending over at least 1,000,000 men by next May."[169] In fact, he added a few days later, future military preparations should be based on sending at least 3,000,000 soldiers in due course to the western front.[170] Three million soldiers! The sheer magnitude of his estimates stunned official Washington; the War Department replied that even by using all available shipping it could dispatch only 634,975 men to France by the following June.[171] Nevertheless, the commander of the AEF essentially gained his purpose: the United States was now committed to deploying a gigantic army in the bloodied and muddied trenches of northern France.[172]

Pershing's request could not have been more antithetical to the convictions of Herbert Hoover. Back in February, in documents submitted to Colonel House and the Council of National Defense, Hoover had vigorously opposed the dispatch of an American expeditionary force to Europe if the United States should enter the war. The creation of a force of any consequence would take too long, he had argued. It would absorb too much scarce shipping and would entail "political difficulties in association" besides. Let the Allied armies recruit American volunteers over here, he had counseled, and let these men then be trained in Europe. In a few months they would be combat-ready, and there would be no need to transport the "impedimenta" of an expeditionary force.[173]

Hoover's proposals had been forwarded to President Wilson.[174] But neither then nor in the ensuing months had he taken part in the decision making that defined America's military role in the war. By summer the die was cast: for domestic and diplomatic reasons primarily, Pershing would create an independent field army under American, not Allied, command.[175]

The implications of this decision—and of Pershing's demand for a fighting force of millions—soon impinged on Hoover's sphere of responsibility. To obtain the multitudes of men that military leaders deemed necessary, the federal government instituted a national system of Selective Service. As the first draftees left their jobs for training camps in late summer, fears of crippling labor shortages rippled across the land. As overseer of the nation's food supply, Hoover was concerned that the drafting of skilled agricultural workers would dangerously reduce the country's food production. On August 27 he asked President Wilson to grant mass exemptions to "key men" of "the foreman, manager and ownership type," and to draft more of "the purely laboring and town classes" instead. One trouble, he added, was that many of these "key men" had "too much patriotism" to apply for deferments.[176]

Wilson referred Hoover's letter to the War Department. Already besieged by similar requests for exemption for particular classes, Secretary of War Newton D. Baker politely rejected the appeal. Let the local draft boards exercise their discretion, he advised. If he started to grant exceptions for certain categories of workers, he would not know where to stop.[177] General Enoch Crowder, crusty administrator of the Selective Service system, was more blunt. Hoover's terms were too vague, he declared. If the President ordered deferments for farmers of the "ownership class," there would soon be "a great many new owners of very small agricultural enterprises." As for the supposed reluctance of "key men" to seek release from military obligation, Crowder observed tartly: "Our experience with the Selective Service law is certainly not that patriotic scruples are very materially decreasing claims for exemption."[178]

Hoover's rebuff at the hands of the military was but the first skirmish in an increasingly tense struggle over priorities. As the dimensions of the Pershing plan sank in, war planners in Washington groped for ways to transport a gigantic army to France. On September 24 Secretary of the Navy Daniels conceded that the transport of a vast expeditionary force to Europe and its maintenance so far from home were "clearly beyond the shipping resources available to us at present."[179] Three days later the United States Shipping Board tried to help by announcing that it would requisition all American oceangoing merchant vessels exceeding 2,500 tons capacity.[180] Barely ten days after that, the president of France pleaded that the shipment of wheat be given priority over troops and munitions. The crisis of October was at hand.

At about the time that Painlevé's cable arrived in Washington, Hoover asked the chairman of the Shipping Board, Edward N. Hurley, for a survey of America's tonnage needs and supplies. Hurley's reply was not at all encouraging: If the United States sent a million soldiers to France, it would require 1,500,000 tons of shipping to deliver and sustain them. In fact, to meet its vital military *and* nonmilitary requirements (including food exports), America needed 900 ships with an aggregate capacity of 5,650,000 deadweight tons. At the moment it had only 352 ships with 2,250,000 deadweight tons.[181]

A few days later, at President Wilson's suggestion, Hoover and Hurley conferred with the Secretaries of War and the Navy about the developing crisis. Hoover was eager, as usual, to shift the burden to the Allies. Find out how much shipping they control, he urged, and then force them to reallocate it to "real needs." He also recommended the seizure of neutral vessels anchored in American ports. Nothing, however, came of the conference except an agreement to study the deteriorating shipping situation more carefully.[182] The critical question of priority was evaded.

While Secretary of War Baker waited for better statistics, Hoover pressed him with disturbing data of his own. On October 18 he informed Baker that the Allies would require about 1,800,000 tons of foodstuffs *per month* from the United States and Canada for the next year. While the Allies would transport most of this in their own vessels, American ships would have to carry the rest, as well as import considerable quantities of other foodstuffs from places like Cuba. In all, Hoover calculated that he would need over 1,000,000 tons of shipping to handle the nation's food exports and imports in the months ahead.[183] Meanwhile Hurley notified Baker that even by adding certain Japanese and Scandinavian ships to the American pool, the United States would still fall more than 2,500,000 tons short of its immediate needs.[184]

How, then, could the government hope to satisfy General Pershing's implacable demand for soldiers by the millions? Was the German General Staff's great gamble correct—that America could never mobilize in time, that the war would be over before the Yanks arrived in meaningful numbers? With U-boats still sinking ships faster than the Allies could replace them, would England, Italy, and France have to choose between their stomachs and their soldiers in the field?[185]

Convinced as ever that food (not men or weapons) was the key to victory, Hoover now made a daring maneuver. On October 27 he gave another memorandum to Colonel House as the presidential envoy prepared to sail for Europe. In the blunt, self-assured manner that was his trademark, Hoover declared that all American and Allied shipping should be allocated according to this scale of priority: first, the transport of food and munitions; second, the dispatch of "special services" such as engineers across the Atlantic; third—and only third—"the movement of our armies to France." To House, Hoover confessed his "great apprehension that a proper co-ordination and statesmanlike handling of this whole situation does not permit of the third undertaking." The available shipping, he said, was insufficient "if future losses are allowed for."

Hoover emphasized the "critical necessity" of transporting food from "the more remote markets in preference to the movement of armies." If America put 1,500,000 men in France, he warned, a "great danger" could loom up here at home: there would be so little shipping left over that the Allies would have to turn "wholly" to America for food, and the food supply could become "entirely insufficient." It was not enough to feed only our expeditionary forces, he contended. The civilian population of the Allied countries must also be supplied, "or our Army may be enveloped in the social cataclysm in Europe, and its retreat absolutely cut off."

Still smarting, one suspects, from his failure to win draft deferments for "key men" in agriculture, Hoover told House that "the assembling of millions of men under arms" was "undermining the foundation of our productive capacity." This was where "the safety of the world must rest," he argued: in American "productivity of food and munitions." He even asked House to consider whether America should send *any* troops to France except "special services." In effect, Hoover was calling for abandonment of the huge American Expeditionary Force in the making.

> I have no right to speak from a military point of view, but two years of fairly active mind on both sides of the front have impressed me with the fact that if the western line is impregnable to five million men, it will be no more pregnable by the addition of another million.

We are "in this war," he concluded, not to "create the glory of soldiers, but in defense of the whole world." We should "submit ourselves to the place" of "farmers and mechanics" if we must do so in order to win.[186]

Hoover's audacious memorandum constituted a powerful if covert challenge to General Pershing and to the unfolding plans of the War Department. Having appealed to Woodrow Wilson's alter ego, the Food Administrator proceeded higher still. On November 5 he sent copies of his memoranda directly to the President and begged him to resolve the shipping priority crisis.[187] The commander in chief sent the documents to the War and Navy secretaries and intimated that he would shortly call a conference to discuss the subject.[188]

Meanwhile Secretary of War Baker had been studying the shipping problem on his own—and with far less perturbation and foreboding. The problem, he informed the President on November 3, was "not so much a shortage of tonnage" as "intolerable" delays in loading and unloading vessels. If this obstacle could be overcome, it would significantly enhance the efficiency of existing ships.[189] Baker may have had another reason for his lack of alarm: In October and early November his department began to requisition ships that Hoover had been relying upon to import foodstuffs from abroad.[190]

Hoover was furious at the military's action, and filled at once "with the utmost apprehension." Here he was, trying desperately to alleviate a "sugar famine" in the Northeast, and what was the War Department doing? Seizing steamers that he had been counting on to bring needed sugar from Hawaii. In a letter to Chairman Hurley of the Shipping Board, he declared the "absolute, critical necessity" of importing more than 4,000,000 tons of sugar and other foodstuffs into the United States in the next twelve months, and he requested assurance that he could get the ships to do so. Sugar was crucial to national morale, he asserted. Furthermore, if the American people lost their sugar, they would "simply have to eat the same tonnage of other products" and thereby deprive the Allies of just that much. Thoroughly agitated, Hoover announced that he wanted his letter "to form a record from the Food Administration against failure to provide the American public and the munitions branches with the commodities for which I have responsibility."[191] He promptly sent a copy to the President.[192]

Food or soldiers? In the escalating battle over priorities Hoover remained convinced that his concerns were paramount.

So far as is known, Hoover did not recover his commandeered ships. Nor is there any evidence that President Wilson ever convened a conference to settle the priorities dispute.[193] Instead, in late October and November events in Europe demolished Hoover's strategic analysis and destroyed for good his hope for a war of economic attrition. On October 24 German and Austrian soldiers launched a devastating attack on the Italian front near Caporetto. Reeling back in abject disorder, the Italian army lost more than 300,000 troops in less than three weeks. In early November, Nikolai Lenin and the Bolsheviks seized power in St. Petersburg and promised the people land, peace, and bread. The Russian army as a fighting force was finished. Meanwhile, in the cratered mud and bogs of western Flanders, the British army's four-month campaign to capture Passchendaele petered out in nearly total futility, at a cost of nearly a quarter of a million British casualties.

With Italy on the ropes and Russia essentially vanquished, with the French and now the British armies incapable of any meaningful offensive action, the tottering Allied governments faced a dire prospect: that the Germans would be able to transfer their victorious armies from the eastern front and achieve decisive superiority in the West by spring. The fear of coming catastrophe produced panic in the Western capitals. On the day that Colonel House's mission reached England, the leaders of the three western Allies agreed to establish a Supreme War Council, a belated step on the road to a unified command. The next day came news of Lenin's coup in Russia. Five days later the government of Premier Painlevé fell, and Georges Clemenceau ("the Tiger") took power in France.

Gone now were some of the bickering and machinations that had vitiated the western alliance for years. Gone were the ambiguities of July and August, when the French military had seconded Pershing's request for a huge American army while various British officials, bearing shipping in mind, had advised against it.[194] Now the desperate leaders in London and Paris pleaded, begged, and demanded American troops for their salvation. The Allied leaders would feud with Pershing all winter over whether his Yankee doughboys should be quickly amalgamated into the battle-tested but decimated British and French armies, or whether—as he successfully insisted—they should take to the field as an independent entity. But all now agreed that the New World must send men, more men, and still more men if the trenches were to be held next summer against the Huns.

Back in Washington, Hoover continued to disagree. In a public address on November 9 he asserted that with the final collapse of Russia, the Great War had become "a war simply of endurance"—"purely a question as to who can last the longest." And the key to that, for America and the Allies, was "purely a question as to whether the United States can produce enough food to feed the world." "[T]o me," he said, "the entire problem is one of food."

> If we can continue to produce and stimulate our production to meet the requirements of the Allies year by year, if we can continue to feed ourselves, if we can hold the Western line, and maintain the blockade, we need do nothing more to win the war.

It was a call for victory without offensive military action,[195] the formula of a man who, a year before, had witnessed the gainless slaughter of the Battle of the Somme and who still believed that armed manpower could not be decisive.

There is no evidence that President Wilson, Colonel House, or the military leadership gave any heed to Hoover's unsolicited advice. The tide, at any rate, was running swiftly in the other direction. On November 15 General Pershing wrote to Secretary of War Baker:

> It should be no longer a question of how much tonnage can be spared for military purposes, but only the most imperative necessity should permit its use for any other purpose. To secure this result the whole of our shipping ought to be under War Department control, and as much more obtained as possible from neutral or allied sources.[196]

Three weeks later Army Chief of Staff Tasker H. Bliss, still in Europe with the House mission, notified Washington that the United States should send a minimum of twenty-four divisions to France before July 1918. To transport this incredible armada, 2,000,000 additional gross tons of shipping would be needed—three quarters of it by January 1.[197] "Is such a programme *possible*?" a staggered Woodrow Wilson asked his Secretary of War.[198] It "can only be made possible," Baker replied, "by sacrificing other things, which up to now we have believed to be of equal, if not of greater, importance."[199]

On December 15 General Bliss and the rest of the House mission returned to the United States. In his report to the commander in chief, Bliss warned that a military crisis was impending, that it would break out no later than the spring of 1918, and that the advantage would be with the enemy unless the United States came massively to the rescue. "The one all-absorbing necessity now is soldiers with which to beat the enemy in the field." he said, "and ships to carry them." He renewed his call for the dispatch of twenty-four divisions before it was too late.[200] On December 18 he conferred in person with the President, who decided to send him back to Europe as America's military representative on the Supreme War Council.[201]

Hoover's behind-the-scenes bid to reorient American war strategy had failed.

But if food alone was not going to win the war, a *shortage* of food might very well still lose it. For Hoover, the recent cataclysms in Russia and Italy were dismal proof of what the "lack of food" had wrought and might wreak elsewhere if England and France were not sufficiently fed.[202] Troop movements or no troop movements, shipping priorities or no shipping priorities, his job remained. The necessary food must get "over there."

V

WHILE Hoover was battling to reduce Allied absorption of his wheat reserves, he was simultaneously addressing another foreign threat: unchecked purchases of American foodstuffs by nations that were neutral in the war. In the spring and early summer of 1917, agents of the so-called "northern neutrals"—Holland, Denmark, Norway, and Sweden—joined America's allies in a scramble for grain in the American market. The soaring prices that resulted were, for the Wilson administration, bad enough. Equally galling was the fact that these very same neutrals were in turn trading extensively with Germany. For both economic and military reasons, then, the neutrals' buying spree was a challenge to which the U.S. government, including Hoover, must respond.

From the outset Hoover was convinced that neutral buying of American goods must be controlled.[203] The neutrals' behavior was disturbing our price structure, he informed the President.[204] At least as early as June 1, Hoover envisaged an out-and-out embargo on export of the nation's foodstuffs to nonbelligerents.[205] While willing out of "obligation to humanity" to "food ration the whole neutral world," he insisted that America was fighting for the freedom of the world and must therefore obtain more from neutral governments than mere cash for American food. In no other way, he said, could he justify appealing to his fellow citizens for self-denial.[206]

There was a certain irony in Hoover's stance. For nearly three years the United States itself had been neutral, and it had officially gone to war in part to vindicate neutral rights. Hoover had earned his own reputation—and his place in government—by feeding the oppressed inhabitants of neutral Belgium. For Woodrow Wilson, the transition to hard-nosed belligerent would not be smooth. For Hoover, it appears to have been instant. The shoe was now upon the other foot, and he showed neither hesitation nor anguish.

On June 15 the President signed the Espionage Act, which empowered him to take control of the nation's exports. A week later he created a four-member Exports Council, including Hoover, to formulate policies and recommendations for his approval.[207] Although clearly moving toward export limitation, the chief executive seemed anxious to reassure the European neutrals as well as American business interests. In a statement made public on June 26, he declared that America's foreign trade would not be prohibited—only "directed" to the points of greatest need. While the Allies, he promised, would receive priority, the neutrals who were dependent on the United States for supplies would be treated fairly.[208]

That same day the Exports Council convened for the first time and promptly urged the President to proclaim a total embargo of certain key commodities except under license.[209] The council also voted to create an administrative committee; of its four original members, two were Hoover loyalists.[210] The council further voted to ask a visiting British diplomat, Lord Eustace Percy, to become its adviser—in effect its liaison with London—on export policy toward the European neutrals. As it happened, Percy had been Hoover's principal contact at the Foreign Office during the Belgian relief.[211] Thus by coincidence or (more likely) by a little wirepulling, the nascent American export bureaucracy had been colonized by Hoover's protégés and confidants.

Hoover was eager for swift and drastic measures. For one thing, he reported, the European neutrals were rapidly buying up American fodder for their herds. As a result, the price of feedstuffs was skyrocketing, forcing American farmers to slaughter their cattle because it was too costly to feed them.[212] The longer the Europeans were free to drain the American cornucopia, the worse off America would be. Indeed, at least as early as June 20 he urged the President to impose an embargo as soon as possible.[213] For whatever reason, the man in the White House declined to act that quickly.

Embargoes were not the only weapon that the Food Administrator wished to deploy against nonbelligerent nations. He intended also to charge neutrals an artificially high price for American flour and to use the profits to reduce the price paid by his countrymen.[214] Hoover felt no compunction about thus turning the screws on the Dutch and other neutrals. After all, he noted angrily long afterward, they had been charging "extortionate rates" for their shipping.[215]

The Food Administrator's zeal for an immediate embargo soon ran into complications. Not only did it take time to develop mechanisms of control and enforcement; the representatives of the affected governments lost no time in raising a protest in Washington.[216] If the United States cut them off, they warned, it could drive them into the arms of their German neighbor. Surely the Allies would not want that. If, on the other hand, they yielded to Allied pressure, they risked harsh German reprisals, including the possibility of invasion. The United States was three thousand miles from the Kaiser; the neutrals were at his front door. Surely America must recognize their dilemma.

These considerations undoubtedly made the U.S. government hesitate to declare the embargo that Hoover was demanding.[217] Early in July reports appeared in the press of dissension behind the scenes in official Washington—of proposals by members of the Exports Council for action being overridden and revised, causing delays.[218] Hoover himself was growing more and more agitated. In a letter to the President on July 7, he warned that the shortage of wheat in the United States was becoming perilous, thanks to intensifying neutral purchases, and that the accelerating shipment of fodder to the European neutrals was making it impossible for American dairymen to maintain their herds. He therefore requested an immediate embargo.[219]

In a meeting with Hoover and the Secretary of Agriculture that very day, President Wilson agreed at last to act.[220] Two days later, in a public proclamation, he prohibited the export of all food grains, flour, fodder, meat, and certain other commodities from the United States except under governmental license. Yet even as he did so, Wilson endeavored, through soothing verbiage, to soften the blow. America recognized its "duty" to the neutrals, he declared, and did not wish to "hamper" them at all. Instead, he pledged that the United States would cooperate with them in relieving their food necessities from "our available surpluses." Still, he added politely, America had an "obligation to assure itself" that the neutrals were conserving their own resources and would not ship their American imports directly or indirectly to the enemy.[221]

Wilson's proclamation thrust Hoover even further into the vortex of policymaking. At the request of the Exports Council, the Food Administrator initiated informal discussions with diplomatic representatives of the northern neutrals in Washington. Before the United States could come to terms with the European supplicants, it must learn precisely what food they needed—and what they would do for the United States in return.[222]

On July 24, therefore, the Exports Council dispatched an identical memorandum to the legations of Denmark, Norway, Sweden, and the Netherlands. In each case, Hoover himself delivered the documents.[223] The council pointed out that America's wartime allies were already in need of more food than it could currently supply. If the United States now undertook to feed the neutrals as well, it must either penalize the Allies, force its own people to make further sacrifices, or divert its productivity and manpower from "the necessities of war."

Nevertheless, the Exports Council held out the prospect of future assistance, provided that the northern neutrals rendered "services of equal value." In order to qualify for American food relief, the neutrals would have to stimulate their domestic production, rigorously regulate their consumption, calculate their minimum deficiency in food values and the amount which must come from abroad, and guarantee that any imported American food would not directly or indirectly reach German hands. The council reminded the neutrals that any American assistance in the present emergency could not be "wholly liquidated by the purchase price." The neutrals must provide "some service in return." It was an unmistakable hint at what America most wanted: access to the neutrals' vital commercial shipping. The council asked the four legations to furnish data upon which America's precise level of food allotments to them could be determined. And it warned that any food exports that the neutrals made to Germany before reaching an agreement with the United States would not be replaced from U.S. stockpiles.[224]

The Exports Council's note was the formal opening volley in a negotiating process that consumed many months. Hoover's zeal to implement the tough new policy immediately collided with Woodrow Wilson's lingering solicitude for neutral rights. On July 26, acting without the authority either of the White House or of the Exports Council, Hoover notified the Danish commercial attaché that the United States was terminating all sales of American fodder for Danish cattle since the American supply was so short. Apart from this economic circumstance, Hoover was determined to cut off exports entirely to neutral countries that in turn sold foodstuffs to Germany. His independent behavior angered and alarmed the State Department's counselor, Frank L. Polk, who demanded that the Exports Council consider the issue on July 27.[225] Another State Department official remarked that Hoover was "trying to dominate" the council and "force it to very extreme measures," with the British "egging him on."[226]

When the council met, Hoover unrepentantly stood his ground. Denmark "is more than self-supporting without imports," he asserted. In fact, it was exporting "vast quantities of fat and protein" to the enemy. "Every pound supplied," he thundered, "contributes to the loss of American lives." Furthermore, the cattle fodder that was being used to create this Danish surplus came largely from the United States. Now the Danes were pressuring us to send them at least 80,000 tons more. It was a request he found totally unjustifiable. He therefore vehemently protested against issuing permits for any further American food exports to Denmark.[227] After discussing the issue at length, the council voted to recommend this policy to the President.[228]

Woodrow Wilson, however, was not persuaded. He told Polk that Hoover was going too far and that he, Wilson, had "stood up for [the] rights of neutrals in [the] past and was not prepared to forbid them to trade with Germany."[229] In the eyes of the President, so recently neutral himself, the neutral states had a legitimate right to engage in commerce with whomever they wished, and America had a humanitarian obligation toward them.[230]

The Exports Council was therefore obliged to retreat and mark time.[231]

Despite this setback, the tide of policy was building in Hoover's direction. On August 24, he urged the Exports Council to withhold all licenses for the export of pork products until he was able to work out quotas with importing countries. The council readily agreed.[232] Within this body Hoover continued to advocate the "absolutely radical stand" of telling the neutrals that America would not permit them to send *any* food into Germany.[233] His hard-line stance found support on the newly created Exports Administrative Board, where the brusqueness of his protégés in dealing with neutral diplomats soon earned them the sobriquet "Mr. Hoover's wild men."[234] The British government, too, continued to press Washington to implement a more powerful policy.[235]

Finally, in late August, President Wilson tightened the nation's export control apparatus. The Exports Administrative Committee, hitherto an adjunct of the Exports Council, was replaced by an Exports Administrative Board, with executive power over export licensing.[236] Six days later Wilson expanded the list of licensed goods to include virtually all articles of commerce.[237] Keenly aware of the diplomatic risks, the President once again asserted that his purpose was export control, not prohibition, and that America intended "to minister to the needs of the neutral nations as far as our resources permit."[238] But his gentle and diplomatic language could not conceal the trend. Three days later the Exports Administrative Board decided to withhold all licenses for the export of controlled commodities to Denmark, Norway, Holland, and Sweden for an indefinite period.[239] In effect, the northern neutrals would receive no further food from the United States until they came to a precise agreement over amounts and terms.

On October 12 President Wilson replaced his existing export control machinery with a new agency called the War Trade Board.[240] Five days later Secretary of State Lansing disclosed that the northern neutrals still had not provided the data that the Exports Council had requested of them on July 24. Moreover, despite the council's warning of the consequences, some of the neutrals were continuing to send crucial supplies into Germany. The Secretary of State therefore announced that the United States would continue to refuse all export licenses to the offending neutrals so long as they failed to hand over the requested information and persisted in aiding the enemy.[241]

Although Hoover as Food Administrator had a representative on the War Trade Board, he was not at the center of the negotiations with the neutrals that now ensued. He did not need to be. His key objective—closure of the American market to untamed foreign purchasing—had been attained. A virtually total food embargo on the neutrals would continue until they acceded to terms satisfactory to the United States. Furthermore, the War Trade Board agreed to license no food for export unless Hoover gave his assent.[242] If the feisty Food Administrator no longer dominated policymaking, as he had done between June and late August, he retained the power of veto in his sphere of concern.

Meanwhile he confronted another thorny problem: What should be done about the huge stocks of foodstuffs that agents of the northern neutrals had managed to purchase in the United States and load onto ships before the President imposed his embargo in July? At the time of Wilson's proclamation, the Dutch alone had filled forty-two vessels with nearly 195,000 tons of grain and fodder.[243] Should they and their fellow neutrals be given licenses to send these cargoes from American ports?

Legally, of course, the food belonged to the buyers. But the U.S. government was at war, and Hoover, for one, saw no reason why the neutrals should be accommodated when they had no urgent need for these shipments.[244] Why, for instance, should the Danes be allowed to forward the 75,000 tons of cottonseed cake that they had bought when it would be used to fatten Danish cattle for slaughter and sale to the Germans?[245]

Still, the neutrals had a case, and the U.S. government was hesitant to push them into the embrace of the enemy. Perhaps for this reason, Hoover broached a compromise to the Dutch in late July: they would be permitted to ship one third of their assembled cargoes of American grain to Europe for their own use if they sold the remaining two thirds at cost to the Commission for Relief in Belgium and delivered it to the commission's storage facilities in Rotterdam. Not only would this assist the Belgians, who were now facing starvation and for whom Hoover continued to have responsibility as head of the CRB. It would also forestall an otherwise untimely drain on America's shrinking grain reserves.[246]

On August 9 the Exports Council asked Hoover to offer each of the northern neutrals a division of their detained cargoes on the basis of his 2:1 formula. The council added that it would "probably approve" such arrangements.[247] The Food Administrator soon negotiated satisfactory agreements with the Norwegians and the Swedes, to the alleviation of the Belgian people's distress.[248] With the Danes it was a different story. Unwilling (according to Hoover) to assign any of their merchant fleet to the United States or the Belgian relief effort, the Danish authorities thereupon suffered the consequences: no export permits and no cottonseed cake.[249]

It was the Dutch, however, who proved the most refractory. On August 3 the Netherlands' minister in Washington agreed in principle to transfer two thirds of existing Dutch cargo in American ports to the CRB.[250] A week later, after conferring with the Exports Council, Hoover informed the minister that the council was "disposed to recommend" the release of approximately 40,000 tons of corn and barley in exchange for the sale and delivery of nearly 60,000 other tons of corn and wheat to the Belgian relief.[251] The Dutch agreed, and the deal—so they thought—was struck.[252]

On August 25 the Exports Administrative Board duly authorized licenses for the first assortment of Dutch cargoes to proceed, some to the Netherlands itself and some to the Belgians.[253] Suddenly complications intervened: inspection revealed that much of the waiting cargo had deteriorated. Anxious to use what he could before it rotted, Hoover abandoned his initial arrangement and agreed to ship all Dutch-held corn at once to Holland. There the corn fit for humans would be divided between the Dutch and the CRB nearly evenly, while rejected corn would go exclusively to the Dutch. The minister for the Netherlands accepted this proposal with alacrity.[254]

When the Exports Administrative Board learned about this change of plan, it was not amused. According to its investigation, *none* of the loaded corn was suitable for human consumption. If the cargoes were allowed to sail anyway, the Dutch in effect would receive a bonanza of cattle feed—to the ultimate benefit of the Germans. The board therefore swiftly rescinded its action of August 25 and voted to refuse licenses for the cargoes.[255]

This sudden reversal caused a sensation in diplomatic circles and left more than one party in a bad temper. The Dutch minister complained at length to the State Department and implied that Hoover and his associates had reneged on a clear commitment.[256] Hoover, for his part, insisted that he had told the Dutch all along that his agreements were subject to approval by the Exports Council. Furthermore, he said, the whole basis of negotiation had been his desire to obtain human food for the Belgians and his assumption that the Dutch vessels contained it. Hoover blamed the Dutch for wasting the CRB's time negotiating over supplies that they must have known were unsuitable for his purposes.[257]

Thwarted in their effort to free their stranded cargoes, the Dutch now attempted to save them from further spoilage. The result was more headaches for Hoover. In Baltimore, where twenty of their grain-filled vessels lay at anchor, Dutch agents began to unload the contents and dry them in elevators on shore. The American facilities were overwhelmed.[258] In New York, after removing the grain from their steamers and reconditioning it, the Dutch reloaded it onto small American harbor lighters. The reason, they said, was that they were negotiating to send their steamers to Australia and did not wish to refill these ships until the issue was resolved. The consequence was a massive tieup of the port's grain handling system. By mid-October no fewer than one hundred lighters were floating around New York Harbor with Dutch-owned grain.[259]

Hoover and Julius Barnes tried frantically to find ways to relieve the strain on the two ports. At times their campaign resembled a guerrilla war. When the Dutch left some of their grain in the Baltimore elevators in the evident hope of obtaining an export license eventually, the Grain Corporation promptly borrowed it and sold it to the Allies, while promising to replace it at a later date.[260] When Dutch agents tried to persuade warehousemen in New York City to sign documents acknowledging that the dried grain in their custody belonged to the Netherlands government, Barnes advised the elevator operators not to do it.[261] The Food Administration also issued a regulation that no lighter could carry grain for more than thirty days.[262] Eventually, after further maneuvers and negotiations, the Dutch gave up and sold their corn to the Grain Corporation and a private manufacturer of glucose.[263] To Hoover's enduring irritation, a great cache of valuable food had been lost to direct human use.

No sooner had the Dutch imbroglio subsided than a challenge to Hoover arose from another neutral nation in Europe. During the summer the Food Administrator had stoutly resisted attempts by the government of Switzerland to acquire wheat in the United States. With America having all it could do to feed its allies, he believed that the Swiss should turn to Australia.[264] Instead, much to his annoyance, the Swiss initiated what he labeled "a great propaganda campaign" to induce America to be their supplier.[265]

In November the Swiss again applied to Washington for wheat.[266] Hoover categorically refused, citing what he said was the virtual exhaustion of America's exportable surplus.[267] Meanwhile, in Paris, his associate Alonzo Taylor and another member of the War Trade Board conferred with Swiss officials over the terms of a rationing agreement for 1918. The Swiss contended that they must import wheat from the United States—and quickly. Otherwise they would have none of it to eat by the coming spring.[268] Wheat from Argentina, they said, could not be arranged in time.[269]

On November 26, under pressure from the State Department, Hoover released 15,000 tons of grain (one third of it wheat) for the Swiss at New York.[270] Otherwise, he was unmoved. "Our wheat situation is such that we simply cannot supply Switzerland," he cabled Taylor. Barley, rye, and corn, yes—but not wheat; the Swiss must go to India or the southern hemisphere.[271] When the Swiss minister at Washington asserted that he had been promised 200,000 tons of American breadstuffs, Hoover accused him of "repeating a lie." The Swiss had received no such assurances whatever, Hoover said: only a "partially formulated contract" that provided this amount without stipulating the source.[272] According to Hoover, the Inter-Allied Conference then meeting in Paris had decided that the Allies must provide the Swiss with wheat from "some quarter other than the United States."[273] On November 30 Taylor confirmed this understanding.[274]

In the last days of November, however, events unexpectedly altered the situation. The collapse of the Italian army at Caporetto raised the specter among the Swiss that the German army would shortly invade their homeland in a drive into Italy from another direction.[275] From the perspective of the State Department and its chargé d'affaires in the Swiss capital, now was not the time to antagonize the Swiss. If the United States was uncooperative about wheat that the Swiss said they desperately needed, the Germans just might offer them food themselves in exchange for safe conduct for the German army through the St. Gotthard Pass.[276]

Even now Hoover did not retreat. He had absolutely no wheat to export, he insisted, and he accused the British and French of trying to foist the burden of feeding Switzerland onto the United States.[277] By the beginning of December, Frank L. Polk of the State Department was so exasperated at Hoover's intransigence that he refused to have any further contacts with the Food Administrator about the Swiss problem.[278]

Behind Hoover's adamancy, of course, lay his ever present fear: that the United States was now "running the most serious risk of a flour famine" before the next harvest. "I do not believe that the American population will remain tranquil for one moment if it is not able to obtain wheat bread," he told Secretary of State Lansing in late November. The Food Administrator refused to take responsibility for exporting wheat to anyone but the Allies, "except on direction" from a Secretary of State fully cognizant of "where this may lead in the United States at a later date." As for the Swiss, so long as they kept open their breweries, Hoover did not "see how we can ask our people to give up their bread to furnish them with grain." If the Swiss were unwilling to travel to Argentina for their wheat, then "they ought" (said Hoover angrily) "to make up their minds to subsist on barley, oats, rye and corn, all of which are perfectly good food."[279]

In Paris, military and strategic considerations now prevailed. On December 5 negotiators for the War Trade Board signed a memorandum with the Swiss government covering a period ending on September 30, 1918. Among other things, the board promised to license for export to Switzerland a maximum of 300,000 metric tons of American wheat and rye, provided that these commodities were not required by the United States or its allies. The memorandum also acknowledged a separate agreement just made at the Inter-Allied Conference that Switzerland would receive a "guaranteed allotment" of 240,000 tons of cereal breadstuffs by next September. Contrary to Hoover and Taylor, the memorandum implied that this quantity would come from the United States. At the same time, the War Trade Board declared that its agreement with the Swiss was not a contract binding the U.S. government but only a declaration of the board's intent regarding licensing.[280]

Despite these loopholes and ambiguities (or perhaps because of them), Hoover immediately protested. The U.S. government, he insisted, had neither the food nor the ships to meet this obligation unless it did so at the expense of the Allies. Let the Swiss hire neutral shipping, he argued. Let them get their grain from Argentina.[281] The British, too, objected that they had no tonnage and fought a rearguard action against the deal.[282] For their part, Swiss "propagandists" (as Hoover called them) claimed that the guarantee of 240,000 tons of breadstuffs was an American commitment on which the United States was now in arrears. Months of delay and acrimony passed before the Swiss (at the insistence of the State Department) received any of their allotments. Even then Hoover objected, citing the lost shipping and supplies that the Allies would suffer. The Food Administrator never accepted Swiss claims that they truly needed American aid.[283]

It was not until well into 1918 that the United States finally consummated food pacts with the governments of Denmark, Norway, Sweden, and Holland. In general, as the price of being permitted to purchase specified quantities of American food, the neutrals were obliged to curb their trading with Germany and to transfer some of their merchant ships to the Allies.[284] In the case of the Dutch, in March 1918, after months of fruitless diplomatic fencing, President Wilson invoked his war powers and requisitioned all eighty-seven Dutch ships languishing in American ports. The owners received compensation after the war.[285] In driving its bargains the United States had been tough but not, Hoover thought, unfair. After all, America was fighting the neutrals' battle for them. And as he pointed out many years later, despite all the outcries and propaganda no one in the northern neutral states actually starved.[286]

Hoover was only peripherally involved in these later episodes. Long before then, the Wilson administration—thanks in considerable measure to his persistence—had plugged the neutrals' hole in America's dike. As he stressed repeatedly, Hoover was prepared to act humanely toward the neutrals, although he did not think they were suffering nearly as much as they professed to be. But he was more than a humanitarian now. He was an officer of the United States government, and in executing his duties the needs of his own people took precedence.

6

"The Benevolent Bogey of the Nation"

I

On September 4, 1917 residents of the nation's capital gathered along Pennsylvania Avenue to honor the first army draftees from the District of Columbia. Two hundred thousand people cheered as the President of the United States led a parade of 28,000 marchers, including 70 U.S. senators, 260 members of the House of Representatives, employees from federal agencies, veterans of the Civil War, units of marines and cavalry, officers from the War and Navy departments, throngs of flag-toting school children, and 900 of the draftees themselves. Fifteen bands added to the fervor. As they passed the reviewing stand in front of the White House, five of them played "Onward, Christian Soldiers."

Among the serried ranks of marchers was a contingent from the United States Food Administration, preceded by a banner carrying its name. Behind it, walking alone, was Herbert Hoover, embarrassed by his conspicuousness in the crowd. Behind him came his associates and staff, including thirty women dressed in the blue uniforms and white caps of the food conservation division. As he strode past the White House reviewing stand, the diffident Food Administrator blushed, dropped his hat, and kicked it as he tried to retrieve it. The President of the United States grinned. It was but a momentary mortification. As he proceeded with his "army" up Pennsylvania Avenue, Hoover received thunderous applause.[1]

All across the nation that September, patriotic parades were commonplace as cities and towns saw their young men off to war. Mobilization of the home front was also the order of the day. The Red Cross beseeched the public for contributions. The Treasury Department prepared to launch a second Liberty Loan drive to persuade Americans to buy more bonds to finance the war effort. And Hoover, a veteran master of publicity, was planning to wage a new campaign of his own.

Stabilizing food prices and guarding food exports were only two of the goals that the Food Administrator had announced on August 10. The third—and the one for which the general public would most remember him—was straightforward: to "stimulate" Americans to conserve food so that they could increase their exports to the Allies.[2] Convinced that compulsory rationing would be expensive, impractical, and un-American, he proposed to achieve his objective by mass persuasion. His midsummer mobilization of 2,000,000 housewives had been a first step. His call for the nation to observe "meatless" and "wheatless" days had been another.[3] As summer gave way to autumn, he prepared to turn his battle against waste and overconsumption into an all-out war.

At the end of September Hoover unveiled a breathtaking plan. In a few weeks, he announced, his agency would conduct a canvass of every single household in the United States with the aim of completing "the enrollment of our forces" in a food conservation army. Every man, woman, and child in America would be asked to "become a member" of the Food Administration and to sign a pledge to carry out its suggestions. The Allies in Europe were "our first line of defense," said Hoover, and they must be fed. Americans could only make this happen by curbing their consumption and switching to substitute foods that were not transportable overseas. "On the success of this unprecedented adventure in democracy," he asserted, "will largely stake the issue of the war."[4]

Preparations for the great campaign now went into high gear, behind the rallying slogan, "Food will win the war."[5] Half a million volunteers, principally women, were recruited to take the pledge cards house-to-house.[6] Hoover asked every school official in the country to teach food conservation in the classroom and to encourage children to write letters to their parents in support of signing the pledge.[7] As in July, he sent letters to 100,000 preachers, this time asking each to appeal for food conservation in church services on the first Sunday of pledge week.[8] The Food Administrator arranged for a national network of 14,000 patriotic public speakers known as "four-minute men" to orate in behalf of his cause.[9] He asked hotels and restaurants to sign up for his crusade.[10] And always, unceasingly, he appealed to American women—"a great army drafted by conscience into what is now the most urgent activity of the war."[11] He may have been the first government administrator in history to organize women for direct war-related service in their own homes.[12]

With relentless passion he pounded away at his message. Americans were "the greatest wasters of fat under the sun," he told a conference of public health officials in mid-October. In fact, he announced, nearly one third of American households were beset by "enormous waste." It would do Americans good to reduce their "over-feeding," and the ensuing surpluses would benefit the Allies.

But could Americans accomplish such a goal voluntarily? Could they reduce their food consumption by 10 percent? This, for Hoover, was "wholly a problem of education"; he had no desire to introduce coercive European methods of conservation over here. Instead, he exhorted his listeners to carry his summons to self-denial across the land. Food conservation was a critical form of national service, he declared. War

> has but few compensations and of them we must make the most. Its greatest compensation lies in the possibility that we may instil into our people unselfishness, self sacrifice, devotion to national interests. We have gone for a hundred years of unbridled private initiative in this country and it has bred its own evils and one of these evils is the lack of responsibility in the American individual to the people as a whole, the unwillingness of personal selfishness to sacrifice to national interest. We are calling upon many of our people to make the ultimate sacrifice, and it is but little to call on those who remain in comparative comfort that they should make some saving in their kitchens and on their tables.[13]

At the President's request Hoover postponed his campaign by a week in order that the Treasury Department could complete its Liberty Loan drive.[14] Then, on October 26, as his great push was set to begin, the Food Administrator made a sensational disclosure. In telegrams to a number of his state food administrators, he revealed that he had been informed of the existence of a "widespread conspiracy" to destroy animals in American stockyards. Citing an unprecedented nineteen fires in stockyards and grain elevators across the nation in the past month, including a blaze that killed thousands of cattle in Kansas City, Hoover urged the governors of several states to place troops at key facilities. The "danger from German plots," he told the press, was "considerable."[15] In Illinois, plans were made to rush the national guard to the Chicago stockyards. In New York City, extra police were assigned to food warehouses.[16] As news of the disastrous fires and other apparent German acts of sabotage spread, the *New York Times* reported that the government was considering a plan to compel all enemy aliens on the east coast to move at least one hundred miles inland.[17]

Hoover's electrifying announcement may have been timed to galvanize the American people into boarding his food conservation bandwagon.[18] In any case, on the same day that he informed the press of the enemy's alleged arson plots against American cattle and grain, he simultaneously launched his national food pledge crusade at a rally in Baltimore. Three thousand women, known as the Maryland Food Conservation Army, assembled to hear him. All wore what the Baltimore *Sun* called the "Hoover costume" of "white shirtwaist and skirt, with the badges of their rank and the Hoover brassard on their arm band." To these uniformed volunteers, who would shortly solicit signatures throughout the state, Hoover issued a stirring call to battle:

> This is the most anxious of days that I have spent since August 10, when the Food Administration was organized. We have worked incessantly to inaugurate the greatest experiment ever undertaken in a democracy, and now it is to be put to the test. . . . We must eliminate waste in this country and send the food we save to the suffering people of our allies. . . .
>
> Tomorrow you take hold of this work, a part of a great national army of 500,000 women. We claim your services for the period of the war. If you succeed, you will have saved the lives of millions, and you also will have saved the cause of humanity and democracy.

Mrs. Hoover joined her husband at the rally and spoke briefly; the female army gave her a military salute.[19]

For the next two weeks Hoover's legions of volunteers knocked at the doors of households from coast to coast. To those who signed a pledge to carry out Hoover's "suggestions" to the best of their ability, canvassers gave a Food Administration membership card and a card entitled "The War Creed of the Kitchen."[20] In a supporting message, President Wilson promised that if the American people did as Hoover requested, they would not only be able to feed the Allies but also attain "reasonable prices" at home.[21]

Between promise and fulfillment, however, lay a trough of apathy and even sullenness, as Hoover's eager volunteers soon discovered.[22] In only four states did they succeed in enrolling at least 80 percent of the families; in some states the figure was less than 10 percent.[23] In many areas housewives signed the pledge cards perfunctorily, with little comprehension or sense of obligation.[24] In Missouri, where Hoover's state food administrator wanted a million signatures, including those of children over ten, many schoolteachers merely enrolled their classes in toto.[25] From Maine to the Middle West to New Mexico, canvassers battled rumors that the government intended to commandeer the home-canned goods of women who signed the pledge.[26] The Food Administration promptly denied this "pro-German propaganda," which the *New York Times* attributed to enemy aliens.[27] Mrs. Hoover was so incensed by reports that certain persons were asking housewives for lists of the contents of their pantries that she declared, "Anyone who does that should be locked in a cupboard till a policeman comes."[28] Still, in Iowa and elsewhere, forged documents about planned confiscation were circulated, including a letter bearing Hoover's supposed signature.[29]

Despite these signs of indifference and resistance, by the end of the two-week campaign Hoover's canvassers had collected signed pledge cards from more than 10,200,000 women representing (it was said) nearly half the nation's 22,000,000 families.[30] The number of enrolled households eventually exceeded 13,000,000.[31] Although this was far short of his professed goal of universal coverage, Hoover appeared satisfied by the overall result.[32]

Certainly his agency was determined to give the statistics a favorable interpretation. Even before the drive was over, the Food Administration asserted that if just half the nation's families cooperated in food substitution, it would yield "far more tangible" results than most people realized.[33] Hoover himself expressed pleasure that 90 percent of the "first-class hotels" in the country signed his pledge card and were complying with its restrictive recommendations.[34]

The Food Administrator lost little time in summoning his augmented "army" to its duty. In mid-December, he sent out more than 10,000,000 "home cards" with instructions elaborating upon his "gospel of the clean plate." He asked Americans to consume no meat of any kind on Tuesdays and no wheat products on Wednesdays, and to eat one meatless and one wheatless meal on other days. He counseled his fellow citizens to serve smaller portions and use substitutes for the wheat, meat, fats, and sugar most needed "over there." And he warned that American behavior on the food front in the coming winter would determine whether we as a people were "capable of voluntary individual self-sacrifice to save the world."[35]

II

HOOVER was too much of a realist to expect such self-denial to well up spontaneously, or in response to a single exhortation. If the American people were to modify their lifestyles without coercion, they must be persuaded, unremittingly, to do so. While the food pledge drive of mid-autumn was the centerpiece of his mobilization strategy, it was only one phase in a perpetual frenzy of salesmanship. Between mid-September and mid-October 1917 his Washington headquarters mailed out an average of 285,000 documents (mostly information circulars) per day.[36] It was just the beginning of a propaganda blizzard that would blanket America without letup until the end of the war.

To coordinate this effort, Hoover relied principally upon what became known as the Food Administration's educational division, directed by his de facto press secretary, Ben S. Allen. The division contained fourteen different sections. The states' section furnished bulletins and daily press releases to state food organizations. The illustrations and plate section supplied photographs for newspapers and magazines, lantern slides for lecturers, and materials for all sorts of publications. The religious press, farm journals, trade and technical journals, black press, and foreign-language press: each could turn to a specific section of Hoover's apparatus for an avalanche of articles and news items especially prepared for their use.[37] All this in addition to an unending barrage of Food Administration press releases—1,400 of them by war's end—aimed at the nation's daily newspapers.[38]

Meanwhile the magazine and feature section, headed by the editor of the *Woman's Home Companion*, Gertrude B. Lane, strove to rally the distaff side of the nation's households. With the assistance of the home conservation division, and of leading home economists from several universities, Lane and her colleagues developed and disseminated recipes, advice on canning, and other useful information for women. Her branch of Hoover's agency sent speakers into the field to demonstrate food conservation menus and techniques. The section's employees prepared five stories a week for the women's pages of nearly three thousand publications. Each month during the war the *Ladies' Home Journal* published up to sixteen articles on food conservation, all drawn from material supplied by the Food Administration. Every outlet, it seemed, was utilized to teach America's women how to "cook the Kaiser's goose on their own stoves."[39]

The Food Administration also took its "gospel" to the farm. It encouraged farm journals to offer prizes for articles on food conservation. It touted rabbits as an alternate source of meat. It supplied slogans and newspaper fillers:

> Food is sacred. To waste it is sinful.
> Don't let your horse be more patriotic than you are—eat a dish of oatmeal!
> Wheatless days in America make sleepless nights in Germany.
> U-Boats and wastefulness are twin enemies.
> Serve beans by all means.
> The Battle Cry of Feed'Em.[40]

No medium of advertisement, no vehicle for dissemination of information, was overlooked by Hoover and his lieutenants. The Food Administration asked outstanding artists to produce multicolored conservation posters, which it then distributed by the thousands throughout the country.[41] It produced lantern slides for exhibit in movie theaters and commissioned films with titles like "Practical Hooverism."[42] It persuaded advertising companies to install huge outdoor signs bearing the slogan "FOOD WILL WIN THE WAR—DON'T WASTE IT" on billboards, railroad depots, city halls, post offices, and other buildings from coast to coast.[43] The Food Administration was the first wartime agency to ask advertisers for such help; the industry complied at no charge to the government.[44] In many cities electric light companies provided free illumination so that the signs could be seen by anyone throughout the night.[45]

The Food Administration displayed 50,000 signs on railroad coaches and another 120,000 in streetcars—all at no cost. The advertising value was calculated in the millions of dollars.[46] It distributed hundreds of thousands of pamphlets, posters, and other materials to 10,000 public libraries, many of which set up special bulletin boards and other food-related exhibits.[47] The library section's crusading chief urged the "great libraries of the country" to "put Shakespeare in the alcove" for a spell and "feature 'Food Conservation' " instead.[48]

American businesses cooperated eagerly with Hoover's crusade. Two leading insurance companies sent food conservation flyers to their policy holders. Theater managers hung food posters on their drop curtains. The American Chicle Company inserted food slogans in its chewing-gum wrappers. One railroad company published the text of a Hoover speech on the front of its timetable.[49]

Children, too, were embraced in the cause. The Food Administration prepared outlines of food talks for youngsters and devised a special pledge card entitled "A Little American's Promise":

I'll eat corn-meal, oatmeal and rice
And nice sweet hominy;
Cornflakes and mush with lots of milk
Are good enough for me.
At table I'll not leave a scrap
Of food upon my plate.
And I'll not eat between meals but
For supper time I'll wait.
I make the promise that I'll do
My honest, earnest part
In helping my America
With all my loyal heart.
This is a promise and I hope
All children make the same
I'll be a good American
And hereto sign my name.[50]

For toddlers not ready for such an appeal, Hoover's employees rewrote nursery rhymes:

Little Boy Blue, come blow your horn!
The cook's using wheat where she ought to use corn!
And terrible famine our country will sweep,
If the cooks and the housewives remain fast asleep!
Go wake them! Go wake them! It's now up to you!
Be a loyal American, Little Boy Blue![51]

Some months later Ben S. Allen proudly looked back upon his division's work as "the greatest and most inspiring propaganda campaign ever conducted in this country. . . ."[52] Truly there had been nothing like it in American history. "No war board at Washington was advertised as widely as the United States Food Administration," one observer remarked.[53] No other agency of the government touched the home as regularly. By untiring persuasion, by omnipresent publicity, by ingenious wartime appeals to head and heart, Hoover sought assent to policies that he neither cared nor perhaps dared to impose upon his fellow citizens by force of law.

And as his hurricane of publicity swirled unabatedly, the Food Administrator himself became the object of adulation. Ever since the "Miracle-Man" embarrassment of midsummer, he had tried to exclude his name from his agency's literature.[54] It did not matter. Newspapers and magazines abounded with references to the man one writer dubbed "the benevolent bogey of the nation."[55] Another wrote that Hoover's was "the biggest war job west of the trenches."[56] Perhaps most tellingly of all, in the autumn of 1917 the word "Hooverize" (meaning "to save or economize") entered the American vocabulary, as people cheerfully spoke of "Hooverized" meals.[57] For millions of Americans, "Hooverizing" became a daily passion.

At times the Food Administrator's single-mindedness evoked friendly satire. In the *Ladies' Home Journal*, a versifier "warned" her readers:

> The darned old Hoover pledge has
>   come to our house to stay;
> To frown our breakfast bacon down, and
>   take our steak away;
> It cans our morning waffles, and our sausage,
>   too, it seems,
> And dilates on the succulence of corn, and
>   spuds, and beans.
> So skimp the sugar in your cake and leave
>   the butter out,
> Or Hoover's goin' to get you if you
>   Don't
>   Watch
>   Out![58]

At one point some of the Food Administration's staff joined in the fun by circulating an anonymous spoof of the government's incessant appeals for conservation:

> My Tuesdays are meatless,
> My Wednesdays are wheatless;
>   I am getting more eatless each day.
> My home it is heatless,
> My bed it is sheetless;
>   They're all sent to the Y.M.C.A.

The barrooms are treatless,
My coffee is sweetless;
Each day I get poorer and wiser;
My stockings are feetless,
My trousers are seatless;
My! How I do hate the Kaiser![59]

Of course, not everyone found the serious, round-faced "bogey" so benevolent. In uncounted homes across the continent, parents used the fear of Hoover's displeasure to induce their children to clean their plates. When one mother told her son that Hoover would be very disappointed if a single bite was left uneaten, the awed little boy asked: Is Hoover God?[60]

While the Food Administrator left most of the media blitz to his subordinates, he, too, assiduously cultivated the press. He kept in touch with Frank Cobb, editor of the powerful New York *World;* one of Cobb's deputies acted as intermediary and even worked directly for the Food Administration for a time.[61] Once a week Hoover held news conferences with newspaper correspondents—a practice that quickly established him as one of the most knowledgeable and accessible public officials in Washington.[62] The Food Administration provided reporters a press room in its building, along with telephone service, typewriters, and tickets to the agency's cafeteria.[63] Grateful for this attention and impressed by Hoover's accomplishments, the Washington press corps openly admired and praised him.[64] So willing was it to serve as his instrument that its wartime relationship to him became "practically a partnership."[65]

Such a whirlwind of activity could not persist without organization, an imperative much on Hoover's mind in the early months of his service. By the time the Lever Act took effect in August, his infant administration was already scattered in six locations around the capital, and in need of doubling its space within three months.[66] In mid-September the President authorized him to construct a temporary building to house the entire agency.[67]

Meanwhile Hoover labored to perfect his organization in the forty-eight states, a task fraught with delicacy and political peril.[68] Although Hoover was scrupulously nonpartisan, each nominee he selected for state food administrator was screened by the chairman of the Democratic National Committee and personally approved by President Wilson.[69] Once appointed, the state food administrators in turn had to develop their organizations down to the county and district levels, with the aims of interpreting and enforcing Hoover's policies, directing "educational work in food conservation," and serving as liaisons between national headquarters and the people. Centralized policymaking, decentralized execution: this, said Hoover, was his theory of administration.[70]

From the outset the engineer-turned-executive strongly resisted bureaucratizing tendencies. In a memorandum to his Organization Committee on

July 26, he declared that he wanted his agency to be one of "extreme elasticity, expanding and contracting as occasion arises, in a way that seems to me impossible for a rigidly charted organization to do."[71] He wanted his staff to be oriented toward ad hoc problem solving, not to preconceived divisions of authority.[72] Thus, when a problem arose, he would simply assign someone to solve it. This person in turn would draw upon his relevant colleagues for assistance.[73] When the task was done, the staff members involved would turn to other challenges under whoever was appropriate for that job. The "essence" of his approach, said Hoover, was "Voluntary Leadership."[74] The "best way to organize anything," he remarked, "is to pick the person, give him a box of pencils, a wastebasket, and a place to work and say 'go to it.' "[75]

The Food Administrator therefore detested organization charts.[76] On one occasion, when an ambitious underling prepared one, Hoover tore up the paper in disgust and put it in the trash.[77] Nor was he any more enamored of time-consuming Civil Service procedures for hiring employees for his new government agency. At his request President Wilson issued an executive order authorizing the Food Administration to employ personnel for the duration of the war without reference to Civil Service laws and regulations.[78] It was a way not only of hiring the people he wanted, and hiring them quickly, but also of securing their undivided loyalty.[79]

He did not have to work hard to obtain it. Many of his closest associates in those early months—such as Ben Allen, Ray Lyman Wilbur, and Mark Requa (his chief assistant)[80]—were friends of long-standing devotion. Others soon acquired similar bonds to the Chief. Unconsciously, it seemed, Hoover engendered such sentiments. On one occasion he was reluctantly persuaded to address the Food Administration's growing staff, some of whom had not yet caught a glimpse of him. Entering the assembly hall from the rear, he quietly took a seat in the back row. When called upon to speak, he went down the aisle, and, instead of taking the stage, simply faced his audience from the foot of the platform. He declared that as Food Administrator he would inevitably become unpopular and would sooner or later be obliged to resign. He urged it to be loyal to his successor and expatiated extemporaneously on themes of service and sacrifice. When he was through, he turned at once to leave. As the hall resounded with applause, he walked back up the aisle and out of the building into a waiting automobile.[81] Such acts of self-effacement cemented loyalties for life.

In mid-November 1917, Hoover and his colleagues moved into their new quarters: a block-long, two-story building on D Street, between 18th and 19th Streets. It contained more than three hundred rooms and had been constructed in fewer than sixty working days.[82] The Food Administration had come a long way since early May, when it had consisted of three bedrooms in the New Willard Hotel.[83] By December 1 the Washington office comprised more than eleven hundred employees. About two hundred held executive positions; eighty-one of these individuals, including Hoover, received no compensation whatsoever for their work. Many others were reimbursed only for expenses.[84] At its peak in 1918, the Food Administration had nearly two thousand employees in Washington and another nine thousand or so (mostly unpaid) in the states.[85] Beyond them, and numbering perhaps three quarters of a million, was the mostly female army of volunteers who gave what Hoover called "part-time service."[86]

By Christmas 1917, then, the Food Administrator's general staff and field organization were in place, and his three-pronged offensive had begun. He had implemented his machinery for price stabilization, he had put a brake on exports to Europe, he had marshaled housewives and businesses into a drive against excess and waste. But not everyone in America wanted "stabilized" prices. Not everyone welcomed his "guidance." Not everyone liked "the benevolent bogey of the nation" or applauded his "steadying hand." Even as he achieved regulatory success, Hoover's consumer-oriented policies were bringing him new trouble from the one sector in the population that did *not* want lower prices: the producers of food, the men and women on the farms.

7

The Politics of Pork

I

In his statement of Food Administration objectives on August 10, 1917 Hoover said nothing about encouraging agricultural production. One reason, no doubt, was practical: with the crops of 1917 already in the field, it was too late for exhortation to make an immediate difference. A second reason was political: by an agreement between himself and David Houston, the stimulation of farm production was to be the responsibility of the Department of Agriculture.[1] Nevertheless, Hoover soon realized that this bureaucratic division of labor was artificial. It was not enough for him to regulate middlemen, check the grain drain to Europe, and alter the daily diets of consumers. If he was to feed the Allies and repress the surge in prices, he must manage both sides of the supply-and-demand equation. He must, in short, extract more output from the nation's farms.

As the Food Administrator confronted this imperative, several hurdles to success stood in his path. For all his prestige as the saviour of starving Belgium, Hoover was not, nor had he ever been, a farmer. Nor were any members of his inner circle. His chief deputy, Mark Requa, was a petroleum engineer; Ben S. Allen a journalist; Ray Lyman Wilbur a university president. Many of the rest were mining engineers and businessmen. Fortunately for Hoover, his rival at the Department of Agriculture was not exactly the idol of agrarian activists.[2] The result was a vacuum that the energetic Food Administrator might hope to fill.

A second obstacle lay in Hoover's method of formulating his regulatory policy. Time and again in 1917 he assembled conferences in Washington of influential executives who represented their specialized lines of endeavor. From these gatherings came practical suggestions for the bureaucrats as well as assent to the rules that Hoover wished to impose. Such a technique of government-business cooperation worked well with highly organized food handlers like grain millers, sugar refiners, and wholesale grocers. The millions of American farmers, however—geographically dispersed and individualistic by temperament—were not so effectively mobilized. Unlike many food processors and distributors, farmers in 1917 had no overarching national trade association that could represent them in Hooverian conference rooms.[3] In the game of interest group politics, the farmers were at a competitive disadvantage.

The Food Administrator's selection of personnel to enforce his rules only compounded the problem. Relying heavily upon volunteers drawn from the ranks of the financially successful, Hoover quickly created an organization staffed by some of the most capable business leaders in their fields. From an administrative point of view, it made considerable sense. Who better understood the intricacies of the wheat trade, for example, than Julius Barnes, the principal grain exporter in the country? Who could better supervise food distribution than men who had devoted their careers to commerce in the affected commodities? But to many farmers it soon appeared that Hoover's agency had been colonized by the very price gougers he was supposed to be disciplining. As one uneasy farm state journalist put it, Hoover, by "insisting that his helpers must be volunteers," was effectively excluding farmers from his organization and limiting his "membership" to middlemen, the historic enemy of producers.[4]

Despite the formal constraints on his sphere of power, Hoover attempted early to reach out to farmers. In early June he retained Charles McCarthy, an ardent Progressive and head of the Legislative Reference Bureau for the state of Wisconsin, as a member of the Food Administration's senior staff. McCarthy was a student of European food policies. More significantly, he was a vigorous advocate of government price supports as a necessary stimulus to increased wartime food production. In April he had helped to push a convention of farm state officials in the direction of this radical break with precedent. The resulting ferment contributed directly to the shaping of the Lever Act.[5]

Upon McCarthy's recommendation, Hoover chose a prominent Texas cattleman named E. C. Lasater to head the Food Administration's livestock and animal food products division.[6] As a leading member of the American National Live Stock Producers Association, Lasater shared his cohorts' traditional antipathy to the meat-packing industry centered in Chicago. Partly in response to his and their agitation, President Wilson, earlier in the year, had requested the Federal Trade Commission (FTC) to investigate the much-despised packers.[7] In the same month that Lasater joined Hoover's team, the FTC's inquiry got under way.[8] For the livestock interests of the West, Lasater's appointment offered an opportunity to tilt government policy against their historic enemy.

Another agrarian activist recruited by Hoover was Charles W. Holman, who took charge of the farm journals section of the Food Administration's educational division.[9] Still another (and again at McCarthy's urging) was Gifford Pinchot, chief forester of the United States under President Taft and a Bull Moose Republican.[10] During the summer, even as they worked in or around the Food Administration, Pinchot, Holman, and McCarthy helped to found a potentially powerful lobbying group called the Federal Board of Farm Organizations. Their action evoked hostility from the Department of Agriculture.[11] Perceiving themselves as not merely brokers but advocates, these four men were firmly within Hoover's entourage by mid-August. And as the Food Administrator shortly discovered, two of them had an agenda of their own.

Hoover, in fact, was initially hesitant to hire Pinchot. As the protagonist in a sensational political controversy (known as the Ballinger / Pinchot affair) that had rocked the Taft administration, Pinchot was a distrusted figure in much of Washington. When the United States entered the war, he was apparently unable to obtain a position in any government department.[12] Nevertheless, despite warnings that Pinchot would be disloyal to him, Hoover offered the fiery Pennsylvanian a job working with Lasater.[13] In Hoover's mind, Pinchot's abilities and standing with farmers and livestock breeders made him an asset.[14]

From the start tensions simmered between the farmers' new in-house advocates and the remainder of Hoover's organization. In his very first conversation with Mark Requa, Lasater excitedly proposed that the Food Administration take over and operate the meat-packing plants.[15] Requa, at this point virtually Hoover's alter ego, rejoined that this would be both illegal and unwise. It was not the purpose of the Food Administrator, he said, to resolve the age-old enmity between producers and middlemen.[16] Besides, the packers could run their business more efficiently than the government could.[17] To McCarthy it seemed that every interest group except farmers was represented in the Food Administration and that few of Hoover's men had either knowledge of, or sympathy for, the producers' viewpoint. Indeed, permeating the organization, McCarthy believed, was an angry suspicion that the nation's farmers were both greedy and disloyal.[18] It did not help matters that Hoover's agency and the Department of Agriculture were in a constant state of what Pinchot called "suppressed hostility" toward each other—a rivalry hardly conducive to good policymaking.[19]

Most of these conflicts essentially revolved around a single question: How could the U.S. government best promote an increase in agricultural production during the war? To the agrarian interventionists whom Hoover had recruited, the answer was plain: The government should guarantee farmers a profit on the needed commodities. The key, to Pinchot and his allies, was price. Unless farmers knew that they would make money on their augmented output, they would refuse to make the effort and take the risk. This advice ran smack into Hoover's paramount priority of reducing or at least capping the price of food for urban consumers. How could he reconcile these seemingly contradictory objectives? How could the farmers get more for their product while housewives simultaneously paid less? Simple, said certain farm activists: squeeze the middleman. For reasons that gradually became apparent, Hoover was not impressed by their panacea.

As the Food Administrator searched for ways to enhance the supply of critical foodstuffs, he turned to an area where quick results seemed attainable: the stimulation of the raising of livestock, especially hogs. In 1917 pork comprised more than half of all meat produced in the United States. It was a staple both for laboring people and for soldiers[20]—and a product that easily could be shipped overseas. Perhaps best of all, from Hoover's perspective, hogs were a rapidly renewable resource. It was possible to breed and fatten them in a comparatively short period if farmers opted to do so.

Yet in the late summer of 1917 the nation's hog population was believed to be only around 60,000,000, down more than 5,000,000 head in just twelve months.[21] As a result (said Hoover) of excessive exports to the Allies, the price of hogs, like the price of wheat, had soared.[22] On August 21 arriving hogs in the Chicago stockyards sold for $20.00 per hundred pounds—the highest price ever recorded.[23]

That same day Hoover and Secretary of Agriculture Houston issued a joint public statement drafted by Lasater. The two officials disclosed that, because of the wartime demand for meat and the accelerating slaughter of European livestock herds, American farmers could expect a robust market for their meat products in Europe for years to come. The two men therefore appealed to American producers to expand their stocks of cattle, sheep, and hogs, and promised that farmers would receive "a fair share of a fair price paid by the consumer." To assist in a nationwide campaign to increase meat production, Hoover and Houston announced the formation of the United States Live Stock Industry Committee, embracing one hundred farmers and experts from around the country, including Lasater and Pinchot. The latter became part of a small executive committee as well.[24]

But what precisely should this huge new committee do? How could Hoover hope to "maintain remunerative and stimulative returns to the producer" yet permit only "reasonable" profits along the chain of distribution? How could he fulfill his announced objective of eliminating "unnecessary cost between producer and consumer"?[25] How, in short, could he translate his fine intentions into policy?

Gifford Pinchot thought he had the answer. Although Hoover apparently expected Pinchot to become a propagandist who would work to stimulate production "in a patriotic way,"[26] the new employee had a far more expansive conception of his job.[27] Within two weeks of joining the Food Administration, Pinchot presented Hoover a drastic plan for increasing the American meat supply. First, Hoover should arrange and then announce that all U.S. government and Allied purchases of American livestock products would be made at prices "large enough to allow the producer a liberal profit." The Food Administration should simultaneously announce that it would take measures to "insure" livestock producers "an attractive margin of profit" for the next three years. It should then proceed to establish a "livestock arbitration board" in Chicago with power to approve or disapprove on a daily basis the prices that meat packers offered for arriving livestock. If the board disapproved the packers' bid, it could then "determine" the "range of prices" itself. Pinchot also proposed that Hoover license the packers, limit their profits, and set "fixed differentials" between what the packers paid for live animals and what they charged consumers for the corresponding processed meat.[28]

According to Pinchot, Hoover's first reaction to his plan was that it was not radical enough.[29] According to Hoover, Pinchot's ideas on "financial measures" seemed both "visionary" and "practically all outside the powers of the Government."[30] Whatever the truth of the matter, it was not long before the two men's perspectives diverged radically.

Meanwhile Hoover was mulling over a somewhat different strategy aimed at encouraging hog production and steadying the notoriously erratic hog market. The Food Administrator had become aware of research by Henry C. Wallace, editor of *Wallaces' Farmer* in Des Moines, demonstrating a close historical correlation between the price of hogs and the price of corn required to raise them.[31] Wallace's data indicated that for the past thirty-six years American farmers had maintained the supply of hogs whenever the price of one hundred pounds of live hog equaled the price of between eleven and twelve bushels of cash corn sold in Chicago: a ratio (as colloquially put) of more than 11 to 1.[32] If the price of hogs per hundredweight exceeded this ratio (that is, if the price was greater than that of eleven or twelve bushels of corn), hog raisers profited and had an instant incentive to breed more. If, however, the ratio fell *below* 11 to 1, hog production plummeted, for under these conditions farmers could do better by selling their corn outright instead of feeding it to their swine.

In the existence of the corn / hog relationship, Hoover discerned the foundation for a policy that would both yield more pork and end the severe price fluctuations that hurt consumers and discouraged farmers from increasing their herds. On September 4 he submitted a tentative proposal to Woodrow Wilson. According to Hoover, the "corn price ratio to hog" appeared to be roughly ten to eleven bushels to a hundred pounds. In addition, eight months were required to fatten a hog. If, therefore, he took the "weighted average price of corn" over this eight-month period and simply multiplied it by 10 or 11 (or whatever the precise figure turned out to be), he would arrive at a price for hogs that would provide "absolute assurance" to producers of a fair return for their effort. If "some instrumentality" made such a calculation once a month and then fixed the resultant figure "as the price to be paid by the packers" for hogs marketed during that month, the arrangement would guarantee producers against loss. It would also eliminate daily speculative fluctuations in the stockyards—an uncertainty factor that livestock breeders hated. As a further method of stabilizing prices, Hoover suggested that the Food Administration might negotiate with the packers for "the fixing of a differential" between the raw materials (hogs) and their finished products, just as it was already doing with the wheat millers and sugar refiners.

There was, however, one potential flaw in this scheme. If Hoover was to force the packers to buy hogs at a predetermined price beneficial to the farmers, someone, he said, would have to "assure the packer" of a market for *his* products "at the agreed ratio to the price he buys hogs." But where? For Hoover, following the advice that Pinchot had just given him, the solution was simple: "a contract with the Allies to take the whole production in excess of domestic demands at the price above arrived at." Hoover knew, of course, that the Allies needed fats badly and could no longer import them from America's shores except on his terms.

The Food Administrator's plan, then, entailed a tripartite arrangement. The hog producers would be promised a satisfying return based on the corn / hog ratio. The packers who paid them would be protected by guaranteed export sales to Europe. The European Allies would get the benefit of stimulated American hog production, albeit at a price which they could not control. To put this machinery in motion, Hoover declared that he would need a commission to set hog prices from month to month. Before opening negotiations with the interested parties, he asked for President Wilson's approval.[33]

The next day the United States Live Stock Industry Committee appointed by Hoover and Houston convened in Washington, D.C., for the first time. While Hoover waited for a reply from the White House, he outlined his hog production plan to the assembled producers. The Food Administrator seemed eager to please them. Asserting at one point that "the one and final stimulus of the live stock industry" was "to put it on the basis of assured profit," he contended that his scheme would do just that. It is price that stimulates, he told the livestock committee. "He would be a madman [who] would suggest that patriotism would stabilize production."[34]

If Hoover thought that the lure of an "assured profit" would instantly satisfy his listeners, he was wrong. Despite his words of promise, all was not serene in the conference hall. The livestock committee's deliberations began only days after President Wilson announced the price at which the government would purchase the 1917 wheat crop, and wheat growers across the country were hopping mad. It was all very well to talk about putting a protective floor under farmers' prices, but what if the government's floor became a ceiling? When the livestock men convened in Washington on September

5, it turned out that they, like their wheat-raising brethren, were almost unanimously opposed to governmental price-fixing.[35]

In the face of their strenuously noninterventionist sentiments, the Food Administrator apparently decided to retreat. Thus, even as he put forth a plan that (by his own admission to President Wilson) entailed the monthly setting of the price of hogs by some kind of commission, Hoover endeavored to allay his listeners' fears. Repeatedly during the conference he denied that his Food Administration had either the power or the intent to fix prices.[36] Repeatedly he drew a distinction between price-fixing, which he said he opposed, and price *stabilization*, which he enthusiastically favored:

> Now it is stabilization which we require in this country. Stabilization is not the fixing of prices. Stabilization is a sufficient interference of prices that it ought to affect the value due to demand and supply in the long run or do it gradually over weeks and months instead of having it done over days and hours. . . .[37]
>
> . . . Stabilizing a price is an effort to prevent wild speculation in the market, in order to more or less curtail speculation. Stabilizing does not mean at all the fixing of price in the long run over and above a month or two months. . . .[38]
>
> . . . Price fixing is the fixing of prices, which we do not contemplate doing, but the real constructive thing is price stabilization, which is another thing entirely.[39]

Hoover also denied that his hog plan would "fix" the price of these animals. Linking the price of hogs to the price of corn, he insisted, would constitute stabilization, not fixing, for the price of hogs would vary with the price of corn.[40]

Hoover's disavowals and distinctions, whether real or semantic, apparently mollified the conservatives in his audience who objected to governmental price-fixing.[41] But for those present who did want the government to intervene, his performance was downright exasperating. Henry C. Wallace found Hoover "evasive" and swiftly concluded that "there was nothing to be hoped for from him in the way of constructive production work."[42] Pinchot, too, was startled and dismayed. Before the conference he had asked Hoover what he wanted the livestock industry committee to do. I want it to ask the Food Administration to guarantee prices for livestock, Hoover replied. Pinchot thereupon started to lobby for Hoover's program among key committee members and was making headway until Hoover abruptly undercut the effort by announcing that *he* was opposed to price-fixing, too. In Pinchot's view, Hoover's subsequent discussion of price "stabilization" only compounded the confusion and led to debilitating uncertainty among the livestock men about what he really desired.[43]

Probably in consequence, the livestock committee's final resolutions on the hog question were innocuous. The assembly called for increased production of pork products, suggested a few uncontroversial means of doing so, and asked that "careful consideration" be given to establishing a "definite relation" between the values of corn and hogs.[44] The committee appointed five small subcommittees to confer further with Hoover and Houston on livestock issues and (as Hoover put it) "to evolve some method that will stimulate the farmers to greater development." The chairman of the subcommittee on hogs was to be Henry C. Wallace.[45]

For the disappointed Pinchot, Hoover's behavior under pressure at the livestock conference was evidence of what he later called Hoover's "supersensitiveness to temporary clamor."[46] But what Pinchot construed as cowardice may well, to his chief, have been prudence. Having already antagonized one powerful bloc of farmers (the wheat growers), Hoover had no desire to offend the skeptical stockmen. Already, too, members of Congress were accusing him of brazen usurpation—of fixing prices under a law that conferred no such power. Anxious to control prices if not literally stipulate them, he must proceed warily indeed. What to Pinchot looked like tergiversation was in all likelihood, in Hoover's eyes, a political necessity.

Then, on September 7, came a development that made Hoover hesitate still more. Instead of endorsing his ambitious hog production plan, Woodrow Wilson unexpectedly asked him to consult with David Houston.[47] To Hoover's chagrin, the President was "not enthusiastic." In fact, having talked to Houston, he was opposed.[48] The Food Administrator was now out on a limb.

Rebuffed by the White House and the Department of Agriculture, Hoover soon found himself under new pressure from the agrarian interventionists. In mid-September, at his invitation, the chairmen of the five subcommittees of the United States Live Stock Industry Committee returned to Washington.[49] Hoover asked them to analyze proposals for licensing the meat packers and to offer a specific program for stimulating livestock production. If Hoover hoped that the livestock industry leaders would steer a cautious and moderate course, he was quickly disillusioned. On September 18 the five subcommittee chairmen submitted their recommendations, prepared for their adoption by none other than Gifford Pinchot.[50] There was very little that was moderate in their package.

Among other things, the five committeemen now asked the Food Administration to initiate stringent controls upon the nation's meat packers, including regulated accounting and restriction of packers' profits to "reasonable" levels. The livestock men called for an investigation of public stockyards and the adoption of appropriate reforms. They asked the Food Administration to arrange a "government guarantee" that the price of pigs farrowed next spring would not fall below "the actual cost of production plus a reasonable profit." This guarantee, they said, should apply to all fattened hogs marketed for eight months after August 1, 1918. Under no circumstances, said the committee members, should the price of hogs be permitted to fall below the cost of production in the next five months. The Food Administration should enforce packer compliance with these price policies by rules imposed as a condition of holding a license. The committeemen acknowledged that they might appear to be overemphasizing the need to assure a profit to producers. But if substantially increased farm output was to be attained, they argued, such an assurance was required.[51]

Hoover promptly rejected the livestock men's report. He told Pinchot that it was "not constructive"; he told Lasater that it contained nothing "creative" or "worth while."[52] Although neither Hoover nor his assistants recorded his objections, three were probably uppermost at this point. For one thing, it was highly uncertain whether President Wilson would accede to such a policy. For another, having just begun to negotiate with the packers, Hoover was undoubtedly reluctant to lose their goodwill by endorsing the radical controls sought by their agrarian enemies. His third objection was probably legal. If the Lever Act (as his critics claimed) did not empower him to fix prices, how could he impose price-fixing for hogs on the packers as a condition of holding a license? And if he could not *order* the packers to pay a certain price for live hogs (as the livestock men clearly wanted him to do), how could he then effect a price guarantee? Only one avenue appeared to remain open: voluntary agreement, a device that would necessitate cooperation from the packing industry. The livestock committeemen's report, however, contemplated little such teamwork. On the contrary, it amounted to an all-out assault on an ancient foe.

Instead of mandating the price-based production policy demanded by his livestock advisers, Hoover resorted to exhortation. In a letter to the chairman of the Federal Board of Farm Organizations on September 24, he announced his agency's intention "to the fullest extent of its powers, through the influence of export buying, to maintain a price for animal products that will give a reasonable return to the producer, for it is our conception that stimulation of production is vital to the Nation and must be encouraged in every way." The increase of livestock production was in "the farmer's own interest," he added; the market for livestock would be profitable "long after peace is declared." But beyond these generalized assurances and optimistic projections, he gave no specific, ironclad guarantee.[53]

A few days later, in a letter to his food administrator for Iowa, Hoover entreated his native state's farmers to increase their hog output at once. He stated that it was his "duty" through export buying and other means to maintain remunerative prices for producers, but again he offered nothing more concrete than his good intentions.[54] On September 29, in a public address in Philadelphia, he announced the existence of a worldwide shortage of fats and declared it to be in the farmers' "immediate interest" to "raise hogs, and more hogs, and still more hogs." Increased animal production, he asserted, was "the greatest national service" that farmers could give. Yet still he pledged no governmental safety net.[55]

As the Food Administrator attempted to talk farmers into breeding more hogs, out in Iowa the editor of *Wallaces' Farmer* was growing perturbed. Wallace had signed the livestock committee members' report on September 18.[56] Six days later he warned Hoover in a letter that "appeals to the producer on the ground of patriotism will not bring an adequate response. It will take the economic appeal. . . ."[57] Inside the Food Administration, Pinchot kept up a similar drumfire. In a memorandum to the Chief on the twenty-sixth, he listed fifteen different reasons why small livestock growers would not increase output "of their own accord." He warned that, unless "vigorous action" were taken very shortly, livestock production would plummet in 1918.[58]

The increasingly badgered Food Administrator, however, apparently wanted political protection in the form of an appeal emanating from farmers themselves.[59] On September 25, therefore, at Hoover's suggestion,[60] Pinchot telegraphed Wallace from Washington:

> Hoover hesitates to act without specific request from hog producers that he establish guarantee price for hogs in corn equivalent[.] Could you secure attendance of say . . . two hundred growers at Waterloo or Chicago making national meeting and if you did would they ask Hoover to act as above[?] I see no other chance of getting action to increase hog production[.][61]

Unfortunately for Pinchot and his boss, Wallace was in no mood to cooperate and promptly told Pinchot so by telegraph:

> Do not wish to call meeting suggested. Waste of time and money. Hoover is now as fully informed as he can be. . . . He must decide.[62]

In a follow-up letter, the editor amplified his complaint: "I feel that we have done everything we can to help Mr. Hoover, until he determines on a definite, clearcut policy. . . . These conferences get us nowhere." Furthermore, Wallace feared that if a meeting of farmers did publicly request Hoover to guarantee a price for hogs, it would give the nation's press a chance to accuse farmers of being the only class in the country "demanding excessive profits" and "threatening to reduce their production if they don't get them." As far as Wallace was concerned, Hoover was the man in charge, and, "like a general leading an army," he should make the decisions. Until he did, Wallace did not care to attend any more conferences.[63]

Pinchot agreed with Wallace but immediately begged him by telegraph to reconsider:

> Your position is absolutely right[.] But we are dealing with man nervously overwrought seeking excuses to avoid action and supersensitive to criticism. . . [.] I strongly urge you to call your meeting. . . [.] With request from such meeting we can force action secure increase save situation[.]

Pinchot now disclosed (September 26) that he had Hoover's "definite promise to take action" if a meeting of hog growers made the desired request. He also reported that he now had a statement written by Hoover himself "specifying just what he wants" and that it was consistent with the livestock committee members' report of eight days before.[64] Despite these inducements, there was no response from Des Moines.

With Wallace reluctant to call a conference until Hoover set a policy, and with Hoover unwilling to set a policy until requested to do so by a conference, an embarrassing deadlock appeared to be in the making. Then, on September 30, an excited Pinchot telegraphed Wallace in Des Moines again, this time with E. C. Lasater as co-signer:

> By Hoovers authority we request you as chairman of hog committee to call meeting of your committee for Wednesday morning October third at Waterloo [Iowa] and invite presence of representative hog men to meet us there[.]

The meeting was necessary, they said, as a "step toward increasing hog products."[65] "By Hoovers authority": Wallace could hardly refuse to respond. The prairie journalist immediately asked seventy-five prominent hog producers from several states to convene as requested in Waterloo.[66]

The Food Administration's two livestock specialists now hastened out to Iowa. Pinchot carried with him a handwritten memorandum from Hoover, probably the statement cited in Pinchot's telegram to Wallace four days before. In it Hoover specified what he desired:

> Want the hog producers to propose to the Food Administration that they would like for the Food Administration to make such arrangements as will fix the price of hogs from month to month based upon the weighted average price and consumption of corn at Chicago quotation for cash corn. The weighting of the consumption and price to be determined by a commission appointed by the Administration. The price to be fixed to be calculated in terms of bushels of corn and in such a manner as to cover the cost of production and profit.[67]

Pinchot also had, he believed, something more: a definite oral promise from Hoover to act upon the request that he wanted the nation's hog producers to make. According to Pinchot, Hoover made this pledge twice in the same conversation in which he penned his memorandum.[68]

But if Hoover appeared to be yielding to his zealous lieutenants, his heart and mind were far from committed to their cause. All through September (according to Pinchot), Hoover in private conversations had bitterly accused the nation's farmers of greed and lack of patriotism.[69] According to Charles McCarthy, Hoover could not understand their psychology.[70] On September 29, in a private address delivered in Philadelphia, the Food Administrator lashed out again:

> We have met the statement almost universally that in order to induce our farmers to undertake this changed strategy in production, we must secure for him some positive definite guarantee of profit. This suggestion grates upon my intelligence and upon my patriotism. It seems to me that with the above facts so well founded—so eveidently [sic] in the farmer's best interest—he should, of his own volition, undertake such a policy even were there no patriotic call. Beyond this, however, it is now vital for every farmer in the United States to take unto himself an additional five or ten hogs, a few sheep, or a few calves, in the national interest. It is necessary for the winning of the war. I cannot but believe that every farmer in the United States has the patriotism to do so.

In words tinged with sarcasm, he then declared:

> I do realize that there are certain members of our community to whom there is no inducement to service except money, and, therefore, to these people I wish to make the following positive statement—that so far as the Food Administration is able to influence the purchase of pork products for export, it will do its level best, through this implement, to see that a price of pork is so maintained in ratio to feed that will not only cover cost, but ample remuneration to the producer as well.

"I am offtimes accused of being an idealist," Hoover continued—of believing that great things can be accomplished

> by service and self-sacrifice in the daily routine of life. I believe that, when our boys willingly sacrificed their lives freely to make this world an endurable place for us and our children, we are not going to stand by and demand a promissory note before we undertake to support our sons in war and their Allies in the field. If, however, Democracy has brought our people by the free play of individual initiative to such a materialism that they would refuse to do their patriotic duty unless guaranteed a profit—if it has increased this sense of miserly greed, a grasping after coins and property amongst our people—then I should prefer autocracy. . . .
>
> My vision of war is not of an academic problem to be solved by discussions and guarantees of profits. To me it is a vision of brave dying men

and suffering women and children, for service on whose behalf demands of cash sound ill to good omen.

The American farmer who sees war as I see it, needs no inducement, no inspiration but the thought that every spadeful of earth turned is lessening human suffering and guaranteeing the liberty of the world.

From the three years contact with the German Army I have come out of this horror with the conviction that autocracy is a political faith that endangers and jeopardizes the future of our race. It has, however, proved to command a complete organization of devotion and self-sacrificing people to the interest of the nation. The German farmer in the name of the Fatherland supports a nation two-thirds as large as ours and holds the world at bay on an area as large as Texas. If we cannot find this same devotion in a democratic faith without compulsion and without payment in guarantees, I, for one, am prepared to abandon Democracy and to accept autocracy for Democracy will have demonstrated its inability to defend itself.[71]

Hoover's speech was in stunning contrast to what he had told the United States Live Stock Industry Committee barely three weeks before: that the only way to stimulate livestock production was to "put it on the basis of assured profit," and that only a "madman" would think that "patriotism would stabilize production." The remarks in Philadelphia seem doubly strange coming from a man who had just given Gifford Pinchot a memorandum offering to set the price of hogs at a figure that would guarantee hog farmers a profit—if the farmers would only ask the Food Administration to intervene. But on reflection, the anomaly disappears. What Hoover really wanted, in his heart of hearts, was increased food production without having to subsidize it. His anger on September 29 came from his resentment of farmers and their spokesmen who were inexorably driving him in the opposite direction.

Four days later Henry Wallace and his representative hog producers assembled in Waterloo, Iowa, to hear Hoover's emissaries, Pinchot and Lasater. After learning that the nation's hog supply was now 10 percent below normal yet must be increased to 15 percent above normal to meet wartime exigencies, the swine growers unanimously adopted resolutions asking the Food Administration immediately to assure hog producers a remunerative price. The convention declared that such a guarantee was the "only way" to obtain such an enormous leap in output. In other words, price—not patriotism—was the key. In keeping with Hoover's memorandum, the gathering asked the Food Administration to appoint a commission to ascertain the cost of hog production in terms of corn and then to establish the price of hogs on a monthly basis at principal markets.

And then, having said all this, the Waterloo meeting took a giant further step. Instead of waiting for a commission to determine the price, the assembled stockmen boldly advanced a recommendation of their own. To stimulate production by the vast amount that the Food Administration deemed necessary, the price of a hundred pounds of live hog should at least equal the value of fourteen bushels of cash corn fed into it prior to marketing: a ratio of 14 to 1. This was far indeed from the 10 or 11 to 1 ratio that Hoover had mentioned to Woodrow Wilson. The assembly asked that the 14 to 1 ratio be instituted at once and publicized before the start of the breeding season.[72] Two days later, with Pinchot and his colleague in attendance, a convention of the National Swine Growers' Association in South Omaha overwhelmingly endorsed the Waterloo appeal.[73] Hoover had gotten the appeal he wanted—and then some.

Pinchot and Lasater were delighted by this outcome and immediately sought ways to prod Hoover into action.[74] Pinchot thought that it might be possible to "bring pressure to bear" on their boss "through persons influential in the [Wilson] Administration."[75] Probably as part of this effort, on his way back to Washington, Pinchot called upon Colonel Edward House and told him that Hoover was on the verge of a nervous breakdown. According to Pinchot, Hoover insisted on "retaining all the authority," to the detriment of his cause. The President's confidant promised to investigate the matter.[76] More and more, Pinchot was behaving as if Hoover were his adversary.

Meanwhile Wallace, probably the leading voice of agriculturalists in the corn belt, was doing his best to maintain the heat on Herbert Hoover. In a letter to Charles McCarthy of the Food Administration on October 4, the Iowa editor gloomily confided that the "hog situation" looked "very bad" and that "large guarantees to insure production" were "absolutely the only way out." With corn at sky-high prices, he noted, farmers were asking themselves: why should they take on the burden of raising more hogs?[77] In a letter to Hoover's deputy Mark Requa the same day, Wallace predicted "still fewer hogs next year unless something very unusual happens to encourage farmers to breed their sows during the next two months and a half."[78] Meanwhile, inside the Food Administration, Pinchot's ally McCarthy told Requa that the Food Administration would not succeed in stimulating the producer "unless far more strenuous efforts are made than at present."

> Our organization is composed of business men, and to my mind is too much influenced by the point of view of the business man and the consumer. After all, we have to get the material and a lot of it and we cannot get it except by paying high prices. . . . It is fatal, absolutely fatal, to our food policy to allow anything to occur today which will in the least discourage the producer, already suspicious and distrustful.[79]

And how could Hoover effectuate such guarantees? It was simple, said Wallace in his publication on October 12: although Hoover had no authority to fix the price of hogs directly, he could do so *indirectly* by regulating the packers. He could "absolutely control the prices the packers pay for live stock," Wallace asserted, under the licensing system that was to take effect in a few weeks.[80]

Yet even as Pinchot and Lasater were prompting midwestern livestock men to solicit price supports from the government, events elsewhere were arousing suspicions in the corn-and-hog belt. On October 5, after discovering evidence of "bull speculation" in corn on the Chicago market and of plots by certain traders to "engineer a pinch," Hoover asked his state administrator for Illinois to prevent it. If any "wild speculation" occurred in corn, Hoover warned, it would be necessary to "absolutely suppress trading on the Board of Trade."[81] In a separate letter to a member of the board, he declared that higher prices for corn should be discouraged, for they tended to impede an increase in the number of livestock. Any attempt by traders to increase the price of corn, he said, would be unpatriotic.[82] When he heard that some farmers were feeding wheat instead of high-priced corn to their hogs, he remarked that the "real remedy" for this problem would be a fall in the price of corn.[83]

And that, not surprisingly, riled Henry C. Wallace, who mounted his editorial pulpit to denounce the idea. If Hoover "proposes to arbitrarily keep down the price of corn, with the thought that this will result in an increase in the supply of livestock," there was "great danger" that farmers would simply plant less corn.[84] For Wallace, the solution to the unfavorable corn / hog price ratio was not to lower corn prices but to raise hog prices relative to corn.

Then, on October 6, a mysterious incident occurred in the heartland. On that day a Chicago trade journal published an article apparently based on an interview with E. Dana Durand, a noted statistician who had recently joined the Food Administration. The journal reported that Durand was now working for Hoover in Chicago on "a scientific scheme of market control" that would reduce hog prices to a mere $10.00 per hundred pounds. According to the article, the Food Administration considered ten-dollar hogs and one-dollar corn—a ratio of 10 to 1—to be "the one which ought to prevail."[85] On the day that this news item appeared, the cost of raising the hogs then being marketed stood at $18.00 and more.[86]

The shocking dispatch from Chicago triggered an immediate panic among swine producers. Evidently fearful that Hoover might reduce the price of their animals to ruinous depths, livestock growers dumped unfinished hogs upon the market in record numbers, thereby precipitating a sharp decline in the price.[87] For farmers, the effect of their premature selling (in lost revenue) was bad enough. Even worse was the lost confidence that it engendered as they attempted to make plans for the coming year.[88] By the middle of October farmers in the Midwest (in Wallace's words) were "boiling hot" at the plummeting price for their hogs.[89]

On October 17 Hoover officially repudiated the "ten dollar hogs" story as "absolutely untrue."[90] Professor Durand also denied making such a statement.[91] In telegrams to his state food administrators, Hoover affirmed that he would use all his powers to maintain his own and Allied governments' meat purchases at a price level that would assure meat producers a profit.[92] But Hoover's disavowal of the Chicago news dispatch did not come until nearly two weeks after it was published.[93] By then the market damage had been done. Nor did his renewed pledge to support "remunerative prices" to beef and pork producers sway many minds. For frustrated farmers it was just more of the same: nice words, but no guarantee.

Publicly, Hoover branded the "ten dollar hogs" report an instance of "pro-German" propaganda designed to deter livestock growers from enlarging their production.[94] Privately, he accused an executive of the Cudahy Packing Company of putting out the story for the purpose of breaking the market.[95] Indeed, during October a number of packing house officials did opine publicly that the price of hogs was excessive and that it either should (or shortly would) sink to $10.00 per hundredweight. Their bearish statements hastened farmers' unloading of half-grown hogs.[96] Since hog prices before the break had been hovering around $18.00–$19.00, the sudden stampede to market and its downward pressure on prices were not unwelcome to the packing industry.

But among Hoover's increasingly angry critics in the corn belt the suspicion grew that the devastating Durand story had been "inspired" not by nameless pro-Germans, and not by self-interested packers, but by the United States Food Administration itself.[97] To Wallace on October 11, the Chicago report and other concurrent happenings suggested that Hoover was deliberately "maneuvering to hand the producers the hot end of the poker."[98] The excitable Lasater wondered why—if a leading packing house magnate was known to have instigated the outrageous tumble in livestock prices, through a newspaper report falsely attributed to the Food Administration—Hoover had not brought the perpetrator to account. Why had Hoover stopped with a mere statement that the report was untrue?[99] Eventually Lasater concluded that Hoover *wanted* lower hog prices—lower even than the cost of production—and that the Durand incident was part of a calculated "conspiracy" to achieve this end.[100] Such allegations Hoover, of course, denied.[101]

No one ever established that Hoover or his associates deliberately planted the "ten dollar hogs" story in the Chicago press. But his curiously belated denial makes one wonder whether he was unhappy with the effect. The Food Administration's counsel, William A. Glasgow, Jr., later told a Congressional committee that the record price which hogs had reached in the late summer of 1917 "was deemed undesirable," and that "with the consent of the producers themselves an effort was made to reduce that price." Glasgow did not explain just how or when this adjustment occurred, nor did he identify the producers who "consented" to it.[102] If Hoover did not directly leak the press report, more likely than not he approved the swift decline of hog prices that it caused: a decline to what he—thinking first of consumers and the Allies—surely considered a more reasonable level.

Two days after the Durand story hit the Chicago press, Pinchot and Lasater reported to the Chief about their midwestern trip. According to Hoover, Lasater demanded that the Food Administration immediately announce a "complete" guarantee for hog prices at the staggering ratio of 14 to 1. To the consternation of his two lieutenants, Hoover refused. To make such a positive assurance (he later recalled that he said) would be dishonest without financial backing from either the Allied governments or his own. And that was something that he did not yet have. It would take an appropriation from Congress, he asserted, or a firm commitment from the Allies, with whom he was still negotiating.[103] According to Pinchot, Hoover appeared ready to drop the guarantee plan entirely and rely instead upon "patriotic" exhortation to augment the hog supply.[104] According to Lasater, Hoover thought that the 14 to 1 recommendation revealed a willingness by farmers to "exploit the country"—something to which he, the Food Administrator, would never be an accessory.[105]

Pinchot was livid with fury. As he saw it, he had gone out to Iowa and had secured what Hoover wanted: an appeal by representative hog producers for a fixed and remunerative price for their product. Now, after all this earnest effort, Hoover was reneging on his pledge to implement it.[106] To Pinchot, this failure to keep a clear promise was evidence of "the stupidest mistake in policy I have ever seen a man in high office make, namely, Hoover's continual bitterness against the producer." Were it not for this "deep-rooted antipathy," Pinchot claimed, "an antipathy which with the exception of a few individuals seems to color the whole Food Administration, the recommendations of the Waterloo meeting would have been carried out long ago."[107]

But the Pennsylvania firebrand may have misinterpreted Hoover's oral promise. Hoover had wanted midwestern hog farmers to make a general request for the Food Administration to act. He had not asked for them to recommend a *specific* corn / hog ratio, still less 14 to 1.

And there, in substantial measure, lay the rub. On October 6 Mark Requa—more likely than not with Hoover's knowledge—initiated a debate-by-correspondence with Henry C. Wallace. "It strikes me that the 14 to one asked for is rather laying it on pretty heavy," Requa declared.[108] Wallace agreed but urged him to face the facts:

> The truth of the matter is that there are a lot of farmers who would rather sell their corn at a dollar a bushel, than bother feeding it to hogs, unless the price of hogs offers a handsome profit. There is no use arguing about

> the right and wrong of this. The one thing to remember is that too many of them are likely to follow this policy and consequently increase the shortage of pork.

Wallace admitted that hog farmers would make more money next year, even if the Food Administration did nothing to influence prices. But if the government really needed increased pork production, it must proceed along the path of incentives and guarantees, as urged at Waterloo and elsewhere.[109]

Requa, almost certainly reflecting Hoover's views, was unpersuaded. "What is to happen to the poor in the tenement districts[?]" he asked.

> Frankly, I don't know, if the farmer is going to exact a price that appears to me to be more than he can justify. The vital question is of course increasing production, but do we have to bribe the American Farmer? My opinion of him is such that I frankly don't believe we do. Give him a reasonable profit and a bonus, and he ought to come through. Twelve is a reasonable profit; 12½ gives him a bonus. Why should it be beyond that figure?[110]

Because, Wallace replied, you must "enlist the marginal producer, the fellow who produces under less favorable conditions and consequently must have a higher price." "You ask what is to happen in the tenement districts," he wrote to Requa. "Let me answer by asking, What is to happen to them if production decreases?" The Food Administration "is sinning away its day of grace in this meat production matter," he warned.[111] Privately, he told Pinchot that neither Requa nor Hoover "seem to understand what must be done to encourage the *marginal* producer"—"the key to the situation."[112]

Hoover's grievances now extended beyond what he clearly perceived to be extortion-minded farmers. Unknown as yet to Pinchot or Lasater, the Food Administrator had been informed that it was none other than Pinchot who had induced the farmers' meeting in Waterloo to request the obnoxious 14 to 1 ratio. The producers would obtain this, he had allegedly told them, if they demanded it.[113] When Pinchot heard this charge, he insisted that the resolutions committee in Waterloo had proposed the 14 to 1 plank without his knowledge and that he had then tried unsuccessfully to delete it.[114] Pinchot later obtained corroborative letters from the chairman of the resolutions committee and from Wallace—both absolving him of any responsibility for, or even approval of, the 14 to 1 platform.[115] But by then it was too late to matter.

Yet if Pinchot may not have been the culprit in Waterloo or Omaha, his behavior in Washington was increasingly veering toward insubordination. Unwilling to accept Hoover's arguments at face value, the Pennsylvanian scurried about the capital doing all he could to intensify the pressure on his chief. On October 10 he met the British representative of the Allied Provisions Export Commission (APEC) and apparently won his hearty assent to the guarantee scheme.[116] When Hoover asserted that he could not act because he was unable to obtain data from the Federal Trade Commission about the packers' handling costs for hogs, Pinchot (with Hoover's permission) went to the commission himself and arranged for it to produce the figures "without delay."[117]

Most daringly of all, on October 15 Pinchot took his case directly to Thomas E. Wilson, one of the leading meat packers in the nation and chairman of a committee set up to confer with the Food Administration. After listening to Pinchot's arguments, Wilson apparently declared that he saw no reason why the packing houses could not voluntarily agree to buy hogs at whatever prices the Food Administration might determine along the lines of the Waterloo plan. Two or three days later Pinchot met Wilson again, only to find that the corporate executive had changed his mind. According to Pinchot, Wilson gave as one reason for his turnabout the fact that Mark Requa had advised him in the meantime that the packers "could not afford to take the risk."[118]

Pinchot did not record Wilson's other reasons for his reversal nor why Requa had so upset the applecart. For the Bull Moose Progressive it appeared to be self-evident proof of the Food Administration's solicitude toward big business.

Lasater, meanwhile, had also been trying to overcome what he scornfully called Hoover's "dilatory tactics."[119] Shortly after returning to his office in the Food Administration on October 8, the Texas rancher drafted a telegram for Hoover to send to Henry C. Wallace. In it Hoover would announce his intention to appoint a seven-member commission that would "have supervision of all matters" relating to livestock production and marketing, including the licensed meat-packing industry, stockyard companies, and livestock exchanges. This body would also determine the corn / hog ratio. For Hoover, his aide's proposal was nothing more than an ill-disguised power grab by the livestock interests. "I won't place a bunch of live-stock producers in control of the packers," he remarked brusquely—and said no more.[120]

Instead, the Chief had another idea. On October 10 he informed Pinchot and Lasater that he had decided to appoint a commission to establish the corn / hog ratio.[121] Hoover asked Wallace's subcommittee on hogs of the United States Live Stock Industry Committee to select the members of the investigative body.[122] Privately, Wallace considered it a "foolish stunt, but I suppose Mr. Hoover thinks it wise to have such a report to fall back on."[123] Within a few days the hog subcommittee recommended, and Hoover approved, the personnel of the new commission.[124]

More and more, Hoover was behaving like a man who did not want to act alone. On October 16 he asked the Secretary of Agriculture for an official statement of "the cost of producing pork in terms of corn." If the department would do this, Hoover wrote, "I have some reason to believe I might get the packers to guarantee this as a minimum price of hogs for the next twelve or eighteen months." This would not be "a case of fixing the price of hogs to corn," he quickly added, "but a question of giving a minimum guarantee, and a guarantee based only on an actual cost. . . ."[125] Ten long days later, Secretary Houston replied with a letter that not only failed to give Hoover the data he sought but objected to his entire plan as "unwise." It would be "exceptionally difficult" to come up with a statistically valid corn / hog ratio, Houston claimed. Furthermore, in much of the country hogs were not fattened with corn. Any attempt by the packers to set prices for producers would likely be "misinterpreted" and "deeply resented." As for augmenting the meat supply, Houston declared that the existing programs of his own department, plus Food Administration oversight of hog-packing plants, would be quite sufficient to yield the desired result. Indeed, according to him, the meat situation was "not as unsatisfactory as some seem to believe." In short, for these and other reasons the Secretary of Agriculture refused to provide Hoover the slightest cover and instead tossed the hot potato back into his lap.[126]

With Pinchot and his faction predicting catastrophe unless the swine producers received guarantees, and with the Department of Agriculture denying that any meat emergency existed, Hoover could be forgiven for feeling agitated. "We were heading into the worst world famine in fats known to modern history," he later wrote.[127] What should he do? Out in Iowa, Wallace was accusing him of "almost criminal carelessness" in dealing with the hog problem—if America's need for enhanced meat production was indeed as critical as Hoover portrayed it.[128] In Illinois, on the other hand, his state food administrator was predicting a massive harvest of corn. If this corn remained cheap, farmers would feed it to hogs and boost hog production anyway, without an artificial stimulus from the government.[129]

At some point in October—perhaps during a visit to the White House on the twenty-third—Hoover raised the subject directly with Woodrow Wilson. The President, it turned out, leaned toward Houston's position but said: "The responsibility is yours."[130] The Food Administrator was running out of maneuvering room.

Meanwhile the mutiny from within Hoover's ranks was reaching a crescendo. On October 20 Lasater submitted his resignation from the Food Administration on the grounds that its policies were "harmful to the common welfare."[131] In a long conversation Hoover managed to dissuade him after criticizing the Chicago meat packers and announcing that the Food Administration would now toughen its policy toward them. Thus mollified, the Texas cattleman left on a private business trip to his ranch.[132]

While Lasater was taking his complaints to the Chief, Pinchot was taking his to Colonel House. In a ten-page letter written on October 20, Pinchot laid out his version of recent events within his agency. It was a tale of "needless delay," broken promises, and incredible hostility toward producers. "The Food Administration," he charged, "seems to have believed from the beginning that it must act by persuasion upon the speculators, middlemen, packers, and other large food interests, whom it has the widest legal powers to command, and that it could impose it commands on the farmer, who is legally beyond its reach, and whom in fact it can only hope to persuade." "I have done my level best to get action from Mr. Hoover," he asserted, "and no action has resulted."[133] By going directly to the President's confidant, Pinchot undoubtedly hoped to get the White House to intervene. Perhaps he even hankered to depose the man from whom he was nominally working.

Clearly this deteriorating relationship could not go on. Two days later, on October 22, Pinchot submitted to Hoover a memorandum defining the duties of the division of live stock and farming in sweeping terms.[134] For Hoover, it was the last straw. You have completely misunderstood the organization of the Food Administration, he charged. In this agency men are assigned to work on problems, and when these problems are solved, the men move on to others. Later that day Hoover informed his lieutenant that the livestock work of the Food Administration was being transferred to a separate division in Chicago and that Pinchot's involvement with this matter was therefore at an end. Hoover thereupon offered Pinchot (who spoke French) a chance to assist in the introduction of thousands of tractors into France. To Pinchot it seemed like a transparent attempt to get rid of him, but he promised to think it over.[135]

On October 25 Hoover summoned Pinchot to his office. "How about the work in France?" he began. In response Pinchot handed him a letter of resignation:[136]

> Because of the continued failure of the Food Administration to take effective action for increasing the production of meats, which failure is certain to result in higher prices to our own people and a shortage in the food supplies needed to win the War, I hereby resign.[137]

According to Pinchot, Hoover immediately asked: Do you think this is fair? I think it is "absolutely fair," Pinchot shot back. Hoover declared that he had been "warned on all sides" that Pinchot would not be loyal to him. Pinchot countered with examples of what he considered to be Hoover's disloyalty to *him*. After a long argument the feisty subordinate refused to withdraw his resignation. His service in the Food Administration was over.[138]

Such, at least, was Pinchot's account of his climactic confrontation with his chief. Hoover's version, recorded long afterward, was quite different. According to him, the Food Administration's censor had intercepted correspondence disclosing that Pinchot and Lasater had initiated a conspiracy to launch a "publicity campaign" with the objective of ousting Hoover from his office and replacing him with none other than Wallace. Furious at Pinchot's treachery, Hoover (so he later recalled) confronted him with the evidence and demanded his resignation. At first Pinchot objected, only to change his mind and leave after Hoover threatened to publish the letters.[139]

Hoover's recollection, written down forty years or more after the event, was probably erroneous. While Pinchot, Lasater, and Wallace did discuss the idea of driving out Hoover in their correspondence with one another *after* Pinchot resigned, there is no evidence that they did so before.[140] And while Pinchot, by writing to Colonel House on October 20, may have hoped thereby to engineer Hoover's downfall, there is no evidence that this letter, written on Pinchot's private stationery, ever came within the orbit of the censors. Hoover's later story of demanding—and finally securing—Pinchot's resignation also conflicts with Pinchot's contemporary account of a protracted argument culminating in Pinchot's refusal to retract his resignation. Unless Pinchot immediately concocted an elaborately self-serving version of the encounter, it seems likely that his fresh memory of the event was more accurate than was Hoover's four decades later.[141]

Still, whether or not Pinchot actually plotted to remove his own employer, there is little doubt that in Hoover's mind his headstrong lieutenant had passed the bounds from dissent to disloyalty. In any event, the very next day—October 26—Hoover composed a stinging reply to Pinchot's letter of resignation:

> . . . You have urged insistently during the past two months that we should announce to the American farmer some firm, definite monetary guarantee for all hogs marketed within the next twelve or sixteen months, the price to be such as would stimulate production. I have as repeatedly informed you that, while I should indeed be glad to see a guarantee that protected both producer and consumer, any promise or assurance of this kind would be absolutely dishonest to the farmer, unless it is backed by an absolute monetary undertaking from responsible quarters. This would involve responsibility for $1,000,000,000, and the only quarters for such a guarantee would be the United States Government, or a contract with the Allies to take the whole excess production, or a guarantee by the Packers under which they take the risk. You know we have no power or appropriation from Congress to give the first assurance; that the Allies insist upon a limitation of their liability to the per cent of the production they require, and that the Packers decline unless one of the two others stand behind them.
>
> Your retort is that we could bring moral pressure upon the Packer to make him do it at his own risk, or that, if we "take a chance," Congress must come to our rescue. Because we are not willing, as you state, to "take a chance" and possibly involve somebody for $1,000,000,000, you resign.
>
> In any event, I am simply not going to give assurances to the American farmer that are not honestly protected, no matter how great the objective. I have gone the utmost limit in assuring him that we will do our best with our control of export buying to maintain a fair price. . . .

And as for one other point, "you have not convinced me that the American farmer requires a promissory note from the Government in order to stimulate his patriotic exertion in the national interest in this crisis."[142]

Pinchot was exasperated by these arguments. Why, he asked, did not Hoover at least *try* to get the packers to pay fixed prices for farmers' hogs? Why didn't he make the packers agree to these terms? Under the law the Food Administration could even seize and operate the packing houses itself and buy and sell hogs at its own prices. For Pinchot, just one motive could explain Hoover's stubborn refusal: "tenderness for big business."[143] The Pennsylvanian seemed unable to appreciate Hoover's belief that he needed the packers and that it would be impossible for him efficiently to run the plants on his own. What (Hoover apparently feared) would happen if the leaders of this critical industry balked at his requests and said to him, "*You* run the plants"? Pinchot and Lasater insisted that the much disliked packers would never be so recalcitrant. In the circumstances of war they wouldn't dare.[144]

Even as Hoover and Pinchot wrangled in Washington, out in Chicago the head of the Food Administration's nascent meat division, Joseph Cotton, was attempting to persuade the packers to offer farmers a guaranteed price for marketed hogs. Earlier in the month Cotton had worked out a system of consolidated export buying with the Allies' purchasing cartel, known as APEC. Under this arrangement APEC would pool its buying orders for processed meat with the Food Administration, which in turn would allot the orders among the packers.[145] The Allies also agreed to pay for these orders at prices sufficient to permit the packers to buy hogs above a stipulated minimum.[146] To coordinate this process, Hoover's agency created a special division on October 24.[147] As long as the Allies were desperate for American pork, they would have little choice but to buy it at prices that the Food Administration deemed sufficiently high to carry out any guarantee to the farmers. The first part of the triangular scheme was now in place.

But the Allies were under no obligation to buy more than they needed—a loophole that the packers could not abide. As late as October 24 their representatives resisted any formula for a guarantee—an attitude of intransigence evidently encouraged by Mark Requa.[148] The packers were worried: What if the prospective guarantee actually succeeded? What if it elicited a gigantic surge in hog production—a surge that they would have to buy at an artificially high price? How could they be sure of processing and disposing such swelled output at a profit? From Hoover and his negotiators came the answer: By controlling meat purchases for the army, navy, Allies, and neutrals, the Food Administration in effect could dictate the sale price of 40 percent of the packers' products. To the packers this amount appeared sufficient to dominate and shore up a potentially volatile market. On October 25—the very day that Pinchot resigned—the packers agreed in principle to Hoover's plan.[149]

But Hoover was taking no chances on voluntary agreements. He soon arranged with the War Trade Board that all would-be exporters of American pork and pork products to Europe must first obtain a certificate that their exports were being sold at a price that Hoover's agency approved.[150]

Attention now turned to the corn / hog ratio commission which Hoover had created in mid-October. Upon its findings the precise guarantee would presumably be calculated. If Hoover hoped, by appointing this body, to appease militant farm activists, he also apparently desired to obtain from it a protective document that he could brandish at urban consumers. This in fact was the *purpose* of the committee, he claimed to a farm state food administrator on October 25. Its purpose was to give advice "in order that we may clearly demonstrate to the American consumer the increased cost of production and the necessity for increased prices over prewar normals."[151] As with the price of wheat, so now with hogs: the Food Administrator wanted such a sensitive question to be resolved by someone other than himself. To his friends it was evidence of administrative fairness and faith in experts. To his detractors it was proof of political cowardice.[152]

As Hoover awaited the commission's findings, he turned a final time to exhortation and to a solemn yet unspecific pledge to sustain a remunerative price for hogs. On October 25, 1917 the Food Administration published the text of his private address of late September in Philadelphia—minus his angry attack on greedy farmers. In it Hoover reviewed the European animal shortage, the grave necessity for increased hog production, and the plenitude of available feedstuffs, and urged farmers and nonfarmers alike to respond. Even suburbanites, he asserted, could help by raising hogs on domestic garbage as the Germans were doing: "We need a 'keep-a-pig' movement in this country—and a properly cared for pig is no more unsanitary than a dog." In fact, said Hoover: "Every pound of fat is as sure of service as every bullet, and every hog is of greater value to the winning of this war than a shell."[153] It was a dramatic claim, which underscored his belief that his was the most important job in wartime Washington.

But time was running out for ingenious appeals to hearts and minds. Hooverian exhortation might work with urban, middle-class housewives. It might work with licensed businesses which were subject to coercion if they did not cooperate. It would not work with unregulated farmers. To them Hoover would have to offer a tangible financial reward for their risk taking.

The next day Hoover's "swine commission" (as it called itself) convened in Chicago under the chairmanship of Professor John M. Evvard of Iowa State College.[154] One day later it signed a report declaring that immediate, "definite stimulative action" was imperative to generate sufficient hogs for the nation and its allies. The commission found that "the approximate, equivalent value of 12 bushels of No. 2 corn" was "necessary to produce 100 pounds of average live hog under average farm conditions"—a ratio, in other words, of 12 to 1. But conditions at present were not average, the commission reported. The present hog population was millions below normal. To return hog production to ordinary levels would require a "stimulative market" paying at least the equivalent price of 13.3 bushels of corn per one hundred pounds of "average hog." And if production were to be induced to rise 15 percent above normal, a corn-to-hog price ratio of 14.3 to 1 would be needed.

The commission did not specify which ratio the government should adopt. But it urged that one be promulgated immediately, to take effect on February 1, 1918. In the meantime, it declared, the government should stabilize the *current* live hog market—reeling from uncertainty and the recent tumble in prices—by establishing a minimum emergency price of $16.00 per hundred pounds for good-to-excellent butcher hogs. The hog market was in a state of "marked depression," the commission concluded. For the Food Administration to obtain more output under these unpropitious circumstances, it should give producers "definite assurance of a fair price."[155]

If Hoover had hoped that the Evvard commission would be more moderate than the farmers who had met in Waterloo and Omaha, the report that now reached him must have been a shock. Instead of scotching what Mark Requa (and probably Hoover himself) considered an egregious ratio of 14 to 1, Professor Evvard and his colleagues had mentioned one even higher. If Hoover now repudiated their findings, he would be playing with political dynamite. Nor could he afford to procrastinate in the hope that patriotic farmers might yet respond to his appeals for more production. As marketings of unfinished hogs and of breeding stock continued unabated, fear was rising in the Food Administration that disconsolate farmers would cease raising hogs altogether and switch to grain.[156] The Durand story of early October had unleashed much more than a downward plunge in hog prices.

Several days of public silence now passed while farmers, packers, and others awaited the Food Administrator's fateful decision. Visiting Joseph P. Cotton in Chicago on the morning of November 3, Wallace became convinced that Hoover was still reluctant to go as far his own division head wished in implementing a price support plan.[157] Hoover's explanation for the delay was different. It took several days, he later wrote, to win the consent of all affected government agencies for the "unification of all official buying" under his control.[158]

At last, at noon on November 3, 1917, after receiving final clearance from Hoover, Cotton announced the Food Administration's hog policy.[159] He declared that the agency would seek to increase hog production, to provide a "fair price" to producers at all times, to limit the profits of meat packers and middlemen, and to eliminate speculation. To these ends it would institute "rigid control" of the packers and use its "full control" over most exports and military purchases of meat to provide equitable prices to farmers. In order to stabilize current hog prices and stop the "sudden break" in prices at central markets, Cotton announced: "The prices so far as we can affect them will not go below a minimum of about $15.50 per hundred weight for the average of the packers' droves on the Chicago market until further notice." This was 50 cents a bushel less than the Evvard commission recommended, but $1.50 more than the packers had wanted to pay.[160]

Cotton then turned to the vexatious corn / hog ratio. Omitting all mention of the 14 to 1 figure (evidently still distasteful to the Chief), he noted instead the Evvard commission's finding that "to bring the stock of hogs back to normal under present conditions the ratio should be about thirteen." (The actual figure was 13.3.) Therefore, he continued,

> as to the hogs farrowed next spring, we will try to stabilize the price so that the farmer can count on getting for each 100 pounds of hog ready for market, thirteen times the average cost per bushel of the corn fed into the hogs.
>
> Let there be no misunderstanding of this statement. It is not a guarantee backed by money. It is not a promise by the packers. It is a statement of the intention and policy of the Food Administration which means to do justice to the farmer.[161]

Relieved that the protracted struggle was finally over, Cotton promptly fled his office for a golf course.[162]

Despite the general lucidity of the Food Administration's announcement, it contained one fateful ambiguity. The Evvard commission had recommended that the Food Administration's stabilization policy be based upon the price of corn *in Chicago*. So, too, had the farmers' meetings in Waterloo and Omaha. Cotton's statement, however, was silent—deliberately silent, he later claimed—on this subtle point.[163] But since his announcement gave the impression that he was adhering closely to the Evvard group's report, farmers and their advocates could easily infer that the Food Administration would calculate the corn / hog ratio on this basis. Before the war was over, they would bitterly rue that inference.

For the present, though, the response of the agricultural community to the unprecedented policy was favorable.[164] Although the monetary incentive was far less definite than that which Congress had bestowed on the wheat farmers, for most hog producers it appeared to be enough. The government of the United States had pledged its word. Within two weeks Cotton reported a movement of pigs from central markets back to the farms for fattening—a trend helped along by an abundance of unsaleable, frost-damaged, soft corn.[165] Mother Nature, it seemed, had intervened on the side of Hoover.

Even Wallace, while still wishing that Cotton and Hoover had gone further, editorialized that the government's announcement "should be satisfactory."[166] Pinchot, now on the sidelines, consoled himself with the belief that his resignation had forced the issue and had obliged a stubborn Food Administration to accept the principle for which he had resigned.[167] Lasater contended that Hoover had had no choice; the Evvard report had made further "evasions" politically impossible.[168]

For his part Hoover quickly notified Wallace that "we are taking just as much risk as we dare in the matter" and claimed that his new policy was arousing "a great deal of opposition" from consumers. Especially in the larger cities, he asserted, "the Socialist and Pacifist classes" were seizing on the issue to agitate against the government. Once more Hoover was walking—or wanted Wallace to think he was walking—on a tightrope.[169]

On one point, though, Hoover was undoubtedly sincere: He was taking a risky leap into the unknown, a consideration that seemed never to occur to his critics. Frequently that autumn he remarked in private that if the hog stabilization program failed, it would mean his downfall as Food Administrator.[170]

On November 9 Lasater, just back from Texas, angrily resigned, convinced that there was "no foundation" for Hoover's anti-packer statements that had induced the cattleman on October 20 to stay on.[171] In Lasater's opinion, Hoover had converted the Food Administration into "a means of really taxing the producers of the country."[172] Ten days later Hoover reported the loss of his two assistants to the President. Instead of "confining himself to stimulation of production in a patriotic way" and to other aspects of the original livestock program, Pinchot—Hoover charged—"took upon himself to advise me" about "financial measures" and to advocate various "radical measures" like seizure of the packing plants.[173] Woodrow Wilson's reply was crisp and reassuring: "Thank you for your memorandum about Mr. Gifford Pinchot. The same thing happens wherever he is involved."[174]

The aftershocks, however, were not yet over. In the months ahead, an embittered Lasater vented his grievances before sympathetic Congressional committees. He charged that Hoover had deliberately conspired in 1917 to force down producer prices in order to get cheap food for the Allies. Lasater even challenged the statistical foundation of Hoover's entire livestock policy: the alleged long-term decline of European herds. Citing Department of Agriculture data issued in early 1918, the Texan testified that Allied and neutral herds had actually increased since the war began and that there had been no European livestock shortage in 1917 at all. Hoover, he claimed, had knowingly disseminated false statistics in 1917 in order to deceive livestock men into producing more, thereby pushing their market prices down. It was all part, said he, of Hoover's intent upon taking office of "exploiting the producers of live stock of America."[175] Pinchot, meanwhile, though disinclined to stage a public vendetta, privately accused Hoover of inability "to deal with masses of people" in a democracy, and of harsh, unreasonable hostility toward farmers.[176]

Hoover's view of his two detractors was no higher. Lasater, he asserted, had shown himself to be an impatient, selfish, narrow-minded zealot, unable to transcend his personal and sectional interests.[177] He was an "impossible team worker," a purveyor of numerous "misrepresentations," a man of "total unreliability."[178] Years later, Hoover labeled Lasater a "dupe" of his co-conspirator Pinchot.[179] As for that "demagog" (as Hoover disgustedly labeled Pinchot in 1920),[180] the Food Administrator no doubt agreed with his press spokesman Ben S. Allen, who later accused Pinchot of "megalomania," "flagrant disloyalty," and usurpation of power that he had not been assigned. According to Allen, while working for the Food Administration Pinchot had been "more concerned with destroying the packers than the Germans" and had conspired to use the agency for this purpose.[181] Years later Hoover wrote that it was "one of the mistakes of my public life that I did not expose them both [Lasater and Pinchot] at the time as they carried on their campaign of misrepresentation and smear for years."[182] Indeed, the reverberations of this imbroglio were to haunt Hoover politically for more than a decade.

The fate of the other agrarian militants in the Food Administration was less sensational but equally definitive. In 1918 Charles Holman, who had been Hoover's liaison to farm journals, was sent on a "fact-finding" mission to Manchuria. He was away from the United States for several months. As for Charles McCarthy, who had recruited Lasater and Pinchot in the first place, this feisty son of Irish immigrants remained with Hoover's organization until late 1918. Suspected by Hoover's entourage of disloyalty to the Chief, McCarthy discovered that his mail was opened for many weeks and that his office telephone had been tapped by what he called a "secret service organization" within the Food Administration.[183] Although McCarthy continued to serve Hoover and remained at least outwardly friendly with him, the Progressive gadfly became essentially an outsider.

With Pinchot and Lasater out of power and McCarthy marginalized, the Food Administrator's internal "farm bloc" disappeared. After the clashes of November 1917, Hoover took little notice of the episode. In the late autumn of 1917 he could not long be distracted by the angry departure of his two frustrated livestock specialists. He had a concurrent battle on his hands with the packers.

II

In the autumn of 1917 Hoover confronted in the meat-packing industry one of the most strategic elements in his unfolding design of food control. Although hundreds of packing companies existed in the United States, the industry was dominated by the so-called "Big Five": Wilson, Armour, Swift, Morris, and Cudahy. Together these giants processed more than 80 percent of all cattle, and more than 60 percent of all hogs, entering interstate commerce. They also controlled more than seven eighths of the branch houses that marketed fresh meat to retailers.[184]

The very economic success of the "Big Five"—and the importance of the packing industry generally—posed a delicate political problem for Hoover. For more than a decade, since the publication of Upton Sinclair's muckracking novel *The Jungle* (1906) and the ensuing enactment of federal pure food legislation, the leading packers had been the object of vehement attack. In an era rent by crusades against "trusts" and monopolies, the emergence of a highly concentrated "food trust" seemed especially sinister. No business interest, Mark Requa later wrote, was more disliked in the nation's capital than the packers.[185] None was more widely distrusted by the American people.

Hoover was well aware of the packers' unsavory reputation; he told Lasater that it "smelled to heaven."[186] In mid-August the Food Administrator privately bemoaned the absence of packing house executives as broad-minded and dependable as his conduit to the grain dealers, Julius Barnes.[187] Yet if Hoover seemed unable to identify industrial statesmen in this branch of the food trade, he was unwilling to embrace the drastic alternative of government control. "We can not administer the food law in this country if we approach it from any other point of view than the one of coordination and cooperation on a patriotic ground," he told the United States Live Stock Industry Committee on September 6. "We are not here for the purpose of dictating what is to be done to industries. We are here attempting to ameliorating [sic] conditions amassed by the war."[188] The next day he was even more explicit. We have come together not "to try any one for any of the crimes that we hear of," he warned, but rather to attempt "to do something positive and constructive and to get through the war . . . with the least national disturbance to our commercial life that we can provide."[189]

Hoover's initial preference, then, was for collaboration, not coercion—a desire that he believed the packers shared. At the beginning of September he told the President that the packers were "disposed to show the utmost good will in carrying out any programme of national interest."[190] Indeed, in the early weeks after passage of the Lever Act the principal packers evinced eagerness to work with the government. At Hoover's request they quickly organized a committee to represent them in parleys with the Food Administration.[191] When, on September 12, Hoover announced that he would shortly place the entire packing industry under license, the committee instantly expressed its approval and offered to help.[192]

At this juncture each side seemed to be acting from a perception of relative weakness. Like Mark Requa, Hoover evidently believed that the government lacked the ability to operate the packing plants itself if the owners failed to cooperate—as he feared they might if he tried to govern them too stringently.[193] The packers, on the other hand, knew that Hoover had virtually limitless power to regulate them and that it was hardly prudent to offend him or inflame public opinion by brusque defiance. With the Federal Trade Commission already investigating their business practices, the Big Five were under increasing constraint. If Hoover believed himself to be at an *economic* disadvantage in his dealings with them, the packers undoubtedly felt themselves to be at a *political* disadvantage. Both sides, then, had reason to seek an accommodation.

On October 8 President Wilson ordered all packers whose gross annual sales exceeded $100,000 to obtain a license from the Food Administration as a condition of remaining in business.[194] To formulate the licensing requirements and supervise their enforcement, Hoover selected Joseph Cotton, a distinguished New York City attorney and a counsel to the Federal Reserve Board, as head of his meat division. Cotton had no direct connection to the packing industry—under the circumstances, an asset more than a liability. But he knew his way around both business and government and came to his assignment with the apparent recommendation of Justice Louis Brandeis.[195] During most of October Cotton was preoccupied with the APEC negotiations and the corn / hog ratio. But by the beginning of November he and Hoover were free to focus on devising the terms under which the licensed packers would operate for the remainder of the war.

At once the two men faced a serious dilemma. One of Hoover's primary objectives was to ensure that the nation's food handlers and processors—the middlemen between producers and consumers—received only "fair" and "reasonable" profits for their services. The Big Five were middlemen par excellence. If the government now permitted them to make inordinate profits as a consequence of the mounting wartime demand for meat, it could enrage rural America, discourage livestock production, and drive up the retail prices paid by suffering consumers.[196] On the other hand, the packers controlled a vast and intricate economic organism, whose efficient—indeed, expanded—functioning seemed crucial to victory. If Hoover for compelling political reasons must regulate and presumably limit the packers' profits, he must for compelling economic reasons allow these same companies sufficient earnings to enlarge and modernize their plants. On the determination of an equitable profit structure for the packing industry hinged the provision of further meat for the Allies and conceivably the outcome of the war.

As the Food Administration and the packers' representatives in Chicago got down to serious discussions, the earlier mood of patriotic cooperation abruptly vanished. When Cotton, negotiating for Hoover, proposed to confine packers' profits to 2 percent of total annual sales, the industry's conferees vehemently resisted.[197] "Packers are kicking terribly. . . ," Cotton telegraphed Washington on October 30.[198] On November 1 he was obliged to report: "I have had a bad day with the packers who are very sulky and unwilling to play."[199] Hoover was not amused: "They are unwise if they do not cooperate with us absolutely," he replied. "For years they have contended that two percent was their maximum profit[;] now they had better concede it."[200]

The industry leaders, however, refused to capitulate.[201] On November 10

Cotton learned privately from the chairman of the packers' committee that his conferees were unlikely to cooperate with the Food Administration unless Cotton permitted a more "liberal" profit margin. The packers wanted 2.5 instead of 2 percent.[202] A few days later he reported that they now demanded 3 percent net on their meat sales—and no limit whatever on so-called "specialties" and "byproducts."[203]

With Hoover's approval, Cotton invited representatives of the Federal Trade Commission (FTC) to review his proposed regulations and listen to the packers' complaints.[204] Since the FTC was already investigating the packers, Cotton was eager to receive its advice—and even more eager to forestall any criticism by it of his impending decision.[205] But his ploy immediately produced complications. Instead of endorsing Cotton's proposed regulations, the FTC officials who came to Chicago rejected his approach entirely and proposed an alternative form of profit control that Cotton deemed impossible to implement. Already casting a jaundiced eye at the Big Five, the FTC representatives believed that regulation would "crush the small hog dealer." If attempted at all, it should encompass the packers' byproducts as well as their meat.[206] Not for the last time, the FTC cast a skeptical shadow over the Food Administration's policies.

If the Federal Trade Commission was disinclined to cooperate,[207] so, increasingly, were the putative objects of all this attention. On November 17 Cotton informed Hoover that it was "out of the question to get the packers to agree to anything except 2½% or 3% on meat business" and no restraints whatever on byproducts. Yet if the Swift company, for instance, were permitted such a high return on sales, it would yield the corporation an annual profit of more than 20 percent on its own invested capital—a margin that would undoubtedly evoke a political howl.[208] Cotton therefore proposed to Hoover a two-tier system of profit regulation: a maximum of 2.5 percent on annual sales for small packers, and 10 percent on capital invested in the meat business for the Big Five.[209] On November 20 the head of the meat division reported that the "large packers" seemed satisfied and should cooperate "provided I can go as high as indicated . . . on terms."[210]

Hoover promptly accepted Cotton's overall scheme, except for the proposed 10 percent return on invested capital permitted to the Big Five. A margin of 9 percent "would excite much less opposition in the country," he asserted; no doubt he sensed the psychological impact of the number 10.[211] When Cotton wavered on this point, the Food Administrator emphatically reiterated his preference.[212] As always, Hoover had his eye on public opinion.

At a final conference with the packers' representatives on November 23, Cotton dutifully announced the decision for 9 percent. At once a storm of anger lashed the meeting room. The representatives of the five giants insisted that 10 percent was the "absolute minimum" they could accept. After the meeting, Cotton advised Hoover by telegram to "keep to nine" but to offer the protestors the possibility of higher earnings later if the government compelled them to make unremunerative wartime capital expenditures. "The situation is nasty," Cotton wired, "but I think we can get away with it."[213] In a separate telegram that same evening, however, Cotton advised that it would be difficult to get the leading packers to cooperate "on allies business . . . without concession." If, he added, Hoover thought that the American people would be "satisfied with ten it would make life a good deal easier for me. . . ."[214]

The Food Administrator was in no mood for further bargaining. His agency—he telegraphed Cotton on November 24—was "stabilizing the packers' business as never before," and in setting a limit on earnings of 9 percent he was

> convinced we are offering everything that the good judgment of the community will ask for and even at this figure the administration will be subjected to acute criticism in view of public feeling towards the packing industry. The professed earnings of the packers in peace times did not exceed this figure and to ask more now is to ask for a profit from the war. The figure works out above normal manufacturing profits. It does seem to me that the packers should be glad to demonstrate to the public a willingness to public service and to ask in these times only a normal commercial profit. My final view is nine percent and I trust the packers in their own interest will willing[ly] agree.[215]

Hoover intended the packers to see this telegram. In a separate message to Cotton he said pointedly: "I am sure it is in their interest and if they do not agree the public will support us both."[216]

Hoover immediately authorized Cotton to announce the profit decision. Even if the packers disagreed, he said, "it is a good thing to issue it on this basis and let them prove to the country that it is wrong."[217] Later on the twenty-fourth, Cotton promulgated the policy in the press. For the small packers: 2.5 percent profits (maximum) on total annual sales. For the Big Five: the same, plus an additional cap of 9 percent on the "average capital" used in their meat business. For specialty products such as leather and soap, Cotton permitted a higher ceiling of 15 percent. For a third category of packer business not subject to the Lever Act, the Food Administration, lacking legal jurisdiction, imposed no limits at all.[218]

The owners of the principal packing houses were furious. The day after the Food Administration's announcement appeared in the newspapers, a buffeted Joseph Cotton telegraphed Hoover: "Packers spent many hours with me to-day hollering that I am a socialist." The packers contended that they must constantly expand their operations in order to remain efficient. But how, they asked, could they do that unless they generated investment capital from profits?[219] The Big Five therefore decided to appeal directly to the Food Administrator in Washington.[220]

Hoover was ready for the onslaught. On November 27, at his request, President Wilson issued an executive order defining "just, reasonable, and fair" profits under the Lever Act to be the "normal average" profits under free competition prior to July 1, 1914. Wilson authorized Hoover to determine these margins for licensed food industries and "to prohibit the taking of any greater profit."[221] The Food Administrator promptly notified Cotton of the President's decision. I "do not want to give [the order] publicity," Hoover said, "but you can use it as a club if you need it."[222]

On December 1, 1917 a delegation from the Big Five converged on Hoover's office. Abjuring all desire to increase their personal profits or corporate dividends, the packers argued that Hoover's plan courted disaster. The nation was at war, the government was stimulating livestock production, the packing industry must now expand its slaughtering and storage facilities as never before. But how? Such items cost far more now than in 1914, and a dollar—thanks to inflation—was worth only half what it was then. By limiting the packers' profit margin to its prewar level, Hoover was shrinking the earnings available for plant expansion and impairing the companies' ability to borrow money for the same purpose under war conditions. The packers pledged to do their best but warned that if they were unable to prepare their products efficiently in the months ahead the responsibility would lie with Hoover, not them.[223]

Hoover was unpersuaded by their pleas. He noted that the Big Five had actually earned less than 9 percent on their investment before the war and had managed to build their plants nevertheless. He also dismissed the claim that prospective moneylenders would lack confidence in the packers' earning capacity under his regulations. Far more importantly, Hoover was troubled by the political and ethical implications of the packers' demand. If he now granted them a higher profit level during wartime than they had received while at peace, would this not be "a toll from the country's losses"?[224] And would he not in effect be taxing the public to pay for "equipment for private enterprise"? Such an action would raise "a serious question of public policy" beyond his power to resolve.[225]

The Food Administrator also invoked an argument that he seemed to reserve for militant capitalists. "We have got to keep an eye on" public opinion "to our common interest," he told the packers.

> We have a good example in the condition of Russia where radical public opinion was allowed to go rampant and where public industry did not respond . . . resulting in the entire collapse of property values. We are doing our best here to try to hold public opinion, and for us to come out . . . on a basis of . . . over the pre-war normal and that the expansion was

> going to be carried on at public expense,—it is a thing that would excite public opinion beyond anything that I can think of.[226]

He urged the owners to proceed "on the 9% basis" and to expand their plants at their own expense—in other words, to accept his plan for now. "I think in doing that," he added, "I am acting in the good of the packers themselves."[227]

The Food Administrator did offer his visitors one consolation. If in the future the packers should become "absolutely unable" to secure capital for expansion "deemed by the Government to be necessary," the Food Administrator would "endeavor to secure aid or alternatively adjust profits by some measure to meet the situation."[228] He thereupon informed President Wilson of his course of action; the President soon gave his approval.[229]

Somewhat grudgingly, perhaps, the packers declared their acceptance of the principle that "no industry should seek to earn larger profits out of war needs." So, at least, Hoover immediately informed the press.[230] Cotton, for his part, considered that he had allowed the packers "liberal profits"—generous enough to maintain ample credit from the banks.[231] The time would shortly come when the packers' enemies would challenge the industry's compliance with these rules as well as Hoover's sincerity in enforcing them. But for the moment, as Cotton drew up and implemented detailed regulations, the furor in the great stockyards subsided, as it had in the corn-and-hog belt a few weeks before.[232]

III

By early December 1917 Hoover's apparatus of food control had evolved into a formidable wartime agency. Farmers, middlemen, housewives, Allied and neutral buying agencies: all were touched by his expanding web of voluntarism and constraint.

Hoover had reason to be gladdened by his handiwork. He had wanted first to check the inflationary spiral in food prices; by late autumn it appeared that he was succeeding.[233] By December, too, the wheat farmers were submissive, the hog producers more or less satisfied, the packing houses acquiescent, flour millers and uncounted others on the distribution chain subjected to his watchful supervision. And not an atom of grain—as he himself might have put it—could leave America's shores without his sanction.

Yet all that he had thus far accomplished—"guiding" the food trades, "guarding" exports, mobilizing conservation campaigns, encouraging the production of meat—was fundamentally preparatory. His policies were formulated, his system in place. Now he must do more than "stabilize": he must convey the requisite foodstuffs to Europe. Winter was coming—and a crush of troubles that would test him to the limit.

8

The Winter of Trepidation

I

As the nation's farmers completed their harvest in the late autumn of 1917, Hoover turned increasingly to his next challenge: fulfillment of his promises to the Allies. Early in December he agreed to ship a minimum of 1,100,000 tons of breadstuff cereals per month from Canada and the United States to Europe during December as well as January and February 1918.[1] The Allies, of course, would have to carry this grain in their own vessels, for the United States lacked shipping of its own. The Allies would also have to borrow from the American government in order to pay for these purchases. This left Hoover one task: He must secure the required grain at interior markets and then move it to port facilities on the coast, where Allied steamers would assemble the cargo and sail.

Yet even as Hoover expressed confidence that he could meet the Allies' cereals needs for the winter,[2] circumstances were conspiring to thwart him. By the beginning of December America's overburdened railway system was approaching paralysis. The government had failed to coordinate its mounting shipments of soldiers, munitions, food, and fuel to the eastern seaboard. As New York, Chicago, and other railroad hubs became snarled in slow-moving traffic, more and more carriers were unable to empty their freight cars and return them to needy points in the West and South. The consequences were far-reaching and ominous. Lacking railcars on which to load coal, many coal mines were obliged to slash their production.[3] Farther west, the growing shortage of boxcars threatened to impede the transit of frost-damaged soft corn to drying plants.[4]

Compounding the crisis was the Wilson administration's decision back in the summer to fix the price of bituminous coal at $2.00 a ton—a figure too low for many marginal mines to survive on. It was another governmental blunder, and not surprisingly, coal production plummeted. Although the administration eventually permitted some selective upward revisions in coal prices, the lost output was quickly felt by a nation still dependent on coal for industrial and home heating.[5]

At the end of November the deepening congestion on the railways, along with an outbreak of coal shortages in New England and parts of the Midwest, touched off a bureaucratic battle in Washington.[6] On November 28 Hoover's friend Harry Garfield, now the government's Fuel Administrator, asked Robert S. Lovett, the government's Director of Priority, to issue an order giving preference to the movement of coal and empty coal cars on the country's railways.[7] Garfield was apprehensive. For weeks various agencies of the government had been dithering over what to do about the developing fuel emergency.[8] Now the city of Detroit was on the brink of a coal famine, and Garfield was convinced that "a fire [must be] built under somebody" to distribute fuel at once across the country.[9] Without waiting for Lovett's decision, he asked the private operating committee of the eastern railroads to issue such an order itself to the lines over which it had control. The railroads' committee quickly complied.[10]

Garfield's unilateral action incensed Herbert Hoover, who immediately protested to Lovett against giving priority to "coal or anything else" over "the movement of essential foodstuffs." Not content with this, Hoover immediately carried his complaint to the press.[11] But if Garfield appeared to be doing an end-run around the federal bureaucracy, it soon became known that Hoover, too, had recently done the same thing. Just a few weeks before, his agency had gotten the railroads to give it 1,400 cars to transport drought-threatened cattle out of Texas and New Mexico—without approaching the Priority Board for an order.[12]

Hoover's public display of displeasure prompted a flurry of rumors around Washington of a quarrel between himself and Garfield, something that the two men quickly denied.[13] But the disagreement between them could not be finessed or avoided, and when Lovett issued a general priority order for rail transport on December 7, it was Hoover, not Garfield, who prevailed. In the competition for railcars, food received preference over coal.[14]

Meanwhile, anxious to free up railroad boxcars for western farmers and ease the growing bottleneck in the East, Hoover persuaded the Commission on Car Service of the American Railway Association to prohibit all further rail shipments of corn or oats to the entire Northeast and much of the Midwest. The extraordinary embargo took effect on December 8. From now on, the most populous parts of the country must make do with the corn and oats grown within their region.[15]

Despite these measures, the nation's rail system continued to flounder and groan. By December 24 Garfield was complaining that Lovett's recent priority order had accomplished nothing to alleviate the congestion.[16] Hoover, for his part, was adamant in his commitment to "food first"—an attitude that irritated even his patron, Colonel House. After meeting the Food Administrator on December 26, House confided in his diary:

> I find with Hoover, as with others, that the matter he is working on is the most important in the world. Hoover believes that food should be moved at the expense of coal or other necessary commodities. He does not think it matters much if the people are a little cold just so the Allies have food. I find this characteristic in nearly all self-centered individuals having a particular specialty.[17]

By now the worsening transportation problems on the eastern seaboard had begun to disquiet America's European allies. Shipments of grain from American ports were falling short of projections, and Allied reserves were correspondingly shrinking. It appeared that Great Britain, France, and Italy would obtain only 800,000 tons of cereals in December from North America, far less than Hoover had been sure of early in the month. On December 16 the inter-Allied body known as the Wheat Executive issued a somber warning from London: Unless it received a minimum of 1,100,000 tons per month from America in January and February, "it will not be possible to carry on."[18]

Hoover was shocked. Upon receiving this staggering message, he immediately transmitted it to President Wilson and minced no words. "I need not dilate on the gravity of this situation," he commented. "It is simply one of railway transport."[19]

Within a few days, however, as the Allies intensified their clamor for more food,[20] Hoover's perspective changed radically. The reason for the prospective shortfall in cereals exports in December, he now concluded, was not the struggling American supply effort but the failure of the Allies to provide enough shipping. To Hoover it now appeared that the Wheat Executive was "trying to load off its inefficiency on us and make us bear responsibility for their shortcomings."[21] The angry Food Administrator was not going to take this lying down.

Hoover therefore cabled London that he would load all the vessels that the Allies had actually allotted for December—if their ships reached American ports on time. He also promised that if the Allies provided the requisite vessels in January, he would fill them with 1,100,000 tons of cereals without difficulty, "barring of course unforeseen incidents of war."[22] If any deficiency occurred in December or January, in other words, it would be the Allies' fault, not his.

Despite Hoover's assurance on December 23 that shipments of Allied foodstuffs were now receiving "every precedence" on America's railways,[23] the British government was increasingly disturbed. If the United States was to export the vast amounts of foodstuffs that Hoover had assented to, His Majesty's Government wanted more than an iteration of good intentions. On December 26 it requested the U.S. government to grant "preferential movement" on the rails to food bound for export to the Allies.[24]

Two days later the Wheat Executive's principal representatives in the United States conferred with Hoover and Julius Barnes in New York.[25] Here Hoover renewed his pledge to ship 1,100,000 tons of cereals across the Atlantic in January 1918 and again in February.[26] Day by day, however, the situation was becoming grimmer. In the month of December the Allies managed to obtain only 492,000 tons of "human foodstuffs" from North America, far less than either they or Hoover had contemplated.[27] Whatever the cause, this was a failure that must not be repeated.

And now, once again, events beyond his domain intervened to shape the context for Hoover's coming struggle. On December 28, by order of President Wilson, the government of the United States nationalized the railroads. The commander in chief appointed Secretary of the Treasury McAdoo to be Director General of Railroads and head of a new agency that would administer them for the rest of the war.

For Hoover the presidential decree held out the prospect of ending the transportation paralysis at last. He predicted that the government takeover would "materially better conditions."[28] This was the good news. The bad news was something that no official edict could alter: in the very week that the railroads passed under government control, the worst winter weather in memory descended on the eastern half of the country.

II

By December 29, from the upper Mississippi Valley to the Atlantic seaboard, a massive cold wave held millions of Americans in its grip.[29] In New York City, the premier port of the nation, the temperature on December 30 fell to −13°F, the lowest ever recorded.[30] The next day the port of Boston experienced its coldest weather in 105 years.[31]

The ravages of winter quickly aggravated the coal shortages and rail congestion already bedeviling the industrial Northeast. From New England to Virginia, ships were unable to sail to Europe for lack of bunker coal. In New York City alone, by early January, more than 125 loaded steamers were stranded for this reason.[32] So frigid was the temperature that coal shipments reaching tidewater in northern New Jersey were frozen solid. Desperate rail workers had to steam the lumps apart before loading them onto barges bound across the icy harbor to New York. It was awful work—and slow. The supply of fuel to the nation's largest city shrank to a trickle.[33]

To avert a threatened fuel famine in eastern cities, the new Director General of Railroads ordered that coal now be given first priority on the rails.[34] In an attempt to conserve the dwindling coal supplies already in stock, the state fuel administrator of New York banned the use of outdoor electric signs for six nights each week.[35] Still, it was not until January 6, 1918 that New York, for the first time in ten days, received enough coal to meet its immediate needs.[36]

As McAdoo and Garfield grappled with the fuel and rail crisis, Hoover observed its ripple effects with alarm. On January 6 he informed McAdoo that the eastern railroads now held as many as 40,000 boxcars that belonged to railways in the grain belt. Unless these cars were returned to western carriers "at once" and put to the task of hauling cereals, it would jeopardize Hoover's promise to deliver a vast tonnage of foodstuffs to the Allies before April. Such a failure, he warned, would threaten "the entire Allied cause."[37]

Hoover also contended that the shortage of boxcars had caused a severe decline in the marketing of corn. As a result, "vast" quantities of corn were threatened with spoilage, the price of corn (and other foods) was soaring, and it was becoming more economical to consume wheat than corn. If this last trend persisted, said Hoover, it would "paralyze" his wheat conservation measures and bring about a flour famine by June, with resultant risks to the "tranquility" of the "industrial population." It was not necessary to choose between corn and coal, he argued. Corn required boxcars, not open tops. Besides, there were plenty of "non-essential commodities" which could be set aside to create more storage cars for grain.[38]

McAdoo replied that he was doing "everything possible" to move the needed boxcars from East to West and that "moderate weather for a time" should relieve the shortage.[39] He also designated January 14–21 as "Freight Moving Week," during which the nation would make a "supreme effort" to unload the stationary freight cars clogging the nation's principal cities and terminals.[40]

Unfortunately for McAdoo, the weather did not improve. On January 6 Chicago was hit by its worst snowstorm in years.[41] In New York Harbor, between January 5 and 8, twenty-four coal barges sank after colliding with ice floes; 360 additional barges could not even be loaded because of the difficulty of extricating frozen coal from incoming railcars.[42] By January 11, more than 40,000 carloads of supplies bound for Europe were tied up on land around six Atlantic ports—victims of the interlocking shortages of coal and ships and of the near gridlock on the rails.[43] In New York City, where 136 ships now waited for bunker coal, it was reported that there was not enough coal either at tidewater or on its way from the mines to supply the crippled armada's needs. Even if there had been coal, it could not have been loaded.

The nearby port of South Amboy, where most of the bunker coal accumulated, was blocked by a three-foot wall of broken ice.[44]

And so it went. In the winter of 1918, for the first time in memory, it became possible to walk from Staten Island to Sandy Hook, New Jersey, across five frozen miles of Raritan Bay.[45] In Baltimore Harbor, far to the south, the ice at one point was three feet thick.[46]

Then, on January 12, an immense and brutal blizzard assailed the Midwest. Temperatures fell far below zero while winds whipped a snowfall of up to twenty inches into phenomenal drifts. Chicago was cut off and overwhelmed; coal and milk deliveries ceased; not a train could get into or out of the Windy City. Downstate, in Cairo, Illinois, the Ohio River froze solid for the first time that anyone could recall.[47]

The storm moved east, stopping vital rail traffic in all directions. The transportation centers of Pittsburgh and Buffalo were paralyzed. For miles, along the tracks, the snow was piled as high as the tops of freight cars. The railroad industry in the Middle West had never experienced a blizzard like this. For three days something like 200,000 railcars could not move.[48]

Was God on the side of the Kaiser? In one stroke nature had undone the initial efforts of the Railroad Administration to facilitate transport. Now the tieup was more widespread than ever.

Fearful that New York City might run out of food and fuel, McAdoo immediately issued priority orders for rail movements to the metropolis: first, coal for homes and public utilities; then food; then coal for ships headed overseas. A massive shutdown of "non-essential" industry loomed.[49] In the city itself, on January 14, scores of cargo-laden ships were still unable to leave for Europe because they could not obtain needed fuel.[50] Meanwhile, not far away on the Jersey shore, 300,000 tons of coal lay largely beyond reach. Government officials and railway executives squabbled over who was responsible for transferring it in barges through the treacherous harbor ice.[51]

As tales of coal shortages and suffering multiplied across the East and Middle West, Harry A. Garfield decided to intervene. For several days in mid-January the Fuel Administrator had been contemplating drastic measures to effectuate fuel conservation in the East.[52] On the evening of January 16 he disclosed how extraordinary his intentions had become. With the approval of the President, he ordered that for five consecutive days beginning January 18 nearly all manufacturing plants east of the Mississippi River (and in the states of Minnesota and Louisiana as well) must burn no fuel whatsoever. Even if individual factories had ample coal on hand, said Garfield, they would not be permitted to use it. In this way, he asserted, everyone would be "placed on an equal footing." In effect, the great bulk of America's factories must shut down.

Nor did Garfield stop here. He also announced that on ten consecutive Mondays beginning January 21, nearly all businesses east of the Mississippi (including department stores and professional offices) would be obliged to burn no fuel except the minimum necessary to prevent injury to property. Unless they chose to operate on these days without heat and electricity, they, too, would have to close their doors and take the economic consequences.[53]

Garfield asserted that his order would save 30,000,000 tons of coal. More importantly, it would provide a "breathing spell" for the nearly paralyzed railroads.[54] As Garfield saw it, the cause of the crisis was an "excess of production" that was overwhelming the Atlantic ports and freight yards. Why were hundreds of ships lying at anchor, unable to sail for Europe? Because, he said, they lacked coal for their bunkers. And why did they lack coal? Because it was stalled behind "the congested freight that has jammed all terminals." To Garfield it was "useless" to continue manufacturing goods at the current pace under these circumstances. His solution to the transportation emergency, therefore, was to force America's factories to produce less by cutting off their fuel supply.[55]

Garfield's totally unexpected order was one of the most draconian edicts ever promulgated by an American government official. That very evening, January 16, in Colonel House's words, "bedlam broke loose" in Washington, D.C.[56] On the streets of the city one Congressional wife detected "almost revolutionary" excitement as crowds of amazed working people contemplated the loss of fourteen days' wages in two months.[57] On Capitol Hill, where criticism of Wilson's war management was reaching volcanic intensity, the Senate by a vote of 50 to 19 requested Garfield to postpone his order for five days pending an investigation.[58] Before the Senate's resolution could reach him, Garfield signed his official order.[59] For his part, President Wilson defended the fuel decree as "absolutely necessary."[60] Privately he acknowledged, "There was nothing to do but retire to the cyclone cellar."[61] Around the nation, incredulous businessmen, labor leaders, and editorialists condemned the impending closure of industries as unnecessary, disruptive, and disastrous.[62]

Among those who were staggered was Hoover, who had received the news from Garfield himself at supper on the sixteenth.[63] The next day, as protests flooded into Washington, Hoover told Garfield that he had not understood "the whole scope" of the fuel order the night before and now had "the gravest possible fears" about its success. Although Garfield had exempted manufacturers of perishable goods from his decree, Hoover was worried about its impact upon related industries. How could he keep the flour mills going, for example, unless the makers of flour sacks were also able to stay open? To Hoover, the best approach would be to grant "exclusive loading rights" for four days to coal, food, and certain other industries, and to deny all other industries access to railcars. In effect, he was proposing a complete if temporary embargo on nonessential rail traffic.[64]

Garfield did not take Hoover's advice. But he did order all food industries to receive coal, and he immediately granted the Food Administration the right to determine which "collateral industries" should also be supplied.[65]

Hoover promptly notified the public that Garfield's decree did not include bakeries, grain elevators, meat-packing houses, sugar refineries, "or any other form of food industry."[66]

Having protected his priorities, Hoover left Washington by train on the evening of January 18 for a previously planned vacation weekend in Pinehurst, North Carolina. His wife and three close friends traveled with him.[67] Ironically, they departed in a snowstorm and had to endure both chilly cold and a bleak landscape in North Carolina.[68]

Meanwhile, from the Canadian border to the Gulf of Mexico, tens of millions of American citizens adjusted to Garfield's commands. For five days, most factories fell silent; well over a million workers lost pay. On January 21, the first of the "heatless Mondays," nearly all businesses except banks and stock exchanges closed down in twenty-eight states. Street lights were turned off, streetcars operated only on reduced schedules, and office buildings that remained open did so without heat or artificial light.[69]

The effect of the unprecedented "holiday" was problematic. Although Garfield subsequently asserted that his action helped to free nearly five hundred waiting ships, he soon requested McAdoo to institute what Hoover advocated: a general embargo on rail shipments except food and fuel.[70] Until now the fledgling Director General of Railroads had apparently been averse to such a step.[71] But on January 23 McAdoo finally authorized a limited embargo excluding everything except food, fuel, and government-approved war materiel on three key eastern railways.[72] Slowly, fitfully, agonizingly, the authorities in Washington were developing a sensible policy.

Despite McAdoo's action, it was now apparent that American exports of grain in January would fall substantially below what Hoover had promised the Allies in late December.[73] In fact, for the two months together the shipments would be a whopping 900,000 tons less than the amount fixed by the Inter-Allied Conference in Paris in November.[74] For the Allied governments, it was appalling news. At a meeting of the British War Cabinet on January 24, the secretary of the Royal Commission on Wheat Supplies reported that by February 1 Great Britain would have only a twelve-week reserve of cereals, half of it still out on the farms. By May 1 this would diminish to a scant four-week supply (aside from what was left on the farms)—a margin deemed insufficient for safety.[75]

Even before this, Allied nerves had been growing frayed. The chairman of the Royal Commission on Wheat Supplies, Lord Crawford, was so upset by Hoover's America-first policies that he suspected him of being a German agent—a suspicion fortified in Crawford's mind by Hoover's "shifty hangdog manner . . . his refusal to look one in the face, and . . . [his] general craftiness of manner and phrase which are most discourteous and extremely unsavoury."[76] If Hoover suspected the Allies of trying to pin responsibility for the growing exports debacle on him, in at least some Allied quarters the feeling of distrust was reciprocated.

By now the Allies had begun to worry about American grain commitments for February. As usual, Julius Barnes was more optimistic than his chief. He notified Hoover on January 16 that he had "no doubt" that if the Food Administration Grain Corporation acquired 30 percent of the February output of American flour mills by the tenth of the month, he could "make the Feby program of the allies."[77] Hoover promptly replied that the Allied demands were "infeasible" and inconsistent with the "previous understanding." If Barnes was prepared to satisfy the Allies, Hoover had something more on his mind. "We cannot," he said, "risk [the] civil population of this country."[78]

On January 22, 1918, fresh from his chilly holiday in North Carolina, Hoover conferred with H. T. Robson and K. B. Stoddart of the Allies' New York-based Wheat Export Company. The situation that they discussed was grave. According to the two Allied executives, shipments of grain from North America in February would once again fall far short of the agreed quota; in fact, the accumulating deficit was now so large that a food "crisis" in Europe was at hand. The two men asserted that it was imperative that the Allies receive 1,100,000 tons of cereals from the New World in March. They asked that they obtain as much of it as possible in the form of bulk grain, which took less time to load on ships than sacked flour.[79]

Two days later Robson and Stoddart recapitulated the essential points of their conversation in a follow-up letter to Hoover: a letter that seemed intended to keep his feet to the fire. They noted that the Food Administrator had arranged to commandeer 30 percent of the flour output of all controlled American mills for delivery to the Allies. They asked for more corn and warned that the short shipments of grain now destined to last through February would deplete Allied food stocks to the "danger point." Indeed, they concluded, "the slightest failure on our part to ship the quantities mentioned can only have the most disastrous results."[80]

Although Hoover was rarely hesitant to exert pressure on others, he was not amused when others did the same thing to him. When he received Robson and Stoddart's letter of January 24, he was considerably annoyed. For one thing, he was convinced that the Allies had greater grain reserves than they were admitting and that their circumstances were less threatening than they alleged.[81] For another, he told Barnes:

> No one can charge me with not being prepared to make every possible effort to meet the Allied necessities. On the other hand, I do not propose to be put in a position by correspondence out of which a case is to be built up against me and this Government for the performance or non-performance of things that are physically impossible in this situation.[82]

According to Hoover, neither the British, the French, nor the Italians were restricting their cereals consumption to the degree that he was now attempting in the United States. In fact, he claimed, the new British and French bread rations were at least as great as American "normal consumption." Just as Alonzo Taylor had lectured the Allies in November, so now Hoover berated them to Barnes. He asserted that Allied food consumption had risen greatly because of war prosperity, and that there must be "universal repression" if America and its allies were to "pull through until the next harvest." "I will want to see more evidence of repression in England and in France than I have seen heretofore," he said irritably, "before I am confinced [sic] that we should take undue and greater risks than those which are now in course." As for the 30 percent of American flour production now promised to the Allies, Hoover told Barnes that he expected a rising "spirit of unrest" at home in the next two months which would force him to divert some of "our thirty per cent" to affected cities "if we are to maintain public order."[83] In other words, the commitment of commandeered flour that Robson and Stoddart thought they had won on January 22 was in Hoover's mind not a certainty at all.

Hoover, then, was in a combative mood when he replied to Robson on January 28. The Food Administrator asserted bluntly that his agency was doing—and would do—its utmost to assist the Allies, but that he was "not disposed to undertake any more specific promises." He claimed that his conservation efforts were attempting to reduce American wheat consumption to a level below that of the British. He declared that if he were thinking "primarily" of his own people, he would embargo *all* exports of corn until its price came down and would even postpone wheat shipments until he knew for certain that the amounts exported "had been actually saved from consumption." Still, he insisted, he was making every exertion possible "to expedite movement at the most extreme risks of maintaining tranquility in this country."

Then, abruptly turning the tables, Hoover proceeded to blame the Allies for their current predicament:

> It does appear to me that if Allied shipping had been directed to the Argentine at the first of January, supplies would in turn have been available from that quarter during the month of March. That the Allied shipping authorities have failed us in this particular should not, I think, make us responsible.

While pledging to do what he could to "correct" this Allied "failure," Hoover admonished Robson not to think that even 30 percent of American flour was "at your disposal until we have had a month's experience with the operation of our new plans. . . ." The Food Administration might have to use some of it "to prevent absolute shortage to our own populations."[84]

Hoover's reaction here was a curious one. Publicly, in his food conservation propaganda, he had been highlighting the privation of the Allies as a spur to American self-denial. Now he seemed to be saying that in the crucial area of bread consumption the Allies were actually faring better than the Americans.

Hoover's analysis, however, was incomplete and misleading. It was certainly true that the British and French normally ate more breadstuffs per capita than Americans did; on the other hand, bread was much more crucial to the European diet. As Hoover himself was aware, the Allied peoples were now eating far less meat and sugar than were the Americans.[85] Thus, even if American bread consumption were reduced to a level below that of Europe, Americans could compensate by relying on other foods. The Europeans had no such flexibility.

Hoover's animadversions about Argentina were similarly less than fair. The Allies had been striving for months to acquire the Argentine wheat crop but had been hindered by financial and political obstacles in the South American country.[86] Only in mid-January did the Allies finally succeed.[87] Of course, if they had sent ships to Argentina in *anticipation* of a successful negotiation, this would have saved them precious time. Perhaps this was all that Hoover meant. Unfortunately, the Allies apparently felt that they could not direct extremely scarce shipping to South America without being certain in advance that the coveted wheat was theirs and that Argentina had not sold it in the meantime to other customers.[88]

In any case, Hoover's response to the growing pressure on him was revealing. Instead of being conciliatory, he had counterattacked, even uttering dubious assertions and half-truths, all while clothing himself in a prickly garb of offended righteousness.

Before Hoover replied to Robson on January 28, the chairman of the Wheat Export Company wrote him a second letter, on January 26. Robson, too, was under intensifying pressure—in his case, from his principals in London, who told him that disaster loomed unless he could fulfill his import quota to the limit. In his letter of the twenty-sixth, Robson renewed his request for 1,100,000 tons of "human foodstuffs" from North America in March, including 850,000 tons from U.S. ports. Unless most of the American contribution came in the form of bulk grain rather than bagged goods, he warned, the needed amount of food could not be loaded in time. Robson specifically asked that as much as 200,000 tons of America's contribution be in the form of bulk wheat. If Hoover could not assure this, "the matter must be referred to the highest quarters." Robson noted pointedly that Hoover had siphoned off 16,200,000 bushels of Canadian wheat at Buffalo during the preceding autumn (in order to keep American flour mills working through the winter). Although Julius Barnes had promised to return an equivalent amount in the form of flour later on, Robson saw the result to date as 16,200,000 fewer bushels than the Allies would otherwise now have.

Robson warned further that the "danger of bread panics, either in Europe or here," could cause the price of wheat to soar above $2.20 a bushel. And in a paragraph that seemed certain to rankle Hoover, he observed:

> The newspapers in this country frequently contain paragraphs with regard to quantities of grain to be supplied to the Allies. The public have the general impression that the Food Administration is providing for the wants of the people in Europe. We are sure that they are quite unaware that the net quantity of wheat and flour supplied [to the Wheat Export Company by the Food Administration] between 1st October and 31st December is only 273,000 tons, and that the Food Administration have been recently unable to fulfill their guarantees to us. We think that it is desirable that the public should remain in ignorance of these facts, and we have done, and shall continue to do, our best to keep this information from the public, but it is perfectly clear that unless the supplies for February and March are forthcoming the food panics which will arise in Europe will be of such a nature that attention will be drawn to the short supplies from this country.[89]

In one respect Robson's letter was misleading. Between October and December the United States had provided the Wheat Export Company much more than 273,000 tons (approximately 10,000,000 bushels) of wheat and flour. Robson obtained his "net" figure by deducting from the actual amount exported the 16,200,000 bushels of Canadian wheat that the Wheat Export Company had given up in Buffalo. The United States, however, was pledged to replace this wheat later on, in the form of flour. If the Food Administration kept its word, this was hardly a lost supply.

Perhaps Robson no longer trusted Hoover to redeem this pledge. Perhaps he was trying to scare Hoover into cooperating. Perhaps he was trying to appease the bureaucrats in London who were breathing down his neck. Whatever his motive, the British grain agent's letter of January 26 now went forward to Washington.

Hoover apparently did not read it until after his reply of January 28 to Robson's letter of January 24. This first letter had made Hoover irritated; the second made him downright furious. To Julius Barnes, he complained that the "whole tone and attitude of Robson and Stoddart" were "positively disgusting":

> What these two men are obviously trying to do is by sucking material from us that we cannot afford to give, to prove that they are right and that Taylor, acting on my instructions, was wrong in acting on the original programme in London. I feel sure that they are trying to convince their governments that they should pull the stuff out of this country and that they could thereby avoid assigning shipping from [to] the Argentine.[90]

Hoover immediately dispatched a stinging five-page rebuttal to Robson. The Food Administrator requested information about Allied cereals imports from Canada and asserted, incredibly, that *his* data showed that the United States had fulfilled its export commitments for December and January. He told Robson that it seemed "impossible" to supply more bulk wheat in March. Moreover, to ship wheat instead of bagged flour would reduce American "mill employment," increase the cost of flour, and deprive the American dairy industry of "critical" feedstuffs. For Hoover, all this evidently took precedence over the Allies' receiving their full March quota. As for Robson's fear that the price of wheat in the United States might skyrocket, Hoover warned that if it did, "it would be due to over-shipments" to the Allies, and that he would then embargo "all further exports" until the price was "restored."

The Food Administrator accused Robson of threatening a "propaganda" campaign against the U.S. government in order to "expose to the American public what you call failure on our part." In fact, he added acidly, Robson's recent letters now "confirm in my mind the necessity of reservation on my part in making any promises whatever." Hoover averred that he had done everything "humanly possible" to aid the Allies and would send them "every atom" of food that he could spare. He would meet his share of the program formulated at the Inter-Allied Conference in November. But he also expected the Allies to fulfill *their* obligations, particularly to buy specified quantities of cereals from other parts of the world, and not to try "to heap the blame on us for their failure to do so."[91]

As it happened, President Wilson had just forwarded to Hoover a letter urging the export of cereals to the Allies in the form of coarse grain rather than packaged goods. According to the letterwriter (who had evidently been talking to British officials in New York), the United States was now more than 30 percent behind on its commitment of food bound for England.[92] Hoover promptly sent the President a long list of reasons why wheat shipments to Great Britain should be in the form of flour. Never one to be understated in discourse—especially in the face of adverse criticism—he told Wilson that the Food Administration's "firm policy" on this point was "entirely approved" by "the whole country." Still steaming at Robson's second letter, Hoover sent the President a copy of his rejoinder and declared:

> The Government is not behind in any obligations it has undertaken. The English have made demands far beyond our original undertakings and we are doing our best to fulfill them. So far as the English are concerned, we have now reduced our wheat consumption to a lower level per capita than they have in England.[93]

The first of these statements was false. The second contained a modicum of truth which was irrelevant.[94] The third, while perhaps technically true, conveyed an impression of American sacrifice at variance with the facts.

If Hoover was resorting to bluff and even misrepresentation, he did have some reason to be irked. *He* was not responsible for the weather, nor for the transportation breakdown that had so disrupted the food supply. Why should the Allies put the onus for faltering exports on him? Thoroughly incensed at the Wheat Export Company, he cabled his agent in London (in "the most secret code") for statistics on current British and French stocks of wheat, barley, rye, and flour. He also requested detailed information on Allied food imports from India and Argentina, and the extent to which these shipments had "failed of realization."[95] No doubt he hoped to prove that the Allies' food condition was not as desperate as they alleged it to be or, alternatively, that they had only their own incompetence to blame.[96]

Several days previously, Julius Barnes had urged his boss to be certain that the Allies did indeed possess a sufficient grain reserve. Hoover, he warned, could not "afford" to let Senator Reed "or any one else . . . make the claim that the Food Administrator declined to believe the representatives of our Allies and jeopardized the food supply" upon which continuation of the war depended.[97] But this motive did not appear to be animating Hoover now. What he wanted was data upon which "we will make up our minds as to what they are to be allowed without any regard to Robson and Stoddart."[98]

On February 2 Hoover's man in London responded. In Britain, grain stocks in the preceding month had plummeted because of "small shipments" and the "heavy diversion of British tonnage" to its allies. From France, Hoover's agent could obtain no reliable data. Even more discouragingly, the Allies had purchased "practically nothing" in Argentina because of the unsettled negotiations. No doubt for this reason, Allied imports from Argentina in December and January had been far less than the Inter-Allied Conference had mandated. Imports of food from India and South Africa had also failed to meet projections—a state of affairs for which Hoover, at least, could not be chastised.[99]

Meanwhile, apparently intimidated by Hoover's scathing rejoinder, H. T. Robson rushed to make amends. In yet another letter to the Food Administration, he earnestly denied that he had intended to threaten the U.S. government with "propaganda" against it. He had only wished to point out that if the "imminent" food famine in Europe did occur, the public there would want to know why shipments from North America had been so "deficient." Robson insisted that he had written his letter in order to forestall the famine and the inevitable, ensuing outcry back home. He professed his "utmost desire" to cooperate with Hoover and promised to take "no step" without consulting American officials.[100]

Beyond these propitiatory gestures, however, Robson did not yield. In a separate letter he reminded Hoover that grain exports from the United States in December and January had been nearly 500,000 tons less than the Allied program called for. In answer to Hoover's queries about Canadian shipments in the same period, Robson conceded that these, too, had been less than the Allies had requested. But, he added, this was largely because the Wheat Export Company had "handed over to the U.S. Food Administration the whole of the stock of our Canadian wheat at Buffalo at the close of navigation." Once again Robson pleaded for bulk grain—if not in the form of wheat (which Hoover refused),[101] then of corn. Robson coupled his request with flattery, thanking Hoover for his "very great efforts" in behalf of the Allies. But he reiterated that without bulk grain of some kind he could not possibly fulfill the inter-Allied program.[102]

There now occurred a denouement that illuminated another aspect of Hoover's approach to controversy. Evidently both he and Robson realized that their heated exchange of January 26 and 29 did not look good on paper. The two men therefore immediately devised a way to sanitize the record. Robson now wrote Hoover a new letter dated January 26, similar to his original letter of that date but without the passages that Hoover found offensive. Hoover's secretary then wrote Robson a bland, one-line letter of acknowledgment dated January 29—the date of Hoover's initial feisty reply. The two men thereupon arranged to place these polite letters in their files as substitutes for the originals. Hoover's secretary then returned to Robson his original letter of the twenty-sixth, and Robson returned Hoover's original reply. This arrangement, said Hoover's secretary, would "keep the matter in order and clear the files of any objectionable material."[103]

Not quite. Unknown, in all likelihood, to Robson, Hoover retained a photostat of Robson's original letter of the twenty-sixth.[104] The clever and ever vigilant Food Administrator thus possessed both the true documentary record and the official one.

Hoover and Robson might paper over their anger, but the controversy that agitated them could no longer be contained. At the end of January the prime ministers of Great Britain, France, and Italy gathered in Versailles for a meeting of the Supreme War Council. There they learned from the Wheat Executive that the cereals import schedule approved back in November was not being met.[105] Ignoring Hoover and Robson, on February 2 the three prime ministers intervened directly with President Wilson.

The Allied leaders cabled Washington that the export of cereals from North America in December and January had been nearly a million tons below the quota fixed in November and that the deficit portended an "especially serious" condition in the months just ahead. The Allied heads of government did not fault Hoover. Relying on the analysis of the Wheat Executive, they attributed the failure to American rail congestion, a shortage of railroad cars, and a shortage of coal, all aggravated by the harsh winter. The Wheat Executive in fact praised Hoover and declared that if it was to secure the minimum grain necessary, the Railroad and Fuel administrations must make "no less" of an effort than he. The Wheat Executive requested—

and the three prime ministers concurred—that President Wilson grant "absolute priority" to the sending of 1,000,000 tons of grain to them in the months of February and March. The "need of cereals in Europe cannot be exaggerated," they said. Acutely aware that food shortages had led to revolution in Russia, the Allied premiers declared that "the dearth of wheat" in their own lands, and the risk this posed to public morale, now constituted "the greatest danger threatening the allied nations of Europe."[106]

This extraordinary cable, coming only days after Hoover had told the President that the United States was not behind in its obligations, must have been embarrassing to the Food Administrator. On February 9, in response to a presidential request for comment, Hoover replied. He now acknowledged that the Allied cereals importation program adopted in November was not being met and that the United States bore some responsibility for the deficit. According to the table of figures that he submitted, there would be a failure in deliveries to the Allies from all sources of 1,444,000 tons for the three months of December, January, and February. Having admitted this much, Hoover immediately tried to shift the blame elsewhere. He told the President that only 37 percent of the deficit was attributable to the United States. The rest, he said, was the consequence of short shipments from Canada, Argentina, and elsewhere.

Hoover did not disclose that Canada's own deficit was substantially due to the Food Administration's borrowing of 16,200,000 tons of Canadian wheat in transit in order to keep American mills operating through the winter. Nor did he mention (though the figures he gave revealed it) that the United States was actually responsible for nearly 60 percent of the deficiency in December and January—without counting what it had diverted from Canada. Moreover, by adding projected deliveries in February to actual deliveries in the previous two months, Hoover made his three-month total look much better for himself. He did so by assuming that the United States would virtually meet its February quota while all other countries would fail to meet theirs. At this early point in the month, with the American railroad muddle still unresolved, it was a very optimistic assumption.

But if Hoover had once again tried to disguise American responsibility for the Allies' desperation, he was on firmer ground in analyzing the cause. In the remainder of his letter, he told the President that a "great degeneration in transportation" was impeding the movement of critical foodstuffs at home. As a result, vast quantities of corn were in danger of rotting, the domestic distribution of wheat substitutes was stalled, and the "consuming centers" of the nation were suffering "growing areas of short supply." The "fundamental dislocation," said Hoover, was a shortage of railroad cars in the grain belt—a condition resulting from the blockage in the East. In other words (though he did not say it directly), the crisis was neither his fault nor within his power to resolve.[107]

Wherever the responsibility might lie, the need for effective action was imperative. As January yielded icily to February, the battle line shifted. It was no longer a case of Hoover versus Garfield, of Hoover versus the Allies, or of everyone against the numbing weather. The Food Administrator now came into conflict with another embattled bureaucrat: the President's own son-in-law, William G. McAdoo.

III

THE confrontation between the Food and Railroad administrations had begun to develop several weeks earlier. In late December Hoover learned of yet another unforeseen crisis: industry was groaning under an unexpected avalanche of pork and beef. Officially Hoover and his associates attributed the glut of pork to "transportation difficulties in the East," and the superabundance of beef to the success of his campaign for "meatless" days.[108] But other, less publicized factors also contributed to the congestion in the stockyards. Since November, the Allied meat-purchasing agency known as APEC had been so strapped for dollars that it was unable to place significant orders in the American market.[109] Complicating matters further was the U.S. Department of Agriculture's discovery that on January 1, 1918 the nation actually had about 71,000,000 hogs, nearly *eleven million* more than the department had estimated just four months before.[110] It was a disconcerting commentary on the reliability of the government's statistics, the fecundity of hogs, or both.

Hoover now confronted an emergency that threatened to overwhelm the packers and wreck the stabilization plan that he had just instituted. In mid-December, as the stockyards in Chicago reeled from the heavy run of live hogs, the Food Administration took the extraordinary step of publicly exhorting farmers to withhold their hogs from the Chicago market.[111] It was, at best, a temporary palliative. In the last analysis, the only solution to Hoover's difficulty lay in coaxing or compelling his European allies to purchase the American packers' surplus.

Would the Allies—could the Allies—come to his rescue? On January 6, 1918 Hoover dispatched a cable to London, offering 50,000,000 pounds of beef and 150,000,000 pounds of pork over the next two months. America's storage facilities were crammed with frozen beef, he reported, and unless he could "get relief," he would be obliged to abandon his conservation efforts. This, he declared, would be a "disaster" for the Allies, for it would "greatly destroy the psychology of saving" among the American people.[112] Hoover boldly promised that, if the British found the necessary ships to carry his excess beef and pork, the Food Administration would "give its support to such financial arrangement as may be necessary."[113] In other words, Hoover would exert pressure on the U.S. Treasury to cover the Allied purchases.

The British were willing to accept Hoover's surprising bonanza but estimated that they would have to borrow an additional $61,000,000 from the U.S. government to pay for it. They soon sent word of their need to the custodian of such loans: Secretary of the Treasury McAdoo.[114]

McAdoo was very annoyed. Not only had the British sprung a major new request for money upon him when he was already having "extreme difficulty" meeting all the demands upon his funds. To make matters worse, it seemed to him that Hoover was goading the British into seeking supplies that they did not immediately require. Even more irritating was the fact that Hoover had instigated the British appeal without first consulting the Inter-Allied Council, which was supposed to advise McAdoo on how to allocate his monthly loans. McAdoo asked President Wilson to have Hoover represented on this council, where, presumably, the Food Administrator would be bound by its recommendations.[115]

The President forwarded McAdoo's complaints to Hoover, along with the opinion that McAdoo's general position was correct. We must "avoid every ounce of additional" strain upon the Treasury at this juncture, the chief executive cautioned, and there ought to be "coordination of the most intimate sort in big transactions of this kind." Gently but unmistakably, the President was advising his Food Administrator not to be a lone wolf.[116]

With both McAdoo and his father-in-law thinking in tandem, Hoover scrambled to justify his action. He told the President that the $61,000,000 loan which Great Britain now sought should be considered not as a new burden on American finance but merely as an "advance in time" that would enable the British to benefit from the present temporary surplus and cut down on their pork purchases later. Trying hard to blunt the implication that he had dealt with the British outside of channels and behind McAdoo's back, Hoover asserted that he had recommended to McAdoo a month before that the Treasury set aside a "regular and definite" amount of its loans for Allied food purchases made in the United States. Had McAdoo done this, Hoover seemed to suggest, there would be no crisis now. Above all, Hoover emphasized what he said the British had not disclosed: that the real purpose of the loan was to maintain the stability of American hog prices at a level high enough to encourage farmers to raise more pigs. Unless "our temporary surplus is absorbed by the foreign demand," Hoover argued, the price of hogs in the American market would slump, producers would become discouraged from breeding more hogs, and Hoover would be compelled to abolish his conservation measures in order to dispose of the unanticipated surplus. Soon, of course, the glut would vanish, but no surge of hog production would replace it. The American people would then be short of meat, and "stabilized prices" would disappear. He did not need to mention the social turmoil that might ensue.[117]

Hoover's reply proved convincing and catalytic. The necessary loan money materialized, APEC began purchasing bacon and ham in large quantities, and a smash-up of the domestic hog market was averted.[118] But Secretary McAdoo did not retreat gracefully. He told the President bluntly that the U.S. Treasury could not "arbitrarily stipulate" the amount of loan money that Allied borrowers must spend in America on foodstuffs (as Hoover requested). The Allies, after all, were "entitled to a voice" in deciding their own priorities. Nor, said McAdoo, was it possible to permit Hoover and the Allied food controllers to "determine their programs without reference to the other war necessities and the financial problems." As for Hoover's reasons for having Great Britain "buy food in excess of [its] immediate requirements"—reasons "not stated" by the British themselves—McAdoo declared sarcastically: "I am glad to have the very convincing reasons for these extraordinary demands upon the United States Treasury thus made a matter of record."[119]

In the end Hoover got his way. But his manner of doing so left a residue of antagonism at the Treasury.

It was not pork, however, but the domestic transportation crisis that did most to set Hoover and McAdoo on a collision course in the weeks after Christmas 1917. Late in December one of Julius Barnes's colleagues at the Grain Corporation notified Hoover that 40,000 railroad cars were needed to move grain from farms to terminals in the corn belt.[120] Barnes concurred with this assessment.[121] A few days later, during McAdoo's very first week as railroad administrator, Barnes proposed that the Grain Corporation control the allocation of railcars for the distribution of cereals. He argued that his agency's precise knowledge of grain stocks and movements would yield unprecedented efficiency in transportation.[122] On its face Barnes's proposal made sense. Hoover himself soon advised McAdoo that the Food Administration's existing network of agents, with their contacts at rural grain elevators, could, in cooperation with the railroads, "greatly minimize the haulage" of corn and oats.[123] Struggling to create his own bureaucratic base, McAdoo may have suspected that Hoover was trying to encroach upon his turf. Still, McAdoo politely acknowledged the Food Administrator's offer and promised to direct the western units of the nascent Railroad Administration to cooperate with Hoover's men.[124]

Despite this pledge, and despite McAdoo's hiring of Hoover's transportation director as an assistant, little effective cooperation developed. By late January Hoover could restrain himself no longer. At a special meeting of the Council of National Defense on the twenty-third, he predicted that unless the railroads sent 20,000 boxcars to the West *immediately* for the movement of wheat and corn, the United States would be unable to provide the Allies the food needed to sustain their armies on a minimal ration.[125] Upon hearing his dismal assessment, the council arranged for Secretary of War Baker to press McAdoo to take immediate action.[126]

The Food Administrator did not confine himself to behind-the-scenes maneuvering. Three days later he went public, asserting in the press that the congestion on the rails had virtually suspended the law of supply and demand. The shortage of railcars, he charged, had created an artificial famine in corn and a consequent surge in food prices. Don't blame me, he seemed to be saying, for the government's failure to control inflation and adequately succor the Allies.[127]

On January 26 a delegation of Allied diplomats warned McAdoo that the food needs of Europe needed "diligent attention" from American authorities.[128] That same day, still another brutal blizzard paralyzed the Middle West. By one uncontrollable act of nature the efforts of the past three weeks to unsnarl the railroads had been negated.[129]

Two days before this latest turn in the weather, Julius Barnes informed Hoover bluntly "that we are facing a possible catastrophe, and that in self-defense you should put the responsibility where it belongs, which is on the management of our railroads."[130] On January 28 Hoover attempted to do just that. In a six-page letter to McAdoo, he asserted that the "railway demoralization" was worsening and that the government faced the "imperious necessity" of transferring not 20,000 but 30,000 boxcars at once to the western lines. Because of the continuing "failure in freight movement," the food supply in the East was degenerating, prices were spiraling, and "acute local famines" were either imminent or under way. Hoover denied that he was writing in "a spirit of criticism"; after all, the weather had been "beyond all human control." But he pleaded with McAdoo for "much more drastic action," including a suspension of westbound passenger service and a complete embargo on all but essential, war-related freights in "the critical sections of the country." The time had come, he concluded, for more than merely local embargoes and priority orders.[131] It was a measure of his growing fears and desire for self-protection that he sent a copy of his letter on to President Wilson.[132]

By now the crisis on the railways was interfering with more than the shipment of grain. On January 28 Hoover announced to the press that the eastern portion of the country was about to face "a temporary scarcity of fresh meat" and that the cause was "difficulty in transporting" it. The Food Administrator was worried that the nation's sellers of meat would take advantage of the confusion and raise their prices out of all proportion to their costs. "This must not happen," he thundered. He thereupon ordered America's meat packers and retailers not to sell their products at prices exceeding "a normal average margin above cost." If any retailer "violated this instruction," his licensed suppliers would be told to cut him off.[133]

If Hoover was feeling the unpleasant consequences of the transportation mess, the Director General of Railroads was not enthralled by the growing chorus of demands upon him. According to McAdoo, the cause of the railcar problem had been the excessive shipment of grain to port cities in the Northeast. If more of the food bound for the Allies had been routed to southeastern and Gulf ports, the grain belt would have many more railcars now.[134] McAdoo implied that the difficulty lay not with his railroads but with the Food Administration. If it would provide him precise data on the location of grain awaiting shipment, he said, his organization would duly supply the cars.[135] "What I want," he wrote to the Secretary of War, "is to be told where the stuff is and we will furnish the cars to take it; but someone with authority must force the loading of the cars with the grain or commodities and must tell the railroads where to deliver them."[136] To this end, McAdoo and Hoover announced a car distribution agreement on January 30.[137]

Within three days, under this new arrangement, the Food Administration Grain Corporation conveyed to McAdoo's agency requests for nearly four thousand railcars—all stipulating exactly where a car should be sent.[138] The Director General could hardly protest that he lacked the detailed information on which to act. But then, just as the government's machinery seemed finally to crank forward, some of the worst weather ever recorded hit the East and Middle West. Ice and drifting snow closed rail lines; freight handlers refused to work in the dangerous cold. In Pennsylvania coal production halted and cities ran short of fuel, as trains strove in vain to deliver empty cars to the mines. By February 5 most of the populous East had only a twenty-four-hour supply of coal in its bins. That day, as temperatures plunged below zero in New York City and elsewhere, the railroads in much of the nation were reported to be in their worst condition of the winter.[139]

Hoover became increasingly disturbed—and increasingly willing to vocalize his apprehensiveness. On February 6 he told a meeting of the Council of National Defense that he "could not get food for our allies for lack of cars" and that he had urged McAdoo to take decisive measures, "without result." Garfield chimed in that he could not move coal for the same reason. The council decided to appoint a committee to call upon the Director General of Railroads.[140]

The next day a delegation of high government officials, including Hoover and two Cabinet secretaries, duly vented its frustration on two of McAdoo's lieutenants. Hoover demanded that the railways immediately supply cars to the country grain elevators in the West so that corn could be amassed in primary markets for expeditious transport to Europe.[141] After learning of this plea, McAdoo ordered that preference on the rails temporarily be given to supplying boxcars for the movement of grain in twelve states of the Middle West and Great Plains.[142] It was one of his most sweeping priority orders yet.

But McAdoo was growing irritated by Hoover's tactics. It was "not merely the movement of cars that determines the supply or movement of grain," he reminded Hoover. "The impression must not be created . . . that this matter rests entirely with the railroads. The responsibility of inducing the farmers to send their grain to market does not rest with the railroad companies and cannot be assumed by them." He called upon Hoover and the Secretary of

Agriculture to persuade farmers and grain elevator operators to release their products.[143] The implication was obvious that somebody other than McAdoo was answerable for the obstructed flow of grain.

Mindful, perhaps, of McAdoo's relationship to Woodrow Wilson, Hoover at first professed to be satisfied. He told the President on February 9 that he "entirely agree[d]" that the "efficacy" of the new preference scheme "should be tested for a few days."[144] But Hoover also remarked that he had wanted even stronger measures, and to Colonel House he complained on the tenth that McAdoo was "merely a megaphone" for his railway experts.[145] On February 11 Hoover disclosed to the House Committee on Agriculture that, a few days before, he had sought an order that all railroad cars in the country should be used "exclusively" for the shipment of food. But McAdoo and his assistants "were not able to see eye to eye with me on that," he testified, "and finally we compromised on a preference."[146]

The Food Administrator, however, was not about to settle for a compromise—not when catastrophe seemed to be staring him in the face. On February 12 he wrote to the Director General once more. The situation was "critical," Hoover contended. A billion bushels of corn and over 100,000 carloads of potatoes were at risk. It was "of absolutely transcendent importance" that the soft corn be moved to drying facilities before April; otherwise it would rot and be lost. "There is no question whatever," Hoover asserted (in rebuttal to McAdoo's last letter) of the willingness of farmers to market their crops. The problem was "the failure of the railways." Hoover thereupon pointedly renewed his weeks-old request for more drastic action, including partial suspension of passenger service and the use of all suitable railroad cars exclusively for the movement of food.[147] Once again he was asserting that his priorities mattered more than anyone else's.

By now the worried Food Administrator was becoming frantic. On February 14 he notified McAdoo that bakeries in the Northeast had run out of flour while flour mills in Minneapolis were operating at but a fraction of capacity—all because of a crippling dearth of railroad cars. Visions of urban violence and administrative failure haunted him. ". . . I can see no way in which we can load the Allied boats," he said, "and at the same time prevent disturbances in our eastern cities." He begged McAdoo to do something efficacious.[148]

That same day, at Hoover's request, McAdoo issued an embargo order affecting nine grain-producing states in the nation's heartland. He decreed that until "the urgent movement" of grain to primary markets had been completed in these states, he would permit no railroad boxcars to be used to ship grain from these markets to points east of Ohio.[149] It was a way of accelerating the flow of grain into major interior terminals, where it could be dried out and accumulated for Allied purchase. The order may also have been McAdoo's way of trying to funnel more grain to ports along the Gulf of

Mexico, away from the clogged Northeast. For Hoover, campaigning relentlessly for even tougher measures, it was a belated step in the right direction.

By now echoes of the emergency were reverberating at the White House. On February 14 the new British ambassador, Lord Reading, explained to the President the "urgent necessity" of conveying more food to the seaboard. The President replied that the U.S. government was doing all that it could.[150] A few days later Hoover wrote to the President in a tone of even greater alarm. While acknowledging that McAdoo's preference order had brought some improvement, Hoover declared that the movement of railcars to the East had been insufficient either for domestic or Allied requirements. As a result, he now confronted a "renewed failure in Allied shipments" coupled with an ever-shrinking supply of foodstuffs in the heavily populated East.[151] President Wilson quickly sent Hoover's letter on to McAdoo with a cover note stating that Hoover was not exaggerating. Wilson also added pointedly that he knew that McAdoo would "make every possible effort to get cars into the West."[152]

Meanwhile, on February 13, Harry Garfield had bounced back into the news by announcing the suspension of "heatless Mondays." It was a consequence, he claimed, of a "vast improvement" in "coal and transportation conditions." With the exception of New England, businesses east of the Mississippi were free at last to operate without fuel restrictions.[153]

For Hoover, gloomy as ever, this development did little to dispel his intuition of impending calamity. On February 18, at a meeting of the Council of National Defense, he again criticized McAdoo.[154] On February 20, in a story carried on its front page, the *New York Times* reported that the railroads were unable to deliver enough supplies at Atlantic ports to fill the cargo space of waiting British ships.[155] This embarrassing allegation may well have emanated from Hoover himself.[156] The Railroad Administration, in any case, denied that the disclosure was true.[157] When, on February 21, the Council of National Defense discussed the emergency, Hoover, Garfield, and Edward Hurley of the Shipping Board joined in a chorus of discontent. Everything now "depended upon transportation," they argued; there was "no use of meeting" unless McAdoo or his representative were there. The council decided to invite him to its future sessions.[158] Another opportunity to resolve the emergency had slipped away.

For Hoover, it was apparently the last straw. Late on February 21 he issued an extraordinary statement to the press. For the first time he acknowledged publicly that since December 1 the Food Administration had "fallen far behind" in its deliveries of essential supplies to the Allies. In fact, it would be short by 45,000,000 bushels of cereals alone by the end of February. This "deficiency," he announced, was "due solely" to "railway congestion." But the debacle, he went on, involved much more than shipments to the Allies. During the past three months the distribution of food to America's own cities and storage centers had also lagged severely, thereby imperiling perishable foodstuffs, disturbing prices, and nearly exhausting the food reserves in many "large consuming areas." As a result of the accumulated delays in transport, said Hoover, "The next sixty days will be the most critical period in our food history."

Hoover urged the public to cooperate in every way to lessen the burden on the railroads. He asserted that at least 8,000,000 bushels of grain must be loaded daily for the next two months—a rate the nation had not yet come close to reaching. Most boldly of all, he declared without qualification that "no solution exists" except expanded efforts by McAdoo's agency to move foodstuffs "in every direction to the exclusion of much other commerce of the country."[159] It was a radical prescription, one he had been advocating for weeks. It was also one that McAdoo's experts considered both impractical and unnecessary.[160]

The next day the newspapers of America reported Hoover's statement in a blaze of stories. Whether from reasoned alarm, excessive gloom, exasperation, fear of political failure, or other motives, he had gone public in a way meant to shock. And shock he did. "Hoover Warns East of a Food Shortage," ran a typical headline.[161] The simmering dispute between the Food and Railroad administrations had finally, spectacularly, boiled over.[162]

McAdoo and his associates were infuriated. Not only was Hoover badgering them again; he was doing so in a public and hair-raising manner. To be sure, Hoover in his press release had refrained from criticizing the railroad directorate overtly and had even acknowledged the "considerable progress" it had been making in recent days. He had also noted that the weather in January had been "insuperable."[163] To the Director General of Railroads these gestures did not compensate for Hoover's incitement of "a blurred but all-pervading notion [in the public] that the railroads have been and still are broken down"—an impression both "incorrect and unjust."[164] Moreover, by imputing all food supply problems to the railroads, Hoover, in McAdoo's view, had absolved all other relevant agencies from their responsibility for meeting the difficulty.

If Hoover thought that his sensational press release would prod McAdoo into an outright ban on certain kinds of rail traffic, he miscalculated. McAdoo was a southerner—and of partial Celtic ancestry to boot. Instead of capitulating, he counterattacked. In a letter to Hoover on February 22, he asserted that Hoover surely must know the precise location of food he obtained for the Allies, as well as the domestic ports to which he wanted these purchases sent.

> If you will notify me from time to time of the location of the specific supplies and the port or ports in the United States to which you wish to have such supplies transported, I will guarantee the necessary transportation, subject alone to interruptions from blizzards and floods.

In plain contradiction of Hoover's warning of a sixty-day food crisis, McAdoo gave his assurance that "so far as transportation is concerned, there is no danger of suffering from a serious food shortage in the eastern part of the country."[165]

The next day the Director General's retort appeared in the press, along with a Railroad Administration statement that the railways were making "an extraordinary effort" and were already loading 6,000,000 bushels of grain per day, a figure that would increase with improving weather.[166] The newspapers also reported that Railroad Administration officials did not believe Hoover's pessimism to be supported by the evidence.[167]

In the opinion of one Cabinet official, Hoover was "tenacious in carrying out his views but not willing to go fully to bat."[168] In response to McAdoo, Hoover now lent some credence to this theory. Apparently taken aback by McAdoo's rejoinder, Hoover and his staff sought cover in ill-feigned politeness. On the evening of the twenty-second, the Food Administration, on Hoover's authority, issued a statement calling McAdoo's letter "very reassuring" since it presaged more cars for the western grain terminals and an end to the shortage of shipments from West to East.[169] The next day, in a letter to McAdoo, Hoover declared himself "grateful" for McAdoo's note. He expressed his "great relief" at obtaining McAdoo's "assurance" that supplies for the Allies would move "promptly" and that no dangerous delays in home distribution would occur. Hoover concluded loftily that McAdoo's "assurance" would "greatly quiet the growing apprehension in the country of the last few weeks."[170] In short, Hoover had slyly chosen to interpret McAdoo's note as an unqualified promise to deliver the goods.

McAdoo, however, had made no such blanket assurance, and he may have detected a whiff of sarcasm in Hoover's reply. In any case, the irate Director General immediately fired back:

> I am just in receipt of your letter of the 23d. You do not, however, touch the points of my letter. I should like to enumerate and reemphasize them.
>
> (1) You are, as I understand it, the sole purchaser in this country of food supplies for the Allied Governments.
>
> (2) You must, therefore, know the location of the food supplies which you from time to time purchase and the ports in the United States to which you desire such supplies shipped.
>
> (3) If you will notify me from time to time of the location of the specific supplies and the port or ports in the United States to which you wish to have supplies transported, I will guarantee the necessary transportation, subject alone to interruption from blizzards and floods.
>
> I am eager to cooperate with you to relieve all anxiety about food supplies for the Allies. Will you cooperate with me by promptly furnishing me with the essential information called for in items 1 and 2 above? If you do, the transportation will be provided.

Then McAdoo added, with scarcely veiled sarcasm of his own, "You can readily understand that generalizations will not accomplish the object in view and that we must be specific in order to get results."[171]

The next day Hoover's and McAdoo's letters appeared verbatim in the press.[172] Meanwhile the Director General complained angrily to President Wilson that Hoover's letter of February 19 to the White House had been "far from accurate" and his press release of February 21 "unjustifiably alarming." McAdoo accused Hoover not only of unfairly blaming the railroads but of stimulating panic-buying and thus an artificial food shortage by claiming that a "desperate domestic food shortage" was at hand. McAdoo charged that Hoover's statement would encourage farmers to withhold their crops from the market in the hope of obtaining higher prices and would give "genuine aid and comfort" to the nation's enemies if they should learn of it. McAdoo insisted that he wanted to cooperate with Hoover, "but I do think that constant statements unduly alarming the country and inexcusably inaccurate ought to be stopped." He added that he was not embroiled in any controversy with the Food Administrator but was merely trying "to pin Mr. Hoover down" to specifics, the basis of "real cooperation."[173]

Despite this disavowal, and despite his and Hoover's attempts to deny that they were feuding,[174] the two men's associates in government knew a row when they saw one. For several days the highly publicized exchanges between the two administrators were the talk of Washington. At the State Department, where Hoover's abrasiveness had more than once ruffled diplomatic feathers, Third Assistant Secretary of State Breckinridge Long hoped that McAdoo would put the Food Administration in its place. "Hoover," said Long, "has a habit of blaming other people for failures in his own operation. He tries to make a written record for future reference and lay the blame for all failures, of record, on other people. He has tried it with this Dept. & with others."[175] At the Navy Department, Secretary Josephus Daniels felt that Hoover "had been the aggressor" and should retract a statement based upon incorrect information.[176] On February 25 Secretary of Agriculture Houston—long resentful of the Food Administration's very existence—entered the fray by contradicting Hoover outright. The secretary told a Congressional committee that there was no reason for the American people to be alarmed about the food supply. A number of surprised congressmen began to suspect that someone in the executive branch was passing the buck.[177]

But Hoover had his defenders, notably his longtime booster, Secretary of the Interior Franklin K. Lane.[178] The Food Administration's recently retired counsel, Curtis Lindley, also sided with the Chief. To Lindley, McAdoo's "insistence upon pointing out exactly where things are, and promising to immediately ship them" did not seem completely sincere.[179] For Hoover and his associates, McAdoo's demand for specifics was a self-serving ploy.

Whatever McAdoo's motive, it was Hoover who now retreated. On February 24 his agency announced that in two or three days it would have in place an organization that would keep McAdoo "completely informed" of the nation's "car necessities" for food. Under this new arrangement, the Food Administration would collect daily reports from Allied purchasing agents as to their requirements and would then convey these data directly to the Railroad Administration.[180] Hoover also abandoned his stunning prediction of a sixty-day food crisis. The Food Administration officially ascribed its new confidence in the future to McAdoo's "assurances as to the supply of cars, if brought to his attention."[181] On February 25 Hoover sent McAdoo a politely worded memorandum on their problems and suggested that their lieutenants get together to resolve them.[182]

That same day Hoover, McAdoo, and several associates met in conference. According to the *New York Times*, they made "definite progress . . . toward a satisfactory solution" of their differences. McAdoo promised that his transportation system would satisfy the nation's and the Allies' food requirements if Hoover's agency furnished the necessary information. McAdoo also flatly asserted that there was no danger either of "severe shortages" or a food famine because of transportation problems and that he would supply all railcars needed for food conveyance if a "definite program" were available. Hoover agreed. After the conference, the Director General appointed a commission of experts to cooperate with the Food Administration. The *Times* reported that a "satisfactory understanding" had been attained and that "the hatchet had been buried."[183]

The process of burial may have been a bit more colorful than this—at least if McAdoo's later recollection was correct. In his memoirs, McAdoo recalled that Hoover did not answer his second, pointed letter demanding specifics. Instead, the Food Administration's counsel, William A. Glasgow, Jr., telephoned McAdoo with a request for an interview. According to McAdoo:

> They [Glasgow and Hoover] came to my office. Glasgow did all the talking. Hoover sat with downcast eyes, like a diffident schoolboy. Beyond the greeting as he came in, and his good-bye when he left, I do not recall that he had anything to say. Glasgow told me, on Hoover's behalf, that the Food Administration wanted to coöperate with me in every possible way; that Mr. Hoover regretted his statement [press release] that had appeared in the "Times"; that the publication was a mistake and he hoped it would not interfere with our cordial relations.
>
> I said that I had been giving the Food Administration preference all along in transportation and that I would continue to do all I could to help, but that I thought Mr. Hoover should make his complaints to me and not to the public through the newspapers. Mr. Glasgow said, while Mr. Hoover made a minute examination of the floor, that Mr. Hoover would do that in the future. Mr. Glasgow finished his say, Mr. Hoover completed his inspection of the floor, and they took their departure.

Such was McAdoo's version of the showdown.[184] Hoover did not mention this incident in his own memoirs. But privately, when McAdoo's memoirs appeared in 1931, Hoover denounced the story as (in his wife's words) "a plain lie and invention." According to Hoover, he had never set foot in McAdoo's office in his life.[185]

McAdoo's account may well have been tendentious. Elsewhere in his autobiography he asserted, quite inaccurately, that Hoover had never complained to him or the Railroad Administration along the lines of the "sixty day food crisis" press release.[186] In fact, Hoover had peppered him with similar warnings for weeks. McAdoo also claimed in his memoirs that the transportation problem "was being solved rapidly, day by day" by late February and that Hoover must have known it.[187] This was not—in Hoover's eyes—a true statement of the situation. Despite the very recent improvement on the rails, Hoover drew attention to the enormous backlog of goods to be moved and the continuing shortage of cars. Moreover, the problem for Hoover in late February was not one of failure to give priority to the transport of Allied foodstuffs from big interior markets to the coast—a point which he explicitly conceded and which McAdoo seized upon. What worried Hoover was the sluggish movement of food products from farms and remote rural locations into the interior markets and terminals.[188] *This* was where the rail system was deficient, said Hoover. If we could not first get the food to these central markets, the Allies would be unable to buy and accumulate it, and the eastern cities would eventually run short as well. McAdoo, at least in his memoirs, seemed not to grasp the gravamen of Hoover's complaint.

Whatever the respective merits of their positions, Hoover and McAdoo now settled into a posture of uneasy cooperation. In the weeks ahead they exchanged a number of superficially polite letters containing enclosures that tended to impute responsibility for troubles to the other man's agency.[189] Looking back on the dispute that had flared briefly but dangerously in late February, Secretary of the Navy Daniels suspected—perhaps rightly—that what had occurred was a clash between two rival aspirants for the presidency.[190]

Skirmish or not, Hoover never forgot his humiliation. Years later, in an unpublished portion of his memoirs, he denounced McAdoo as a demagogue, a "promoter," and a "complete 'phoney' " whose "high offices," marriage to President Wilson's daughter, and "personal, but government-paid, publicity bureau" had made him "the most arrogant person in Washington." McAdoo, he charged, had used the war "to build for the Presidency" and had mostly surrounded himself with "politicians." His own wife "ultimately could not stand him," said Hoover, "and secured a divorce." According to Hoover, McAdoo's "shoddy character" eventually undid him—a reference, no doubt, to McAdoo's postwar embroilment in the Teapot Dome scandal.[191]

Despite their lasting mutual detestation, neither McAdoo nor Hoover could afford to indulge in prolonged public bickering. The fate of the Allied food supply, and perhaps of the war itself, was in the balance. On February

20 H. T. Robson of the Wheat Export Company in New York pleaded with Hoover's organization for 1,100,000 tons of grain in the month of March. The Allied agent disclosed that he had not yet secured 300,000 tons of it, and he begged that this deficit be filled in the form of bulk wheat. Nothing else would do, he argued. The crisis was "so extremely grave" as to permit no substitutes.[192]

Two days later the British ambassador to the United States, joined by high-ranking Italian and French representatives in Washington, seconded Robson's appeal in a letter to Hoover himself. The situation was "most critical," they warned; it could be resolved only by his releasing bulk wheat from his reserves. A "failure to make adequate shipments in March," they added, "may produce events of incalculable gravity in both Europe and America." The Allies also put pressure on McAdoo and emphasized that they had the ships to carry the food if it got to the seaboard.[193]

Hoover's supervisor of the grain trade, Julius Barnes, was reluctant to accede totally to the Allied request. For one thing, American reserves of wheat were shrinking rapidly, and no one knew whether cantankerous farmers, again hoping for a higher wheat price, would market the remainder of their 1917 crop.[194] Furthermore, Barnes contended, the Food Administration needed bulk wheat at home to keep the flour mills running and avert a shortage of bread.[195] Nevertheless, faced with the second Allied diplomatic intervention in a month, he and Hoover tried to fill the March quota in some fashion. Within a few days they managed to line up enough grain from various sources to meet the Allied tonnage requirements. In a break with Hoover's hitherto unyielding policy, the designated cargo even included 125,000 tons of bulk wheat.[196]

Hoover was not enthusiastic about this result. He informed President Wilson that the coming shipments constituted "a very considerable diversion from our domestic demands," and that it would "sooner or later precipitate us into difficulties with our own supplies. We felt, however, that it was your wish that we should take care of their pressing necessities."[197] In this subtle way, Hoover hinted that if trouble arose at home because of these exports it would not be *his* fault. He was only doing what the President wanted.

The Director General of Railroads also hastened to allay the Allies' distress. He declared that he was prepared "to go to any length" to convey food to the seaboard, and he promised them—as he promised Hoover—to provide the requisite railcars if he were kept properly informed. More concretely, on February 21 McAdoo announced that for the next month six special trains filled with meat and pork products for the Allies would leave Chicago daily for the east coast.[198]

Such were the promises. This time—thanks to improving efficiency, better interagency coordination, and, perhaps most crucially, warmer weather—the U.S. government was able to keep its word. In late February and March a tremendous aggregation of foodstuffs descended by rail on the principal port facilities of the Northeast. Storage depots up and down the east coast were overwhelmed.[199] During March the United States and Canada finally succeeded in shipping about 1,100,000 tons of foodstuffs to the Allies—three quarters of it in the form of grain and grain products. It was a substantial improvement over February's dismal showing.[200]

For the anxious Allies, the worst was over. Although total North American grain deliveries to Europe between December and March had fallen considerably short of projections,[201] the amount shipped had been enough to avert the Allies' worst fear: hunger and mass privation on their home front. At least one British observer in Washington gave much of the credit for this to Hoover, who, he said, "stands head and shoulders above the other American war executives."[202]

But every solution, it seemed, left a new problem in its wake. On March 1, 1918 American wheat reserves were 78,000,000 bushels fewer than those of a year before and were dwindling daily.[203] As the sun crossed the equator in March, Hoover repeatedly had to ask himself how much more of the precious grain he could let go. Would his countrymen make it to the next harvest without depleting their remaining stocks too soon? Complicating his task, as we shall now see, was a new commitment he had made to export still more wheat and flour if he could conserve it.

The winter emergency was over, but the spring emergency was not far behind.

9

"The Hour of Our Testing"

I

ON December 28, 1917 Robson and Stoddart of the Wheat Export Company met with Hoover and Julius Barnes in New York.[1] Stoddart was just back from London, where the Wheat Executive had handed him a revised schedule of projected cereals imports until the next harvest. He warned that unless this program was fulfilled, "it would mean disaster for the Allied cause."[2]

The table that Stoddart carried with him must have brought satisfaction to Hoover. In response to Alonzo Taylor's hard bargaining in his behalf, the Wheat Executive had drastically scaled down the amount of wheat and flour it expected the United States to deliver by July 1918. The new table asked for only 900,000 tons, or about 33,000,000 bushels, to be shipped between December and February.[3] Hoover, as we have seen, had already agreed to this request earlier in December. At his conference with Robson and Stoddart on the twenty-eighth, he even pledged to exceed the target for total North American cereals exports that the Wheat Executive had set for the next two months.[4]

For the nervous officials of the Wheat Export Company, Hoover's assurances must have been music to their ears. The very next day they received still more. Ever since mid-autumn Hoover had been insisting that the United States had no statistical surplus of wheat left to export. The country, he had contended, had already shipped overseas all the available wheat that it could spare, based upon its normal requirements before the next harvest.[5] On the other hand, by his own calculations America must supply 75,000,000 more bushels than it had already committed if the Allies were to pull through.[6] On December 29 he tried to square the circle. He informed the Wheat Export Company that despite his statistically exhausted reserves, the United States would nevertheless provide the Allies 1,565,000 tons of wheat and flour between January and April, a quantity that he thought he could save through conservation measures. But—he added—he would permit these deliveries (equivalent, he said, to 70,000,000 bushels) only with a significant "reservation": all such exports must be considered an advance, to be replaced later upon demand from *Canadian* stocks if the United States needed these to maintain its own wheat supplies before the next harvest. Uppermost, as always, in his mind was the conviction that his countrymen must not run short of flour in the spring. No doubt to soften the blow, he assured Robson that he would not dip into the Canadian surplus unless it were "critically necessary."[7]

Hoover's unilateral "reservation" went far beyond his recent undertakings with the Allies. Early in December, before agreeing to fill the Allied cereals program through February, he had wanted it understood that if America supplied the Allies with "deficiencies" of wheat which Canada could not deliver during the "closed season" on the Great Lakes, he would expect "corresponding amounts" from the Canadians later on.[8] Now, less than a month later, Hoover insisted not merely on recovering whatever he loaned against immovable Canadian stocks during the winter. He now demanded the right to seize up to 70,000,000 *additional* bushels from Canada any time before the next harvest. This represented more than half of what the Canadians were supposed to ship to Europe during the entire 1917–18 crop year.

From Hoover's point of view, it was a reasonable bargain. After all, he did not have to promise 1,565,000 tons of American wheat and flour at this juncture to the Allies—an amount he might not truly be able to part with. In his eyes, his "reservation" was only prudent, a safeguard against a domestic bread famine and urban disorder. In any showdown between foreign and American wants, Hoover, as ever, was determined that his country's interests would prevail. No "Sir Herbert," he.

On the other hand, Canada was a part of the British empire, and the Allies were counting on Canadian wheat for themselves. Indeed, they had already purchased the entire Canadian crop. Robson, stationed in New York, therefore could hardly commit his principals to Hoover's new offer all by himself. No doubt Hoover assumed that Robson would clear the deal with London. In any event, Robson apparently acquiesced in Hoover's stipulation.[9] So far as the Chief was concerned, the deed was done.

Hoover's intention to use Canadian wheat as an American insurance policy soon precipitated an international row. But for the moment, his turnabout of late December committed him to something else: a renewed crusade for domestic food conservation, a crusade more comprehensive than anything he had yet attempted. Even as he struggled to keep his promise to ship 33,000,000 bushels of surplus wheat and flour to Europe between December and February, he began to work on the concurrent project that now transcended it: the saving and sending of far more wheat than this.

To all appearances it was a daunting challenge. By January 1, 1918 the United States had already exported more than 60,000,000 bushels of wheat since the previous July.[10] According to Hoover this completely exhausted the amount that could be spared from the 1917 harvest, *unless the American people curtailed their consumption.*[11] The cautious Food Administrator was not willing to bet that they would do so of their own untutored accord. They would need, he believed, an infusion of Hooverian guidance, and this he now prepared to give them as never before.

II

ALL during the autumn Hoover had been beating the drums for voluntary food conservation. "Meatless" Tuesdays, "wheatless" Wednesdays, and "Hooverized" meals had become popular customs as much of the public responded to his "gospel of the clean plate." In mid-December, after warning that the European food crisis was "far graver" than previously believed, he asked holders of Food Administration home cards to restrict their diets further by abstaining from pork products on Saturdays and by reducing their consumption of candy and soft drinks.[12] Publicly, Hoover claimed great success for his summonses to self-denial. He praised the hotels and restaurants of New York City for vigorously adhering to his conservation rules and saving many tons of food as a result.[13] On December 5 he announced that "for the first time" the national observance of "meatless days" had generated sufficient meat to "partially fulfill our duties to the Allies."[14] A few weeks later he asserted that the American people had saved up to 50,000,000 bushels of wheat in the past five months.[15]

Privately, however, the Food Administrator was not so sanguine. Contrary to the drift of some of his press releases, Hoover no longer believed that voluntarism would be enough. As early as October 22, on the eve of the great pledge campaign that enlisted nearly half of America's families under his banner, he told a friend that the completion of the drive would mean "the ending of an era," and that "stronger" steps would be necessary to get Americans to "consume less."[16] By mid-November—indeed, even before the pledge drive was under way—he had concluded that the introduction of compulsory "war bread" was unavoidable.[17] And when, not long afterward, the President asked him to recommend legislation that the new session of Congress might adopt,[18] Hoover's reply was unequivocal. The Congress, he said, should give the President "general powers"—"enforceable by executive order"—"to control waste, to require substitution of one commodity for another in consumption, and to limit actual consumption of commodities." However much Hoover might publicly espouse the virtues and results of voluntary self-restraint, he now advised the President that "forced food conservation" in manufacturing, distribution, and public places was a "necessity."[19]

What had gone wrong? Despite the fact that 90 percent of what the Food Administration called "first-class hotels" had voluntarily signed its pledge card by early November,[20] large numbers of public eating places in the United States had failed to comply with Hoover's admonitions. Many of these establishments were owned and patronized by the foreign-born, who were often indifferent to or hostile toward Hoover's patriotic propaganda. In New York City alone, out of 18,900 public eating outlets only 8,000 were English-speaking—another obstacle to the propagation of the Food Administrator's "gospel."[21] Frustrated by his inability to stop the "waste" being committed in "pro-German" and other facilities beyond his legal reach, Hoover began to agitate for a new law that would make wheatless and meatless days compulsory in all hotels, restaurants, and railroad dining cars in the country.[22]

By the time Robson and Stoddart came calling, then, in late December, Hoover had long since decided that strictly hortatory devices would not yield him all the wheat that the Allies craved; certainly not the 70,000,000 bushels that he now proceeded to promise them.[23] A new and more coercive effort must be tried.

In early January Hoover laid the groundwork for the coming battle. On January 6 he released a cable from his British counterpart, Lord Rhondda, warning that the British and French food situation was "critical" and that compulsory rationing in England was likely.[24] On the tenth, the Food Administration announced that it would buy up to 30 percent of the output of every flour mill in the United States during 1918 in order to meet the needs of the army, the navy, and the Allies.[25] If the mills did not offer their flour at prices that the Food Administration deemed satisfactory, the agency would requisition what it wanted.[26] The next day Hoover revealed to the country for the first time that the Allies needed 75–90 million additional bushels of American wheat (despite the exhaustion of the exportable surplus) and that he would unveil "a further programme of saving" in a few days. He called upon his fellow citizens to curb their consumption of wheat products still further. At the same time—anxious not to trigger a nationwide hoarding spree—he promised to export only as much as Americans actually saved. He also insisted that no rationing would be necessary. As for enforcement, he was taking, he said, "a line unique among nations" by asking his millions of female followers "to see that our new proposals are carried out on every side." He expressed confidence in the power of the American press to create "public opinion greater than among any other people on earth."[27]

The Food Administrator, however, was not about to rely upon the media to accomplish such a purpose unaided. At once he turned to England for a catalytic expression of anxiety. On January 14 he informed London of his impending drive to conserve 75,000,000 bushels of wheat and asked Lord Rhondda to dispatch him a cable "expressing the imperative necessity of this provision."[28] The British food controller obliged in ringing terms:

> Unless you are able to send the Allies at least 75,000,000 bushels wheat over and above what you have exported up to January 1st and in addition to the total exportable surplus from Canada I cannot take the responsibility of assuring our people that there will be food enough to win the war. Imperative necessity compels me to cable you in this blunt way. No one knows better than I that the American people regardless of national and individual sacrifice have so far refused nothing that is needed for the war, but it now lies with America to decide whether or not the Allies in Europe shall have enough bread to hold out until the United States is able to throw its forces into the field. I have not minced words because I am convinced that the American people if they know the truth will not hesitate to meet the emergency.[29]

Hoover, gratified, cabled back that he would "export every grain of wheat the American people save from their normal consumption," and he recorded his conviction that his countrymen "will not fail to meet the emergency."[30]

Then, in mid-January, just as Hoover was about to initiate his national food conservation appeal, the nation's coal crisis roared to center stage as Harry A. Garfield closed nearly all factories east of the Mississippi River. In the ensuing hurricane of public anger, Hoover could not hope to command media attention for his crisis and was compelled to postpone his campaign for several days.[31] Finally, on January 25, he released Lord Rhondda's cable to the press and informed his fellow citizens that a new conservation drive was imminent. To fulfill foreign needs, he said, Americans must "rigidly reduce" their wheat consumption to "30% below normal until next harvest." They must also cut their pork consumption by 20 percent until the country's hog population increased and must save about 10 percent on sugar. These were not "large percentages," Hoover insisted; "there is no privation in them." Ever fearful of working-class discontent, he added that he would "protect the food supply of our own people," and that the burden of saving must largely fall on the "more fortunately situated." "Those who have most must save most," he concluded.[32]

Despite these dulcet reassurances, it was now apparent that Hoover was seeking an immediate and massive revision of the American diet. The next day he unveiled the details of his plan, along with a supportive proclamation drafted by himself and signed (with minor revisions) by President Wilson.[33] The new regimen was to take effect on January 28. Many of Hoover's "suggestions" (as the presidential proclamation called them) were precisely that: suggestions (or, as Hoover separately labeled them, "rules"), which depended upon voluntary adherence for their efficacy. Thus Hoover asked homes and public eating places to observe two wheatless days a week instead of one, and to maintain the practice of meatless Tuesdays as well as a meatless and wheatless meal every day. He urged consumers, when buying wheat flour, to purchase an equal amount of other cereals simultaneously. When buying bread, they should buy only loaves containing a 20 percent admixture of nonwheat flour.[34] He denounced hoarding as "both selfish and unnecessary"[35] and appealed to his "one police force—the American woman" to organize to ensure obedience to his rules by "that small minority who may fail."[36]

Just what he expected his distaff constabulary to do, Hoover did not explain. But he listed the rules that housewives should follow in their own homes—and why. "There is simply not enough food in Europe," he declared; "North America must furnish the food." With undiminished conviction that his was the most important sector in the war effort, he wrote:

> The whole great problem of winning the war rests primarily on one thing: the loyalty and sacrifice of the American people in the matter of food. It is not a Government responsibility. It is the responsibility of each individual. . . .
>
> If we are selfish or even careless, we are disloyal, we are the enemy at home. Now is the hour of our testing. Let us make it the hour of our victory; victory over ourselves; victory over the enemy of freedom.[37]

All this was a familiar reprise of the Food Administration's conservation drives of the previous summer and autumn. But amidst these idealistic and voluntaristic themes Hoover now injected another element: a sweeping set of compulsory regulations for licensed businesses. He ordered the nation's millers to raise the extraction ratio of flour from wheat to 74 percent—an increase of 2–4 percent from the year before. He ordered bakers of wheat bread to mix their wheat flour with a minimum percentage of other cereals—5 percent immediately, and 20 percent by late February. After that, all commercially made wheat bread in the country would have to contain at least 20 percent nonwheat flour. Such products, he announced, would be known as "Victory Bread."

Hoover also decreed that manufacturers of breakfast cereals, crackers, pastry, spaghetti, and certain other foods must henceforth buy no more than 70 percent of the wheat flour that they had used in 1917. Wholesalers in wheat flour must similarly reduce their purchases from millers. Most stringently of all, Hoover instituted what became known as the 50–50 rule. Under its terms, wholesalers must sell wheat flour to retailers "in the proportion of one pound of wheat flour to one pound of other cereals." Retailers must sell their wheat flour to consumers on the same basis. Thus if a housewife entered a grocery store and asked for ten pounds of wheat flour, the grocer could not sell it to her unless he simultaneously sold her ten pounds of some other cereal flour (made out of ingredients such as corn, barley, or rice).[38]

Once again Hoover had skirted the edge of the law. Under the Lever Act he had no authority to impose direct rationing upon the American people. "The adoption of compulsory rationing" was for Congress to decide, he remarked in late January.[39] But by severely limiting the freedom of businesses which dealt with consumers, he could, by administrative fiat, accomplish much the same result. From now on, if the American people wanted wheat flour, they must purchase an equivalent amount of government-approved substitutes, thereby, he hoped, reducing their consumption of wheat products by 50 percent. And if they wanted to buy a loaf of wheat bread, they would soon discover that it contained at least one fifth of some substitute. Hoover could not prevent housewives from baking 100 percent wheat bread at home if they chose. But in a roundabout way he had moved effectively to constrain them.

The Food Administrator quickly followed up with other coercive acts. Until now, only bakeries that used ten or more barrels of flour per month had been subject to his supervision. On January 31 the President ordered all establishments using as few as three barrels per month to obtain a license.[40] In this way thousands of small bakeshops, restaurants, hotels, and clubs came into Hoover's regulatory orbit.[41] The Food Administration immediately ordered all bakers of cakes, cookies, crackers, pies, and pastry to reduce their use of wheat flour to 70 percent of their comparable 1917 usage for the next six months.[42] It ruled that pies, cakes, and doughnuts would be known as Victory pies, cakes, and doughnuts if (and only if) one third of their flour came from something other than wheat. Nothing less could legally carry the Victory label.[43] On February 15 the Food Administration ordered all licensed public eating places in the United States to serve Victory products only.[44]

No detail, it seemed, eluded Hoover or his associates. The Food Administration decided that all waffles served by its licensees must contain 75 percent wheat substitutes.[45] It announced that public eating places should serve patrons no more than two ounces of bread, or two one-ounce rolls, per meal unless the bread was made entirely from wheat substitutes. In that case, the customer would be permitted four ounces.[46]

Occasionally Hoover had to modify his stringent policies. On February 7 he allowed pies and doughnuts to be sold in public eating places on wheatless days after he learned that his ban on them had caused financial hardship to lunchroom owners in New England. But, typically, he bent his rules as little as possible. He announced that he would countenance such sales only if the products sold were Victory pies and doughnuts, and only if these were made exclusively throughout the week.[47]

Far greater problems attended his imposition of the 50–50 rule, which caught the entire baking industry by surprise. In many areas in the East, retailers lacked sufficient substitute flours to put the measure into effect immediately.[48] The Food Administration's New York branch therefore delayed full implementation of the rule in that state until March 1, thereby giving local businesses time to adjust their inventories.[49]

The Food Administration's sudden and enforced switch to wheat substitutes led to other complications. Bread dealers in New York City claimed that barley, corn, rice, and other cereals cost just as much as wheat flour, and sometimes more, and that the price of Victory bread would surely increase unless the government controlled the price of substitutes.[50] Almost immediately the Administration received complaints that handlers of wheat substitutes were taking advantage of its new wheat policy to hoist the price of the government's touted substitutes.[51] In effect, Hoover had created a sudden market for alternative cereals. The result, he learned a few days later, was that the prices of the alternatives were "rapidly rising."[52]

Hoover was outraged. There was no justification, he argued, for the price of either substitute cereals or Victory bread to go up. "The supply of substitutes is ample to meet our needs," he asserted. Once the winter's transportation bottleneck disappeared, the price of wheat substitutes, such as superabundant corn, would fall.[53] On January 28 the Food Administration declared that it would immediately investigate any attempt by businesses to raise the price of Victory bread and would take what one newspaper called "summary action" if the increase were unjustified.[54] A few days later Hoover warned that he would harshly punish any licensed or unlicensed food dealer who sold goods at more than a "reasonable profit."[55] The Food Administration's struggle against the law of supply and demand was intensifying.

But Hoover did not rely entirely upon threats. As always, he preferred voluntary concordats with responsible businessmen—the gentleman's agreement rather than the cudgel. Before promulgating his 50-50 rule, he obtained a promise from leading wholesalers and manufacturers not to exploit the new commercial conditions.[56] Publicly, at least, he was satisfied with their compliance. On February 11 he told a Congressional committee that there had been "no consequential rise in the price of substitutes" since his issuance of the 50-50 order, nor was there likely to be. The trades, he claimed, were "cooperating very well."[57]

Such, at least, was Hoover's public and typically optimistic posture. Only later did he admit to a U.S. senator that the high price of wheat substitutes did "for a short period" cause "hardship" in several sections of the country. But—and this was typical, too—he blamed this problem "entirely" on "the shortage in railway transportation during the winter months."[58]

Meanwhile he had begun to lobby the Congress for a massive expansion of his regulatory authority. On January 15, at his behest and with his approval, Representative Lever introduced a new food control bill in the House.[59] The proposed legislation would give the President (and, through him, Hoover) the power to make wheatless and meatless days obligatory in public eating places—an objective much emphasized by its proponents.[60] But Hoover's eyes were now set on far more than this. As written, the bill authorized the President—by simple proclamation and the issuance of regulations—to modify, limit, or prohibit outright the sale, use, manufacture, or distribution of any foodstuff in the United States, not just by proprietors of public eating places but by any food producer, manufacturer, distributor, carrier, "or other person" in the country. Anyone who disobeyed could be fined and sent to prison.[61]

Despite its endorsement by President Wilson and the Council of National Defense,[62] the Lever bill immediately hit a snag. Within hours of its introduction, Fuel Administrator Garfield issued his own sensational plant-closing edict. Shocked by this unbridled exercise of executive power, many legislators speedily developed doubts about granting still more authority to the President or his surrogates. The chances for passage of the Lever bill suddenly dimmed.[63] Even Representative Sydney Anderson, until now one of the Food Administration's staunchest allies, declared on January 23 that he could not consent to granting the "vague, indefinite, unqualified, and unlimited powers" that Hoover sought. The Minnesota Republican told Hoover bluntly that the language of the bill was "broad enough to include practically every article the mind can conceive of, and every activity of the human race." Such a general delegation of authority, he added, was both unnecessary and politically unattainable. Instead, the representative offered a rough draft of a bill of his own that would clothe Hoover with only a limited number of specific new powers.[64]

Hoover quickly responded that Anderson's substitute would not "meet the emergency." It was not enough, the Food Administrator argued, to repress food consumption in public places. Such measures could not supply the margin that the Allies required. Asserting that the American people consumed or destroyed 30 percent more food than they needed, Hoover now requested more drastic authority than ever to shrink this loss and funnel the savings to Europe. He asked for power to control the use of food in manufacturing in order to curb production of "non-essential" items like soft drinks. He asked for governmental "control of distribution" in order to prevent "unnecessary consumption" and ensure that "all classes and localities may fare alike" during shortages. "Voluntary conservation," he acknowledged, had been helpful, but the demands upon America's food supply were now "greater than can be borne on a purely voluntary basis." Although Hoover hoped that his intensified "voluntary methods" would succeed, he warned Anderson that if they failed, "the grave responsibilities cannot be left upon my shoulders, if

Congress should consider that nothing further is necessary by way of legislation."[65]

As if in counterpoint, on February 3 the *New York Times* reported that Hoover's "first mild conservation programme" had failed and that the pending Lever bill would "compel by law the saving that the appeals to patriotism have not produced." The *Times* noted also that the language of the bill was so broad that it could encompass every housewife in the country.[66] For many suspicious congressmen, opposed to rationing and executive branch aggrandizement, this was precisely the bill's intolerable flaw.[67]

Eight days later Hoover took his case to the House Committee on Agriculture, where he testified in executive session on behalf of the bill. Once more the Food Administrator laid out the sobering facts: For the Allies to maintain their "bedrock" rations until July 1, the American people must cut their own consumption of wheat by 25 percent, of pork by 10–15 percent, and of sugar and beef by 10 percent. At the same time—aware of Congressional sensitivities and of the waters so recently roiled by the unpopular Garfield—Hoover declared forcefully that he did not intend to impose compulsory rationing on consumers. The object of the bill was "indirect conservation," through such methods as "compulsory handling of the public eating places," compulsory restraints on "nonessential" food manufacturing such as candy, and "restriction of supplies through the control of distribution." Hoover was not very specific about how he would actually translate these elastic expressions into policy. But he did acknowledge that the bill would enable him, through power over "distribution" and "control of sales," to regulate hitherto hard-to-control retailers. All of these approaches, he contended, plus "purely voluntary action in homes," would produce the desired surplus without resort to rationing.[68]

In short, Hoover was proposing ever more restrictive and coercive conservation of food supplies—but from the top down, not the bottom up. "It is no use legislating things you can not do," he testified. He had no desire to apply the bill either to farmers (at one end of the food chain) or consumers (at the other). *His* target, he said, was the food manufacturers and distributors.[69]

The committee decided to give Hoover the powers he sought. But instead of conferring blanket authority on him (through the President), as he originally wished, it drafted an entirely new bill carefully defining the powers to be granted and withholding authorization for compulsory rationing of consumers. The bill also mandated that any presidential proclamation on the subject of food conservation could not take effect for at least five days after its promulgation. War or no war, the committee wanted no more bolts from the blue like Garfield's, or like Hoover's recent wheat conservation directive.[70]

On February 23 the new bill was reported and referred to the House calendar—and was never heard from again.[71] Most likely the opposition was too strong. The proposal may also have become enmeshed in a developing fight in Congress to force the government to raise the price of wheat. Whatever the cause, Hoover had no choice but to carry on, wielding his existing powers as inventively as he dared.

Certainly there was no time to pause in his struggle to conserve critical foodstuffs, nor was there any thinning of the obstacles in his path. At the beginning of March he unexpectedly found another glut of pork upon his hands. Something had clearly gone wrong. Back in January, when he had sold 150,000,000 pounds of excess pork to the Allies, he had justified the sudden strain on the U.S. Treasury by asserting that the surplus was temporary. By April, he had asserted, American beef and pork production would fall.[72] He had even predicted "a long and desperate period to face as to our meat supply" after the coming spring.[73] Late in January he had announced that pork supplies were "below normal" and that Americans must reduce their consumption at least 20 percent.[74] But now, just four weeks later, he discovered to his alarm that American meat production was actually soaring and again threatening to destabilize the market.

What had happened to throw his confident predictions so awry? According to a Food Administration announcement in mid-March, the "backing-up" of meat on the farm was "largely" the result of the agency's own appeals for "increased production and decreased consumption."[75] The Food Administration's campaign for meatless meals, it seemed, had evoked a large decline in pork consumption, while its price floor of $15.50 per hundredweight had simultaneously encouraged the breeding of more sows.[76] Not surprisingly, Hoover himself stressed other factors: bad weather during the winter, transportation snarls in the corn belt, "delays in Allied purchases," and "contraction" of Allied shipping. In addition, farmers were now fattening their hogs early with large amounts of soft corn left over from the last harvest—corn that would otherwise soon spoil. As a result, the hogs that were coming to market were much heavier than normal. All these factors, said Hoover, had created a tremendous logjam that was about to break.[77]

The Food Administrator hurriedly searched for ways to dispose of this unforeseen bounty before it swamped the packing houses and perhaps disposed of him. As in January, he turned first to the Allies. On March 1 he appealed to the British ambassador, Lord Reading. "We cannot allow the result of this glut to break the price to lower levels than at present," Hoover warned, "or we will discourage our farmers and demoralize the whole of next year's production." There were only two possible solutions, he said with characteristic certitude. Either he must lift all his restrictions on American consumption of meat—thereby destroying "the whole sentiment for food conservation" and leading to reduced meat exports to the Allies later on—or the Allies must make a "blanket order" for all American excess pork until the end of April: a total (he said) of up to 450,000 tons.[78]

Having unilaterally determined what he wanted the Allies to do, Hoover tried to spur them into an instant response. He told Reading that America's meat packers were in financial peril—and all because the Allies were making huge demands for pork, yet stretching out payments over a long period. The Food Administrator opined ominously that the packers would either be forced to stop taking orders from the Allies altogether "unless they can get some advances," or would be compelled to stop buying hogs from farmers "until the present stocks are diminished." If the latter happened, he warned, it would "stifle further supplies" eventually. Pressing Reading for an "immediate solution" on March 3, Hoover declared starkly that only one measure would suffice: the Allies must "make an advance of 80 per cent against all unexecuted orders" for American pork in the next two or three months.[79]

The British ambassador, however, was not to be stampeded, and so on March 4 Hoover stepped up the pressure. He announced publicly that the American people would no longer be asked to observe "porkless Saturdays" or eat a meatless meal every day. He did, however, urge his fellow citizens to continue to abstain from beef and pork dishes every Tuesday.[80]

The Food Administrator tried to make the best of this breach in his conservation dike. He told the American people that he was easing his restrictions on meat because meat was temporarily plentiful and because eating more of it would help reduce consumption of bread.[81] To his representative in London, however, he cabled irritably that he had been forced to act as he did because a "delay in securing some definite expression from Allied governments" had threatened him with an "acute crisis in prices of livestock which would be disastrous to the whole Allied cause."[82] No doubt Hoover intended his European associates to read this version of his rationale for his decision. No doubt, too, he did not want the general public to think that he was trying to bail out the packers or shore up the price of live hogs. Not for the first time, Hoover was tailoring his explanations to his audience.

On March 4 Lord Reading replied favorably to Hoover's offer, provided that satisfactory storage and financial arrangements could be made.[83] The Allies, in fact, were more than amenable to the idea. In the words of a British food ministry official, his agency "reacted like a starving man at a Lord Mayor's table."[84] The British, the French, and the Italians joined to buy heavily—with American credit.[85] During March, accordingly, a tidal wave of American pork swept across the Atlantic: more than 308,000,000 pounds of it in all.[86]

And yet, for a worried Hoover, it was not enough. By mid-March the Food Administration acknowledged that as of the previous January 1 the United States actually had several million more live hogs on the farms than at the same time a year before.[87] As the rush of live animals to market accelerated, storage facilities for pork products became jammed. The amount of pork and lard in storage reached a billion pounds for the first time ever.[88] Hoover's relaxation of curbs on pork consumption did little to lessen the glut.[89] Worried hog producers feared a break in the market price.[90]

Then, on March 28, the head of Hoover's meat division received a telegram from Thomas E. Wilson, chairman of the packers' committee cooperating with the Food Administration. The packing executive was thoroughly alarmed. He and his competitors were now "carrying maximum stocks"—indeed, the most in history—yet agents for the Allies were unlikely to purchase more for at least a week. Wilson warned that unless the Allies quickly placed larger orders, it would be "impossible" for his industry to continue to handle incoming hogs. The packers desperately needed the space as well as money with which to pay farmers. Wilson begged the Food Administration to provide "relief"—including complete abolition of "meatless" days—and uttered words which must have chilled Hoover's spine: "I cannot see how the price can be maintained on hogs if these conditions continue."[91]

With the leading meat packers apparently on the brink of going under, Hoover instantly suspended "meatless" days for an entire month. His food conservation "army" was now released from its moral duty to abstain from pork and beef. In announcing his decision, Hoover attributed the current "over normal run" of hogs to "supplies [being] dammed back during the winter months' car shortage"—an oblique attempt, perhaps, to pin the blame on William McAdoo. Trying once more to detect a silver lining, Hoover declared that the increasing availability of meat, potatoes, and milk should enable Americans to eat fewer breadstuffs.[92]

The crisis of late March soon subsided. In the next two months the United States exported tremendous amounts of pork to its western Allies—nearly 400,000 tons in all between March 1 and the end of May.[93] It was enough to extricate Hoover from a debacle. The British, too, were much relieved and grateful. During the winter as many as 1,800,000 Britons had queued up daily in front of meat shops; by late spring the queues had virtually disappeared.[94] Thanks to what it called America's "splendid response," the Ministry of Food was able to restore to normal levels a meat ration that it had previously been compelled to cut to virtually nothing. The effect on British civilian morale was profound.[95]

For Hoover, though, the hog problem would not go away. Again and again it defied his expectations. At the beginning of March, in his zeal to unload pork, he predicted that his surplus would only last two or three months. From June to September, he prophesied, there would be a "shortage in arrivals" of meat.[96] By late May, no such dearth was in sight, and Hoover began to press the Allies to buy far more than they thought necessary.[97] The disposition of America's hog production had become a headache that would vex him repeatedly in the months to come.

At least with pork Hoover had food that he could spare. Wheat was quite another matter. By the beginning of March the remaining American wheat supply was only two thirds of what it had been on the same date in 1917.[98] Despite all the conservation propaganda with which Hoover had bombarded the country, per capita consumption of wheat had actually *increased* in the past eight months, compared to the same eight-month period in the preceding crop year.[99] Clearly many Americans were paying little attention to "wheatless Wednesdays" and other Food Administration recommendations, as the *New York Times* publicly (and Hoover privately) acknowledged.[100] While many middle- and upper-class citizens had responded enthusiastically to his belt-tightening appeals, many working-class Americans had not.[101] Thanks to the war-induced surge in wage levels, men and women at the lower end of the economic ladder were consuming more food, and better-quality food, than ever before.[102]

With large numbers of Americans failing to restrict their diets, Hoover now tried to force the Allies to alter theirs. On March 1 he informed Lord Reading that America was "entirely short of breadstuffs" and that he did "not see how we can go on exporting at the present rate per month." This was the letter in which Hoover offered instead a mountain of pork. As usual, he did not waste time on diplomacy. "It does appear to me," he told Reading pointedly, "that, in this situation, food is food and that the natural thing would be that the Allies should take the whole of our excess production where we have an excess and not drain our shortages deeper in other directions."[103]

Reading and his associates were shocked. Did Hoover really mean that he would have no breadstuffs whatsoever to ship to them in April except any residue left over from March? On behalf of the Allies, Reading immediately requested clarification. He pointed out that, while "food is food," beef and pork were not adequate substitutes for bread. The French, Italians, and British, said Reading, must have bread.[104] He did not need to add that, like Hoover, the British government was reluctant to ration the staple of its working class.

Taken aback, perhaps, by Reading's reply, Hoover appealed directly to the White House. He informed President Wilson that the American people would normally consume 40,000,000 bushels of wheat in each of the next four months but that the actual monthly supply would only be 25,000,000 bushels. Under the circumstances, he told the President, "it seems to me it is a matter that requires your decision."[105]

Instead of siding with his apprehensive Food Administrator, Woodrow Wilson threw the issue back into his lap:

> I am not sure what it is you think I ought to decide. I suppose you mean that I ought to decide whether we are to continue our present scale of shipment of breadstuffs across the seas and so incur the shortage for our own people to which you refer. I am afraid there is no choice in the matter. The populations across the sea must be fed and have, as I understand it, no available substitutes for wheat, whereas our own people have at least substitutes and have them, I believe (have they not?) in adequate quantities. Personally, I feel confident that the spirit of our people would rise to the sacrifice and that, if there are adequate quantities of the available

> substitutes, they would be willing to use them. Is this not your own judgment?[106]

Despite this rebuff by the President, Hoover was more determined than ever to restrain the flow of American wheat to the Allies. If the Allies would not accept beef and pork as substitutes, he would find some other way to modify their behavior. In a forceful cable to London on March 12, supplemented by a separate cable from the Wheat Export Company, Hoover requested fresh data on Allied food stocks and conveyed the impression that the British and French, in his opinion, were consuming altogether too much bread.[107] He disclosed that America's remaining wheat supply comprised less than 50 percent of its "normal consumption," and that "under these circumstances" it was "utterly impossible" for the Allies to continue to try to "maintain their stocks."[108] The United States would have to "totally exhaust" its wheat supply by August, said Hoover. He saw "no reason why Allied countries cannot walk parallel with us."[109] So serious was the American "cereals position," in Hoover's judgment, that any further Allied purchases of American wheat were to be "deprecated."[110] Although his cable did not mention the point, the Wheat Executive concluded that, in order to meet American requirements, the United States might decide to import wheat from Argentina—wheat that the Allies had been expecting to acquire for themselves.[111]

Hoover's message caused consternation across the Atlantic. After meeting twice in special session to consider his cable, the Wheat Executive implored him not to touch the crop in Argentina but, if necessary, to go to Australia instead. It pleaded for every grain of cereal that Hoover could spare. It warned that his projected cereals exports were so low that they would threaten the Allies' ability to "maintain distribution to armies and big centres of population."[112] As for Hoover's charge that the Allied governments were not doing enough to curb their people's consumption of bread, the British food controller replied that his government had already diluted the bread loaf by more than 20 percent and had only refrained from actual rationing because of doubts about its efficacy.[113] From the earnest tone of these communications, it was clear that the Allies were upset by Hoover's news and quite unwilling to lower their demands.

Meanwhile Hoover's problems at home were multiplying. From the latest crop reports it now appeared that the wheat harvest of 1917 had been 40,000,000 to 50,000,000 bushels lower than previously estimated. To make matters worse, many wheat farmers were hoarding their remaining supplies in the hope that Congress would decide to set a higher price. In milling centers that ground wheat for the "industrial population," said Hoover, the supply of wheat was "dangerously exhausted," while across the country the demand for substitute flours was threatening to outrun supply. Added to these stresses was his continued "total lack of adequate authority to impose a competent control of distribution." "For all these reasons," Hoover reported to the President on March 22, "I feel we are not only taking great risks but asking the last mite from our own people."[114]

For the second time in fifteen days Hoover had laid his fears for America's wheat supply before the man in the Oval Office. But if Hoover still hoped that the President might relent and permit him to export less wheat to Britain and France, he was disappointed. Once again Woodrow Wilson turned him down. "I see how serious the situation is," the President replied, "but there is no choice, I believe, but to go forward as best we can."[115]

Hoover's two preferred policy options—curtailing American wheat exports and forcing the Allies to consume less bread—had died aborning. Only two alternatives were left, both of which he was already pursuing. During March the Food Administration redoubled its efforts to bring about increased conservation of wheat products by the American people. It revoked all exceptions to the 50-50 rule.[116] It ordered bakers to make "Victory bread or close."[117] It organized a national educational campaign against waste and even banned the use of icing on hot cross buns.[118]

Privately Hoover wondered whether the time was at hand for something he dreaded: the introduction of compulsory food rationing. In mid-March he and several lieutenants began to investigate possible rationing plans.[119] With wheat becoming ever scarcer, the Food Administration was finding it impossible to maintain an adequate supply for the all-important flour mills of Minneapolis, Kansas City, and Buffalo.[120]

Then, on March 23, a sensational public announcement came from Hoover himself: In order to meet the Allies' "military necessity," his fellow citizens must reduce their consumption of wheat to just one half of normal until the next harvest. In words that made front-page news from coast to coast, the Food Administrator spelled out what must be done. He asked every American to eat no more than one and a half pounds of wheat products per week. He asked public eating places to serve guests food containing in the aggregate no more than two ounces of wheat flour per meal. He asked retailers to sell urban customers no more than one eighth of a barrel of flour at a time. It would be a barrier, he thought, to waste and panicky hoarding. He asked bakers and grocers to sell three-quarter-pound loaves of Victory bread where they had once sold loaves weighing a full pound.[121] That same day, March 23, the Food Administration ordered that, as of mid-April, the proportion of substitutes for wheat flour in commercially baked Victory bread must be increased to 25 percent.[122]

Hoover's newest conservation drive occurred against a backdrop of frightening news from Europe: on March 21 the German army had launched its long-awaited, supreme offensive in the West. In the last days of the month the enemy's forces smashed across the trenches of northern France and nearly broke through to Paris. The desperate Allies tried to hold on and asked the United States to rush reinforcements. For America and its associates, it was the most dangerous moment of the war.

On March 29 Hoover addressed a gathering of leading hotel executives whom he had summoned to Washington from the principal cities of the country. He told them that it was "probably the most serious day in our national history since the Battle of Gettysburg." America's wheat supply was less than estimated; shipping was becoming scarcer; grain from Argentina was delayed and less than expected; the supply of breadstuffs in Europe was "at its lowest ebb." And now the Allies were pleading for reinforcements—a request that would inevitably draw shipping away from South America. Only the United States, Hoover declared, could save the Allies. To do so, "we must cut our own consumption [of bread] by one-half." Only wheat would serve the Allies now. Only wheat, at this time of year, would "stand shipment." Less than a month before, Hoover had bitterly accused the Allies of eating *too much* wheat. Now, to a different audience, he stated that the Allies' diluted war bread was "as nothing" compared to American bread, "neither in palatability nor luxuriousness." Now he said that if the Allies were to be fed, "they must be fed on wheat bread, or none at all."

But how? If America was to resolve the problem, Hoover asserted, "it must be accomplished by the voluntary effort of the intelligent people, the influential people of the community": people like his audience and himself. The "one antidote" to "social unrest"—an antidote that "was never applied in Russia"—was "a willingness for us to sacrifice more than we ask of those who have less to give." Hoover thereupon asked "every well-to-do" and "independent person" in the United States to "abstain from the use of any wheat in any form until the next harvest." And he asked the businessmen before him to "abolish the use of wheat and wheat products in every first class hotel and restaurant" until September. Standing with their right hands raised, the representatives of five hundred major hotels took the pledge.[123]

Hoover immediately cabled this news to the Allied food controllers; it was an electrifying tribute to his faith in American idealism.[124] But the Food Administrator was taking no chances that these or similar renunciatory gestures would be enough. Even as he mobilized hotelmen and orchestrated American public opinion to a fever pitch, he was simultaneously exploring his final alternative to domestic privation: his ace-in-the-hole, the unshipped wheat of Canada.

In mid-March Julius Barnes made the first move. He informed the Wheat Export Company that the United States had now exported, or contracted to export, almost 100,000,000 bushels of wheat or equivalent flour since the last harvest. But the waning American reserves were now "unevenly distributed," said Barnes, and he was finding it more and more difficult to keep the critical flour milling centers at Buffalo and Minneapolis properly supplied. He therefore asked the Wheat Export Company for "definite reassurance" against any additional American deliveries of wheat and flour before the next harvest. He sought, that is, a promise that he could draw upon the Wheat Export Company's Canadian supplies, if he needed them, to prevent a disruptive shortage at American mills. Specifically, he requested the right to acquire up to 25,000,000 bushels of Canadian wheat in the spring and summer as a replacement for flour that America, in the meantime, sold to the Allies over and above its completed and existing commitments.[125]

In effect, Barnes was drawing the line at 100,000,000 bushels. If America now went beyond this mark and sold the Allies additional flour before the next harvest, he wanted the option to get it back in Canadian wheat. From Barnes's and Hoover's point of view, the proposal made sense. North American wheat, they argued, should be treated as a unit.[126] Besides, why should the United States continue selling its dwindling stocks at the risk of disrupting its principal flour-making mills?

Barnes's proposed "replacement principle" applied to future transactions, not to the existing arrangements negotiated by Hoover in late December.[127] Probably for this very reason, the Wheat Export Company was "very loath" (said Barnes) to agree. It claimed that it needed wheat, not flour, for its own mills, and it especially required the Manitoba wheat that Barnes was trying to reserve exclusively for possible American use.[128] The Allies' real objection, however, was no doubt more fundamental. If they granted Barnes his option, it would render entirely conditional all further American flour sales to them in the current crop year. At any time he chose, Barnes in effect could negate these transactions to the equivalent of 25,000,000 bushels of wheat—*Canadian* wheat that the Allies would otherwise obtain. No wonder, then, that the Europeans were decidedly cool to Barnes's initiative. It was not much of a deal for them.

On March 20 Barnes reported the problem to Hoover.[129] The very next day the Chief intervened by letter—not to the mere underlings at the Wheat Export Company but to the British ambassador, Lord Reading, himself. Hoover began by noting that the Inter-Allied Conference attended by Alonzo Taylor in November 1917 had agreed that the United States would export 900,000 metric tons (approximately 33,000,000 bushels) of wheat to the Allies between December 1, 1917 and the following August. Hoover now asserted that the conference had also agreed that this amount "was to be considered an advance to be liquidated from Canada later in the year." Hoover then presented statistics indicating that the United States had considerably exceeded this 900,000-ton quota, although its deliveries of other promised cereals showed a deficit. After reviewing Canadian exports and commitments, Hoover emphasized his deepening problems at home: his discovery that the 1917 wheat crop had been overestimated, his "very hard" restrictions on domestic wheat consumption (to a point that Americans must now eat, he said, far less wheat bread than the Allies), and, especially, the maldistribution of wheat supplies across the country. For the Food Administrator, there was only one way "to rectify this situation": consolidation of Canadian and American reserves.

Hoover therefore boldly proposed that, from April 1, 1918 until the end of June, for every two bushels of wheat that he exported to Europe, he "should draw from Canada one bushel at such times and places" as he directed. He calculated that this would come to 525,000 tons, or more than 19,000,000 bushels. It was virtually half of what Hoover believed to be the remaining Canadian surplus. Hoover seemed to intend that this wheat would eventually go to the Allies as American-made flour. But, like Barnes, his overriding immediate objective was to keep American mills operating, producing flour that Americans might need.[130]

Lord Reading and his associates were aghast. "Neither I nor my French or Italian colleagues," he replied, found "any trace" in the Inter-Allied Conference documents of an agreement that America's promised 900,000 tons were a mere loan, to be replaced in toto by Canada. In fact, the ambassador asserted, Hoover's claim was "inconsistent with the figures of the programme then set out." The data demonstrated plainly that "at that time there could not have been any intention of repaying from Canada the 900,000 tons to be exported from the United States." The question of repayment, he pointed out, had only arisen several weeks later, on December 29, in Hoover's letter to H. T. Robson with its notable "reservation." Reading did not add—though he might well have—that Hoover's unilateral reservation (which the Allies evidently did not contest) applied to *future* American exports of up to 70,000,000 bushels, not to the 900,000 tons prescribed by the Inter-Allied Conference and already agreed to by Hoover in early December.

The British ambassador was also disturbed by Hoover's statistics, which appeared both to overstate American exports of wheat during the winter and to understate the American export deficit in other cereals. In preparing his data, Hoover (Reading pointed out) had not included 430,000 tons of wheat that the Allies had sent down from Canada some months before. This was evidently the amount that the Wheat Export Company had loaned to the Food Administration in December in order to keep America's flour mills operating through the winter. Under the agreement that Julius Barnes had negotiated at that time, the United States was obliged to provide the Allies an equivalent amount of flour in due course. Reading now declared that if this commitment (and other unmet obligations) were taken into account, the Americans' "net deficiency" on their portion of the inter-Allied cereals program was not (as Hoover claimed) 298,880 tons but a staggering 1,128,000 tons—nearly four times as much. The British ambassador also thought that Hoover was exaggerating the size of the remaining Canadian wheat surplus, but on this issue he declared that he awaited more definite data from north of the border.[131]

Lord Reading politely disclaimed any intention to be critical, but there was no concealing his challenge to Herbert Hoover. Stung by his assault, the

Food Administrator struck back. Fortified by a memorandum from Alonzo Taylor, he declared that he was "somewhat astonished" at Reading's statements about America's commitment of 900,000 tons of wheat back in November. Perhaps, Hoover suggested, their difference of interpretation had arisen because the meetings of the Inter-Allied Council "had been confined to general terms," while the "detailed discussions" on the subject had occurred with the Wheat Executive. In any case, Hoover claimed now to have "abundant evidence in memoranda of the Wheat Executive of last autumn" that his understanding of the November agreement was correct—"and furthermore, as you rightly state, it was confirmed in my letter to Mr. Robson of January 1." (Reading, of course, had stated no such thing.)

Hoover was not content to reiterate in the teeth of the evidence that the 900,000 tons he had agreed in early December to export by the end of February had really been only an "advance." According to him, American wheat exports to the Allies in the past four months had actually exceeded 1,000,000 tons, and *all* of it was returnable to the United States upon demand. He informed Reading that, so far, America had received an "actual replacement" of 430,000 tons of Canadian wheat, leaving "a deficiency in returns to us" of more than 700,000 tons. In making this astounding calculation, Hoover ignored the fact that the 430,000 Canadian tons in question had been an Allied loan to the United States. Now, in disregard of Julius Barnes's promise to return it to the Allies as flour, Hoover defiantly construed it as a partial repayment on a gigantic debt to him!

Every particle of wheat that the United States had shipped to Europe since early December, then, had really only been a loan: this was the claim that Hoover was now making to the British ambassador.

But then, in an abrupt reversal, Hoover drew back: "I am however making no claims for replacement of this amount [the remaining 700,000-ton "deficiency"] as we take it that we have saved this amount from consumption and therefore in accord with our assurance that we would ship everything we could save, the matter is ended." With this apparent gesture of magnanimity, Hoover abandoned his claim to 900,000 tons of Canadian wheat. But as for what that the Allies had already loaned him, he showed no signs of surrendering it. "The matter is ended." Having pocketed these 430,000 tons, he in effect told Lord Reading to back off.

Hoover also counterattacked on other fronts. He told Reading sharply that "I do think it is desirable that we should have some reliable figures" on Canada's export surplus, and he hinted that the Canadian government's current statistics were egregiously inaccurate. (In this he again relied on Taylor's memorandum.) Hoover also took another jab at Allied rationing policy. He intended to ship every grain he could "extract from our population," he announced. "We must assume Canada will do the same." "In this connection," he added, "I would commend to the Allies the action of our leading hotels in stopping the use of wheat entirely. . . ."

And always he kept his eye on his objective. "The main point," he informed Reading, was that the proposed new imports from Canada would permit the Food Administration "to ship unreservedly from all points, which we cannot do without such assured distribution to and consequent preservation of tranquility in our industrial population." That, for Hoover, was the bottom line.[132]

Hoover's rejoinder contained some dubious assertions. He claimed that he had "abundant evidence" that the Canadians were supposed to repay the entire American "loan" of 900,000 tons, but he did not produce the documents. He claimed that he had "confirmed" this understanding in his letter to Robson at the end of December, but the letter in fact included no such statement. The "replacement principle" enunciated in that letter referred to *future* American wheat exports, not to those previously agreed upon.

Certainly Hoover, in the autumn of 1917, had wanted protection for his own wheat exports in the form of later Canadian replenishment if he made up for a temporary slack in Canadian deliveries during the winter.[133] In mid-November also, the Allied food authorities had agreed with Alonzo Taylor that, "if the necessity arose," the United States might be able to arrange to export wheat to the Allies in excess of the existing American and Canadian surplus (133,000,000 bushels), "in view of the possibility of meeting the deficiency thus created in America by Wheat from the Argentine or Australia, provided that it could not be made good by economy in America."[134] In other words, future American wheat exports, over and above the combined American and Canadian surplus already spoken for, could be construed as a loan if the United States failed to conserve the extra amounts exported. But the Allied officials and Hoover's representative identified only Argentina and Australia as possible sources of such replacement wheat. The Inter-Allied Conference imposed no requirement to repay on Canada.[135] Nor did it stipulate that Canada was to replace any of the *existing* American wheat (900,000 tons of it) that America promised in late autumn to export by the end of February 1918.

Conceivably, in the pressure of work, the confusion of trans-Atlantic cablegrams, and his zeal to protect his country's food resources, Hoover misunderstood this distinction. In any case, the Canadian replacement option did not emerge in a document until his letter to Robson on December 29. Hoover may possibly have believed that it was retroactive, and thus applicable to the 900,000 tons he had already started to ship, but the plain words of his letter did not say this.[136]

In his quest in March and early April for a Canadian "reassurance," then, Hoover erroneously conflated three separate agreements with the European Allies: the unconditional, 900,000-ton, American export commitment made in November and early December 1917; his conditional pledge of additional wheat on December 29; and the Allies' loan of 430,000 tons of wheat to him in December for wintertime use by American flour mills. In Hoover's defense, it must be recorded that his reply to Lord Reading was based on a somewhat confusing memorandum from Alonzo Taylor.[137]

On one point, though, Hoover had a case: whatever the agreements made some months before, the wartime coalition partners needed now to confront conditions as they found them. On April 11 he, Lord Reading, and various associates conferred in Washington about the problems of Canadian wheat.[138] Hoover was greatly agitated. The Food Administration, he disclosed, was having "extreme difficulty" in "maintaining internal distribution" of wheat to American flour mills. If the mills should not supply enough flour to the "industrial districts," the likelihood of "serious trouble" was great. Hoover was especially worried about the mills of Buffalo (the key suppliers of flour to the industrial East) and requested 2,000,000 bushels of Canadian wheat to keep them operating in May. If the Allies failed to do this, he announced, he would be "forced to reconsider" his distribution program and to take back some of the flour en route to the east coast and already designated for the Allies.[139]

According to one of Hoover's deputies at the meeting, the "English authorities" did not appear much disposed "to meet our views."[140] For some weeks, in fact, the British had been uncooperative. "Evidently," said the head of Hoover's milling division, "they want all the Canadian supplies and our own as well."[141] The conference of April 11 adjourned without result.[142]

A few days later, however, after consultations in London, the Allied representatives reluctantly came to terms. In behalf of Hoover, Julius Barnes promised to "make an effort not to interfere" with the Allies' program of wheat imports from the eastern seaboard in the month of May.[143] For its part, the Wheat Executive agreed to provide 2,000,000 bushels of Canadian wheat to the Buffalo flour mills during that month.[144] But the Allies were unwilling to yield any more. Reading informed Hoover in mid-April that these 2,000,000 bushels constituted "a final allocation of Canadian wheat for this cereal year," an assertion that irritated Barnes.[145] The Grain Corporation president intended to ask the Allies to "contribute whatever was necessary after June 1st" to supply American mills, and he contended that the Allied negotiators had explicitly agreed that this question was "open to discussion."[146] Siding at once with his lieutenant, Hoover told Reading that the 2,000,000 bushels were *not* a "final allocation" of Canadian wheat for the current crop year, since "the whole question after June 1" remained "open."[147] More friction and rancor appeared to loom.

In the end, the Food Administration's Grain Corporation purchased 17,358,832 bushels of Canadian wheat during the 1917–18 crop year—a figure that apparently included the 430,000 tons (or nearly 16,000,000 bushels) that the Wheat Export Company had let Barnes have for the winter.[148] If so, the total was far indeed from the 19,000,000 or so additional bushels that Hoover had requested in his March 21 letter to Lord Reading. According to one of Hoover's associates, the "major portion" of the Grain Corporation's

Canadian purchases "was returned to the Allies in the form of flour."[149] It seems that, after all the antagonism and arguments, the Allies recovered most of their loan. For the rest, they had to accept money.

Why, however, did Hoover desist in his attempt to scoop up more Canadian wheat after May? The principal reason, it appears, was that he did not need it. During the spring his tremendous drive for food conservation gained momentum, with results that the Food Administration pronounced as a great success. In Arkansas, for example, families returned to dealers more than 2,500,000 pounds of flour in excess of their "patriotic portion" after the Food Administration made an appeal against hoarding.[150] From Texas came reports of flour shipments being turned back and given up for export.[151] From Indiana and Montana came news that these entire states had adopted a totally wheatless diet until the next harvest.[152] Toward the end of May the press reported that three quarters of the householders in New York State had pledged themselves to abstain from wheat products until summer. The Masons, Knights of Columbus, and other fraternal bodies passed resolutions committing their members to this regimen.[153]

Some of these reports were obviously exaggerated. In Montana, Hoover's state food administrator declared the state "absolutely wheatless until July first" after his county administrators unanimously voted that the people were ready for this step.[154] The people of Montana themselves did not vote. Still, there was no gainsaying the considerable grass-roots popularity of Hoover's campaign, particularly (it was said) in the South and the West.[155]

Sometimes, in fact, popular enthusiasm ran to excess. Back in December, the Oklahoma City government had adopted an ordinance making violations of wheatless Wednesdays an act of sedition.[156] In Birmingham, Alabama, in late May, a mob wrecked a restaurant after its owner refused to eliminate wheat products from its menu.[157] In their patriotic fervor many Americans refused to eat sauerkraut, which Hoover considered a valuable substitute for exportable staples. The Food Administration felt obliged to announce with a straight face that sauerkraut was said to be of Dutch, not German, origin.[158]

Hoover was, or at least professed to be, pleased by the public response to his great crusade. He told a U.S. senator in mid-May that he was convinced that at least 20,000,000 Americans had voluntarily stopped eating all wheat or wheat products.[159] Later he put the figure at 25,000,000, or nearly one fourth of the entire population.[160] More significantly, on May 4 he cabled a heartening message to London:

> Our reduction in wheat consumption now amounts to 60 per cent of normal and will I believe hold until harvest. This should permit our continued shipment of present programme of flour until July 1.

For the Allies it was some of the best news in months.[161]

Nevertheless, Hoover did not relax his pressure on the home front. He beseeched farmers to market their remaining stocks of wheat, even including some ordinarily reserved for seed.[162] In a message read in the nation's churches on May 26, he announced that his country's consumption of wheat must now be reduced to just one third of normal until the new harvest and entreated all who could do so to eat no wheat or wheat derivatives whatsoever.[163] "Normal American consumption" exceeded 40,000,000 bushels per month, he said, but for the next two months together only 26,000,000 bushels would be available for home consumption.[164] During May, meanwhile, his Grain Corporation increased its purchases from domestic flour mills to a mandatory 40 percent of their total output.[165] The screws were turning tighter and tighter.

In the end Hoover and the country made it, but by the most narrow of margins. A year before, the nation had entered the 1917 wheat harvest season with a carryover from the preceding crop of about 50,000,000 bushels. On July 1, 1918 the carryover amounted to just 17,000,000 bushels—the smallest margin in years.[166] By this slim amount Hoover had avoided an absolute, if temporary, wheat dearth, with economic and social consequences he cared not to contemplate.

III

On July 11, 1918 an unusually cheerful Food Administrator wrote a letter to President Wilson. Hoover had reason to be in a celebratory mood, for he had a success story to tell. In the past twelve months, the United States had exported more than $1.4 billion worth of food to Europe for the use of the Allies, the American military, the Belgian relief, and the Red Cross. Most of this had been purchased "through or with the collaboration of the Food Administration." The shipments included more than 3,000,000,000 pounds of meat and fats as well as 340,800,000 bushels of cereals. These aggregate figures constituted an enormous increase over the year before.

Hoover was proudest of his record in exporting wheat. He informed the President that since the Allied request in January 1918 for 75,000,000 additional bushels, he had actually shipped or set in transit nearly 85,000,000 bushels, despite the fact that as of January the available surplus had been "more than exhausted." The successful provision of this amount, he said, was a magnificent accomplishment of the American people. In fact, he now asserted, so poor had the 1917 harvest been that America had barely had enough wheat for "normal" consumption. Thus the total American shipments to the Allies for the past year represented (he claimed) "approximately savings in our own wheat bread."

All this and more, he exulted, had occurred because of the "effort and sacrifice" of his compatriots. All across the country, "in every direction," food consumption and waste had been "greatly reduced." It had been achieved "voluntarily and individually," he contended, and predominantly by American women.[167]

Hoover's letter was promptly published (with White House permission) in the press, as he had intended.[168] It was a glowing testimonial not only to the American people but to his own leadership. Yet had Hoover's wheat conservation drive—the centerpiece of his interventionist policy—been as successful as he confidently alleged? And was it successful for the reasons he publicly adduced?

In the 1917–18 crop year the United States exported 132,578,633 bushels of wheat, a *decrease* of more than one third from the 203,573,928 bushels it sent abroad the year before.[169] The percentage of the wheat crop exported also decreased, from 32 percent to just 20.8 percent.[170] In the all-important area of wheat and flour, the United States helped its allies less in Hoover's first year as Food Administrator than it had in the year before it entered the war.

Yet this statistic bore little relevance to Hoover's claims. In 1917–18 he could only administer what he had: a national supply of wheat nearly 100,000,000 bushels below that of the previous crop year.[171] While the 1917 crop itself was no smaller than that of the year before, the carryover was substantially less, giving Hoover much less room to maneuver.

The evaluation of Hoover's performance thus revolves first around a statistical question: How large was the American wheat surplus prior to his conservation crusade? At once the waters become muddy. Hoover evidently had no reliable figure, and his estimates varied considerably as the year went on. In August 1917 he put the exportable surplus from the new wheat crop at 80,000,000 bushels.[172] By December 1 his agency had reduced its estimate of the exportable surplus to 70,000,000 bushels, while Hoover himself, in a letter to the President on November 15, submitted data implying that the surplus was under 30,000,000 bushels.[173] Then, in a press release on January 25, 1918, the Food Administration placed the "normal surplus from the last harvest" at 60,000,000 bushels.[174] Two months later, after learning that the 1917 crop had been overestimated, Hoover told the White House that he had "really had no export surplus at all."[175] This was probably the basis for his claim to Wilson in July that the entire amount of wheat exported during the preceding twelve months had been a measure of Americans' self-denial.[176] But a few months later he told the President's secretary that there *had* been a surplus after all: 25,000,000 bushels.[177] The smaller the original surplus, of course, the greater and more impressive the subsequent acts of self-restraint.

One problem confronting Hoover was that he could not very well calculate his surplus without knowing how much wheat remained in stock or circulation, including wheat held back on the farms. In 1918 this was not an easy computation. During Congressional testimony that winter, he stated that the wheat available for consumption on January 1 had been as little as 251,000,000 bushels (according to one accounting method) and as much as

303,000,000 bushels (according to another).[178] Another complication was that projections of the size of the wheat surplus depended heavily on estimates of normal consumption. But what was "normal," and were the American people now eating normally or not? In mid-November 1917 Hoover informed the President that the "average yearly domestic consumption [in the United States] for the past three years" had been about 615,000,000 bushels.[179] A few months later his own statisticians estimated that it had been nearly 87,500,000 bushels less.[180] Such discrepancies raise the possibility that Hoover deliberately understated American wheat reserves and overstated domestic wheat requirements in order to provide himself a cushion against disaster.[181] Certainly on these issues he seemed consistently less optimistic than Julius Barnes.[182] On the other hand, even if the American people were consuming less wheat than in previous years, how could Hoover be sure that they would continue to do so?

All of this underscores the excruciating perplexities that Hoover faced as a policymaker and the difficulty of determining the proportions of his success. The United States exported about 132,000,000 bushels of wheat to the Allies in the crop year 1917–18: that much is knowable and certain. But just how much of this amount was generated by Hoover's food-saving campaign obviously depends on whether the pre-campaign, "natural" surplus stood at 80,000,000 bushels, or zero, or somewhere in between. It is a statistical puzzle that probably cannot be solved.

On one point, though, after late October, Hoover did not waver: that the United States had by then exported all of its existing wheat surplus based on "normal" (pre-1917) consumption. Since the highest official estimate of the 1917 surplus was never more than 80,000,000 bushels,[183] and since America as of December 31 had already exported over 62,000,000 bushels from the 1917 crop,[184] Hoover could not be faulted for thinking, on the basis of the information available to him, that his conclusion was essentially sound.

In January 1918 Hoover's conservation drive accelerated. During the next six months the United States exported more than 70,000,000 additional bushels of wheat. If one assumes (reasonably) that the bulk of this reflected reduced American consumption, was the reduction ascribable to Hoover's efforts? Or did he, in taking credit for it, commit the fallacy of *post hoc, ergo propter hoc?*

Once again perplexities arise. First, as noted earlier, during the winter of 1917–18 (and for several months beforehand) American consumption of wheat actually rose, in defiance of all the propaganda that Hoover unleashed. Adherence to the Food Administration's voluntary conservation rules varied widely among social and ethnic strata. Middle- and upper-class Americans were much more observant of "meatless" and "wheatless" practices than working-class and foreign-born individuals.[185] Secondly, as economists subsequently pointed out, Hoover's wheat policy was somewhat self-contradictory. While he feverishly entreated Americans to consume less, his price policy simultaneously encouraged more consumption. By keeping the lid on the price of wheat, flour, and bread, while the prices of other, uncontrolled foods increased, Hoover in effect made wheat products relatively more attractive to consumers. His stabilization measures thus became an incentive to eat more wheat rather than less. Just how significant this factor was, we may never know. But at least in theory his selective price controls undercut his pleas for "wheatless" dining.[186]

Despite these countervailing pressures, in the final months of the 1917–18 crop year American consumption of wheat products fell substantially.[187] Yet here, too, the story is more complicated than the numbers suggest. Time and again, in early 1918, Hoover publicized the claim that Americans normally consumed 40,000,000 or more bushels of wheat per month.[188] Since the United States obviously lacked the reserves to permit the continued use of wheat at this level, the Food Administrator implored his fellow citizens to cut their consumption by 50 percent or more. Once again, however, the government's statistics proved deceiving. It was not true that America's "normal consumption" of wheat was 40,000,000 bushels every month of the year. What Hoover evidently did not know was that American wheat consumption traditionally declined—and declined substantially—in the months of *March, April, May, and June.*[189] From 1914 to 1917, in fact, national wheat consumption during these months averaged only about 26,500,000 bushels, barely half that of the other eight months of the year.[190] With the advent of spring, it seems, many Americans customarily switched to newly available fruits and vegetables. Thus when Hoover, with a flourish of publicity, asked his fellow citizens to lower their wheat consumption by one half in the spring of 1918, he asked them to do what, to a great extent, they had always done without instruction. In the spring of 1918 the American people made fewer sacrifices on the "food front" than Hoover apparently realized.

Had his whole food conservation campaign, then, been a redundancy? Such a conclusion would be too extreme. It belies the evidence that millions of Americans did obey Hoover's injunctions during the winter and spring of 1918. Their behavior surely made some difference.

But here, as well, a distinction must be made. In his letter to the President on July 11—a letter intended for public perusal—Hoover asserted that the American people's food sacrifices in the preceding months had been voluntary. This, no doubt, was effective propaganda for a nation in the midst of a war. It presented a morale-boosting contrast to the ways of Kaiser Wilhelm and his Prussianized subjects. It was also good advertising for Hoover. But just a few weeks later, in another (and unpublicized) report to President Wilson, Hoover submitted data indicating that nearly all of the savings of wheat that occurred in the United States between January and June 1918—a figure he put at 65,687,000 bushels—had actually resulted from *compulsory* measures, notably the 50-50 rule and the enforced commercial baking of Victory bread.[191] Herein lay the real key to Hoover's victory. It was a conclusion that one of his Food Administration associates also reached.[192] It was not, of course, the conclusion that a man who abjured the label "food dictator" would want to disseminate.

The volume of wheat savings that Hoover effected, then, derived less from voluntary self-denial than from coercion. The popular response to his campaign was also selective. But it cannot be inferred from this that his voluntaristic rhetoric had been inefficacious. In 1917–18 the United States was far less accustomed than its European allies and enemies to the governmental interventionism required by total war. Hoover's repeated summonses to the food control "barricades" did not win universal acceptance. But they did help to explain what had to be done and to elicit public tolerance for the belt-tightening. A spoonful of voluntarism, so to speak, helped the regimen go down.

Even more importantly, the Food Administrator's unremitting calls to self-sacrifice helped to cancel out the powerful wartime economic pressures for increased food consumption—and without resorting to an untried system of universal rationing. If many Americans ate more and better food in 1917–18, millions of others—in obedience to Hoover—ate less. At the very least, his mobilization of restaurateurs and middle-class housewives into a food conservation "army" helped to preserve a wheat surplus created mostly by other means. This in itself was a valuable achievement.

In the final analysis one must ask: What would have happened if Hoover had done nothing? What if there had been no appeal for conservation at all? Even if American wheat consumption would have fallen seasonally anyway, Hoover could hardly be blamed for taking no chances. He was not living in normal times. The United States was in mortal combat, and its allies needed wheat for the staff of life. One statistic above all validated his actions: on July 1, 1918, at the beginning of a new crop year, his country had but 17,000,000 bushels of wheat remaining in storage—less than one month's supply.

If there had been no organized conservation campaign, if there had been no Hooverian barrage of exhortations to save, in all likelihood the United States would have exhausted its most precious staple well before the summer of 1918. Then would have come shortages, spiraling prices, and urban unrest at home, and incalculable consequences for the Allies abroad. The American people would not have starved—there was other food available—but they would at a minimum have suffered great inconvenience. The impact on their associates in war might have been worse.

Hoover as a policymaker could not be nonchalant about such possibilities. He had seen what had happened in Russia. The future was unpredictable. The German armies were driving for victory in northern France. The fate of the war conceivably rested on his ability to keep the Allied populations supplied with meat and bread.

And of this much he could, by July 1918, be certain: the wheat shortage that had harassed him for a year was over. A new and larger harvest was under way. Food was flowing to Europe in gigantic quantities. The United States had "the largest area under cultivation" in its history.[193] America was finally becoming the cornucopia upon which the Allies might draw with confidence.

Yet nothing was ever easy in the enterprise of food control. During the winter and spring of 1918 Hoover had had to resort to draconian edicts in order to pull America through to the next harvest. While doing so he had been obliged to fight a series of angry domestic battles, to which we now turn. Even in war, not everyone was yielding willingly to his leadership.

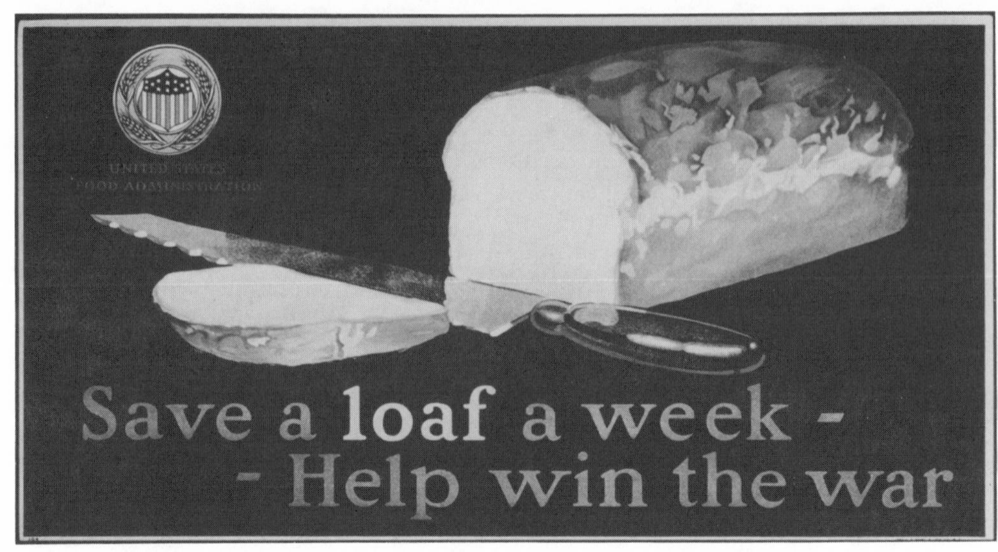

6–10. *Some propaganda posters of the U.S. Food Administration.* Poster Collection, Hoover Institution Archives.

Little
AMERICANS
Do your bit
Eat Corn meal mush-
Oatmeal-Corn flakes
Hominy and rice with
milk. Eat no wheat
cereals.
Leave nothing on your plate

UNITED STATES FOOD ADMINISTRATION

UNCLE SAM
THE LID'S DOWN!
FAMILY SUGAR BOWL
OBEY ORDERS!
U. S. Food Administration

11. *Official uniform of the Food Conservation section of the U.S. Food Administration. Patterns could be obtained by sending 10¢ to the agency in Washington, D.C.* U.S. Food Administration Collection, Hoover Institution Archives.

12. *Official window card of the U.S. Food Administration.* Poster Collection, Hoover Institution Archives.

13. *Atlantic City, New Jersey, supports Hoover.* U.S. Food Administration Collection, Hoover Institution Archives.

14. *An unofficial food conservation display.* Herbert Hoover Presidential Library-Museum.

15. *Enforcement of the Food Administration's rules.* National Archives.

16. *An outdoor food conservation sign.* Herbert Hoover Presidential Library-Museum.

17. *Placard used by restaurants which adhered to Hoover's regulations.* Poster Collection, Hoover Institution Archives.

18. *The Biltmore takes the pledge (Spring 1918).* U.S. Food Administration Collection, Hoover Institution Archives.

10

Ambush on Capitol Hill

I

ON November 28, 1917 President Wilson asked a number of his closest associates to suggest legislation that he might propose at the forthcoming session of Congress.[1] Herbert Hoover was quick to respond. It was time, he declared, to vest a "general price-fixing power" either in the President or the Federal Trade Commission. Despite all the government's controls over exports, imports, and purchases, and despite "making first one voluntary agreement after another, we are playing around the fringes of the problem," said Hoover, "and setting up great currents of injustice." The nation's farmers in particular were "justly" complaining that the government was restricting their income while doing nothing to restrain the price of goods that they must buy.

Hoover argued that the federal government must acquire the power not only to determine the "fair price" of a few "primary raw materials" but also to "fix the profits or differentials" obtained by manufacturers and distributors. Furthermore, the government should have the authority to buy and sell "primary commodities" if that were necessary to "maintain regular and seasonal flow." By direct government involvement in marketing operations, Hoover hoped to bring under control the multitudes of pestiferous small retail businesses that were beyond the direct reach of his regulatory apparatus.[2]

A few days later President Wilson incorporated the thrust of these recommendations into his message to Congress. The executive branch, he said, must receive additional powers to "set limits to prices." Relying heavily on Hoover's own words, Wilson declared that the "law of supply and demand" had been "replaced by the law of unrestrained selfishness." And, like Hoover, the President acknowledged the justice of farmers' complaints.[3]

In the next several weeks Hoover and other members of the Wilson administration formulated a bill that would give the President of the United States blanket authority to fix prices through any agency he chose.[4] The timing of their effort could not have been less opportune. By the middle of January 1918 the Wilson administration was under ferocious assault from Congressional critics who accused it of nearly criminal incompetence in managing the war. As fusillades of criticism emanated from Capitol Hill, the chances of persuading Congress to grant unprecedented new powers to the "college professor" in the White House (as Theodore Roosevelt castigated him) seemed to dwindle. So poisonous and unpromising was the political atmosphere that when the bill was finally ready to be submitted, Representative Lever himself declined to introduce it.[5]

Nevertheless, throughout the winter Hoover continued to advocate governmental control of the prices and distribution of every commodity rendered scarce by the government's military requirements.[6] The United States must do this, he insisted, "in order to protect the civil population." Just leaving the market alone under these circumstances and allowing prices to rise "until consumption ceases at some class in the population" was, for him, unacceptable. That, he said, was "conservation for the rich and not for the poor, and [it would] stimulate profiteering and upset wage levels."[7]

Hoover's push for ever more extensive price controls, like his concurrent request for sweeping power to enforce food conservation, provided additional proof that by early 1918 the voluntaristic emphasis of his work was weakening. Yet as Hoover—impelled by the demands of modern warmaking and the logic of economic interventionism—moved in increasingly "extra-constitutional" directions,[8] a vocal chorus of critics rose to challenge him. The winter of 1917–18 brought not only the severest weather in decades, monumental rail tieups, the closure of eastern factories, and a dangerous interruption of food shipments to the Allies. It also witnessed an explosion of discontent aimed at the Food Administrator himself and his regulatory system. For Hoover, the war at home was to be nearly as stressful as the war abroad.

II

It was on the sugar front that the gathering opposition to Hoover struck first.

During September and October 1917 the Food Administrator had implemented a complex set of voluntary agreements and other devices designed to stabilize the price of sugar to American consumers. But as he had done so, a great shortage of sugar had arisen along the eastern seaboard, forcing refineries to close and many customers to do without. By early December members of Congress—notably Senator Henry Cabot Lodge of Massachusetts—were wondering why.

Scrambling to meet the emergency until a new harvest became available in Cuba and elsewhere, Hoover initially blamed the shortage on the failure of the American people to curtail their consumption and on his need to send "unusual shipments" to beleaguered France that autumn.[9] The Republican senator from Massachusetts, however, was unpersuaded. On December 11 Lodge introduced a resolution directing the Senate committee on manufactures to investigate the sugar problem. The Senate agreed to his proposal without debate.[10]

It quickly became apparent that this was to be no ordinary inquiry. The chairman of the Senate's committee on manufactures was none other than Hoover's bitterest Congressional critic, James A. Reed. When Reed—no friend of Woodrow Wilson, either—appointed a subcommittee (headed by himself) to hold hearings, it turned out that all but one of its members were anti-administration.[11] Sensing that an inquisition was in the making, Hoover requested that the Food Administration's counsel be permitted to cross-examine witnesses.[12] It was an extraordinary demand, which the subcommittee unanimously rejected. Only the senators would be allowed to interrogate witnesses, although other parties could submit questions for committee members to ask.[13]

Despite Reed's promise of impartiality and his assurance that the Food Administration was not on trial,[14] Hoover soon had reason to think otherwise. On December 14 the subcommittee on the sugar shortage called as its first witness Claus A. Spreckels, a wealthy German-American sugar refiner who was a critic of Hoover's policies. In three days of sensational testimony Spreckels asserted that there was no genuine scarcity of sugar in the United States at all. On the contrary, the "localized" shortages in the Northeast had been "created" by the Food Administration itself. Under the "voluntary agreements" that Hoover had negotiated with American sugar interests in the summer and fall, domestic refiners had surrendered their right to import sugar independently of the Food Administration. Instead, they had agreed that Hoover's International Sugar Committee would "arrange" their imports for them. According to Spreckels, on October 1 Hoover's committee imposed an embargo on further imports of sugar from Cuba despite (he said) a considerable amount of sugar remaining there. Why? Because the committee did not want to pay the high price demanded by Cuban owners. The committee was anxious to protect the domestic price control structure for refined sugar just worked out by Hoover and to keep down the price of sugar for American households. But the result, charged Spreckels, was that

American refineries were obliged to shut down for lack of Cuban imports—and consumers in the urban East soon had little or no sugar to consume.

The German-American tycoon did not stop here. Another motive for the untimely embargo, he asserted, was to protect the financial position of a refining company in which George Rolph, the head of Hoover's sugar division, was interested. In fact, Spreckels testified, Hoover's International Sugar Committee was a mere "adjunct" of the American Sugar Refining Company, popularly known as the "sugar trust," which controlled about 40 percent of the sugar business of the United States. Hoover had named George Babst, president of the "trust," to this committee. According to Spreckels, Babst had thereupon staffed it with his own employees and used his influence to advance his own self-interest. Among other things, said Spreckels, Hoover had permitted Babst virtually to corner the Louisiana cane sugar crop in secret negotiations sponsored by the Food Administration in October, at a time when competing refiners would have dearly loved to obtain some of this commodity.

Spreckels alleged further that during the recent sugar famine, George Rolph's company in California had refused to send its huge stockpiles to the rescue on the dubious ground that its supply was needed on the west coast. Western sugar beets had also been available for shipment east, Spreckels contended, but had not been sent because refiners and sellers of cane sugar did not want their market "invaded by a cheaper product." Spreckels's complaints were various, but their essence was simple and explosive: the great sugar famine of 1917 had been entirely artificial, a result of bureaucratic interventionism and egregious conflicts of interest.[15]

For the next few days Babst and Rolph, on the witness stand, angrily contradicted Spreckels's claims. The eastern sugar shortage of 1917 was real, they insisted. It was the consequence of (among other things) a shortage of railcars to move sugar beets from the West. The crisis had not been caused by the International Sugar Committee's decision to embargo further Cuban sugar imports in October. The committee had done this to avoid enriching Cuban "speculators," who wanted a price for their product that would have forced up the price of table sugar to American families. Even if the committee had imported all of the Cuban crop still available, there was so little of it left that it would not have fed the American people for more than a few days. An unrestrained scramble for this small amount would only have driven prices through the roof and yielded no significant quantity of sugar.

As for the Louisiana deal, Babst asserted that he had been invited to make it because the Louisiana cane growers desired to deal with him. The Food Administration, he testified, was guilty of no preferential treatment. For his part, Rolph heatedly denied that his California company had had anything like the stocks that Spreckels said it had or that it had failed to ship these to the east coast for selfish reasons. In fact, Rolph said, his company had sold it at a loss to alleviate a "famine situation" in the Midwest. Nor had domestic sugar beets been held back for greedy purposes. This western crop, on which Hoover had been relying to tide over the East until winter, had been harvested late and then entrapped in the nationwide breakdown of rail transportation. In the eyes of Babst and Rolph, their accuser was an unreliable witness with grudges and selfish motives of his own.[16]

So, too, said Herbert Hoover in a blistering press release on the second day of Spreckels's testimony. Spreckels was "sore at the Food Administration," Hoover asserted, "and would like to see it destroyed." Why? Because the Food Administration had regulated sugar refiners' profits, had reduced the high prices of last August, and had then prevented the price of sugar from reaching astronomical heights in the midst of a shortage. All this, remarked Hoover caustically, had adversely affected Spreckels's "balance sheets."[17]

The Food Administrator was not the only person to suspect that Spreckels was a far from disinterested witness. According to Hoover's aide Mark Requa, Spreckels "hated Babst beyond measure" and was furious when Hoover appointed Babst (but not Spreckels) to the International Sugar Committee.[18] Yet if Spreckels was as resentful and prejudiced as Hoover alleged, why had the Senate subcommittee made him its very first witness? Senator Reed later asserted that he had summoned Spreckels and other men to Washington "practically at random" and that Spreckels had testified first because "he happened to be the first witness appearing." Reed claimed that he had never met Spreckels in his life and did not know in advance what "the character of his testimony" would be.[19] It is doubtful that Hoover accepted this explanation. *He* later asserted that Reed's own law firm had received retainers from certain food processors "who objected to the prospect" of regulated wartime profits. It was a broad hint that Reed himself had a financial stake in besmirching Hoover's agency.[20]

Relations between Hoover and the subcommittee's ranking Republican, Senator Lodge, were no better. Lodge was incensed when he heard that Hoover had called him "pro-German," a label tantamount to traitor.[21] Behind the scenes the British ambassador to the United States tried to effect a "truce" between the two men. Unfortunately for the ambassador, Hoover (he noted) was "a natural fighter" with "very bitter enemies"—an "uncompromising" man with "no parliamentary arts."[22]

Hoover could not be content with a single press release against Spreckels. The refiner's assault had been too comprehensive and widely publicized for that. Fearful that Spreckels's denial of a sugar shortage would undercut the government's campaign for sugar conservation, Hoover appeared in the Senate subcommittee's hearing room on December 17 in the hope that he could immediately rebut Spreckels's testimony. Chairman Reed paid him no attention. Hoover's counsel, Curtis H. Lindley, asked Reed to let Hoover testify quickly; Reed promised to consult his committee colleagues. But when the subcommittee returned from lunch, Reed said nothing. Instead he let

Spreckels, who had not finished testifying, reply to Hoover's blast at him in the press. By the end of the day the subcommittee had not replied to Lindley's request. Hoover, meanwhile, made his way to the White House to confer with the President.[23]

By now the Senate hearing room was "electric with hostility" between most of the subcommittee and Hoover's representatives.[24] The State Department, too, had become embroiled in the fight. On the afternoon of December 17 the subcommittee grilled the department's counselor in executive session about Hoover's negotiations for purchase of the Cuban sugar crop, another issue raised by Spreckels.[25]

The next day Lindley attempted again to have Hoover appear at once before Reed's panel. The attorney pointed out that Hoover was "one of the hardest working men in Washington today" and had been obliged to cancel a meeting in New York in order to be available to testify. Reed, however, refused to alter the "orderly course" of the testimony as it was starting to unfold. The exact timing of Hoover's appearance remained unresolved.[26]

In the next several days, amidst contentious clashes between Reed and pro-Hoover witnesses, the subcommittee probed the causes of the sugar famine. As the hearings proceeded, two competing theories of the crisis emerged. One, propounded by Hoover and his supporters, was that the inaccessibility of much of the world's sugar had compelled the Allies in mid-1917 to focus their purchasing on Cuba, thereby threatening a shortage and galloping prices. By a remarkable series of price-capping arrangements with all major American sugar interests, and by a fair-minded agreement with the Cubans, Hoover had heroically managed to stabilize domestic sugar prices at an acceptable level and forfend a catastrophic tripling of price. The shortage of sugar to consumers that then ensued was the result not of price controls or of manipulations by unsavory sugar men but of unforeseen factors—such as freight congestion—for which Hoover was not responsible.[27]

The other theory—congenial to anti-Wilson senators like Lodge and Reed—was that the U.S. government's own intervention in the sugar market had caused and then exacerbated the crisis. Reed implied that Hoover's well-publicized expressions of "imaginative alarm" in May 1917 about a coming sugar shortage had themselves encouraged hoarding and higher prices.[28] A representative of Spreckels's interests contended that uncertainty about the food control law and Hoover's intentions in the summer of 1917 had prompted many American sugar merchants to hesitate to import sugar at a critical point. Unsure of what their prices and profits might be under Hooverian supervision, the importers fatally held back while the Allies scooped up Cuban sugar at a furious rate.[29]

Hoover was also criticized for closing the sugar futures market and for adopting regulations that prevented refiners from taking steps to minimize the impending scarcity.[30] According to one sugar broker, Hoover made a "too radical peremptory attempt" to reduce sugar prices at the outset, thus intensifying the shortage.[31] The beet sugar price was a case in point: at the figure Hoover and the processors initially agreed upon, very little of the crop came east. But when the Food Administration raised the price of beet sugar in Boston, a shipment speedily materialized from the West.[32] (Hoover blamed this hiatus in shipments on the railroads.) The Louisiana cane harvest was a similar case: at the price that Hoover and others arranged, it was expected that 100,000 tons would be sold to Babst's refining company, with prompt relief for the sugar-starved urban Northeast. Instead, the Louisiana producers found that they could sell their product elsewhere in semi-refined form at a better profit—and largely did so.[33] As a result, the northeastern famine persisted. Once more, it seemed, Hoover's solicitude for the American consumer had backfired.

In short, one theory—Hoover's theory—held that the Food Administration had rescued America from a chaotic market that, unless stabilized, would have yielded runaway sugar prices, urban suffering, and social dislocation. The other theory held that the Food Administration itself, by its heavy-handed intervention in the market, had made matters worse. In the words of Senator Lodge, "the satisfaction of a low price, when you cannot buy anything, seems rather barren."[34]

Meanwhile Hoover was waiting with rising frustration for the opportunity to present his version of events to the subcommittee and the public. On December 20 Senator Reed announced the subcommittee's intention to call Hoover as a witness the next day, as soon as George Rolph was finished.[35] The next day the committee examined Rolph until suppertime and did not hear Hoover at all.

Then, on Saturday, December 22, a new complication arose when a delegation of angry beet sugar farmers from as far away as California appeared on Capitol Hill. Some weeks before, Hoover had negotiated price control agreements with the factories that processed the beet farmers' crops; these arrangements appeared to guarantee the factories a comfortable margin of profit. The beet growers now complained bitterly that in contracts presented to them for the coming year's harvest the factories failed to offer a remunerative price. To add insult to injury, the Food Administration, in its zeal for more beet production, was allegedly siding with the factories and pressuring the farmers with patriotic exhortations. The farmers warned that unless they promptly received a much better offer for the next beet crop—due to be planted very soon—they would refuse to sign the proferred contracts and would curb or even terminate their production. It was a threat that Hoover and his colleagues could not ignore.[36]

With Christmas only three days away and the committee set to adjourn for the holidays, Reed and his colleagues decided (he said) "as an act of common decency" to let the western beet sugar growers, who had traveled so far, testify ahead of Hoover. Their complaints consumed the entire committee session of December 22. In mid-afternoon Chairman Reed announced that

Hoover's appearance would be deferred yet again, this time until the following Friday, December 28.[37] According to Reed, he had asked a representative of Hoover's in the committee room whether this postponement was agreeable and had been told that it would be.[38] The representative, however, remembered this critical conversation differently. According to him, Reed had merely asked him to notify Hoover of the committee's decision.[39] Whichever version was correct, the effect was to deprive Hoover of his coveted pulpit for six more days.

By now Hoover was convinced that Reed and his cohorts were trying to silence him and manipulate the hearings to partisan advantage. On the morning of Saturday, December 22, Hoover sent President Wilson an advance copy of a statement on the sugar shortage that he had prepared for delivery to the Senate subcommittee as testimony. Hoover was anxious to release the document to the press immediately. The President, however—sensitive to the ways of Congress—felt that this might be interpreted as a discourtesy to the subcommittee.[40] Later that morning, after learning of the subcommittee's decision to postpone Hoover's testimony until after Christmas, the Food Administrator forwarded his statement to the panel and requested that it be read at once into the record. In this way, his detailed defense could become public at last.[41]

It was now midday on Saturday. If Hoover's document could be made public that very day, it would guarantee him front-page coverage in the Sunday newspapers—a windfall he was surely aware of.

Hoover's request appeared to be fair and reasonable. For five days he had waited for an opportunity to combat the adverse publicity generated by Spreckels. Now it appeared that he would have to wait six more. If the senators could not promptly call him as a witness, surely they could do him the simple justice of printing his explanation of the sugar famine in the hearing record.

But if the subcommittee now permitted Hoover to do this, it would mean that he would be able to disseminate his story without immediately having to defend it, a turn of events that evidently galled Senator Reed. The erstwhile prosecutor from Kansas City immediately objected to inserting in the record "these ex parte statements that we have no chance to examine about."[42] Over the strenuous protests of Senator A. A. Jones of New Mexico (Hoover's sole sympathizer on the panel), the subcommittee upheld Reed's objection and voted not to receive Hoover's prepared statement because (said Reed) the committee expected "to put Mr. Hoover upon the witness stand [later] and examine him, as other witnesses."[43] According to Hoover, the subcommittee members even refused to state whether they would consider it discourteous if Hoover released the document independently to the press.[44]

The next day the subcommittee's rebuff reverberated across the country. Whatever the technical merits of Reed's position, it was a public relations blunder. "Hoover's Story on Sugar Fight Is Suppressed," ran a typical headline.[45] By chance or by maneuver, Hoover had won a sympathetic response in the press. Still, the Food Administrator was livid at what he considered the subcommittee's blatant "attempt to stifle truth and to leave prejudice in the minds of the public."[46] Hoover announced to the press through his counsel that he did not feel he ought to give his statement to the newspapers "at this moment," lest he appear discourteous to the subcommittee.[47] Instead, he immediately asked President Wilson to release the document from the White House, through the government's Committee on Public Information.[48] The committee's director, George Creel, agreed with Hoover, and told the President that Senators Reed and Lodge were attempting "to keep this report from the public" until their "own lies" could "sink in and take on color of fact."[49] Hoover's counsel, meanwhile, accused Reed of displaying "personal venom" and of refusing to receive from Hoover "information which the committee had specifically invited Mr. Hoover to present."[50]

President Wilson needed little persuading. According to the British ambassador, the chief executive was "bitterly angry" at the coalition of "disgruntled democrats" and "sour republicans" attacking Hoover.[51] On Christmas night Wilson took the extraordinary and possibly unprecedented step of issuing Hoover's blocked Congressional testimony to the newspapers.[52]

For all the fanfare, Hoover's statement was a moderately worded survey of the sugar problem and his agency's response to it. The fundamental cause of the scarcity, he contended, was that the Allies had been forced to quadruple their imports from the western hemisphere in 1917—an action that "denuded" the United States of the 300,000 tons it needed to "maintain normal consumption" in the last quarter of the year. The shortage, he said, had then been aggravated by the "lack of cars to move Louisiana and beet sugar promptly to areas of greatest pressure," notably the Northeast. Hoover also emphasized the critical need to rush 100,000 tons of sugar to France during the autumn in order to bolster that wavering ally's rations and morale. He vigorously denied that there had been, or would be, ample sugar available at home—a claim that, if acted upon by the American people, would wreak "incalculable harm" on the war effort. He denied that he had engaged in price-fixing "in a legal sense." He had had to rely, he said, on the "feeble weapon of voluntary agreement" and various regulations to limit profits. Nevertheless, he declared, these measures had been efficacious. Without them, retail sugar would not cost 8½ to 9½ cents per pound as it did today, but 20 cents or even 25. Thus by Hoover's calculations, the Food Administration had prevented the American public from being "robbed" of at least $180,000,000 a year.[53]

The promulgation of Hoover's statement by the White House was a clever counterstroke that put Reed and his senatorial colleagues on the defensive. Former President William Howard Taft spoke for much moderate and liberal opinion by publicly depicting Hoover as a victim of a maliciously unfair

Congressional investigation. "What is the reason for this discrimination?" Taft asked. Why was Hoover being treated "worse than a criminal under indictment, by denying him the right to cross-examine his accuser, by hearing the evidence for the prosecution and by then postponing his day in court?" The answer, Taft suggested, was the enmity felt for Hoover by James A. Reed. Taft warned that "if the food issue alone cannot win the war, it may lose it for us." The "fear of starvation" threatened to destroy the morale of the French and Italian people and to break the will of their armies to fight. Food was vital, said Taft, and Herbert Hoover was the man "whose words should be law to our people" in conserving it.

> If his prestige is injured, if his motives are impeached, if his statements are questioned, then food conservation and all dependent on it will fail. Then we will be driven to drastic, burdensome legislation and minute compulsory executive action.[54]

Far more than esoteric issues of sugar policy were at stake, then, when Reed's subcommittee reconvened on December 28 to listen to Hoover at last. The reputation and effectiveness of the Food Administrator were in peril. But when the subcommittee came to order, to its astonishment Hoover was not there. Instead, his counsel, Lindley, informed the senators by letter that Hoover had been called to New York the day before to attend "an extremely important conference on the tonnage situation." Noting that the "public press" had reported that Hoover was expected to meet the committee on the twenty-eighth, Lindley stated that he had tried in vain to notify the members in advance about Hoover's sudden change in plans.[55]

The committee was not amused by Hoover's failure to be present, and still less by Lindley's suggestion that Hoover had only learned about its timetable in the newspapers. If this were true, it would make the committee again appear discourteous and again cast Hoover in the role of wounded innocent. The committee therefore immediately put Hoover's personal representative in the hearing room under oath: had he not informed Hoover six days ago that the committee would hear the Food Administrator today? The representative admitted that he had. But to Reed's disgust the representative denied that he had previously told Reed that this alteration of the schedule would be "entirely agreeable" to Hoover. The representative said that he had no such authority to speak for his chief.[56]

Fuming at this twist in his growing feud with the Food Administrator, Reed emphatically defended his committee's conduct. His panel had *not* denied a hearing to Hoover's viewpoint, he declared. While it was true that the leadoff witness (Spreckels) had been unfriendly to the Food Administration, the next two witnesses (Babst and Rolph) had been supportive of it. The Missouri Democrat insisted that the postponement of Hoover's testimony until December 28 in order to accommodate the western beet sugar farmers had been done "with the full approbation and consent of Mr. Hoover's representative."[57] What Reed did not mention was that Babst and Rolph had not received a friendly reception. Whether by accident or design, the hearings to date had been decidedly damaging to Hoover's cause.

With Hoover two hundred miles away, Reed's panel temporarily turned to other matters and sent Hoover a pointed telegram requesting his testimony immediately after New Year's Day.[58] Suddenly the shoe was on the other foot; the subcommittee was pursuing Hoover, not vice versa. Up in New York, Hoover showed no remorse for skipping town and risking reproach for contempt of Congress. Perhaps—one strongly suspects it—he had lost interest in the subcommittee's deliberations. After all, he had now conveyed his story to the public in the best manner possible, under the protective, prestigious cover of presidential authority. Thanks to Woodrow Wilson and a sympathetic national press, he was winning the battle for public opinion. When asked in New York about the senators' anger at his absence from Washington, Hoover replied disdainfully: "I make it a practice never to discuss the feelings of the Senate committee."[59]

Nevertheless, on Wednesday morning, January 2, 1918, the Food Administrator answered the committee's summons. For the next two days, in a hearing room filled with up to two hundred spectators, he fought an acrimonious duel with his critics. Senator Lodge suggested that Hoover's much-publicized predictions, back in the spring, of an impending sugar shortage had themselves caused the price of sugar to increase; Hoover denied it.[60] Lodge wondered skeptically whether governmental price-fixing had ever been a success in history. Hoover replied that in short-term emergencies like the present it had been.[61] Hoover conceded that governmental interventionism never worked perfectly and that purely legal attempts to fix maximum prices would fail, as they had in Europe. But—he insisted—the fixing of maximum prices, *combined with governmental control of the distribution of the affected commodity*, could succeed, at least in the short run. For him this was clearly the lesser evil.[62]

Senator Lodge was not at all convinced:

> *Senator Lodge*. Then a controlled maximum, you think, is successful?
>
> *Mr. Hoover*. I think in the case of sugar we have a controlled maximum, where we have prevented the doubling of the price of sugar.
>
> *Senator Lodge*. But what you have prevented, of course, is what you think you have prevented?
>
> *Mr. Hoover*. I would be very glad if you would take the evidence on what the price of sugar would probably be at the present moment if the precautions had not been taken.
>
> *Senator Lodge*. Any evidence on that is merely what a man thinks it would have been.[63]

To Lodge, Hoover's controls amounted to the fixing of a single "arbitrary price" that was both a maximum and a minimum. Hoover disagreed:

> *Mr. Hoover.* No. We fix a price beyond which any charge will be considered extortion or profiteering and secure an agreement of the trades that they would themselves acknowledge that, in effect.
>
> *Senator Lodge.* You fix an arbitrary price?
>
> *Mr. Hoover.* Competition is free to play below that price. I would not want to say we fix an arbitrary price. If you wish to call it a maximum price I have no objection. . . .

Lodge persisted. Was not Hoover's scheme price-fixing (which under the law, of course, he had no direct authority to practice)?

> *Mr. Hoover.* I rather look on it from my own aspect of mind as profit fixing. It has the effect of fixing price.
>
> *Senator Lodge.* It is practically to fix a price and take it out of the operation of the law of supply and demand?
>
> *Mr. Hoover.* Yes. The law, in my view, is suspended in these cases, anyway.
>
> *Senator Lodge.* Suspending natural laws is always an interesting experiment.
>
> *Mr. Hoover.* I agree with you that it is the most difficult operation that can be conceived.[64]

Still, Hoover the temperamental activist was willing to try. He was convinced that his plan of "voluntary organization of trade to carry out the national interests" could work—and certainly better than by attempting to set prices by legal fiat.[65]

A few moments later Hoover remarked that beet sugar production might decline in 1918 because farmers might be able to make more of a profit by growing beans. Lodge could not conceal his sarcasm:

> *Senator Lodge.* That is another of the natural laws. Can you not set it aside?
>
> *Mr. Hoover.* I am not sure but what it might need to be.[66]

When Hoover asserted that his capping of the price of imported Cuban sugar in September 1917 had saved American consumers a penny a pound, Lodge retorted, "Lowering the price of sugar when there is no sugar is rather unsatisfactory."[67]

Hoover also came under fire for depending upon leading businessmen to administer his "voluntary agreements." Senator James K. Vardaman of Mississippi warned him that it was "pretty hard to serve God and mammon both."[68] Hoover insisted that it was "hopeless" for him to oversee the nation's food trades without "the best and most competent advice" available, and he assumed that the men who actually led these trades—"if they are patriotic and honest"—could render him the best advice of all.[69] His "test" of the fitness of businessmen to serve him was "very simple," said Hoover, "and that is whether or not a man is willing to devote himself to assisting his country to win the war in subjection to all personal and private interests, and if a man stands that test, then I do not care what his associations are." Vardaman rejoined that there was a difference between what men said and what they did. Furthermore, the nation's larger sugar interests had "not been neglected." They had made no sacrifices. Yes, they had, said Hoover; their profits had been reduced to prewar, "normal" levels. For Vardaman that was not enough.

> *Mr. Hoover.* Do you dispute the right of a commercial interest to make its prewar normal profit?
>
> *Senator Vardaman.* As a matter of fact, I do, when the people are suffering so much. The men who are suffering at the front are not making their normal profits, and they are giving up everything. The boy who leaves a thousand-dollar position and takes $350 a year and loses the balance and gives his life is not being protected. I do not think they have any more right to get it than anyone else has to claim it. The men who are suffering at the front are not being protected in that way.
>
> *Mr. Hoover.* I will agree with you in theory that no one should make any profit at all out of this war, but I have serious doubts whether as an economic system the country would revolve 24 hours without it.
>
> *Senator Vardaman.* If it could not revolve 24 hours without it it is because of lack of patriotism.[70]

It was not Lodge and Vardaman, however, whose hostility to Hoover generated the most heated exchanges. That distinction belonged to the committee's acerbic chairman. When Senator Jones attempted to introduce Hoover's recently published statement on the sugar shortage into the hearing record, Reed's anger and scorn boiled over:

> *The Chairman [Reed].* Did you feel that you had to take that statement to the President in order to get it published, Mr. Hoover?
>
> *Mr. Hoover.* It was sent to the President coincident with being sent to the committee.
>
> *The Chairman.* That is not my question. The statement was given to the country. In order to get that statement before the country it was taken to the President, and by his intervention it was published. Did you think it was necessary to do that in order to get this paper published[?]
>
> *Mr. Hoover.* Yes; I thought it was necessary in order to get it done.

> *The Chairman.* Had you had any difficulty in getting your material published?
>
> *Mr. Hoover.* This was a statement to the committee, and I was told that a statement given to the committee could not be released for publication by myself without the committee's approval.

Reed now claimed (without evidence) that he had publicly told Hoover's counsel that Hoover was "at perfect liberty" to print the statement on his own. Hoover replied that he was unaware that Reed had said this. Reed insisted vehemently that the committee had not prevented Hoover from issuing the statement to the press. Hoover countered that he had learned from Senator Jones that the committee had "declined to say whether it was a discourtesy or not if I sent it out," thereby tying his hands. Hoover testified that he had been anxious to release the document in order to counteract the disastrous and erroneous assertion that there was ample sugar in the country. "If I had known that it would have been considered no discourtesy by the committee, I would have been glad to send it out on Saturday [December 22], but I was left wholly uninstructed in the matter."[71]

On and on the two men wrangled. Reed pointed out that two pro-Hoover witnesses had already testified. To Hoover, the words of Babst and Rolph were no adequate substitute for his own. Besides, Babst was no witness in the Food Administrator's behalf. Then did you consider Babst an adverse witness? inquired Reed. "I have no opinion whatever on Mr. Babst's testimony," Hoover shot back, adding, "That is not a fair question." "Do you complain because we put him on the stand?" asked Reed.

> *Mr. Hoover.* I asked to go on the stand at the time that Mr. Babst went on the stand, and I was refused. I wished to get over to the country the true state of the sugar situation in order that there should not be disorganization. . . . My only complaint is that I was not given an early opportunity to come before this committee, either in person or by statement, and 15 days elapsed from December 13th to 28th.[72]

This encounter was only the beginning. The next day Reed cross-examined Hoover minutely about his sugar policies. Hoover had told Senator Lodge that the severe shortage of sugar in the East had been due to a single cause: "Solely and absolutely shortage of [railroad] cars; inability to get cars through."[73] But under questioning from Reed a more complicated picture emerged, one that illuminated the perils of price control.

In an apparent bid to hold down the price of sugar to consumers, the Food Administration had first negotiated a maximum price for refined domestic beet sugar produced in the Middle and Far West. In September and October the Food Administration made no attempt to bring this sugar east of the Allegheny Mountains, lest it undercut higher priced Cuban *cane* sugar then selling (in refined form) on the east coast. Sugar dealers in the East had bought this Cuban sugar "at a higher level," Hoover testified, and he "had no right to impose a loss on the total sugar industry just to level it down with beets."[74] The result was a de facto, two-priced system: one for the East and one for the rest of the country.

Hoover hoped that his price support for eastern sugar would be temporary and that the product would decline in price (presumably to western beet sugar levels) once a new crop from Cuba flooded the market. But before this could occur, the eastern stores of sugar dwindled and vanished, and eastern refineries, deprived of further Cuban imports, had to close.

Desperate for relief, Hoover appealed to the cane sugar producers of Louisiana to sell their product to the Northeast at the same price as beet sugar. The Louisiana men, citing production costs, insisted on a higher price. Hoover eventually gave it to them ("to protect their industry") and arranged for a protected eastern market (meaning no competition from beets). That is, to assure the Louisiana producers a "proper" and "righteous" price for their product, he held the price of east coast sugar up—by keeping cheaper western sugar out. Babst of the "sugar trust" then offered to buy a huge chunk of the Louisiana crop.

But the deal that Hoover and Babst arranged was not good enough. Instead of sending 100,000 tons or more of their sugar to Babst and the Northeast, as Hoover undoubtedly expected, the Louisiana growers sold nearly all of it elsewhere as brown sugar and made more money. "That always happens," Reed commented sarcastically, "when you undertake to do a thing and go against a natural law, when you fix a price that is not satisfactory, and the fellow finds a market for himself."[75]

It was not until mid-November that the Food Administration realized that the Louisiana sugar it was counting on would not be forthcoming in sufficient quantity to rescue the Northeast. Then Hoover attempted to salvage the situation by finally hauling beet sugar east of the Alleghenies. It was too late. The railroads were clogged, and the needed replacement sugar could not get through.[76]

For Reed, all this was evidence not of an honest if fumbling attempt to solve a wartime crisis but of the folly of governmental interference in the free market. The senator was equally outraged at Hoover's interpretation of his powers under the Lever Act. By what right, Reed wondered, did Hoover claim to regulate sugar planters, when the Lever Act explicitly exempted farmers from its provisions? The planter was not only a planter but a refiner, replied Hoover, hence a manufacturer subject to licensing.[77] Hoover also asserted his legal right under the act to regulate planters' profits and to move against "extortionate" prices for plantation-grown sugar.

> *The Chairman.* So that this bill, which undertook to exempt from its operations the farmer as to the prices on his products, and which you said had nothing to do with price fixing, has been so worked out by you that

you do fix the price on the farmer's wheat and on the planter's sugar, and what else do you fix the price on?

Mr. Hoover. Of course, as I told you before, I do not admit the price-fixing theory that you have presented.

The Chairman. No; you come into the house from the other door, but we both get into the same room.[78]

Hoover was unwilling to retreat, however.

Mr. Hoover. We take the bill as the bill reads, and the attempt of the bill in our view is to prevent extortionate prices.

The Chairman. That means price fixing, does it not?

Mr. Hoover. Well, you have got to determine what a price is, sometimes, in order to tell what extortion consists of.

The Chairman. Yes; certainly. Extortion consists in anything that you think is extortion. You decide that question yourself, do you not?

Mr. Hoover. Well, I do not know that we ever have.

The Chairman. You decide what you think is a fair price, and anything that you do not agree to as a fair price becomes extortion?

Mr. Hoover. Allow me to continue. I would have to have legal advice in order to answer that question. It never has been done. Whether I have the right to do it I do not know. All of these prices have been arrived at by consultation with the people concerned as to what would be a fair price.

The Chairman. All of them have been purely voluntary?

Mr. Hoover. They have been voluntary agreements.

The Chairman. And yet you have testified, in answer to Senator Lodge, that these voluntary agreements could not be made if you did not have the power to force their making.

Mr. Hoover. The remaining 5 per cent; 95 per cent agree.

The Chairman. Yes, and you have admitted here this morning on several occasions that, as a matter of fact, these people were in such a situation that they could be compelled to do your bidding.

Mr. Hoover. I do not know that they were. I do not know that the matter ever arose in discussion.[79]

Reed did not stop at suggesting that Hoover's professed voluntarism was a fraud. Turning abruptly to the Food Administrator's control of the nation's wheat, the senator accused him of engaging in out-and-out price-fixing in blatant violation of the intent of Congress. Reed began by eliciting from Hoover an unapologetic admission that he had indeed "stabilized" the price of wheat through government buying and government control of the distribution machinery.[80] Hoover acknowledged, too, that his agency had told the nation that it wanted trading in wheat "to go on at Government prices." It had succeeded, he asserted, "by virtue of the voluntary response of the country." Reed was not persuaded:

The Chairman. Let us see. Where did the farmer have a place to sell his wheat? Where was the farmer's market? . . . The farmer had two places to sell, had he not, one to the grain dealer and the other to the miller?

Mr. Hoover. Yes.

The Chairman. And you have instructed the grain dealers that they must pay just certain prices. That is right?

Mr. Hoover. Yes.

The Chairman. And you have instructed the millers that they must pay certain prices?

Mr. Hoover. We asked them to; yes.

The Chairman. And you have instructed the millers that if they did not do it that something will happen to them?

Mr. Hoover. No. We asked the millers to enter a voluntary contract with us that they would not.

The Chairman. Have they done that?

Mr. Hoover. They have.

The Chairman. So that now you have taken away from the farmer his market for his wheat, except that he may sell it to grain dealers who will give but one price, and to millers who will give but one price. That is right, is it not?

Mr. Hoover. We have stabilized the price in the country.

The Chairman. You know, do you not, that Congress never gave you any such authority. You can not put your finger on a line of legislation giving you that authority, can you?

Mr. Hoover. I consider that the whole sense of the food bill—

The Chairman. Can you call my attention to a clause authorizing you to do that?

Mr. Hoover. The food bill provides for the purchase of wheat by the Government.

The Chairman. That is a different thing. . . .

To Reed, the purchase of wheat by the government was one thing; the ordering of independent grain dealers to pay farmers no more than a certain amount or be "disciplined" was another.[81]

Hoover now attempted to justify his implementation of the wheat price policy. The senator from Missouri was not mollified:

Mr. Hoover. We originally called a commission together—the President called a commission together in which the farmer had a majority, and determined what was a fair price.

The Chairman. For what?

Mr. Hoover. To determine a fair price at which wheat should be bought and stabilized for the country.

The Chairman. I am not asking what the President did. I am asking about this bill, and I want to ask you if, when this bill was before Congress and when you were advocating its passage, you did not repeatedly tell the Congress of the United States that there was no price-fixing in the bill? I mean by that, did you not tell the committees of Congress that?

Mr. Hoover. I do not recollect whether I did or not.

The Chairman. See if I can call your attention—

Mr. Hoover. Wait one moment. I agree that I probably did, and there was no price-fixing in the bill.

The Chairman. And yet you have employed the language of this bill, which you solemnly assured Congress did not authorize price-fixing, so as to fix the price on every bushel of wheat raised in the United States, have you not?

Mr. Hoover. We have, and it has been—

The Chairman. Is not that a direct and an absolute usurpation of authority?

Mr. Hoover. It has been done—

The Chairman. Is it not an abuse of power that would be a criminal act under the laws of our States if it was done at normal times—for any man to employ a legitimate power for the purpose of coercing and compelling a citizen to do something that does not come within that power?

Mr. Hoover. It has been done with the full approval of the President of the United States.

The Chairman. Of course, the President's coat tails are broad and his shoulders are mighty, and his position in the world is unchallenged by anyone, but I insist that I am examining you, not with reference to what the President has done, but with reference to the authority in this law which you told us, which you admitted, did not contain price-fixing power—authority under which you have presumed to fix the price for the wheat of the country.[82]

Hoover, however, refused to give up. A "country at war wishes to get results," he said. "It wishes to protect its producer and protect its consumer." "Who is to judge of that," Reed fired back, "you or the Congress that makes the law?" Hoover responded that the Congress itself, in the Lever Act, stated that one of the Act's purposes was "to establish and maintain governmental control" of certain "necessaries" during the war. You have quoted the preamble, Reed retorted; the preamble "means absolutely nothing in itself. It is not an enacting clause. . . ."

[The Chairman.] . . . Do you pretend to say to us that there is contained in the substantive part of this act any authority on your part to fix the price of wheat?

Mr. Hoover. I pretend to say, or I do say, that, taking the act altogether in all of its phases, its objects have been carried out in the arrangement of the wheat control in this country.

The Chairman. You pretend to say there is price fixing in the act, do you—the right to fix prices?

Mr. Hoover. In the sense it has been fixed in the case of wheat.

The Chairman. I do not care about senses. I am just talking about whether it is done.[83]

Reed now noted that in testimony before Congress on June 19, 1917 Hoover had explicitly declared that the Lever bill was *not* directed against farmers and in fact exempted farmers from every one of its provisions except the wheat price guarantee of $2.00 a bushel—a provision meant to "entirely benefit" and protect farmers. Yet now Hoover was saying that he had in fact fixed the price of wheat for all wheat growers in the United States.

Mr. Hoover. We have stabilized the price.

The Chairman. Yes; stabilized it; and that is to say that by stabilization you mean fixation, is it not?

Mr. Hoover. He can in his local markets obtain more or less.

Reed's exasperation once more came to the surface:

The Chairman. Oh, more in his local market. Mr. Hoover, you are too smart a man, and as weak as I am, I hope you will not pay me the poor compliment of saying that you could for a moment convince me or any one that the local market that is left to the farmer leaves him a price that amounts to anything after you have taken away the great markets for his wheat—that is to say, the market of the grain merchant, the market of the board of trade, and the market of the miller.

Mr. Hoover. I do not wish to quibble with the position. I agree with you; the price of wheat has been stabilized. There is practically a limit to what the farmer can get for his wheat.

The Chairman. Practically a limit, and for all intents and purposes has he not fixed an absolute price on the wheat in the United States?

Mr. Hoover. Practically so.[84]

Yet Hoover—Reed noted a few moments later—had told Congress back in June that the Lever bill contained no provision for price-fixing and that none could be effected under its provisions.

The Chairman. You said that, did you not?

Mr. Hoover. Yes.

The Chairman. And you have carried it out, have you not?

Mr. Hoover. I have not.

The Chairman. You have just told us how you have, have you not?
Mr. Hoover. We have endeavored to stabilize prices, and this statement promised we would do so.
The Chairman. Do not let us quibble about terms. You say you have stabilized prices. What do you mean by that—stabilizing prices?
Mr. Hoover. To maintain a reasonable level of prices.
The Chairman. When you maintain a level of prices, you fix the price, do you not?
Mr. Hoover. Well, you can use the terms as you like.
The Chairman. What is the use of our haggling about it?
Mr. Hoover. You can use them as you like.
The Chairman. Yes.

Hoover now quoted section 2 of the Lever Act, the section that authorized the President to create agencies and enter into voluntary agreements to carry out the stated objectives of the bill, which included government control of necessaries. Once again the strict-constructionist senator and the broad-constructionist bureaucrat clashed:

The Chairman. Then, you say there is price fixing in the bill, do you? Why did you not tell us that when you were over telling the committee of Congress there was no price fixing? Why did you not call attention to that and say, "The language is broad enough so that we can fix prices and we are going to fix prices"?
Mr. Hoover. I do not agree that we have fixed prices. You have not read the whole of my statement. That is a matter of discussion between us as to terms.
The Chairman. Hardly. It is hardly a matter of discussion.[85]

For the conservative Democrat from Missouri, then, Hoover's behavior was nothing less than criminal:

The Chairman. You wanted to protect the farmer. That was your object, was it?
Mr. Hoover. One of our objects.
The Chairman. Your object in protecting the farmer you have carried out by going contrary to the terms in this law.
Mr. Hoover. I do not concede that.
The Chairman. And without authority of this law.
Mr. Hoover. I do not concede that for one moment.
The Chairman. And taking away the farmer's market for his wheat this year and fixing a price at which he must sell it this year, although you told the committee when this bill was under consideration that there was no price fixing in it.

Mr. Hoover. I do not concede your statement for a moment. You are making a statement here that is practically a judicial decision. If anything wrong has been done in the administration of this bill, it is for the courts to determine. I do not assume that you can give judgment on the subject at all. I do assume that the Food Administration—

The Chairman. I am taking your own statement.

Mr. Hoover. I do assume that the Food Administration has remained within the law in everything that it has done, and within the intent of the law.

For Hoover, price-fixing "from a point of a legal regulation that such and such is the price" was fundamentally different from "arriving at a stabilizing price" through agreements with businesses to control distribution.[86]

And on that distinction—real, artificial, or casuistical—Hoover's defense against his bitterest enemy rested. Hoover, in fact, had no choice. The Lever Act did not explicitly authorize price-fixing in a direct, legal sense. But it did permit government buying-and-selling operations and voluntary agreements—devices that Hoover used to achieve substantially the same result. Reed and a number of farm state senators like him felt (or perhaps pretended to feel) tricked. Hoover had not heard the last from these critics.

Reed's examination of Hoover had been as rigorous and as rancorous as official Washington had anticipated. But the senator from Missouri was his own worst enemy. Late on the second day of Hoover's testimony, the sympathetic Senator Jones asked Hoover an easy question: Did the people of the United States generally support the Food Administration's policies? Hoover replied that he had had "an almost overwhelming response of that character." Reed angrily interrupted this colloquy: "Do you think that adds anything to this, Senator Jones, and is a proper manner of examination?" "Oh, I think so," Jones answered sharply, "or else I would not do it." The spectators in the room applauded. That may be, Reed observed, but such evidence "never would be received in any court." According to Reed, Hoover's claim that he had "received encomiums" and "pleased the people" added nothing to "the question under investigation." Jones shot back: "I may lay a foundation for it which I think would make it admissible even in a court of justice, or perhaps a criminal court in Missouri." The watching crowd exploded in laughter.[87]

In truth, Reed's harsh and accusatory manner of examination, his penchant for sarcasm, and his obvious partiality to Claus A. Spreckels lost him the respect of much of the public.[88] When Hoover rose from the witness table at the end of his two-day ordeal, many in the audience applauded and cheered. A furious Reed threatened to clear the hearing room.[89]

In the words of one of Hoover's lieutenants, the Chief had survived the Senate subcommittee's inquiry "with flags flying."[90] Despite two days of unpleasantness, Hoover had been victorious where it most mattered: in the eyes of the urban press and of public opinion. The *New York Times* declared that the attempt to blame the Food Administration for the price of sugar put too much stress on governmental policy and too little on underlying factors of production and Allied need.[91] Although Reed's subcommittee continued its hearings on sugar for several more days, a growing scandal at the War Department, the deepening coal crisis, and Harry Garfield's astounding closing of factories in mid-month deflected public attention and Congressional wrath elsewhere. For the time being, Hoover was off the hook.[92]

The Food Administration did not escape without changing course, however. In response to the dangerous discontent of the western beet sugar farmers (whom Reed had so obliged with a forum), Hoover hastened to appoint a number of commissions to determine the cost of producing sugar beets in various regions and to recommend a "fair price" under those conditions. Although the commissions had no legal power to fix prices or compel acceptance of their conclusions, Hoover hoped that their fact-finding (and the cudgel of publicity) would induce the beet processors and producers to come to terms. In most cases the contending parties did so. As a result, the sugar factories paid the farmers much more for their beets in 1918 than in the year before.[93] The militant producers had forced Hoover and the middlemen to compromise.

Other wounds from the political brawl did not heal so quickly. In February 1918 Hoover's associate, Julius H. Barnes, initiated "certain private inquiries" into Senator Reed's record. An investigator scoured Missouri and Iowa for damaging information about Reed's business connections and private life, including his involvement in a divorce scandal thirty-one years before. The investigation cost Barnes nearly $3,000.[94]

Some years later, Barnes, who was by then in financial trouble, asserted that Herbert Hoover was supposed to reimburse him for this expense after Hoover left public office. Barnes thereupon asked Hoover for the money.[95] Hoover, who appeared to be shocked, denied that he had ever "made any such a transaction."[96] In any case, the investigator's anonymous "Report on R," dated April 20, 1918, at some point found its way into Hoover's papers, where it lies today.[97] There is no evidence that Hoover or any of his colleagues used it to expose or intimidate Reed.

In the case of Claus A. Spreckels, though, Hoover eventually—thanks to his accuser's intransigence—got even. On March 1, 1918 Hoover notified President Wilson that Spreckels, alone among all American sugar refiners, was still refusing to sign the government contract for purchase of 1918 Cuban sugar. Despite Spreckels's raising "one quibble after another," said Hoover, he had supplied Spreckels's company with sugar since January 1 in hopes of reaching a friendly settlement. But the Food Administrator's patience was now gone. The Cuban arrangements that Spreckels was resisting were critically necessary, Hoover reported. He therefore asked that, if Spreckels failed to sign the contract, President Wilson terminate his licenses to import and transport foreign sugar.[98] After reviewing Hoover's enclosures, Wilson agreed that Spreckels's position was insupportable and that it was now necessary "to control the market" without his cooperation. The President thereupon ordered the Shipping Board and War Trade Board to refuse Spreckels all further transportation and licensing for the importation of sugar.[99] The stubborn refiner now paid the penalty for his defiance.

The Senate committee chaired by Reed, meanwhile, never produced a report on its massive hearings. Instead, on February 27, 1918 Senator Henry Cabot Lodge set forth his own conclusions in a speech to his colleagues. Analyzing the data and other evidence, Lodge contended that the great sugar famine of 1917 had been an "artificial" one, caused by the Food Administration's "attempt to establish artificial prices" and by its "interfering to some extent with distribution."[100] About three weeks later Senator Jones took the floor to argue that Senator Lodge was wrong; there had indeed been an "actual shortage" of sugar in late 1917. "The law of supply and demand does not maintain when there is a stricture in transportation," claimed Jones, echoing Hoover. The Food Administration's handling of the sugar crisis had been "masterly."[101]

And then, at last, the controversy abated. By March 1918 the sugar shortage was a stale story, and Hoover had more worrisome matters on his mind. But the issues it raised about governmental interventionism and the ethics of business / government collusion did not die. The sugar hearings were but the opening battle in what, for Hoover and his Congressional critics, had become a widening war.

11

The Perils of Price Control

I

THE Senate's noisy inquiry into the sugar shortage represented no passing spasm of displeasure. By midwinter 1918 anger at the United States Food Administration was reaching dangerous proportions on Capitol Hill. Fueling the outcry was a darkening mood of discontent in rural America.

In a series of hearings before the Senate Committee on Agriculture in February and March, a parade of farmers and their spokesmen poured out their grievances. The witnesses charged that Hoover's endless drumbeating for wheatless and meatless days was demoralizing farmers, destroying their markets, and discouraging increased production. Hoover's conservation propaganda had resulted in a savings of meat, the farmers conceded, but only at the cost of a "damming back of the supplies" and a ruining of "the profitable market to the producer."[1]

According to the witnesses, feeders of beef cattle and sheep had fared the worst. On the one hand, Hoover's agency had exhorted the nation's livestock breeders to enlarge their herds. The stockmen had reacted by raising and fattening substantial numbers of cattle. Meanwhile, however, Hoover had been asking his fellow citizens to observe meatless days. By simultaneously producing more beef while eating less of it, Americans, he hoped, would create a surplus for the Allies.

Alas, his policy had not worked as intended. Hoover's appeal for conservation failed to sway the working classes, whose consumption of low-grade beef actually increased. But upper-class Americans did respond—by sharply curtailing consumption of *high-grade* beef, which the Allies did not want. Faced by a suddenly plunging demand for the better grades of beef, livestock producers who had finished their cattle to this level found themselves unable to sell their product at a profit.

The Food Administration tried to dissuade farmers from fattening their cattle to an unprofitable "finish." But during the winter, bad weather and chaotic transportation forced many stockmen to hold back their animals on the farm. A glut of unsalable, frost-damaged, soft corn from the recent harvest also encouraged farmers to fatten rather than rapidly market their animals. Farmers could not blame Hoover for the weather or the near collapse of the rail system. But many of them felt betrayed when the Food Administration announced in January that it would use its influence to try to prevent a rise in the price of cattle. As farmers saw it, Uncle Sam had asked them to produce more meat "indiscriminately." Now many of them were sustaining heavy losses, thanks in part to the selective effects of meatless days.[2]

With sheep it was a similarly depressing story. In obedience to generalized governmental calls for more production, sheep breeders had dutifully fattened many of their lambs, only to find, at marketing time, that conservation-conscious consumers no longer wanted their product. As a result, the sheep farmers claimed, their prices had fallen below the cost of production, and many sheep growers had suffered "tremendous" financial losses. According to the witnesses, the Food Administration then compounded the tragedy by decreeing that no one should eat mutton or lamb on certain days, despite the fact that America did not export mutton or lamb to the Allies. Hoover hoped by this rule to encourage consumption of mutton and lamb on other days in preference to exportable varieties of meat. His fine-tuning failed to satisfy his critics. Eventually the Food Administration relaxed its restrictions on mutton and lamb.[3]

For livestock farmers and their allies, it was bad enough that Hoover's conservation campaign was forcing down the price of their products. Even more irritating was his failure to control the cost of mill feeds that they bought for their stock.[4] To irate farmers it seemed that only they were making a sacrifice, while their historic antagonists, the milling interests, were being permitted to profiteer.[5] As one farmer declared to the committee, "The Food Administration has taken the farmers' wheat at fixed prices and then allowed the by-products of the wheat to be delivered back to the farmer at unrestrained, extortionate prices. . . ."[6] It was a recipe for political trouble.

Everywhere they looked, disgruntled agrarians saw evidence of the deleterious effects of Hoover's regulations. While the price of stabilized wheat remained rigidly constant, the price of alternative grains, such as corn and oats, did not. Before long, in parts of the grain belt, farmers found it cheaper to feed wheat rather than high-priced corn to their hogs, thereby undercutting Hoover's Herculean effort to save wheat for export to Europe. Thus did good intentions and the all-out drive for conservation yield unintended and sometimes embarrassing effects.[7]

All this and more led many farmers and their Congressional advocates to challenge and increasingly denounce Hoover's policies.[8] The insurgents charged that the Food Administration did not have enough "practical farmers" in its organization and was too sympathetic to urban consumers.[9] The influential *Wallaces' Farmer* declared:

> The trouble with Mr. Hoover is that he does not understand agricultural production problems, and he has not yet come to see that ours is a problem of production as well as distribution. Naturally he hears more from the consumer than from the producer. From every side, people beset him to hold down the cost of living. They can not understand that if the cost of food products is held down below the cost of production, the farmer can not continue to produce.[10]

To the increasingly vocal farmers it seemed that they and they alone were being "squeezed"—squeezed by "artificial control" administered by men who neither comprehended nor cared for their plight.[11]

Unfortunately for Hoover, several of his decisions that winter only intensified the farmers' disquietude. By early February 1918 both the U.S. Food Administration and the U.S. Department of Agriculture had become alarmed at the apparent "disintegration" of the American poultry industry. Battered by the extraordinarily high cost of feed for their chickens, and enticed by the high prices then prevailing for live and freshly killed hens, many poultry producers decided to unload their birds on the market.[12] In Texas alone, between January 1 and early February, farmers sold 160,000 hens that otherwise would have laid millions of eggs.[13]

Convinced that this trend (if unchecked) would soon produce a national egg shortage, the Food Administration decided to intervene. On February 11 it announced to the nation that from February 23 through April 30 all licensed trading in live or freshly killed hens and pullets would be forbidden. In other words, every poultry farmer in the United States would be prevented from selling his laying hens for more than sixty days because he would have no legal outlet. By restricting the marketing of chickens in this way, the Food Administration hoped (it said) to increase egg production and avoid "a very real shortage" of eggs in the spring, with consequent high prices to consumers. The agency warned that failure to comply with its edict would constitute a violation of the Lever Act and would be punishable by revocation of license, a heavy fine, and even imprisonment.[14]

Hoover's order sent shock waves through rural America, especially in New England, where the price of chicken feed had reached phenomenal levels.[15] To poultry farmers already losing money under these conditions, Hoover's intervention to hold down the future price of eggs to consumers seemed one-sided, to say the least.[16] Because of his action, owners of chickens would be unable to cut their losses before spring. Some agrarians even detected a malevolent hand in the Food Administration's new regulation. One reason that live hens had been selling high was a strong demand for them for fattening purposes in anticipation of the Jewish holiday of Passover. But now, because of Hoover's ban on sales, Passover would go by before the nation's hens could again be marketed. After that, demand for hens would decline, and the price that farmers received for them would fall drastically. The beneficiaries would be the meat packers, who would not have to pay farmers so much for their hens. To Hoover's bitter enemy E. C. Lasater, the Food Administrator's poultry decree looked like a covert attempt to benefit the packing industry.[17]

Perhaps with Passover in mind, Hoover announced on March 1 that the sale of lightweight chickens known as broilers would be permitted.[18] Otherwise the Food Administrator was disinclined to budge. His rule had been "a conservation measure entirely," he declared. Without something like it, there would be "a positive crisis in the poultry business six months hence." The poultrymen of Texas, he said, had been marketing "perfectly fabulous quantities of stuff that ought to be held."[19] For Hoover, the long-term national interest, as he perceived it, must take precedence over the short-term self-interest of certain farmers.

Nevertheless, under pressure from a committee of his own agricultural advisors to rescind the controversial order, Hoover announced in mid-April that he would lift the ban on sale of hens on April 20, ten days ahead of schedule.[20] As usual, he made no concession to his critics. He claimed that he was removing the prohibition at this time because weather conditions had produced an "early laying and hatching period" and because his regulation had "served its purpose." In fact, he claimed, it had been "extremely beneficial": more than 3,333,000 egg-laying hens had been saved from a premature demise.[21] As a result, he later reported, the nation's supply of eggs in storage on June 1 was more than 11 percent greater than on the same date a year before.[22]

Hoover's suspension of the free market, then, had proven successful—if an abundant supply of inexpensive eggs for consumers was the overriding desideratum. But for angry farmers the sudden substitution of a distant bureaucrat's judgment for their own was thoroughly unnerving. If Hoover could unilaterally prohibit the sale of hens for an entire season, might he not prohibit the sale of cattle, hogs, or any other farm product?[23] Some observers, including the ever watchful Senator Reed, questioned whether farmers would be willing to raise hens at all if they feared that "a dictator in Washington" might take away their market.[24] Even Elbert S. Brigham, commissioner of agriculture for the state of Vermont and a Hoover sympathizer, warned that when "you force [the farmer] to keep something that it doesn't pay him to keep and confiscate some of his property, I believe it is an entirely wrong principle."[25] In the aftermath of Hoover's astonishing hen ruling, many farmers wondered where he would strike next.

One place, it soon appeared, was the tomato industry. On February 28 a branch of the Food Administration announced that the U.S. Army and Navy would henceforth refuse to purchase tomato products from processors who had paid or planned to pay farmers more than a certain price for raw tomatoes. For Delaware, Maryland, and New Jersey, where half the nation's tomatoes were grown, the army and navy specified a ceiling of $21.00 per ton.[26] This seemingly routine announcement set off a thunderclap in Congress, where, on March 8, senators from the mid-Atlantic tomato belt demanded an immediate investigation. By what authority, the solons asked, and for what purpose, did the government issue such a potentially ruinous document? If the tomato growers of their region concluded that the government was fixing the price for their crop, they would cut back their tomato planting severely rather than accept such an unremunerative price. The Senate ordered its committee on agriculture to investigate.[27]

The Senate's growing discomfiture with Hoover's price controls provided Reed of Missouri an unexpected chance to taunt his colleagues and renew his war on the Food Administration. "Mr. President," he proclaimed sardonically, "there is trouble in the tomato States."

> The Food Administration has sent out a circular so drawn as to leave the impression that the prices of Delaware, New Jersey, and Maryland tomatoes are to be fixed at $21 per ton, wherefore consternation reigns. . . . The Senators from those States, in open-mouth astonishment, are asking, "Is it possible that the Food Administration we helped to set up is about to lay unholy hands upon our sacred tomato patches?" They are wondering if the authority it was expected would be executed upon the wheat fields and cattle ranches of the Middle West is to ruthlessly invade the truck farms of Delaware, New Jersey, and Maryland, where hitherto has reposed in luxurious security the glorious tomato. [Laughter]

I told you so, the caustic Democrat continued. I warned you that the Lever Act would be used "to fix the price of the farmer's products." I told you

> not to turn the prosperity of the great agricultural portion of our population over to a man ignorant alike of farming, stock raising, and of American conditions. I told you that only those who intend to employ power are greedy to acquire it; that the ambition that lusts for power will abuse power. I warned you that the licensing authority would be employed for the purpose of controlling the markets of the country, and that whoever controlled the markets would thereby control prices of the producer as well as the merchant.

Railing at the "arbitrary" Lever Act and its even more "arbitrary administration," Reed predicted a "national calamity" unless Hoover's "indefensible" policies were abandoned. The fundamental mistake that Hoover and his fellow price regulators were making, Reed charged, was to set their "individual and usually uninformed regulations against the common judgment of mankind." The world needed more food production, but what were Hoover and his associates doing? They were endeavoring to "reduce the price of the thing, instead of undertaking to increase the amount of the thing." To Reed price regulation was "as ancient as man's foolishness, as futile and useless a thing as a food administrator."[28]

Heaping scorn on the "tomato order" and—for good measure—on Hoover's prohibition of the sale of hens, Reed predicted that the Food Administrator would retreat.[29] Within days the senator's prophecy came true. Anxious, no doubt, to pacify a hitherto friendly bloc of senators, Herbert Hoover issued a clarification. The Food Administration's tomato announcement, he said, did not fix, and was not intended to fix, the price at which tomato farmers sold their crop. The Food Administration, in fact, had neither the power nor the wish to fix the price of tomatoes. The offending announcement had been a mere information bulletin sent to tomato canners who might want to bid for army or navy contracts. No one was compelled to bid, he pointed out, nor was any "limitation . . . made on the price per ton which anyone might ask for his tomatoes. . . ."[30] In other words, tomato farmers were free to sell their produce on the open market for whatever they could get.

Hoover's explanation satisfied Senator Willard Saulsbury, Jr., of Delaware, who had introduced the resolution for an investigation.[31] But Hoover could not escape the fact that the army and navy were planning to purchase 35 percent of the tomato pack of the country and that their stipulation on prices would have an enormous effect.[32] By refusing to do business with tomato processors who paid tomato farmers more than $21.00 per ton, the government was not only attempting to stabilize bids for its own orders. It was also deploying its economic power in a way that would inevitably tend to hold down the price of the farmers' crop. If this was not price-fixing in a legal sense, the broad effect on farmers was the same. The *deliberate* effect, charged Reed, in a chamber that seemed increasingly willing to believe him.

The tempest over tomatoes soon subsided, but the price for Hoover in Congressional anxiety was high. On March 8 a formerly quiescent senator accused the Food Administration of perverting its licensing powers under the Lever Act in ways that controlled the price of the farmers' crops. Through manipulation of its licensing power, he charged, Hoover's agency had "made it impossible for a farmer to sell a hen to a corner grocery store."[33] No longer was Reed a member of a small, cantankerous minority of anti-Hooverians.

A few days later the Senate debated a special appropriations bill to meet deficiencies in the budgets of federal agencies for the current fiscal year. Seizing his opportunity, Senator Reed introduced an amendment deleting the entire emergency sum requested by the Food Administration: $1,750,000. If the amendment passed, Hoover's agency would be unable to expand its operations in the states. For much of the day, Reed lobbed shell after shell at his favorite target. Never in the history of the U.S. government, he declaimed, had there been "such a saturnalia of wastefulness and of extravagance" as was occurring in Hoover's bailiwick. "A drunken sailor landed in port for the first time in five years and filled up with a bad quality of New England rum never threw money around as the Food Administration is now doing." In the end Reed's amendment was defeated, but not before Hoover's name had been dragged yet again through the senatorial mud.[34]

In the case of chickens and tomatoes, Hoover might plausibly have sought refuge in the argument that his regulations had been devised by expert assistants. But only he could take responsibility for an incident that now disturbed his standing in the House of Representatives, where his support had traditionally been strong. In mid-February, in behalf of a constituent working for the Food Administration in New Hampshire, Representative Edward H. Wason asked the Food Administration in Washington for a copy of President Wilson's executive order appointing Hoover to his position. Upon receiving Wason's letter, Hoover passed it along to the State Department, which, he said, had custody of the document. A few days later the Secretary of State informed Wason that the President's executive order had not been made public and that the department therefore would not supply a copy to his constituent.[35]

The New Hampshire representative now asked for a copy for himself; the State Department turned to the White House for instructions.[36] For some reason, in August 1917 (when the executive order had been issued) President Wilson had directed that it not be printed and that instead it be kept confidential.[37] Wilson was now willing to release the document if Hoover advised that it be published. But after inquiry one of the President's secretaries reported: "Mr. Hoover sees no reason why it should be published and hopes it will not be."[38]

Hoover apparently gave no reason for his curious recommendation. Perhaps he suspected that the inquisitive congressman was a troublemaker. In any case, the President thereupon ordered that the executive order remain confidential. The State Department dutifully declined Wason's request.[39]

The New Hampshire Republican quickly protested to Secretary of State Lansing:

> Mr. Hoover is a public official of this country. The law was passed by Congress creating this position. I desire to ascertain just what responsibilities and authority the order appointing him conferred upon him. As a Member of Congress I am unable to receive that information.

Wason now asked that he be permitted to read the executive order in Lansing's office.[40] At the direct order of the President, Lansing refused.[41]

A few weeks later, no longer able to contain his irritation, Wason took to the floor of the House and demanded that the "mantle of secrecy" be removed from "this sacred and important order." "What subtle magic does this order contain?" he asked. "What secret that the American people or a Member of Congress should not know is therein?" If the document did not include anything detrimental to the war effort, "why should it be a confidential communication between the Executive of our people, the Department of State, and the man who is conserving the food resources of this Nation?"[42]

As in the case of the tomato controversy, this public display of Congressional outrage produced speedy results at the Food Administration. Two days later a member of Hoover's staff notified Wason by telephone that the executive order appointing Hoover Food Administrator was already accessible to the public. It was contained in Hoover's report of January 31 on his agency's 1917 disbursements—a document printed by the House of Representatives itself! Wason was amazed and furious. Why, he asked, had Hoover shunted his original letter over to the State Department when Hoover had included the executive order in his own report barely three weeks before? Why had Hoover neglected to tell him that the order could be found therein? Why had the State Department thrice erroneously asserted that the document had not been made public? To the applause of his colleagues Wason denounced the "denial of the inherent rights heretofore enjoyed by Members of Congress."[43]

In the face of this cannonade, Hoover fought back and tried to outmaneuver his opponents. In a press release issued on February 22 he stoutly defended his system of meatless days as a successful device to create a supply of "absolutely vital" exports for the Allies. If people could hear the "expressions of gratitude" that America's increased meat shipments were receiving in Europe, "they would feel amply rewarded" for their sacrifices. Even the "animal raisers in the west," said Hoover, would feel that the recent meat conservation campaign had been an accomplishment of which to be proud. He also remarked that if anyone had a "more equitable" approach under the law to reducing meat consumption than meatless days, the Food Administration would be happy to consider it.[44]

For the cattle and sheep producers of America, Hoover's rejoinder was unsatisfactory. The meatless days drive might have been good for the Europeans, but it manifestly had not been good for them. The livestock men did not want accolades from Europe; they wanted enough income to survive. They did not want less American consumption of meat; they wanted more—and there was the problem.

Agrarian complaints against meatless days did not abate, and just ten days later Hoover was compelled to retreat—without, of course, admitting it. On March 3 he called upon Americans further to curtail their consumption of bread and simultaneously announced a relaxation of his restraints upon meat. Except on Tuesdays, his countrymen were free to eat meat whenever they wanted. Meatless meals and porkless Saturdays were abandoned. Hoover justified his change of policy on the grounds that by eating more meat Americans would tend to eat less bread, now the more critical commodity. He noted, too, that for various reasons the United States now possessed "considerably enlarged" meat supplies and more than enough for the Allies. Hoover said nothing about the demand of livestock breeders for exemption from his conservation rules, a demand he had rejected less than two weeks before. His press release contained no hint that his meatless regimen for the nation had worked perhaps too well.[45]

Behind his facade of imperturbability, however, Hoover was a worried man. To a meeting of agricultural editors on March 7 he confessed that he did not know what to do about the plight of the feeder cattle industry. While American beef consumption was soaring at an "extraordinary" rate, nearly all of the increased demand was for cheaper cuts, not the "highly finished" grades. Evidently unwilling to admit that his conservation propaganda might have had unintended results, Hoover ascribed the shifting consumption patterns solely to "economic forces" (such as working-class prosperity) that he could not control.[46]

Why not, then, suspend meatless days altogether for a time and let the nation's hotels buy up finished cattle? This was the advice one editor offered Hoover that day. Such a policy, the editor argued, would absorb the surplus of heavy cattle and improve the morale of livestock producers. The Food Administrator, however, was reluctant to make such a turnabout. To be sure, he himself had just removed most of the "effective restrictions" on meat consumption. And he now conceded to the editor that the remaining rules for meatless days were "really not conservation at all." ("Unless you get conservation every day," he admitted, "you do not get it.") Still, Hoover feared that if he now authorized the American citizenry to "eat all you like," he would "undermine the whole situation from a conservation point of view." And this—the psychology of conservation—he could not bear to sacrifice. Already, he claimed, in just four days since he eased his meatless rules, consumption of meat around the country had risen to undesirable levels, causing "difficulties."[47]

But even Hoover's adamantine will could not resist the deepening pressure to shift course. In a concession to angry livestock producers who descended on the Food Administration in mid-March, he promised to help the feeder cattle industry by having governmental buying agencies purchase larger amounts of high-grade beef.[48] A few days later the head of his own meat division, Joseph Cotton, publicly admitted to a Senate committee that feeders of cattle and sheep were losing money and that the meatless days policy had been "somewhat" responsible.[49] Then, in late March, came word that an unexpected rush of hogs to market was threatening to overwhelm the storage facilities and cash resources of the meat packers. Hoover knew that if the packers were forced to stop buying live hogs from farmers, the price of hogs would crash below the minimum he had promised to try to maintain. Then there would really be trouble in rural America. On March 29 he announced that meatless days would be suspended across the country for the next thirty days.[50]

Hoover's hand had finally been forced, not by wails of agrarian protest but by a glut of pigs. But significantly, after the immediate crisis was over, he did not reinstate meatless days. When, on May 2, he again exhorted the nation to economize on meat consumption, he issued only a vague appeal for elimination of waste and for consumption of smaller portions of meat at each meal. Such a course, he said, would avert the "inconvenience" caused by meatless days. In this quiet way he dispensed with a once-cherished program that while successful with urbanites had become a red flag to livestock interests and a political liability to himself. The policy of meatless days never returned.[51]

Meanwhile Hoover attempted to answer a crescendo of complaints that flour millers and sellers of mill feeds were shamelessly profiteering at farmers' expense and that his agency was doing little to prevent it. The Food Administrator conceded in February that abuses had occurred in "certain cases." But he insisted that the majority of millers were behaving properly and that in recent months "very few" of them had earned more than the maximum profit permitted by his regulations. It takes time to develop a "proper control in inspection and accounting," he pleaded.[52]

Nevertheless, during February his enforcement division extended its domain to include the flour-milling industry, and Hoover himself initiated a preemptive investigation of his grain division by his friend Frank W. Taussig, chairman of the United States Tariff Commission.[53] Such an inquiry, Hoover told President Wilson, would enable the Food Administration to be "armed" in the event of a Congressional "assault."[54] Barely a month later, buffeted by fresh reports of miller profiteering in the sale of feeds to farmers, Hoover asked Taussig to assemble a committee and focus on the profit control regulations of the Food Administration's milling division.[55]

As it happened, another federal agency, the Federal Trade Commission, was just completing its own study of the flour milling and jobbing industry. After submitting a preliminary draft to Hoover and Julius H. Barnes for comment, the FTC released its report in April. The commission declared that, according to information before it, Hoover's regulations had reduced most flour millers' profits to a level below that of 1916–17. Because of this, and because of the government's fixing of the price of wheat, the price of flour to consumers had declined by several dollars a barrel.[56]

For Hoover, the FTC's words must have provided a welcome vindication. But the commission also reported that Hoover's system of setting millers' profits at a fixed margin above cost encouraged "unpatriotic millers" to falsify their accounts and exaggerate their costs.[57] The Food Administrator knew that he would have to do something to bring wayward millers into better conformity with his regulations.

As for the soaring price of coarse grains such as corn (while the price of wheat alone remained fixed), Hoover, in midwinter, had a ready answer. "The distortion in the price of other food commodities is practically altogether a transportation question," he told a member of Congress. Never before had the "margins between the producer and consumer . . . been so wide as they are in these certain commodities," he said—"all because there has been insufficient railway distribution in the community." The "remedy" for the suspension of the law of supply and demand in most cereals was not price-fixing but "curing the transportation."[58] As for the tales of farmers feeding wheat to hogs because corn was too expensive, Hoover cited a Department of Agriculture report denying that this had occurred to any significant extent.[59]

The price anomalies of the winter, then, were the result of bad weather and chaotic transportation, not of ill-administered federal price controls; this was Hoover's argument as protests intensified. Hoover, in fact, had become extremely sensitive about price-fixing, or at least about the political turmoil that the concept evoked on Capitol Hill. And so, only weeks after helping to draft a bill that would have created sweeping new presidential power to fix prices, and even as he continued to lobby within the executive branch for expansion of governmental control over prices, Hoover tried to convince farmers and their spokesmen that this was not what he wanted at all. One problem—he announced to the nation on February 25—was that farmers were afflicted with "misinformation" about his price-fixing policies. The Food Administration was not "a price-fixing body," he stated, except (he now admitted publicly for the first time) "with regard to certain commodities which are today dominated by wholly abnormal overseas commercial relations" and by the dangers that these created. The commodities so controlled, he said, were wheat and sugar. In the case of wheat, he added, his arrangements with the Allies became "absolutely price-fixing." In a lengthy press release Hoover forcefully defended his policies for these two commodities and for pork. "Beyond the above," he asserted flatly, "the Food Administration has no powers or intention to in any way interest itself in price."[60]

Hoover's categorical denials were undoubtedly meant to reassure farmers that he was planning no wholesale intervention in the market for their products.[61] It is unlikely, however, that many farmers believed him, especially when, only three days later, his agency released its bulletin on the price of tomatoes.

Indeed, less than three weeks later one of the Food Administration's own livestock advisers, E. L. Burke, denounced Hoover's explanation in testimony before the Senate agriculture committee. Burke was angered by Hoover's contention that except in limited instances he possessed neither the authority nor the desire to fix the prices of agricultural goods. That, Burke charged, "was not a frank statement, in view of the indirect methods of control that have been exercised and in connection with the destroying of the demand for the product. . . ."

> The word "stabilize," you know, is a very euphonious expression; it sounds good, but it means "control."
>
> That has been the trouble, gentlemen, all the way through; that is really the crux of the situation in regard to the distrust, the discontent of the producers with the Food Administration. They—the Food Administration—say one thing and they mean something else.[62]

To such a depth had relations between the regulators and the regulated fallen.

Having finally conceded that in key areas he *was* engaged in price-fixing, Hoover in mid-April launched a forceful counterattack against his detractors. While emphasizing that the government had "developed no principle of price-fixing as a broad economic policy," he insisted that "the total economic dislocations imposed by the war" had compelled the United States to deal with "conditions and not with theories." In the interest of winning the war, the government now controlled every item exported from America's shores. Abroad, the Allies had found it "absolutely impossible" to rely upon "normal commercial agencies" to handle and transport national necessities; governments, not private individuals, controlled shipping. At home, a single agency was buying goods for 2,000,000 men under arms. Abroad, the Allies had created "single-handed" buying of supplies for 120,000,000 people—"a phenomenon never before witnessed in the economic history of the world."

It was these facts, Hoover argued, that dictated his course of action:

> In order that these two buying agencies should not get in each other's way, it has been necessary to place them under joint direction. In the final outcome, therefore, we find ourselves in the presence of a gigantic monopoly of buying just as potent for good or evil as any monopoly in selling, and in many instances either making or influencing prices. Therefore, not through any theory, but through an actual physical fact, the price made by this gigantic buyer dominates the market.
>
> This is price-fixing in a light never contemplated in economic history or theory, and it is time that economic thinkers denude themselves of their procrustean formulas of supply and demand and took [sic] cognizance of it.
>
> In commodities where this situation arises, the Government must necessarily regulate the price, and all theories to the contrary go by the board.[63]

Besides rebutting specific complaints leveled against him, Hoover tried various measures of containment. On March 7, he and Secretary of Agriculture David Houston assembled thirteen of the nation's leading editors of agricultural journals for a review of issues of concern.[64] Later that month he and Houston created an advisory committee of twenty-four prominent agricultural and livestock producers from across the country under the chairmanship of a recently retired governor of Virginia. Meeting in Washington from March 28 to April 4, the committee received briefings, ventilated grievances, and made a host of recommendations, including abolition of the temporary ban on the sale of hens.[65]

The establishment of the Agricultural Advisory Committee proved to be a shrewd political maneuver. From an initial mood of suspicion and hostility, the body quickly veered to general approval of Hoover's policies.[66] Now, in the face of militancy in the heartland and on Capitol Hill, he could argue that he had listened to leading farmers and that they supported him.

But Hoover's attempts to pacify his critics were frustrating. No matter what he did, it seemed, someone—somewhere—became angry, subjecting him to what he called "mud slinging."[67] In early March he confessed to a friend that the Food Administration was becoming an "impossible job" and that it was only a matter of time "until you hear that I have 'cracked up.' " The "eternal opposition" of producers and consumers—and of politicians like James A. Reed—was making Hoover's task a "burden."[68] But there was even more to his discouragement than that. "Whenever you begin to tamper with a normal course of commerce you have to keep on tampering," he remarked the next day to some journalists.[69] He was learning not only about the orneriness of human nature but also about the pitfalls of interventionism.

Despite the charges hurled against him by aggrieved agrarians, Hoover appeared convinced that farmers were faring far better than they claimed. In a letter on May 4 to a member of Congress on the subject of profiteering in foodstuffs, he asserted that the "real crux of this question" lay in "the balance of rights between the producer and the consumer." Should producer prices now be increased or reduced? Neither, Hoover appeared to answer. The objective should be "stability in price" and the avoidance of "a vicious circle of constant increase" in prices and wages.

But Hoover immediately left no doubt that farmers were the principal obstacle to such an equilibrium. Every effort he had made so far to achieve price "stability," he said, had "met with protest" from producers, even as consumers inundated him with complaints about the high cost of living. Abandoning his posture of impartiality, Hoover now openly urged the creation of a Congressional counterweight to the aggressive and vociferous farm bloc:

> I would indeed be glad to see someone take up the advocacy of the consumer in Congress. So far as I know he has had no vocal advocate there yet, the whole leaning of discussing having been towards the producer.[70]

Only once in these trying months did Hoover permit his exasperation at the farmers' advocates to show in public. In a powerful defense of his policies at the Pittsburgh Press Club on April 18, he rebuked those who sought to benefit financially from the war:

> I do not believe that any person in the United States has a right to make one cent more profit out of any employment than he would have made

> under pre war conditions. I do not care whether this refers to the farmer, to the laborer, to the manufacturer, to the middlemen or to the retailer; to me, every cent taken beyond this standard is money abstracted from the blood and sacrifice of the American people.
>
> I do not believe that extortionate profits are necessary [to] secure maximum effort on the part of the American people in this war. If we are going to adopt that theory, we have admitted everything that has been charged against us of being the most materialistic, the most avaricious, and the most venal of people in this world.
>
> If we are going to admit that the Government, in order to secure the supreme effort of its citizens in production must bribe them with money to this extra exertion, we have admitted a weakness of American character, of American civilization and of American ideals that puts us on a plane below German *Kultur*.[71]

Since the nation's wheat growers at that very moment were seeking an increase in the guaranteed price for their crop, there could be little doubt about the target of his ire.

Privately, Hoover even denounced militant farmers as "bolsheviki."[72] Fortunately for his political standing, his expressions of bitterness did not evidently travel beyond his staff.

In short, after months of consultations, expostulations, exhortations, announcements, and policy adjustments, a chasm of suspicion remained between many of the nation's farmers and the man who (Senator Reed said) held their destiny in his hands. As the winter of 1918 wore on, agrarian vexation settled on two issues, the two most politically sensitive of all: the price of wheat and Hoover's oversight of the meat packers.

II

IN the winter of 1917–18 America's wheat farmers were beginning to wonder about the future. At the moment they were receiving an essentially fixed price for their 1917 harvest, on a scale pegged to $2.20 per bushel for No. 1 Northern Spring wheat sold in Chicago. Under the provisions of the Lever Act, farmers knew that they would receive a government-guaranteed minimum of $2.00 per bushel, on essentially the same basis, for the crop of 1918. But beyond this, all was murky.

Back in November 1917, Hoover had considered asking the President to proclaim $2.00 as the guaranteed price for 1918 wheat—in other words, a reduction of 20 cents per bushel. Hoover and Julius H. Barnes evidently hoped that promulgation of such a price for the next crop would induce farmers to accelerate their sales of their current crop, since they would have no incentive to retain it. But when the railroad car shortage began to interrupt grain marketings in mid-autumn, the usefulness of an early proclamation of 1918 wheat prices became doubtful. At Barnes's recommendation, Hoover abandoned the idea for the time being.[73]

By early January, pressure for clarification of the government's policy toward 1918 wheat was building from another direction. Out in the wheat belt, agents of the Department of Agriculture had been trying, with only partial success, to persuade farmers to augment their acreage. Instead of deciding to grow more wheat for a safe but (in their view) low return, many farmers were considering switching to oats and barley, whose unregulated and rapidly increasing price held out the prospect of a larger profit. Before committing themselves to one crop or another, farmers wanted to know precisely what they could expect to obtain for 1918 wheat.[74]

The mood of uncertainty soon curdled into anger. Wheat farmers and their advocates in Congress began to complain that the fixed price of wheat was incommensurate with the rising cost of living. The cost of farm labor, for example, was soaring, thanks to a scarcity of men brought on in part by the military draft.[75] Many farmers also continued to be annoyed by the government's handling of the 1917 wheat crop. The basic price of $2.20 per bushel applied only to the best (and rarest) grade; all other grades commanded less. The price schedule, moreover, was pegged to a few large interior terminals, not to rural markets where most growers actually sold their crop for much less. To the farmers' representatives in Congress, the Wilson administration's failure to establish a single, uniform price of wheat in all markets was an "injustice."[76]

Undergirding these lingering grievances lay ill-suppressed feelings of betrayal. Many farmers and their champions in Washington had not forgotten how the price of wheat had reached $3.00 per bushel before the Wilson administration had intervened and brought it down.[77] They had not forgotten that the Lever Act said nothing at all about the price of the 1917 wheat harvest and that Hoover had solemnly denied beforehand that the Lever bill conferred price-fixing power over farmers' crops. Nevertheless—and without (said his critics) "the slightest warrant"—Hoover had effected a fixed price for 1917 wheat.[78] In the eyes of senators from the wheat states, the Lever Act was designed to stimulate wheat production in 1918 by providing farmers a safety net in the form of a minimum guaranteed price. Otherwise, the free market was to be unchecked. Instead, Hoover had wilfully destroyed the 1917 wheat market and had made the minimum price a maximum: actions utterly contrary to Congressional intent.[79]

All this, in a way, was water under the dam by midwinter 1918. The crucial question now became: How would the Wilson administration implement the congressionally mandated guarantee for the coming wheat crop? With this query in mind, Senator Gore and other members of Congress from the wheat states conferred with Food Administrator Hoover on February 12.[80] The meeting turned into a disaster. To Gore's dismay, Hoover intimated that the price of *not less than* $2.00 per bushel required by the Lever Act for 1918 wheat was also a *fixed* and *absolute* price—a maximum price as well as a minimum. Furious at this misinterpretation of the law's intent, Gore announced that he would seek a formal opinion of the law's meaning from the Attorney General.[81] The senator also disclosed that he would shortly introduce legislation to compel the government to pay a higher price for the forthcoming wheat crop. Hoover pleaded with him not to do so. The senator from Oklahoma was unmoved.[82]

Hoover soon backed off from his misreading of the Lever Act.[83] But by then it was too late. The very next day, February 13, Gore introduced a resolution to raise the minimum price of wheat to $2.50 per bushel for the 1918 harvest. Not to be outdone, Senator Porter McCumber of North Dakota offered a separate resolution to increase the price to a whopping $2.75.[84]

Hoover was aghast. In an apprehensive letter to the President on February 14, the Food Administrator reported that about 125,000,000 bushels of 1917 wheat were still in the hands of the nation's farmers—wheat upon which he was depending to supply "bread for our people" in April, May, and June. Hoover feared that farmers would now withhold this remaining supply from the market in the hope of "mixing" it later with higher-priced 1918 wheat, thereby gaining a "larger return."

As usual when he was agitated, Hoover depicted the situation in the starkest terms. If the clamor for new price legislation continued, he told the President, the U.S. government would have but two options. It would either have to cease all wheat exports to the Allies "instantly" and forcibly seize wheat from the farmers in order to "complete our domestic supplies" at the current fixed price, or it would have to raise the price of 1917 wheat "at once" to whatever level the Congress set for future wheat. The latter alternative, he declared, would not only be unfair to farmers who had already sold their 1917 wheat at the current price "on the assurance that it was a fixed and constant price for the year." It would also effectively raise the price of millions of bushels of wheat now in the hands of middlemen, in effect taxing consumers up to $200,000,000 "without one penny's benefit to the producer." There was no need for such a stimulus to farmers, said Hoover. The amount of winter wheat under cultivation had recently increased by 2,000,000 acres—proof that the existing guarantee was "ample to produce the results desired." While expressing a wish for "justice" and proper incentives for the American farmer, Hoover asserted that equal "anxiety" should be directed to the condition of the "American consumer," whose loaf of bread stood to shoot up in price if the price of wheat (and hence of flour) were inflated. For Hoover, it was a chilling prospect. Already, he told the President, he was deeply worried about "tiding over our industrial populations . . . without disturbances" at the present price level.[85]

If Hoover was apprehensive, his principal grain adviser, Julius Barnes, was nearly apoplectic. On February 15 Barnes sent Hoover a three-page barrage of arguments against the folly of raising the wheat price guarantee above the basis currently set for 1917 wheat. Such a Congressional act, he warned, would render it "impossible" to obtain the remainder of the 1917 crop. It would be a "breach of faith" with farmers who had "patriotically" marketed their 1917 wheat promptly last autumn at the previously established price. It would be a blatant "repudiation" of "pledges made in the public interest" by Hoover and his colleagues. "We must not forget at all times," said Barnes, "that ninety million consumers in this country are entitled to be heard in Government price influence. We cannot assume that they can properly present their claims for consideration in Congress." Barnes, in fact, was disgusted that Congress, rather than a commission of experts, was now trying to determine the price of wheat. "Congressional legislation substitutes the result of political influence and power in place of intelligent investigation," he said.[86] It was a sentiment with which Hoover thoroughly concurred.[87]

The heads of the Food Administration and its Grain Corporation did not, as it turned out, have to worry about the man in the White House. Woodrow Wilson agreed that "agitation" for legislation to raise the price of wheat would be "a very serious mistake just now," while the existing crop was in the pipeline.[88] In fact, there "could hardly be a more dangerous field of agitation than this."[89] The President asked Representative Lever, chairman of the House committee on agriculture, to attempt to "check such agitation in some kind and tactful way."[90]

The White House could count on Asbury Lever, a southern Democrat and author of the Lever Act. Senator Thomas Gore was another case entirely. On February 14, the day after introducing his wheat resolution, Gore convened his Senate agriculture committee for public hearings on the meat and wheat situation in the United States. For the next six weeks a procession of angry critics of the Food Administration testified before the receptive senator and his colleagues.[91]

To Hoover, already beset by bad weather and a dozen other woes, the prospect of another Congressional siege-by-hearings must have been repellent. Within days came news that was even worse: the Senate Committee on Agriculture favorably reported on Gore's resolution to amend the Lever Act by increasing the government-guaranteed minimum price for the 1918 wheat crop to $2.50 per bushel. On February 19 Gore submitted both the resolution and the report to the full Senate.[92] The revolt of the wheat belt had taken a powerful leap forward.

The Wilson administration quickly disclosed through an "authoritative source" (possibly Hoover) that it would strenuously oppose the measures pending in Congress to increase the price of wheat.[93] Gore countered that he would try to expedite passage of his proposal by attaching it to an appropriations bill for the Department of Agriculture.[94] Meanwhile unnamed Food Administration officials asserted on February 20 that the week-old agitation was already retarding—indeed, was threatening to abort completely—the flow of 1917 wheat from farms to grain terminals and flour mills.[95]

Before the political eruption of mid-February, Hoover had planned to ask President Wilson in June to appoint a commission (like the Garfield commission of 1917) to recommend a price for the 1918 wheat crop.[96] Now, however, Gore's unexpected assault forced the Food Administrator's hand. On February 23, with Hoover's approval, the President suddenly issued a proclamation fixing the guaranteed price of the 1918 wheat harvest on the basis of $2.20 per bushel for the best grade in Chicago—exactly the same figure as at present. Any increase, the President declared, would cause the remainder of last year's crop to be withheld from the market and would "dislocate all the present wage levels," thereby inciting "industrial unrest" that would injure "every industry in the country."[97]

If Hoover hoped that the President's fait accompli would dissolve senatorial sentiment for $2.50 wheat, he had failed to gauge the anger of the wheat states' legislators and the tenacity of the senator from Oklahoma. In mid-March, when the Department of Agriculture's appropriations bill for the next fiscal year finally came before the Senate, Gore, as promised, offered an amendment. It would raise the guaranteed minimum price for 1918 wheat to $2.50—30 cents more than President Wilson had just decreed. It would apply this basic price, not to No. 1 Northern Spring wheat, but to No. 2, thereby raising the farmers' price for this and all lesser grades down the scale. Finally, it would mandate that farmers receive these prices not at a few major interior markets (as at present) but at local elevators and local railway centers near which the wheat was actually grown. In this way, farmers would receive the fixed price without first having to deduct the cost of transporting their wheat to distant primary markets.[98] Thus each provision of the proposed change would yield more money to wheat producers.

Gore's amendment ignited a prairie fire of Congressional debate that lasted for the better part of five days and repeatedly singed Hoover in its flames. Reed of Missouri asserted that the Lever Act contained no authority "to fix the price of a single foodstuff" and that any man who did so was a "lawbreaker."[99] Norris of Nebraska argued that Congress had no intention of interfering with the law of supply and demand beyond establishing a price floor for wheat harvested in 1918. The President's fixing of the 1917 and 1918 crops at below-market prices was "absolutely contrary" to congressional intent.[100] Fall of New Mexico called the Food Administration's fixing of wheat prices an "error."[101] Sherman of Illinois labeled it "incomparable folly."[102] Nelson of Minnesota termed it an "abject failure."[103]

The proponents of the Gore amendment advanced two fundamental arguments. The first was *necessity:* an enhanced price for wheat, they insisted, was essential to stimulate production in the face of mounting costs and alluring alternatives. The second was *equity:* it was manifestly unfair and discriminatory, they contended, to freeze the price of wheat alone while the price of everything else kept on rising. Only the wheat farmer, they declaimed, had to sell his product in a restricted market yet buy his necessities in an unrestricted market.[104]

As the debate raged, Hoover tried from behind the scenes to stem the tide. He supplied arguments and data to Atlee Pomerene of Ohio, virtually the only member of the Senate to oppose the Gore amendment on the floor. Hoover denied that any further price incentive was needed to "secure a sufficient production of wheat" in the coming year. A huge crop of winter wheat—the largest, in fact, ever seeded[105]—was already in the ground, planted there before the President's recent decree. If a still higher price were now established, it would elicit more planting of spring wheat in arid regions, with only marginal results at best. As for the fairness issue, Hoover noted that wheat was "still the highest priced grain in the country" and that, except for "a number of perpetual mal-contents in the dry wheat region," most American farmers accepted $2.20 as a "fair price." The *real* inequity, he suggested, would be "a total disruption of the wage level of the country" that would result from a massive increase in the price of wheat.[106]

The Food Administrator also attempted to promote an alternative to that of his Congressional foes. In mid-February Julius Barnes privately proposed to him that a commercially sounder way of encouraging the planting of more spring wheat would be to offer farmers a bonus per acre sown instead of an increased price per bushel harvested.[107] Such a scheme would obviously eliminate the danger of farmers' hoarding last year's wheat in the hope of a greater eventual return. A couple of weeks later, two high officials of the Grain Corporation floated this idea on a trip to Kansas City with little apparent result.[108]

Then, in mid-March, as the Senate debate reached its climax, a group of restive farmers prepared to convene in Kansas City. Barnes was worried; what could the Food Administration do other than send a representative to the meeting? Hoover ordered Barnes to tell the representative "to stir up diversion quietly onto his acreage bonus."[109] Barnes immediately did so, instructing his agent not to appear "too directly to father the idea."[110]

The bonus proposal never became more than a tactic, in Barnes's words, "to sidetrack the renewed agitation for a higher wheat price."[111] Certainly the "perpetual mal-contents" were unimpressed. On March 21, with legislators from the western states in a nearly solid phalanx, the Senate voted, 49–18, to adopt Gore's amendment.[112]

Hoover was appalled. The continuing "agitation" for a higher price for wheat was "just raising the deuce with marketing in this country," he told Barnes a few days later. Instead of dispatching 7,000,000 bushels per week to market as they normally did at this time of year, farmers were sending only 3,500,000. Hoover saw little hope for a solution until the noxious Gore amendment was disposed of.[113]

Pomerene, too, was stunned. In the final showdown only eighteen senators had stood with the President and his Food Administrator; the Ohio Democrat could not understand it. To Pomerene, "profiteering in bread stuffs by legislation" was profiteering "in its worst form"; he urged the President to veto the bill if necessary.[114] Wilson hinted strongly that he would.[115]

The shocked administration forces now tried to regroup. Within days the press reported that Wilson would not accept the amendment, that it would increase the price of bread by 25 percent, and that no farm organization had protested to the Food Administration against the President's decision to keep the price of wheat unchanged.[116] For his part, Julius Barnes advised Hoover that, if he could not "protect our needs" for the rest of the current crop year by seizing remaining wheat held on the farms, he should "seriously consider withdrawing" from any further attempt to control wheat and flour. Instead, he should publicly blame the culprits: "a group of senators inspired by antagonism to the President and yourself," along with members of Congress more attuned to their constituents' "selfish interests" than to the welfare of 90,000,000 "inarticulate" consumers.[117] Hoover sent a copy of Barnes's letter along to the President.[118]

Fortunately for Hoover and his allies, only the Senate had adopted a wheat price amendment to the Department of Agriculture's appropriations bill. The House of Representatives, which had passed the bill first, had not considered this issue. Before the appropriations bill could be sent in final form to the President's desk, all differences between the two versions must be eliminated. Since the House (with its large contingent of southern Democrats and urban easterners) had always been more sympathetic to the President's food policies than the Senate, Hoover no doubt hoped that the House would hold out.

Now began a protracted and rancorous struggle.[119] On April 1 the House disagreed with the Senate's amendments and requested a conference to reconcile the differences. About ten days later a duly appointed joint conference committee reported that it had reached agreement on everything except the Gore amendment. Unlike August 1917, however, when Hoover had triumphed in the fight over the Lever bill, this time the Senate did not "recede." On April 12 it ordered its negotiating team to insist on retention of the Gore amendment. The scene now shifted to the other chamber. On April 18, after four hours of debate, the House resoundingly rejected the amendment by a vote of 167 to 98. The appropriations bill now returned to conference.

For the next two and a half months the conferees got nowhere. The five-member House delegation, controlled by Representative Lever and two fellow southern Democrats, adamantly refused all compromise.[120] The five-member Senate delegation, three of whom were from western wheat-growing states, likewise refused to renounce its instructions.[121] With each branch of the Congress firmly on record on opposite sides of the question, the negotiators felt little inclination to budge.

As the deadlock deepened, Hoover fortified his lines. At the end of March he laid the wheat issue before his newly created Agricultural Advisory Committee and emphasized that the persisting clamor was impeding delivery of the crop to marketing outlets.[122] Julius Barnes told the committee that the Congressional push for higher wheat prices at this time was "absolutely against [the] public interest." It was inciting farmers to hold back a critically needed resource and was "a real menace to the food supply of this country."[123] Barnes insisted that the United States now had all the wheat under cultivation that it needed for 1918 and that any Congressional action to increase the acreage would, at this point, have little effect.[124]

Despite Barnes's assertion that the wheat price amendment was unnecessary, and despite his claim that its pricing mechanism was so "unsound and illogical" that it would lead to "chaos,"[125] the Agricultural Advisory Committee did not instantly acquiesce. When one of its members offered a resolution declaring that any change in the President's announced price structure for 1918 wheat would be "detrimental to the best interests of the nation in winning the war," several of his colleagues objected. At least one favored the Gore amendment. Others questioned the propriety of injecting themselves so publicly and pointedly into the hottest political controversy in Washington. In the end, the pro-administration member withdrew his resolution, and the committee voted to expunge the discussion of it from its records.[126]

Instead, the committee resolved unanimously that the price of *last* year's wheat should not be changed and that, if necessary, the Food Administration should requisition the remainder of it from whoever held it. Without mentioning the Gore amendment by name, the committee also declared unanimously that a change of the price of wheat at this time would have no appreciable effect on 1918 production.[127]

Upon close analysis, it was clear that the Agricultural Advisory Committee had sidestepped the contentious question of whether the price of wheat should rise as a matter of equity to farmers.[128] Nevertheless, by denying that a boost in price at this point would significantly enhance production, the committee *had* taken sides. It had knocked down one of the two sustaining pillars of the Gore amendment. Herbert Hoover had reason to be pleased.

When word of the committee's action leaked out a few days later, Senator Gore was furious. Taking to the floor, he asked whether this body of "farmers, or alleged farmers"—"hand-picked" by Hoover and David Houston—was qualified "to speak for and to bind the 6,000,000 actual farmers in the United States." The Oklahoma Democrat introduced letters and telegrams showing that the National Grange and other influential farm groups favored his amendment. He also introduced a resolution directing the Secretary of Agriculture to turn over "a full and unedited copy" of the Agricultural Advisory Committee's minutes, including those portions that had been expunged. The Senate promptly adopted Gore's resolution.[129]

There is no evidence that Secretary of Agriculture Houston complied with the Senate's demand.[130] Even if he had, the senatorial sleuths would have found little to embarrass Herbert Hoover. On at least two occasions during the advisory committee's proceedings, its stenographers had deliberately refrained from recording what Hoover said. According to the official version of the minutes, it was "the usual practice" not to report Hoover's remarks at Food Administration gatherings because, "among other reasons," his comments often contained "confidential information on the situation among the Allies."[131] In all likelihood the real reason was a keen desire to protect himself.

During April, in any case, Hoover continued to defend his policies.[132] Then, on April 30, in a speech to a national conference of representatives of the grain trade, he delivered a trenchant explanation for his wheat program and his most biting attack yet on the Gore amendment. In mid-1917, Hoover recalled, the government had confronted a disappointing wheat crop and the necessity to reduce domestic consumption in order to assist the Allies. What had been its policy options? It could have imposed rationing: a method that "bristles with difficulties." It could have simply permitted food prices to rise until consumption fell: a conception "based on conservation for the rich and against the poor." Or it could have adopted an approach "not hitherto applied": the reduction of individual consumption by "almost wholly" voluntary means. According to Hoover, he had taken the last course.

The government had faced another imperative last summer, he continued: the need to eliminate "abnormal speculation" and devise "some substitute for the law of supply and demand." "This law is not sacred," Hoover declared. "It can and has worked the most intense hardship. Its unchecked operation might even jeopardize our success in war." What if he had done nothing? Hoover asked. What if he had allowed "the commerce in wheat to take its untrammeled course" and had done nothing to "stabilize price"? The Allies, he answered, would have bought their wheat from us early in the season, our population would have gone on consuming, and today "all classes of our community would have been totally without wheat-bread." The price of flour, moreover, would cost three to five times as much as at present. And with what consequence?

> If there was suffering in May, 1917, as I am too well aware that there was; if there were food riots in New York in the winter of 1917, what would the position have been in this country in the winter of 1918? I do not wish to indulge in overdrawn statements, but scores of our best observers have informed me time and again that rioting would have been experienced in all our centers of congested population, of a violence that leads to blood in our gutters.

At the very least, there would have been "a total instability in the cost of living," "a total instability" in wage levels, and "an enormous loss in national efficiency" in wartime.

"All disruption of normal commerce is an evil," Hoover added. "We had to choose the lesser evil." And this meant intervention to "stabilize" the price of wheat.

The Food Administrator conceded that various people had criticized his wheat policy as unjust and likely to "stifle" production. He did not believe it. The fact that America's wheat farmers, right now, had more wheat acreage under cultivation "than ever before in our history" was "the final refutation of this hysteria." "Do you suppose," he asked, "this would have been the case if the price were unjust?"

Hoover asserted that the government had stabilized the price of wheat at a level exceeding that of any other grain—a claim that, while true, overlooked the fact that corn had a higher yield per acre. He pointed out that farmers were now receiving 131 percent more for their wheat than they had, on average, obtained shortly before the war. He contended that the price of wheat during the war had increased faster than farmers' costs. He argued that the best way to achieve justice in this matter was not to compare the price of wheat to the price of rye but to determine whether the wheat farmer had obtained "proper compensation for his labor and capital." And in some of his bluntest language ever, he warned farmers against taking "one cent of profit" above their "pre-war normal earnings":

> I agree entirely with the contention of some farmers that they would have received $5 and perhaps $10 a bushel for wheat had it not been for the restraints imposed by the Government, but I would say to these farmers that they would have been taking money not only from the blood of our soldiers and from the suffering of the poor sections in our consuming centers, but every farmer in this country would himself have paid fifty times over in the national damage resulting in reactions from labor and instability in our population that would have thundered at the farm door sooner or later.

Hoover exhorted his listeners—and, by implication, farmers also—to lift their sights and transcend their petty self-interest. To 10,000,000 people in the bread lines of Belgium and northern France—all dependent on imported wheat from the United States and Canada—the grain had become "the symbol of the greatness and charity of America." Because of the war, "enormous populations" were suffering and even starving. For people everywhere wheat had become "the positive emblem of national survival, national tranquility, national ability to continue in the war."

> We have in the distribution of this commodity above all others a duty that far transcends mere commerce: it is a duty in humanity and a duty in our self-defense. Its improper handling can spell more privation, more starva-

> tion, with danger to national efficiency, to failure in war. Its handling must be in a spirit by which our commerce will have passed from gain to that exalted idealism which underlies our national character.[133]

Yet more than idealistic sentiment would be required to pry remaining wheat stocks from the farms. While the prospects for a banner 1918 harvest were steadily improving,[134] the amount of 1917 wheat coming to market was lagging. At the beginning of March, 111,000,000 bushels of wheat were still on the farms. During the ensuing month, weekly receipts at mills dropped to less than half of normal.[135]

Contemplating the havoc brought on (he believed) by Senator Gore, Hoover considered requisitioning wheat directly from farmers—something which, under the law, he had authority to do. On March 23 he authorized the seizure of large stores of wheat in New Mexico that had been held back from the market by two farmers of German extraction. The men had repeatedly refused to sell at the ruling price and had given "no satisfactory explanation."[136] That same day, Julius Barnes urged Hoover to create an elaborate card index listing all farmers in the country who still held wheat, the amount they possessed, and their nationality. Such an index, said Barnes, would enable the Food Administration to identify the "most objectionable" cases (such as "notoriously pro-German" farmers) and, in the event of requisitioning, to move against these individuals first.[137]

Barnes's card index plan was never implemented, possibly because Hoover hesitated to be so draconian.[138] When the press reported on March 28 that the Food Administration was planning "drastic measures" against hoarding and had reminded its state officials that the law permitted grain seizures, Hoover swiftly announced that his agency had issued "[n]o general order requisitioning wheat."[139] The Food Administrator evidently did not want to antagonize farmers with the threat of indiscriminate compulsion.

In the same press release, however, Hoover disclosed that he had ordered his state food administrators to appeal to the nation's wheat farmers to "market their residue" by May 15 at the latest. He also divulged that his state administrators had been notified of numerous reports of "German farmers refusing to market any of their wheat" and had been asked to direct these persons to dispose of it at once. If they refused, the government could then requisition it.[140] Although Hoover tried to make it appear that his only target was farmers with German sympathies, he probably hoped that other wheat growers—fearful of the taint of disloyalty—would now find it expedient to release their crop.

While Hoover was reluctant to be more coercive than necessary, he wanted it understood that he would be coercive if necessary. And such necessity would arise, he revealed, if Senator Gore secured his amendment. On April 5 Hoover disclosed that the Food Administration and Department of Agriculture would recommend commandeering all existing wheat stocks in the country if Congress increased the price to $2.50 a bushel.[141]

To an outraged Gore, this was tantamount to blackmail. With a vehemence equaling that of Senator Reed, the Oklahoma Democrat excoriated the Food Administrator. "I do not see why such a threat should be made," the senator fumed the next day. "I do not see why its execution should be made contingent upon the action of Congress within its appointed and constitutional sphere." The Senate had voted to raise the wheat price out of "a sense of public duty and a patriotic desire to stimulate production." If the House of Representatives concurred, it would do so from similar motives.

> But, sir, if Congress does not behave to suit the Food Administration it is to be rebuked and chastened by the Food Administrator. If the Congress assumes to discharge its constitutional function and its patriotic duty it is to call down upon its offending head the sword of retributive justice in the hands of the Food Administrator. If the Congress acts upon its own responsibility and acts contrary to the views of Mr. Hoover, he is to convert himself into an avenging deity. He is to wreak his wrath not upon the Congress alone but upon the unoffending farmers of the country. He does not threaten to commandeer wheat because it is being willfully hoarded. That would be a sufficient reason. He does not threaten to commandeer wheat because the necessity is impending and is imperious. That would be a sufficient justification. He threatens to commandeer all the wheat in the country if the Congress should slip its leash, should defy the lash, and should decide upon its own responsibility to do justice to the American farmer and, as time will reveal, an act of preeminent service to the American people and to their allies. I must be permitted to say that this threat, if true, is a brazen affront and an unprovoked insult to the Congress of a great and of a free people.[142]

Hoover apparently took no official notice of this denunciation. Nor did he abandon his carrot-and-stick approach to the wheat farmers. On the one hand, in early May he beseeched them to market even wheat ordinarily reserved for seed—so great, he said, had become "the European demand for flour."[143] On the other hand, in mid-April his agency ordered all wheat in North Dakota sold by May 15. If any remained unsold on that date, local officials were to take it to town, sell it, and deduct transportation costs from the farmer's receipts.[144] Hoover undoubtedly hoped that appeals to patriotism, supplemented by a few selective cases of coercion, would overcome lingering resistance based upon pecuniary or "pro-German" motives. The strategy succeeded. According to one of his lieutenants, the government's relatively few outright acts of requisition "had a very salutary effect and resulted in a large marketing during May and June, 1918."[145] Certainly by July 1 there was very little wheat left on the farms.[146]

Meanwhile the political impasse continued on Capitol Hill. On May 16

Representative Scott Ferris, chairman of the Democratic Party's Congressional campaign committee, urged the President to "relent" and fix the wheat price halfway between "the two extremes." The Oklahoma legislator warned that "it would be unfortunate to create a feeling among the wheat farmers of the west that they were being discriminated against," for it would cause a decline in wheat production.[147] Woodrow Wilson, however, declined to yield. The fixing of prices by legislatures, he replied, was a "mistake." If $2.50 was a proper price for wheat, it should be ascertained by the means he had used to determine the price in the first place. To permit legislative "rigidity" to intrude here would "destroy the whole method by which we are dealing with the industries of the country."[148]

A few weeks later the President authorized the Food Administration Grain Corporation to pay farmers more than the guaranteed price for wheat if Hoover approved.[149] Hoover thereupon raised the basic price to $2.26 per bushel to reflect the government's recent increase of railroad freight rates.[150] Since the wheat price had been advanced only to cover increased transportation costs, the net effect on wheat producers was nil.

So, too, was the political effect on Capitol Hill. All through June the legislative deadlock persisted. Near the end of the month the Senate majority leader attempted to break it by asking his colleagues to instruct their conferees to abandon the Gore amendment. The Senate refused by a vote of 46 to 19.[151] As in the protracted battle over the Lever Act a year before, bitterness was rampant. Senators Reed and Gore suspected that the House conferees had deliberately held the matter in conference until spring planting was over in order to nullify part of the rationale for Gore's proposal.[152] On the other side of the Capitol, House negotiators contended that according to the rules governing consideration of appropriation bills it was the duty of the Senate conferees in this instance to "recede."[153]

Yet if one of the principal arguments for the amendment (that it would stimulate spring wheat planting) was now passé, one of the principal arguments against it (that it would stop marketing of 1917 wheat) was also obsolete. By now, too, many Democrats in the West had become alarmed about the political implications of alienating 3,000,000 wheat farmers in their region only months before a Congressional election. When the wheat price amendment returned to the House of Representatives for another vote on July 6, the pro-Wilson, pro-Hoover forces found themselves outnumbered. A representative from Michigan offered a compromise: a minimum of $2.40 per bushel for grade No. 2 at twenty-five primary interior markets around the country. By a vote of 150 to 107, the House accepted it. The Senate concurred and sent the amended appropriations bill to the White House.[154]

Even before the bill arrived, Woodrow Wilson notified Congress that he would veto it.[155] Nevertheless, for the next several days wheat farmers and their advocates bombarded the chief executive with pleas to accept the Congressional compromise.[156] Fearing political disaster, Representative Scott

Ferris begged the President to "spare us the veto." Democratic members of Congress from the West, he reported, believed that it would be "ruinous" to them.[157] For his part, Hoover informed the President that the amendment promised catastrophe of another sort. To implement the $2.40 guarantee as a virtually uniform national price without allowing for transportation differentials (as the amendment mandated) would either require an immediate $500,000,000 in working capital (which Congress had not supplied) or an increase of 43 cents per bushel at every grain terminal in the land. This, he said, would add $2.00 a barrel to the price of flour as well as provide a "gift" to farmers of $387,000,000 for their 1918 wheat harvest. Hoover questioned whether such a gift was necessary. No "responsible body of farmers" had ever complained to him about the price, he said—a price which had already proven "stimulative."[158]

Secretary of Agriculture Houston also objected to the price-fixing measure—and to the "unwise" way in which it had come about. Such subjects, he argued, should be settled by executive rather than legislative determination.[159] Even the Allies entered the controversy. In a letter to the Secretary of the Treasury, the British ambassador pointed out that enactment of the amendment would compel Canada to raise its wheat price also and would cost the Allies an additional $100,000,000 in wheat expenditures—which, he noted, they would have to borrow from the United States.[160] Hoover had already made the same arguments to President Wilson.[161] In fact, Hoover probably instigated the ambassador's letter.[162]

Any lingering doubts about the President's resolve vanished on July 12 when he vetoed the Department of Agriculture appropriations bill rather than accept its wheat price section. Wilson did so "upon principle," he said, because it was impossible to satisfactorily administer "such inelastic legislative price provisions," which established "arbitrary" price levels "quite independent of the normal market conditions" and because "the present method of regulation by conference" was a superior approach. He also vetoed the bill, he said, on the grounds of "wise expediency." The present method of fixing the price had yielded a tremendous increase in production, and the "overwhelming majority of farmers" considered the current price to be "fair and liberal." Following Hoover's analysis closely, Wilson asserted that the foreign and domestic costs of raising the minimum price to $2.40 would be terrific.[163]

Agrarian spokesmen quickly challenged Wilson's statistic (supplied by Hoover) that the amendment would effectively yield farmers an additional $387,000,000 for their 1918 wheat. They charged that this figure was fallacious, for it assumed a jump in the guaranteed price from $2.00 (the current legal minimum) to $2.40. Since the President himself had already set the 1918 price at $2.20, the actual *additional* payment to farmers, under the bill, would be only $180,000,000, and its impact on flour prices would be far less than claimed.[164] Henry C. Wallace publicly suggested that whoever prepared the President's figures had failed to take "reasonable care" to avoid leading him into "grave errors."[165]

Hoover insisted that there was no error in the data at all. The critics, he said, had overlooked the fact that the revised amendment would establish $2.40 as the basic price not just in Chicago (as at present) but in twenty-four other primary interior markets as well. To him this was tantamount to establishing a "universal price" of $2.40 for the No. 2 grade, or $2.43 for No. 1.[166] Since the government's figures showed that the *farm* price for 1917 wheat had averaged just over $2.00 per bushel,[167] his estimate of the amendment's cost may have been more accurate than his critics'.

All this now became moot. On July 13 the House of Representatives attempted to override the President's veto. Whether from awe of the President, respect for his reasoning, or some other medley of motives, the body reversed its stand of a week before. The advocates of higher-priced wheat needed two thirds of those voting to win. They did not begin to come close. Only 73 representatives voted to override; 173 voted against. Another 180 did not vote at all.[168] The five-month battle was over. Woodrow Wilson—and Hoover, too—had prevailed.

III

THE final defeat of the Gore amendment won applause in the eastern press, where sympathy for Hoover was strong. The farmers were "enjoying unprecedented prosperity," the *Washington Post* editorialized. The amendment would have taken hundreds of millions of dollars "out of the pockets of the people" and put it in the hands of the "wheat profiteers."[169]

Certainly Hoover could argue that, despite all their lamentations, wheat farmers had responded spectacularly to his price support system. In 1918 American farmers harvested more than 61,000,000 acres of wheat, an increase of more than 14,000,000 acres over 1917.[170] The 1918 harvest of over 900,000,000 bushels was the second largest in the history of the country.[171] It was potent testimony to the appeal of the government's price incentives. Moreover, on July 1, 1918 the average farm price of wheat in the United States was more than double what it had been just two years before.[172] None of these statistics suggested that the wheat farmer had suffered very much because of the fixed price on his product. In the words of one later student of the subject, "The margin between cost and price was definitely in his favor."[173]

It was harder, however, to combat the perception that the government had arbitrarily imposed a penalty on wheat producers while letting the rest of the country profit freely from the wartime boom. In vain did Hoover argue that wheat was different because so much of it was exported—that in "no other foodstuff" had "the unrestrained play of the law of supply and demand" led to "such an entire distortion of the real functions of distribution."[174] Hoover stressed that he intended to interfere with the market only when it was "imperative" in order to "minimize" Allied and domestic suffering.[175] Senator Gore countered that if it was necessary to supply wheat to the Allies "without price," then the U.S. government and the nation as a whole should "absorb the loss" and not inflict it upon "the most indispensable class of our citizens."[176] It rankled farmers that—in Gore's bitter words—grain millers, elevator owners, and meat packers were earning "fabulous" profits while wheat producers were compelled "to take 30 per cent less for their product than it was worth. Is that 'equal justice'?"[177]

Hoover and Wilson had frustrated the wheat bloc, but the election campaign of 1918 was just beginning. Already Republicans were charging that the Democratic Party—dominated in Congress by southerners—was indifferent to the needs of the West. The Republicans noted that the Democrats had been willing to legislate governmental control of the price of the great western staple—wheat—but had been utterly unwilling to do the same for cotton, whose unregulated price rose to record-breaking heights during the war.[178] Gore himself, although a Democrat, lashed out at southern members of his own party on this very point in mid-July.[179] He predicted that if the next Congress went Republican, it would be due to the President's veto message.[180] The charge of sectional discrimination was to inflict severe political harm on Woodrow Wilson.

For Hoover, too, the political cost of price-fixing was considerable. In the whole five-month conflict, neither he nor the President seemed ever seriously to consider a compromise: a stance that probably widened the rift between themselves and their antagonists in the Senate.[181] Hoover's refusal to countenance what he considered an irresponsible and dangerous piece of legislation fed agrarian suspicion that the Food Administrator was no friend of the farmer. His eloquent idealism, global perspective, and concern for the poor earned him deep respect among colleagues, newspaper editors, and middle-class women. But to much of rural America he seemed an unsympathetic outsider. This negative perception would dog him all the way to the presidency ten years later.

For now, though, he at least had the satisfaction of foiling his senatorial foes.

12

A Dance Along a Precipice

I

THE producers of wheat were not the only farmers whose anger curdled into agitation in the stormy winter of 1918. The livestock lobby, too, had clout in Washington and a deepening determination to use it.

In mid-January the annual convention of the American National Live Stock Association warned the country that an "impending food shortage" was jeopardizing success in the war. Even worse, hard-hit producers of beef and dairy cattle were utterly unable, under current conditions, to increase their output.[1]

The livestock men did not content themselves with passing a resolution. On February 13 a delegation from their trade association called upon President Wilson at the White House. The petitioners declared that their industry was in peril and that livestock producers, no matter how patriotic, could not continue in business at a loss. The delegation asserted that discontent and apprehension were growing among farmers and that meat production would fall disastrously unless the government took immediate, "constructive" action. The industry representatives requested nothing less than a new "national live-stock policy," based upon "sound economic principles" that would stimulate production.[2]

Although moderate in their choice of language, the petitioners did not spare Herbert Hoover from criticism. They charged that the Food Administration was controlling the price of finished beef "in the interest of the consumer" while the price of livestock feed was rising abnormally.[3] According to one of their leaders, the Food Administration, by its control of beef exports, had indirectly fixed livestock prices at levels "unremunerative" to producers.[4]

If Hoover was not faultless in the eyes of the worried livestock men, the principal object of their ire was elsewhere. Why were they losing money on every head of cattle that they raised? Because—they told the President—the mighty meat packers completely controlled the price.[5] To the cattlemen it was an outrage that they, the actual raisers of live animals, were suffering heavy losses while those who handled cattle products were making "enormous" profits.[6] The stockmen's delegation seemed unmoved by the fact that Hoover had imposed a limit on the packers' profit margins. Instead, the petitioners pointedly asked that the Food Administration verify the meat packers' claims about their earnings since being licensed.[7]

Impressed by the sincerity of his visitors, President Wilson asked Hoover for comment.[8] For the embattled Food Administrator, yet another crisis was at hand. For months he had been navigating (as he put it) "between two storms—the producer and the consumer," in a search for commodity prices that would simultaneously encourage production and "preserve tranquility" among the urban poor.[9] Now a powerful group of producers was questioning his handling of the middlemen. It did not help that the protesting stockmen included William Kent, a personal friend of Woodrow Wilson and one of his appointees to the United States Tariff Commission.[10] Clearly here was a challenge that Hoover could not dismiss as the perpetual whining of greedy malcontents.

Yet how could he respond? If he accepted the cattlemen's complaints and shifted course, he would be tacitly conceding regulatory failure—something he never cared to admit. But if he defiantly defended the status quo, he would antagonize still more of the farm bloc and risk the charge of being a patsy of the packers. Already critics on the left had accused the Food Administration of being "dominated by big business."[11] Hoover's staffing of his agency with well-to-do volunteers, and his endless conferences with leaders of regulated food industries, seemed to give credence to this criticism. In the nasty political climate of early 1918, he could not tolerate the perception that the most hated big businesses in America—the packers—were flourishing under his regulatory aegis while raisers of livestock teetered toward bankruptcy.

In a written response to the President on February 21, Hoover attempted to negotiate the political minefield. The Food Administrator was quick to assert that he had "no great love for the packers," who in fact had been "very difficult to deal with." He also admitted that the packers did control the prices of live animals in the sense that all middlemen "operating in large units" controlled prices "to some extent . . . more or less from day to day." But beyond these concessions Hoover did not move. He insisted that even the packing industry could not control supply and demand "in the long run" and that the Food Administration had now imposed effective limits on the packers' profits. In fact, he reported, the packers' "sworn statements" showed the companies to be operating on a very narrow margin or even at a loss in the past two months—a claim that the angry cattlemen plainly doubted. Hoover was willing enough that the packers' data be checked. He asked that the Federal Trade Commission's accountants perform this task. But he added at once that it was "only fair" to record that the packers had been performing "an indispensable service for war purposes." Whatever the industry's past record, Hoover asserted that it had "advanced very far" in "national service" in the three months it had been under his supervision.[12]

In a separate memorandum for the President, Hoover defended his meat policies at every point. The Food Administrator did not deny that the livestock industry was suffering losses, but he declined to take any responsibility for its plight. The industry's problems were the result of "forces set up by war dislocations," he contended, and were "impossible of solution by any authority yet conferred by Congress." Hoover also insisted that the national livestock supply was "not in danger," and blamed the soaring price of cattle feed on the breakdown of the railroads.

As usual when under pressure from agrarian activists, Hoover minimized the extent of his legal powers. The Food Administration, he asserted, had no authority to control the price of cattle or beef. Nor had it tried to exert such authority, with one exception: in placing some recent Allied orders on the American market, it had attempted to "sustain the price of cattle."

The key issue, however, remained packer profits, and in his memorandum for the President, Hoover was unequivocal. His newly imposed restrictions were working; the industry's profits were now "well within the limits" he had set. In fact, thanks to his stringent regulations, the packers' profits were now "more . . . purely an incident in the progress of cattle to the consumer" than ever before.

Hoover therefore saw no need for massive federal intervention in the meat trade. He rejected the suggestion that the government take over the packing houses and fix the price that packers paid farmers for cattle. Such a course, he argued, was fraught with practical difficulties and would lead to "complete disaster." In the end, his reply to the distressed cattlemen boiled down to two fateful assertions: that the meat-packing giants were now behaving themselves and that his agency was effectively supervising them.[13] On this uncertain foundation he took his stand.

If Hoover believed that his rebuttal would quell the agitation to crack down on the packers, he was soon disappointed. Only four days after he sent his memo to the White House, a political bombshell in Chicago exploded his hopes. Early in 1917, in response to pressure from the livestock interests and others, President Wilson had directed the Federal Trade Commission to investigate possible conspiracies, monopolies, and illegal restraints of trade in the nation's food industries. The commission had gotten under way later in the year. As part of its inquiry it had retained as special counsel a flamboyant former prosecuting attorney from California named Francis J. Heney. The FTC's counsel was not just a lawyer with a well-developed flair for publicity. He was also a nationally prominent Progressive with a passionate distrust of big business.[14] On February 25, 1918 he opened the commission's public hearings in Chicago. His subject—nay, his target—was the meat-packing behemoths known collectively as the "Big Five."

Using scores of private letters seized from the confidential files of packing house executives, Heney painted a lurid picture of corporate moguls manipulating the federal government for private gain. He charged that packers had obtained valuable "inside" information on federal food policy before the public did, including word of Hoover's decision to make Joseph Cotton the head of his meat division. Heney charged that the principal packers had assiduously infiltrated federal agencies with individuals "friendly" to their interests. At the Food Administration itself, he disclosed, Swift & Company had placed three of its leading affiliated executives: F. S. Brooks, E. O. Heyl, and W. F. Priebe. Despite the fact that these men were working for the government, Swift continued to pay them hefty salaries.[15]

The next day Heney concentrated his fire on Priebe, head of the poultry and egg section of the perishable foods division of Hoover's agency. Before joining the wartime government, Priebe had been president of one of the largest butter and egg companies in the country, a position he continued to hold. Heney now charged that Priebe's supposedly independent business was actually a subsidiary of Swift and that Priebe was drawing $275 a month in salary from his firm—or in effect from Swift—while working for Hoover. Even worse, Heney alleged that Priebe, the "independent" egg dealer, had set up "dummy" companies in an effort to drive the packers' independent competitors out of business.[16]

Heney's revelations evoked sensational headlines across the country—and a dangerous political headache for Herbert Hoover. It was bad enough that disgruntled cattlemen thought the packing houses were profiteering while farmers suffered. Now it appeared that the agency that was supposed to oversee the packers had itself been "packed" by men with a blatant conflict of interest. If this impression should stand, the Food Administration's reputation for impartiality would be destroyed. Hoover must speedily rebut Heney or risk being labeled a dupe of the Big Five.

In a press release issued on February 26—the day Heney's first allegations appeared in the newspapers—Hoover struck back. He asserted that none of the Food Administration officials named by Heney had "anything whatever" to do with regulation of the packing industry. Nor were they "now paid" by the packers. Each of the individuals named, said Hoover, had served their government at "considerable sacrifice." Each was unquestionably devoted to the "public interest."[17]

On February 27, as Heney's barrage of allegations continued, a seething Hoover prepared a letter and memorandum for President Wilson. The Food Administrator declared flatly that Priebe, Brooks, and Heyl held "subordinate positions" in his agency and had no role whatever in regulating the Chicago packers. (He appeared not to realize that Swift, at least, dealt heavily in poultry and eggs.) Far from being mired in conflicts of interest, Brooks and Heyl had been required to sever their ties to the packers before taking assignments in the Food Administration. As for Priebe, Hoover praised the egg merchant as "a most progressive and public spirited man"—an "independent dealer" who had never had "any relationship" with the packers, save for one "remote exception": one packing company was "a stockholder in one small company" out of five in which Priebe was an officer.[18] Hoover apparently did not know what Priebe had admitted in house the day before: that Swift held a majority of the stock in one of Priebe's companies.[19] Priebe was more beholden to Swift than he and perhaps Hoover cared to let on.

Hoover quickly realized that more was at stake than the possible malfeasance of a single employee. Heney was not merely crying, "Scandal!" He was challenging the very rationale of Hoover's system of government-business interaction. In his letter to the President, Hoover attempted to justify his approach. It was "utterly hopeless," he explained, to run the Food Administration unless he could draw "patriotic and honest" experts from the industries he regulated. "To attempt to intelligently watch the operations of cold storage, flour mills, and a hundred other industries of this technical type, with a sole equipment of doctors and lawyers, would be ridiculous." Hoover emphasized that his Food Administration made a fundamental distinction between policymaking and policy *implementation*. The "entire matter of policy" rested with himself and his division chiefs, all of whom were required to be "entirely independent" of the particular trade they oversaw. Subordinate "technical men" (like Priebe) were "here simply to carry out the detail."[20]

Hoover did not submit his letter and memorandum to the President.[21] Instead, he evidently conveyed his indignation orally. Meanwhile, on the night of February 27, Priebe publicly denied that he was receiving $275 a month directly from Swift. The poultry executive declined to comment, however, on the charge that Swift owned his company. "When Mr. Hoover asked me to become associated with the Food Administration," Priebe said, "I told him all about my business connections and suggested that objections might be raised to me. He told me that if I could stand the guff he could."[22]

Out in Chicago, Francis J. Heney was unmoved. To the crusading attorney, prior employment with the meat-packing giants was in itself sufficient ground to disqualify a person from service in the Food Administration, and he was determined to drive the tainted officials from their posts.[23] On February 27 he elicited testimony at his hearing that Priebe, in his strategic post in the Food Administration, had issued regulations that effectively devastated independent poultry dealers and enriched the big packers such as Swift.[24] It was the most stunning allegation yet of outright corruption within Hoover's ranks.

Eventually the regulations in question became the subject of two Congressional inquiries.[25] Whatever the rules' merits, Priebe's defenders insisted that he had not been responsible for their formulation or enforcement.[26] According to Hoover, Priebe was merely a "go-between," an interpreter to the trade of rules and policies that other, entirely disinterested, men in the Food Administration devised.[27] To Hoover's frustration, critics like Heney seemed not to grasp this crucial point.

Nor, it seemed, did many other Americans. As Heney's relentless pounding continued, Hoover was obliged to retreat. On March 1, at his request, Priebe resigned as president and director of the W. F. Priebe Company, thereby foregoing his substantial monthly salary. (He did not, however, give up his profit-sharing arrangements with his firm.)[28] The poultry executive told Hoover that he hoped thus to terminate the controversy and avoid suspicion.[29]

It was too late. At the beginning of March, Priebe arrived in Kansas City as Hoover's representative to address a convention of poultry dealers. There he was bitterly accused of using his office to destroy the small independents. An angry delegate introduced a resolution condemning Priebe by name and demanding his ouster from the Food Administration. The resolution was narrowly defeated after employees of the big packers registered to vote and after other delegates argued that it would be a discourtesy for the convention formally to rebuke an invited guest.[30]

Francis Heney's headline-grabbing charges of packer infiltration were beginning to hurt Hoover badly. On March 3 one of his lieutenants in Wisconsin telegraphed that the Chicago hearings were causing the Food Administration "great harm."[31] The next day, one of Hoover's closest friends reported from Kansas that people in that state were starting to feel that "as soon as the packers squeal or business interests face a loss the food administration protects them and plays their game."[32] The Kansas editor William Allen White was similarly direct. The Food Administration, he warned privately in a letter to Vernon Kellogg, was "getting in bad" by relying on "dealers big and little" to administer its policies. There was just as much talent in the "professional class" as in the "commercial class," White asserted. Grain millers should not comprise a majority of Hoover's flour managers, "and the packers should not control the meat."[33]

Upon reading White's letter, Hoover exploded. "The whole of this is formulated simply on junk conclusions and prejudice," he fumed. Aside from trade representatives who were in the Food Administration for the purpose of "educating their trades on what we want them to do," fully 80 percent of the Administration staff were professional men already. Hoover said it was "enough to make one sick" to hear people say that Heney's revelations confirmed their beliefs about the Food Administration. "There is no representation of packers in this establishment in any shape or form." Not one employee of his meat division was a packer. Hoover did admit that "our travelling lecturer to the egg trade" (Priebe) had "the misfortune to be connected with a firm in which a packing concern held some shares." Once again he played down Priebe's links to Swift. For the Food Administrator, the whole controversy was bogus. "If there is no more justice in the United States than is evidenced by such paragraphs as this," he exclaimed, "I am prepared to accept German autocracy as being the only hope of the world!"[34]

By now Hoover was convinced that something must be done about Heney. Around the beginning of March, Hoover complained to President Wilson that Heney's publication of the packers' correspondence files was undermining the Food Administrator's influence and jeopardizing his effort to persuade the country to conserve food. Hoover demanded that disclosure of the letters be stopped. Wilson notified the FTC of Hoover's protest and, without giving instructions, expressed his hope that a clash could be averted. The FTC commissioners promptly recalled Heney to Washington. On March 8 he, they, Hoover, and Hoover's counsel, William A. Glasgow, Jr., met at the commission's offices for a showdown.[35]

As usual in such head-to-head encounters, Hoover was in no mood to compromise. When Heney suggested that Priebe be fired, Hoover pronounced himself satisfied that Priebe was beyond reproach. Priebe, he asserted, had given up his salary and had cut his ties with his principal company. None of Priebe's remaining four companies, said Hoover, had any connection with Swift. Furthermore, Hoover claimed, Priebe had just been unanimously endorsed by the poultry leaders' convention in Kansas City.[36]

Taking the offensive, Hoover and Glasgow pressed Heney to cease his public disclosure of the packing house executives' private letters that were allegedly proving so detrimental to the Food Administration. To Hoover it was quite unnecessary to air dirty linen in this way. If a man was crooked or ill-suited for a particular job, he said, he would remove him immediately. The Food Administrator did not need anyone to tell him to take such steps. Heney finally promised not to divulge any more troubling letters relating to Food Administration personnel without first submitting them to Hoover and giving him an opportunity to investigate and act. But the zealous FTC counsel reserved the right to unveil the documents later if he deemed it in the public interest.[37]

Heney did not mention Priebe again in his hearings, but the imbroglio did not end there. Upon returning to Chicago, the counsel investigated the matter further and concluded that Hoover's defense of Priebe had been thoroughly inaccurate. Priebe's four remaining businesses were not independent entities (as Hoover claimed) but were instead mere buying agencies of Priebe & Company, which Swift controlled.[38] Nor had the Kansas City poultrymen's convention given Priebe a unanimous vote of confidence; quite the contrary. On this point Priebe's immediate superior at the Food Administration, G. Harold Powell, had misinformed Hoover.[39]

Heney now discovered evidence that Powell had attempted to intimidate a New York businessman named H. L. Preston, who owned a trade journal that had been hostile to Priebe (as a "Swift man") for months. According to Heney's sources, Powell had threatened to have Preston's publication banned from the U.S. mails under wartime law if Preston persisted in his anti-Priebe editorials. Shortly thereafter, the journal retracted its criticism of Priebe.[40]

When Heney asked Preston to confirm this, however, the New York businessman told a somewhat different story. His journal had indeed altered its stance toward Priebe after being informed by Powell that Priebe had "entirely severed his relations with Swift & Co." Preston denied that Powell had threatened him with loss of his journal's mailing privileges. But the businessman disclosed that Powell *had* made remarks to an associate of Preston that led the associate to infer that "there was some idea" in Washington of asking the Post Office Department "to relieve us of our second-class privileges if it were found that the paper was discrediting the Food Administration and its purposes and subordinates." Moreover, Powell himself told Preston that Priebe had Hoover's complete confidence and that Preston should "keep that fact in mind." Under the circumstances, Preston was well aware—as he told Heney—that the "authorities at Washington" had the power "to entirely ruin my business." Preston now proposed to accept the Food Administration's statements about Priebe unless Heney turned up evidence to the contrary.[41]

To Heney it was obvious that Preston had been "quite well intimidated."[42] Whatever the truth of that judgment, the episode revealed something else. Preston's encounter with Powell had occurred before Heney's electrifying public hearings. The response of Hoover and his lieutenants to a single trade journal's criticisms revealed how sensitive they already were about their dealings with the packers.

Word of Heney's interest in the Preston case soon reached the Food Administration. Powell strenuously denied that he had ever discussed with Preston or anyone else the idea of using governmental power to suppress a publication. The thought, he told Hoover, had never entered his head.[43] Hoover apparently believed him. In a lengthy letter to Preston, Hoover repeated Powell's denials and again defended the Food Administration's reliance on businessmen. In many industries, Hoover argued, the best way to advance the wartime national interest was to elicit "the voluntary effort of the trades themselves." This meant that he must recruit outstanding business leaders to serve as liaisons between himself and the trade—leaders like W. F. Priebe. Hoover had no use for the anti-big business prejudices of muckrakers like Heney (though he did not mention him by name).

> If we are to assume that there is no patriotism and no honesty in the business community of the United States, it is obvious enough that this war is being fought for a futile purpose. I do not hold this view and so long as I hold this position I propose to adhere to my confidence in the honesty of the American business men as a whole and to their patriotism and willingness to make any necessary sacrifice for the objectives of the Government.

To Hoover the affiliations of Priebe with Swift & Co. were beside the point. The sole issue concerned Priebe's "honesty, capacity and patriotism." Of these, said Hoover, there was "ample evidence"—and not "one single atom of evidence to the contrary."[44]

It is hard to know whether Hoover truly believed his vehement words or whether—having gone this far—he was trying to bluff his way through. Certainly his professed confidence in his beleaguered subordinate was not shared by the Federal Trade Commission. Heney now uncovered masses of private correspondence between Priebe and various business associates after Priebe joined the Food Administration. Heney claimed that the correspondence proved that Priebe had tipped off Swift & Co. about his plans for poultry regulation and had used information obtained as a government official to further his business interests: an incontestable breach of public trust. Hoover's counsel Glasgow later examined the same correspondence and concluded that it contained no proof of dishonesty, and thus no grounds for dismissal. To fire Priebe in such circumstances "would have branded him as a dishonest man," said Glasgow, and this the counsel could not do.[45]

Early in April 1918 Heney himself—swashbuckling scourge of the special interests—completed his service as the FTC's special counsel. Hoover was surely delighted to see him go. The commission now turned from headline-grabbing hearings to the preparation of a report on the meat-packing industry. Nevertheless, the issue of Priebe's conduct continued to fester between the two agencies. As late as June—partly at Heney's instigation—the FTC attempted to have Priebe ousted from office. In the eyes of one of the FTC's investigators, Priebe had unquestionably used his office to benefit the "big meat packers" and inflict severe economic damage on independent poultry dealers.[46] Whether from belief in Priebe's innocence or from confidence that adverse publicity was no longer a danger, Hoover resisted the FTC's pressure. Victim or malefactor, Priebe remained at the Food Administration through the end of the war.[47]

Unfortunately for Hoover, his chief poultry and egg expert was not his only associate to come under Heney's unfriendly fire. "I do not question your integrity one iota," Heney told Hoover in their confrontation on March

8, "but I do question your viewpoint, not only in this matter but others."[48] In particular, the FTC's counsel wondered whether Joseph Cotton was the proper man to administer Hoover's meat division. Cotton himself had no personal stake in the packing industry.[49] But he had once been a partner of certain attorneys who at one time or another had represented packing interests or their financial allies. Hoover and Cotton pointed out that Cotton himself did not participate in any of these transactions, some of which occurred after Cotton had left his law firm.[50] But to Francis Heney, such distinctions seemed irrelevant. Cotton, he said, was "a man of the highest integrity but absolutely unfit, because of his viewpoint and environment," to regulate the packers. Cotton was a New York corporate lawyer, and that, for Heney, was enough to condemn him.[51]

It was not Cotton, however, but his principal deputy at the meat division, E. Dana Durand, who became the next to suffer from Heney's barrage. A University of Minnesota professor of statistics and agricultural economics, Durand was already under suspicion among the anti-packer forces for helping to write a 1905 government report on the industry that Heney and others termed a "white-wash."[52] In 1916, after an outbreak of agitation in Congress that ultimately led to the FTC's food inquiry, Durand had agreed to edit a manuscript prepared by Swift & Co. to justify its business.[53] Now, at the beginning of March 1918, Heney ignited two bombshells that called into question Durand's impartiality as one of Hoover's key lieutenants.

Heney's evidence consisted of two letters written by packing house executives to business associates just a few weeks before—letters found among the corporate files that the FTC had seized. The first letter described a secret conference of Big Five leaders with Durand at the Food Administration's headquarters in December 1917. At this gathering Durand allegedly disclosed valuable information about forthcoming export allotments—information that he did not want to leak lest it antagonize small packing houses and destabilize the market for livestock. To all appearances Durand was favoring the industry's giants while keeping their competitors in the dark.[54]

The second letter described another meeting with Big Five representatives a month later. Here Durand revealed that the government was about to place orders for tremendous amounts of beef for export—an operation that would tax the resources of the packers as never before. There was nothing improper about Durand's announcement or his effort to work out a practical plan with the assembled businessmen. But the professor-turned-bureaucrat proceeded to warn them that they must handle their purchases of live animals in such a way as to prevent an increase in cattle prices. An advance in prices "absolutely must not come about, and if it did he would take drastic measures to prevent it."[55]

In effect Durand wanted to keep prices stable despite the sudden, unprecedented demand for live cattle. The Big Five executives unanimously promised that they would not pay more for livestock and would maintain the prices of their own finished products at "normal" levels.[56]

Durand's remarks (as recorded in these two letters) appeared to undercut Herbert Hoover's contention that the Food Administration had no authority to control the price of cattle or processed beef.[57] Technically this was true. Hoover could not *fix* the price. But as Durand's conferences showed, Hoover's agency was using its economic and moral power to achieve essentially that result. Durand's warning against higher cattle prices appeared to conflict with Hoover's public posture in another way. Hoover told President Wilson on February 20 that the Food Administration had not interfered with cattle and beef prices except once, to sustain them.[58] Yet just three days earlier, Durand had instructed the packers to hold those prices down.

Heney's disclosure of Durand's actions infuriated the nation's farmers and their advocates. The Priebe affair seemed to prove that the Big Five had infiltrated Hoover's agency. The Durand revelations seemed to prove that the regulators and regulated were in actual collusion. Amid anger about governmental secrecy and favoritism, Joseph Cotton and Durand were called before the Senate agriculture committee in late March. Rumors flew that the Senate might recommend Cotton's ouster.[59]

In the face of skeptical questioning, Durand insisted that his remarks at the January conference had been misrepresented. The Food Administration, he said, had been fearful that a growing glut of domestic frozen beef would depress the market price of live animals. Hoover's agency had therefore asked the British government to place an unusually large order for American beef precisely *in order to support the endangered cattle market*. The British had agreed to oblige, provided that they could obtain the beef at current prices. Durand had then informed the packers that, if the British order was placed, there could be no advance in the price of cattle (hence the price of beef) while the order was being filled. Otherwise, he now claimed, the British would have canceled the contract and taken their business to a cheaper market such as Argentina.[60]

Durand's defense was plausible if not entirely convincing.[61] Nevertheless, by the time he offered it the damage had been done. To a vociferous chorus of critics, one point stood out: at the very moment in January that the nation's cattle producers were taking a financial beating (in part because of Hoover's campaign to reduce meat consumption), his agency had covertly arranged with the packers to hold cattle prices down. A prominent agricultural editor in Missouri spoke for many when he testified before Congress that Durand's secret "ultimatum to the packers" had been "a most remarkable piece of duplicity."[62] Hoover's standing in the farm belt had been jolted yet again.

For the harried Food Administrator, the new outbreak of suspicion must have seemed unfair. *Of course* his men were cooperating with the principal meat packers. Like it or not, the Big Five were indispensable to the success of his policy.[63] So upset was Hoover by the aspersions being cast upon him that he thought of asking President Wilson to appoint a body of "independent men" to investigate the Food Administration's relations with the meat packing industry.[64] Hoover's travail was emblematic of a larger dilemma that the U.S. government faced in World War I. He needed big business for victory, yet big business remained a pariah to many Progressives.

Indignation at Hoover's handling of the packers added fuel to what, by early March, was a roaring political blaze. On March 9 an alarmed Senator William Kenyon of Iowa informed President Wilson that farmers in the Middle West were athrob with "unrest" and "a deep-seated resentment against the packers." The senator urged the federal government to "restore confidence" by taking over and operating the packing plants.[65] A few days later Senator William Thompson of Kansas made the same request.[66] Wilson hesitated. He told Kenyon that the government was not adequately prepared for such a "very big undertaking" and that the industry might not cooperate.[67] Nevertheless, the pressure on Wilson and Hoover to act was becoming terrific.[68]

Hoover, of course, had argued as late as February 21 that his recently imposed regulation of packers' profits was working well.[69] Presumably, then, no further federal intervention was required. But a month later, in the wake of the Heney offensive, the Senate agriculture committee hearings, and a parade of angry deputations from the farm districts, the Food Administrator realized that he could no longer hold the line. On March 22 he asked the President to appoint a commission to study the meat problem.[70] Such a step, he believed, could help to reduce agrarian "discontent."[71]

Four days later Hoover formalized his proposal in a letter to the President. The Food Administrator declared that he had been "struggling" with an "entire inadequacy of definite policy" over the meat industry. He claimed that he had been "practically powerless" to protect the cattle industry or intelligently direct cattle production. According to Hoover, the government now had but three alternatives in the control of meat. It could abandon its interest in price control altogether by terminating conservation measures and federal direction of war purchases. It could continue, as at present, to guide large-scale meat purchases with "a mixture of partial national policy in production" and ad hoc responses to emergencies. Or it could "stabilize prices" on a cost-plus-stimulative-profit basis to producers and engage in "stabilization to eliminate speculative risks and wasteful practices."

The first option—dismantling the government's existing regulatory apparatus—Hoover rejected. Such a course, he contended, would encourage profiteering and speculation, produce "wage discontent and instability," destroy "systematic saving" of food ("a vital national policy"), and expose farmers to turbulent markets that would discourage production. The second option—the status quo—was equally unpalatable. It was, he said, "an almost intolerable situation for any Government official in criticism from both producer and consumer. . . ." Thus did he admit, with surprising candor, his political discomfiture. Hoover's preferred option was clearly the third: "stabilization." It was one of his favorite terms.

But stabilization by what methods? According to Hoover, the choices available to the government were but two. It could either make a "voluntary agreement" with the packers on prices to be paid to farmers and charged to consumers for meat products, or it could intervene and operate the packing houses itself. In both cases it would inject itself deeply into price control and become the target of buffeting from all sides. To determine the option most conducive to winning the war, and to recommend a national meat policy generally, Hoover proposed the creation of a five-member, intragovernmental commission consisting of himself, the Secretaries of Agriculture and Labor, and the chairmen of the Federal Trade Commission and U.S. Tariff Commission.[72]

Woodrow Wilson accepted Hoover's plan and asked the officials whom Hoover had named to join the task force.[73] It is not clear whether either the President or Hoover consulted with these agency heads before the written invitations went out. Indeed, Hoover's letter to the President appeared in the press (with Wilson's approval) a full day before Wilson formally contacted the other proposed commissioners.[74] These circumstances suggested that Hoover—in good, Hooverian fashion—had staged a neat, interdepartmental fait accompli.

Hoover's proposal was a clever political stroke. "Wilson Initiates New Meat Policy," a leading newspaper reported on April 1. "May Mean Federal Control."[75] The announcement that the government would study possible changes in meat control was sure to assuage some of the discontent that had erupted in recent weeks. More than this, the new commission would instantly preempt the issue from critics like Henry C. Wallace, who had publicly urged in mid-March that a group of agricultural experts be brought in to devise a meat production policy for the government.[76] Hoover undoubtedly wanted none of that, especially if the experts were men with the biases of Wallace. Hoover's proposal for a commission composed exclusively of government officials was probably designed to head off Wallace and his allies on Capitol Hill.[77]

In still another way Hoover's call for a collective evaluation of meat policy at the Cabinet level proved adroit. In his letter to the President, he remarked that he had never felt that a "single individual" should determine "broad policy" regarding particular commodities.[78] Hoover's position was no doubt intellectually sound; no one, after all, had a monopoly on expertise. It was also—and Hoover surely knew it—good politics to shift responsibility to a committee.

And not just *any* committee, but one carefully preselected by Hoover himself. One member, Secretary of Agriculture Houston, was a cautious conservative. A second, the chairman of the Tariff Commission, F. W. Taussig, was a friend of Hoover and in his eyes a dependable moderate.[79] Together with the Food Administrator, they would constitute a majority against any radical proposals that might emanate from the the representatives of the FTC and the Department of Labor.

While Hoover was organizing his advisory commission, he endeavored to defend himself on another flank. On March 29 the Food Administration announced that it had arranged for the FTC to audit the meat packers' accounts, determine their accuracy, and find out whether the packers were keeping their profits within the prescribed maximum.[80]

Early in April Hoover and his colleagues on the new meat commission delegated their assignment to a subcommittee of associates and underlings.[81] Out in Iowa, Henry C. Wallace was not amused. Not a single participant in the meat policy study, he editorialized, represented the corn belt. Not a single one possessed "real knowledge" of meat production and agricultural economics. Evidently sensing a political trap, Wallace declared that the new commission had but two options. It could recommend "such new policy as Mr. Hoover may work out, thereby relieving him of the responsibility for it." Or it could call in some real experts and have *them* devise a national meat policy.[82] There was no sign that Hoover and his associates contemplated the latter course.

Nor was Hoover about to abandon Professor Durand when the embattled assistant head of his meat division came under a new attack. Hoover, who continued to be "absolutely convinced" of Durand's honesty, was nonplussed when a member of the Tariff Commission publicly impugned the professor's integrity in a way that threatened his academic appointment at the University of Minnesota. Hoover asked his friend Taussig to intervene.[83] Taussig responded by defending Durand in a ringing letter to Durand's university president.[84] Like Priebe, Durand rode out the storm.

The meat policy commissioners' surrogates now got down to work. As Hoover probably anticipated, they soon disagreed. The representatives of the Federal Trade Commission and the Department of Labor favored outright government operation of the Big Five packing companies. The representatives of the Food Administration, Department of Agriculture, and the Tariff Commission favored governmental regulation only.[85] At this point Hoover intervened. One argument for nationalization of the packers was that the government had already taken over the railroads, telephones, and telegraph lines. To Hoover, there was no comparison. The government, he said, had seized the railroads and communication systems for war purposes because these had ceased to function well in private hands. The packers, in contrast, were functioning superbly; the only problem was the size of their profits. Hoover warned that if the government actually seized and operated the major packing houses, it would have to fix the prices that packers paid farmers for live animals as well as the prices packers charged consumers for finished goods. In so doing, the government would be ripped apart by the conflict between farmers and nonfarmers over the proper price for food. It was far better, he argued, for the government to *regulate* the packing industry than to own and operate it.[86]

Hoover's analysis won over the Department of Labor team to the "regulate only" position.[87] The representative of the FTC on the panel also adopted this view, although his FTC colleagues did not.[88] Thanks to Hoover's behind-the-scenes persuasion,[89] the meat policy commission was finally unanimous and on his terms.

On May 13 Hoover submitted the commission's report to the White House.[90] Suddenly an obstacle arose that threatened to discombobulate his carefully crafted handiwork. In a memorandum that reached the President's desk a few days later, William B. Colver—an FTC commissioner not on the meat policy body—offered another solution to the packer problem. As a middle ground between regulation and nationalization, he proposed that the government take over one of the Big Five companies and administer it by a committee including Henry C. Wallace. Colver argued that the government could use this experience to "measure reasonable profits" and establish a standard of comparison with the other packer giants.[91]

Colver's "half-way course" (as Wilson called it) struck a responsive chord at the White House. Instead of routinely ratifying Hoover's report, the President withheld judgment, forwarded Colver's memo on to Hoover, and asked him to assess its feasibility.[92] Disturbed by this unexpected development, Hoover responded with his heaviest artillery. He told the President that the packing industry was one of the most "complex and speculative" in the country. If the government now tried to operate even one of the principal plants, it "would at once become the target of pressure on the part of both producers and consumers" concerning prices, and the lightning rod for "confusing and embarrassing" political tension. Moreover, it would be entering into competition with hundreds of packing houses across the country, thereby incurring huge "risks of competition." The rest of the Big Five, for example, if they were willing to do it, could gang up on the government's plant and put it "out of action in a month."

Hoover was convinced that regulation of the packers would entail "less interruption and disturbance" to the wartime economy then any form of governmental operation. "Whatever the sins of the packers have been," he added, the packing companies had more than doubled their exports, while meeting domestic needs, in recent months. For this contribution to the war they deserved credit. "We are not satisfied that we need to despair in the control of their profits," Hoover asserted. "It does seem that if the intelligence does not exist by which the profits of the packers can be controlled, it certainly does not exist by which the packing houses can be operated." If the government wanted to solve the packer problem, it should do so by "permanent legislation," not by "experimental work under emergency powers."[93]

The next several days must have been agonizing ones for the Food Administrator. Just when he thought he had defeated the advocates of radical intervention, along had come William B. Colver to gum up the works. What would Woodrow Wilson do now?

Hoover's arguments apparently convinced the President to toy no further with Colver's suggestion. Instead, a few days later the chief executive approved the meat policy commission's report with minor modifications. Hoover thereupon released the revised document to the press.[94] On the fundamental issue as framed by Hoover—continued regulation of the packers by the Food Administration or outright governmental operation—the commission recommended the former and rejected the latter, unless regulatory devices became unenforceable. The panel did advocate certain additional measures such as federal licensing of the stockyards (which was soon effected).[95] And it urged that the Federal Trade Commission report by July 1 on the "reasonableness" of the maximum profit margins that Hoover had imposed upon the packers. But after all the sound and fury of the winter, the commission's recommendations did not decisively alter the status quo.[96] And that, one suspects, was Hoover's objective all along.

In Des Moines the editor of *Wallaces' Farmer* was disgusted. Where was the new national meat policy which Hoover himself had requested in March? There was *no* national policy, Wallace charged. The meat commission had not even addressed "the great question of animal production." All it had done was "endorse as a committee the general policy which Mr. Hoover has been following. It marched up the hill, looked over the top, and then marched down again."[97]

By clever bureaucratic maneuvering, then, and with the ultimate acquiescence of Woodrow Wilson, Hoover had outflanked his agrarian critics and blocked a risky wartime venture into socialism. Or had he? At the beginning of June 1918 he did not know it, but the FTC was about to strike again.

II

DURING June, in compliance with the meat policy commission's report, the Federal Trade Commission's experts studied the "reasonableness" of the meat packers' profits under Hoover's existing regulations.[98] Neither the accountants nor the FTC's commissioners liked what they saw. On June 28 the commission formally presented its conclusions in a letter to the President. For Hoover, it was another embarrassing blow.

The FTC bluntly reported that the maximum profits being made by the Big Five packers under Hoover's regulation were "unreasonably high." In fact, their rates of profit were 2¼ to 3 times what they had earned in the peacetime years of 1912–14. Since President Wilson had already ordered that the profits of regulated wartime industries not exceed the prewar average, the FTC's findings amounted to a stunning accusation of corporate greed and regulatory failure.

The Federal Trade Commission did not stop there. It told the President flatly that Hoover's system of regulation made "adequate certification" of packer profits "impossible." The commission thereupon recommended seven fundamental alterations of Hoover's scheme. The Food Administration, for instance, should stop segregating the packers' business into different classes subject to varying degrees of profit limitation. Instead, for the current year Hoover should impose a single rate of profit upon the packers' entire business, without exceptions. The Food Administration should also calculate packers' earnings on the basis of the companies' "net worth," exclusive of the sums that the packers borrowed to finance their operations. At present Hoover was permitting the biggest packers to earn profits on their "net investment," a far larger figure including money borrowed from banks.[99] If the FTC had its way, then, the principal packing houses would be forced to make much less money than Hoover was currently allowing them.

The FTC's report was the opening salvo in an all-out offensive against the Big Five. The next day, June 29, the commission submitted a separate report to the U.S. Senate, in response to a request three weeks earlier for information on wartime profiteering by American corporations. The commission charged that many industries were making "unusual," even "outrageous" profits, in part because of "inordinate greed and bare-faced fraud." Of all the enterprises that the commission surveyed, the packers received the harshest criticism:

> Five meat packers, Armour, Swift, Morris, Wilson, and Cudahy, and their subsidiary and affiliated companies, have monopolistic control of the meat industry and are reaching for like domination in other products. Their manipulations of the market embrace every device that is useful to them, without regard to law. Their reward, expressed in terms of profit, reveals that four of these concerns have pocketed in 1915–1916–1917 $140,000,000.

Whatever the definition of profiteering, said the commission, the dominant packers had "preyed upon the people unconscionably."[100]

Unlike its letter to President Wilson, the FTC's report to the Senate immediately became public. Stung by the assault, some of the Big Five hit back. They were not a monopoly, they claimed, but a strenuously competitive industry. They were *not* making extortionate profits but, rather, just a fraction of a cent per pound of product. The packers angrily accused the FTC of grossly distorting and exaggerating their earnings record. And at least one of their leading executives took refuge behind Hoover: according to Louis F. Swift, his firm was "conscientiously" adhering to the Food Administration's profit controls.[101]

Hoover, for his part, remained officially silent. But in a transparently inspired news story in the *Chicago Tribune*, he reminded the public that the packers' profits had not come under his rules until November 1, 1917. Hence the FTC's sensational figures for 1917 included ten months of unregulated packer earnings for which he could not be blamed. According to the *Tribune*, Hoover was confident that his regulations had quelled excessive profit taking since taking effect.[102]

The commission was not cowed by the packers' protests. On July 3 it quietly submitted to the President another report: a 51-page, printed summary of its just-completed, year-long, presidentially ordered investigation of the nation's meat-packing industry. It was a blistering indictment. The FTC declared that it had found "conclusive evidence" of "monopolies, controls, combinations, conspiracies," and "restraints of trade" in violation of the law and public interest. The Big Five, it said, were so dominant that they now controlled "at will" both the market in which they bought their supplies and the market in which they sold their own products. Furthermore, they held "the fortunes of their competitors in their hands." In its summary the FTC cited numerous examples of vicious, unethical, and illegal methods by which the principal packers had built their evil empire.

Still, despite its "amazing and devious ramifications," the FTC was convinced that no complicated remedies were needed to destroy the five great corporations' outrageous hegemony. The source of their power, said the FTC, was their "monopolistic control of the market places and means of transportation and distribution." To break this stranglehold, the commission boldly recommended that the U.S. government acquire and operate as a government monopoly the nation's principal stockyards, all privately owned refrigerator cars, and all rolling stock used to transport meat animals throughout the country. The federal government should also acquire and operate all branch houses, cold-storage plants, and warehouses needed to establish "competitive marketing and storage of food products" in the major cities. The federal government should similarly establish "central wholesale markets" and storage facilities in these same population and distribution hubs. All this, said the FTC, would strike deeply at the "tree of monopoly."[103]

Within one week, then, the Federal Trade Commission had fired three searing volleys at the meat-packing industry—and, inferentially, at Herbert Hoover. At the moment, two of the reports lay unpublicized on the President's desk. But the issue of how to control the unpopular packers was once more very much alive. Just when Hoover thought he had gotten that pot to settle down, the FTC had abruptly stirred it up again.

President Wilson now forwarded to Hoover the FTC's report of June 28 on the Food Administration's regulation of packer profits. Although the FTC later insisted that it had not offered its findings in "a spirit of criticism" or with "an eye to public reading,"[104] Hoover was thoroughly perturbed. Whatever the commission's intent, its unmistakable conclusion was that his attempted constraint of packer profits had been a massive failure. If word should now leak out to the press that the hated Big Five had been raking in "unreasonably high" profits under his vaunted regulations, the ensuing political firestorm could be fatal. Hoover knew that he must not under any circumstances let himself be portrayed as soft on the packers.

As in the Heney affair a few months earlier, Hoover swiftly endeavored to suppress the embarrassing document. He told the President on July 8 that if the FTC's report was made public, then Hoover's reply (which he enclosed) should "in justice" receive "co-incident publicity." The Food Administrator immediately added that he did not believe that "any useful purpose is served by public ventilation of inter-departmental disagreements as to governmental policy."[105] He obviously hoped that Wilson would agree.

Hoover's enclosed response to the FTC's findings also betrayed his anxiety.

> I realize fully [he wrote to Wilson] that in the discussion of this matter, any sentence uttered that can be interpreted as in support of profits to the packing industry subjects one to the charge of corrupt influence and, on the other hand, I recognize equally the easy road to popularity through denunciation of these profits. It is however our duty to separate the emotional aspects in these matters from justice and national necessity to secure war results.[106]

In the ten-page letter that followed, Hoover rebutted the Federal Trade Commission on point after point. He declared that he could not set a single, maximum rate of profit for all classes of the packers' business (as the FTC desired) because the law would not permit it: his writ extended only to the packers' domestic and food-related operations, not their foreign-based and nonfood specialties. He also vehemently rejected the FTC's proposal to forbid the packers from earning a profit on their borrowed capital. If this principle were adopted as a precedent, he thundered, "it would produce an absolute state of panic in the United States." All businesses, he asserted—and especially the packing business so dependent on short-term borrowed money for its expanded operations—simply "must earn a profit over and above interest charges on actual capital borrowed." The packing industry, with its gigantic, war-generated inventories under constant threat of sudden depreciation, was a far riskier enterprise than the FTC understood. Acutely aware that his national "food strategy" had obliged the packers to increase their stocks in storage and hence increase their borrowing, Hoover reiterated that their compensation "must bear some relation to their borrowed capital."

Hoover also minimized the significance of the packers' profits. In 1918, he said, the Big Five, under his regulations, would earn less than a penny a pound. Even if this were now reduced by one third (as the FTC proposed), the benefit to consumers would be negligible.

Nevertheless, on the final page of his lengthy rebuttal Hoover acknowledged that he was "not in disagreement" with the FTC that the meat packers might be earning "too large profits" under his regulations. He did, however, disagree emphatically about the remedy. Instead of fixing a specific ceiling on profits (as the FTC proposed), Hoover suggested instead a continuation of his own regulations, supplemented by Congressional enactment of a tax on "any inordinate earnings that might be secured by the more fortunate manufacturers." According to the Food Administrator, an "advance profit regulation" of the FTC type

> operates, if too strictly drawn, to curb incentive, to destroy production and to limit efficiency. The sound method, if possible, is to give a fairly loose profit regulation, sufficiently strict to prevent speculation, stabilize price levels and then, by taxation, to appropriate to the Government any extraordinary profit that may have arisen.[107]

Hoover therefore asked President Wilson to set aside the "matters at issue" between himself and the FTC pending action by Congress, which was then considering a war revenue bill. If Congress enacts "sufficiently strong excess profits legislation," Hoover asserted, "it will automatically correct the situation and meet the views of both the Trade Commission and ourselves." But if the President felt he could not wait, Hoover had a fall-back position ready. He asked Wilson in that case to turn the dispute over to "some independent person" for advice on "the matters of principle involved." Never one to overlook a crucial detail, Hoover offered two names. Both were men he could expect to rule in his favor.[108]

Hoover was not content with merely appealing to the White House. A bureaucratic warrior par excellence, he immediately moved to box in the FTC and frame the public policy debate on his terms. The very next day, July 9, his counsel conferred with two of the three Federal Trade Commissioners and secured their agreement not to publish their June 28 letter to the President unless he so wished.[109] Objective number one—suppression of the offending document—was achieved, at least for the present. Two days later Hoover himself published a prearranged letter to the chairman of the Senate finance committee on the subject of profiteering and tax proposals currently before the Congress. In this communication Hoover vigorously endorsed an excess profits tax on "extra normal profits earned out of war conditions."[110]

Hoover's recommendation seemed to him the best way out of an economic and moral dilemma. On the one hand, he believed that "[e]xtra profits out of war" were "hateful," particularly when American youth were being "called upon to sacrifice all that they have." On the other hand, some profit was essential to stimulate increased war production.[111] The problem faced by Hoover and other government regulators was that not every business in a particular industry was equally efficient. Corporate giants (like the Big Five packers) could prosper on very small margins of profit, while smaller, higher-cost producers (whose production was just as vital) could not. If Hoover regulated the packing industry too sternly and set a profit limit that was low, he would discourage and even destroy marginal producers. The result would be curtailed aggregate production, to the detriment of the war effort and the ultimate advantage of the bigger, more efficient firms. But if he set a profit limit that was high, it would help small companies, but it would also enable the dominant firms to make a killing. Hoover's solution was simple: Let them make a killing and then tax it away from them.

The excess profits tax undoubtedly appealed to him for another reason. Any such tax would have to be enacted by Congress. The legislative branch, therefore, would have to assume responsibility for the result. In mounting peril of being touched by the packer tar baby, Hoover was eager to drop it into Congress's lap.

Meanwhile, the worried Food Administrator attempted to exert pressure of a different sort on the other side of the equation: the packers themselves. On July 10 he addressed identical letters to Louis F. Swift and to Arthur Meeker, another leader of the Big Five. Writing, he said, as a private citizen, Hoover asked the packing house executives voluntarily to limit their corporations' profits on their regulated food business for the current year to one third of a cent per pound (after taxes) and to announce that their companies would pay any earnings in excess of this amount to "one of the great national war charities." Hoover warned the two businessmen that there was "no question" that they were earning "very large profits" on their American food business. Furthermore, public sentiment against war-generated profits in foodstuffs was becoming "extremely bitter." Such feelings, although "extreme and unreasonable" in some of their manifestations, were nevertheless "fundamentally . . . rightly founded."

Hoover told the two packers that they were "under a great deal of suspicion" and that in their own self-interest they should "take only a just remuneration" for their services. Increasingly fearful of the postwar potential for collectivism, he pleaded with the packers to take a longer view:

> Aside from all of the immediate issues involved, there is an increasing feeling against property as a reaction from the individual sacrifices that are imposed by the war. I do not associate myself with any socialistic views. I do believe that the very foundation of our institutions and our government is based on individual initiative and that individual initiative necessitates the individual ownership and control of property. On the other hand, I cannot associate myself with the view that property or individuals are entitled to any larger payment for an economic service during the course of the war than in ordinary peace times, otherwise they are reaping a benefit from the war itself and in a time when others are making the supreme sacrifice. It therefore seems to me of vital importance if the large businesses of the country are to establish and maintain public confidence that

> they should see that no such advantage comes to them and I cannot but feel it would go a long ways to satisfy the entire public, both producer and consumer, if some such voluntary limitation were expressed by the packers themselves.[112]

Hoover's remarkable appeal got nowhere. The Big Five were apparently unwilling to surrender a dime.[113] The corporate giants may have feared that if they voluntarily restricted their profits in wartime, they might be compelled to continue the curbs when the war ended. Already under relentless political attack, they may well have felt that any concession to the doctrine of corporate social responsibility would fatally crack the protective shield of their economic freedom.

Hoover was disgusted. He told friends a few weeks later that the packers were obsessed with making money and acquiring social position. Even though (in his opinion) the top packing house executives were already earning ten times what they needed to live, they continued to covet high rates of profit for the sake of their prestige.[114] For Hoover, who had amassed a significant fortune of his own by 1914 but had then subordinated moneymaking to public service, such attitudes were atavistic.

While the Food Administrator vainly made his pitch to the packers, the White House forwarded his ten-page letter of July 8 on to the FTC. The commission was not amused by Hoover's response. In a bluntly worded letter to the President on July 20, Chairman William B. Colver, representing the FTC, charged that Hoover's reply seemed "to revolve around a question of publicity," an "unfortunate" development. Colver pointed out that the commission had not asked that its report be made public. It had been invited to evaluate the "reasonableness" of the packers' profit margin under current regulations and had done so, in good faith. Colver vigorously disputed Hoover's claim that, in computing a return, borrowed money should be counted as invested capital—an interpretation that would enormously augment the packers' allowable profits under Hoover's rules. To the contrary, Colver rejoined, borrowed money was the capital of the lender, not the borrower—a principle universally accepted by expert authorities.

The commission was even more agitated by Hoover's assertion that an excess profits tax would "automatically correct the situation" and thus satisfy the FTC. In Colver's words, it "wholly and entirely" disagreed. Before the government could collect an excess profits *tax*, the excess profits themselves would be improperly extracted from consumers "in the form of inflated prices." Such a system would not only be injurious to the American people; it would also encourage tax evasion and wasteful expenditure by businesses eager to reduce their tax burden.[115]

Colver did not send his angry letter to the White House.[116] Instead, in late July, under pressure from Hoover, the commission and the Food Administration made a settlement, as it were, out of court. The commission had submitted with its report of June 28 on Hoover's profit regulations three subsidiary reports by the commission's experts who had actually assembled the relevant data. Hoover took immediate exception to two of these documents, which in his judgment reflected adversely on his administration.[117] The two exhibits, indeed, comprised a powerful critique of his policy and a rationale for alternative methods of control. They showed that on a net worth basis, the Big Five would earn as much as 20.5 percent on their investment in 1918 under Hoover's rules. Such a number would not look good in the newspapers.

At Hoover's and Glasgow's insistence, the FTC agreed to revise its report and suppress the two attached documents that Hoover found so embarrassing. On July 29, therefore, the White House returned the original commission's report and its enclosures to the FTC for alterations. The commission promptly changed the wording of its report, omitting all reference to the two controversial supplements, and sent the corrected report (minus the two supplements) to the White House, where it remained. The revised report was given the same date: June 28.[118]

Once again, Hoover had cleverly created a protective paper trail. Moreover, he had managed to conceal it from the public; the FTC agreed with him that even its revised report should not be published.[119] The original report and the two discomfiting exhibits remained buried in the FTC's files until late 1919, when a Senate investigation pried them out into the open.[120]

The FTC, however, could take consolation on one point: both it and Hoover were now in agreement that the Big Five were earning excessive profits.

Meanwhile the commission's summary of its general report on the meatpacking industry—the third of its blasts of early summer—lay languishing, undisposed of, at the White House. With President Wilson's permission, the FTC released this document to the press on August 8 and at once precipitated a national uproar.[121] No longer was anti-packer agitation confined to disgruntled cattlemen or Progressive zealots like Francis Heney. Now a prestigious agency of the federal government—an agency comprised entirely of Woodrow Wilson's appointees—had formally labeled the Big Five packers a dangerous monopoly. More sensationally still, it had called for government intervention on a scale unprecedented in American history.

The commission's agenda—outright government ownership and operation of the principal stockyards and of much else—now became the subject of vehement debate. Technically, perhaps, this need not have concerned Hoover. As Food Administrator his responsibility was a specific and temporary one: to deal with the food industry as he found it and to do what he could to win the war. The Federal Trade Commission was a permanent agency proposing a permanent solution to a condition unrelated to the war. Still, the FTC proposed to implement most of its reforms initially through McAdoo's Railroad Administration—a temporary, wartime agency—and it wished to start immediately, while the war was still on. For these reasons alone, it was unlikely that the Food Administrator would stay out of the fray.

As it happened, Hoover was in Europe attending a conference of Allied food controllers when the FTC's summary report became public. Moving quickly to keep the Chief from being bypassed, the acting Food Administrator in Washington asked President Wilson to give Hoover an opportunity to comment on the report after his trip if any changes in control of the packers were to be made.[122] The President promised to try to defer his decision on the FTC's proposals until Hoover returned.[123]

On August 23 Hoover got back to the United States and to a growing political storm. Five days later, eager to seize the moment and hopeful that the President himself would take the initiative, the Federal Trade Commission submitted draft legislation embodying its reform proposals to the White House.[124] On Capitol Hill, too, sentiment for swift and drastic action was swelling. On September 5 Senator Gore introduced the commission's recommendations as an amendment to an agricultural appropriation bill. Gore later withdrew his amendment, but only after triggering a noisy debate on the Senate floor.[125] In Washington a report circulated that a coalition of Progressive Republicans and Democrats led by Senator William Borah would fight for the FTC's bill.[126]

Hoover now confronted a political minefield. For months he had fiercely resisted a wartime government takeover of the packing industry, at the risk of appearing soft on the Big Five. Then had come the FTC's finding (which he did not dispute) that the packers were earning egregiously high profits under his regulations. Then, while he was in Europe, the FTC had gone public with its indictment of the principal packing houses and with its call for government seizure of much of their property. Could Hoover afford to align himself with the packers yet again?

Sensing, perhaps, a shift in the political tide, Hoover began to backpedal. On August 30 he told an associate that he actually *favored* three of the FTC's four recommendations: nationalization of the stockyards, nationalization of all privately owned railroad refrigerator cars, and nationalization of all railcars used to transport live animals. But, as always, the Food Administrator had reservations. The government should take over these facilities permanently, he said, and not through a temporary war agency. He also did not approve of the FTC's call for government ownership of packer warehouses, branch houses, and cold-storage plants. That was evidently more socialism than he could bear.[127]

Hoover now told the President that he generally agreed with the FTC's conclusions. Such, at least, was Wilson's impression after a conference with his Food Administrator sometime before September 6.[128] But there is reason to question the totality of Hoover's commitment. On September 6 he wrote to the President that while the FTC's "theoretical views" were "the ultimate desiderata," there were "some practical difficulties that might subject the program to a great deal of criticism."[129] Two days later the *Chicago Tribune* reported that a "bitter feud" had erupted in the Wilson administration over future policy toward the packers. The newspaper asserted that Hoover was "so violently opposed" to the FTC's proposed legislation that he had threatened to resign if it became law.[130]

Whatever the truth of this report, by September 6 Hoover still had not submitted a comprehensive written response to the commission's recommendations. Perhaps playing for time, he informed the President on the sixth that he was postponing his report until he could confer with some independent packers who had "hewn their way up by sheer ability against a good deal of tyranny." Hoover appeared to be striving to avoid any imputation of excessive solicitude for the Big Five.[131]

As it turned out, Wilson had already made up his mind about his response to the FTC. On September 6 he notified the commission that *after conferring with Hoover* he was convinced that "no real material advantage would result from the action proposed by your bill, at any rate at this time." The President appeared to evaluate the bill as a war measure, a perspective probably abetted by Hoover. The chief executive noted, for instance, that Hoover had told him that the packers' branches and distributing agencies were already operating at full capacity and that a government seizure of these would therefore be "of no real service to the public."[132]

For the members of the FTC, the President's refusal to endorse their legislative agenda was a devastating rebuff for which they clearly blamed Hoover. Replying to the President, the commission suggested that Hoover could not possibly have been "sufficiently acquainted" with its findings and purposes to "finally present" them to the chief executive. The commission declared that it had not proposed *any* war measures (as Wilson mistakenly seemed to think). And while it was true that the big packers' branches and distributing agencies were filled to capacity (as Hoover said), these were being used (according to the commission) *to the exclusion of other meat packers*, an injustice that the commission desired to remedy. It clearly rankled the FTC commissioners that Hoover had gained access to the Oval Office while they had not.[133] To the commissioners' bitter frustration, the Food Administrator had won another round.

Unaware, perhaps, of the President's decision in his favor, Hoover continued to try to justify his supervision of the packers' profits. On September 9 he sent Wilson a letter just received from an Armour & Co. executive complaining that the giant packing house was not making any money at all at present, mainly because of "the conditions imposed upon us by the Food Administration." The executive claimed that Armour's profits under Hoover's rules amounted thus far to less than half of what the Food Administration had projected, and he asked for a meeting with Hoover to discuss ways "to compensate us for this condition."[134]

Hoover was probably delighted to furnish evidence of packer dissatisfaction as a counterweight to the FTC. But on this occasion President Wilson was unimpressed. "My fundamental trouble about all of this matter," he replied, "is that I do not trust the information which these men give us."[135] Clearly Hoover would have to do better than this to defend himself against the Federal Trade Commission.

On September 11—five days after Wilson declined to support the FTC's proposed legislation—Hoover responded in writing to the commission's summary report and proposals. The Food Administrator began by telling the President that there was indeed "a growing and dangerous domination of the handling of the Nation's foodstuffs," a view that he said he had expressed to the President nearly a year before. Hoover added at once, however, that this domination was not necessarily due to "wrong doing on the part of the proprietors" (as the FTC believed) but to "the natural outgrowth of various factors which need correction." Hoover proceeded to analyze the history of the packing industry and the forces which had led to the Big Five's primacy. Although he was convinced that the industry's leaders had "developed great economic efficiency," the question now at issue was whether this "expanding domination" could be replaced by an equally efficient system "of better social character." The packers' monopoly, he predicted, must eventually lose some of its efficiency and, "like all monopolies, begin to defend itself by repression rather than by efficiency." To Hoover this was the greatest menace of all. "The worst social result of this whole growth in domination of trades," he said, "is the undermining of the initiative and the equal opportunity of our people and the tyranny which necessarily follows in the commercial world."

Hoover, then, accepted the need for corrective federal intervention in the packing industry, without, however, sharing the Federal Trade Commission's moral posture and its unfeigned hostility toward the leading packers. But when he turned to the FTC's specific suggestions, his response became highly qualified and even ambiguous. Hoover declared himself "in full agreement" with the commission's proposal that the Railroad Administration take over all animal and refrigeration car services. In fact, he said, he himself had proposed something similar months ago, when the Railroad Administration was created. Hoover then added that if the FTC's reforms were to be "of any value," they must be permanent and not just for the war. Unless Hoover misunderstood the FTC's report, this was an unnecessary observation, since that was exactly what the FTC was proposing. But on this, the crux of the matter—*permanent* government ownership of the meat-related railcars—Hoover equivocated. Whether these services should be operated by the government itself or by private enterprise regulated as a public utility was a question, he said, that required "further thought." It also depended on what the government ultimately did with the railways it had seized during the war. On that question—the future of the railroad system—he offered no opinion.

On the FTC's next recommendation—federal takeover of the stockyards—Hoover was similarly vague. The Food Administrator agreed in principle that the stockyards should be "entirely disassociated from the control of the packers." But here, too, he argued, the nature of the solution would depend on whether or not the government held on to the railroads or returned them to private ownership after the war. If the government nationalized the railways, then it could nationalize the stockyards as part of the same arrangement. Or it could simply regulate the yards (if they remained privately owned) through the Interstate Commerce Commission. But again, on the specific issue thus posed—government ownership versus regulation of the yards—he expressed no preference.

Hoover did, however, object flatly to the FTC's final recommendation: that the federal government immediately take over the packers' warehouses, branch houses, and cold-storage facilities. Such a course, he argued, would be fraught with difficulty and would yield "no permanent values." It would also "disrupt distribution" at this juncture in the war. "Altogether," he declared, "I do not consider that the prime objective of maintaining the initiative of our citizens and of our local communities is to be secured by this vast expansion of federal activities."

In one area, though, Hoover ventured where the FTC had not. Disturbed by the packers' "invasion" and "absorption" of food industries outside their specialty, he asked for study of whether these great corporations should be "confined to more narrow and limited activities" directly related to the slaughter and processing of animals. (Eventually, after the war, the government adopted this approach and compelled the packers to agree.)[136] And, once more, Hoover urged that the Railroad and Food administrations—creatures of the war emergency—not be made the instruments of packing house reform. The permanent solution of this problem, he argued, should be the responsibility of Congress.[137]

Hoover's letter to the President was thoughtful and nuanced. It was also brilliantly obfuscatory. No one reading it could accuse him of being an apologist for the big packers. Yet with every specific recommendation made by the FTC he had either disagreed outright or diluted his professed agreement to virtual meaninglessness. The FTC wanted *immediate*, *permanent*, and *massive* federal intervention in the meat-packing industry, largely through the wartime Railroad Administration. Hoover wanted *no* immediate intervention (while the war was on), *no* involvement by temporary wartime agencies, and *no* federal ownership of the packers' branch houses and storage sites. As for the rest—permanent government ownership of the railcars and stockyards—he called for further study and neatly sidestepped a choice between nationalization and more limited regulation.

Hoover's letter, then, was a masterpiece of bureaucratic jujitsu, designed to derail the FTC's proposals without incurring the stigma of being pro-packer. Not surprisingly, a few days later he sought presidential permission to publish his document, which, he audaciously claimed, "supports the critical recommendations of the Commission."[138] Alas for the ever combative

Food Administrator, Wilson declined. He wanted, he told Hoover, "to avoid even the appearance of a controversy between two agencies which really trust oneanother [sic] . . . ."[139] It is impossible to know whether the President was being naive or ironic.

Once again, in any case, Hoover had checkmated an internal challenge from the Left. This did not mean, however, that he had leaped into the camp of the capitalist Right. On September 12 an anxious delegation of senior executives of the Big Five converged on his Washington office. They told him that their companies were now earning far less profit than permitted by his regulations—so much less that it would soon jeopardize their credit. Hoover was unmoved by their alarm. He told them to submit any specific proposals for change in writing, and he warned that it was "not to their advantage to make other than conservative profits" in the present climate. The Food Administrator also suggested that they confine their business to their traditional meat-processing activities and "divorce themselves" from other lines of business that incurred public distrust.[140]

Once again Hoover had posed as the reasonable regulator and the packers' enlightened friend. Once again the industry took no heed. During the autumn of 1918 one packing house leader, Arthur Meeker, even asked the Food Administration to compensate his company for nearly $2,000,000 in losses that he said his company had sustained in beef transactions involving the government.[141] Hoover would have none of it. The FTC's figures, he replied, showed that the packers would earn "a large return" on their invested capital in 1918, "even if some departments fall below the maximums set."[142] Thus the Food Administrator, who had just tried to undermine the FTC's claim that the packers were earning excessive profits under his rules,[143] now used the same FTC data to keep the packers in line.

By refusing to let Hoover publish his September 11 analysis of the FTC's reform proposals, President Wilson managed to preserve the illusion of peace between the commission and the Food Administration. Behind the scenes, however, the battle raged without letup. For some months the commission, at Hoover's request, had been auditing the accounts that the packers had submitted to the Food Administration. The FTC had also been struggling to devise a uniform accounting system for ascertaining the packers' true profits. In its letter to the President on June 28, the FTC complained that Hoover's three-class system of regulation made proper certification of the packers' accounts impossible. In its place the FTC recommended a single profit ceiling applicable to all of the packers' business activities. Hoover resisted, and President Wilson did nothing. On September 13 the commission again appealed to the White House for a ruling.[144]

The President apparently returned the issue to Hoover and the FTC for negotiation, which, predictably, made little progress. The FTC continued to argue that if its investigation of packer profits was to have any value it must audit *all* the packers' business activity, not just portions of it. Otherwise the crafty packers could shift their profits from regulated to unregulated classes of business in a multitude of ways and make it impossible to determine whether the companies had truly adhered to Hoover's limitations.[145] Hoover responded that under the law he could regulate the packers' food-related business only, and nothing more.[146]

Nevertheless, on November 1, 1918 Hoover did amend his regulations. He reduced his classification of the packers' business interests from three categories to two: (1) domestically produced food (and certain food-related business), and (2) all other activity. The former was subject to regulation; the latter, including overseas operations, was not. On the former, Hoover retained his profit ceiling of 9 percent. On the latter, over which he said he had no jurisdiction, the packers were free to earn whatever they could. Hoover made his edict retroactive to November 1917.[147]

Hoover's revisions failed to appease the FTC. On December 14 the commission bluntly informed Hoover's counsel that it was unable to verify *any* financial statements submitted by the meat packers under the old or the new regulations. The commission was incensed that Hoover expected it to "certify the accuracy" of the packers' profit sheets when the rules governing the accounting process were so flawed.[148] While the FTC's accountants continued to assist the Food Administration in various ways, the commission itself never formally certified that the packers had earned what they said they had.[149] For it, Hoover's two-class system had rendered the truth about packer profits "impossible" to ascertain.[150]

The commission's refusal to give its seal of approval to the packers' profit claims did not prevent Hoover's aides from suggesting that the FTC had done just that. In February 1919 William A. Glasgow, Jr., submitted data to a Senate committee concerning the Big Five's actual profits in 1918 under the Food Administration rules. According to Glasgow, the statistics he submitted (which showed profit margins well below Hoover's ceiling) were the Federal Trade Commission's own, audited figures.[151] The FTC angrily retorted that Glasgow was wrong: it had *not* audited the packers' profits for 1918, it had *not* prepared Glasgow's figures, and it had "no knowledge" of the accuracy of the packers' reports that it saw.[152]

A few weeks later Hoover's deputy, Edgar Rickard, submitted the Food Administration's annual report for the year 1918 to the President. In it Rickard announced that the controlled meat packers' "audited accounts" for the regulatory year 1917–18 showed a "net profit on the total investment" of just 5.6 percent, much less than the allowable maximum under Hoover's rules. In all likelihood, the "total investment" included "borrowed capital." Rickard further asserted that "supervision over the accounting" had been "exercised by the Federal Trade Commission," thus implying that the FTC corroborated his claims.[153] The commission, of course, had done no such thing.

Ultimately, in 1919, when the guns in Europe had fallen silent, Hoover's year-long feud with the FTC came to light, and his wartime supervision of the meat-packing industry was subjected to an acrimonious Congressional investigation. But in the short run—during the war itself—he successfully blunted every significant challenge. He limited or avoided publicity that could have impaired his effectiveness and political future. He kept his approach to packer regulation largely intact, despite fierce assault. And he helped to forestall a plunge into socialism that might have resulted in enduring government ownership of the railroads and other large businesses.

It is interesting to speculate what would have happened in mid-1918 if Hoover, as one of President Wilson's trusted advisers, had thrown his influence behind the drive to convert the food-processing giants known as the Big Five into a permanent, government-owned monopoly. It is not too much to suggest that the shape of American history would have been different. The year 1918—not later—was socialism's moment in the United States, even though those who called themselves socialists were divided and in some cases in jail. No matter: war is itself collectivistic, and the Great War briefly provided a chance for certain Progressives to win their own war against big business. That the Wilson administration did not embark upon massive federal ownership of "the means of production" at this juncture was attributable, in considerable part, to the resourceful resistance of Herbert Hoover.

III

YET if Hoover skillfully opposed all-out socialism, his own brand of market regulation became more encompassing as 1918 wore on.

One target was the grain-milling industry, whose pricing practices had infuriated farmers for months. According to Food Administration rules adopted in 1917, individual flour mills were entitled to receive cost of production plus a maximum of 25 cents per barrel for flour, and cost of production plus 50 cents per ton for feed. Any profits in excess of these limits were deemed unreasonable.[154] It did not take long for unscrupulous millers to evade these regulations by padding their expense reports and engaging in creative accounting. Some even established phony jobbing departments in order to claim separate profits both in milling and jobbing.[155] It did not help matters that, unlike all other departments of the Food Administration, Hoover's milling division consisted of men selected by the trade and still engaged in it. To an extraordinary degree, the industry was regulating itself. While the milling division's personnel were untainted by fraud, they were initially slow to investigate abuses of their regulatory system or challenge the ethos of business-government cooperation upon which it was built.[156]

Although Hoover gradually tightened his controls over the millers in ensuing months, by the spring of 1918 he was convinced that his method of capping their profits was quite unsatisfactory.[157] After hearing from his task force on milling regulation, he decided on a radical overhaul.

In late June the Food Administrator abolished his milling division, replaced it with a milling section less tied to the industry, and terminated all contracts between "agreement" mills and the Grain Corporation.[158] Henceforth, instead of earning a maximum "net profit" per barrel of flour, all millers would be limited to a margin of $1.10 between the selling price of a barrel of flour (and attendant mill feed) and the cost of the wheat required to produce it.[159]

Hoover's plan was a stunning new assertion of federal power. Until now, the millers had been free to sell their flour for as much as they wanted, so long as their profit did not exceed 25 cents per barrel. This had given them every incentive to exaggerate their costs of production in order to maximize and disguise their true earnings. Now this would not matter. Since the price of wheat was already essentially fixed, the new formula effectively fixed the price of flour also.

Hoover went still further. Because he controlled the price of wheat in all sections of the country, and because he could calculate freight costs to and from all points, he could easily determine the maximum allowable price for flour and feeds at every milling site in the United States. Accordingly, during July 1918 the Food Administration sent out individually tailored "fair price" schedules to several thousand American grain mills. Each list specified the precise maximum that this particular operator could charge his customers for flour and related products.[160]

Once again, Hoover, if challenged, could claim that he had not indulged in price-fixing in a legal sense. Grain millers were always free to sell their product for less than he allowed. But his new system amounted to price control on a gigantic new scale. Gone were the evasions, voluntary agreements, and hortatory rhetoric of 1917. Hoover was more confident now. His guiding hand was steadily becoming more interventionist.

Meanwhile the Food Administrator had been cracking down on another impediment to his regulatory goals: the multitude of small food retailers who were exempt from his licensing power. Back in the autumn of 1917 he had attempted to put pressure on these businesses—and on licensed larger dealers, too—by encouraging his state food administrations to draw up and publicize officially approved "fair price" lists for selected food products. This program, however, was voluntary, and despite repeated exhortations from Washington it was implemented in only a few major cities.[161]

By the spring of 1918 it was evident to Hoover that tougher price control measures must be tried, despite the refusal of Congress to grant him additional authority. From all across the country he was receiving reports that local retail food prices were soaring, and out of all proportion to production costs.[162] Nor was his supervision of distributors who were subject to license—the wholesalers and very largest retailers—working well, either. Each month tens of thousands of licensed dealers were required to submit elaborate, written reports to the Food Administration. It was a procedure that was cumbersome at best.[163]

In May, Hoover and his colleagues decided to modify their oversight system in ways that would effectively "protect the consumer from unreasonable price advances." On June 7 they publicly unveiled their plan.[164] In another sweeping extension of its authority, the Food Administration announced that it would develop and publish "fair price" lists in nearly every American city, town, and village. In every community it would establish "price interpretation committees" comprised of representatives of wholesalers, retailers, and consumers. These bodies would determine "fair margins of profit" for local retailers and "fair retail prices" on basic foods. The committees would then publish weekly lists of acceptable "maximum selling prices" for these goods in local newspapers.[165]

Hoover hoped that the regular dissemination of such data in the press would empower the general public to "police" the situation.[166] The Food Administration, in fact, explicitly requested consumers to report to it the names of any stores that charged more than the government's announced price.[167] But Hoover and his associates were not going to rely merely on tips received from housewives. The Food Administration announced that it was appointing "retail price reporters" in every county in America. These investigators would report to local food administrators any dealer who sold goods at prices above those that the government had determined to be fair.[168]

Legally, neither the Food Administration nor its price interpreting committees had any direct power to fix prices.[169] Nevertheless, Hoover announced on June 7 that his local administrators would punish any dealer found, after a hearing, to have violated the agency's fair price maximums. He reminded the nation that he could exercise "indirect control" over unlicensed retailers by ordering licensed *wholesalers* to "sever business relations" with firms that charged their customers more than a "reasonable" price.[170]

The next day Hoover's shift in policy made headlines across the nation. "Hoover to Control Retail Food Prices," the *New York Times* proclaimed.[171] As if to underscore this get-tough attitude, the Food Administration announced two days later that it had imposed more than eight hundred penalties for violation of its rules governing licensed food dealers in the past ten months. It pointed out that it had ordered about 150 companies and individuals to close their businesses for varying periods because of their offenses.[172] In the summer and autumn of 1918 the Food Administration issued numerous press releases announcing punishment for violators of its regulations.[173] The message could not have been more clear.

Thus as with the flour millers, so now with local grocery stores and other retail food outlets: the carrot was making way for the stick. At the outset of his tenure as Food Administrator, Hoover had rejected the label "dictator" and had emphasized the voluntary features of his program. He had done so partly from idealistic faith in most of the American people, partly from worry about Congressional antagonism, and partly from fear of imposing unprecedented regimentation on a libertarian populace, many of whom resented the war. But now, a year later, under pressure from inflation, agrarian critics, and complaining consumers, Hoover made another leap of intervention, shifting from imperfect oversight of business profits to ever more overt control of retail prices.[174]

To be sure, Hoover did not completely jettison his appeals for voluntary compliance. But even here, failure to "join the ranks" carried a penalty. Early in October he launched a drive to induce every retail grocer in the country to sign a pledge to adhere to the "rules and regulations" of the Food Administration. The grocers were requested to charge "fair and moderate prices" *regardless of market conditions*, to discourage hoarding, and to cooperate with the government's food conservation program. Grocers who took the pledge would receive from the Food Administration a "fair price certificate" which they could display in their store windows. In this way, customers could identify "loyal" grocers and presumably put pressure on the rest.[175] No one was required by law to sign the pledge. But any who refrained had to risk the suspicion of their neighbors that they were not in support of the war.

As Hooverian voluntarism yielded increasingly to coercion, another momentous change was occurring for the nation and its food regulator-in-chief. Thanks to the usually supportive Woodrow Wilson, the applause of the vast majority of the nation's press, and the loyalty of the urban middle class, Hoover had outmaneuvered his agrarian enemies, his disparagers in the Senate, and critics like Francis Heney and the FTC. But scarcity—the fundamental challenge of the 1917–18 crop year—was now giving way to abundance. Soon solutions would become problems, creating snares and pitfalls of another kind.

13

A Trip to Europe

I

IN the spring of 1918 Hoover's thoughts turned increasingly to the future. In a few months the United States and its allies would harvest another cycle of crops, and early signs pointed to a substantial improvement in yield. A new phase in inter-Allied food control was at hand.

In mid-May, Hoover decided that he should travel to Europe during the summer to "consider the whole situation" with his European counterparts.[1] In a letter to President Wilson on June 13, he explained that it was necessary to devise a joint American-Allied cereal program for the coming year. It was also necessary to "improve the organization" of the Allied food purchasing agencies known as the "Executives." In addition, Hoover was anxious to persuade his European colleagues to switch their American meat purchases from scarce beef to plentiful pork—something that the Allies had been reluctant to do.[2] The matter was becoming urgent; by mid-June the United States had amassed more than a billion pounds of surplus pork.[3] Hoover candidly informed the President that he intended to obtain some "cooperation" on this issue if he went to Europe. Otherwise, he prophesied, an unmarketable glut of American pork would "discourage our producers" and risk "a national calamity in production."[4]

Hoover's final reason for his mission was frankly psychological. He asserted that it would substantially affect the "psychology" of "American production and consumption" if he could inform his fellow citizens that their food resources must be pooled with those of the Allies and if he could then stipulate to his countrymen a "definite program we must fulfill." He also believed that the morale of Allied civilians would benefit hugely if he could declare in Woodrow Wilson's name that the American people would "make any necessary sacrifice to maintain [the Allies'] food necessities."[5]

President Wilson immediately assented to Hoover's trip.[6] In a second letter to the President two weeks later, Hoover amplified his purposes. He now proposed to develop with the food controllers of Great Britain, France, and Italy not just a cereals program for the coming twelve months but a "general programme" for allocating all leading food commodities among the four nations, including "the distribution necessary at each point." To this end he proposed to create an intergovernmental committee on which the United States would be formally represented; "our interest in distribution" (he told Wilson) "extends outside the United States." As for boosting morale, he now asked the President for authority to announce to the Allies that Americans "are, in fact, eating at a common table with them," and that the United States would make any sacrifice in food production and consumption "short of damage to our own efficiency in the war" in order to sustain the Allied populations. The Food Administrator proposed to dramatize this commitment by instituting, with his fellow controllers, a universal war bread containing 20 percent cereals other than wheat and available to all in unlimited quantities. It would "have a great moral effect in Europe," he told the President, and it would discourage the German enemy besides.[7]

Hoover's letters to the White House did not fully convey the intensity of his motivation. Behind his low-key references to Allied food distribution, in fact, lay an inter-Allied quarrel of increasingly bitter proportions. For some months the French and Italians had been complaining that the British were shortchanging them of food purchased by the Allied "Executives" overseas. Instead of distributing these precious commodities equitably, the British—who controlled most of the shipping—appeared to be diverting the "lion's share" to themselves. As a result, by the early summer of 1918 Italy was facing privation in breadstuffs, and several French cities had already endured bread riots. Meanwhile in England, where bread was unrationed, the government had stockpiled a reserve of breadstuffs sufficient for fifteen weeks' consumption. The consequence of this inequality in supplies was a deepening popular resentment of Britain among its battered allies, along with the danger of a collapse (so narrowly averted in 1917) of the French and Italian will to fight.[8]

The British, of course, believed that they were not acting unfairly at all. Great Britain, after all, was an island, under constant siege by German U-boats. It was far more dependent on food from abroad than France and Italy were, and it was far more vulnerable to starvation-by-blockade if the German armies broke through to the Channel ports, as they nearly did in the spring of 1918. Back in 1917, as the enemy's submarine campaign mounted, a frightened British Cabinet had vowed to maintain a substantial strategic reserve of wheat. To the British, it was only prudent to do so, especially now that more than four hundred British merchant ships had been assigned to transport American troops and equipment across the Atlantic. To the irritated British, it ill behooved the French to cast aspersions against them, when it was common knowledge that the French government's own food regulations were unenforced and widely flouted. While the British were willing to divert food to France in emergencies (and did so in late 1917), they continued to resist any systematic pooling of food and ships with their ally.[9]

Nevertheless, by the late spring of 1918 the British Cabinet had become convinced that the time had arrived for a more coordinated Allied food policy and administrative structure. In mid-June it informed Washington of its decision.[10] The plaints of the Italians and French had made their mark. But inside the British government, opposition to pooling Britain's food supplies with those of its continental allies remained fierce, particularly at the Ministry of Food. Fearful of loss of British power (and its own) under a multinational arrangement, the ministry's staff did nothing to carry out the Cabinet's intent.[11]

By now the British knew that Hoover was coming and that "coordination" of Allied food policy was very much on his mind.[12] Furious at what he perceived to be Britain's selfish treatment of Italy and France, Hoover was determined to effect a change. This, he later told his secretary, was the principal "inside" reason for his trip.[13] Behind the noble rhetoric of the "common table" lay Hoover's desire—endorsed by Woodrow Wilson—to coerce Great Britain into treating the table as truly common.[14]

Hoover's eagerness to carry a morale-boosting message from Woodrow Wilson may also have had a deeper motive than he let on. In a private conversation with Colonel Edward House on June 17, Hoover excitedly disclosed that both the United States and the Allies now had ample food for the next twelve months. House urged him to exploit this fact in propaganda to buoy the Allies and depress the Germans. Hoover replied that he planned precisely such a campaign. "In outlining it" (House noted afterward in his diary), "I could see he needed no suggestions in this direction."

> He contemplates . . . to go to England, have a banquet given in his honor at the Mansion House, with the Prime Minister, the Food Commissioners of England, France and Italy and other dignitaries present, with himself as the center of interest. It is then that he expects to give out the news that the Allies need not restrain themselves any longer in their food conservation.

Long a friend and patron of the U.S. Food Administrator, House appeared to be somewhat taken aback:

> Hoover may think the plan is for the purpose of maintaining the morale of the Allies and depressing that of the Germans, and I do not like to hint that he is the greatest living advertiser.[15]

If House's suspicion was accurate, Hoover intended to advertise not only his successes but himself.

And only on his terms, if he could manage it. He informed Louis P. Sheldon in London that since he would be traveling there "purely on matters of common administrative interest," he did not wish to "undertake any public functions" except the event at the Mansion House.[16] Eager as he was to trumpet good news and receive credit for it, he realized that it would "never do to convey the impression that this is any kind of a junket."[17]

On July 8 the American Food Administrator left Washington for New York, from which, a few days later, he and several associates embarked for Europe. On board the *Olympic* with them were six thousand American troops headed for France. For most of the crossing the huge, crowded vessel plied the treacherous Atlantic without escort. The passengers were told to wear life preservers at all times, and the portholes were kept sealed.

Despite the constant strain, the voyage had its lighter moments. When Hoover addressed a mammoth Sunday evening religious service on deck, two thousand soldiers who could not see him boisterously greeted the Food Administrator with a complaint: "Feed us on seagulls, we're tired of tripe!" "Seagulls, Mr. Hoover!" "Please, Mr. Hoover, seagulls!" The Chief grinned and proceeded to give a spellbinding extemporaneous speech about his work.[18]

On July 19 "the Great Dispenser" (as one British official called him)[19] arrived in Southampton, where a special train was waiting to take him to London.[20] That very morning American newspapers carried a just-released letter from Hoover to President Wilson disclosing that the United States had exported $1,400,000,000 in foodstuffs to the Allies in the fiscal year that had ended on June 30. The shipments included more than three billion pounds of meats and fats, and 340,800,000 bushels of wheat and other grains. In both cases, said Hoover, the figures substantially surpassed those of the preceding year.[21] In a statement to the British press on his arrival, Hoover was similarly upbeat. "There is no danger of our losing the war through lack of food—till next harvest, anyhow," he said.[22]

Riding through the British countryside toward London and rooms at the prestigious Savoy Hotel, Hoover savored the irony. The British had not always received him so warmly. Earlier in the war, some British officials had opposed his Belgian relief commission and had even suspected him of being a German agent. When asked on the train now how he liked being the guest of the British people, he replied, "It's different from the time I used to slink through here like a hunted dog."[23]

Some of this British attitude may not have been dead yet. A few weeks before Hoover's arrival, Prime Minister Lloyd George, on the prompting of the Minister of Food and his deputy, had asked King George V to bestow the Order of Merit on Hoover in recognition of his services to humanity and to the Allies as chairman of the Commission for Relief in Belgium.[24] The

British monarch unequivocally refused. He informed the prime minister that Hoover was not at all an appropriate candidate for the order, even if American law were to permit him to accept it. The king also reminded the prime minister that under the rules governing the order all recommendations for it were to be initiated by the sovereign.[25]

George V did not indicate why he regarded Hoover as unsuitable for the O.M.[26] Whatever the reason, it was one distinction that Hoover would not receive when he reached London.

The royal refusal turned out to be inconsequential. If Hoover was looking for adulation, His Majesty's Government was quite prepared to lavish it upon him. As the British food controller publicly admitted, Hoover was "the man who could deliver the goods."[27] On July 21, just two days after the Great Dispenser's arrival, King George himself summoned the visiting American to Buckingham Palace. There both the king and queen thanked the American people, through Hoover, for the tremendous voluntary effort that had enabled Great Britain to obtain enough food to survive the winter.[28]

Two days later came the event that Hoover had eagerly coveted and probably instigated: a lunch in his honor hosted by the Lord Mayor of London at the Mansion House. Hundreds of British and foreign dignitaries, including Foreign Secretary Balfour and the Archbishop of Canterbury, turned out to acclaim their Yankee saviour. To the cheers of his audience, Hoover announced that the Allied food crisis of 1917–18 was over. American meat and cereal supplies were ample, he said. So successful had been the exertions of America's farmers and "agricultural authorities" that there need be no restriction on the quantity of breadstuffs that his country could ship to its European allies in the coming year.[29]

Hoover had reason to be proud. In the fiscal year that ended on June 30, 1918 the United Kingdom, France, and Italy had imported more than 22,600,000 tons of foodstuffs from around the world.[30] According to Hoover, nearly half this amount—approximately 10,000,000 tons—had come from the United States. In the coming year, he revealed, the United States would be able to export 18,000,000 tons to the Allies if necessary, and the Canadians would add another 3,000,000. No wonder he believed—and gladly informed his luncheon audience—that "all anxiety as to the great essentials of food is now past."[31]

In his eagerness to proclaim the news of American beneficence, Hoover did not shrink from a dollop of exaggeration. He told his listeners that his country had just exported 10,000,000 tons of food despite the fact that the United States ("except under pressure of this war") was "not normally a food exporting country of consequence."[32] In fact, as he himself later reported to President Wilson, the United States had been a significant food exporter even before the war. In 1912–14 it had exported an average of more than 5,000,000 tons of food annually.[33] In some commodities, moreover, notably wheat, American shipments to Europe in 1917–18 had *decreased* from the year before. Still, no one could gainsay the fact that in the cereal year just ended, the United States had supplied the Allies the "vital margin" between sufficiency and suffering.[34]

Two nights later, at a dinner for the four Allied food controllers, it was Lloyd George's turn to utter the accolades. The British prime minister declared that Hoover did not merely represent "the great Republic of the West"; he represented Providence. What Hoover had accomplished "in coming to the rescue of Europe" in recent months was a "notable triumph" both for himself and for the people of America.[35]

Not all the encomiums showered on Hoover were so transparently tinged with flattery. One morning a British food ministry official arrived at the American embassy with 200,000 letters from British schoolchildren thanking Hoover for sending them food. The man who had accepted—and even sought—the praise of the powerful now looked on in embarrassment as the simple thank offerings were presented. When he posed with two children for photographers, his face turned brilliant red.[36]

Meanwhile the other, and harder, work of his sojourn had begun. On July 23 the three Allied food controllers—Silvio Crespi of Italy, Victor Boret of France, and J. R. Clynes of Great Britain—conferred with their American benefactor in London. Hoover was in an optimistic frame of mind. In the past year, he said, American had exported its 10,000,000 tons of food to Europe despite the lowest supply of food at home in American history. This happy result, he asserted, had been achieved "largely by a reduction in [home] consumption." Now, he declared confidently, the tide was turning. In the year ahead a food surplus would prevail. Still, Hoover impressed upon his colleagues the need for greater "consolidated effort" along lines already taken in the management of shipping, munitions, and military strategy. He therefore proposed the creation of a Food Council consisting of the four food controllers, along with a separate body of representatives to carry out the day-to-day work.[37]

Crespi, Boret, and Clynes quickly agreed in principle to Hoover's scheme.[38] Implementation, however, proved to be quite another matter. For the next several days Hoover, his counterparts, and their aides haggled over the precise structure and staffing of the new arrangement.[39] It soon became apparent to Hoover that the British Ministry of Food was not at all pleased at the prospect of being displaced from its previous dominance over its continental allies.[40] The key antagonist was the ministry's permanent secretary, Ulick Wintour, a career bureaucrat who dominated his new boss, J. R. Clynes, who had been in office less than three weeks.[41] Hoover had little respect for Clynes, a Labour Party Member of Parliament whom he regarded as a mediocre, self-seeking politician.[42] As the days went by, Hoover developed even less respect for Wintour, whom he perceived as an obstructionist.[43] It did not help when Hoover discovered that Wintour had repeatedly snubbed W. A. M. Goode, a Hoover friend and loyalist who was the Ministry of Food's liaison with the Food Administration.[44]

Part of the battle centered on the critical question of personnel: who would serve on the committee of representatives which would actually carry out the Food Council's policies? Hoover, the Italians, and the French wanted Great Britain to appoint as its representative Sir John Beale, the energetic and ambitious chairman of the powerful Wheat Executive. A hard-driving and able British businessman who nevertheless got along well with the Allies, Beale was just the sort of person to impress Hoover. Anxious to maneuver Beale into the desired slot, Hoover apparently discussed his design with Lord Northcliffe, proprietor of *The Times* and confidant of Lloyd George. The next day *The Times* printed an editorial lauding the Wheat Executive's efficiency and success under Beale's leadership.[45]

Unfortunately for Hoover, Beale and Wintour were bitter rivals. In the opinion of some at the Ministry of Food, Beale had not been loyal to his superiors.[46] When the French food controller attempted to force Clynes to appoint Beale to the committee anyway, Clynes retorted that he intended to appoint Waldorf Astor, M.P., the food ministry's new parliamentary secretary.[47] For Hoover, who hoped to create a powerful and efficient inter-Allied food mechanism, Clynes's choice of a fellow politician was ludicrous. When Clynes refused to select Beale, Hoover announced that he would appoint Beale as an *American* representative! Hoover then let his intentions be known to Lloyd George, who sympathized with Hoover but did not immediately intervene.[48]

After several days of vexatious intrigue and delay—caused, entirely, in Hoover's opinion, by the British[49]—the food controllers accepted a compromise propounded by Hoover: Each country would appoint two delegates to the committee of representatives, of whom Beale would become independent chairman without a vote.[50] For Beale the result was evidently far short of the role he wanted, and he acceded to the arrangement only with reluctance.[51] For Clynes and the anti-Beale faction at the British food ministry, it was evidently a humiliating surrender to Allied pressure.[52] Hoover later told a friend that Beale's appointment had occurred under duress.[53]

With the fight over personnel settled, on July 29 the food controllers formally created the Inter-Allied Food Council (consisting of themselves), along with its agent, the Committee of Representatives. The controllers declared that the purpose of the new arrangement was to coordinate their respective food programs, preserving a "proper balance" among their needs, and to purchase and transport their overseas supplies. In order to do this, the Committee of Representatives would develop, and the council would ratify, a consolidated "general food programme for all foods and all allied countries." Such an import schedule would embrace the needs of all members of the wartime coalition.[54] From now on, in other words, Great Britain would not be able to distribute food to its continental partners as it saw fit. Instead, the wants of each Ally, including Britain, would be scrutinized and adjudicated by a multinational body on which each would have an equal vote. Of course, as Wintour and others like him fearfully realized, the senior partner in this entity would be the man who could deliver the goods: Herbert Hoover.[55]

By now Hoover was more convinced than ever that a drastic change in inter-Allied food allocation must occur. According to his investigations, since last autumn the Italians had fallen short by 30 percent on the agreed-upon import program, the French by 20 percent, and the British by a mere 4 percent. The consequence, he informed the President, had been "great hardship" and embitterment "of a very dangerous character" in Italy and France.[56]

Under the circumstances, Hoover was in no mood to let Wintour and his ilk meddle in the machinery. On July 30 the Food Administrator complained frankly about Wintour's behavior to Lord Northcliffe. Rising to the bait, the influential press lord promised to take the matter to Lloyd George.[57] But if Hoover hoped in this way to drive Wintour out at once, he was disappointed.[58] Despite the prime minister's own concern about the senior bureaucrat,[59] the crisis did not end. For the next several weeks resentment at the new scheme smoldered at the Ministry of Food, along with an escalating feud between Wintour and Beale.[60] At least one senior ministry official warned that continued British foot-dragging might alienate Hoover to the detriment of British interests.[61] In the end, after a nasty row and the intervention of the War Cabinet, Wintour was forced out, shunted off to the Stationery Office, and replaced by none other than Beale.[62]

Long before then, Hoover and his foreign colleagues had turned from procedural and personnel issues to a consideration of food policy for 1918–19. Hoover quickly won assent to the creation of a uniform Allied war bread containing 80 percent wheat and 20 percent other cereals.[63] In response to his disclosure that the United States had virtually unlimited quantities of pork to export, the British food controller immediately ended his country's rationing of bacon and ham.[64]

These were easy steps; much harder decisions were soon to follow. Despite Hoover's prediction of plenty for the beleaguered Allies in the year ahead, another fateful crisis was building. In the first year of American co-belligerency, a mediocre harvest and a scarcity of wheat had limited the United States' exportable reserves. Now, one year later, a man-made impediment threatened to intervene just as dangerously between American supply and Allied demand: a steep and worsening deficit in available shipping.

Hoover realized, of course, that his ability to deliver the developing American surplus depended on his finding sufficient vessels to carry it over. Publicly, he did not seem concerned. "We can give you all the pork products you need," he told the British press as soon as he landed. "It is only a question of ships."[65] But a few nights later, at a food controllers' dinner, Prime Minister

Lloyd George delivered a far less sanguine message. "The great American Republic is sending over its sons by the hundreds of thousands every month," he warned, as well as enormous quantities of ammunition and other supplies. No shipbuilding program would be equal to the burgeoning military demand for ships, he declared, "unless we get firmly in our minds the essential need for economy in food and in every other commodity."[66]

If Hoover did not know the statistics beforehand, he learned them now. Despite the fact that in the month of June 1918 Allied production of ships exceeded losses at sea for the first time, on July 1 the European Allies possessed 2,000,000 tons deadweight *less* than they had twelve months before.[67] The British mercantile fleet had shrunk to 11,000,000 tons, down from 18,000,000 tons before the war. Much that remained was being used to transport American soldiers to Europe.[68] More than half the American Expeditionary Force, in fact—a million strong by early summer—had thus far been carried across in British vessels.[69]

To be sure, America's own shipbuilding program was accelerating. But so, too, were the shipping demands of the U.S. Army. At least in the short run, the United States would need every new ship it could launch to transport soldiers, munitions, and military supplies, not Allied food.[70]

The morning after Lloyd George's sobering admonition, Hoover and his European colleagues convened and passed a resolution that considerably attenuated Hoover's message at the Mansion House. The four food controllers declared that while increased food production in America permitted a relaxation of "some of the restrictions which have borne with peculiar hardship on all our peoples," it was nonetheless "absolutely" imperative to maintain "rigid economy and elimination of waste." Only by so doing could the shipment of the necessary troops and supplies from North America to the battle zone be effected. In a further challenge to complacency, they added: "We cannot administer the food problem on the basis of one year's war; we must prepare for its long continuance if we are to ensure absolute victory."[71] Hoover quickly sent the warning home, where, at his request, it received wide publicity.[72]

At this point another inter-Allied agency, the Allied Maritime Transport Council (AMTC), entered the scene. Created in late 1917 to coordinate and allocate the wartime coalition's shipping resources, the council was responsible for adjusting the Allies' import programs to the tonnage available.[73] Hence as soon as Hoover and his associates formulated their import schedule for the coming year, they would have to submit it to the AMTC for its approval.

On July 30—only a day after the Food Council was formally created—the AMTC apprised its infant colleague of the alarming facts. The European Allies had suffered a net loss of shipping since January 1. Neither present nor prospective tonnage was sufficient to convey to France all the American troops that the military leaders wanted. The trade-off between food and men could be reduced to a formula: Every increase of 5,000 tons of imports meant 1,000 fewer Americans sent to France. Under the circumstances, the AMTC asked the Food Council to prepare an import program for 1918–19 that, in conjunction with domestic European production, would maintain the European Allies' food consumption at the same level as during the past year. If home production should exceed last year's figures, imports should be reduced correspondingly. If home production should fall, imports should accordingly increase. The objective, said the AMTC, was to cap Allied consumption at its current volume, with reserve stocks "above, but not unnecessarily above, the point of danger."[74]

Hoover and his fellow food controllers were aghast. For the American Food Administrator especially, who had just proclaimed that happier days were ahead, the AMTC's proposal to perpetuate the status quo must have been a thunderclap—not least because it imperiled his ability to dispose of his soaring stocks of wheat and pork. Within minutes of receiving the AMTC's letter, the Food Council emphatically protested. If British, French, and Italian imports were to be based on last year's program "less increase of production," the council declared, the food difficulties of 1917–18 would simply be repeated and the morale of the civilian population would be "most seriously endangered." The Food Council asked instead for access to the "same ship ton mileage" as it had employed in the past twelve months.[75]

While Hoover and his cohorts waited for the Transport Council to respond, they ordered their Committee of Representatives to prepare a comprehensive import plan for 1918–19 and submit it to the Food Council within two weeks.[76] The food controllers now prepared to return to their respective capitals, except for Hoover, who decided to fill in the time with a "hasty journey" to France and Italy. The Food Administrator notified the White House that he wished to demonstrate that "we are equally concerned with all."[77] But if his later recollection is correct, he had more than fraternal symbolism on his mind. Whatever the various experts might decide in London, Hoover believed that the real determinant of his shipping allocation would be the intentions of the American and Allied army commanders on the western front. The quantity of food he could export to Europe, in other words, would depend on the extent of the U.S. Army's demands on the shipping pool. He was therefore anxious to learn, if he could, the Allied military leaders' strategic and logistical plans for the year to come.[78]

II

On the morning of August 1 Hoover, Boret, Crespi, and their staffs left London for France. After crossing the English Channel under escort and spending the night in Boulogne, the American Food Administrator was motored on to the French capital.[79]

For the next few days, the humble and the great of Paris acclaimed "the man who made it possible for France to eat."[80] At the Elysée Palace on August 2, he lunched with President Poincaré and most of his Cabinet.[81] The next day he visited the Citroën munitions plant, where more than three thousand workers greeted his remarks with a thunderous ovation.[82] Later that afternoon, the government of the city of Paris honored him with an official ceremony at which prefect after prefect eulogized him ad infinitum.[83]

Much as Hoover loved public praise and at times maneuvered to get it, the flow of Gallic oratory strained his patience. He went to the city of Paris's reception "with his usual grunt" (as a friend put it) "and came home grunting still more heavily."[84] On August 3 he had to endure no fewer than fifteen speeches. That night he went to bed, in the words of his secretary, feeling "gassed."[85]

In between the official courtesy calls and ceremonial tributes, Hoover pursued his intelligence gathering. He conferred with General Tasker Bliss, the American representative to the Supreme War Council, which periodically met to formulate joint war strategy.[86] According to Hoover, Bliss told him that the four Allies had not yet fixed their military plans for the year ahead.[87] Hoover was also disturbed by reports of a food shortage among the civilian population of Bordeaux—and determined to force the British to do something about it. According to his information, the British had plenty of wheat stocks with which to alleviate the distress of their suffering ally. In a typical Hooverian maneuver, he asked the U.S. Army command to pressure the British into releasing wheat to the French.[88]

The trip to France included more than ceremonies, however, and more than consultations with the American military. Late in the evening on August 1, the Germans staged an air raid on Boulogne. Hoover was at his hotel when the attack began: a weird melange of bombs, machine-gun fire, antiaircraft barrages, searchlights, shrapnel, and the drone of the enemy airplanes overhead. Suddenly a tremendous explosion erupted nearby; flames leaped hundreds of feet into the air. A German bomb had hit a munitions dump on the waterfront. The force of the explosion shattered the windows in Hoover's room and in much of the hotel. Instead of taking refuge in the basement, Hoover and his traveling party watched the battle from his room until the "all clear" signal sounded after midnight.[89]

It was a close call but not the only one. For some weeks the Germans had been shelling Paris from afar, using a powerful new long-range cannon that the Allies nicknamed "Big Bertha." Day after day the distant artillery piece inflicted random destruction on the populace. No one knew when or where a projectile would land. On the afternoon of August 7, a shell blasted the Hôtel de Calais as Hoover was walking nearby. Fourteen people died. Unfazed by the commotion, the Food Administrator picked up a shell fragment for a souvenir and carried it back to his hotel.[90]

Such incidents, though potentially deadly, were but a sideshow compared to the titanic struggle raging not far away. Early on August 5 Hoover and his party left Paris in six Panhard automobiles for an all-day visit to the western front. It was a day filled with numbing and awful sights. They passed hundreds of *camions*, some carrying the wreckage of aircraft. They passed thousands of French and American troops returning to billets. They drove through little villages reduced to rubble by shell fire. They reached Château-Thierry, where hastily deployed American Marines had thwarted the enemy from breaking through toward Paris in the perilous early days of June. The visitors passed a field where fifty mounds held the bodies of some of the first Americans to die.

From Vaux, destroyed completely, Hoover and his companions motored to Belleau Wood, where, between June 6 and 25, untested Marines had driven back the Germans in ferocious combat and proved that the U.S. Army was for real. They had proved it in blood as well as valor; the victory had cost 5,200 American casualties. By the day of Hoover's visit, the battlefield had been cleared of the dead and the wounded but of nothing else. The visitors saw rifles, helmets, boots, debris of every description, and graves marked by rifles with bayonets thrust vertically into the earth. On the butts of the rifles lay helmets identifying the nationality of the soldier interred beneath. Not all the fallen had been so formally buried. Some lay in the woods and in shell holes, "hidden from the eye but not from the nostrils."

Hoover and his party pushed on to other scenes of recent devastation. To Dormans, where dead and bloated horses littered the roadside and made it almost impossible to breathe. To Epernay, "shelled into a smother of bricks." Near Rheims, late in the day, Hoover and his friends climbed a camouflaged observation tower on a hill called Mt. Sinai and observed the frontline trenches through a telescope. From time to time, falling artillery shells churned the earth.[91]

Hoover did not yet know it, but he had just seen the mute, horrific sites of the turning point of the war. For months the Germans had held the initiative on the western front and had attacked again and again in the hope of defeating the weary French and British before the Yanks could arrive in sufficient numbers to reverse the tide. On July 15 the Germans launched their fifth and, as it turned out, final offensive of 1918. It failed almost before it began. Seizing the initiative, the Allied armies counterattacked. Between July 18 and August 5 they closed the Marne salient from which the Germans had threatened Paris since March. In three terrible weeks of fighting the Allies recaptured much of the territory that had been lost earlier in the year. More importantly, they were on the offensive for good.

Hoover had not come from Paris, however, merely to sight-see. After spending the night of August 5 in a town well back from the front, the next morning he drove to the general headquarters of the American Expeditionary Force (AEF) for lunch with its commanding general, John J. Pershing.[92] Still irritated by the failure of the British to send food to Bordeaux, Hoover raised the issue directly with Pershing. Although doubting that the British had many reserves on which to draw, Pershing nevertheless took Hoover's word for it and promised that the AEF would "stand ready to assist."[93]

The question of prying wheat from the stingy British was a trivial one compared to the topics that the Food Administrator and the general evidently discussed during their two-hour lunch.[94] According to Hoover many years later, he informed Pershing that the Allied "food situation" was "much improved" while that of the enemy was deteriorating badly. But Hoover also disclosed (so he later recorded) that he was "in a fog" about "food strategy" because he had been unable to learn what the Allied coalition's military plans would be for the coming year—plans that would inevitably dictate the amount of shipping left over to transport food.[95]

If the future was on Hoover's mind on August 6, it was also decidedly on Pershing's. On June 23, in the wake of recent German offensives which had come within a whisker of victory, the American general had joined the commander in chief of the Allied armies, General Ferdinand Foch, in a staggering recommendation to the U.S. government: To win the war in 1919, the Allies must achieve numerical superiority over their foe. To obtain it, the United States must place one hundred divisions of American troops in France by July 1, 1919.[96] One hundred divisions! At the time of this request, the American Army in France comprised about a million men. Pershing and Foch now proposed to quadruple this number in just twelve months.[97]

Pershing's estimate of his requirements was based on several factors. In late June 1918 the German army was anything but defeated. To the contrary, it was still on the offensive. Having knocked Russia out of the war earlier in the year, the Germans were massing their forces on the western front. Time and again between March and early summer, the Hun seemed on the verge of shattering the Allied lines.

Nor did the future seem more promising. Pershing feared that if the war dragged on, the Germans might replenish their army by conscripting soldiers in Russia. He believed that the French and British armies, and their civilian populations, were approaching exhaustion and that the burden of combat would increasingly fall on the Americans. He argued that only the "continuous arrival" of American troops could restore the tottering morale of the Allies. All these considerations undergirded his request for a gigantic American army in France—a force sufficient to strike in the autumn and then conclude the war in the summer of 1919.[98]

For the next several weeks the military authorities in Washington studied the hundred-division proposal, while carefully warning Pershing and General Bliss to hold out "no expectation" to the Allies of American ability to implement such a program "until you are informed so from here."[99] The implications of the Pershing-Foch plan were mind-boggling. Aside from the challenge of drafting and training several million more American men for combat, and manufacturing the equipment and munitions that they would need, where on earth would the United States find the ships to transport them? And would the already clogged ports in France have room for such an armada?[100] Undeterred, Pershing kept up the drumfire. On July 19 he demanded that at least 500,000 tons of vessels "now employed in other trades" be transferred to military service. He also requested that the steel tonnage equivalent of all newly built ships be allocated immediately and exclusively to the army.[101] In a letter to the army chief of staff in Washington in July, Pershing asserted that there was "nothing necessary to win this war too stupendous for us to undertake." He added that "unless we carry out the program that has been outlined for next year the war will drag on interminably. . . ."[102]

Meanwhile the European Allies were also pondering the Pershing-Foch plan. On July 2 the Supreme War Council asked General Bliss to find out just how much shipping the United States could provide for its contemplated one hundred divisions. After learning this, the War Council continued, the British government would "examine to what extent it can make up any deficiency."[103] Despite the ambiguity of these words, Pershing was not worried. On July 3 (he later reported to Washington), Prime Minister Lloyd George privately assured him that Great Britain intended to provide "all the shipping possible, showing that they fully appreciate the situation."[104]

In mid-July the U.S. Army's chief of staff, General Peyton C. March, concluded that placement of one hundred divisions in France by the summer of 1919 was an unattainable objective.[105] Instead, on his recommendation, President Wilson approved a plan to have a total of eighty divisions on French soil by that time. This scaled-down program contained several crucial provisos, notably, that Great Britain would continue to furnish the requisite troop and cargo ships to "supply our deficiency" until the American shipbuilding program could meet the need. The War Department calculated that the eighty-division program would make America dependent on the British for troop ships indefinitely, and dependent on Britain for military cargo tonnage until March 1919.[106]

The War Department did not appear to be concerned about troop ships. The British had evidently promised to continue to furnish these at present levels—enough, the Americans believed, to "take care of that deficiency."[107] Cargo ships were quite another matter. After specifying America's projected needs in this category for the next seven months, General March noted that cargo tonnage in use in the current month had fallen short of the amount required properly to supply American forces already in France.[108] Here, potentially, was a lethal hurdle to the eighty-division plan. If cargo shipping for the army was deficient right now, where would the alliance find additional vessels that would be needed between now and next February?

On July 23 General March informed General Bliss by cable of Washington's provisional adoption of the eighty-division program.[109] Curiously, however, neither the chief of staff nor the Secretary of War directly notified General Pershing. Perhaps they assumed that Bliss, in Paris, would pass along the news. In addition, because the plan was contingent on securing additional British shipping, the authorities in Washington were waiting for Bliss to consult the British and obtain their response.[110] As a result, having received no formal notice of the President's decision, General Pershing felt free to continue to agitate for his rejected one hundred-division plan.[111]

It is impossible to say how much, if any, of this behind-the-scenes struggle was familiar to Hoover when he called on Pershing at AEF headquarters on August 6. But in the next two hours the general evidently gave him an earful. By the time lunch was over, the Food Administrator had become an enthusiastic supporter of Pershing's position. Afterward, in a dispatch to Washington, Pershing reported that Hoover concurred with him that "the extreme maximum program thought necessary to end the war [in 1919] should be undertaken for next July." By the "extreme maximum" Pershing meant one hundred divisions, not eighty.[112]

Many years later, in his own account of this conversation, Hoover stated that Pershing disclosed that Allied civilian agencies were resisting his "full power" program on the ground that there was insufficient shipping available to send such an enormous military force to France and simultaneously transport necessities like food to the Allies. According to Hoover, he (Hoover) thereupon offered to divert more than two thirds of the inter-Allied "food fleet" to military use for several months and let the Allied populations live off their new harvest in the meantime.[113]

Be that as it may, the next day, in a conversation with General Bliss back in Paris, Hoover discovered that the Allies were not the only ones who had reservations about the Foch-Pershing plan. According to Bliss, America's own "military people" were inclined to pare down General Foch's huge demands for Allied shipping before notifying civilian agencies. Hoover the reborn war strategist was indignant. In the words of a friend who was present, the Food Administrator told Bliss

> that there was no use trimming down a particle of the demands; that we were now using our tonnage in a way that was certainly susceptible of being scaled down; that we and the Allies wd have to get along without things that we now considered necessary to our normal life and that we cd be made to do so if it was a matter of life and death. The difference between giving Foch what he asks may readily prove to be another year of the war and the lives of a million American soldiers. We *cannot* stand for this no matter what deprivation the civil population is called upon to make, and if the need is made clear enough the civil population will increase its output of ships and reduce its demands upon them until the big job has been put over. If there is not enough resiliency in our whole system to

make up the full budget of what Foch wants we had better make up our minds now that we cant win and make such a peace as we can get in the fall.

Hoover therefore urged Bliss to "stand tight for the full list" and encourage Foch to demand all that he deemed necessary.[114]

Later that evening (August 7), after Bliss departed, an aroused Hoover codified his thinking in a confidential, handwritten letter to General Pershing.[115] Years later Hoover would claim that he did so reluctantly and only at Pershing's request the day before.[116] It seems at least as likely that the Food Administrator composed his letter eagerly, and quite possibly on his own initiative. In any case, Hoover's message was unambiguous:

I learn that Gen'l Foch will present to the Supreme War Council within a few days a programme; that this programme will be based upon of some hypothesis of strength against Germany on this front next year; that there are a number of programmes short of the maximum; that the voice of civilian necessity may temper these demands.

Could I suggest something to you? The programme that will give so far as human vision can foresee a finish of this business in 1919 is the only programme that we are justified in receeving for the American people. No doubt a hundred civilian agencies will say it cannot be done; but if the program is put forward on this basis of full power; if anything short means a certainty of another years war and the sacrifice of another 1000000 of American lives then we must put over the full power programme. If the full power programme is 100 divisions of U.S. troops we want that programme.

As between full power and part power there does not stand *more* than 3,000,000 tons of shipping; perhaps at most 2000000 tons; if we stand in a position where there is not this margin of resiliancy [sic] between 1919 and 1920 then we will never win for if we cannot find self denial in these 220000000 people amounting to 10% of our present total imports we will never last until 1920. Furthermore no group of civilians like myself can get anywhere in our complex problems unless we have a *definite* positive issue to hew at. Nothing but a positive demand backed by a definite statement of the tonnage, supplies and men that is needed—against the alternative of which stands the loss of 1000000 lives will bring these negotiations bickerings and higglings to an end.

I believe there is more margin in this transport situation than the mass of aggregated views of officials zelous [sic] for their own jobs will indicate.

I am for the final and maximum blow and any tampering should be done after its demands have been fully stated not before.[117]

The next day, August 8, a close friend of Hoover delivered the Chief's letter to General Pershing in person. The commander of the American army "snorted with pleasure" when he read it, reaffirmed his support for the "full program," and vowed not to be a party to "scaling it down on this side." The general remarked that Hoover had given him "some fresh ammunition."[118]

The head of the AEF soon found occasion to use it. On August 17 he renewed his demand on Washington for one hundred divisions by the following July. He boldly cited Hoover as a backer of his request. According to Pershing, one hundred divisions were "the very least American force that will insure our victory in 1919." Apparently building upon Hoover's arguments, the general asserted that the European Allies would "more freely concede additional tonnage and supplies" if they believed that the United States truly intended "to make the maximum effort."[119] In a separate letter to the Secretary of War, Pershing insisted that the problem of finding food for the one hundred-division army "should not frighten us off." There were, after all, 220,000,000 people in the European Allied countries, and the provisioning of "2,000,000 or 3,000,000" American soldiers in France was unlikely "to bring us anywhere near the danger point of starvation." Besides, French and British food supplies "would always tide us over" in an emergency.[120]

In making this argument, Pershing was thinking only of food for his own soldiers. He was trying to overcome the War Department's reluctance to send over a gigantic army without the shipping in sight to keep it supplied with food.[121] To Pershing, this objection was nonsensical. France was not "a barren country," he said; his army was not crossing the Sahara Desert.[122] In his single-minded zeal to win his objective, the general seemed unworried by the possibility of *civilian* privation and unrest behind the lines as a consequence of the "considerable sacrifice" he called for.[123]

It was not surprising that Pershing, locked in a bureaucratic battle to secure one hundred divisions, should welcome and perhaps even recruit Hoover as an ally. What is puzzling is why Hoover was so willing to become one. The Food Administrator was not known as a friend of the military. Less than a year before, he had strenuously opposed sending a multi-million-man army to France. Victory by offensive action was impossible, he had argued. At that time he had advocated a defensive war of endurance based on holding the line, feeding the Allies, and starving the Germans into submission. Then and later, he had stressed the intimate relationship between food and civilian morale. Now, however—and only two weeks after his Mansion House speech—Hoover was prepared to countenance a new round of civilian self-denial and a 10 percent reduction in Allied food imports, all on the uncertain premise that the war could be won next year.

Why? One reason—probably the decisive one—was starkly simple: A shortened war might save *one million* American lives. Put in these terms, further belt-tightening on the home fronts seemed a meager price to pay. Hoover also evidently judged that the Allied "food front" had improved sufficiently to withstand the shock of additional deprivation. Beyond this, another factor undoubtedly reinforced his change of attitude: a deepening anger at, and suspicion of, Great Britain. Already during his trip he had discovered that the British had been diverting a far greater portion of joint Allied imports than he had known.[124] Clearly the British, at least, had an ample margin of foodstuffs for the present.[125] The Food Administrator's skepticism also extended to the Allied shipping supply, which he considered to be in less desperate straits than Allied officialdom asserted.[126] Two weeks in London and France had convinced him that the European Allies' capacity for sacrifice was not exhausted. Eager to end the war, whose ghastliness he had just witnessed with his own eyes, and incensed at the self-centered stinginess of the British, Hoover was emotionally ready to line up emphatically, even impulsively, on Pershing's side.

As he conferred with the American generals in France, Hoover was unaware of a new bombshell from across the Channel. The British shipping controller had been studying Washington's plan to transport eighty divisions of soldiers to France by mid-1919—with considerable assistance from British vessels. By the beginning of August the Americans seemed confident of receiving the necessary aid.[127] But on August 2, in a cable to the premier of France, Prime Minister Lloyd George indicated otherwise. The British, he announced, would be unable to carry any more military cargo for the Americans and would be obliged to reduce troop transport as well. The constraints on British shipping, he said, were too great.[128]

Sometime in the next few days someone gave a copy of this document to General Pershing, who relayed its startling contents to Washington on August 7.[129] It is not known whether Pershing had it at hand when he met Hoover on the sixth or whether he shared its stunning news with Hoover. In all probability he did not.[130] But if he had, it would only have intensified Hoover's distrust of the British.

Meanwhile the Food Administrator busied himself with promoting another cause while in Paris: improved coordination of the civilian side of the American government's war effort in France. On his first day in the French capital, Hoover met with his loyal diplomat-friend Hugh Gibson, then on assignment at the U.S. embassy. Gibson told him that an "interallied diplomatic council" was badly needed in Europe, or "failing that," an American high commissioner "with the full confidence of the President." Hoover agreed, but feared that such a reform could not be "put over."[131] Perhaps he suspected that Woodrow Wilson would be reluctant to invest so much power and prestige in someone who, if the war went well, might easily become his rival and successor.

Nevertheless, in ensuing days Hoover broached with Pershing and others "the need" (in Gibson's words) "for some central control over American [civilian] representatives in France."[132] According to Gibson, finding a solution to this problem had been Hoover's "chief reason in coming over."[133] By August 7 Hoover thought he had a solution: (1) daily meetings of the American representatives to the numerous governmental bodies; and (2) a "personal delegate of the President" who could coordinate their efforts and resolve most problems without referring them to Washington. Hoover said that he would present the matter to President Wilson upon returning home.[134]

Gibson and the others probably did not realize it, but this was not the first time that Hoover had advocated that a supreme coordinator be sent to administer the civilian side of the American war effort in Europe. In February 1917 he had recommended precisely the same step to Colonel House if the United States entered the war. Hoover's own desire for this position had been transparently obvious on that occasion.[135] Did he covet the same job now?

On the surface it seemed not. Hoover told General Pershing that the coordinator should be the Secretary of the Treasury, William McAdoo.[136] Moreover, at the time he made this suggestion, it still seemed possible that Hoover might be sent on a humanitarian mission to Russia.[137] Nevertheless, it is hard to believe that Hoover's nomination of McAdoo, of all people, was entirely genuine. Did Hoover secretly hope that by self-effacingly recommending a rival he might induce Pershing to recommend Hoover himself? Did he really think that Woodrow Wilson would dispatch his own son-in-law to Europe as the civilian equivalent of Pershing? We cannot say. But Hoover would not have been Hoover if the thought did not occur to him that *he* should be America's civilian overlord in France.

To General Bliss, the Food Administrator floated a different idea: the creation of a single agency that would have "supreme control over all of the various Allied and Inter-Allied agencies now existing," including those which handled the food supply and shipping. Hoover believed that such a coordinating body would greatly reduce the demand for food and other goods and thereby release valuable shipping for the military. Hoover apparently did not suggest who might represent the United States on such an all-powerful entity, but it did not matter. Bliss rejected the idea as impractical. What was needed, the general advised Washington, was not another agency but an "absolutely paramount" objective, to which all other questions would be subordinate. For Bliss, the goal should be the victorious termination of the war in 1919. This would solve Hoover's coordination problem and motivate the Allied peoples to make the "supreme effort."[138]

One primary objective—total victory in 1919—and all "secondary" interests sacrificed to it: Bliss's advice was consistent with Hoover's simultaneous request to Pershing for the same objective and for "a *definite* positive issue" for civilian agencies "to hew at."

Because of the illness of his fellow food controller Victor Crespi, Hoover canceled his plan to travel to Italy.[139] Instead, on August 8 he returned from Paris to London.[140] As he drove across the French countryside to the Channel, British troops were launching a counteroffensive east of Amiens. Taken by surprise, the Germans retreated in confusion. War-weary soldiers surrendered by the thousands. General Ludendorff later called it "the black day of the German Army in the history of this war." Knowing that the war was lost, a few days later he tried to resign his command.[141]

Hoover, of course, did not know this, nor could he foretell how soon the enemy would collapse. He had enough to ponder, including a massive reversal in his own policy. Three weeks after promising unlimited breadstuffs for the Allies, he was now committed to constraining them anew in order to permit an enlarged American army to come and get it over "over there."

III

BACK in London, Hoover turned his attention to settling the Allies' food import program for 1918–19. During his absence the Allied Maritime Transport Council had firmly rejected the food controllers' attempt to receive the same allotment of shipping tonnage as in the previous year. The AMTC reiterated that total Allied food consumption in the year ahead should not surpass that of the year just ended. In other words, if home production increased, food imports (and allotted shipping) would be reduced.[142]

Despite this unambiguous rebuff, the Food Council's Committee of Representatives proceeded to draw up an import program exceeding that of the previous cereal year. In the twelve months ending June 30, the British, French, and Italians had collectively imported more than 22,600,000 tons of food.[143] The committee now boldly recommended that this be *increased* to more than 27,000,000 tons for 1918–19.[144] On August 12 Hoover and his European counterparts reassembled in London and swiftly approved the augmented program.[145]

Why, in view of his change of attitude in Paris, did Hoover not oppose this radical new impingement on the inter-Allied shipping pool? Probably he considered the new program to be a mere "wish list" that the AMTC would never approve. Probably, too, he did not feel free to introduce military considerations that were far from definite. The Supreme War Council had not yet met to consider the "full power" program that he had just confidentially endorsed. For the moment, he was obliged to go on record in favor of more food for the Allies.

But if the American Food Administrator did not openly veto the new food import plan, he did attempt immediately to shrink it. At their last meeting in July, he and his fellow food controllers had approved a priority test for importation of Allied foodstuffs. The list included bread grains (the first priority) and various other commodities. It did not include fodder for farm animals other than dairy cattle, whose milk was deemed essential for children.

To Hoover the British government's continued importation of fodder for nondairy animals was indefensible. On both humane and military grounds, he contended, the people of Europe must be fed before "meat animals," and he was disgusted by the "self-interest of certain classes" who would "rob the vital food of human beings in order to maintain the class industry."[146] Hoover's reasoning was practical as well as moral: fodder consumed much more cargo space than finished meat and fats.[147] By eliminating an estimated 2,000,000 tons in fodder shipments to England, he could—he said—economize on precious shipping, for he would need to export only 400,000 tons of American pork to England as a substitute.[148] Thus moral and practical motives neatly coincided with his own self-interest: by dropping fodder he could dispose of that much more surplus pork. Hoover did not seem to care that his policy could ruin Britain's domestic meat production, for British farmers might have to slaughter their herds as a result of a cutoff in foreign feed. "More shipping!" was the cry of the hour. Shipping was what he needed most. If this meant the end of a nonessential British industry, so be it.

And so on August 12 Hoover moved to revise the Food Council's priority schedule for its new import plan. Hoover proposed a three-tier scale of priority, with sugar (which the British badly wanted) in the second category of preference and fodder in the third or lowest class. He further proposed that any monthly deficiency in deliveries of the highest-priority goods (category #1) would be taken care of in the subsequent month before any country received any goods from categories #2 and #3.[149]

Hoover's demands ignited a bitter row. The British were furious. They had already accepted a substantial reduction in their original demand for animal fodder—and only then after a long and difficult argument.[150] Now "the Great Dispenser" was maneuvering to take even this away. The British were also upset about the relegation to second-rung status of imported sugar, which they had been trying (over Hoover's resistance) to put into the highest-priority class.[151] The Italians and the French, after all, had some sugar sources of their own. The British had none and feared that they would get none if Hoover got his way. To the men at His Majesty's Ministry of Food, the Yankee food controller's proposal looked thoroughly unfair.[152]

The Committee of Representatives, to whom Hoover's hot potato was referred, proved unable to agree on a detailed priority schedule. Instead, the next day it recommended a British scheme based not on categories of food but on tonnage. The three European Allies would be allocated sufficient priority tonnage to import 18,500,000 tons of nonmilitary food in the coming year. Up to this limit, each country would be free to import whatever it wanted.[153] The British immediately made it known that they would include some sugar and feeding stuffs "in the first priority," and they reserved the right to revise the arrangement in December if it appeared that they would receive less food or feeding stuffs in toto than the year before. As for the remainder of the Allies' food program, this would be delivered "as shipping serves" in proportion to each country's remaining share of designated imports.[154]

Hoover was not pleased. Instead of accepting "principles," he grumbled, the Committee of Representatives had fiddled with the figures.[155] In the end, the four food controllers accepted the committee's handiwork, subject to a reservation insisted upon by Hoover: that it was vitally necessary "to the prosecution of the war and the safety of America's Armies in Europe" that "human feeding in Allied Countries should proceed upon a basis of comfort and maintenance of morale." Furthermore, no imports "to preserve animal life, except dairy interests, should transgress upon the breadstuff, meat fats and edible oil imports in any country. . . ."[156] With this proviso, the Inter-Allied Food Council authorized the dispatch of its "programme of priorities" to the Allied Maritime Transport Council for approval.[157]

Hoover was now nearly ready to go home. But just before he left, still another rancorous dispute arose with the British. During the 1917–18 cereal year, the British had controlled the assembling and shipment of Allied grain purchases from facilities in the United States. Hoover decided to change this, as he explained by cable to Washington on August 13:

> I have resisted all pressure English Shipping Control to delay our plan of conveying cereals to all shippers at seaboard. I have informed them that plan is already in operation. . . . It is vital to us to control all exports of cereals in order to guarantee the righteous disposal of these cereals amongst the Allies, if for no other reason. Present situation of breadstuffs in France endangers our whole military situation, and could not have resulted if we had dominated destination of export shipments, which I propose we shall do during the forthcoming year.[158]

Hoover told an associate that while Britain would still largely control shipping, *he* would control loading in the United States. If food shipments for Europe were not "destined" in a manner he considered equitable, or if the British did not divide the food fairly on the other side, the U.S. government could simply stop the loading.[159]

Hoover's decision led to a nasty spat with an official in the British shipping ministry. In an attempt to patch up the rift, the British shipping controller himself, Sir Joseph Maclay, invited Hoover to visit him at the ministry at 3:30 P.M. Hoover was "quite busy," his young secretary replied, but he would adjust Hoover's schedule if Sir Joseph wished to come to Hoover's hotel that evening. Maclay came.[160]

By the time he left London on August 16, Hoover was in a thoroughly anti-British mood.[161] In addition to the irritations and arguments of recent days, he was now convinced that the British government was opposing a decisive military breakthrough on the western front in 1919 because of unwillingness to make the necessary domestic sacrifices.[162]

Still fuming at what he judged to be British selfishness, Hoover hoped that the Food Council's Committee of Representatives would be able to control allotments of food. He appeared to have faith in Sir John Beale, the chairman, who had opposed his own government's earlier policy and had a reputation for fairness.[163] But the angry American Food Administrator was taking no chances. Leaving Joseph Cotton behind to be his chief representative in Europe,[164] Hoover spelled out his instructions in unambiguous terms. We must not allow the Allied Maritime Transport Council to encroach on the sphere of the food controllers, he declared. We must create "a solid structure of priorities" for European consumption in every area; it was the "only logical solution" to the problem of underproduction and the shortage of transport. We must never again permit the food supplies of France and Italy to "degenerate" to the perilous point they had done in the past year. Just last month, he said, the great majority of the French people had been "without bread," while England held 2,000,000 tons of breadstuffs in reserve. For our own "national safety" we must "exact a fair division of food supplies."[165]

Hoover also remained in a truculent mood about animal fodder. He instructed Cotton that "our entire policy" must be to provide Europe the established monthly quantities of bread grains, meats, and fats "before feed stuffs are imported." If this did not occur in the months ahead, "it will be necessary for me to dictate this issue peremptorily from the United States as a matter of seaboard loading of foodstuffs."[166]

If Hoover was in a disgruntled frame of mind, so, too, were some of the British. What, for them, had been the result of his visit? An Inter-Allied Food Council which he, not they, would dominate. Public promises of bounteous food from the New World—coupled with an attempt to impose a priority scheme that could wreck the domestic British meat industry. The Earl of Crawford, chairman of the Royal Commission on Wheat Supplies, was particularly disturbed and recorded in his diary:

> Interview about American breadstuffs with [Lord] Reading. He quite confirmed my fears that the USA is frankly out for plunder, Hoover aiding and abetting. We were fleeced last year, this year we shall be stripped naked, and Hoover all the time is chattering about altruism.[167]

What Crawford, perhaps, did not fully understand was that Hoover's perspective had radically changed during his European visit. Because of the intensifying shipping shortage, Hoover's promised era of plenty had abruptly receded into the future. The theme of sacrifice had returned to his lips. What rankled the British was the impression that "the Great Dispenser" seemed all too willing to make *them* sacrifice, and in ways that might benefit America economically after the war. What rankled Hoover was the conviction that the British were looking out for their own interests to the point of jeopardizing success on the field of battle.

In mid-August Hoover sailed back to the United States. The voyage across the Atlantic was uneventful.[168] Gone from his propaganda arsenal was the slogan that had helped to make him famous: "Food Will Win the War."

He had abandoned it in June lest it appear to suggest that his agency's activities were equivalent to the bloody sacrifices of the doughboys under fire in northern France. Now he had a new slogan, a new overarching theme for the final phase of the struggle. It was: "Win the War in 1919."[169]

For all his exasperation with the British, Hoover was content with the outcome of his negotiations in London. He had gotten nearly everything he wanted.[170] But the inter-Allied battle, it soon transpired, was not over. The British had one great weapon left and were about to use it: their control of the shipping needed by the U.S. Army.

IV

On August 23 Hoover landed in New York and took a train to Washington, where he quickly urged his "full power" views on Secretary of War Newton Baker.[171] When Hoover arrived at the War Department, he found Baker in conference with a young member of the general staff named Douglas MacArthur. The subject was the size of the American army to be sent to France. Baker turned to his visitor and asked: How many soldiers did he think could be shipped to Europe and supplied there? Hoover's answer was instant and apodictic: As many millions of troops as were necessary.[172]

But how? Washington still did not know. On August 14, while Hoover was still in England, General Bliss recommended to Baker that the U.S. government force the issue at the next meeting of the Supreme War Council. "The time has come to plan a campaign with reasonable hope that it will be the last one," Bliss cabled.

> If Marshal Foch will state that the 80 division program gives reasonable assurance of a final campaign next year I feel sure that United States can demand and secure the necessary tonnage. . . . If the United States gives its money and blood the others can diminish their secondary demands and give the necessary ships. The peoples will not sacrifice much without a definite object; with a definite object they can sacrifice a good deal more.[173]

Three days later Baker informed the President that he agreed. "There must be a show-down on this subject," he said. "The tremendous effort America is making, and the vast force which we will have in 1919 will win the war, if our allies want it won, and are willing to make any correspondingly devoted effort."[174] The commander in chief thereupon authorized his Secretary of War to travel to Europe and negotiate an end to the troops-and-tonnage impasse. Herbert Hoover was not the only American official losing patience with the British government.

Back on the scene in Washington, Hoover soon learned of the presidential decision, made while the Food Administrator was on the high seas.[175] With the crucial military issue in abeyance for the moment, Hoover proceeded to lobby for his other policy recommendation: consolidation of the civilian side of the American war effort in France under a single head. On August 26 he conferred with President Wilson about "coordination of economic effort in Europe" in order to secure "sufficient tonnage to fill the American army program."[176] It was apparently in this conversation that Hoover recommended Secretary of the Treasury McAdoo for this task. Wilson replied that he could not spare McAdoo but intended to send Newton Baker instead. Hoover (so he told a friend later) objected: "Mr. President, I am sorry. Baker wins his points, but he wins them by persuasion and the time is too short to persuade people."[177]

The next day Hoover returned to his theme in a letter to the President. Hoover strongly urged Wilson to appoint a "personal representative," who could "coordinate directly with the Prime Ministers of Europe," "head up all of the American economic representatives in Europe," and—above all—remain in Europe continuously for the next twelve months. The problem at hand could not be solved by "a temporary negotiation or declaration of principles," he asserted. It required "continuous effort and adjustment" by someone who could "coordinate the views" of the Allied governments "with ourselves" and "present a consolidated front of economic action as we have now on the military side." Because of Newton D. Baker's "large responsibilities," said Hoover, the Secretary of War's upcoming visit to Europe could only be "temporary." Hence Hoover urged the selection of an economic coordinator who could accompany the secretary on his trip.[178]

In effect, Hoover asked the President to appoint an individual whose powers and prestige would be rivaled only by General Pershing's among Americans in Europe. Who should this civilian generalissimo be? Hoover offered no names in his letter, but it is hard to resist the conclusion that he had just composed a job description for himself. If this was indeed his intent, Woodrow Wilson failed to oblige. Instead, the President politely acknowledged his letter and then asked Baker to suggest someone "who can keep the adjustments going" after his return from Europe.[179]

Was Hoover angling yet again for the post of supreme economic commander in Europe? Curiously enough, at just this moment a young journalist in uniform named Walter Lippmann was on assignment in Europe for the War Department and Colonel House. As a founder of the *New Republic* magazine, Lippmann was already well known in Washington political circles. He was also an acquaintance of Hoover and had dined with the Chief's secretary in early August.[180] A few weeks later Lippmann told an American embassy official in Paris that Hoover would make an excellent high commissioner to Great Britain. Hoover, he opined, should be able to oversee readjustments in Europe in conjunction with his ordinary duties. Lippmann's suggestion quickly made its way to the State Department and the White House.[181] Was it a coincidence? Perhaps. But perhaps not.

In any event, it was Baker, not Hoover, who sailed for Europe at the beginning of September. And it was Baker, not Hoover or anyone else, who became the de facto head of the American war apparatus in France upon his arrival.[182]

Meanwhile, across the Atlantic, the Allied Maritime Transport Council—the Great Dispenser in the shipping realm—had been meeting on August 29 and 30. It was not a relaxing two days. The AMTC was shocked to discover that Hoover and his fellow food controllers had requested a 4,500,000-ton *increase* in British, French, and Italian imports for 1918–19—a request that, if granted, would absorb more shipping than in the year before.[183] Nor was this the only dismaying news. The AMTC now learned that the U.S. Army's eighty-division plan would require a substantial additional assignment of Allied tonnage—at the outset, more than a million tons *per month*—until next March.[184] The menace to food, munitions, and other competing imports was plain.

The AMTC finally permitted the Food Council to initiate its import program. Not, however, on the basis of the 27,000,000-ton request that it had submitted, but on the basis of the "priority" figures that Hoover and his colleagues had agreed upon: a total of 18,500,000 tons for the year (excluding military oats). But the Transport Council was loathe to sanction even this. It warned that its authorization was "purely provisional" and that the figures would be reconsidered as soon as "full information" became available concerning the U.S. Army's transport plans.[185]

If the multinational AMTC was in a touchy mood, the British members of it were even more so, and they did not hesitate to add conditions of their own. The new priority system would force them to divert ships to meet French and Italian deficiencies. The British announced that they would comply, but only if France and Italy made satisfactory shipping arrangements with them, and only if the United States included its *own* import program "on equal terms at an early date."[186]

Now, more than ever, the Allies—especially the British—were upset. On August 30 the British ambassador to the United States, Lord Reading (who was then in England), warned the U.S. government by cable that American absorption of additional Allied cargo tonnage for the eighty-division program would force the European Allies to reduce their imports of goods that had formerly been deemed essential, both for military purposes and for sustaining civilian morale. Reading noted that there was a limit to the sacrifices that the Allied peoples could make. More pointedly still, he declared that it was "vital" that the four associated governments "be able to assure that the sacrifices [for victory in 1919] are imperative" and "made in pursuance of a common policy" followed by the Allies and the United States alike. He therefore asked the U.S. government to send over those officials who were responsible for allocating American tonnage and for limiting American imports so that the question of allocating shipping for Uncle Sam's army supply program could be expeditiously settled.[187] The French and the Italians supported the British.[188]

Behind Reading's request was an upsurge in Allied anger at the United States. The Allies were now being asked to curtail their own imports in order to make room for the U.S. Army, but it seemed to them that the United States was showing no disposition to do the same. The Europeans therefore argued that the United States must submit its imports to the same standard of necessity as the Europeans had agreed to do. They also asked the United States to disclose its import data for Allied criticism, just as America had criticized Allied imports in the past. The British intimated that they would more willingly curb their own imports if the United States agreed to these requests and inaugurated a tonnage conservation program of its own. According to Hoover's chief representative in London, an American declaration of intent "to cut its own trade to the bone" would generate "prompt action" by the Allies on the U.S. Army's request for more of their ships.[189]

Hoover was not impressed by the Europeans' pleas for reciprocity. Except for "some minor liner space" and two oil tankers, he rejoined, the United States was using "no transatlantic tonnage for food imports." "Therefore," he cabled London, "our food import programme cannot interest Allies and should be sufficient evidence of our stripping to the bone." In other words, American employment of small coastal vessels to import food from the Caribbean was none of the Europeans' business. He did add, however, that the desired public assurances of American belt-tightening were being issued by two other government agencies.[190]

Hoover's reply must have seemed ironic to the Europeans, coming as it did from one who had just preached the doctrine of the "common table." While it was probably true that curtailment of American imports from the Caribbean would not release much oceangoing tonnage, Hoover seemed oddly oblivious to the psychology of the situation. What the Allied governments in part wanted was a gesture of American solidarity in suffering—a gesture that they could cite in an effort to make their people accept more pain.

Instead, Hoover took their request as a challenge. And, as usual when challenged, he became defiant. Relaying the Europeans' views and his reply to the White House, he declared that there was only one food import for which the United States could be criticized: bananas, which did involve the use of vessels "capable of trans-Atlantic use." Absolving himself of any responsibility for this anomaly, Hoover asserted that he had opposed the importation of bananas for eight months.[191]

It was now up to Newton Baker to find a way out of these entanglements—Baker the smooth negotiator, so unlike the abrasive Food Administrator in temperament. The Secretary of War arrived in France on September 7. A little over two weeks later he reported to Washington that the British had agreed to divert 200,000 tons of additional shipping to the

Americans.[192] This was much less than the U.S. Army needed, but it was something. The British, however, were worried that any tonnage they surrendered to the Americans would mean a reduction in "essential" Allied imports and a possible dangerous shortage later on. Such a deficiency, they argued, would have to be met with American aid later in the cereal year when the United States finally would have sufficient ships of its own.[193]

While Baker waited for Lord Reading to recover from an illness and resolve the cargo issue definitively, he turned to another source of difficulty: the commander of the American Expeditionary Force in France. Pershing had not given up his quest for a one hundred-division army. After learning in August that Baker was coming over, the general had met with Foch and Tasker Bliss. Each remained committed to the one hundred-division program.[194] By September Pershing was well aware, though not officially, of the War Department's eighty-division alternative. To Baker's surprise, it now turned out that Pershing and his staff interpreted this to mean eighty *combat* divisions plus sixteen depot divisions besides. The upshot was that whereas the War Department contemplated placing 3,760,000 American soldiers of all kinds in France by mid-1919, Pershing contemplated receiving nearly a million more.[195] It was not until September 25 that the army chief of staff in Washington, on Baker's prompting, informed Pershing directly that Pershing's plan was "impracticable," that the eighty-division program was the official program, and that it embraced eighty divisions of all kinds, and no more.[196]

At long last the struggle over the future size of the AEF had been resolved. But what about shipping? On September 30, October 1, and October 2, the Allied Maritime Transport Council convened in London. Speaking for the European Allies, the chairman of the council declared that since America's increasing production of ships should exceed the needs of its army by mid-1919, it might be possible for the Europeans to divert some of their tonnage to the U.S. Army in the meantime *if* the resulting European deficit in food and other imports "could be met by American assistance later in the cereal year." Speaking for the United States, Newton Baker pledged to participate fully in the work of the council and to replenish European food stocks when the Americans developed a shipping surplus. The United States also agreed to disclose and submit its shipping and import programs to the AMTC and another inter-Allied agency and even to be guided by their recommendations. Baker stipulated, however, that "in the last resort" the United States would retain "ultimate control" of its own tonnage.[197]

Baker's concessions were the quid pro quo that the Allies were looking for. The Allied Maritime Transport Council now proceeded in effect to endorse the Americans' eighty-division plan by recommending a diversion of 300,000 additional tons of Allied shipping to the U.S. Army. The council decreed that during the late autumn and winter of 1918–19 the transport of munitions and army supplies should be given preference over food, and that next spring and summer food should then take precedence. As for the food imports themselves, the AMTC now turned the food controllers' "priority" program into a ceiling: 18,500,000 tons for the year. The council promised to give food shipments greater priority if a food shortage should threaten to occur after the winter.

When military oats were added to the food program, the total authorized importation for 1918–19 rose to approximately 22,000,000 tons. This was 5,000,000 tons fewer than Hoover and his colleagues had requested, but it was close to what the three European Allies had imported the year before. The AMTC had won its point: aggregate Allied food imports were frozen at approximately the level of 1917–18. The projected civilian portion of these imports was actually reduced by nearly 2,000,000 tons.[198] When all was said and done, the noncombatant populations of England, France, and Italy were now scheduled to receive less food from abroad than they had in the preceding crop year.

In making these decisions, the AMTC counted on an estimated increase of nearly 2,000,000 tons in cereal harvests in Britain, France, and Italy to compensate for its retrenchment on imports.[199] Still, Baker and his cohorts were taking a considerable gamble, not only that Allied civilians would endure another year of hardship but also that the available ships could meet any food emergency in time in the spring of 1919. Years later Hoover remarked that there might have been a "debacle" if the war had not been won before then.[200] But it was a risk that he, too, was willing to take in order to end the war quickly and avert a million American deaths on the battlefield.

The prolonged and agonizing debate over priorities was finally over. Or was it? Late in October Baker discovered that the British were lagging in their promised diversion of additional tonnage to the U.S. Army.[201] Apparently the British had received what embarrassed American representatives in London had just received: data from Washington showing that America was using more than 2,000,000 tons of commercial shipping in excess of what it needed for essential imports.[202] The British were evidently unpersuaded by Hoover's assertion that nearly all this shipping was unfit for trans-Atlantic service. Fortunately for all concerned, the war ended before a new altercation could erupt.

Hoover was on the sidelines in Washington when Baker negotiated the shipping concordat in Europe. But the Food Administrator was hardly immune from unsettling developments across the sea. In mid-September he learned that the American army intended to increase its use of Allied shipping immediately, thereby forcing him to reduce and delay his projected exports of cereals. Hoover was seized with alarm. His grain-storage facilities were "full to the roof," he told the army's chief of staff on September 21. The situation was so bad that he had had to embargo grain shipments by farmers, thereby causing "financial difficulties in every direction." To relieve the glut, Hoover had urged the Allies to step up their imports of American grain in the next three months. Instead, thanks to the army's mounting diversion of Allied vessels, he was facing a devastating contraction in his cereals exports to fewer than 500,000 tons per month. Yet if information from the chairman of the U.S. Shipping Board was correct, the army would not have sufficient material "ready for transportation" to fill all of America's "cargo tonnage" during the next three months. Sensing a disaster in the making, Hoover warned that if his cereal shipments to Europe were confined to 500,000 tons monthly or less, "the whole of the Allied countries will be filled with food riots by the first of April."[203]

Hoover's expostulations did not sway General March. The army's chief of staff replied bluntly that the chairman of the Shipping Board had been misinformed. The army needed all the American tonnage that it had so far received—and more.[204]

Not surprisingly, Hoover was in a "dispirited" mood when he visited Colonel House on September 23. Once more the Food Administrator stressed the need for "better coordination of our economic forces" in Europe. By now the colonel was used to this. Hoover "was in his normal pessimistic frame of mind," House recorded in his diary. "I cheered him and he left feeling better."[205]

While Baker labored in London to secure ships for the ever-swelling U.S. Army, Hoover, at home, adjusted his food policies to the new exigencies of the war. At the end of August, the Food Administrator had relaxed some of his restraints on American wheat consumption, in keeping with his announcement in London of ample supplies. Wheatless days and meals were abolished, while the stringent 50-50 rule gave way to an 80-20 rule for retail sale of wheat flour and substitutes.[206] But the war was not over yet, and Hoover had no intention of returning to a policy of culinary laissez-faire. On September 22 he released his food conservation program for the coming year to the American people.

"There is no prospect of a proper ending of the war before the campaign of the Summer of 1919," he began. To achieve victory, the United States must send 3,500,000 soldiers and vast amounts of equipment to France. In order to accomplish this feat, and keep Allied armies and civilians properly fed, America must increase its food exports to Europe by 5,730,000 tons, nearly 50 percent above 1917–18 levels. Although the Allies were about to receive less food in toto from abroad than in the year just ended, Hoover explained that Allied dependence on the United States itself was increasing. Because of the continuing scarcity of Allied shipping, the United States was the Allies' most convenient food source.

The Food Administrator therefore summoned his fellow citizens to another season of self-denial. He asked Americans to reduce their consumption of breadstuffs as well as meats and fats by up to half a pound per person per week. He asked the better-off segments of the populace to practice "even greater simplicity of living than last year." He asked the owners and employers of "public eating places" to institute even stricter conservation measures.

Conspicuously, Hoover did not institute general rationing. "This is not rationing," he announced—"a thing we will never have if our people continue to support us as in the past." He insisted that America could "accomplish the necessary ends by voluntary action of our people."

> The willingness to assume individual responsibility in this matter by the vast majority is one of the greatest proofs of the character and idealism of our people, and I feel it can be constantly relied upon. Our simple formula for this year is to further reduce consumption and waste in all food.

Except for "a moderate substitution of other cereals in bread," Hoover hoped that it would not be necessary "to substitute one foodstuff for another," or to return to the wheatless and meatless days he had abandoned.[207]

Privately, Hoover believed that a policy of voluntarism resonated well with the American people. He also feared that rationing—which would necessarily entail an elaborate apparatus of government control—would encourage collectivist tendencies that he, as an individualist, opposed.[208] In mid-1918, as the nation's sugar shortage worsened, he did impose on businesses a stringent certificate system that eventually forbade retailers from selling families more than two pounds of sugar per family member per month. But here, too, he avoided the direct issuance of ration cards to consumers.[209]

Still, in the final weeks (as it turned out) of the war, Hoover did not hesitate to impose further restraints upon the eating habits of a significant portion of the American people. In mid-October the Food Administration issued a set of mandatory "General Orders" governing all "public eating places" in the United States. The eating establishments, where nearly 9,000,000 Americans took at least one daily meal, were forbidden to serve any bread or bakery product that did not contain at least 20 percent wheat flour substitutes. They were forbidden to serve bread under meat, bread or bacon as a garniture, or more than half an ounce of butter per person per meal. They could not place sugar bowls on tables or lunch counters or use more than two pounds of sugar for every ninety meals served.

In promulgating these regulations, Hoover's agency acknowledged that public eating places were not presently under federal license. A year earlier, Hoover and his colleagues might have found this a deterrent to drastic action. Not now. On October 11 the Food Administration announced that failure to adhere to any of its "General Orders" would be deemed a "wasteful practice" forbidden by section 4 of the Lever Act. If the "patriotic co-operation of such public eating places can not be secured by other means," the Food Administration warned, the agency was ready to "secure compliance . . . through its control of the distribution of sugar, flour and other food supplies."[210]

Hoover, in short, was willing to crack down on food distributors and small business people, a relatively limited group which he could oversee and discipline. But he continued to shy away from all-out conspicuous repression of the populace at large. Direct coercion (if need be) for the business classes; exhortation and indirect coercion for the "masses": this was Hoover's strategy for wartime success. It was a formula born of philosophical conviction, administrative prudence, political necessity, and a keen desire to survive on the public stage.

Yet even as Hoover unveiled his new conservation program, events in Europe were overtaking him and all other war planners. During August and September the news from the battlefield became increasingly favorable to the Allied cause. On September 26, 1918, just four days after Hoover's conservation announcement, the American and Allied armies launched the great Meuse-Argonne offensive. One million two hundred thousand American soldiers took part.[211] By early October the German army was in retreat all along the line. When Secretary Baker met General (now Marshal) Foch on October 4, he asked the supreme Allied commander how many divisions he needed to win the war in 1919. Foch replied, "Forty." Baker could not believe his ears. He repeated the question. The Marshal of France again answered: Forty. But, Baker argued, there are already nearly that number in France now, and Pershing wants one hundred in 1919. Foch was unmoved. "I win the War with forty," he said.[212]

In the end, 2,084,000 American soldiers—not the 3,760,000 called for by the 80-division plan or the nearly 5,000,000 requested by Pershing—reached France before the Great War ended.[213] No one anticipated the swiftness of the German collapse.

But it was coming, and with it a new panoply of problems. On October 6 the German government asked Woodrow Wilson for an armistice. By then the U.S. Food Administrator had new reasons for trepidation. The wheat glut of mid-September had been his first inkling of the future. As the American and Allied armies fought their way toward victory, surging surpluses of food at home were driving Hoover toward yet another emergency.

14

The Bittersweet Fruits of Success

I

IN early July 1918, as Hoover was preparing for his voyage to Europe, a recurrent problem arose again to vex him. Across America farmers were beginning to harvest wheat that they had planted earlier in the year, wheat which the government had pledged to buy at a guaranteed price. This guarantee, however, applied only to the present crop. Soon farmers would be planting winter wheat that would mature in 1919, and before they determined how much acreage they would sow, they would want to know the terms of any guarantee. Even before the 1918 harvest had been gathered, President Wilson was coming under pressure to issue a proclamation concerning the next one.[1]

To Hoover, the solution was obvious: the guaranteed minimum price for 1919 wheat should be precisely the same as in 1918. A higher price would encourage farmers to hoard their current wheat in the hope of selling it for more next year. Furthermore, Hoover believed that the existing price scale was sufficient to "secure the desired acreage" again.[2] The farmers, in other words, needed no extra inducement.

There was but one complication: at the moment, Congress was deadlocked over Senator Gore's attempt to legislate an increase in the price of wheat. The annual appropriation for the Department of Agriculture had been delayed in the process. Hoover therefore advised the President to say nothing about a 1919 price guarantee until Congress had completed all legislation relating to the Department of Agriculture. Otherwise, the chief executive would merely toss "another bone of contention" to the hostile Senate.[3]

In mid-July, while Hoover was en route for London, President Wilson successfully vetoed Gore's proposal, and the Congressional appropriation for the Department of Agriculture was finally released. The way was now clear for the White House to announce its policy for the coming year's harvest. At this point, Secretary of Agriculture Houston made a move that gave Hoover a headache. Houston agreed with Hoover that the government's guaranteed price should not be raised.[4] But the secretary suggested that before his department and the Food Administration made their final recommendation to the President, it might be wise to consult their Agricultural Advisory Committee.[5] Back in the winter, Hoover and Houston had created this body after agrarian leaders had complained that the Food Administration was not receiving enough input from "practical farmers." It would hardly be politic now to ignore this committee on an issue as critical and controversial as wheat prices. President Wilson agreed, and on August 5 the farm advisory panel duly convened in Washington.[6]

At the committee's first meetings in March and early April, Hoover had easily dominated the proceedings and had persuaded the group to endorse most of his policies. But now, with the Food Administrator out of the country, the assembled agrarians manifested signs of independence.[7] Despite a strongly worded cable from Hoover and the arguments of Julius Barnes and other Food Administration officials, the advisory committee immediately revealed a disposition to raise the guaranteed price of wheat for next year.[8] In a desperate bid to head off such an outcome, Barnes and his colleagues tried to get the committee to endorse a continuation of the 1918 price in exchange for a Food Administration promise to consider increasing the price later if an investigation proved that an increase was justified.[9] The farmers' panel refused to be tempted.[10] Instead, citing a variety of rising production costs on the farm, the committee voted unanimously on August 8 that the minimum price for the 1919 wheat crop should be increased by 20 cents per bushel.[11]

To Julius Barnes, the committee's decision was lunacy. The nation already had enough wheat, he exclaimed, thanks to a record acreage planted in response to last year's guaranteed minimum price. Why raise it? The existing guarantee was quite sufficient to produce the same acreage again. Furthermore, if the price of 1919 wheat was pegged at a higher level than for 1918 wheat, growers and dealers would have a powerful incentive to hold the current crop and sell it later under false pretenses at 1919 prices. The result would be massive fraud as well as dislocation of the grain markets. Nor was this all. Barnes warned that an advance in the American wheat price would compel a boost in the Canadian price as well—a double whammy for the European Allies. And he warned that at the first opportunity the Allies would import less expensive wheat from elsewhere, thereby leaving the United States with an overpriced, unmarketable surplus.[12]

Still aghast at the Agricultural Advisory Committee's recommendation, Barnes vented his alarm in a lengthy message to Hoover on August 10. "Irrational that organization farmer representatives should influence action involving commercial and political phases they cannot comprehend," he cabled.[13] Barnes did not have to worry about the Chief. From London Hoover cabled back that he was "strongly opposed on many grounds" to the advisory committee's recommendation. He urged the White House to defer action until he returned.[14]

When Hoover finally reached Washington in late August, he faced a delicate dilemma. Privately, of course, he was strenuously against raising the controlled price of wheat. But if he openly repudiated his own Agricultural Advisory Committee, he risked alienating further the wheat growers and their Congressional allies. Hoover also must have been aware that the Congressional election of 1918 was less than three months away and that across the wide wheat belt of America farmers were restless. How could he do what he wanted to do and minimize the political cost?

In a letter to the President on August 26, Hoover proffered his answer. He first warned that any guaranteed price for wheat for the coming year entailed "considerable national risk." After all, he argued, the United States would surely have enough wheat for its domestic needs. The only purpose of a guarantee, then, would be to obtain a surplus to send to the Allies. But if the war should end before next year's surplus could be exported, the Allies would immediately draw upon the vast and previously undeliverable stores of "much cheaper wheat" that had accumulated in the southern hemisphere. The U.S. government would then be trapped by its obligation to purchase wheat from its farmers at a guaranteed price that would be artificially high. All such wheat, of course, would be unsalable, except at a loss. Hoover calculated that in these circumstances the guaranteed price could cost the government up to half a billion dollars.

Nevertheless, the Food Administrator recommended retention of a guaranteed price for wheat. The arrangement did promote price stability, he said, and it did remove "speculation from our prime food." If wheat were now deregulated, the ensuing fluctuations in its price, coupled with the threat of competing supplies in Australia and South America, could subvert the "confidence" of American farmers and lead them "to relax their efforts in grain production." It could also cause speculation in breadstuffs, to the detriment of farmers and consumers alike.

Hoover therefore urged Wilson to guarantee the 1919 wheat crop "upon the present price basis" (in other words, no change), pending a "searching inquiry into the true costs of production" by an independent commission. If the results of the inquiry warranted an increase in the minimum price, the President could then increase it. Such a "preliminary guarantee," said Hoover, "and the possibility of an entirely fair readjustment of prices upward," should motivate farmers to maintain the desired level of planting.[15]

Lest there be any doubt about what Hoover did *not* want, later that day he passed along to the President a lengthy letter from Julius Barnes objecting vehemently to raising the guaranteed price of wheat from its current $2.26 basis to $2.46 per bushel, as the Agricultural Advisory Committee had proposed.[16]

Woodrow Wilson was immediately persuaded by his Food Administrator's strategic advice.[17] On September 2 the President issued an executive order fixing the 1919 wheat price guarantee at 1918 levels. The chief executive simultaneously announced (in a memorandum drafted by Hoover) that next spring he would appoint a "disinterested commission" to obtain the facts "by that time disclosed" concerning the increased cost of farm labor and supplies. Using these data, he would determine whether—and if so, by how much—to increase the 1919 wheat price "in order to maintain for the farmer a good return."[18] This was not at all the specific assured increase that Hoover's advisory committee wanted, but Wilson's promise conveyed at least the appearance of openmindedness.

It is not clear how seriously Hoover or Wilson construed this pledge. No commission was ever appointed. Moreover, Barnes, at least, believed that it was impossible to ascertain justly the "cost of production." The Department of Agriculture, he said, had tried in vain to do so and had consequently avoided the issue for several years.[19] According to Barnes, the commodity price index showed that the price of wheat had risen faster during the war than the price of anything that farmers had to buy.[20] With all of this Hoover probably agreed.

But whatever the future might hold, for the time being Hoover had outmaneuvered his opposition. His proposal of a "preliminary" guarantee plus a study commission was a clever delaying tactic, and it worked.[21]

So the deed was done. Barring any upward revision after inquiry, the government's price for wheat would remain frozen at current levels until June 1, 1920, the deadline for marketing of the 1919 harvest. Except for a slight adjustment in June 1918 to cover increased rail transportation costs, the designated price of wheat had not changed since August 1917, when President Wilson had implemented the recommendations of the Garfield committee. Hoover was gambling that the unvarying price was still high enough to induce wheat growers to maintain their current acreage.

The Food Administrator had reason to be hopeful. Despite the protests of agrarian leaders that wheat growers had been victimized by their government, out in the country farmers had been behaving differently. Julius Barnes was right. In response to the congressionally mandated guarantee of 1917, farmers had planted more wheat than ever before.[22] Call it patriotism; call it the lure of a guaranteed return on investment. The result was a harvest nearly 50 percent above that of 1917.[23]

Even before the colossal harvest was in, Herbert Hoover knew what was coming: a large and very early marketing of the crop.[24] Since the price was already known and invariant, farmers had no incentive to hold back. To the contrary, they might as well sell their product as speedily as possible and collect their reward. This was precisely what now happened. Beginning in August, and for three months thereafter, an unprecedented volume of fresh wheat descended on American's grain markets.[25]

By mid-September the country's storage facilities were bursting with wheat.[26] Even worse, the money to buy the crop was running out. Under the law, Hoover's Grain Corporation was obliged to purchase every bushel of grain offered to it, and at the guaranteed price. In the summer of 1918 it possessed $150,000,000 for this purpose—the maximum possible under the Lever Act. But as the tide of wheat surged off the farms in late summer, even this enormous sum was not enough. By mid-September the Grain Corporation had exhausted its capital and had begun to borrow heavily from banks.[27]

Hoover and Barnes knew that if the government were forced to suspend payments for wheat, the economic and political consequences would not be pretty.[28] During September, therefore, the Food Administrator scrambled for ways to avert the looming debacle. He asked for assistance from the Treasury Department and the War Finance Corporation (WFC).[29] But the WFC's lending power was limited by law; in the end, it loaned the Grain Corporation a mere $25,000,000.[30] On another front, Hoover's agency and the Railroad Administration announced in September that no one would be allowed to ship grain to eleven key markets without a permit, which must be approved by a government committee. It was a way of reducing congestion and probably the financial pressures as well.[31]

On October 1 Barnes delivered more bad news to the Chief. The Grain Corporation had now spent $250,000,000 on wheat purchases, including $100,000,000 borrowed from banks. Barnes estimated that he would need to borrow another $100,000,000 at least. Acutely conscious of his growing vulnerability, Barnes feared that some "untoward event" might cause "a general refusal of credit to us by the banks" and instantly compel the government to cease its required grain purchases, with disastrous results.[32]

What options remained open to Hoover? He could, of course, ask Congress for the substantial sums still needed to carry out the guarantee.[33] But if he did, "political demagogues" would undoubtedly make the appropriation contingent on an increase in the price of wheat. It was a trade Hoover was completely unwilling to make.[34]

At this point, stimulated by a suggestion from Barnes,[35] Hoover hit upon an alternative: Why not have the Allies buy a stock of American wheat in advance? If the U.S. Treasury could not directly provide him the $100,000,000 or more that he needed, it could loan the money to the Allies for the purpose of buying wheat immediately from the Grain Corporation. This would give Barnes the cash to weather the storm—and without having to involve the U.S. Congress.

In cables to London on October 1 and 2, Hoover broached his idea to his

European partners. He attributed his financial difficulties not to American farmers' flooding of the market but to the "curtailment" of his overseas transport. In his initial cablegram, Hoover asked the Allies to buy 50,000,000 bushels from the Grain Corporation for cash. In his second cablegram, he said he wanted the purchase to be a reserve, held in storage at American facilities until America's surplus was exhausted. The U.S. Treasury approved the transaction, he said, and would loan the Allies the requisite funds. Hoover was in a hurry and, as usual when he was in a hurry, he turned on the heat. The "whole wheat policy" of the American government was "directed solely to support [of the] Allies," he declared, "and I do not assume there will be any difficulties in securing this cooperation."[36]

By October 4 the Grain Corporation's plight—or perhaps just Hoover's willingness to exploit it—had intensified.[37] The Food Administrator calculated that the Grain Corporation's total liability for wheat purchases could reach $385,000,000, or $235,000,000 in excess of its exhausted capital.[38] Hoover was more convinced than ever that it was up to the Allies to bail him out. "The whole of this wheat operation is conducted" for their benefit, he asserted. "The guarantees have been issued purely to stimulate production" for them.[39]

Abandoning his proposals of October 1 and 2, Hoover now asked the Allies to buy 100,000,000 bushels of his wheat immediately and to carry it in storage in the United States until next spring. This reserve would be separate from *another* 100,000,000 bushels that would be shipped to the Allies in the meantime.[40] Hoover figured that by having the Allies buy and store 100,000,000 bushels now at their expense, he would reduce his Grain Corporation's own purchase-and-storage burden to manageable proportions.[41]

Secretary of the Treasury McAdoo immediately agreed to loan the Allies the money to effectuate the scheme.[42] In a separate cable to London, McAdoo asserted that American banks were being "loaded up with paper to carry the wheat which is being held back" because of the "lack of available shipping." America's "whole financial situation," he warned, was being "imperilled" by the Allies' "failure to take their share of the wheat." This was, of course, a highly tendentious explanation of the peril; the Allies were not responsible for the shipping crunch. But McAdoo, echoing Hoover, wanted results. The Treasury Secretary requested an answer to his cable that same day. When it came to high-pressure salesmanship, he could be nearly as peremptory as the Food Administrator.[43]

The sudden barrage of cables from Washington startled London. While the French and the Italians apparently had no objections to Hoover's scheme, the British reacted tepidly. The British Treasury was reluctantly willing to borrow money from the United States in order to buy 50,000,000 bushels of American wheat immediately (Hoover's initial proposal).[44] But Hoover's subsequent proposal for a massive wheat *reserve*, to be stored for months at Allied expense in American facilities, was quite another matter. The British already owned an enormous reserve of wheat in Australia—wheat that they currently lacked the ships to transport. Why, they wondered, should they accumulate still more untransportable wheat?[45]

It was not the present dearth of shipping, however, that really concerned the British. It was a question becoming more acute with each day's favorable battle reports from France: What if the war should end before next summer? At that point, presumably, the world's shipping shortage would end. Why, therefore, should the British tie themselves down now to a long-term wheat deal with Hoover when they might soon be able to draw upon more than 2,000,000 tons of wheat already purchased and waiting for them in Australia?[46]

Not surprisingly, then, the British response to Hoover's 100,000,000 bushel contract proposal was conditional. British Treasury officials insisted that the Allies' Wheat Executive must be free to resell the wheat anywhere it liked, if necessary. The British also demanded that the contract be voided for any part of the 100,000,000 bushels not actually shipped to Europe by mid-1919.[47] The British were determined not to get stuck with a mountain of unwanted American wheat.[48]

For Hoover, this was not good enough. On October 11 he and the Wheat Executive's representative in New York concluded their own agreement, which the authorities in London eventually approved. Under its terms, the Wheat Executive agreed to buy 100,000,000 bushels of wheat from Hoover's Grain Corporation at a provisional price of $2.00 per bushel. (The final price, reflecting carrying costs, would be decided at time of shipment.) This entire supply would remain in storage in the United States until February 1919; after that, the buyer would be free to ship it abroad. The Wheat Executive promised not to resell this wheat to anyone other than the Allies or the Grain Corporation. (Hoover evidently did not want the Allies to dump such wheat later on the world's markets, to the possibly injury of the United States.) In exchange, the Grain Corporation pledged to buy back, if asked, any of the 100,000,000 bushels that had not actually been dispatched to Europe by September 1, 1919.[49]

Not long afterward, the U.S. Treasury duly released $200,000,000 to the Allies to make the purchase. Buoyed by this roundabout infusion of funding, the Grain Corporation managed to avoid financial disaster.[50]

Despite this outcome, Hoover could not be pleased. The Allies had agreed to buy 100,000,000 bushels of wheat *if it were actually shipped by the following September*. Whatever the Allies did not ship, the Americans must repurchase. Hoover had no assurance that the Allies would ever complete the transaction, especially if cheaper Australian wheat became accessible in the meantime. Next September he might be faced with the awkward necessity of buying back a substantial part of the wheat that he thought he had sold.

By October 16 Hoover was in an angry mood. Privately, he accused the British of reacting with "bad grace" to a sale "solely in the interest of the

Allies." In fact, he told an associate, the British had always displayed the attitude "that they are being extremely kind and condescending to us in all matters connected with acceptance of foodstuffs, which we must be extremely glad to sell to them." The Food Administrator was not going to put up with this any longer.

> Hereafter I think we shall take the attitude that we wish to export *nothing* and that whatever they get is a favour and that they must get it on our terms or do without. I do not think anyone is more possessed than myself with the desire to handle the whole food problem with broadmindedness and generosity, but the "down east Yankee" attitude which they have in these matters gives me no comfortable feeling.

On all sorts of issues, he claimed, the British had engaged in "the very lowest form of merchant trading and I am getting very weary of it all."[51]

And if the British were beginning to ponder the implications of any early peace, so, too, was the U.S. Food Administrator. On October 16, with Germany already seeking an armistice, Hoover told his chief representative in Europe that he wished "to take no commitments to the Allies for foodstuffs" after the end of hostilities. "I am convinced that we will have to feed the Central Empires [Germany and Austria-Hungary] if we are to preserve anything like stability of any government throughout the winter, and that we must be in position to deal justly with all people." Hoover was now sorry that his domestic financial problems had forced him to sell 100,000,000 bushels to the Allies. He would have been "glad," he said, "to hold it out in order that we might be in position to doll [sic] out foodstuffs to the entire world, as an implement to enforce justice all the way round."[52]

Still annoyed at the British, Hoover now attempted to negotiate a second agreement that, among other things, would nail down the Allied purchase of 100,000,000 bushels of grain and fix the price. Immediately he ran into trouble. For some time the Grain Corporation had been charging neutral countries $17.00 per barrel for flour, compared to $12.00 per barrel for the Allies. Hoover justified this practice with the argument that the neutrals were charging exorbitant prices for their shipping. He used this profit to help cover the expenses of his Grain Corporation.[53] Here, probably, was one reason why he did not want the Allies to have the right to resell the 100,000,000 bushels to neutral countries. It could undercut American's flour sales in the same market.

The Wheat Executive's agent in New York now contended that America's profits from grain sales to neutrals should be used to cover the *Allies'* cost of carrying American grain. Hoover was outraged:

> This would simply mean that we are presenting them [the Allies] with money and I propose that every transaction in grain shall stand on its own

foundation, pay its own cost of handling and that the Allies shall pay this cost. If they do not wish to accede to this proposed working arrangement, our alternative is that we will make a price on all grains in such dimensions as will cover the issues as we are endeavouring to obtain under this memorandum, and will do so without regard to their feelings.[54]

For the next several weeks—and then months—Hoover and his colleagues labored to replace the initial wheat agreement of October with a more favorable and ironclad contract. It was to be an embittering struggle.[55] But at least for the moment the Food Administrator could take comfort in the knowledge that the effects of his price support system had not been politically ruinous. One way or another, he had paid his nation's farmers for their wheat.

II

THE U.S. Food Administrator's other great experiment with price incentives was not so successful or so lucky. In the autumn of 1918 it nearly engulfed him in a debacle.

For some months Hoover had been casting a nervous eye over the nation's growing population of hogs. America was overrun with pigs, he had told a British audience in July, even more than Australia was overrun with rabbits.[56] In response to his exhortations and financial incentives of the previous autumn, American farmers had begun to breed hogs in record numbers.

Late in the spring, Hoover had urged the British government to import much more American pork in the coming months, both to dispose of his present surplus and to absorb the surplus looming on the horizon. The British had agreed to take increased amounts, though not enough to satisfy Hoover.[57] The British explained that the price of Hoover's pork was so high that there was no way their populace would consume all that he offered.[58] As the summer wore on, the problem worsened. Unable to dispose of its imported pork at once, the British government was compelled to find storage. Because of a shortage of refrigeration, the government had to salt the pork heavily, rendering it even more unattractive to British palates. To make matters worse, some of the arriving products were unfamiliar cuts and had deteriorated during long and delayed voyages across the Atlantic. The upshot was that domestic British demand did not keep pace with Hoover's supply. By the end of the summer he had nearly saturated the British market for his pork.[59]

Despite British complaints at his high prices, Hoover refused to bend. The Allies, he insisted, must pay the same price for American food as American consumers and the U.S. government did. He declared that the high American cost of living was the Allies' fault. They had caused it by their "wildly foolish and competitive bidding" for American goods in the three years before the United States entered the war.[60] But whatever the cause of the disparity in consumer price levels between the New World and the Old, Hoover in mid-1918 believed he had no choice. If the price of American exports seemed high, this was the ineluctable consequence of his offering strong financial incentives to American farmers to boost their production for the Allies' own benefit.[61] It seemed not to occur to Hoover that the U.S. government might buy food from its farmers and resell it abroad at a loss. Hoover was running the Food Administration on business principles and was adamant that Allied purchases must cover his costs.

It was not the residue of processed pork that most concerned Hoover by late summer, however. It was the coming "harvest" of live hogs that had been bred in the previous winter and early spring. These would shortly enter the market under the terms of the grand bargain that he had struck with farmers and the meat-packing industry in late 1917. In order to stimulate hog production, he had prevailed upon the packers to offer farmers a minimum average of $15.50 per hundredweight for live hogs. He had also promised to do his best to manipulate the market in such a way that for each one hundred pounds of hogs bred in early 1918 farmers would receive a price equal to the average cost of thirteen bushels of corn fed into them. This was the so-called ratio of 13 to 1. To induce the meat packers (who would actually do the buying) to pay this price, Hoover offered them a guaranteed export market: the meat purchases, which he controlled, for the Allies, the U.S. Army, and the Belgian relief. Hoover promised to set the prices for these purchase orders sufficiently high to enable the packers to make a profit after paying the hog breeders according to the 13 to 1 ratio.

Although Hoover's scheme was not legally binding, he had nevertheless taken a gamble, and he knew it. For his policy to work, the price of live hogs could not rise too far above $15.50. Otherwise the packers might be unable to market their own products at a profit to resistant consumers. Hoover could always peg the export price at a level certain to bring the packers a profit—*if the Allies thereupon bought at this price*. But by the summer of 1918 the British, at least, were balking. Like it or not (and Hoover did not like it at all), he had been forced by pressure from farm groups to tie his policy to a formula based on research by Henry C. Wallace. But what if complications occurred? What if the price of corn and / or hogs should soar?

In the late summer of 1918 Hoover's worst fears began to materialize. Instead of falling (as the Food Administration no doubt hoped),[62] the price of corn on the futures market rose to $1.67 3/8 per bushel in mid-August and stayed well above $1.50 through much of September.[63] It did not take a mathematical wizard to draw the inference. At the beginning of September, *Wallaces' Farmer* announced that on the basis of the 13 to 1 ratio which the government had adopted, the price of hogs at Chicago in October should top $20.00 per hundred pounds: an all-time record.[64]

Why was the price of corn so stubbornly high? For one thing, the impending crop had been seriously damaged by heat and drought.[65] But another factor was probably more influential: in 1918 America's farmers reduced their planting of corn by more than 12,000,000 acres, while increasing their planting of wheat by more than 14,000,000 acres.[66] The lure of a guaranteed price for wheat caused the diversion. While Hoover was anxious to secure more wheat, the prospective lower harvest of corn presaged high corn prices, just as he was about to implement the 13 to 1 corn-to-hog ratio.

For the consumer-conscious Food Administrator, this was a most unwelcome development. Nor was it the only unintended consequence of his interventionism. At the beginning of July 1918 the price of live hogs also began to climb. During August and early September, the average price in Chicago reached the giddy level of $19.00 per hundred pounds, far above the floor of $15.50 established nearly a year before.[67] Here, too, governmental policy had caused complications. Back in June, in the face of a shortage of beef for home consumption, Hoover had publicly summoned the American people to switch to pork.[68] Millions of patriotic households apparently did so. The sudden surge in consumer demand for bacon, pork, and ham sent hog prices soaring.[69]

By mid-September the price of hogs had reached unprecedented levels, and the Food Administration was increasingly alarmed. The meat packers would never be able to pass along such prices to the Allies, and sooner or later American buyers would rebel as well. If the packers bought the hogs anyway and converted them to products placed temporarily in cold storage, in all likelihood the packers would have to dispose of the accumulation later at a terrific loss. How long would the Big Five and their smaller brethren put up with that?

Yet Hoover's options were distinctly unpleasant. If he intervened again and urged his countrymen to eat *less* pork (in order to reduce the demand and thus tame the price), he stood to be accused of "too much changeability of plan and purpose."[70] The nation's hog producers would also loudly object. But if he let the market adjust itself, it would eventually crash, destroying his stabilization mechanisms in the process.[71] Hoover knew that if the packers refused to buy more hogs at current prices, farmers would soon be driven to settle for less. The market would plummet, and hog producers would be enraged. This was Hoover's great fear: that the packers in desperation would bargain the market price precipitously downwards, even below the $15.50 floor he had pledged to try to maintain. His 13 to 1 promise—and his reputation—would be in tatters.

On September 16 the average price of hogs in Chicago passed $20.00, the highest figure ever recorded.[72] Three days later it nearly reached $21.00 and appeared to Hoover to be threatening to go to $25.00.[73] Desperate to restrain the spiraling market, Hoover cabled London for help. On September 19 he asked the Allies to postpone their October orders for American hog products until November and to defer additional orders for another month or six weeks. By thus abruptly shrinking the export demand, he hoped to rein in the runaway price.[74]

Risky as his maneuver was, it did have one political advantage. When the hog market slumped, Hoover could always put the onus on the Allies. If the Food Administrator dared not ask American consumers to refrain from eating pork,[75] he had less hesitation about asking the Allies.

The British government was amenable to a temporary postponement of its American orders, and the Food Administration proceeded to "choke" the export demand.[76] Although the head of Hoover's meat division later claimed that the deliberate withholding of Allied orders helped to break the "upward tide" in the market,[77] the reversal was not instantaneous. The price of hogs in Chicago continued to hover around $20.00 and averaged $19.65 for the month of September.[78]

Even before turning to the Allies for assistance, Hoover had begun to explore another path out of the deepening morass. Early in September he decided to bring the livestock subcommittee of his Agricultural Advisory Committee to Washington to "advise on hog questions."[79] Out in Des Moines, Henry C. Wallace sensed trouble. There were only two things to be done, he responded: announce at once that the 13 to 1 ratio would be implemented, and make the same guarantee for next year.[80]

Hoover had no such intention. On September 25 his livestock subcommittee and a small number of invited hog producers (but not Wallace)[81] gathered in Washington. The Food Administrator bluntly informed them that application of the 13 to 1 formula on the basis of Chicago prices was out of the question. It would mean $21.00 for hogs, he said—a figure impossible for the Food Administration to sustain. The price of hogs in October, he announced, must not exceed $20.00 per hundredweight.[82] Hoover's new meat division head, F. S. Snyder, was equally emphatic. A "temporary extreme price" for hogs, Snyder warned, would inevitably lead to a reaction, a "smash in the market," and a price of hogs that would go down, down, down.[83]

Hoover's startling declarations now ran up against a problem: How could he square his new attitude with the solemn assurances of the Food Administration to hog producers a year before? In the autumn of 1917, a commission which he had appointed had told him that to restore the nation's supply of hogs to normal levels, the ratio between the value of corn and the value of hogs should be about 13 to 1. The commission had explicitly recommended using the Chicago price of corn and hogs as the basis for any price stabilization. In response to this report, Hoover's meat division chief at the time, Joseph Cotton, had made a public declaration with Hoover's approval:

> Therefore, as to the hogs farrowed next spring [1918], we will try to stabilize the price so that the farmer can count on getting for each 100 pounds

of hog ready for market, thirteen times the average cost per bushel of the corn fed into the hogs.

Cotton qualified his statement by warning that it was neither "a guarantee backed by money" nor "a promise by the packers." It was a declaration of intent.[84] Or, as Hoover later remarked, "a sort of informal assurance."[85] Still, it was a pledge of best effort by the U.S. government itself.

Cotton's official announcement, however, was not as unequivocal as it appeared. How, precisely, would the government determine "the average cost per bushel of corn fed into the hogs"? What did 13 to 1 really mean? Unlike Hoover's study commission, neither he nor Cotton explicitly committed themselves to a Chicago-based price ratio. Years later Cotton claimed that his silence on this point had been deliberate. He had not wanted, he said, to tie Food Administration policy to a single market that might prove difficult to control.[86] Cotton also indicated that his decision on this point was clear at the time to the leading advocate of the corn-hog ratio, Henry C. Wallace.[87] It was not, however, equally clear to the readers of the announcement.

Cotton's calculated ambiguity did not escape the notice of *Wallaces' Farmer*. In the early summer of 1918 the journal pointedly noted that the Food Administration still had not disclosed which corn values it would use in calculating the ratio.[88] But Wallace's uneasiness was undoubtedly exceptional. Since Hoover's study commission had expressly recommended using Chicago prices, and since Cotton had not expressly rejected its advice, thousands of farmers evidently assumed that when the time came to sell their fattened hogs, they would be compensated according to Chicago market quotations. It was a plausible presumption.

It was not, however, Hoover's presumption, as he made plain on September 25, 1918 to his livestock advisory panel. Apparently for the first time, he disclosed that the Food Administration had never intended to carry out the ratio on the basis of Chicago prices. Instead, he now proposed to work out the formula using the cost of each bushel of corn *on the farm*—a very literal reading of his pledge indeed. The livestock subcommittee objected strenuously to this interpretation. In the end, in the face of what one member of the subcommittee considered a virtual ultimatum by the Food Administration, the advisory group and Hoover compromised. The subcommittee agreed to recommend that in setting the price of hogs, the "average cost per bushel of corn" should be a weighted average of the *farm value* of corn, or its selling price at local railroad stations, in the eight leading corn- and hog-producing states. This would be more remunerative to the farmers than Hoover's original proposal. But since the "farm value" of corn was 20 cents per bushel less than the Chicago price, it meant that farmers would receive $2.60 less for each one hundred pounds of hogs than they would have gotten if an all-Chicago ratio had been used. By construing his 13 to 1 promise of a year ago in this way, Hoover had deftly reduced the amount of money that packers would be expected to pay for live hogs.[89]

For the month just ahead, Hoover's clarified formula would yield hog prices of $18.50 per hundredweight at Chicago, a dramatic decline from existing market quotations and an even more dramatic departure from the 13 to 1 formula as farmers had understood it. But Hoover told his subcommittee that $18.50 was the best he could accomplish under the circumstances.[90] Unable or unwilling to challenge him, the subcommittee agreed to recommend $18.50 as the "fair price interpretation of the ratio" for October.[91] On only one point did the panel hold out. Worried by the specter of a sudden collapse of the hog market, it urged Hoover to announce his intention to maintain a minimum price of $15.50 for the rest of the war.[92]

Late on September 25 the Food Administration issued a press release containing the livestock subcommittee's report.[93] Nowhere did the press release mention that most of the panel's recommendations had arisen in response to heavy pressure from Hoover himself. The Food Administrator had gotten what he wanted: a seemingly independent request by a group of representative hog producers for a change in policy that he had largely predetermined.

Having obtained his protective document from his farmer-advisers, Hoover now proceeded to exploit it. A few days later, he published his response in the form of a letter to the chairman of his Agricultural Advisory Committee. In it Hoover warmly thanked the livestock subcommittee for its "helpful and intelligent recommendations" and once again concealed his role in extracting most of them. With President Wilson's approval, he now promised to try to extend the existing $15.50 minimum to hogs farrowed in the autumn of 1918. He also pledged to try to stabilize hog prices in accordance with the subcommittee's interpretation of the 13 to 1 formula. In a transparent bid to deflect agrarian criticism, he noted that the new "farm value" standard for corn would remunerate hog producers more than the "cost of corn" standard that (he implied) had been his original commitment. Even so, he said, he was not "disposed to quarrel with just profits to the farmer. . . ." Hoover said nothing about his repudiation of the still more profitable Chicago basis of calculating prices.[94]

The Food Administration, of course, had no money of its own to enforce the $15.50 minimum or the 13 to 1 formula. It could only effect its objectives by persuading the meat packers to buy hogs from the farmers at the government's prescribed prices. To ensure the packers' compliance, Hoover convened a conference of representatives of forty-five packing firms at the Food Administration's offices on October 3. To the assembled executives he explained his plan and appealed for support.[95]

The packers immediately objected. Hoover's target price of $18.50 for October hogs was too high, they said. The foreign price for their own products was too low, and domestic demand was now too weak, to enable them to make a profit on this basis. Many packers had deep reservations about the workability of the 13 to 1 formula. During the day-long meeting they tried to ditch it altogether in favor only of a $15.50 minimum.

For Hoover and F. S. Snyder, such a wholesale breach of the Food Administration's promise to the hog producers was "manifestly impossible." The average price of hogs in October, said Snyder, must "correspond" to past Food Administration assurances, and that price, he insisted, must be $18.50. Throughout the day, he used both the carrot and the stick to bring the stiff-necked packers into line. He told them that the newly interpreted 13 to 1 ratio put matters "upon a very much more favorable basis." He told them that the Food Administration wanted the market price of hogs to decline steadily and rapidly, down to "the price which we have been after for some time." He promised that, if the packers cooperated, the Food Administration would place export orders for their products at prices that would guarantee the packers a profit. He asserted that the government could dispose of one half of all packer output in this way—surely enough to enable them to pull through. When the packing executives still showed signs of resistance, he warned them that it was in their interest to protect the hog producers. He did not need to explain that the packers were the most hated industry in the country and that their postwar future was in doubt.[96]

At the end of the day the packers grudgingly capitulated. In a formal letter to the Food Administration, they warned that droves of hogs would soon be deluging the stockyards and that it would be exceedingly difficult to maintain the market price that Hoover and his associates demanded. Moreover, the 13 to 1 plan was fraught with difficulty. Nevertheless, the packers pledged to do their best to pay a minimum of $15.50 per hundredweight for average droves during the heavy packing season. And they agreed to pay a "minimum average" of $18 per hundredweight in October.[97] This was 50 cents less than Hoover had just requested, but in a concession to the industry the Food Administrator acquiesced. According to Hoover, the "minimum average" would yield "substantially the same result" and be "more practical in operation."[98] It was "easier," he said, "to work a minimum than an average."[99] It was a debatable rationale for diluting the 13 to 1 ratio still further.

Although it was now obvious that the government and the packers were about to engineer a controlled slide in the hog market, Hoover seemed anxious to disguise their objective. At his request the packers modified some of the language of their pledge in order to make it more suitable for release as a public document. The packers had originally promised that "in order to stabilize the market" they would "endeavor not to lower hogs too rapidly." In its revised form this became a promise to "endeavor to hold the usually sharp decline to a gradual change."[100] In this way the packers avoided admitting their intent to cause a sharp decline with Hoover's blessing.

With the packers now on board, Hoover released the Allied purchasing orders that he had withheld from the market in late September. For the month of October the Food Administration let out export contracts for 130,000,000 pounds of pork products to fifty participating packing companies. Hoover saw to it that the price the Allies paid for these products was high enough to permit the packers to buy hogs for slaughter on the basis of his newly defined 13 to 1 ratio.[101]

A few days after the packers' meeting in Washington, their pledge to Hoover and his decision concerning the 13 to 1 ratio appeared in the press—and evoked an explosion in the corn belt.[102] Henry C. Wallace, who had sensed what was coming, was livid.[103] Wallace conceded that the Food Administration in 1917 had not explicitly promised to link its hog policy to "the value of No. 2 corn on the Chicago market." But that, he now asserted, had been "clearly implied, because the whole theory [of the ratio] is based on that assumption."[104] In a scathing editorial on October 11, *Wallaces' Farmer* accused the Food Administration of repudiating a perfectly plain, "fair-and-square business deal" with the farmer. The Food Administration was altering "the terms of the contract to suit its own notion" after the farmer had carried out the terms "in good faith." "When the plan was adopted, the price of No. 2 corn at Chicago was taken, and the price of hogs at Chicago. Now it is proposed that instead of taking the price of corn at Chicago, the price will be taken on the farm." The cost of this change to hog producers, said Wallace, would be $5 to $10 million during October alone.[105]

Wallace was not the only outraged agrarian. The *Prairie Farmer* accused the Food Administration of surrendering to the packers and of throwing the 13 to 1 policy overboard.[106] In Iowa, the Corn Belt Meat Producers' Association demanded that the corn-hog ratio be "carried out in good faith and in accordance with the original intent." If there were now too many marketable hogs in response to the Food Administrator's earlier pleas, and if the Administration could not keep its prior promise, then the agency should frankly say so and stop agitating for increased production of hogs.[107] In Illinois, the Agricultural War Board complained that the government's announced price for hogs in October was at least $1.00 below what it should be. It charged that the Food Administration's failure explicitly to reaffirm the 13 to 1 ratio was a breach of faith.[108]

To his critics, Hoover's interpretation of the meaning of the ratio was infuriating. Nearly as aggravating was the method he now used to determine the "farm value" of corn fed into marketed hogs. In its report on September 25, his livestock subcommittee had urged him to compile a weighted average of corn prices for the five months preceding marketing at various locations in "the eight leading hog and corn producing states." But which *were* the eight leading hog- and corn-producing states? Instead of simply looking at production figures, Hoover introduced other, less obvious criteria. As a result, he came up with a list of states that included South Dakota and Minnesota yet excluded Kansas, whose corn and hog output dwarfed that of these two states.[109]

Why had Hoover passed over Kansas? To his critics, the answer was simple. In mid- to late 1918, the "farm value" of corn in Kansas was 20 cents per bushel higher than it was in Minnesota and South Dakota. The exclusion of Kansas from the database—and the inclusion of the two less expensive states—thus had the effect of lowering the government's average price for corn and hence the price that would have to be paid for hogs. All this, in the eyes of Wallace, was no happenstance. It was an act of statistical manipulation that permitted Hoover to drive down the price of hogs while pretending that he was fulfilling his 13 to 1 commitment.[110]

Stung by the charges of betrayal coming out of the heartland, Hoover fought back. In a telegram to several of his state food administrators on October 18, he denounced as "wholly unwarranted" the editorial assault upon him by Wallace a week earlier. Hoover asserted that it was his advisory committee, together with invited hog producers, that had "unanimously recommended" in late September the "basis of calculation" now being used to carry out the 13 to 1 ratio. The Food Administration, he insisted, was merely implementing "these recommendations of the farmers themselves." While Hoover was eager to disseminate his defense, he advised his state food administrators to avoid tangling with Wallace. According to Hoover, Wallace "simply represents the [Gifford] Pinchot group in its campaign among farmers to attack the government for political purposes."[111]

With the Agricultural War Board in Illinois Hoover was equally unyielding. The board's interpretation of the 13 to 1 formula, he declared, was "entirely contrary to the promise made by the Food Administration and even of the interpretation given by the Producers in Conference last month in Washington. I cannot entertain the suggestion of bad faith of this administration nor do I believe such a suggestion will be entertained by any single one of the gentlemen who have attended the conference. . . ."[112] Once again, he was using his advisory committee as a shield.

For the embattled Food Administrator, open attacks on his integrity were bad enough. Even worse—and more dangerous—was the behavior of the corn and hog markets. Hoover had undoubtedly hoped that his 130,000,000 pounds of export orders would be the great stabilizer, enabling the packers to purchase hogs at a "fair" price to producers.[113] Even assuming that the packers kept their promise, Hoover's plan depended on the lack of surprises. There was one factor in particular that he had not anticipated: the response of the angry hog producers themselves.

Early in October a tide of live hogs began to descend upon the stockyards of the Middle West. By mid-month the run had become a stampede. Hogs—hogs by the tens of thousands—jammed the markets in record and near-record numbers for that month of the year.[114]

As hog receipts soared, prices tumbled, adding further fuel to the panic. On October 1 the average price of hogs in Chicago was $19.50. Barely three weeks later it had plummeted below $16.00.[115] The average price for the month was only about $17.50—50 cents less than the minimum the packers had said they would try to sustain.[116]

As bitter farmers pondered their vanished profits, a question rankled: Why? Why the sudden tumble in prices? Why the flood of hogs onto the market in the first place—a flood more than 25 percent larger than in 1917?[117] Here another factor entered the picture, or so Hoover soon and insistently asserted: in early autumn, the price of corn suddenly plunged. Late in September, Germany's ally Bulgaria surrendered to the Allies. From then on, rumors of an early peace buffeted the American grain markets. On September 26 the price of corn in Chicago (for October delivery) was more than $1.47 per bushel; only two weeks later, it had sunk to $1.13½.[118] Traders knew that if the war should now end quickly, a bottled-up surplus of Argentine corn, which was selling for only 63 cents per bushel, would enter the world market and depress the price.[119]

As the turmoil in the hog markets worsened, Hoover ascribed the producers' panic to the falling price of corn. The peace negotiations with Germany had alarmed owners of corn, he said, and thereupon precipitated a drop of 30–40 cents per bushel. The decline in corn had in turn frightened hog raisers, who (he said) feared that peace would send hog prices tumbling, too. Furthermore, since hog prices were dependent on corn prices under his 13 to 1 plan, the plummeting value of corn foretold "a continuously falling price of hogs." In anticipation of lower hog prices to come, the producers had panicked and flooded the market with their animals.[120]

Hoover's explanation was plausible. It also absolved him of any responsibility for the battering that hog growers were taking in the market. If anyone was to blame, he seemed to suggest, it was the farmers themselves for "overshipping" their product.[121]

The Food Administrator's enemies had another explanation for the farmers' panic. According to Wallace, the price of hogs began to fall in late September when word circulated that Hoover did not intend to carry out his original 13 to 1 promise in good faith. Faced with the likelihood of lower prices, farmers had reacted by attempting to cut their losses by cashing in on their hogs as fast as they could.[122] It was not farmers who broke the price, said Wallace. The panic was the direct result of Hoover's September meeting with his livestock subcommittee, shortly after which Hoover's intent to evade his promise became known.[123]

Who was right? Certainly Hoover was largely correct about corn. The increasing possibility of an early peace triggered the break in the corn market; knowledgeable financial observers agreed about that.[124] Hoover was also correct that a fall in corn would eventually be reflected in lower hog prices under the 13 to 1 policy. But Wallace was at least partly right about hogs. Farmers did not have to ponder the future price of hogs under the ratio as the price of corn slid downward; they need only reflect upon the price of hogs right now. On the basis of Chicago corn values, they should have received more than $21.00 per hundredweight for their hogs in October. Instead, they were promised an "average minimum" of $18.00 and got even less. Under the circumstances, it was not surprising that many farmers rushed their animals to the stockyards in order to make as much money as they could. The "average minimum," after all, was valid only for October. Who knew where it would go after that?[125]

Ironically, one of the participants in Hoover's conference with the packers on October 3 had speculated that this would be the effect of the Food Administration's plan. If farmers concluded that the government intended to keep lowering the hog price, why should they hold onto hogs and fatten them? Why not sell them immediately at a better price?[126] Hoover and his associates apparently tried to counter this possibility by announcing a target price for October only and by saying nothing publicly about their intention for the months ahead.[127] But the packers' very pledge to maintain a minimum price of $15.50 (when the price was still well above that figure) implied that *somebody* anticipated that hog prices would continue to fall.[128] It was not just the price of corn or the prospects of peace which unsettled farmers in October 1918. It was the thrust of the Food Administration's own policy.

Whatever the reasons for the panic, in mid-October Hoover tried to contain it. If falling corn was causing jittery farmers to dump their hogs (as he claimed), perhaps he could check the tide by shoring up the price of corn. On October 14 he had his Grain Corporation openly purchase "a large amount of corn" for export on the Chicago market. The price per bushel shot up 10 cents within minutes.[129] Ten years later, during Hoover's successful campaign for President, a former Chicago Board of Trade official would assert that Hoover's dramatic intervention had saved the corn market from collapse and had saved thousands of American farmers from ruin.[130] The price of corn did indeed rebound significantly for ten days.[131] Farmers, at least briefly, were encouraged.[132]

The next day, October 15, Hoover tried a similar maneuver on the hog front. He informed four hundred packing firms that they must send 2,600,000 tons of meats and fats to the U.S. Army, the Allies, and neutrals by next July 1. He said that it would mean an increase of more than 1,000,000 tons above shipments in 1917–18.[133] Despite this bullish assessment of the industry's prospects, the demoralization of the hog market intensified. A wave of virulent influenza added to the havoc by reducing the packers' work force by 25 percent.[134] By October 24 the packing houses were—or said they were—overwhelmed.[135] That day, hog prices in Chicago fell steeply to $15.85, a decline of $1.80 in a single week.[136]

By now the packers were protesting that they lacked the plant capacity to continue to handle such an avalanche.[137] Nor, they claimed, could they hope to "find a market" for the resultant increase in their output.[138] Certainly not—they undoubtedly felt—if they had to charge prices reflecting Hoover's minimum for their raw materials. On the other side of the political divide, a leading farm journal wondered why, if the packers were so surfeited in October, they did not return live hogs to the countryside. Why did someone not try to "stay the run" by some means other than slashing prices? Why did not the Food Administration urge farmers to hold back their hogs?[139]

Hoover, too, was distressed. In a long letter on October 24 to the chairman of his Agricultural Advisory Committee—a letter no doubt intended "for the record"—he defended his policies and blamed his difficulties on unforeseeable causes: over-marketing by panicky farmers in response to peace rumors and the falling price of corn. Hoover insisted that his "one desire" was "to do justice to the producer," and that his "whole plan" of a few weeks before had been "designed purely for this purpose." He declared that he was prepared to allocate export orders for 170,000,000 pounds of pork products in November on a basis commensurate with the 13 to 1 ratio. But, he warned, if hog producers continued to "flood the market," he did not think that even this arrangement would "assure any stability to price." In short, success was up to the farmers. The key was normal marketing and an end to "the panic among producers."[140]

It was against this backdrop that the livestock subcommittee of Hoover's Agricultural Advisory Committee, and a committee of packers' representatives, came to Washington for a joint meeting in late October. In agreeing earlier in the month to uphold a "minimum average" of $18.00 per hundredweight, the packers had indicated that this price would apply to October receipts only and had requested a separate conference to determine policies for after that.[141] The packers had also asked that the farmers' representatives attend this next meeting. It was a suggestion more than agreeable to Hoover, who told certain farm advisers that he wanted hog producers present as a counterweight to the unhappy packing house leaders.[142] Hoover also undoubtedly realized that if agrarian representatives participated in a meeting in which price levels were changed and huge export contracts were determined, such individuals could provide valuable political cover for him in the corn and hog belt.[143]

The Food Administrator therefore asked the chairman of his Agricultural Advisory Committee to supply the names of those hog producers who had been most "constructive" at the September meeting which defined the 13 to 1 ratio.[144] Hoover wanted these men back. He did not want any obstreperous rebels.

In the end, he did not have to worry. On October 25, after three days of conferences in an atmosphere of crisis, the Food Administration, the packers, and the livestock subcommittee of Hoover's Agricultural Advisory Committee agreed to abandon the 13 to 1 formula altogether. The agrarian representatives, led by Professor Evvard of Iowa State College, had become convinced that implementation of the vaunted ratio on the basis of Chicago prices was utterly impossible and that the best alternative was to discard it completely. A year before, John Evvard had chaired the commission that had recommended 13 to 1 (Chicago basis) to Joseph Cotton. Now, despite his past disagreements with Hoover's "methods," Evvard declared his "utmost faith" in the Food Administrator; indeed, "more faith now than I have ever had."[145]

What had turned Evvard around? Realization, he said, that twenty-dollar hogs were impossible under present market conditions for hog products, in Europe as well as at home. According to Evvard, Allied buyers had been adamantly opposed even to paying $17.50 for hogs and had yielded only after Hoover had threatened to go over their heads to the Allied heads of government.[146]

It is not clear whether Hoover truly threatened the Allied buying agency or whether he merely staged a "confrontation" with it for the benefit of his livestock subcommittee. The Food Administrator was exceedingly adept at playing off one faction against another. One point, however, was incontestable: the 13 to 1 formula was dead.

In its place, the packers participating in the foreign export trade pledged to pay an average "daily minimum" of $17.50 per hundredweight for live hogs marketed in November.[147] In no case (except unsuitable animals known as "throw-outs") would the packers buy hogs for less than $16.50. The packers' committee agreed to these terms after working out a detailed price schedule for November export allotments with the Food Administration. The conferring parties also decided jointly to determine future prices for export orders on a month-by-month basis, as they had just done. In effect, having abandoned the free market and the corn-to-hog ratio device, Hoover had settled for ad hoc monthly price-fixing by a committee.[148]

The Food Administrator immediately announced the new policy and strove to put the best face possible upon it. In a seven-page press release, his agency contended that "uncontrollable factors" (notably the fall in corn prices and the increasing talk of peace) had caused the hog panic and necessitated "an entire alteration in the plans of price stabilization." Hoover contended that the new price plan "should work out close to $18.00 average"—in other words, not so far from October's levels. He appointed a committee to execute the plan in the various hog markets and asked independent "commission men" not to undercut the established minimum price. He asserted that the postwar demand for pork products should increase. Hence there was no need to take alarm at the possibility of peace. And, yet again, his agency joined in pledging to make "every possible effort" to sustain "a live hog price commensurate with swine production costs and reasonable selling values."[149]

But Hoover did not stop here. In his press release and elsewhere, he boldly asserted that the discarded 13 to 1 ratio had proved "disadvantageous to the farmer upon any interpretation."[150] In abandoning it, he implied, he had done farmers a great service. After all, the falling price of corn, when incorporated into the ratio, would "obviously result in a continuously falling price for live hogs."[151]

However true in theory, Hoover's arguments about the ultimate price of hogs did little to mollify farmers whose immediate earnings had been sharply reduced. And it was the farmers on whom Hoover now depended. Would his new price controls work? Both he and the packers warned that they would not if the current flood of hogs to market did not subside.[152]

Although Professor Evvard and his fellow livestock committeemen believed that the new arrangement was the best possible under the circumstances,[153] it did not go down well with Hoover's opponents in the corn belt. Wallace noted sourly that if the 13 to 1 ratio "promised last fall" had been "fairly applied," the November price of hogs should be $19.25, not $17.50.[154] Wallace also criticized Hoover's monthly price-setting plan as a "hand-to-mouth" policy. How, the editor asked, could farmers "make an intelligent guess" about prices in the remainder of the market season? But the fiery farm journalist took grim satisfaction from one thing: since Hoover believed that he could not keep his promise of last November, it was "just as well that he abandon all pretense of doing so."[155]

And that, as much as the policy oscillations, was what infuriated Wallace and his allies: the belief that Hoover had acted deviously and dodged his responsibility. The editor of the *Prairie Farmer* was blunt:

> The October hog market was the bitterest pill farmers have had to swallow for a long time. We do not appreciate attempts to super-coat it by going to Minnesota and South Dakota for corn prices in an attempt to make us think that the $18 average was really based on the 13 to 1 policy. We do not like the statement put out by the Oct. 24 conference that it was feared that with lower corn prices the 13 to 1 ratio might be unfair to the farmer. As long as the corn market is unmanipulated, the 13 to 1 ratio, honestly applied, can never be unfair to the swine grower.
>
> We know that the 13 to 1 ratio was abandoned because Mr. Hoover felt he could not maintain it, and not because he felt that it might be unfair to pork producers. We would feel better if he would tell us so frankly.

The October panic had occurred, the editor continued, because farmers had had no faith in the hog market.

> There was no reason why they should have any faith in it. The 13 to 1 agreement had been discarded. The $18.50 price had been abandoned. The packers' own price of $18 had been shot full of holes. If these things would not start a panic it would be hard to know how to start one.[156]

Despite their indignation, there was little that agrarian spokesmen could do now but hope for the best. Then, in November—to the surprise, perhaps, of nearly everyone—the crisis abated. The packers' promise not to buy hogs for less than $16.50 evidently had a calming effect. Although hog marketings continued to be heavy, the Food Administration succeeded in stabilizing the market, and at a level above the target price.[157] Even Wallace acknowledged that hog producers that month made a profit, although much less (he added) than they would have received under the original 13 to 1 proposition.[158] In mid-November, after consulting its farm and packer advisers, the Food Administration announced that the November price for hogs would be extended, unchanged, through December.[159] The panic of 1918 had passed.

But Wallace neither forgot nor forgave the Food Administrator's handling of the crisis. In the eyes of the Des Moines editor, Hoover was "more responsible than any other one man for starting the dissatisfaction among the farmers in the corn belt"[160]—dissatisfaction that fueled, among other things, the creation of the American Farm Bureau Federation and the so-called farm bloc in Congress. In 1920, 1926, and 1928, *Wallaces' Farmer* excoriated Hoover for doing all in his power to "squirm" out of his 13 to 1 assurance while hypocritically maintaining the "superficial appearance" of adherence. Instead of being fair and frank with the farmer, Hoover had resorted to deliberate deception, "methods of evasion," "barefaced juggling of figures," and a business philosophy of the "ends justify the means." All this at a cost to hog producers of $50,000,000 in lost earnings.[161] As late as 1931, Henry A. Wallace (son of Henry C.) accused the Food Administration of having "deliberately tried to double cross the hog farmers" in 1918. Hoover, he exclaimed, was "such a mixture of crooked and idealistic impulses that he is almost impossible to work with."[162]

If the politically powerful Wallace family was unrelenting in its criticism, Hoover, with his eyes on the White House, was equally determined in his defense. In 1920, 1926, and 1928, he and his defenders shot back with unwavering reiterations of the arguments he had begun to make in 1918. He had carried out the 13 to 1 ratio in good faith; he had defined it in accordance with recommendations by "a committee of corn-belt farmers." He had changed course only after collapsing corn prices had precipitated an "over-marketing" of hogs. He had abandoned the ratio when it had proved to be "no longer in the farmers' interests." In its stead, he had established a monthly "arbitrary price" which had protected farmers from a crash that would have sent hog prices catastrophically down. All in all, then, Hoover had behaved honorably toward the farmers and had even rescued them from economic disaster: so he and his surrogates tirelessly proclaimed. It was a measure of his sensitivity to the accusations against him that he had a former Food Administration colleague named Frank Surface engage in polemics with *Wallaces' Farmer* and write a book defending Hoover's pork policies at every point. When it came to constructing a defense (or, his enemies believed, an alibi), Hoover spared no effort and expense.[163]

What, finally, can be said about this great controversy that dogged Hoover all the way to the White House? On one issue, he was technically right: He did not break his promise to implement the 13 to 1 formula using Chicago prices because technically he never made such a promise. Joseph Cotton's announcement of November 3, 1917 nowhere explicitly mentioned *Chicago* corn and hogs. Moreover, Henry C. Wallace himself knew that the Food Administration had made no such commitment. In June 1918, three months before Hoover decided to use farm values for corn as the basis for the ratio, Wallace speculated in an editorial that the Food Administration might do just that—a policy, he at once added, that would be "unfair."[164] It would be ironic indeed if Wallace was the person who first put this idea in Hoover's head. In any case, it seems clear from the record that Hoover and Cotton intended to keep their options open.

Nevertheless, the context for their 1917 announcement had undeniably been Chicago prices. A Chicago-based ratio was what Hoover's study commission had recommended; the Food Administration had not disagreed. Fairly or not, the impression arose that Hoover would carry out his promise on a Chicago basis—the version most favorable to hog producers. Naturally this was the version preferred by Wallace, who claimed that Cotton's announcement had been "based on" the study commission's report.[165]

But if Hoover was not bound to a Chicago-based ratio, the ratio that he eventually did devise—and the manner in which he formulated, promoted, and then discarded it—cost him dearly in public trust in the farm belt. In terms of policy, Hoover had a strong case. Unlike Wallace, who was free to beat the drums loudly for his interest group, Hoover, as a government official, was obliged to consider competing pressures from many "constituencies": farmers, the packers, the Allies, the U.S. Army, and American consumers. He could not force housewives in the cities to buy high-priced pork. He could not necessarily count on making the Allies purchase ham and bacon at any high price he set. Nor could he compel packers to buy hogs from farmers at prices that bore little relation to consumer demand. In the last analysis, as he informed President Wilson in September 1918, his hog policy was a statement of intent "within our abilities arising from purchases under government control." Circumstances could arise, he added, "under which we could not make good."[166] Given his opposition to governmental operation of the packing industry, and his fundamental decision not to let the free market seek its own price level in wartime, Hoover had little alternative but to balance conflicting interests as best as possible. It was a strategy subject to constant improvisation and inconsistent with ironclad assurances.

Still, it is hard to avoid the conclusion that Hoover in late 1918 would have been better off had he been more forthright in his explanations for his decisions. Instead, out of fear of antagonizing farmers and their advocates, he resorted to tactics that seemed designed primarily to protect himself from political assault. Alas, the tactics became more damaging to him than the policies themselves. Never admit the justice of a criticism: this had been his approach to wheat farmers when he insisted that he had not manipulated the market downward or "fixed" prices. As in the case of wheat, so with hogs:

Hoover's actual policy was more defensible than his strained and dogged defenses of it.

If the long-term political fallout for Hoover was substantial, by mid-November 1918 his immediate economic problem was under control. Hoover had mastered another emergency. But in the 1918 calendar year America's farmers delivered more hogs to the principal markets than ever before in the history of the United States.[167] Purchase of this unparalleled output at prices remunerative to farmers was now contingent upon continued shipment of hog products in huge quantities overseas—and at prices that the Allies already thought excessive. More than ever, Hoover's price support mechanism was hostage to Allied cooperation.

During 1918, with the outcome of the war in the balance, this had not been too difficult to achieve. But by the beginning of November the end of the Great War was near. Soon Hoover would be embroiled in an epic battle with the Allies to absorb the hog surplus that he—for their sake—had done so much to create.

III

ALTHOUGH the battle over hog prices was Hoover's principal headache that autumn, it was hardly the only subject on his mind. In little more than a year the United States Food Administration had become a bureaucracy. More than 9,000 people, mostly volunteers, worked for it in the states. At its headquarters in Washington, more than 1,900 men and women labored. Of these, about 120, including Hoover, took no pay.[168]

At the apex of this expanding pyramid stood the man whom the Food Administration staff revered as "the Chief." It was no empty epithet conferred by sycophants. There was "hardly an administrative or policy detail connected with" the agency that did not "come up for final review before him" before being implemented, an awed associate remarked.[169] "I do not think there is any Government Department or any big commercial organization in the world where the head has such an intimate knowledge of every detail as Hoover has of the Food Administration."[170] F. S. Snyder of the meat division marveled at Hoover's "extraordinary ability to grasp with great facility and rapidity not only the fundamentals, but the details of merchandising of any type."[171]

Certainly there was no dearth of perplexities to occupy his hyperactive mind as the war reached its climax. There was the supreme challenge of finding 17,530,000 tons of foodstuffs to ship abroad in the year ending next July 1.[172] There was the need to negotiate a price for the next Cuban sugar crop. There was the need to maintain momentum for conservation.

Despite the Food Administration's growing problems with its price supports for farmers, in mid-October Hoover proudly informed the White

House that his price stabilization policies had succeeded. He sent the President a collection of statistical tables indicating "an appreciable stabilization in the price of food" during the first year of the Food Administration. Wholesale prices had fallen, farmers' prices for their crops had risen, and the profits of middlemen had been reduced by 16 percent. Hoover admitted that *retail* prices had gone up "in congested areas," but he noted at once that "Congress gave us no control in this matter."[173]

Whatever the validity of Hoover's statistics (and he sometimes eagerly leaped to unwarranted inferences),[174] there was no mistaking his confidence that he had been a success. Through a blend of hortatory voluntarism and ingenious coercion, through brilliant public relations and daring regulation, through relentless managerial drive and clever wirepulling, he had created "the greatest experiment in economic organization the world had seen."[175] Having established a dominant role for himself on the home front, he was once again beginning to think on a grander scale.

For the peace talk of October was not delusory. Victory truly was almost at hand. Even before the guns fell silent, Hoover had begun to prepare for the aftermath.

15

Politics in Wartime

I

LONG before the armistice, it was evident in Washington that Herbert Hoover was a rising political star. Nowhere were the feelings of admiration and anticipation more pronounced than among the burgeoning staff of the Food Administration. To his awed subordinates, Hoover was a "miraculous" figure, "a man of Napoleonic leadership."[1] To the Food Administration's chief counsel, Hoover was a person of "remarkable intellectual power" . . . "the most ingenious man in the devising of ways and means to meet a very difficult situation that I have come in contact with."[2] It was not cheap flattery for such men and women to call him "the Chief."

Hoover's associates were amazed by his "extraordinary vitality" and capacity for work.[3] "He could work indefinitely and not get tired," one remembered; another remarked that his capacity for work appeared to be "unlimited."[4] Then and later, his associates found him to be the most indefatigable worker they had ever met.[5] Spurning exercise, looking perpetually bleary-eyed, he aroused fears in his staff that he would suffer a nervous breakdown.[6]

Hoover's colleagues were also struck by his exceptional ability to concentrate, to the point of sheer obliviousness to all that went on around him. One friend called it Hoover's "outstanding characteristic."[7] One day in the winter of 1917–18, for instance, the Food Administrator and an aide were being driven by a chauffeur through downtown Washington. The streets were glare ice; suddenly the automobile skidded and crashed onto a curbstone. Most passengers would have been a bit rattled; not Hoover. Absorbed in a discourse about food policy, he simply left the damaged car and proceeded to walk down the street without so much as a comment to the chauffeur. According to Hoover's companion in the back seat, Mark Requa, the Chief resumed talking without skipping a word or even momentarily interrupting his train of thought.[8]

Yet if Hoover seemed a marvel of dedication and of almost superhuman efficiency, he was no impersonal machine. To the contrary, some who observed him detected a "nervous and high strung" individual behind the executive's mask.[9] He smoked expensive Havana cigars incessantly, as many as ten to twenty per day.[10] When angry, he swore "like a Turk,"[11] usually denouncing some irritating individual as a "bloody fool."[12] In private he was surprisingly emotional; one close associate, his aide Charles McCarthy, frequently saw him cry when discussing the plight of the Belgians.[13] Sometimes, according to this same aide, Hoover's intensity was a handicap: when trying to "put over anything" in an interview, he would betray himself by "the nervous motion of his feet or hands." Consequently he would conceal his hands in his pockets. Still, his toes would twitch.[14]

For Hoover every moment of time, every ounce of energy, seemed focused on the multifarious challenges of his job. One assistant compared him to an athlete in training.[15] Even the Food Administrator's personal habits seemed subordinated to the imperatives of efficiency. Every day he wore identical suits and neckties.[16] For breakfast he invariably ate bacon and eggs—until his own regulations altered his routine.[17] At lunch he consumed very little,[18] much less than anyone else. Why? an associate asked. Because, Hoover replied, "I'm an engineer, and I'm not using my body. An engineer does not stoke the engine unless there is a considerable amount of power to be exerted. So, I eat as little as I can to get along."[19] Hoover, of course, *was* using his body—at one level, he was in constant overdrive—but his abstemiousness was surely wise for someone so sedentary.

Such devotion and apparent selflessness cemented the loyalty of Hoover's organization to its leader. Quietly dignified, rarely voluble, never breezy or flamboyant, he impressed many as a man of great modesty.[20] In staff meetings, his colleague F. S. Snyder noted, Hoover never used the pronoun "I." It was always, "The Food Administration has aimed to do this, or has accomplished this."[21] His habitual self-effacement, along with a "boyish diffidence" when addressing groups, endeared him to his followers all the more. Men and women alike, they sensed in his shy demeanor a vulnerability that evoked a passionate urge to protect him.

The loyalty that Hoover engendered was remarkable since he rarely complimented his subordinates on their work or offered gestures of bonhomie. Even at the informal staff lunches where many of the Food Administration's problems were discussed, he never told a joke, although he would smile "somewhat benignly and paternally" if someone else tried.[22] Yet if the Chief was far from chummy, the utter totality of his commitment forged unshakable bonds. "We would have done anything for that man," one of the Food Administration's attorneys, Harvey H. Bundy, remarked long afterward. He "established a form of devotion that I've never seen equalled by a leader anywhere."[23]

Very different, however, were Hoover's relationships with those in wartime Washington with whom he dealt on terms of equality. His advent to the nation's capital in the spring of 1917 had touched off one of the bitterest legislative fights in memory. Although Hoover had won out in the end, the price of passage of the Lever Act had been the enduring enmity of more than a few U.S. Senators. To be sure, Hoover had his defenders on Capitol Hill (usually Wilsonian loyalists), and he was by no means the only object of Congressional wrath. But among the often embattled executive officers of the Wilson administration—men like Secretary of War Baker and Fuel Administrator Garfield—Hoover stood out for the vehemence and persistence of the anger, even hatred, that he evoked from certain denizens of Congress.

Such feelings—or, as they seemed to him, such petty posturings—repeatedly nonplussed the thin-skinned Food Administrator.[24] One day the chairman of his Agricultural Advisory Committee, a former governor of Virginia named Henry C. Stuart, tried to console him. Congress, said Stuart, was like a "worm fence," whose rails are fitted diagonally without the use of nails. "In the first place, a worm fence is crooked. In the second place, it takes a long time to get where it's going. But it fairly well serves its purpose and there are many stout oak rails in it."[25] Hoover enjoyed this definition and liked to retell it. Still, the peculiar ways of Washington continued to vex him.

The Food Administrator's difficulties were not confined to Capitol Hill. As a newcomer to Washington, with no political capital other than his reputation, Hoover had few intimates in the Wilson administration. In the Cabinet only his old patron, Secretary of the Interior Lane, could be called a friend.[26] While Hoover and Secretary of Agriculture Houston cooperated politely on the surface, relations between their two departments were in "a state of suppressed hostility."[27] The same could be said of Hoover's relations with Secretary of the Treasury McAdoo after their public quarrel in the winter of 1918. At one point Hoover clashed sharply with the army's Provost Marshal General over draft deferments for Food Administration personnel.[28] On another occasion his tough-minded dealings with the Swiss government so exasperated a senior official in the State Department that the official would have nothing to do with him.[29] Hoover also crossed swords with the powerful head of the War Industries Board, Bernard Baruch. Hoover accused the board of trying to poach some of the Food Administration's best men and of encroaching on its sphere of responsibility. Baruch airily denied the charges and accused Hoover of seeking "to hang me first and try me afterward."[30]

Not all these disputes were of lasting importance. Nor was Hoover the only abrasive administrator in the crowded and gossipy hothouse of wartime Washington. The higher echelons of the Wilson administration were no haven of brotherly love. Still, the evidence is plain that the comparatively youthful "food czar" was not especially popular among his peers.

Why? Outright jealousy no doubt accounted for much of their animosity. Certainly it underlay the attitude of the turf-conscious Agriculture and Labor departments, which never cared for the energetic interloper in their midst.[31] Hoover's flair for publicity bred further resentment. "No war board at Washington was advertised as widely as the U.S. Food Administration," one scholar remarked shortly after the conflict ended.[32] By the winter of 1918 Baruch and certain other Washingtonians agreed privately that the nation was being "drugged by Hooverism, by being told every day that food would win the war." Military force would win it, they insisted; "economic measures" alone would not suffice.[33] Of course, if Hoover was correct—if food was indeed more critical than any other requirement for victory—then it followed that the manager of the food front was more important than any other war leader. Hoover was probably aware of the self-promoting implications of his propaganda. So, too, were his envious colleagues.

Eventually, in June 1918, Hoover himself banned the further use of his slogan "Food Will Win the War," lest it appear to equate civilian sacrifice with mounting American casualties in Europe.[34] But by then the impression in political Washington was strong that the Food Administrator was a man who craved the limelight.

Bureaucratic rivalry and envy did not alone explain the simmering tension between Hoover and various other government officials. To David Houston, Hoover's word could not be trusted, for he "never said [the] same thing twice."[35] Moreover, for all his winsome diffidence before admiring subordinates, Hoover could be belligerently tactless with his peers. One night in the spring of 1918, at a dinner party for the Secretary of War, the Food Administrator sat next to the army's chief of staff, General March. Hoover made a remark about some event that day on the western front; March told him he was mistaken and corrected him. Hoover was not pleased. "General March," he said, "when you know me better you will find that when I say a thing is a fact it is a fact." March retorted, "Mr. Hoover, when you know me better you will find that I am not ashamed to say, 'I do not know,' when asked anything. But when I tell as a fact something about the military progress of the war, it is a fact."

The two men did not converse again that evening. But that night, after the dinner, Hoover went to his office and checked his files on the point in dispute. The next morning he sent March a note admitting that he had been wrong and the general right. For this gesture, Hoover promptly went up in the general's estimation.[36]

In this instance, without directly apologizing, Hoover conceded that he had been mistaken. But such admissions were rare, probably because he rarely felt that he was in error.

Clearly the taut and aggressive Food Administrator lacked the social graces of more conventional public figures. This was part of the problem, in the eyes of his lieutenants. "He is a puzzle to the pothouse politicians," said one. "He is so straight that they do not understand him."[37]

Others, however, saw him differently. "Writing about Herbert Hoover," declared a leading Wilsonian, George Creel, "is like trying to describe the interior of a citadel where every drawbridge is up and every portcullis down, thus leaving nothing for inspection but a stretch of blank wall."[38] Wary and reserved, Hoover did not initially greet Washington officialdom with hearty hellos. "If we had been carrying tin cups and wearing the blue glasses of mendicancy," said Creel, "our reception could not have been colder."[39]

The Food Administrator's extraordinary ability to concentrate was another source of provocation to those who did not know him well. When deep in a virtual trance of cogitation, he would give visitors "scant consideration." However innocent, such behavior made him enemies.[40]

One Hoover trait, above all, aroused suspicion: his peculiar habit of never looking at people directly while talking to them. Instead, he would stare at his desk or at his shoes.[41] To friends, it was a sign of shyness, a residue of the trauma of his early orphanhood. To less friendly observers, it was proof of his deviousness and insincerity. Secretary of Agriculture Houston deemed Hoover "very shifty—could not look you in the face."[42] George Creel, head of the government's Committee on Public Information, had similar feelings of revulsion. "It must be," he told the President, that Hoover "looks on all of us as politicians, and therefore not to be trusted."[43]

Creel soon discerned greatness in the Food Administrator. Hoover, he declared in 1919, "had one of the most difficult jobs ever assigned to a human being" and was "one of the great organizing geniuses of the war."[44] Bernard Baruch also recognized Hoover's talents. Of all the men he had ever met, said Baruch, Herbert Hoover had the greatest capacity for absorbing and organizing facts, determining the course of action implied by them, and accomplishing the desired result. Hoover's brain, he said, was like a sponge, absorbing facts into "every tiny interstice."[45] Still, these were tributes more to Hoover's ability than to his personality, which continued to puzzle and offend. "It is a pity he has so little personal charm," Colonel House sighed, "for he could go further than he will with the lack of it."[46]

Sometimes Hoover himself seemed to wonder how long he would survive in an environment so uncongenial to his temperament. Inveterately pessimistic, he professed to be convinced that the days of wartime agency administrators were numbered. Thus, in one of his first addresses to Food Administration personnel, he asked them to be loyal to his successor![47] "Someone has to be the first to hang on the barbed wire," he said one day to Baruch.[48]

Nevertheless, as the months wore on, Hoover's fears of failure proved groundless. Thanks in part to his skillful propaganda, he became a hero to millions of housewives, middle-class professionals, liberal intellectuals, Washington journalists, and well-to-do businessmen inspired by his idealistic summons to national service. More importantly, he had earned the complete confidence of his boss. To be sure, at least once the gloomy Food Administrator got on the President's nerves. After a meeting with Hoover in February 1918, Woodrow Wilson complained to Colonel House that it was disagreeable to talk with Hoover because of his "excessive pessimism. Nothing was ever being done right."[49] Yet when it came time for a decision, the chief executive rarely overruled his Food Administrator or refused his requests. What stands out in their relationship between the spring of 1917 and the armistice was that Hoover nearly always got what he sought.

The best evidence of Hoover's growing stature within the Wilson administration appeared in March 1918 when the President invited him to join a select coterie of advisers who soon became known as the War Cabinet. During that fierce and fretful winter, the White House came under enormous pressure to improve its coordination of the war effort, which to friend and foe alike appeared to be sputtering. Hostile members of Congress even attempted to force the President to accept creation of a War Cabinet or Council—comprised of "three distinguished citizens of demonstrated ability"—a humiliating measure that Wilson vehemently and successfully resisted. Instead, he pushed for sweeping power to reorganize the executive branch himself, power that Congress finally granted him in May.[50]

Politics aside, the need for some kind of "War Board" could not be denied. On February 25 Colonel House presented to the President a plan for such a body, to be composed of various Cabinet officials and the leaders of certain temporary wartime agencies. House proposed that the group meet with the President once a week.[51] Wilson agreed, and in mid-March invited Hoover and several other agency heads to the White House for a conference.[52]

Hoover later claimed that it was he who suggested and initiated the process which led to the creation of the War Cabinet.[53] If so, he was partially responsible for an innovation that yielded great dividends to the hitherto fragmented war administration. Meeting in the President's study for the first time on March 20, and then on successive Wednesdays until the end of the war, the informal council became an invaluable "clearing house of facts and policy."[54] One participant, Edward N. Hurley, likened its sessions to "conferences of executives of large corporations reporting progress of their work to their president and submitting ways and means to carry on further."[55] At these gatherings, which at times lasted two hours or more, the assembled executives discussed problems, argued earnestly, and accepted the immediate decisions of the commander in chief. Whatever their differences outside the "cabinet" room, inside it the participants were polite and cooperative. In thirty years as a businessman, said Hurley, he had never been "associated with a group of men who worked so harmoniously and effectively."[56] Hoover agreed.[57]

Eight men comprised Woodrow Wilson's War Cabinet: the Secretaries of War, the Navy, and the Treasury, and the heads of the Shipping Board, War Industries Board, War Trade Board, Fuel Administration, and Food Administration. Of these eight, only Hoover was not already a close personal friend of the President.[58] It was a tribute to his ability and usefulness that as a comparative stranger he should rise so fast and so high.

Let the gossips, then, and those whom Hoover had shoved aside, say what they will. In less than a year he had ascended to the pinnacle of the Wilson administration. He was an insider now.

II

As the Food Administrator's press releases blanketed the land in 1917 and 1918, some in Washington began to wonder whether winning the war with food was his only ambition. Was the master of publicity a self-publicist as well? Was he seeking not just results but the presidency of the United States?

Certainly not a few in his entourage held precisely this dream for him. The thought of Hoover as a presidential possibility had long been discussed by his eager admirers in and around the Commission for Relief in Belgium.[59] In April 1917, when Hoover returned to the United States, one of his closest British colleagues in the relief effort told an influential British figure visiting America: "You will find him a remarkable man in every way, in fact so remarkable that I think if he really makes his mind up, he will become President of the United States."[60]

It was not long before similar speculation floated through the corridors of the Food Administration.[61] As early as July 1917, an observant Democratic Party activist from California who was helping Hoover set up his new agency concluded that the men around Hoover were going to make him a presidential candidate—"with them it is the dominating thought."[62] As early as September, an article in the *American Review of Reviews* proclaimed that Hoover had "the biggest, most vital war job in the world" and openly suggested that if he succeeded, he might eventually occupy the White House.[63] Only two months later no less a political sophisticate than Colonel House told a friend that Hoover (in the friend's words) had "got it into his head to be Republican candidate for President" and that his relief organization was being made into a political machine. If Hoover succeeded as Food Administrator, he would run, said House. But if Hoover failed, he would blame Woodrow Wilson.[64]

House apparently gave no evidence for his startling assertions. But the President's confidential adviser was not alone in his assessment. When Hoover returned to the United States from Europe in 1917, a prominent mining engineer and friend of his remarked: "Hoover has got presidential aspirations. I don't see how he is going to make it."[65]

All this may have been merely conjectural. What was incontestable—and, to politicians, more than a little significant—was that Hoover, a man not yet in his mid-forties, was the subject of growing popular adulation. In influential magazines, flattering articles about him proliferated, some written by close friends and associates.[66] He was the darling of the Ivy League and elite colleges in the East. In 1917 alone, Harvard, Princeton, the University of Pennsylvania, Oberlin College, and Williams College conferred honorary degrees upon him. In 1918 Yale University followed suit.[67] Millions of housewives looked to him for instructions. All this would be enough to make almost any man in public life dream of someday inhabiting the White House.

Hoover himself was publicly mum about his plans. But the increasingly lionized Food Administrator was surely aware of the murmurings around him.[68] Moreover, he had long been intrigued by the lure of public service. In 1910 he had sought, through a friend, to become the first director of the U.S. Bureau of Mines. In 1912, as a progressive Republican, he had contributed financially to Theodore Roosevelt's presidential campaign. In 1914 he had unsuccessfully attempted to purchase a newspaper in California as a launching pad for his long-contemplated entry into the "big game." In early 1917 he had endeavored eagerly to obtain a high position in the Wilson administration if the United States should enter the Great War. Thanks in part to the patronage of Colonel House, he had succeeded.[69] Having come this far, he had no compelling reason to forsake going higher up the ladder.

Then, in the summer of 1917, Hoover made an interesting decision: he resigned from the Republican Club of New York City, to which he had belonged since 1909.[70] The Food Administrator did not advertise his act, and, like so much of his behavior, it is subject to conflicting interpretation. Three years later, when his withdrawal from the club became known to the public, friends suggested that he had resigned because he considered such a partisan affiliation to be inconsistent with government service in wartime.[71] In 1917 Hoover was also evidently under fire from some Democrats for appointing Republicans to most key posts in his agency.[72] By renouncing his formal Republican ties, he apparently hoped to enhance his credibility as a nonpolitical administrator.[73] So his supporters believed (or wanted the public to believe) in 1920, when Hoover, by then a Republican presidential aspirant, was trying to refurbish his party credentials.

Such was the "idealistic" interpretation of Hoover's motives in 1917. But was it the accurate one? Despite his Republican background and affiliation, Hoover had apparently approved Woodrow Wilson's reelection in 1916.[74] By severing his Republican affiliation some months later, was he merely trying to be scrupulously nonpartisan during the war? Or had he deliberately decided to expand his political options? No conclusive answer is possible, since Hoover, then and later, was silent. But the question of motivation illustrated the ambiguity surrounding the sphinxlike Food Administrator. What admirers and underlings construed as lofty disinterestedness, skeptics and rivals saw as calculating ambition.

Happily for Hoover, there was no inconsistency between the two as he strove to carry out his duties. For the moment he had a job to do and a war to win. But the youthful Food Administrator undoubtedly realized that if he succeeded he would become, in the words of an adviser, "the great American figure," with the presidency itself as the prize.[75]

Perhaps for this reason, Hoover's organization seemed to become more protective of him as the war went on. Within the Food Administration a "secret service" kept watch on the activities of certain personnel, notably Charles McCarthy.[76] Hoover himself, McCarthy noticed, "changed completely" as the months passed. At first the Chief had an office opening directly onto a hallway where crowds of people lay in wait. Hoover enjoyed the hustle and bustle, so much so that when his harassed secretary moved his boss to a more remote room at the end of a hall Hoover insisted on moving right back, because, he said, it was "too damn lonely down here." By the end of the war this informality had vanished. Hoover had become increasingly inaccessible, his office guarded on either side by his secretary, Lewis Strauss, and his trusted aide, Edgar Rickard. Newspaper reporters especially were held at bay.[77]

Anxious to avoid mistakes and uncontrolled publicity, Hoover was also careful to sidestep political entanglements that might impair his effectiveness or prestige. During the spring of 1918 an old friend, the novelist Mary Austin, urged the Food Administrator to use his office to promote certain "spiritual" and social reforms. Hoover bluntly refused. "In my capacity as Food Administrator," he replied, "I have no general reforms, no spiritual movements to undertake, but simply a purely practical end to attain. If I succeed in the practical end, that is what I shall be judged by, not by any outside attitude towards citizenship which I may hold." For Hoover, winning the war was paramount, and his role in winning it was

> simply a question of intelligent handling of the supplies which we have available, and doing so with the very least interference in the normal life of our people.
>
> There are infinite injustices and wrongs in the United States and an infinite amount of social evils. Like every other citizen who loves his people, I would truly like to see these things remedied. But it is a job that I cannot undertake and at the same time successfully fill my niche in prosecuting the war.[78]

Reservations of a different sort guided Hoover in June when the founder of the *New Republic*, Herbert Croly, invited him to serve on the "organization committee" of a proposed "School of Social Research" in New York.[79] Hoover's response was cautious. Although pronouncing himself "glad to be of any service I can in this direction," he emphasized that he did not wish to be affiliated with

> any institution which might degenerate into a school of some special character of political or economic thought. I am not a Socialist and I am opposed to the whole theory, root and branch, and I believe that the worst disaster that could come out of the war will be any rush of public opinion for some panacea of this kind. On the other hand, I am not a believer in the use of property to impose either political or economic power over fellow-men.

He could "not sit easily," Hoover continued, "in a group where even freedom of thought led to stamping an institution as advocating either of these extremes." Instead, he said he liked educational institutions "devoting themselves to research in determination of truth as distinguished from a shelter for advocacy."[80]

So far as is known, Hoover had no further contact with Croly's project, which eventuated in the New School for Social Research (established in 1919). But his brief exchange with the *New Republic*'s editor was illuminating. A newcomer to the "big game" of politics, Hoover saw himself as a prudent progressive, eschewing both the radical Left and unyielding Right.

It was easy for Hoover to fend off would-be reformers like Mary Austin and "advanced" thinkers like Herbert Croly. It was not so easy to dodge the more dangerous snare of Prohibition. Initially, he had advocated a complete ban on brewing and distilling for beverage purposes during the war, on the grounds that this would save grain for more vital uses. But the prospective Food Administrator had quickly retreated into ambiguous silence while "wet" and "dry" forces battled over the issue in Congress.[81] As finally written, the Lever Act banned the production of whiskey and gin for the duration of the war but left it up to the President whether to impose similar curbs upon beer and wine.[82]

In keeping with a promise that he had made several months earlier, Hoover proposed in August 1917 that the President now establish a committee to determine "whether we should interfere with the brewing trade in any fashion."[83] Such a body, of course, could provide him the "facts" that he needed. It could also serve as a useful screen against political criticism. Woodrow Wilson, however, was uninterested. He instructed his food controller that "we had better leave the brewing trade alone until the situation develops more clearly."[84] If Hoover was walking a tightrope, so was his boss. The President knew well that laboring men in the shipyards and other critical industries liked their beer, and he was naturally reluctant to risk their discontent.

The Lever Act as finally passed was an open invitation to the Prohibition lobby to pressure Wilson to take drastic steps against beer and wine. It was not long before he and his Food Administrator felt the heat. In mid-November Hoover informed the White House that dry "agitation" for further action against alcohol under the Lever Act was so intense that some Americans were refusing to conserve food so long as other foodstuffs were going to the breweries.[85]

Hoover was uncomfortably on the spot. On the one hand, he averred that he had "utmost sympathy" with the "ultimate ends" of the "temperance advocates." (Just what he meant by this was unclear, since Hoover during the war enjoyed daily cocktails.)[86] Moreover, the brewing industry was undeniably consuming significant quantities of critically needed barley and was tying up 15,000 cold-storage cars desperately needed for other purposes. On the other hand, if the federal government suppressed the brewing of beer entirely, he feared that it would arouse the anger of the "labouring classes," drive Americans to consume more wine and leftover whiskey (which had a higher alcohol content), and cause severe "dislocation" of business. Not surprisingly, the worried Food Administrator opted for a "medium course." He asked the President to limit the amount of grain used by breweries and reduce the allowable percentage of alcohol in beer. Limit, but not prohibit. If the American people wanted complete Prohibition for the war, then Congress, said Hoover, should enact it.[87]

President Wilson accepted most of Hoover's recommendations and in early December issued an executive order submitted by the Food Administrator.[88] The edict required brewers to curtail the use of foodstuffs in beer production by 30 percent from 1917 levels and to reduce the alcohol content of beer to a maximum of 2.75 percent.[89] The effect of the two regulations was that breweries would still be able to manufacture the same volume of beer as before but that it would be weaker. Hoover calculated that the restriction would save the country 18,000,000 bushels of grain in the coming year.[90]

Having worked out his delicate compromise, the Food Administrator resolutely defended it. The Lever Act had outlawed the further manufacture of distilled spirits (such as whiskey and gin). It had not, however, banned the sale of existing supplies of distilled spirits, supplies sufficient (said Hoover) to last for two or three years. The Food Administrator therefore warned that if the government now totally suppressed beer making, it would place the country "on a whiskey basis" with far worse moral effects.[91]

It is not certain whether Hoover truly believed this argument or merely found it a handy retort to the dry lobby. What was certain was that he wanted as little to do with the thorny question as possible. "I have taken the attitude from the beginning," he told a leading Prohibitionist member of Congress, "that my business was simply under the direction of the President to give administration to the Food Law, and that it was not my business to advocate either one way or the other, legislation for the furtherance of moral or economic questions:—that this is solely the job of Congress."[92]

Yet even as Hoover attempted to throw "moral" and "economic" questions into the lap of Congress, behind the scenes he was contemplating the very policy that he publicly opposed. Late in November 1917 he became alarmed at the Allies' rising purchase of American barley for their breweries. He asked his representative in London to find out whether the Allies themselves would stop brewing. "If Allies lead off," he cabled, "we could secure this country dry for the war. Without it matter is impossible. . . ."[93] A couple of months later he again quietly raised the question of a mutual "cessation of brewing on both sides of the Atlantic." The continuing Allied demand for U.S. barley was driving its price to record levels, he said, just when it was needed as a substitute for wheat in the making of bread. He also claimed that his countrymen were making a "great outcry" against his "drastic" conservation measures "while barley is going to England for beer."[94]

Hoover's suggestion—made for war-related, not moral, reasons—died aborning. Although the British government soon stopped the use of home-grown and imported barley for malting purposes, the British food controller warned Hoover that the imposition of "any sweeping measure of prohibition" on the working class would be dangerous.[95] At home President Wilson opposed all-out wartime prohibition for the same reason. When Senator Morris Sheppard of Texas, an ardent dry, presented him draft legislation for this purpose, Wilson rejected it, asserting that it would "introduce a new element of disturbance in the labor situation which I should dread."[96]

Nevertheless, the pressures for more stringent measures against alcohol continued. In the Congress, Prohibition forces were irritated at the President's refusal to use his clear authority under the Lever Act to end the manufacture of beer and wine altogether.

Then, in May 1918, Hoover abruptly encountered a political crisis—precipitated, ironically, by his own propaganda. All through the spring, as America's wheat reserves steadily dwindled, the Food Administrator feverishly exhorted the nation to conserve the precious grain. In May he even issued an appeal to be read in the churches asking all who could to refrain from eating any wheat or wheat products whatsoever.[97]

Hoover's pleas had an unexpected consequence. If wheat was so essential yet so scarce, why not prohibit its use in the manufacture of alcoholic beverages? Suddenly the "liquor question" was back, and Hoover was inundated with letters from throughout the country.[98] Even worse, on May 21 Representative Charles Randall of California, a militant Prohibitionist, introduced an amendment to a pending agricultural appropriations bill. The amendment would forbid the expenditure of $6,100,000 until President Wilson issued a proclamation under the Lever Act prohibiting the use of foodstuffs in the production of beer and wine for the rest of the war.[99] The House of Representatives promptly adopted Randall's amendment.[100]

Although Hoover had been exploring ways to stop brewing (if the Allies would join him or go first), the sweeping Randall amendment was more than he could stomach. The Food Administrator therefore drafted a rejoinder for the White House (not himself) to issue. In it he pointed out that the nation's stocks of distilled spirits were large and that the Lever Act did not close saloons. Thus if President Wilson now banned the brewing of beer as the Randall amendment demanded, the saloons of America would simply serve whiskey, "the most deleterious of all the drinks," instead. If Congress really wanted the country to "go dry," said Hoover, it would have to enact "an entirely new act" prohibiting the sale of alcoholic beverages.[101] President Wilson agreed with Hoover completely, but decided that it was unnecessary to "fire this [memo] off just now."[102]

Meanwhile Senator Sheppard of Texas seized upon the Randall amendment to ask the President whether he had changed his mind about wartime prohibition.[103] Wilson quickly indicated that he had not—and then took refuge behind Hoover. The "wise and statesmanlike thing" to do, Wilson told the senator, was "to let the situation stand as it is for the present, until at any rate I shall be apprised by the Food Administration that it is necessary in the way suggested still further to conserve the supply of food and feed stuffs." The Food Administration, he added, "has not thought it necessary to go any further than we have in that matter already gone."[104]

Wilson's response neatly shifted the onus onto his Food Administrator, who now found himself the unwanted object of Senator Sheppard's attention.[105] In a letter to the Texas lawmaker on June 4, Hoover attempted to escape from the political quicksand. Proclaiming himself "a life-long believer in national temperance," he nevertheless asserted that as "a purely administrative officer of the Government," he believed he should not "enter into any contentious matters." He could "only compromise in this situation pending definite action by the American people or by Congress to whom the ultimate responsibility in such questions belongs." Hoover also argued that abolition of wine making would add "no consequential amount of food to our national supplies," while the abolition of brewing would create "moral and physical dangers" far outweighing the savings in food that would be effected. Such issues, he plainly believed, were up to the Congress to resolve.[106]

Hoover's letter deftly tossed the problem back to Capitol Hill.[107] Lest anyone misread his intent, he immediately made public his letter to Sheppard along with an explanatory press release. Hoover asserted that "from a strictly food conservation point of view," he would like to suppress the use of foodstuffs in all beverages, hard *and* soft. But this, he insisted, was not "the whole story." If the government lowered the boom on beer, the patrons of saloons would switch to gin and whiskey. "If the American people want prohibition," he declared bluntly, "it should prohibit by legislation to that end and not force the Food Administration to the responsibility for an orgy of drunkenness." If Congress terminated the sale of distilled liquors, he added, he would "find no difficulty in stopping brewing."[108]

Yet if Hoover wanted Congress to decide the Prohibition question (if it must be decided), he carefully refrained from publicly saying what he himself would like Congress to do. Committed (so he said) to "national temperance," he nowhere defined what he meant by this term or addressed its ethical dimensions. In a conversation with Senator Sheppard, he evidently suggested that something be done to end the sale of whiskey.[109] Yet he also told Sheppard that (in Sheppard's words) the Randall amendment would wreak "needless hardship on a large number of business men in certain parts of the country, and would therefore do more harm than good."[110] Supportive of a dry (or at any rate drier) America, at least in the abstract, Hoover nevertheless discerned a host of hurdles in the way—hurdles that he, at least, did not care to leap. This was not necessarily cowardice or hypocrisy. Determined, above all else, to win the war, he did not wish to be tormented by divisive social issues which were not properly his to resolve.

If Hoover thought that passing the buck back to Congress would relieve the pressure on himself, he was mistaken. The day after he released his letter to Senator Sheppard, a *New York Times* headline told the story: "Wilson and Hoover Kill Bone Dry Bill."[111] The administration's action angered the anti-liquor forces, and this time they did not retreat. Instead, debate on the Randall amendment and various alternatives to it raged in Congress during the summer.

On August 29 the Senate voted to ban the use of foodstuffs in the manufacture of beer and wine, beginning the following spring. The Senate also voted to ban the sale of beer, wine, and distilled spirits, thus meeting Hoover's persistent objection to closure of the breweries. On September 6 the upper house then sent its handiwork to the House of Representatives for concurrence.[112]

Meanwhile, under a directive from the President, Hoover's and other temporary war agencies had been conferring about ways to curtail "non-essential" industries, including—they quickly agreed—the nation's breweries.[113] On September 7 (after a conference with the President), the Food, Fuel, and Railroad administrations and the War Industries Board announced a dramatic decision: on December 1, 1918 the entire brewing industry of the United States would be closed until further notice. Ignoring moral arguments and the ongoing debate in Congress, the Wilson administration based its action solely on wartime necessity.[114] Some days later, President Wilson signed an executive order implementing the new policy.[115]

What, however, of Hoover's much-expressed concern that the disappearance of beer would drive thirsty drinkers to whiskey? On this point Hoover admitted to his state food administrators that he had changed his mind. Last year, he pointed out, there had been a surplus of fodder grains, hence no problem in the use of these grains to manufacture beer. Now there was a shortage. He could no longer, therefore, "justify a continuation of brewing," even though one consequence would be the engendering of "some moral difficulties in the population."[116]

It is hard to know whether the Wilson administration's decision to shut down the nation's breweries was taken to head off the more stringent measures making their way through a dry-dominated Congress. Hitherto, Wilson had been reluctant to interfere with the wartime drinking habits of millions of workers. Now, as the election of 1918 approached, he was warned by advisers that enactment of the looming "bone dry" legislation would devastate the Democratic Party's chances in eastern states.[117] Perhaps, then, a preemptive strike at the brewers would sidetrack even worse actions by Congress.

Whatever the motivations of the President, the impending proscription of brewing up executive order did not appease the drys. In November 1918 Congress enacted, and the President reluctantly signed, a bill prohibiting the manufacture and sale of *all* alcoholic beverages after mid-1919 "until the conclusion of the present war, and thereafter until the termination of demobilization."[118]

Ironically, the fighting in Europe ended ten days before the bill became law. But since the legal state of war continued, the "wartime" Prohibition law took effect anyway.

Thanks in part to his astute straddling of the issue and to his dogged adherence to win-the-war nonpartisanship, Hoover survived the fierce wartime storms over Prohibition without harm. There is little evidence that he deliberately acted out of concern for his postwar career. But political neophyte though he was, Hoover was shrewd enough to recognize a quagmire when he saw one. If he could avert noisy, no-win imbroglios over side issues, the better off (now and later) he would be. This was the beauty of his position: his agency's success and his own self-interest were in harmony.

III

HOOVER managed, then, to steer past the stubborn shoals of Prohibition. The vortex of the 1918 election campaign proved more perilous.

Americans like to think that when the United States goes to war all partisanship dissolves in a glow of national unity. This was not the case in World War I. Although Congress declared war by overwhelming majorities, and although President Wilson famously announced that "politics is adjourned," the Congress of 1917–18 was riven by partisan antagonisms of an intensity not seen since the Civil War.[119] In each house, Democrats held vulnerable majorities. With control of the Congress—and power to shape the postwar world—in the balance, the election of 1918 promised to be fervidly contested.

In no section of the country were Democratic candidates more at risk than in the West, where the Wilson administration's wheat policy was increasingly unpopular. Wheat farmers had been furious when Food Administrator

Hoover had used his powers to push the price of their 1917 crop well below its previous market levels. They had been incensed when President Wilson, in July 1918, vetoed a Congressional attempt to raise the guaranteed price of wheat. Nor were they mollified a few weeks later when Wilson, at Hoover's urging, announced that the government price for 1919 wheat would remain unchanged. To angry wheat growers, it was bad enough that the price of their staple remained frozen while the prices of most other commodities were soaring. What galled them further was that only wheat, the great crop of the West, had been subjected to such government control, while cotton—the staple of the South—remained exempt from mandatory price restraint.

The Republican Party was quick to capitalize on the West's discontent. Time and again, in the rancorous campaign of 1918, Republicans castigated the southern-dominated Democratic Congress for imposing price controls on wheat while failing to control cotton, whose unregulated price had more than quintupled since 1914. "The South is in the saddle," Republican orators charged; the Democratic Congress had permitted the South to profiteer. The allegation was devastatingly effective in the wheat belt.[120]

As the uproar over price controls escalated, Hoover was drawn into the fray. In September Representative Jouett Shouse of Kansas, a Democrat in a desperate fight for reelection, asked Hoover for a detailed explanation and defense of the Food Administration's policies on wheat. Shouse, a pro-Wilson member of Congress, clearly wanted the information for use in his campaign.[121] Hoover immediately obliged with a six-page letter arguing, among other things, that *without* government intervention the price of wheat would now be less than $1.00 a bushel.[122] On another occasion President Wilson's secretary, Joseph Tumulty, asked Hoover for ammunition to use against public criticisms of administration wheat policy by Senator John W. Weeks of Massachusetts, one of Wilson's most hated political enemies.[123] Hoover quickly sent Tumulty a letter cataloguing the senator's "errors."[124]

While the Food Administrator was willing to accommodate endangered Democrats in this way, he showed no disposition in the early autumn to inject himself otherwise into the partisan slugfest. Nor could he be accused of publicly tilting toward the Democrats. His policies, after all, were under attack, and he could hardly refrain from defending them when requested, particularly when his arguments were made in unpublished correspondence. But then, in the waning days of the campaign, events conspired to shatter his above-the-battle posture.

For some weeks President Wilson had been contemplating a written appeal to the American electorate to return a Democratic Congress in November. Besieged by candidates of his party for assistance, furious at the Republicans who had fought him on Capitol Hill, and anxious for a free hand to shape the imminent peace, the President finally released his message on October 25.

The chief executive did not confine himself to a simple appeal for a continuation of "unified leadership" under the Democrats. Instead, in bluntly worded prose, he lashed out at the Republican chieftains on Capitol Hill:

> At almost every turn, since we entered the war, they have sought to take the choice of policy and the conduct of the war out of my hands and put it under the control of instrumentalities of their own choosing. This is no time either for divided counsel or for divided leadership. Unity of command is as necessary now in civil action as it is upon the field of battle.

If the Democrats lost control of the House or the Senate, Wilson warned, "an opposing majority" could force all legislative action "to be taken amidst contest and obstruction." Furthermore, if the Republicans won majorities in either house, it would be "interpreted on the other side of the water as a repudiation of my leadership." The Allies knew as well as Americans, he added, that "the Republican leaders desire not so much to support the President as to control him."[125]

Wilson's extraordinary and intemperate plea unleashed a new wave of political frenzy. Republican leaders accused the President of besmirching their patriotism. The chairman of the Republican National Committee called the appeal an "insult."[126] To outraged Republicans it was additional proof that the man in the White House was an imperious autocrat whose "only test of loyalty" was "loyalty to one man no matter what he does."[127] Less partisan Americans were also stunned. Writing years afterward, Hoover recalled that Wilson's appeal had come as a "shock."[128]

One by one the members of the President's Cabinet publicly endorsed their leader's call for a Democratic Congress—all except Secretary of War Baker, who desired "to keep the Army out of politics."[129] Angry Republicans fired back in kind. The campaign now reached a crescendo of vituperation that threatened to obscure the fact that the end of the war was very near.

Not everyone joined in the bitter cacophony. In New York City Frederic R. Coudert, a prominent lawyer, was distressed. A political independent and advocate of a postwar League of Nations, Coudert feared that this great cause would be hindered if the coming election produced "a divided government."[130] As it happened, Coudert was acquainted with Hoover. On October 29 the New York attorney asked the Food Administrator for a chance to discuss "some matters" in Washington on November 1.[131]

Lunching together that day in the capital,[132] Hoover and Coudert discovered that they shared common concerns. Both men agreed (wrote Coudert afterward) that the impending victory in Europe gave the United States a "unique opportunity" to "advance human progress" and create an improved world order. Both, too, feared that if the legislative and executive branches of the American government came to be held by different political parties, "disorganization and paralysis" would ensue. To achieve "beneficial results" from the war, "unity of direction" was essential.[133]

Finding Hoover in agreement with his analysis, and knowing his friend's great national prestige, Coudert asked the Food Administrator to write him a letter for publication expressing their mutual concerns. Hoover agreed.[134]

The Food Administrator now proceeded to write a first draft of his response. "I have no politics," Hoover began. His hopes for America were three: to "win unconditional surrender," establish "a representative government in Germany as a real assurance of world peace," and heal "the world['s] wounds." In pursuit of the second objective, the President was even now succeeding "beyond all hopes." As for the third, if the President was to nurse Europe back to health and away from an all-consuming "flame of bolshivism [sic]," he, "the acknowledged leader of the world," would need "undivided support."[135]

Meanwhile, and apparently without Coudert's knowledge, Hoover was coming under pressure from another source to speak out: frightened Democrats, anxious to counteract the bitter backlash against the President's appeal. On November 2 Vance McCormick, chairman of the Democratic National Committee and a fellow member of the War Cabinet, conferred twice with Hoover at the Food Administrator's offices.[136] On these occasions, if a later *New York Times* account was correct, McCormick told Hoover that the election of a Democratic Congress was imperative and that it was Hoover's duty, in light of the world situation, publicly to support the President's appeal. According to the *Times*, Democratic leaders believed that such an endorsement would turn the tide. Hoover was apparently hesitant. But finally, after an argument, he yielded.[137] Years later McCormick asserted that it was he who obtained Hoover's letter endorsing Wilson's call.[138]

McCormick's solicitation may have occurred independently of Coudert's. Or perhaps McCormick instigated Coudert's visit.[139] In any case, the Food Administrator's endorsement now took the form of an exchange of letters between Coudert and himself. Both communications were dated November 2, the same day that McCormick made his visits to Hoover's office. Hoover reportedly insisted that his endorsement be issued not as a Democratic Party document but in the form of a letter to a private citizen.[140] If so, Hoover was still skittish about identifying himself too closely with a political maneuver.

In the first communication, Coudert asked Hoover whether the United States, "so united in the prosecution of the war," could now maintain its unity in achieving "a just and enduring peace." Indeed, was such a peace possible "unless we are as a unit" in fundamental policy? "It seems to me that divided counsels now may imperil the fruits of victory," Coudert continued. He asked Hoover, with his "unique experience" in Europe and his "great knowledge" of economic forces, to address these questions, which "naturally transcend all matters of party politics."[141]

Hoover's reply was unequivocal:

> My own views are summarized in a word—that we must have united support for the President. In the issues before us there can be no party policies. It is vital that we have a solid front and a sustained leadership.
>
> I am for President Wilson's leadership not only in the conduct of the war, but also in the negotiation of peace, and afterward in the direction of America's burden in the rehabilitation of the world.

The Food Administrator extolled President Wilson's "genius" in conducting the armistice negotiations that were now nearing a climax. By his "conduct and word" the President had helped the German people and their allies to realize the "debauchery" into which "militarism" had led them. If the German people themselves could now overthrow their autocracy, the President would "save the lives of a million American boys and countless innocent women and children" and attain a "more complete victory and a more permanent guarantee of peace than [by] any other means." Wilson's leadership, declared Hoover, "has gained gigantic strides in this course."

Looking to the future, Hoover concluded that the United States must rescue Europe from a threatened "conflagration of anarchy" by restoring it to "industry and self-support," while avoiding American "entanglement in the process." This, "the greatest problem that our Government has ever faced," could be overcome only by "this same leadership which has the confidence of the great mass of people in Europe": the leadership of Woodrow Wilson and no other.[142]

Neither Coudert nor Hoover explicitly alluded to the shrill political campaign raging around them. Both men eschewed "party politics." The words "Republican" and "Democrat" did not appear in their letters. But Coudert's reference to "divided counsels" and Hoover's appeal for "united support for the President" could mean only one thing just days before the election: Vote Democratic. On November 4 their letters appeared in full in the *New York Times* under the headline: "Hoover Calls for Support of Wilson."[143]

The President was both moved and delighted:

> Your letter to Mr. Coudert has touched me very deeply [he wrote to Hoover], and I want you to know not only how proud I am to have your endorsement and your backing given in such generous fashion, but also what serious importance I attach to it, for I have learned to value your judgment and have the greatest trust in all your moral reactions. I thank you from the bottom of my heart.[144]

Herbert Hoover never stood higher in the esteem of his chief than he did on that November day.

The Republicans, however, were outraged. The chairman of the Republican Congressional Committee accused Hoover of "prostitution of official station three days before the election" and hinted darkly that the Food

Administration would be investigated by the next Congress.[145] Senator Henry Cabot Lodge, who had clashed with Hoover in the sugar hearings, was also annoyed: "He has been appealing to Republicans and Democrats alike and has received from both great support, and it did not lie with him to come out and make such an appeal as he made for a Democratic Congress."[146] Theodore Roosevelt, who had publicly lent his prestige to Hoover's food conservation efforts, told a friend that Hoover had "showed himself in a very contemptible light," and added, "I shall never feel the same toward him again."[147]

In a sense, Hoover had written the letter that President Wilson should have issued: dignified and thoughtful, with no direct criticism of the opposition. Yet if nervous Democratic leaders hoped that Hoover's document, published only a day before the election, would tilt the electoral balance, they were disappointed. On November 5, the resurgent Republicans captured the House of Representatives by a substantial majority and the Senate by a margin of two seats. Although many factors contributed to the outcome, the nation's newspapers overwhelmingly interpreted it as a stinging rebuke of the President's harshly partisan appeal.[148]

For Hoover, the entire episode was an embarrassment, whose reverberations would haunt him for several years. Just which side of the political fence was he on? If he did have presidential ambitions—and by now some in Washington thought he did[149]—it would be difficult for him to pursue his quest through the Republican Party whose leaders he had just antagonized.

In the aftermath of the Democrats' debacle, and off and on during the next two years, Hoover's admirers endeavored to control the damage. Only six days after the election, Hoover's intimate friend Edgar Rickard pointed out to a correspondent that Hoover's letter had not endorsed any political party and had specifically rejected "party politics." Ignoring the political context in which the letter appeared, Rickard contended that the letter was "a personal tribute to President Wilson's policy and expression of Mr. Hoover's loyalty to him." Since Hoover had "absolutely no thought" of entering politics, said Rickard, it was "quite natural" that he should express his approval of a President whose conduct of foreign policy he considered masterful.[150] For his part, Frederic Coudert—unaware of Vance McCormick's part in the incident—insisted that neither Hoover nor himself had been "thinking of politics or of helping the Democratic party or the President as such."[151] In their lunch on November 1, Coudert claimed, "no question of partisanship or local political concern" was ever discussed.[152]

Hoover himself characteristically kept silent. When he did offer explanations much later in his life, he betrayed a lingering defensiveness. In a draft of his memoirs, he asserted that he had issued his statement because he "considered it my duty to support in the 1918 election the Congressmen who were loyal to Wilson and his objectives." Despite the "abuse" he thereupon drew from Republican politicians, Hoover continued, he "had to be content with the satisfaction of knowing that I had stood firm on the fundamental principle of loyalty to my superior. And loyalty is doubly important in war."[153]

When he published his *Memoirs*, however, Hoover subtly changed this passage. Deleting the references to loyalty to his superior, he now asserted that he had acted out of duty to support "the Congressmen who were loyal to Wilson's objectives whether Republicans or Democrats."[154] He did not explain how his letter to Coudert, appearing the day before the election, could have helped any Republican candidates. Still later, in 1958, in a book entitled *The Ordeal of Woodrow Wilson*, Hoover claimed that Coudert was a Republican and that Hoover had written to him in support of Wilson "because I believed that the President's hand in the Treaty negotiations would be greatly weakened if the election went against him."[155]

Curiously, in all of these explanations Hoover never mentioned the role of Vance McCormick. In 1920, in fact, when Hoover was a Republican presidential candidate, he went to considerable lengths to have Coudert deny in writing a published report that McCormick had instigated Hoover's letter.[156] Fighting to reestablish his Republican credentials after the misstep of 1918, Hoover could ill afford to admit that he had embraced Wilson's appeal at the direct behest of the chairman of the Democratic National Committee. It would be more expedient for Hoover politically, and more consistent with his reputation as a man above politics, to assert instead that in 1918 he had merely responded to the query of an independent-minded gentleman named Frederic Coudert. Having established his alibi, as it were, by 1920, Hoover never wavered from it thereafter: he had been a partisan in 1918 for only the best and most nonpartisan of reasons.

Yet if Hoover did succumb to political pressure in 1918 and then concealed the fact, his stated reasons for his endorsement of Wilson were nevertheless genuine. In November 1918 he *did* admire the President and did enthusiastically approve his foreign policies. In all likelihood he sincerely believed that a Democratic defeat in the Congressional election would weaken both his commander in chief and America's power at a critical moment in world history. Hoover's eloquent letter to Coudert was no act of hypocrisy. Probably, too, the Food Administrator felt obliged to stand loyally by his leader when the case was put to him in these terms. He may also have feared the consequences if he, a member of the Wilsonian inner circle, should refuse a request to rally to the President's side.

Were Hoover's undoubted convictions mixed with personal calculation? There is no evidence that he issued his letter to Coudert in order to ingratiate himself with the President or Democratic Party bosses. If anything, he entered the fray with reluctance. But like his resignation from the Republican Club of New York City the year before, his encomiastic gesture in support of Wilson raised a question: Could any man in public life be that nonpartisan, that guileless, that devoted to nothing but the public weal? Or was he pursuing ambitions of his own? It was hard for awestruck admirers to believe he was. It was even harder for veteran politicians to think he was not. By the end of the war, the aura of inscrutability that enveloped Hoover when he first came to Washington still had not disappeared.

16

Gains and Losses

I

THE crises of war and the machinations of politics were not the only challenges Hoover faced in the nation's capital in 1917–18. Maintaining some semblance of a private life was another.

In the spring of 1917, after staying for a time at the New Willard Hotel, Hoover rented a furnished home at 1628 Sixteenth Street. In the overcrowded conditions of wartime, it quickly became a boardinghouse. Many of Hoover's closest associates had left their wives at home when they came to Washington to join the Chief's crusade. By midsummer no fewer than ten of these "bachelors" were living with Hoover and his wife Lou.[1] One newspaper called it "[t]he busiest household in America."[2]

As Washington groaned under the oppressive heat (air conditioners not yet having been invented), Mrs. Hoover was more than willing to provide her husband's senior aides the comparative comforts of a private home.[3] Still, the arrangement could only be temporary. In mid-August Hoover signed a lease for the home of Charles Francis Adams at 1701 Massachusetts Avenue.[4] Into this elegant brick dwelling the Food Administrator and his family eventually moved.[5] Here, with the aid of a cook, nannies for their two children, and other servants, the family resumed the lifestyle that had graced their beloved Red House in London.

The following spring the Hoovers concurrently leased a second home: a secluded estate called "In the Woods" in the Maryland suburb of Chevy

Chase.[6] For Hoover's wife, though not for the overworked Chief, it became a summertime getaway from the sultry dews and damps of downtown Washington.

While the acquisition of more ample living quarters gave the Hoovers a modicum of privacy, it did not mark any withdrawal from society. The war—and their own preferences—saw to that. Rare was the evening when the Food Administrator and his wife had supper alone. To the house on Sixteenth Street and then to the Adams mansion, an unending stream of guests came to dine: visiting dignitaries like Lord Reading, Arthur Balfour, Ignacy Paderewski, and Marshal Joffre of France, as well as countless Food Administration officials and representatives of other wartime agencies.[7] On at least one occasion, Hoover's guests included Assistant Secretary of the Navy Franklin Roosevelt and his wife Eleanor.[8] Although Hoover and Roosevelt had little direct contact officially, they did meet socially during the war and became, in Hoover's words, "good friends."[9]

Dinners at the Hoover table were not occasions for idle chatter. The Food Administrator had neither aptitude nor tolerance for small talk, certainly not when affairs of state needed to be addressed. For Hoover and his guests, the line between work and recreation was rarely drawn. One topic—the war—was all-consuming. Discussion of its infinite ramifications frequently lasted late into the evening.[10]

When the habitually taciturn Hoover chose to talk at length about these issues, the effect on his listeners could be profound. During the summer of 1917 he occasionally visited the "House of Truth," a popular nearby rooming house where a number of brilliant young men, including Felix Frankfurter and Walter Lippmann, lived and incessantly entertained.[11] Hearing the Food Administrator discourse to this group about the war and European politics, Lippmann was fascinated. Never, he said, had he encountered "a more interesting man."[12] Hoover, he concluded, "had the greatest gift for exposition of anybody I'd met."[13]

Only on Sundays—and sometimes not even then—did Hoover permit himself a few hours of recreation. Although born and raised a Quaker, he had not attended a meeting for years. As in England before the war, so now in Washington in 1917–18: the Hoover family's Sundays were devoted not to Sabbath observance but to automobile excursions into the countryside with friends. Almost invariably the picnickers would stop near a stream. Then, after lunch, "the great engineer" (as Hugh Gibson once called Hoover) would lead them in diverting the stream from its course by digging canals and building dams with stones. By late in the afternoon, everyone was wet and muddy, and their leader looked "like a tramp." It was one of his favorite forms of recreation.[14] At the end of the day the little motorcade would return home in time to entertain the Hoovers' guests at their Sunday suppers.[15]

Once in a while, Hoover's lifestyle became the subject of public attention. In May 1918, amid concern over the growing labor shortage in war industries, the Food Administrator announced that he had sold his large automobile, discharged his chauffeur, and had begun to drive a smaller car himself. "I could not think of witholding a man from industry who should be building ships," he said.[16] As it turned out, the loss of a chauffeur was Hoover's recreational gain. His new car was a Cadillac Roadster, which he took to driving with "boyish delight."[17] For his passengers, the experience was less relaxing. Edgar Rickard advised a friend to "hold tight" when Hoover was "at the wheel . . . for he is a reckless and speedy driver."[18]

The Hoover family's eating customs also came under public scrutiny—a development they did not entirely welcome. In the summer of 1917 Hoover's two young sons, on vacation in Palo Alto, California, were seen to be consuming plenty of ice cream sodas at a local hangout for Stanford students. Soon the story spread that the Food Administrator could not control his own children and that he was letting them eat all the sweets they desired. When Mrs. Hoover hired a celebrated black cook to prepare meals in the Hoover household, similar rumors circulated. The cook was not known for the simplicity of her creations. No doubt because of undercurrents like these, in the winter of 1918 the *Washington Star* and *Ladies' Home Journal* published articles insisting that the Hoover household had been "thoroughly Hooverized." Young Herbert and Allan, it was said, had not eaten a single piece of candy since coming east. As for the cook, after "a time of sorrow and stress of wounded professional pride," Mrs. Hoover had converted her to the most stringent practices of food conservation. According to the press, every day at the Hoover home was completely porkless and almost entirely wheatless. The Chief, it reported, had been obliged to do without his breakfast bacon for months.[19]

The *Ladies' Home Journal* emphasized that Lou Henry Hoover was "entirely" responsible for the "food-conservation regime" at her bustling home.[20] The resourceful wife of the Food Administrator had even more on her mind. In the autumn of 1917, along with the wives of certain other of her husband's associates, she established a Food Administration Club for the hundreds of women who had taken jobs in the new agency. The purpose of the club was to provide an opportunity for a social life for these mostly young and single women in the difficult wartime conditions of Washington. To this end, Lou and her colleagues leased a house on I Street to serve as a headquarters and "rest-house" (as she put it) for the women. By the end of the war the club had rented two more houses on the same street. The buildings contained living quarters, a reading room, a parlor for guests, and a dining room in which club members could obtain their daily meals. Lou poured money as well as energy into the project. Between late 1918 and mid-1919 the three club buildings consumed more than $8,000 in rent which she herself paid, evidently out of the Hoovers' own pockets.[21]

Like her husband, then, Lou immersed herself in purposeful wartime activity. In her own sphere she, too, was an executive.

Yet for all the satisfactions of their daily lives, the Hoovers' continuing residence in Washington exacted a price. When Bert arrived in New York City in May 1917, his wife and sons were not there to meet him. They had preceded him from London and had gone directly to Stanford University, where Lou had rented the home of a professor.[22] This in itself was not unusual. Years before, Hoover and his wife had acquired the habit, during visits to California, of temporarily leasing homes from faculty friends on or near the Stanford campus, which Hoover had long considered his spiritual abode.[23] Now, however, the prospective Food Administrator faced an indefinite stint of war service three thousand miles away. What should his family do?

Worried about health conditions in the East,[24] Lou telegraphed her husband in mid-May that the boys "cannot go east till cold weather" and that she did not think she should leave them for the entire summer.[25] Bert telegraphed back to do whatever she considered best for herself and their sons.[26] But Hoover was struggling to establish suitable living arrangements in Washington, and the next day asked his wife to come east for a little while.[27] And so, at the end of the month, leaving her boys in the care of California friends and relatives, Lou took a train across the country to Washington, where she promptly became the efficient manager of the "boarding house" on I Street.[28] She did not see her sons again for three months.

Late in the summer Lou returned by train to Palo Alto, rounded up her boys, and took them with her back to Washington, where they were reunited with their father for the first time since the preceding winter.[29] The next nine months were happy ones for the family. Herbert, Jr., now fourteen, and Allan, now ten, enrolled at the Sidwell Friends School (a Quaker academy in Washington) and frequently joined their parents on Sunday outings.[30] For Hoover, it was a chance to "gain more association" with the sons from whom he had so often been separated since the war began.

In the spring of 1918, however, the old family pattern of unsettledness reasserted itself. Young Herbert, who had developed ear and tonsil problems, was sent to Duluth, Minnesota, where he entered a boys camp and then stayed with the family of Hoover's associate, Julius Barnes.[31] Mrs. Hoover hoped that exposure to the outdoors would cure the boy's condition.[32] In May, Lou herself journeyed to California for a brief visit after addressing the national convention of the General Federation of Women's Clubs in Hot Springs, Arkansas. Allan remained in the care of household staff in Washington.[33] During most of July and August, the Chief was in Europe on government business. By then, Lou was back home with her younger son. But in late August she once again set out for the West, probably to fetch young Herbert in Minnesota.[34] When the school year opened in the autumn, Allan matriculated at the Sidwell Friends School and his brother at the Taft School in Connecticut.[35]

Then, in the expectant autumn of 1918, as Allied armies pressed toward victory in France, a pandemic of Spanish influenza swept over much of the globe. It was the worst eruption of disease since the bubonic plague of the Middle Ages. Striking the east coast of the United States in early September, the scourge spread steadily south and west. By the time it subsided, more than 20,000,000 people had died around the world, including half a million in the United States.[36]

Of the approximately 1,600 men and women in the Food Administration's Washington offices, more than 300 became afflicted with influenza. Eight died.[37] Hoover and his wife escaped, as did Allan, who was confined to "In the Woods" for safety.[38] Up at the Taft School, Herbert, Jr. was not so fortunate, and his mother journeyed anxiously to his side.[39] Although the boy survived, his hearing did not recover.[40] He was now partially deaf—a handicap that would plague him for years.

If a "somewhat disconnected" family life was one casualty of Hoover's wartime service in Washington, his hope of immediately building a home in California was another.[41] For several years he and his wife had been planning to construct a "dream house" in the Golden State. At first they had intended to do so in San Francisco; then they had decided upon the Stanford campus itself.[42] But when? That was the question.

On May 14, 1917 Lou, in Palo Alto, telegraphed her busy husband in Washington: "Do you think it advisable build fifty thousand dollars house or five thousand or none at all."[43] Hoover immediately telegraphed back: "You can build any sort of house you wish but if it is to be the ultimate family headquarters it should be substantial and roomy. The cost is secondary."[44]

The Hoovers soon hired Louis C. Mullgardt, a distinguished San Francisco architect who had recently designed the first official residence for the president of Stanford University. The Hoovers' plans called for a two-story, twenty-one-room, $50,000 house on San Juan Hill, overlooking the campus and San Francisco Bay. But when Mullgardt indiscreetly announced their intentions (and his own selection as architect) in the press, his clients were mortified and angry. Ever prospective of their privacy, the Hoovers hated uncontrolled publicity. They particularly disliked it now. Here was the U.S. Food Administrator, the nation's premier preacher of self-denial, preparing (or so it seemed) to build a magnificent edifice for himself in wartime. Furthermore, Mullgardt's preliminary design was in the same Portuguese Gothic style as the university president's house then going up—a structure that the Hoovers found distinctly pretentious. The result came swiftly: Mullgardt was paid off and dismissed.[45]

Unfortunately for Hoover, the cat was out of the bag. Before long he came under criticism for allegedly diverting scarce wartime labor to construction of a large home, even though the project had not gotten beyond the planning stage. Hoover's wife tried to minimize the damage. During the winter and early spring of 1918, she denied to friends that her husband planned to build a mansion on San Juan Hill. He had simply asked an architect to develop (in the words of a newspaper account of her remarks) "some rough plans for a little home in the hills" sometime after the war—only to have the architect mistakenly come up with "elaborate plans for a veritable regal mansion." At this point, according to Mrs. Hoover, her husband had dropped the matter. So the Stanford University and Palo Alto newspapers reported to their readers in early April 1918.[46]

When Lou Henry Hoover saw the Stanford newspaper's story, she swiftly wrote a letter to the editor. The wife of the Food Administrator did not deny the report's general accuracy.[47] Instead, she now asserted that her husband had never considered building a house "on the campus." Rather, *she* had intended to build a "cottage" on San Juan Hill—had intended, in fact, to do so in the autumn of 1914, only to have the war intervene. Since then, she had been unable to give the subject "more than an occasional passing thought" while on campus. According to her, "the whole matter" must now wait until she had "the time and inclination for such peaceful contemplation."[48]

Mrs. Hoover's explanation was implausible. By hiring an architect in the first place, she showed that she had obviously devoted more than "an occasional passing thought" to the project. Her claim that her husband had never planned to build on campus was equally implausible, unless she was making an irrelevant distinction between the central campus and San Juan Hill, a mile or so away. While Mrs. Hoover may have intended to construct a cottage on this hill in 1914, in 1917 Hoover himself had expressly authorized her to spend $50,000, if she wanted to, for their "ultimate" family home. Surely this was the Hoovers' purpose when they hired Mullgardt. Why else would they have retained someone so eminent to draw up their plans?

Lou's letter was deeply revealing. Sensitive, like her husband, to public criticism, and anxious to end the embarrassment caused by Mullgardt's unauthorized disclosure of her intentions, Lou now strove to convey the impression that she had never had such intentions at all. Like Bert, she was finding that public life could be nettlesome.

Clearly for political reasons (if no other), the Hoovers could not build their "dream house" as long as the Great War raged. The family's quest for rootedness must be deferred. In mid-1918, therefore, Mrs. Hoover purchased the nearby campus home of Professor Albert C. Whittaker for $10,000. This became the Hoovers' California residence, pending construction on their lot on San Juan Hill.[49]

II

A PERMANENT home in California was not the only Hoover dream to suffer from disruption by the war. Across the Atlantic, circumstances were slowly driving him toward a final bittersweet farewell to his prewar mining empire.

When Hoover returned to America in the spring of 1917, his London-based business career was nearly over. He had no time for making money any more. Only three years before, he had stood at the pinnacle of his profession: a director of eighteen mining and financial companies having a total authorized share capital of more than $55,000,000.[50] In the ensuing three years, as the Belgian relief effort absorbed his energies, he had gradually let his business interests go. By early 1917 he had largely divested himself of his directorates and stockholdings—with one great exception: the Burma Corporation, Ltd., where he retained not only his seat on the board but a bloc of stock exceeding 100,000 shares. It amounted to at least a one-seventh interest in the multi-million-dollar enterprise, a portion second only to that of one other stockholder.[51]

Hoover's unwillingness to part with his Burma investment was understandable. The Burma Corporation was the holding company for Burma Mines, Ltd., a British-registered enterprise that was developing an abandoned Chinese silver mine known as Bawdwin in the jungles of upper Burma. Hoover had launched this undertaking in 1906, and in 1913 workers at the site had finally confirmed his conviction: beneath the old surface workings was one of the richest silver-lead-zinc deposits on earth. With ultimate success more or less assured, Hoover had promptly reorganized the venture's finances and had made plans for development on a colossal scale.

The mine's owners had thereupon concentrated on what Hoover and his technical committee considered crucial for systematic exploitation of the vast deposit: construction of a 1.4-mile horizontal tunnel, complete with a narrow-gauge railway, into the side of the ore-bearing mountain. It was a daring and extraordinarily laborious undertaking. But in late 1916 the "Tiger Tunnel," as Herbert Hoover named it, was essentially completed. With at least 3,240,000 tons of proven and probable ore reserves at the Bawdwin site, the long-awaited era of gigantic ore production—and commensurate profits—seemed at hand.[52]

Meanwhile, in London, where the board of directors of the Burma Corporation sat, all was not nearly so promising. For some time the board had been riven by bitter policy disagreements between R. Tilden Smith, the company's principal shareholder, and a faction led by Hoover and a British financier, Francis Govett.[53] By the summer of 1917 the strife was so intense that Govett had had enough. We must either buy out Smith, he told an ally (a difficult feat that would require American money) or we must sell out our own interests, an alternative he clearly preferred.[54]

As it happened, Hoover had been thinking along similar lines. In March 1917, while on a trip to the United States for the Belgian relief, he had approached potential investors in New York City for the purpose of organizing "a business here that will let me out of a part of my holding and build up the probable control of the [Burma] Company on this side" (the American side) of the Atlantic.[55] Hoover's initiative was "extremely confidential";[56] just whom he contacted is not known. But little seemed to come of his action.[57] By early October 1917 he, too, was ready to sell out and so instructed his London representative.[58]

Now, however, a new and formidable actor entered the scene. By 1917 the British government was thoroughly alarmed by the power which German metallurgical companies had exerted over mining enterprises in Great Britain and the British empire before the war. At the outset of hostilities in 1914, for instance, the Zinc Corporation in Australia—another of Hoover's great enterprises—had been encumbered by a long-term contract requiring it to sell its zinc concentrates exclusively to a German smelting firm. As the war intensified, the British government grew determined that never again would Germany dominate the vital base metals industry of England and its overseas possessions. In 1915 and 1916 the British government adopted numerous measures to this end.[59]

In 1917 it considered still more. In April the Board of Trade (a government department) proposed to the nation's War Cabinet that exports of "important ores and metals" produced in the empire be "controlled" for a time after the war.[60] In June, citing the dominance of the world's base metal industry by German companies and their American affiliates, the Board of Trade went further. It now asked the War Cabinet for permission to draw up a measure that would prohibit British subjects who owned mining properties abroad from selling these to "foreigners" without the prior consent of the government.[61] Later in the year the War Cabinet created an interdepartmental Economic Offensive Committee. Among its task was to investigate means of protection (in its chairman's words) against "being at the mercy of any German monopoly at the end of the war."[62]

The Board of Trade was not the only British government agency to entertain such fears. In May 1917 the India Office, which supervised affairs in Burma, asked the Board of Trade for advice about the best way to secure and safeguard British control of mining concessions held by British-registered companies that had "a proportion of foreign (though not enemy) directors and shareholders."[63] In making this inquiry, the India Office was almost certainly thinking of Hoover's mighty silver-lead-zinc enterprise emerging in the Burmese jungle. In reply, the Board of Trade suggested that the India Office could bring pressure on companies in its jurisdiction to enact Articles of Association ensuring permanent British control of their enterprises. As a way of achieving this, the Board enclosed a copy of a document that it had devised to enforce the Trading With the Enemy Amendment Act of 1916. This document was a model form of additional provisions of Articles of Association that the Board required formerly enemy-controlled companies to adopt when selling their shares to British subjects.[64]

The India Office's concern about the fate of Hoover's Burma company was not illogical. Before the war a German firm had tried unsuccessfully to buy it, and in 1914 a scientist apparently representing German interests had joined the Burma Corporation's technical committee.[65] He was still a member in 1917.[66] The India Office may not have known these things, but it certainly knew that the property in Burma was a glittering prize. Not long after receiving the Board of Trade's model clauses, the India Office apparently asked the Burma Corporation to insert them in its Articles of Association.

Around the beginning of October, Hoover, now in Washington, received a copy of the model clauses from London, along with an "order" (as he described it) that the Burma company alter its Articles to comply with them.[67] Reading the model clauses, Hoover was stunned. The document did not merely forbid *enemy* individuals and corporations from holding shares in British companies without the Board of Trade's consent. It stipulated that *foreigners* could not, without permission, collectively hold more than 40 percent of a company's share capital or 25 percent of its voting power. If, at any time, foreign participation in a company exceeded these figures without the British government's consent, the company's board of directors "may at any time and shall at the request of the Board of Trade" require "the holder of the Shares in question" to "retire from the Company" and sell his shares. Furthermore, at all times at least three quarters of the board of directors, including the chairman, must be "British subjects resident in the United Kingdom." Although ostensibly aimed at the Germans and their accomplices in other countries, the model clauses were so broadly drafted that they would affect all foreigners, including Americans.

To Hoover the proposed revision of the Articles of Association of the Burma Corporation along these lines must have looked like a dagger aimed at his heart. To be sure, he himself did not own 25 percent of the corporation's shares. Nor, so far as one can tell, did the aggregate foreign interest surpass this threshold.[68] But he was one of at least two Americans on the company's seven-member board of directors—a ratio that exceeded the Board of Trade's recommendation. He had also served as the company's chairman and may have hoped to hold this command post again. Most importantly of all, perhaps, if the Burma Corporation now accepted the British government's "suggestions," this would forever prevent Hoover and his American associates from increasing their shareholdings to the point of establishing effective control of the enterprise on the American side.

In an angry letter to the State Department, Hoover denounced the British government's action:

> I make no appeal to the Government to take care of my private business, for I am thoroughly able to take care of that myself, but I do want to call your attention to the fact that these regulations, and this attitude towards

> Americans doing business in the British Empire, is the most vicious form of trade war, and is deliberately designed to break down any possibility of American enterprise within that country. With all the devotion that I have for the English people, yet if the result of our expenditure of a few dozens of billions of dollars and a few hundred thousand lives is to provide for us this sort of eventuality in trade and commerce after the war, we had better have kept out of it, because we will find ourselves, when it comes to peace treaty, sitting on the same side of the table with the Germans, endeavoring to get the right for the free activity of our countrymen in trade, whereas we have gone to war in an endeavor to preserve their right to travel the seas.[69]

Hoover decided not to send his letter to the State Department. Instead, he took up the issue with the President.[70] Persuaded by the protests of his Food Administrator, Woodrow Wilson in some way threatened the British with retaliation. A few weeks later a British Cabinet official, after conferring with the President of the Board of Trade and the Parliamentary Under-Secretary of State for India, recorded in his diary:

> Talked with Stanley and Islington on the question of the Burma Co. Hoover has got Wilson to interfere. Burma must be open to American capital or else America wont play.[71]

Meanwhile the British government's campaign against foreign economic interests was accelerating. Back in May the government had issued an Order-in-Council forbidding British subjects to transfer any shares or interests in mines in the United Kingdom to aliens or "foreign controlled" companies without official consent.[72] On October 23 a new Order-in-Council extended the prohibition to "mines wherever situated."[73] No British subject, in other words, could sell his stock *in any mine in the world* to a foreigner without first obtaining permission from the British government. One week later, a high official at the India Office contacted the Board of Trade about certain issues of policy arising from the proposal to insert the Board's model clauses in the Burma Corporation's Articles of Association. The official warned that while the Government of India was "willing to consider alternative Articles," it would "hesitate on agreeing to a scheme which would allow an American house to obtain control of the Burma Corporation" without the government's consent.[74]

Across the Atlantic, Hoover, for his part, was mounting a strenuous campaign for an "open door" in Burma. One instrument of his counterattack was Thomas Lamont, a senior partner in J. P. Morgan & Company, who raised the issue on a visit to London in the autumn of 1917.[75] By this time, the Morgan firm had evidently become a significant investor in the Burma enterprise—and an ally of Hoover in the struggle for control of its destiny.[76] One way or another, Hoover made his objections known to the British in no uncertain terms. "We represented strongly," he later wrote, "that we had developed a great imperial raw material assett [sic], that we were not at war with them, that most of us were giving our time to war work[,] that such a property was unsalable in war times etc. etc. It was obvious that the acts were formulated to get rid of Americans as well as Germans—or to get properties cheap."[77]

In the face of President Wilson's intervention, the India Office temporarily retreated from its insistence that the Burma Corporation alter its Articles of Association. Instead, at a meeting of the British government's Economic Offensive Committee on November 23, the Under-Secretary of State for India, Lord Islington, alluded to the newly formulated British policy of controlling imperial exports and raw materials after the war. Because of this policy, he said, the Indian government might be able to be more "lenient" on the issue of limiting foreign control "in such a case as that of the Burma Corporation." Probably heaving a sigh of relief, the Economic Offensive Committee agreed that temporary postwar export controls "might make it more possible for the Government of India to meet the American difficulty by a concession."[78]

The India Office's backpedaling was brief. Just one week later, the Undersecretary of State for India returned to the Economic Offensive Committee with a blunt message: In the case of the mines at Bawdwin, the "national interest" was at stake. The Government of India deemed it "essential" that the Burma Corporation's zinc ores be "available for smelting in India" and that the company be operated in accord with "the requirements of the British empire and especially of India." If "an American house" got control of the company, this might not happen. The ores might instead end up in the hands of "some great international Trust," with no "security that the mines would be worked in the interest of India."

Confronted with Islington's appeal, the Economic Offensive Committee gave in. It decided that if the Indian government could persuade the Burma Corporation to adopt the model clauses, there was "no sufficient reason for hanging up the matter" now. But the committee noted pointedly that if "Messrs Morgan" or the U.S. government objected to the clauses, the India Office would have to handle the issue. Plainly anxious not to antagonize the Americans, the committee stressed that its decision in this "exceptional" case did *not* establish the principle that American capital would henceforth be excluded from participating in or controlling mining enterprises in the British empire.[79] Of course, the India Office's expressed fear that an American "house" might gain control of the Burma mines confirmed Hoover's accusation that the target of the model clauses was not only Germany but the United States.

With a green light from the Economic Offensive Committee, the India Office now proceeded to exercise its powers of persuasion. In March 1918, at a special meeting of the stockholders, the Burma Mines, Ltd. formally amended its Articles of Association by adopting in entirety the Board of Trade's model clauses. The company incorporated the clauses under the heading: "Prevention of Foreign Control."[80] This change had no immediate effect on Hoover, since his shares and directorate were in the parent Burma Corporation. But at some point in 1918, the Burma Corporation, too, agreed with the Secretary of State for India to amend its Articles of Association "for the same purpose": insurance of a permanent "preponderance of British representation."[81]

As the noose tightened, Hoover again raised a protest. In a letter to Secretary of State Lansing on May 10, he declared: "The Indian Government has issued instructions by which alien ownership of stock and alien participation in any enterprise dealing with raw materials is reduced to such a minority as to practically make American enterprise in that country impossible." The Australian government, he added, had enacted "even more drastic" legislation of a similar character.

> In taking up the matter, I of course do not wish to have my own name put forward personally but I do think as a matter of national interest some recognition of the world right of citizens to trade should be arrived at at an early date. This line is entirely consonant with our ideals and intentions in this war and a monopolization of raw material industries is fundamentally one of the things which has given rise to the present strife and is in a fair way to make peace impossible.[82]

There is no indication that Lansing intervened in Hoover's behalf.[83] Meanwhile, in London, the Burma Corporation's internal problems had continued to fester. In December 1917 an ally of R. Tilden Smith came to the United States in an effort to buy Hoover out. Hoover was amenable—for the right price—but the negotiations soon collapsed.[84] On the board of directors itself, the warfare between Smith and his colleagues went on unabatedly.[85] To thwart any surprises by Smith at the company's annual meeting, Hoover and his allies carefully pooled their proxies.[86] They also explored the possibility of having the newly founded Anglo-American Corporation of South Africa—in which Hoover had considerable influence—acquire control of the Burma Corporation and buy out the "Hoover Morgan interest." Hoover's price was $20.00 a share, or a total of about $2,500,000.[87]

All this was in ironic contrast to the development work proceeding at the Bawdwin site itself. By June 30, 1918 the mine's proven ore reserves amounted to nearly 3,900,000 tons, enough eventually to yield a lucrative string of dividends.[88]

With the board enmeshed in strife, with no time to devote to the company's affairs,[89] and with the likelihood that the Burma Corporation would soon accept the British government's proposed restrictions on aliens, Hoover finally crossed the Rubicon. In the autumn of 1918 he sold virtually his entire shareholding in the Burma Corporation, thereby ending his mining engineering career.[90] Not long afterward, he resigned from the board of directors.[91]

Legally, of course, Hoover was not obliged to get out. Even if the Board of Trade's model clauses had been in effect, he could have remained a prominent shareholder, mover, and shaker in the Burma Corporation. And even if his—or the combined foreign—holdings in the company had come to exceed 25 percent of the voting power, one wonders whether the board or the British government would have dared to move against him. On the other hand, Hoover must have asked himself: Why risk it? Why should he put up with the hostility to Americans that the India Office and the model clauses betrayed? Why should he devote his energies to a company he could never hope to control? Why should he accept a position of permanent inferiority to the likes of R. Tilden Smith?

So Hoover reluctantly relinquished his association with the increasingly promising Burma mining venture in which he had invested "practically the whole of my saving" for almost ten years.[92] It was a considerable transaction. Some time afterward, in a set of handwritten notes on what he had accomplished in his life, he wrote that he realized about $2,500,000 from his Burma "interest."[93] In 1940, in an unpublished portion of his memoirs, he stated that he "got about $3,500,000 out of it."[94] Whatever the precise figure, it was more than enough to fulfill what had once been his dream: the making of a fortune by the time he was middle-aged.[95] The money he made from the sale of his Burma holdings, he wrote more than two decades later, "constituted the family fortune—less the great wastage from public service benevolence beyond my means and the violent shrinkages since."[96]

Years later Hoover looked back on his Burma adventure with nostalgia and a hint of ruefulness. "It was a great enterprise," he wrote; "took it as bare jungle and left it with 25,000 men employed and a new town on earth."[97] He pointed out that his "interest" in Burma had represented "a profit in sight" at the mine of around $10,000,000—"the net savings and energy of 15 years of my life."[98] During the 1920s and 1930s the Burma Corporation finally yielded handsome dividends, but Hoover did not receive them. By selling out when he did for the price he received, he parted with his holdings at a fraction of their value.[99]

Yet it Hoover knowingly gave up a prospective immense fortune, he did gain enough to live comfortably for the remainder of his life. (Two and a half million dollars in 1918 was the equivalent of more than $20,000,000 in the mid-1990s.)[100] More importantly, he gained his freedom: freedom to devote himself, if he wished, entirely to altruism and public life. And this, by 1918, was his desire. His final farewell to private business that year was not entirely caused by the British. It was one more manifestation of where his deepest dreams were already taking him.

19. *Herbert Hoover and associates on a trip to London in the summer of 1918 (left to right: Hoover, Alonzo Taylor, Lewis L. Strauss, E. Dana Durand, Louis P. Sheldon, James F. Bell, Joseph P. Cotton).* Herbert Hoover Presidential Library-Museum.

20. *Julius H. Barnes.* Herbert Hoover Presidential Library-Museum.

21. *Woodrow Wilson and his "War Cabinet," 1918. (Seated, left to right: Benedict Crowell, William G. McAdoo, President Wilson, Josephus Daniels, Bernard Baruch. Standing, left to right: Herbert Hoover, Edward N. Hurley, Vance McCormick, Harry A. Garfield).* Herbert Hoover Presidential Library-Museum.

22. *Herbert Hoover's office at the U.S. Food Administration. A photograph of President Wilson is on the mantel, under the official emblem of the Food Administration.* National Archives.

23. *Herbert Hoover, Jr., in 1918.* Herbert Hoover Presidential Library-Museum.

24. *Allan Hoover in 1918.* Herbert Hoover Presidential Library-Museum.

25. *Lou Henry Hoover at "In the Woods," Bethesda, Maryland, 1918.* Herbert Hoover Presidential Library-Museum.

26. *The Chief, cigar in hand, at work, circa 1918.* Herbert Hoover Presidential Library-Museum.

17

"Ami de la Nation belge"

I

HERBERT Hoover was never one to cast off burdens willingly accepted, or to surrender power once he had acquired it. When he returned to America in the spring of 1917 to join the Wilson administration, he did not leave his previous responsibilities behind. For the remainder of the war, he simultaneously served as U.S. Food Administrator and as chairman of the Commission for Relief in Belgium, or CRB. The succor of the civil population of German-occupied Belgium and northern France—a mission to which he had already given nearly three years of his life—continued to weigh upon his shoulders.

As a neutral, humanitarian enterprise, the CRB was responsible not only for importing food into German-held territory, but for supervising its distribution and verifying that the helpless populace (and not the German army) received the aid. Until the spring of 1917 this critical function was performed almost exclusively by American CRB volunteers. When the United States entered the war, the Americans, no longer of neutral nationality, were obliged to withdraw from Belgium and northern France. Citizens from neutral Spain and Holland took their place. Outside Belgium, however, the administrative structure of the CRB remained largely unchanged. Hoover, as chairman, simply moved to Washington. He selected William B. Poland, an American civil engineer and longtime relief associate, to take over the CRB's London office and become the organization's chief of European operations.[1]

In one respect the American character of the CRB now became more pronounced than ever. Until the spring of 1917, the CRB had received 90 percent of its funding—about $266,000,000—from the governments of Great Britain and France.[2] (Much of this was money that the British and French had loaned for the purpose to the Belgian government-in-exile, which had then passed the sums along to Hoover's organization.) The rest had come from charitable contributions, including $12,000,000 from the United States.[3] But on May 9, 1917, after months of behind-the-scenes campaigning by Hoover, the U.S. government announced that it would take over financial responsibility for the relief for the next six months. No longer would the British and French governments be creditors to the Belgians. Instead, the United States would lend $12,500,000 per month—$7,500,000 to Belgium and $5,000,000 to France—or a total of $75,000,000 over six months, all of it earmarked for relief in these two countries. Although recorded on the books as government-to-government loans, the sums would actually be spent by the Commission for Relief in Belgium.[4] Gratified by this outcome, Hoover immediately suspended further charitable appeals.[5]

Hoover had good reason to be pleased. He would not now have to seek more funding from the financially strapped British and French. Although the American loan was only for six months, Hoover believed that the "way is open" for him to apply for further assistance in due course.[6] Having publicly committed itself to massive pecuniary support for the CRB, the U.S. government was not likely to reverse itself later on.

But if the American loan brought Hoover's commission financial stability, as well as the official American "recognition" that he had "long desired,"[7] the travails of his benevolent enterprise did not subside. Sadly and ironically, the first year of American belligerency was a period of ever-deepening trauma for the trapped citizens of Belgium and northern France. Time and time again the overworked U.S. Food Administrator was obliged to turn his attention to their piteous plight.

In the spring and summer of 1917 the German enemy's unrestricted submarine warfare campaign reached its deadliest intensity. Even the CRB was not spared. Although the Germans promised not to molest the commission's ships if they followed a narrowly defined route across the North Atlantic, twenty-two CRB vessels were nevertheless lost to mines and U-boats in 1917.[8] Moreover, the Germans adamantly refused to grant safe-conduct passes to CRB ships traveling directly across the English Channel from Great Britain to the neutral Dutch port of Rotterdam. As a result, the commission was unable to deliver a large quantity of food that it had assembled at English ports.[9] Complicating matters further, the CRB's little fleet—mostly ships requisitioned and donated by the exiled Belgian government—was too small to carry even half of the supplies needed per month.[10] To make up the deficit, the commission chartered neutral vessels, which were neither cheap nor easy to obtain. As the war at sea grew more desperate, many neutral shipowners refused to lease their vessels to the relief effort. Meanwhile the British government competed for these same ships for its own needs.[11]

The consequence of all this was only too plain. To keep their Belgian and French dependents alive, Hoover and his associates calculated that the CRB must deliver a minimum of 110,000 to 120,000 tons of food to Rotterdam every month.[12] Alas, from February 1917 through the following September, deliveries plummeted to a monthly average of less than 50,000 tons.[13]

The CRB tried frantically to compensate by drawing upon its reserves and by increasing food purchases in nearby Holland.[14] It was not enough. From Brussels, Emile Francqui, executive head of the Belgians' own relief agency, known as the Comité National, sent pleas to Hoover for help. "The famine is extending," he cried. Four million people were now "wasting away" because of "insufficient nourishment." Mortality and malnutrition were rising; tuberculosis was spreading; in many places weakened people were fainting in soup lines. Francqui warned that a terrible calamity would occur unless his country and northern France soon received the "strict minimum" of 100,000 to 110,000 tons of imported food per month.[15] In London, William Poland agreed. "If most desperate situation Belgium and France is to be avoided combined with discredit relief and American protection," he cabled Hoover in early August, the CRB must obtain at least 60,000 tons of "additional cargo capacity" immediately.[16]

Three thousand miles away, in Washington, Hoover strained to do just that. His target was the shipping of the "northern neutrals"—Holland, Denmark, Norway, and Sweden—who were engaged in a precarious balancing act between the Allies and the Germans. Hoover knew that the neutrals had bought substantial amounts of food for themselves in the United States and now wanted permission to ship it. Very well: let them allocate some of their vessels to the CRB as part of the bargain. It was time, he said bluntly, that the United States secure "some definite service from these people of a character which does not jeopardize their ships but which leads them into the path of a little humanity." For Hoover this meant conveying foodstuffs to Belgium.[17]

Late in the summer of 1917 Hoover obtained six charters for the CRB from Norway as a condition of releasing Norwegian-owned grain embargoed in the United States.[18] In the same way he extracted a few charters from the Swedes.[19] He also prevailed on the U.S. Shipping Board to give the CRB several recently seized vessels belonging to something called the Wagner fleet.[20] In fact, he told Poland, there was "absolutely nothing that my mind can invent that we have not tried within the last month" in the effort to find sufficient cargo tonnage to save Belgium from mass starvation.[21]

Still, the going was slow and filled with frustration. When the CRB announced in September that it had chartered two Norwegian vessels for several consecutive voyages, the British government vetoed the arrangement on the ground that charters could be approved only for one voyage at a time.[22] "[D]readfully short of ships" themselves,[23] the British evidently hoped to use the two Norwegian ships for their own purposes. With Hoover's approval, Poland protested vigorously to the Foreign Office.[24] Two weeks later the British let the relief commission keep its Norwegian charters.[25]

Was this humanitarianism, or was it a war-within-a-war? Hoover must often have wondered as the never-ending trials of the CRB taxed his energy and time. For a brief time in October he actually began to think that he should give it up. On the evening of October 9 he urged the American Red Cross to assume the CRB's duties.[26]

The next day the Red Cross official with whom Hoover spoke replied that the organization would be willing to replace the CRB, but only if Hoover and his relief colleagues continued to negotiate and handle financial transactions involving the U.S. government. For Hoover, this was not much of a deal; it was precisely the time-consuming handling of money and shipping that was most onerous. If he could not transfer these functions to someone else, why bother to reorganize the relief at all, particularly when the Red Cross seemed to think of it as a "merely managerial job"? Hoover knew that keeping the vulnerable enterprise alive would require much more than good management. His proposal to the Red Cross fell through.[27]

Meanwhile, at the Comité National's offices in Brussels, and at the exiled Belgian government's headquarters in France, anxiety for the future had curdled into anger at Hoover. In late August Hoover received what he considered a "very insulting" cable from Emile Francqui. Apparently Francqui and the Belgian government questioned whether Hoover and his government were doing enough to save the Belgian populace from a deathly debacle. Furious at this challenge to his leadership, Hoover replied coldly that the Belgians "had better take over the business themselves if they thought they could do it any better." The Belgians promptly apologized (according to Hoover), but the chairman of the CRB was disgusted for days. America was providing millions of dollars per month to the Belgian cause, he told a friend. It was doing everything in its power, "even to the prejudice of our people," by ceasing "absolutely essential imports" in order to free up shipping for Belgium and by reducing domestic food consumption. "It is about all they have a right to ask from any Nation."[28]

If Hoover's anger was laced with righteous indignation, it was not the first time he had clashed with certain Belgians. Repeatedly in 1915 and 1916 he had fought bitterly with Francqui and other Belgian leaders, to the point of threatening more than once to withdraw from the relief effort altogether. Nor was the formidable Francqui his only critic. The exiled Belgian government's finance minister, Aloys van de Vyvere, detested Hoover. It was only with great reluctance, and under heavy Hooverian pressure, that the Belgian government-in-exile had agreed in 1917 to ask the United States for the $75,000,000 relief loan that commenced in June. The Belgians would have preferred to borrow the money from Britain and France, as they had been doing, rather than from the United States, which might actually force them to repay the loan after the war.[29]

And now these same Belgians—or so Hoover believed—were insolently accusing him of not doing enough for them. The chairman of the CRB was not about to tolerate such behavior.[30]

It was apparently around this time that Hoover, fed up with the "pin pricks" emanating from van de Vyvere, among others, suggested that the entire relief project be turned over to "an international governmental commission." Hoover was not really serious. "It was," he told Poland later, "the usual reply that we have to make periodically to some people in order to maintain a reasonable decency in our relations and never went farther than suggesting to some of them that if they did not like it they could tackle it themselves." Unfortunately for Hoover, his bluff worked almost too well: Poland and the French government became concerned that he really meant it.[31] The effect on the Belgians was evidently more what he intended.

Then, in mid-October, Hoover heard that the Belgian government-in-exile was thinking of diverting one or more of its ships, which the CRB was using, to some other purpose. Furious all over again, he dispatched a stinging telegram to his New York office:

> Inform Mali [Belgian honorary consul-general in New York] that if the Belgian Government divert any single vessel from the Relief I will prevent the sailing of such vessel from American ports.
>
> If the Belgian Government has no consideration for her own people the American Government has and will enforce it.[32]

The Belgian consul-general must have wondered just who was sovereign over his native land: the king and his Cabinet or Herbert Hoover.

The chairman of the CRB was in no mood for conciliation when, just three days later, King Albert of Belgium cabled a personal appeal to President Wilson. In language no doubt approved (and probably prepared) by his government, the monarch asserted that the CRB's food deliveries to his country had been "inadequate" for several months and that the beleaguered populace was now confronted with "actual famine." Only "immediate and energetic action" could save the lives of many of his people in the coming winter. The king declared that his government had provided "all available ships" to the CRB and had no more to give. For "additional transports," cargoes, and financing, "Belgium must rely entirely upon the United States." He asked President Wilson to give Hoover "full power to meet the present emergency with adequate measures."[33]

According to Hoover, Woodrow Wilson was "somewhat nettled" by the king's message. After all, Wilson knew well the "Herculean efforts" that the CRB was making to save the people of Belgium from a ghastly fate.[34] If Wilson was irritated, Hoover was outraged. To him it seemed that the Belgians were once again trying to blame the United States—and him—for the present suffering and the suffering to come. Hoover therefore resolved that the President's response to the king (in an associate's words) would "for once and all settle the question of the responsibility which the C.R.B. has shouldered and the little support we have had from the Belgian Government itself."[35]

In a letter to the President, Hoover conceded that in the preceding eight months his commission had delivered less than half of the 880,000 tons of food required under its program. The result was "the most appalling suffering" inside Belgium. But this was not the fault of the CRB, he insisted. Some of its cargoes had been sunk by the Germans. Others had been stranded in England because the Germans would not let relief ships cross the Channel unmolested. Still other vessels had been delayed by war-related factors that the CRB could not control. Were it not for these circumstances, he asserted, the commission would have met its quota. Hoover also granted that the CRB needed more shipping and money. But the solution, he implied, did not lie with the United States. It was a question, he said, of the Allies' fixing *their* priorities.[36]

Hoover did not stop here. He now prepared a cable for the President to dispatch to the Belgian king. In it, the CRB chairman staunchly defended America's posture toward the relief effort. He explained precisely why the commission's food deliveries had fallen short and why the CRB had been "powerless" to prevent this. He stated bluntly that one cause of the shipping shortage was that the exiled Belgian government itself had taken ships away from the CRB at critical points. He pointed out that the U.S. government had recently contributed 40,000 tons of shipping to the relief fleet and had leaned hard on neutral governments to provide tonnage for the CRB in exchange for American food supplies. The United States, he concluded, would do everything it could to assist the Belgian people. But if it was "unable to render them the full measure of services to be desired," this would not be because of "lack of effort or sympathetic understanding." Woodrow Wilson approved Hoover's draft and cabled it in his own name on October 26.[37]

By the standards of diplomacy, Wilson's ghost-written reply was unusually frank. But it was tepid indeed compared to a separate message that Hoover prepared for the State Department to send to America's minister to the Belgian government, Brand Whitlock. Hoover had long considered Whitlock a weak and gullible dilettante, all too easily duped by Emile Francqui and other Europeans. (Whitlock, although originally an admirer of Hoover, had begun to regard *him* as an abrasive egotist.)[38] In any event, Hoover now obtained the President's consent for Secretary of State Lansing to send Whitlock the following unequivocal instructions—drafted, but not signed, by Hoover himself:

> It is desired that you take an opportunity to impress upon the Belgian Government the fact that this Government has not only done all that could

reasonably be expected of it to provide food for the civilian population of Belgium, but has exacted from neutral nations additional foodstuffs for the Belgians in return for concessions as to food and supplies. This has been done by Mr. Hoover with an insistence and severity that we have not exercised on our own behalf, and has caused some resentment which we have willingly accepted in the interest of Belgium.

Furthermore, we have given Belgian food shipments from the United States priority over all the Allies.

Neither this Government nor Mr. Hoover has any obligation other than good will in the matter, and Mr. Hoover has repeatedly asked the Belgian Government to take over the purchase and transport of supplies.

For your confidential information, I may say that the tone of implied criticism in messages from Belgian sources and the apparent attempts to load responsibility on individuals and this Government are difficult for us to understand. It is hoped that by taking every occasion to create an understanding of the true situation, and the difficulties before the Commission, you will succeed in ending the influence of those who apparently are seeking to convey an impression that the inadequacy of the food supply in Belgium is in any way attributable to negligence or lack of sympathetic understanding on behalf of this Government or its officials.

On October 26 Lansing dutifully dispatched this message, under his own name, to Minister Whitlock.[39]

Startled by the verbal barrage from Washington, the Belgians hastily retreated. Their prime minister declared that he had the highest regard for Hoover and his work, and that both the king and his exiled government were grateful for America's sacrifice. The prime minister also averred that his government did not intend to requisition the CRB's ships, and he promised to try to squelch the criticisms emanating from certain Belgians.[40] As for King Albert, in a rare and propitiatory gesture he sent Hoover an autographed photograph of himself and expressed the hope to Whitlock that Hoover would not desert the Belgian people or become too offended by inconsiderate comments. In Whitlock's presence the king even admonished his minister of finance, van de Vyvere.[41]

The Belgian tempest quickly subsided. It was well for all concerned that it did, for by late October Hoover had another emergency on his hands. Early in the month his European operations chief, William B. Poland, conducted a survey of the CRB's import requirements for the year ahead. Because of deteriorating crop conditions inside Belgium and northern France (among other reasons), Poland found that the CRB would need to augment its monthly deliveries to Rotterdam by 20 percent. Not only would this necessitate a substantial and unforeseen increase in shipping tonnage; it would also entail a tremendous leap in commission expenditures, to a level more than double the current monthly U.S. government subsidy. Thoroughly alarmed, Poland reported in mid-month that the CRB's financial condition was "grave."[42]

The commission's woes, however, were even more serious than that. Although most of its expenditures occurred in the United States, where the bulk of relief foodstuffs was bought, the CRB also spent substantial sums in Europe on such items as shipping insurance and chartering of vessels. According to Poland, this amounted to the equivalent of more than $10,000,000 a month.[43] Suddenly, in mid-September, the London office of the CRB received a devastating message from its New York colleagues: Under the terms of the $75,000,000 American relief loan that had gone into effect in June, all of this money must be spent solely within the United States.[44]

This constraint may not have been as ironclad as it seemed. At times Hoover gave the impression that it was an absolute legal requirement.[45] Other evidence, however, indicates that the restriction was merely a rule or policy of the U.S. Treasury, which was not at all "disposed" (as Hoover put it) to grant exceptions.[46] In any case, neither Hoover nor the Treasury showed any inclination to modify or circumvent the regulation. As a result, it now became necessary to ask the European Allies to subsidize the CRB's expenditures on their side of the Atlantic.

In London, Poland and the American ambassador were appalled by this news. Only a few months before, they protested, the U.S. government had announced to the world that it would assume the entire relief burden and that the European governments "would be spared further expense." Now the United States was reversing itself, an act sure to jeopardize its (and Hoover's) reputation. Nor was it at all certain that the Europeans would consent to underwrite what amounted to 40 percent of the CRB's expenditures, particularly when they had so recently been led to believe that the American loan had lifted this weight completely from their war-swollen budgets.[47]

Fortunately for the commission, during the summer and early autumn it held cash reserves that it could freely expend in Europe.[48] But by the end of October this unencumbered money had run out. The commission must now either find new funding for its European operations or suspend its vital purchases there at once. For the people of Belgium and northern France, the consequences of the latter course would not be pretty.

Despite the anguish of his European director, Hoover firmly refused to change course. He bluntly told King Albert (through President Wilson) that since the U.S. government was unable to provide money for expenditures outside its borders, Albert should "interest" himself in contacting the Allies.[49] "There is no reason why European Governments should not renew advances to the Belgian Government for relief purposes," Hoover cabled Poland on October 30. "The terms of American loan do not permit remittance of these moneys abroad," and he was not going to "participate" in any "evasions of the American law on this subject."[50] Since the U.S. government was unwilling to alter its loan policy, Hoover took the only option remaining. On October 30 he asked the Secretary of State to ask the British and the French to come to the CRB's rescue.[51]

While Hoover attempted to force the Europeans to pick up more of the commission's tab, he also sought to win concessions on food and shipping. On this front he soon achieved success, at least on paper. At the end of November, at the Inter-Allied Conference in Paris, the French and the British formally agreed that the CRB's recently increased import program would have first claim on the Allies' supplies. The Allies also promised to supply all additional tonnage necessary to carry it out.[52] This guarantee of priority appeared to resolve Hoover's shipping crisis at long last. Whether the Allied governments would adhere to their pledge, however, remained to be seen.

The financial battle proved far more vexatious. Around the beginning of November, Hoover learned that the British and French had just arranged a large war loan to the Belgian government-in-exile. As it happened, the six-month American relief loan was due to expire at the end of the month. Seizing his opportunity, Hoover turned the screws on the Allies. He disclosed that the United States would probably increase its Franco-Belgian relief subsidy from $12,500,000 to $15,000,000 per month—provided that the Belgians took $5,000,000 per month from their Allied loan and used it to defray the CRB's European expenses.[53] Since the Belgians could not divert their Allied loan money to this purpose without the lenders' permission, it would be necessary to win the consent of Paris and London.

It now became William P. Poland's duty to wield Herbert Hoover's big stick. Under prodding from Poland and the Belgian finance minister, the French government offered on November 23 to pay all the European costs for French relief, and half the European costs for Belgian relief, provided that the British paid the other half.[54] The British, however, hesitated and stalled. On December 7 Poland informed Hoover that he was certain that Great Britain had acceded to the French proposal.[55] He was wrong. Two weeks later an agitated Poland told the Chief that the British government had taken "no action whatever."[56]

The British government's indecision—or recalcitrance—pushed the CRB to the brink of disaster. To tide the commission over, Poland obtained an overdraft from the London office of a Belgian bank, only to be told by a nervous bank official on December 22 that he must reimburse the entire sum (as much as £700,000) by the end of the month.[57] For its part the French government authorized Poland to float a relief loan in Holland, where the CRB's funds would run out by January 1. The British, who were having monetary difficulties with the Dutch, did not respond to the French proposal, thereby tying Poland's hands.[58]

Convinced that the commission's plight was "absolutely desperate," and that bankruptcy and dishonor were but days away, Poland appealed to the French and British prime ministers for assistance.[59] On December 27 the

French promised a temporary loan of £1,000,000 to cover the bank overdraft.[60] The next day an embarrassed French financial agent in London declined to honor the pledge; the end-of-the-year drain on his resources was too great.[61] From Prime Minister Lloyd George, meanwhile, there came no answer at all.[62]

By now the CRB's European bureau chief was nearly frantic. On December 27, and apparently at Hoover's instigation, Poland notified Lloyd George by telegraph that the CRB's European funds were exhausted and that the commission had suspended all food purchases in Holland and Great Britain. The loss to the French and Belgian people, he said, would be 28,000 tons of imports per month. Poland warned that unless the Allies reached an "understanding" by the beginning of January 1918 on financing the CRB's European expenditures, the CRB would "announce to the world" that it could no longer feed the Belgians because of a "lack of funds."[63]

This time the British paid attention. Lloyd George quickly turned Poland's plea over to the Foreign Office and the Chancellor of the Exchequer.[64] Shortly thereafter the British Treasury transferred £750,000 to the Belgian government-in-exile to eliminate the CRB's overdraft at its bank.[65] Better still, on January 2, at a conference in Paris, the British Chancellor of the Exchequer finally agreed in principle to the French proposal of November 23: the French would absorb all the European costs of the relief of northern France (one third of the total) and would evenly split the remaining two thirds (the Belgian share) with the British.[66]

The British capitulation was far from gracious. His Majesty's Government insisted that the monthly Belgian expense be limited to £1,000,000 instead of £1,500,000 (as the French had earlier proposed). [67] Moreover, the British Treasury refused to implement this arrangement until an inter-Allied agency known as the Commission Internationale de Ravitaillement (CIR) had investigated the CRB's operations and needs—a process that consumed several weeks.[68] Alarmed by the CRB's mushrooming requirements, and angered by its refusal to return certain unexpended Allied subsidies after the United States took over the financing, the British government was evidently determined to keep a tight leash on this voracious little beast. From now on, Hoover's commission was forced to subject itself to the intrusive oversight of the CIR.[69]

Although bureaucratic constraints continued to plague the CRB for several more months, its harrowing financial ordeal was finally over. Once again the French and reluctant British were paying a significant part of Hoover's bills. In return, the U.S. government increased its own advances for the relief to $15,000,000 per month.

Despite this victory, Hoover dared not relax his "constant solicitude" for the CRB. "The next six months are the most difficult period that we will have to face," he told Emile Francqui in January.[70] The head of the embattled relief commission was more prophetic than he knew.

For words were one thing, deeds another. Between November 1917 and March 1918 the CRB managed to deliver only 408,000 tons of food to Rotterdam—267,000 tons short of the barebones program that the Allies themselves had sanctioned.[71] The commission's temporary inability (for financial reasons) to buy food in England and Holland was part of the explanation, as was a general tightening of the world's food supplies. But one factor was paramount: despite the Inter-Allied Conference's promise in November to grant the CRB priority in assignment of food and ships, the British government did not implement the pledge. Certain British government departments were not even aware of the priority declaration. Others were—and willfully ignored it.[72] With the war approaching a fearful and uncertain climax, harried Allied officials had more pressing things on their minds than the fate of the Belgians.

As the CRB's food deliveries faltered, the consequences for its beneficiaries became dire. On March 15, desperate relief officials inside Belgium reduced the population's daily bread ration by nearly 25 percent.[73] Eight days later, the CRB's London office confessed that it had "miserably failed" to meet its import quota for five months, thanks to the Allies' failure to grant it priority in food and ships. The commission pleaded with the Allies to supply the requisite tonnage and make the "principle of priority" a reality.[74]

The CRB's request could not have come at a worse time. Two days before, on March 21, the German army had launched a terrific offensive in northern France. Flushed with victory over Russia, and buttressed by massive reinforcements transferred from the east, the Germans hoped to overwhelm the French and British before the Americans could appear in sufficient numbers to tilt the balance. In late March and early April the Germans came perilously close to success. And although the western front then stabilized, the initiative still belonged to the German foe. To the frightened Allied leaders, only the early arrival of American troops in huge numbers could save the day. And that meant ships, ships, and more ships diverted to the transport of Yankee troops.

Not surprisingly, then, the CRB's appeal for additional ships for itself fell on deaf ears in London.[75] In Washington, Hoover fared no better. For some time the CRB had expected to acquire a significant portion of neutral Dutch shipping interned in American waters. But on March 20 the U.S. government, invoking the international law of angary, seized the Dutch vessels for its own military purposes.[76] The CRB did not obtain a single vessel from this transaction. Hoover appealed to the U.S. Shipping Board for other vessels, only to learn that the board had already given the CRB all the available neutral shipping it controlled.[77] Unable to extract more assistance from his government, Hoover urged his London office to persuade the British government to assign Swedish and Norwegian vessels under its control to the CRB fleet.[78] For William B. Poland, this was not much of a reed to lean on.

With the CRB facing collapse within a month (according to Poland) unless it somehow acquired more tonnage,[79] Hoover suddenly found himself battling on a new front. On March 4, the redoubtable General Peyton C. March became chief of staff of the U.S. Army. March was appalled that, ten whole months after declaring war, the United States had delivered fewer than 250,000 men to France. March concurred with Generals Pershing and Bliss that the U.S. Army must henceforth transport two divisions, or 90,000 soldiers, to France *per month*—nearly double the current rate.[80] On this, the military representatives to the Supreme War Council agreed, the safety of France in 1918 would depend.[81]

Soon after assuming his duties in Washington, March held a meeting with the heads of the major war agencies, including Hoover. Getting right to the point, March announced that "the most necessary and important" task that America now faced was "the shipment of men to France." The general therefore proposed to "divert from trade" every single American ship "so occupied" that was capable of carrying troops or cargoes across the Atlantic. Hoover objected that President Wilson had promised him a number of vessels for the Belgian relief. March was unfazed. "Mr. Hoover," he replied, "if we do not get the men to France there will be no Belgian Relief problem." The crusty general then added, "I am going to get the men to France if they have to swim."[82]

On March 26 the War Department's advisory group known as the War Council declared that the two-divisions-per-month-to-France program was unattainable unless the United States and its allies took "drastic action" to overcome a tremendous "deficit" in shipping tonnage. The War Council asked President Wilson to set aside "all American tonnage suitable for trans-Atlantic service" for the exclusive use of the army.[83]

The War Department brass were not the only ones pressuring the President to expedite American troop deliveries. From Europe, where the British army had suffered 120,000 casualties in the first week of the new German offensive, Prime Minister Lloyd George sent pleas for American troops to replace them.[84] In a conference at the White House on March 30, the British ambassador to the United States, Lord Reading, obtained (or so he reported) a presidential promise to rush 120,000 American infantrymen to Europe per month for the next four months, provided that the requisite shipping could be found.[85]

President Wilson later denied that he had consented to any specific figure, and it took much of April to dispel the resultant confusion.[86] One person who was not confused was General March. On April 3 he cabled General Tasker Bliss that the President had in fact committed himself to 120,000 troops per month. To March, the implications of this decision were plain: it could only be carried out if all tonnage "owned or controlled by the United States" were devoted to troop transport and supply. "We cannot divert any additional tonnage," he added, "without impairing the military program" that the President had now authorized.[87]

Within days March's assertion of priorities collided with those of Herbert Hoover. In view of the shipping emergency, Hoover offered to reduce the CRB's import program temporarily from the ideal minimum of 120,000 tons monthly to just 90,000 tons. But to fulfill even this shrunken quota in April and May, he declared that he would need nine additional ships, or about 65,000 tons.[88] For the ship-hungry military planners, this proposal was unacceptable. In early April the War Department demanded that the U.S. Shipping Board refuse to allocate the CRB *any* tonnage beyond its current holdings.[89] Hoover feared that under pressure from the army the Shipping Board might even take back three Norwegian steamers it had recently assigned to the CRB.[90]

On April 8 Hoover informed the President that the War Department's War Council had "apparently decided that no [additional] shipping can be afforded to the Belgian Relief Commission." Sensing, perhaps, that a purely humanitarian argument at this moment would not suffice, Hoover emphasized the political risks in Europe of jeopardizing the relief. The Flemish portion of Belgium (which the Germans had long cultivated) might break away and form a pro-German state. The Belgian army and government-in-exile might decide that their country's civilian "sacrifice of life" was too great a price to pay for staying in the war. The French people and army might suffer a terrible blow to their morale if they witnessed a "debacle" among their brethren whom the CRB was feeding behind German lines. Two million Belgian workers, who had hitherto survived on CRB food and refused to work for the Germans, might be obliged to yield and work for German rations. Hoover therefore asked the President to review the War Department's decision and at least refer the question to the Supreme War Council in Europe for a decision. The chairman of the CRB implied that his needs were modest: no interference with the CRB's current fleet, and a total of just nine extra ships during April and May.[91]

After conferring with Hoover on April 10, President Wilson decided to turn the matter over to the Allies. He instructed Hoover to have the State Department ascertain which course the French and British preferred: Should the U.S. government allocate 60,000 tons of shipping to the Commission for Relief in Belgium in order to carry out Hoover's scaled-back program, or should the government devote this tonnage to "military purposes"?[92] From Paris and London the answer quickly came: Military purposes. This was "of paramount importance," said the British. The French explicitly asked that the ships be used to carry American troops across the Atlantic.[93]

Perhaps to soften the blow to Hoover (and appease the exiled Belgian government as well), the British added that they would not object if the CRB tried to charter ships in neutral Sweden.[94] The French added that they "fully appreciated" the need to provide relief for Belgium and northern France.[95] Several days later the British expressed their hope that the United States would be able to find the ships to meet both its military needs *and* the "minimum requirements" of the CRB.[96] Much as the Allies wanted American troops, they did not want to take responsibility for what this might mean for the Belgians.

For its part, the Belgian government-in-exile was horrified that Hoover had offered to reduce the CRB's monthly food deliveries from 120,000 to 90,000 tons. Such an action, it declared, would imperil the populace and weaken its "moral resistance." The government announced that it was unable to consent to the American proposal.[97]

Hammered and rebuffed on all sides, Hoover now retreated to the sidelines while William B. Poland made yet another appeal to the Allies to redeem their priority pledge of the preceding autumn. On April 18 Poland submitted a memorandum detailing the CRB's shipping shortage to the Allied Maritime Transport Council (AMTC). He requested that it take all necessary measures to give effect to the Allies' promise that the CRB would have a prior claim on shipping. Poland explained that the situation inside Belgium and northern France was now "the most serious since the war began."[98] He was not bluffing. Just three days earlier, word had come via Rotterdam that the Belgium supply of bread would be gone in less than two weeks.[99]

On April 25 the Allied Maritime Transport Council, meeting in Paris, gave Hoover and Poland a victory, at least on paper. The council declared that all food necessary for feeding Belgium and northern France would be "included in the program of the Wheat Executive if that body consents" and would be given the priority promised months earlier. The council also decided that any shipping needed by the CRB beyond its own resources would be "allocated by the Wheat Executive from the tonnage provided by the Associated Governments." The Council ordered its secretariat to "arrange for" the additional ships needed to implement this decision.[100]

Once again, however, words were one thing, deeds another. While apparently willing to accept the new directive, the Wheat Executive had no fleet of its own.[101] Nor did the AMTC, which was only an advisory body. If the council's resolution was to have any practical effect, the officials in the Allied governments who did control the ships would somehow have to be persuaded to part with some.

While Hoover waited to see whether the AMTC's gesture would yield him anything tangible, he turned in desperation to Sweden. The CRB chairman was not optimistic; all previous efforts to charter Swedish vessels for relief work had failed.[102] Instead of contacting Stockholm directly, therefore, Hoover came up with an idea: let King Albert of Belgium make a personal appeal to the king of Sweden. On May 3 Hoover cabled his proposal to the American minister to the exiled Belgian government, Brand Whitlock. As usual when he had a brainstorm, Hoover was breathlessly emphatic. "Under the present pressure for American troops to France there is no hope of saving Belgian relief except in one direction," he said: acquisition of 120,000 of the

300,000 tons of Swedish shipping lying idle in Swedish ports. Hoover promised "full guarantees" for the safe return of these vessels after at least six months' service to the Belgian relief. "This is," he concluded, "our only hope."[103]

As Hoover put it in a separate message to his lieutenant, Poland: "I cabled King of Belgium telling him fate relief hangs absolutely on his personal intervention King of Sweden. . . ."[104]

Although Whitlock relayed Hoover's proposal to the Belgian authorities, the fastidious American diplomat was shocked. Whitlock had long since grown tired of Hoover's brusque and peremptory ways. He was also now aware that Hoover had conspired to oust him from his post in 1916.[105] To Whitlock this latest cablegram was "but one of Hoover's bombs, bluffs—always trying to force, to blackmail, to frighten people into doing things his way. . . . What a bully! He would even bully a poor exiled King!"[106]

Hoover no doubt would have rejected this accusation. In his view, he was simply stating his case in the only way likely to get results. If his tone was aggressively authoritative, he did not care—not when the alternative was mass starvation.

Instead of complying at once with Hoover's virtual diktat, the Belgian government-in-exile took seventeen days to respond. When it did, its nervousness was apparent. It pointed out that a similar attempt to obtain Swedish shipping had been made in 1917 and had been vetoed by the British. Before trying again, the Belgians wanted to know whether the British would object to Hoover's proposal and whether the U.S. government would support it. (The Belgians evidently did not know that the British had already given Hoover their approval.) The Belgians also pointed out that the Allied Maritime Transport Council had decided that the Wheat Executive would provide the requisite tonnage for the relief. The Belgians did not want to upset this arrangement by an ill-timed approach to the Swedes.[107]

The Belgians' reluctance to take the initiative irritated Hoover, who considered the exiled government "entirely too diffident, to say the least, about their requests" for the relief.[108] But in one respect his Swedish gambit made no difference. In early May, Emile Francqui reported that malnutrition and even famine conditions were pervasive inside Belgium. Daily, he said, people were dying of hunger in Brussels.[109] Hoover now realized that even if he successfully negotiated a shipping deal with Sweden, its vessels could not be put into service in time to resolve the current emergency.[110]

Frantic to find the needed vessels somewhere, Hoover decided at the beginning of May to withdraw 40,000 tons of American shipping from the Cuban sugar trade, load it immediately with food bound for Belgium, and impose a rationing system on American confectionery manufacturers who would thus lose a portion of their raw sugar. Hoover estimated that his action might throw 100,000 Americans out of work. Nevertheless, he was prepared to risk this in order to "save the lives of a much larger number" of Belgians.

But when Hoover notified the U.S. Shipping Board of his decision, the board informed him that if he had such surplus ships in the Cuban sugar trade he must hand them over for military purposes. Hoover was not amused. The shipping that the CRB required, he asserted, would not maintain 20,000 soldiers at the front. The "military damage" caused by collapse of the relief would be "infinitely greater" than the strength provided by these 20,000 men.[111]

Hoover was now thoroughly fed up with the delays and ineffectual pronouncements about priority coming from Europe. More than two weeks had passed since the Allied Maritime Transport Council's meeting in late April, and still the council had not completed its promised arrangements to provide more ships to the Wheat Executive to convey CRB food.[112] The Commission for Relief in Belgium needed 120,000 tons of additional shipping, he told Secretary of State Lansing on May 10. In order to produce "actual ships," "some Government" must give "specific instructions" to its shipping authorities to release "neutral charters" to the CRB.[113]

Some government, yes, but whose? The United States did not want to assume the burden. Nor did the British, who insisted that Uncle Sam fill all of the CRB's shipping deficit.[114] To Hoover's disgust, the British persisted in asking the United States to "do something" when it was "clearly obvious" (said Hoover) that the U.S. government lacked enough ships "to handle its own prime necessities." In a cablegram to William B. Poland on May 7, Hoover laid down the law: If the Allied governments "really intend" to implement their months-old promise of priority to the CRB, the British must order their shipping agent in the United States "to turn over to Belgian Relief instantly specific neutral ships."[115]

It is difficult to know whether Hoover's plain speaking had any effect. But a few days later news of a breakthrough came from an unexpected direction. For some time Raymond B. Stevens, the American representative on the Allied Maritime Transport Council, had been quietly trying to reach a "temporary working agreement" on the issue with the British Ministry of Shipping. On May 12 Stevens cabled Washington from London that after "great difficulty" the British had finally agreed in principle to his proposal that the United States and Great Britain each provide one half of the additional shipping needed by the CRB.[116] The Belgian prime minister and William B. Poland quickly endorsed the 50-50 scheme.[117]

As Stevens's compromise made its way to Washington for official action, the Belgians stepped up their own pressure on the Allies. The Belgian government had learned with alarm that its countrymen's daily per capita bread ration—already reduced by nearly 25 percent in March—would be reduced yet again, from 250 grams to a mere 180, on May 15. With outright famine apparently only days away, the Belgian prime minister beseeched Lloyd George by cable on May 13 for "immediate measures" to "assure the execution" of the Allies' "contract" to "furnish the tonnage and food products for the famished population." The government of Belgium and its king, he added, "decline all responsibility for the moral and material disaster" that would occur if effective steps were not taken at once. The prime minister sent a similar appeal to President Wilson and one to Prime Minister Georges Clemenceau of France, who transmitted it, with his full support, to Washington.[118] The issue had now reached the highest level of the allied governments.

Seemingly unaware of Stevens's 50-50 agreement in principle with the British, Hoover now escalated his thus far unsuccessful campaign to win more relief shipping from American sources. The head of the CRB wanted nothing less than an assignment to his relief fleet of ships previously given to the War Department.[119] On the afternoon of May 16, he made his case directly to the President.[120] To Hoover's chagrin, Wilson was inclined to the view that military necessity must take precedence over Belgian relief.[121]

Hoover was not deterred. "I fully appreciated the military need," he later wrote, "but I was responsible for ten million helpless people."[122] And so, on the evening of May 16, Hoover took an extraordinary step. Writing not as a U.S. government official but as head of the CRB, he appealed to Prime Minister Lloyd George to intervene. The relief "cannot be saved" otherwise, Hoover declared by cable. A "pitiable" amount of shipping was all that was required. He asked the British leader, who had given the CRB crucial support in the past, to issue the appropriate orders and convey his approval of the "necessary diversions" to President Wilson.[123]

Private citizen or government official, Hoover had just gone around his commander in chief. But the CRB's protector did not stop there. The next day the *New York Times* reported that Hoover had told the President that Belgium was starving and that some of the Allies' supply ships must be "diverted" to the relief.[124] As the obvious source of this story, Hoover in effect was attempting to mobilize American public opinion against his own boss. Meanwhile, on the morning of the seventeenth, Hoover persuaded the chairman of the U.S. Shipping Board to assign to the CRB any ships removed from the Cuban sugar trade.[125] Later in the day Hoover sent President Wilson a copy of his message to the British prime minister.[126]

Meanwhile, in London, William B. Poland and a delegation of Belgians led by their prime minister had been holding a virtual summit conference with Lloyd George. The visitors asked the British leader explicitly to affirm as a war policy that the provision of food and ships for Belgian relief would have "priority over all other Allied requirements" and to instruct his shipping authorities accordingly. More specifically, the Belgians asked that the British and Americans split the burden 50-50 and immediately hand over three ships each.

Lloyd George needed little persuading. At the first conference, on May 15, he declared unequivocally that the relief must go on and that the present crisis must not be permitted to continue. Taking their cue, British food and shipping officials, who were also present, pledged their complete cooperation with the relief organization and announced that they had assigned the CRB four ships in the last two days! This allocation was apparently contingent, however, on the American government's matching it. Before Lloyd George would agree to cable Wilson (as Clemenceau had), he decided to await Washington's reply to the British offer—that is, to Stevens's 50-50 proposal.[127]

By May 17, when Lloyd George held a second meeting with the Belgians and Poland, no reply from Washington had come. Instead, during the meeting Hoover's private message of May 16 was presented, with its dramatic claim that only Lloyd George could save the CRB. The British leader must have been somewhat puzzled, for he declared that Great Britain had already announced its readiness to supply half the needed ships and that the United States should do likewise. Instead of immediately cabling the President, as Hoover desired, Lloyd George decided to take counsel with his advisers. Evidently he felt that the ball was already in Wilson's court.[128]

As it turned out, Lloyd George never intervened with Woodrow Wilson. Instead, on May 20, after learning of the British government's 50-50 offer and its conditional immediate allotment of four ships to the relief operation, Hoover himself asked the President to agree.[129] Two days later the commander in chief assented, and Hoover promptly announced the decision in the press.[130] Each government, Hoover disclosed—the United States and Great Britain—would find one half the shipping required to "restore the volume of foodstuffs" needed to keep nearly 10,000,000 people alive and well.[131] Hoover's relief was palpable. "A ghastly situation in Belgium" had been averted, he told Poland; "one of the most difficult crises" ever endured by the CRB was over—and in the nick of time.[132]

Never again would the Commission for Relief in Belgium come as close to failure as it did in early 1918, when its prolonged inability to obtain sufficient shipping charters and meet its monthly import quota nearly led to a horrible catastrophe. Later in the year, as a result of a comprehensive Allied agreement with Sweden, the CRB obtained the use of 200,000 tons of Swedish shipping, thus ensuring full food deliveries to Rotterdam at last.[133]

Years later Hoover credited Lloyd George and Clemenceau with saving the CRB in the climactic crisis of May 1918.[134] He might also have cited Raymond B. Stevens, a dogged and unsung hero whose 50-50 formula proved to be the way out of the impasse. But in apportioning praise Hoover might justifiably have saved some for himself and his faithful director in Europe, William B. Poland. Their tireless lobbying, even badgering, of harassed and preoccupied Allied warmakers ensured that the lives of nearly 10,000,000 helpless civilians were never ignored. How easy it would have been to overlook them in the harrowing spring of 1918, as the mighty German army came closer to victory than at any time since the first month of the war. That Belgium, even then, commanded Allied resources was attributable in considerable part to Herbert Hoover.

It was not surprising, therefore, that when Hoover traveled to Europe for the Allied food controllers' conference in the summer of 1918, the Belgian government gratefully acknowledged his benefactions. Upon arriving at the French port of Boulogne on August 1, Hoover was immediately driven north to the seaside Belgian town of La Panne in a tiny corner of Belgian territory unconquered by the German invader. There, in a cottage amidst the sand dunes, King Albert and Queen Elizabeth now lived. In these modest surroundings, Hoover had lunch with his royal hosts.

It was a simple meal, its very simplicity underscoring the king's determination to spend the war on Belgian soil and in solidarity with his people.[135] Later in the day, Hoover described the event in a letter to his eleven-year-old son Allan:

> Sir: Today I had lunch with His Majesty the King of the Belgians, Her Majesty the Queen, the Crown Prince and the Princess Royal. The Princess is about 11 years old and is a busy collector of the pieces of shell that explode every night or two in the little garden of the Kings house here. She gave me a piece of the biggest one to be sent to you specially from her to you. This place is 4 miles from the Front line and the guns sound as if they were 1/2 mile away. The shells drop in here every once in a while, specially the arero bombs that they try to drop on the Kings cottage. The Princess says "it makes you feel small in your bed." Her bed is in the "abris"—Bub [Allan's brother] could translate that for you.
>
> Your Dad[136]

While in La Panne, Hoover conferred about relief problems with the Belgian prime minister and three members of his Cabinet.[137] For nearly a year the Belgians had been attempting to confer decorations on the CRB chairman and his colleagues in recognition of their meritorious work.[138] Although many CRB veterans would have welcomed such an honor, the Chief repeatedly objected.[139] "As to European decorations," he told Brand Whitlock on one occasion, "I have a complete abhorrence of all such toys. I do not want any distinction of this kind whatever and have often expressed myself to this end. . . . I value the personal note and photograph of the King of the Belgians and the expression with it much more highly than all of the brass buttons possessed by the Belgian people."[140]

Nevertheless, the Belgians persisted, in part because Hoover did accept another European decoration—Commander of the National Order of the Legion of Honor—after the French government conferred it on him in 1917.[141] (Hoover explained to Whitlock that the French did this "without consulting me and I could not, without appearing discourteous, refuse to accept it.")[142] And so, on August 1, at the end of Hoover's conference with the Belgian Cabinet officials, the foreign minister told him that the king and Cabinet wished to offer him the highest decoration of their government: the Grand Cordon of the Order of Leopold.

While deeply appreciative of the proffered honor, Hoover declined it, explaining that it was impossible for him as a U.S. government official to assent. (No doubt he was thinking of the fact that the U.S. Constitution forbids American government officials, without the consent of Congress, to accept titles of any kind from kings, princes, or foreign states.)[143] To clinch the matter, and perhaps also to assuage any hurt feelings, he added that he would be satisfied if it were recognized simply that he was a friend of the Belgian people.[144]

To the foreign minister and his colleagues, Hoover's offhand remark provided an opening. That evening at the royal cottage, King Albert hosted a dinner for his American guest; the visiting Belgian Cabinet officials also attended. At the end, as Hoover was about to leave for Boulogne, the king suddenly addressed him. The monarch declared that he wished to express a "debt of gratitude" that could never be repaid. The Belgian people, he said, would always turn to Hoover as their saviour in times of national calamity. Albert thereupon stated that he had created a new order and that Hoover would be its only member. He then conferred upon Hoover the title "Ami de la Nation belge"—"Friend of the Belgian Nation."[145]

Nearly overcome with emotion, Hoover struggled to express his thanks. The Belgian prime minister then announced that as head of the government, he confirmed this title "for all time to come." The king and his staff escorted Hoover to his waiting automobile. As the chairman of the Commission for Relief in Belgium was driven off into the twilight, the king and his staff saluted.[146]

A few days later Albert and the Belgian government-in-exile duly formalized the unprecedented honor. In a report to the king, Prime Minister Cooreman acknowledged that because of Hoover's governmental status, and out of "respect for American tradition," the Belgians could not bestow on him a symbolic recognition of the customary sort. It therefore asked the king, by this new title, to reserve for Hoover a place of honor in the Belgian family, whose "Providence" he had been.[147]

Four years before, Hoover had been a successful mining engineer searching for an entrée into public life. Now he was being treated like a head of state, and in a way he was. This "strong personality" (as the Belgian Cabinet called him) was captain of a "colossal" enterprise.[148] Hoover might at times seem curt and imperious, but as the exiled government realized, he had been their conquered nation's "Bienfaiteur."[149]

II

BELGIUM was not the only country whose plight was the focus of Hoover's thoughts in the spring and early summer of 1918. Far to the east, in Russia, Nikolai Lenin and the Bolsheviks had overthrown the pro-Allied government the previous November. In short order the revolutionary regime appealed for a worldwide proletarian revolution, repudiated hundreds of millions of dollars' worth of debt owed by previous Russian governments to the Allies, called for a general armistice in the war, and violently dispersed the newly elected Russian Constituent Assembly, in which the Bolsheviks were a small minority. Lacking any political legitimacy beyond the barrels of their guns, Lenin and his fellow militants shocked and angered Allied leaders. Then, in March 1918, under pressure from advancing German armies, the Bolsheviks signed a separate treaty of peace with Germany. Under its terms, Russia lost a quarter of its territory and population. Even worse from the Allied point of view, the Russian capitulation made it possible for the victorious Germans to transfer hundreds of thousands of seasoned soldiers to the western front in the hope of delivering a quick knockout blow.

As the German threat in the west intensified, worried Allied leaders pressed the United States to relieve their danger by attempting to reconstitute the eastern front. The Allies proposed that an expeditionary force consisting largely of Japanese troops land in Siberia and make its way west. The Allied leaders argued that such an intervention could rally Russian resistance to the Germans and tie down German divisions in Eastern Europe, thus lessening the force of the German assault in France. Woodrow Wilson was not convinced. To him and his military advisers, the idea of recreating an eastern front in this way was impractical, even preposterous. Military intervention, he argued, might throw the Russians into the arms of Germany if the Japanese (whom the Russians hated) dominated the invading force. Deeply distrustful of Japanese ambitions in Siberia, and of French and British motives as well, Wilson resisted armed intervention for months.[150]

On this issue, as on most others, Hoover concurred wholeheartedly with his chief. At some point in the winter or spring of 1918, the President asked Hoover what he thought of inviting the Japanese to enter Siberia. Hoover replied that it would unite many Russians behind Lenin and the Bolsheviks; such was the "Russian racial hatred toward the Japanese." Furthermore, said Hoover, the Russian people would resist; it would take the Japanese army at least a year—and maybe ten—"to subdue Russia to such a point as to threaten Germany." And that, after all, was the pivotal issue. Not only would intervention in Siberia fail to harm the German army; in the end the Japanese would "demand Siberia for a reward."[151] Woodrow Wilson could not have agreed more.

Still, the Allied pressure for military action was unremitting. In part because of it, during the spring Wilson and a number of American policymakers began to explore an alternative: a strictly American economic expedition to Siberia for the purpose of organizing relief and reconstruction projects. In Wilson's eyes, such a commission could help the demoralized Russians organize their food supplies, rebuild their railroads, and restore domestic trade.[152] Early in June, already vocal public agitation for American aid to its former wartime ally grew rapidly. On June 5 the War Trade Board urged the President to appoint a "Russian Commissioner," who would "take charge of all matters pertaining to Russia."[153] During this same week, former President Taft and a prominent Republican senator publicly demanded immediate action on the Russian question. The tangled issue of whether—and how—to intervene now threatened to explode in political controversy.[154]

At this point—on June 12, to be exact—Colonel House's son-in-law Gordon Auchincloss, who was working in the State Department, had an idea: Why not appoint Herbert Hoover to head the proposed relief mission to Russia? Auchincloss quickly telephoned his father-in-law, who approved the thought and told Auchincloss to see the Food Administrator.[155] Tell him, House advised shrewdly, that he has been "so entirely associated with food problems, that for his own sake, it would be a good thing to show the world that he [is] capable of just as good work in other directions."[156]

The next morning Auchincloss visited Hoover and found him willing to serve wherever the President and Colonel House deemed best.[157] Indeed, according to House (who received a report on the conversation soon afterward), Hoover heartily agreed that Auchincloss's suggestion was "the best solution of the Russian problem."[158] Hoover even asserted that his Food Administration was now in such a satisfactory state that he could easily hand it over to somebody else.[159]

Auchincloss was greatly impressed by the Food Administrator's "sane view" of the Russian situation. "Hoover knows Russia as he has interests there," Auchincloss noted shortly afterward, alluding to Hoover's vast mining interests in the Ural Mountains and Siberia prior to 1917. Furthermore, in Auchincloss's opinion, Hoover was "one of the best organizers that this country has produced." The State Department official was more certain than ever that Hoover could do a "splendid" job as Russian aid administrator.[160]

With House's approval Auchincloss immediately broached his proposal to Secretary of State Lansing, who had him embody the suggestion in a draft letter to the President. Later in the day (June 13), Lansing signed and sent the letter. The Secretary of State noted the growing agitation, both at home and abroad, for a "constructive" American "plan for meeting the present chaotic conditions in Russia." He therefore asked President Wilson to create a "Commission for the Relief of Russia," to be led by Herbert Hoover and "organized generally along the same lines" as the Commission for Relief in Belgium. Hoover's appointment, said Lansing, would quell domestic restiveness over Wilson's Russian policy by showing America's determination "to assist the Russian people towards the establishment of an orderly Government independent of Germany." Creation of a relief expedition would also, "for the time being, dispose of the proposal of armed intervention." Concerned that the President would be reluctant to let his Food Administrator go, Lansing disclosed that he had learned that "another man could easily step in" and run the agency.[161]

In a separate letter to the President the same day, Colonel House endorsed

Lansing's proposal. "The Russians know Hoover and Hoover knows the East," said House. If Hoover leads a "Russian Relief Commission," he added, "it will typify in the Russian mind what was done in Belgium, and I doubt whether any Government in Russia, friendly or unfriendly, would dare oppose his coming in." House also emphasized Hoover's personal prestige, his "ability as an organizer," his replaceability at the Food Administration, and the fact that his selection would "settle the Russian question" so far as Woodrow Wilson could settle it at the present time.[162]

Auchincloss's suggestion, now formally ratified by Lansing, evoked an enthusiastic response within the State Department and from the chairman of the War Trade Board.[163] It also pleased Sir William Wiseman, head of British counterintelligence in the United States, who was visiting Colonel House on June 13.[164] But whereas the Americans construed their Russian relief plan as a *substitute* for armed intervention, Wiseman saw it as a promising first step toward the Allies' objective. In a secret cable to his government, Wiseman reported that Hoover would need a protective military force for his relief-and-reconstruction mission and that additional troops might be dispatched later if he requested them. Hoover "is by no means a sentimentalist, but an ambitious and energetic man," said Wiseman, and could probably persuade the President to approve armed intervention if he (Hoover) recommended it.[165]

Eager to take charge of the proposed Russian relief enterprise, Hoover journeyed up to Colonel House's summer home in Massachusetts a few days later.[166] According to Hoover's account of their conversation, he told the colonel that the United States must give up all hope of reestablishing Russia as a "fighting element" in the war. Instead, America must work to prevent Russia from becoming either an ally or an economic vassal of Germany. Achievement of these goals would require not a "military expedition" but reconstitution of Russia "along lines of peaceful and commercial endeavor"—a task entailing only a small "body guard." According to Hoover, House completely agreed and declared that Hoover was the only man for the job.[167]

After sketching out the plan in detail with House, Hoover returned to Washington, where he conferred with Secretary of State Lansing and Justice Louis Brandeis. Both men expressed their support.[168] At some point Hoover also discussed the matter with President Wilson himself, who expressed interest in the relief plan but was silent about who should administer it.[169] For his part, Colonel House, on June 21, urged the President to announce creation of the relief commission (and Hoover's appointment to lead it) in an address to the Congress. "This program will place the Russian and Eastern situation in your hands," House counseled the President. Moreover, the British ambassador (Lord Reading) was "enthusiastic" about the project.[170] Indeed, Reading was, for the same reasons as his compatriot Wiseman.[171]

Unfortunately for Hoover and his promoters, one man did not fully share their enthusiasm. That man was the President of the United States. For some weeks the President had been contemplating placing the Russian relief mission under the direction of his friend John R. Mott, general secretary of the international committee of Young Men's Christian Associations. Widely esteemed at home and abroad, Mott had served by presidential appointment on the Root Mission to Russia in 1917. Aware that the YMCA leader had been slated for the new post but under the impression that he had declined to accept, House told the President on June 13 that Hoover was a far better person for the job.[172] But at a meeting with members of the Cabinet some days later, Wilson turned to Secretary of Commerce William Redfield and asked him to designate the individual most qualified to lead the relief expedition under Mott.[173]

When Hoover, who by now was evincing what an aide called "tremendous interest" in the Russian issue,[174] heard about what had transpired in the Cabinet meeting, he protested to Secretary of State Lansing. As usual in such situations, Hoover disclaimed any personal ambitions. He pointed out that the relief scheme was a great gamble, which might totally fail and "cook him." Furthermore, there was a good possibility that if he went, he would be killed by a Bolshevik bomb. Nevertheless, Hoover argued vigorously that he should be the one to lead the relief expedition. By sending the U.S. Food Administrator, he contended, the President could give proof of his desire to prevent a famine and to help the Russians solve their food problem—objectives that had nothing to do with Russia's military involvement in the war.[175]

Curiously, Lansing (who just a couple of weeks earlier had strongly advocated a Commission for Relief in Russia) now objected that the plan looked too much like the Commission for Relief in Belgium. If the Russian expedition were perceived as merely another CRB, he said, the effect would not be good. Hoover disagreed; "on the contrary," he believed (in the words of his confidant Hugh Gibson), "it would be the best possible cover for the sort of work we want to do."[176]

If Hoover hoped that Lansing would intercede in his behalf with the President, there is no evidence that the Secretary of State obliged. The Food Administrator's appeal had been in vain. Meanwhile, on June 27, John R. Mott withdrew from consideration for the Russian relief assignment.[177] The way seemed clear at last for Herbert Hoover, but no call came.

Why did Woodrow Wilson not now turn to the man in his administration who most personified practical idealism and whose international relief experience was sans pareil? The President evidently had several reasons. On June 29 he told Vance McCormick that he "did not like to put Russia in the same class as Belgium."[178] The President apparently did not elaborate. But given this attitude, it would hardly be appropriate for him to send to Russia the founder and chairman of the Belgian relief commission. Nor did the President think it wise to choose for this assignment an individual who had had extensive mining interests in Siberia. It would introduce a "capitalistic element"[179]—hardly a reassurance to the anti-capitalist Bolsheviks in Moscow.

More surprisingly, Wilson told McCormick that Hoover's temperament was unsuited for the Russian aid undertaking.[180] Once again the chief executive did not elaborate. Still another factor may have been the most important one of all. When Bernard Baruch added his voice to those urging Hoover's appointment,[181] the President demurred. I cannot spare him, he replied, "without dislocating some of the most important things we are handling."[182]

Then, in early July, American policy toward Russia lurched in a startling direction. For reasons that are still debated by historians, President Wilson decided to dispatch seven thousand American soldiers to Siberia in conjunction with a similar number of Japanese. Officially the purpose of the mission was to protect a legion of around 50,000 pro-Allied Czechoslovak soldiers (formerly part of the Russian army) who were fighting their way across Siberia. The Czechs were supposedly under attack from armed contingents of former German and Austrian prisoners-of-war. In reality, the Czechs were fighting the Bolsheviks and had already routed them from much of the region.[183]

In an aide-mémoire for the western Allies on July 17 and a statement to the American press in early August, Wilson presented the rationale for his intervention. On both occasions he announced his intention to dispatch to Siberia at "the earliest opportunity" a "commission of merchants, agricultural experts, labour advisers, Red Cross representatives, and agents of the Young Men's Christian Association," who would be able to render "educational help of a modest sort" and "relieve the immediate economic necessities of the people there."[184] Thus even as Wilson resorted in a limited way to the sword, he held out the promise of technical assistance. But precisely who would administer it he did not say.

Hoover was in Europe for the Allied food controllers' meetings when Wilson make public his explanation of his Russian policy. Despite the fact that Hoover had heard nothing from the White House on the subject, he had not lost interest in heading the proposed economic mission to Siberia. While in Paris on August 4, he told Hugh Gibson that he intended to "follow it up" when he returned home. Once more he professed to have little enthusiasm for the venture since (as Gibson put it) "from a personal point of view the chances are very poor of ever coming home alive."[185] Such gloomy thoughts, however, did not cause Hoover to drop the matter.

Hoover returned to Washington in late August to discover that the President still had selected no one to lead the much-touted commission. Indeed, he seemed in no hurry to do so, evidently preferring to let his military expedition unfold.[186] On August 31, in response to a presidential request for suitable names for the Russian aid project, Paul Reinsch (the American minister to China) suggested Hoover. The Food Administrator, said Reinsch, had "unequalled qualifications."[187] From the White House there came only silence.

In the end the Commission for Relief in Russia never materialized.

Instead, in mid-September, President Wilson authorized the chairmen of the War Industries Board, War Trade Board, and the U.S. Shipping Board jointly to supervise the funneling of economic assistance to Russia. The Food Administrator was not named to this interagency committee. Nor did he become involved with the War Trade Board's Russian Bureau (created in October), which quickly superseded the tripartite entity. Ultimately, Vance McCormick, not Hoover, became the overseer of the administration's Russian economic policy.[188]

For Hoover, it was probably just as well that the relief expedition he sought to lead did not occur. Siberia was a long way from the world's power centers, where he wanted to be. On August 27, in fact, Hoover—with himself almost certainly in mind—asked Wilson to appoint a "personal representative" who would control all of America's economic missions to Europe.[189] Nothing came of this suggestion either, but it abundantly illuminated the soaring wings of Hoover's ambition.

And that was probably the most revealing aspect of Hoover's involvement in the abortive campaign to replicate on Russian soil the achievements of the Commission for Relief in Belgium. Many years later Hoover claimed that he had been "greatly relieved" when he learned that the President had told Baruch that the Food Administrator could not be spared from his current duties.[190] Hoover's behavior at the time indicated otherwise: far from shrinking shyly from opportunities, he avidly sought to turn them his way. It reflected his growing passion for public service and for even greater prominence on the world's stage.

III

THE Russian aid commission plan had barely gone aglimmering when another set of circumstances propelled Hoover toward a new plane of responsibility. Once again his Belgian relief post provided the launching pad.

On September 23, 1918 Hoover announced the CRB's import program for the next twelve months, a commitment that would cost $280,000,000. As before, loans from the United States to France and Belgium would cover the cost of supplies purchased in the United States, while expenditures by Great Britain and France would cover shipping costs in Europe as well as foodstuffs obtained outside the United States.[191] The CRB's projections were for an entire year. Although the Allied armies had recently gained the initiative on the western front, neither Hoover nor many others anticipated that the war would cease before mid-1919.

Three days later, on September 26, the Allied forces in France launched their greatest—and, as it turned out, final—offensive. By early October the German army was in retreat, armistice negotiations had begun, and the problem of feeding liberated populations in Belgium and northern France had suddenly become critical. As the Allied armies advanced, a quarter of a million French and Belgian civilians in German-held areas fled toward the Dutch frontier.[192] Amidst the mounting confusion, Hoover and his relief organization scrambled to make provision for assistance in the newly evacuated territories.[193]

Hoover also attempted to deter the retreating Germans from acts of vengeful despoliation. When, on November 2, he learned that the Germans had issued orders to destroy Belgium's coal mines, he swiftly urged President Wilson to protest. The loss of this "absolutely vital necessity" would cause "enormous loss of human life" in the coming winter, Hoover exclaimed.[194] President Wilson promptly protested to Germany.[195] The Germans did not flood most of the mines.[196]

The increasing likelihood of an early peace now brought to a head an issue about which Hoover had been thinking for some time: How would Belgium and northern France be rehabilitated when the war was over? As early as the summer of 1916 Hoover had proposed that any cash surplus held by the CRB at the end of the war be used to create a Belgian foundation for "the stimulation of scientific and educational research."[197] He had also proposed to establish an organization to raise funds in America for the postwar reconstruction of cities and villages in Belgium and northern France.[198] Little had come of these ideas while the conflict raged.[199] But Hoover, typically, had not abandoned his vision. The "re-building in Belgium and Northern France" is "the one job that I would like to have," he told Brand Whitlock in January 1918.

> I believe that it contains usefulness and sentiment beyond any other occupation after this War is ended, and there is nothing that would appeal to me so much as to join with you in a mission of this kind on a basis of proper organization that would reflect credit and satisfaction to us for our remaining days.[200]

Certainly there could be no doubt that Belgium faced a challenge of staggering enormity. Four million of its people—more than half of the population—were destitute, dependent on the soup lines for their daily food. More than 80 percent of the industrial work force was unemployed. At least 50,000 homes lay in ruins. While starvation—thanks to the CRB—had largely been averted, "under-nourishment" (as Hoover termed it) had not. At current rations, the "industrial class" was "too weak" for "hard physical labour." In 1917 and 1918, moreover, the Germans had systematically dismantled entire Belgian factories and shipped them (along with other materials) to Germany, in a deliberate attempt to weaken future Belgian competitiveness. The famous Belgian spinning industry was completely destroyed. In the final weeks of the fighting, the withdrawing Germans wrecked railways, destroyed 350 railway bridges, seized whatever manufacturing equipment they could, and took Belgian livestock with them on a massive scale. To the millstones of four years of economic paralysis and disrepair were now added new physical destruction, depletion of capital goods, a shortage of work horses, a famine in milk, and the prospect of privation for months, even years, to come.[201]

Yet if Belgium was more "thoroughly despoiled" than any other industrial country touched by the war,[202] it was not yet clear how the battered kingdom would be restored to economic viability. At the most basic level—food relief—both France and the Belgian government-in-exile wanted the CRB to continue to operate in their liberated regions until the two governments could restore effective order, a process that might last well beyond the armistice.[203] Indeed, when Hoover, some time in October, ordered the CRB to begin preparations to turn its work over to the Belgian authorities, the Belgian minister to Washington was aghast. Hoover was "moving too rapidly," he protested, and was making a "great mistake." The diplomat asked the U.S. State Department "to stay Mr. Hoover's hand."[204]

Hoover was willing enough to oblige—on his terms. Even before hearing the Belgian pleas, he cabled William B. Poland that the Belgian government might ask—and the American government might insist—that the CRB "continue through reconstruction period. If so, will ask have all relations precisely defined by President."[205]

Immediate relief, however, was one thing; long-term reconstruction another. But here, too, new opportunities were thrusting themselves upon the Chief, as his lieutenant, Edgar Rickard, told a friend on October 24. According to Rickard, both the British Treasury and the Belgian government-in-exile were demanding that the CRB continue in existence "on a very much larger scale than was ever conceived." If "these people have their way," Rickard opined, the CRB "will embrace the whole of the reconstruction of Belgium and extend for many years after peace is declared." Rickard added that if Hoover could be persuaded "to put his whole attention into work of this kind," it would become "one of the unique accomplishments" of the era.[206]

Despite Rickard's claim, it is not clear that the British or the Belgians were putting any such pressure on Hoover at all. Rickard's letter was typical of many that Hoover and his closest aides wrote over the years—letters depicting the Chief as a self-effacing and passive consultant, responding only reluctantly to the pleas of would-be clients. Rickard was wrong: Hoover needed no pressure or persuasion. Three days earlier, in fact, he had boldly offered himself for the mission of rebuilding Belgium.

Hoover's initiative came in the form of a letter and memorandum to President Wilson on October 21. The chairman of the CRB asserted that the French government would be able to take care of its liberated territories—embracing only 7 percent of the country's population—without further outside support. Belgium, however, was another matter entirely. To restore its people to a "self-supporting" condition, he declared, would require an immediate doubling of American and Allied governmental aid from $15,000,000 to $30,000,000 per month for the next twelve to eighteen months.

How should such a rehabilitation program be organized? According to Hoover, certain Belgians wanted the CRB to be liquidated and surrender its functions to the restored government, which would then rely upon the European Allies for assistance. Other Belgians wanted the CRB to continue to operate but under the Belgian government's control and definition of its duties. Still other Belgians wanted the CRB itself to "undertake the great problem of economic restoration" in cooperation with nongovernmental Belgian bodies and with Allied and American subsidies.

As ever, Hoover disavowed any ambition for the job. He claimed that "the selfish view" of his colleagues and himself lay "entirely" with the first policy option: outright liquidation of the CRB. "We would like to have relief," he added, "from this especially poignant anxiety that has now extended over four years." Nevertheless, Hoover contended that Americans in general, and the CRB in particular, should organize the rehabilitation effort. He argued that Belgium had "little hope" of recovery unless "the major help" came from the United States. He asserted that the challenge offered "an opportunity for further service," which could yield America significant "moral rewards." He warned that Americans could not garner these rewards unless it was through the "bond" of a "definite American organization" participating in the great undertaking. And he suggested that American involvement "in organization and administration" could "more effectively" guarantee the "security" and efficient use of the funds "without religious, political or racial bias" than if the Belgians alone were dispensing the money.

Hoover also insisted that a "single channel" of expenditure of charitable sums from abroad was necessary to avoid "enormous waste and corruption," and he contended that the Belgians would be better off in their quest for ships and supplies if they were under the American—not the Europeans'—"wing." What could be more "logical," he asked, than to funnel "American participation" in Belgian renewal through the already existing CRB?[207]

Hoover's letter was a clever, even brilliant, document. His invocation of the theme of "service," his allusion to the "moral" advantages of foreign aid, his call for a "distinctly American organization" to administer it, his contrast between American efficiency and European rivalries—all were arguments likely to strike home with Woodrow Wilson. Hoover's contention that his CRB merely needed "larger resources" to accomplish its redefined mission was also probably designed to reassure the commander in chief. For on its face, Hoover's proposal was an audacious one. The CRB, after all, had but two hundred people in its ranks, and had never stationed more than three dozen of these inside Belgium at any one time. It was one thing to supervise and monitor the tightly organized feeding of a hungry and demoralized country in wartime. It was something else to reconstruct its entire trade and industry in a time of economic freedom and peace.

On October 24 Hoover discussed his proposal with the President at the White House.[208] Evidently Wilson was amenable, or at least interested, for two days later Hoover sent him two "memoranda." One was a draft letter to Hoover to be signed by Wilson, authorizing the CRB and its leader to take charge of American efforts for the "economic rehabilitation" of Belgium. The other "memorandum" was evidently a draft letter from Wilson to various members of his administration instructing them to cooperate with Hoover.[209]

While the chairman of the CRB awaited Wilson's decision, he attempted to make certain that the European Allies would not be permitted to interfere. In a conversation at the State Department on October 28, an anxious Hoover urged the department to make no agreement with other countries about Belgian reconstruction. There should be no "joint conference," he said, for this would tie America's hands.[210] Hoover wanted a free hand, and he wanted that hand to be his.

Not everyone was ready to agree. In mid-October, certain of the Allies approached the U.S. Treasury about financing Belgium's impending reconstruction. The Treasury immediately contacted Hoover, only to learn that he had already taken the matter to the White House. Hoover did not disclose what he had recommended.[211]

Furious at being left in the dark, Secretary of the Treasury McAdoo immediately asked President Wilson to "take no action" on Hoover's letter until McAdoo had a chance to present the views of his department.[212] In a separate letter to Hoover, McAdoo asserted that it was "essential" for Great Britain and France to share the financial burden of restoring Belgium. If they were to do so, he added, they would be "entitled" to "a voice in determining the form of administration"—precisely what Hoover did not want. With ill-concealed irritation, McAdoo observed that the Treasury was "necessarily interested' in this matter, and that its "financial aspects" should be "fully discussed" with his department before any plans were officially authorized.[213]

McAdoo's sally did not sit well at the Food Administration. Hoover quickly retorted that McAdoo must be unaware that the British and French had "long since obligated themselves to undertake the matter." As for American action, Hoover loftily offered his rival a civics lesson: "No obligation of this government can or will be entered without the authority of the President and no doubt without every department expressing its own views."[214] Hoover did not reveal that he had already asked the President to *order* McAdoo, among others, to do what Hoover wanted for Belgium.

Meanwhile, at Le Havre, the Belgian government-in-exile had been formulating its own scheme for the postwar reconstruction of its homeland. The plan called for creation of an inter-Allied commission composed of delegates from each country participating in Belgium's restoration effort. The inter-Allied body would examine programs submitted to it by the Belgian government and then "distribute the execution of these programs among the Allied countries." In each of these countries there would be national commissions of "prominent men," who would facilitate delivery of resources from their countries to Belgium. In all of this there was no mention of the CRB or of Hoover. When the Belgian minister to the United States transmitted the proposal to the State Department on October 29, he asked the U.S. government to "designate someone, now in Europe" to discuss it. Herbert Hoover, conspicuously, was in Washington.[215]

McAdoo and the Belgian minister were too late. On November 6—without, apparently, consulting either of them—President Wilson notified McAdoo and several other administration officials by letter that he had invited Hoover

> to expand the activities of the Commission for Relief in Belgium to cover the entire relationship of this government, and possibly that of other governments, together with all American public charity, to the whole business not only of food but also clothing, raw materials, tools, machinery, exchange and other economic relief involved in the reconstruction of Belgium.

The President directed the recipients of his letter to give Hoover "all support and cooperation in this matter" and to "refer to him for guidance in all questions of an economic order that arise in any connection between Belgium and this country."[216] For Hoover (who had ghost-written the draft of this categorical directive), it was a sweet and sweeping victory.

The next day Wilson sent Hoover a slightly edited version of the "memorandum" that Hoover had drafted for his signature on October 26. In it, Wilson declared that the "all important work of reconstruction and rehabilitation" of Belgium "should be organized under a single agency," an entity which would "coordinate the whole effort of the American people and government, in the furnishing of supplies, machinery, finance, exchange, shipping, trade relations and philanthropic aid." This agency, he said, should be the Commission for Relief in Belgium.

Wilson expressed his understanding that the British and French governments wished "to participate in carrying this burden." He therefore authorized Hoover—in words that Hoover himself ghost-wrote—to ask these governments to "continue and enlarge their present support to the Commission to these ends, so that we may have a comprehensive and efficient agency for dealing with the entire problem on behalf of all." In other words, the CRB would be the *only* Belgian reconstruction agency, and the Allied role in it would be confined to writing checks. Like Hoover, Wilson was quite willing to relegate the British and the French to the status of bit players in a drama in which Americans would be the heroes.[217]

Hoover swiftly consolidated his mandate. With the President's approval he created a CRB executive committee, chaired by himself, with representatives from several government agencies. Of the nine members, eight were Hoover loyalists.[218] On November 9 he informed the White House that any Belgian assistance program would require at least $200,000,000 "to pay for the food and reconstruction materials necessary to be shipped from the United States, pending the restoration of trade conditions" and possible legislation. He asked that the U.S. Treasury loan this sum to the Belgian government with the stipulation that the entire amount be spent in the United States through the CRB. Ever in a hurry, he asked that, "in order to avoid a debacle in the relief" in case peace came suddenly, the Treasury should commit itself to furnish this amount "at once."[219]

In this case, Hoover did not immediately get what he wanted. Instead, at a meeting of the War Cabinet four days later, the President approved an increase in the CRB's subsidy to a maximum of $20,000,000 per month for the purchase of food and clothing.[220] Expenditure for reconstruction was deferred.

Hover also took steps to assure "an orderly development of re-construction" after the Belgian government was reestablished on its own soil. He declared that no licenses should be granted for American exports to Belgium without approval of the CRB's executive committee. He declared that no credits or monetary transfers to Belgium should be permitted without the executive committee's assent. All food purchases in America for Belgium should be made solely by the Food Administration. "All attempts of private traders to establish credits in the United States" for Belgium should be "discouraged."[221] Clearly Hoover intended to keep every facet of the Belgian project under his vigilant control.

Over at the U.S. Treasury, Secretary McAdoo could do little about Hoover's presidentially sanctioned steamroller. But McAdoo did object to some of the details. He reminded Hoover sharply that under the law the responsibility for establishing governmental credits rested with the Secretary of the Treasury and that he did not intend to delegate his authority to the CRB's executive committee. McAdoo also protested Hoover's "suggestion" that private credit operations *vis-à-vis* Belgium be discouraged. To the contrary, McAdoo argued, "individual initiative and direct commercial relations" should be restored as quickly as possible. The U.S. Treasury, he made it plain, intended to "encourage private financing of foreign trade and the reduction of governmental aid to a minimum."[222] The stage was set for clashes with Hoover for months to come.

If McAdoo was miffed by Hoover's control of Belgian rehabilitation, the Belgian government—according to Brand Whitlock—was "deeply disappointed" by Washington's rejection of its proposal for an inter-Allied commission. Hoover might believe that the Belgians would be better off under America's (and his) benevolent patronage, but Belgium could hardly ignore its neighbors, Great Britain and France. Whitlock blamed the American rebuff of the Belgians' scheme on Hoover "and his desire to monopolize, to have all the credit."[223]

Alarmed by the signals now emanating from Washington, the Belgian Foreign Office addressed an appeal to the United States, through Whitlock, on November 9. The situation inside Belgium, the cable asserted, was "grave." Within two weeks a million workers, about to be freed from German control, would be demanding employment. If they did not find it, severe "social disturbances," even revolution, might occur. The despairing Belgian government beseeched America and Hoover to provide help.

The exiled government did not stop here. It again asked that Belgium receive priority on all orders for industrial machinery placed in the United States, with the financing to be arranged "according to the program already submitted at Washington." If this program was unacceptable, the Belgians asked that Hoover or some other American official criticize it, suggest an alternative program, or select "some competent person now in France to discuss the details."[224] Badly as they wanted American aid, the Belgians were clearly nervous about becoming completely dependent on their "Bienfaiteur."

Hoover was irritated by the Belgians' message and by Whitlock's readiness to serve as their mouthpiece. Five days later the CRB chairman replied crisply by cable that there was "every sympathy and desire to assist the Belgians." "Every priority has and will be given," he asserted. At this very moment his government was expanding its food and clothing assistance "to a very remarkable degree." As for tools and machinery, however—the very heart of a rebuilding effort—he now announced that these could be provided only after "we have accurate knowledge of what is required, a thing impossible until [German] evacuation." Moreover, appropriate credit arrangements would have to be devised. Badly as he wished to be Belgium's rebuilder, he was not going to let himself be stampeded into ill-conceived ventures.

Hoover pointedly ignored the Belgians' request that he delegate someone in France to talk to them. Instead, he announced that the President had asked him to "take charge" of the American "interest" in Belgian rehabilitation and that he would arrive in Brussels for consultations in about a month.[225]

It was no idle promise. On November 11 an armistice had been proclaimed in Europe. The fighting was done. Now the restoration of ravaged Belgium could really begin.

But not just Belgium was in need. From the Atlantic to the Urals, the two Horsemen of War and Death (as Hoover later put it) had passed on, only to be replaced by two others: Famine and Pestilence.[226] With characteristic foresight, he was already preparing to meet them.

18

"Food Will Win the World"

I

IN October 1918 Hoover had much more than the impending rehabilitation of Belgium on his mind. On every front in Europe, events were rushing toward a climax. On September 29 Germany's ally Bulgaria signed an armistice ending its participation in the war. A week later the German government itself asked Woodrow Wilson for an armistice and peace negotiations on the basis of his Fourteen Points address of January 8, 1918. The next day Germany's ally, Austria-Hungary, followed suit.

There now ensued what Hoover later called "the greatest drama of intellectual leadership in all history,"[1] as President Wilson attempted to maneuver the Germans (and the Allies) into acceptance of peace terms consistent with his vision of a new world order. While the exchange of diplomatic notes proceeded between Washington and Berlin, the Allied armies hammered forward steadily against their foes. To the east the Austro-Hungarian empire tottered and crumbled, as the Czechoslovaks and Yugoslavs proclaimed their independence. On October 31 Germany's ally Turkey agreed to an armistice. On November 4 what remained of Austria-Hungary did the same. Now Germany was fighting alone.

By mid-October Hoover had begun to prepare for the possibility that the war might end much sooner than previously anticipated. Convinced that America would have to feed the people of Germany and Austria-Hungary in the coming winter in order to preserve "stability" there,[2] on October 17 he suggested to the President's War Cabinet that America begin shipping food to Europe immediately.[3] The Food Administrator informed the press that the coming victory in the war would actually increase the pressure on America's food supply and would necessitate continued conservation and controls. Otherwise, the soaring postwar demand for better rations in Allied and enemy countries would drain the United States of its stocks. According to Hoover and his associates, the world food situation was poor if one took into account conditions in enemy nations. The Food Administration warned that if peace should descend upon Europe during the winter just ahead, the continent's food problems would give Hoover his greatest challenge yet.[4]

As if to underscore this message, sometime in October Hoover's agency prepared new information cards, probably for use in an upcoming national appeal for food conservation. "After the War," the cards said, "180,000,000 people in hungry lands will look to America for food which no other people can give them." Belgium, northern France, central Russia, Serbia, Montenegro, Poland, Romania, and Armenia "will cry to us." "From us food must come," the message continued. "We must save that we may give. It is America's mission, our opportunity to serve. FOOD WILL WIN THE WORLD."[5]

Hoover was by no means the only senior American official who believed that massive food relief would be needed to preserve stability abroad in the months ahead. At a meeting in the White House on October 17, President Wilson quoted a preacher who had said that the Lord's Prayer began with the words "Give us this day our daily bread" and that "no man could worship God on an empty stomach." Hunger in Europe, the President added, would lead to Bolshevism and anarchy.[6] Secretary of State Lansing emphatically agreed. Deeply alarmed that the coming enemy collapse would produce conditions favorable to violent social upheaval, Lansing wrote on October 28:

> Food is the real problem. Empty stomachs mean Bolsheviks. Full stomachs mean no Bolsheviks. The feeding of Europe must take place as rapidly as possible to defeat the chaos which threatens society.

Wherever the social order is "broken by famine, idleness and penury," he warned, "the possibility of revolution and Bolshevik domination" would exist. For Lansing, as for Wilson, American food was the key to saving Central and Western Europe from the bloody terror and suffering that were even now ravaging Russia.[7] Herbert Hoover shared these views completely.

By October 26 Hoover, in the words of his secretary, was "working on Relief plans for the whole of stricken Europe on an immense scale."[8] Yet even as the Food Administrator contemplated pouring American assistance into enemy lands as soon as the fighting stopped, he was far from feeling well disposed toward those who would presumably assist him. Hoover had not forgotten how the British, in his view, had shortchanged the French and Italians in the division of imported food until he had rectified matters during the past summer. He had not forgotten how certain British officials had resisted his creation of the Inter-Allied Food Council and had fought his assertion of priorities. He had not forgotten how the British-dominated Allied Maritime Transport Council had clipped the Food Council's projected program of imports for 1918–19. Nor was he pleased by British reluctance to snap up the 100,000,000 bushels of wheat he offered the Allies early in October. By mid-month he even wished that it had not been necessary for him to sell them the wheat at all.[9]

The Food Administrator was therefore in no collegial mood when, around October 23, he learned that certain members of the Inter-Allied Food Council were promoting "international control of world distribution of food after peace."[10] More specifically, on October 21 the powerful Allied Maritime Transport Council had drafted a proposal to turn itself into a "General Economic Board" with complete control of all inter-Allied bodies created to handle food, munitions, and other commodities during the war. The AMTC recommended that this "whole inter-Allied organisation" be maintained not only during any period of armistice but in certain respects after the signing of a peace treaty.[11]

Hoover was immediately suspicious. In a letter to the President on October 24, he declared that his "instinct" was "entirely against any such agreements or entanglements." From a moral point of view, he warned, "any international body" on food in which the United States participated "would involve us in acceptance of their views." From a practical point of view, it would entail American "acceptance of their distribution of our supplies."

Hoover therefore proposed a radical alternative. Since the United States would have "the dominant supplies" if peace "arrives at any time during the next few months," America should "maintain a complete independence" and distribute its resources "so as to fill in the gaps in supplies that are not secured by the various nations from other countries." The United States, that is, could employ its food supplies to "level up, in a rough manner," the "deficiencies" that would eventually result from "the general grab for the balances of the world's food." Hoover was acutely aware of the political advantages of such a deployment of American bounty. "If we maintain our independence," he told Wilson, "we can confer favours instead of complying with agreements and we can use our resources to make economic exchanges which will maintain justice all round."

Hoover was candidly specific about what he meant. After the war, he pointed out, the U.S. Army in Europe would require "rapid transport home." By keeping independent control over its foodstuffs, the United States could require Great Britain, France, Germany, Austria, and the neutral countries to supply "a certain amount" of shipping for our troops in exchange for "every ton" of American food. Similarly with raw materials: these, too, said Hoover, "could be used to maintain some sort of justice." Germany, for example, had "wantonly destroyed the entire spinning industry" of Belgium, Poland, and northern France in order to capture the markets for this industry after the war. Hoover suggested that the United States "ration" its postwar exports of raw cotton to Germany in such a way as to allow Germany's despoiled competitors to "get back on their industrial feet."[12]

Although he did not openly say so, Hoover was advocating nothing less than a reversal of American policy toward its co-belligerents. Until now, the thrust of the inter-Allied war effort had been toward ever-increasing coordination of policy. The Supreme War Council, the Allied Maritime Transport Council, and a host of lesser entities had been expressions of an imperative driven by necessity. Hoover himself had contributed to this trend by creating the Inter-Allied Food Council just three months before. Then his rhetoric had invoked the comradely image of "the common table." Now, however, in October, with the end of the war nearly at hand, he was boldly proposing that the United States break free of such constraints and go it alone.

And more than that. Prior to April 1917 Hoover had earned international acclaim as Belgium's saviour, as an intercessor for hungry innocents in a world of hardened militarism and hate. For Hoover then, the claims of humanity had been transcendent. Now, however, with the war almost over, he was frankly urging his President to use food as an instrument of policy, a means of "conferring favours" on certain nations.

What had happened? Had Hoover changed? Not really. He had always been willing to exert high pressure to gain his objectives. In his "Belgian" days he had invoked "the club of public opinion" and had even threatened to terminate the relief if he did not get his way. At the Food Administration he had repeatedly used coercive regulations and tough tactics to bring domestic and foreign recalcitrants into line. Now, in the impeding postwar "grab" for the world's food, he intended to use his supplies as a weapon with which to achieve what he considered justice. Implicit in his proposal was the assumption—by now a settled conviction—that America's wartime allies could not be trusted to pursue justice as righteously as the United States.

Hoover was apparently unsure how Woodrow Wilson would react. He asked the President for a response and promised that "if you hold the view that we shall entertain no entanglements whatever I shall take steps at once to maintain such a stand."[13] Wilson did not reply immediately—at least not in writing. But Hoover soon found that the two saw eye to eye. Like his feisty Food Administrator, Wilson was increasingly distrustful of the British and angered by what he deemed to be their selfish policies. And like Hoover, Wilson was quite prepared to marshal America's formidable economic power—including food—as a force for equity in postwar Europe.[14]

Even as Hoover sent his letter to the White House, he knew that the end of the war might come quickly. Just the day before, on October 23, he and other members of the President's unofficial "War Cabinet" had assembled in the President's study for their weekly conference. There the President had reviewed the latest diplomatic note from the Germans and had asked his advisers for comment. On paper, at least, the enemy had agreed to everything he had demanded (including democratization of its autocratic government) as a prelude to acceptance of an armistice. But were the Germans sincere? Should they be granted an end to hostilities short of total capitulation? Could they be trusted to adhere to the terms of a cease-fire while a formal peace treaty was negotiated? Would the American people, who were clamoring for an unconditional German surrender, be satisfied with anything less? What effort would seeking an armistice have on the Congressional elections less than two weeks away?

On the other hand, if Wilson did not accept an armistice, how much longer might the fighting go on? What would be the effect inside Germany? Rebuffed in its bid for peace, would the enemy turn Bolshevik, engulfing Central Europe in bloody chaos? Indeed, if the war continued much longer, would there even be a stable German government with which to make peace? And if America and its associates proceeded to vanquish the Germans utterly, would not this outcome weaken Wilson's hand in his *other* "war"—the struggle against the Allies over the postwar settlement? Was the unconditional surrender and severe punishment of Germany truly in America's best interest?[15]

For Hoover and nearly all of the War Cabinet present, the answer to this last question was negative. Two years ago, Hoover declared, he had expressed the hope that Germany would never make peace in London nor the British in Berlin. Such a result would mean another war in ten years. America now held the balance of power, Hoover asserted. If President Wilson did not now deal justly with the German people, who were evidently trying to effect constitutional reform, Wilson's altruistic ideals would be "shattered."[16] Hoover urged the President (in one of the participant's words) to send a "note of encouragement to Germans who were trying to encourage self government in Germany."[17] As for his colleague Vance McCormick's call for unconditional surrender and the occupation of Berlin, Hoover demurred. "I remarked," he wrote later, "that I wanted to see a quick end to the war and that I took no stock in a triumphal march down the Unter den Linden."[18]

In the end, with Hoover and all but one other member of the War Cabinet in agreement, President Wilson made the fateful decision for an armistice.[19] Later on October 23 he submitted his recent diplomatic communications with the German government, including its request for an armistice, to the Allies and invited their response. One week later the three Allied premiers gathered in Paris with the President's representative, Colonel House, for the tortuous task of negotiating the precise terms of the armistice to be offered Germany.

The prospect of an imminent end to hostilities triggered a development that was to anger Hoover no end. On October 28 the permanent representatives of the Allied Maritime Transport Council and the Inter-Allied Food Council unanimously adopted a recommendation for the inter-Allied authorities who were about to consider armistice terms. The representatives asked that, as a condition of the armistice, all German and Austrian merchant ships be placed under the control of the AMTC and that any post-armistice food for the enemy be acquired only through "the existing Allied organisations" on such terms as they imposed. The representatives asserted that it would be economically "disastrous" if either enemy or neutral countries were now to enter the world's markets and purchase critically needed commodities "in competition, but without co-operation, with the Allies."[20] Forwarding this document to Washington on October 30, Hoover's chief European representative, Joseph Cotton, stressed the need for immediate action and indicated that he was inclined to acquiesce. Certainly, he reported, "better cooperation could be obtained from representatives of existing Allied organizations than by attempting to create new machinery" in which Allied representation might be "weaker."[21]

Hoover was aghast. The AMTC/IAFC proposal was precisely the opposite of the free hand that he wanted. Cabling Cotton on November 2, the Food Administrator declared sharply that "policies outlined [by you are] entirely against views here." He ordered Cotton "[u]nder no circumstances [to] take any pledges until instructed."[22] Perhaps for this reason, when the British foreign secretary proposed to Colonel House in Paris that the German merchant fleet be seized as a condition of the armistice and turned over to the AMTC, House put him off. The colonel suggested instead that the issue be considered immediately after the armistice was signed. The British foreign secretary went along.[23]

While House in Paris apparently played for time, Hoover in Washington endeavored to kill the Allied scheme. Hoover did not feel that he could veto it solely on his own authority. On November 4, therefore, he sent Cotton's dispatch on to the White House for "urgent consideration."[24] Two days later, at a meeting of the President with his War Cabinet, Hoover got the sanction that he sought. Soon afterward, he bluntly notified Cotton: "For your general advice and not to be communicated. This government will not agree to any programme that even looks like interallied control of our economic resources after peace." Hoover pointed out that with the arrival of peace, "over one half of the whole export food supplies of the world will come from the United States and for the buyers of these supplies to sit in majority in dictation to us as to prices and distribution is wholly inconceivable."[25]

Hoover's factual claim was exaggerated. His own data, compiled just days before, showed that the American portion of the world's exportable food before the next harvest would not be "over one half" but more like 42 percent, including sugar exported from Cuba.[26] But the Food Administrator was less concerned with statistical accuracy than with power: power to allocate the immense food reserves that the United States had amassed under his direction. "Our only hope," he told Cotton, "of securing justice in distribution, proper appreciation abroad of the effort we make to assist foreign nations and proper return for the service that we will perform will revolve around complete independence of commitment to joint action on our part." Clearly more than the saving of lives was on Hoover's mind. Justice, "proper appreciation," and a "proper return" for his country's service were all among his desiderata.

Yet something obviously would need to be done to organize relief in Austria, Bulgaria, and elsewhere in the event of an armistice. How should the victors proceed? For Hoover the answer was obvious. To handle the "commercial aspects" of the coming effort, he told Cotton, "the efficient thing" would be to "organize a duplication" of the Commission for Relief in Belgium. "Such machinery," he declared, could "determine the needs," secure credits, operate shipping, buy and distribute food, and take "independent action" of a commercial kind that the existing inter-Allied food and maritime transport councils never could.

Hoover had no intention that Allied representation on such a body would be equal to that of the United States. Instead (he informed Cotton), it could be *proportional:* "proportional to the actual resources" in food, shipping, and finance that the Allies contributed to the commission's tasks. Since Hoover expected to control most of the world's food surplus in the months ahead, and since the United States was already the Allies' chief creditor, his principle of proportional representation would necessarily mean American hegemony over postwar relief.

Hoover was determined, in fact, to protect American interests from what he plainly feared would be Allied encroachment. He notified Cotton that the proposed relief commission's food purchases inside the United States would be "co-ordinated" with those of other buyers by the Food Administration. Outside the United States, the new entity's purchases would be handled in cooperation with "existing agencies." In this way, Hoover asserted, the "international disorganization" proposed in Cotton's cable of October 30 would be averted, "and above all the extension of the functions and life of Inter-Allied food and maritime councils either now or after peace will be prevented."

Clearly he hoped to eliminate these if he could. As for delegating neutral countries' food purchases in the United States to these same inter-Allied councils, Hoover was unalterably opposed. "We cannot consent" to this, he thundered. "We must continue to act with entire independence in our commercial relations with all neutrals and Belgian Relief."[27]

Hoover therefore ordered his London representative to "discourage any attempts" to implement the Allies' proposals.[28] The wary Food Administrator did not know it, but he had just precipitated a bitter row that would pit him against the Allies for nearly two months.

Hoover did not stop here. After preparing his cabled instructions to Cotton, he forwarded a copy to Woodrow Wilson[29] and asked the President to send it to Colonel House with Wilson's endorsement. Hoover also asked the President to tell House that "I will be leaving within the next few days for Paris and that no arrangements looking forward to the handling of food for liberated populations should be undertaken until after my arrival and consultation with him."[30] The President swiftly complied with Hoover's requests.[31]

Hoover's reference to an imminent trip to Paris was no impetuous act of impertinence. Only three days before, at Colonel House's initiative, the inter-Allied summit conference at Versailles had unanimously affirmed its readiness to provide as much food as possible to the civilian populations of defeated Austria, Bulgaria, and Turkey.[32] The news of this momentous decision reached Washington on November 5. That same day, Secretary of State Lansing and one of his senior advisers discussed the possibility of Hoover's traveling to Austria, presumably to ascertain that country's needs.[33] It was hardly a startling thought. Who, after all, had more standing as an authority on food and relief? Nor was Hoover, apparently, indifferent to the prospect. On November 5 he himself called at the State Department to review the European food crisis with one of Lansing's deputies.[34]

Desire quickly became official policy. On November 6, at the President's meeting with his War Cabinet, it was decided that Hoover would indeed go to Europe to examine food conditions—particularly in Austria, where starvation loomed.[35] Hoover told the meeting that since the United States would either have to provide money for relief work directly or loan it to Great Britain and France, the United States itself should perform the mission "and let it have our brand."[36] It was an argument that met with presidential favor. Hoover's suspicions of the Allies, in fact, were mirrored by Wilson's own. "I intend to carry as many weapons to the peace table as I can conceal on my person," the President told his advisers on November 6. He would, he promised, be "cold and firm."[37]

The chief executive was not the only person who envisaged a widening European role for Hoover as soon as hostilities stopped. From his perch in Paris, Colonel House perceived that conditions in Central Europe were deteriorating. In a cable to the President on November 8, House warned that "[p]robably the greatest problem" to confront the United States at the cease-fire would be the provision of food and other necessities to Austria, Bohemia, Germany, Serbia, Belgium, and northern France. Like Hoover, but independently of him, House had concluded that such a relief enterprise would "have to be done almost entirely through American effort." House was also wary of the British attempt to have the Allied Maritime Transport Council take control of Germany's merchant fleet. Instead, he urged that as soon as an armistice with Germany was signed, President Wilson should propose immediate creation of an "International Relief Organization" to be headed by Herbert Hoover. This organization—not the AMTC—should operate the German merchant marine for relief purposes.[38]

When House prepared this cable, he was not yet aware of the decisions reached by the War Cabinet on November 6 or of Hoover's subsequent dispatch to Joseph Cotton. It did not matter. On this issue the President and his emissary in Paris were in accord. On November 11 Wilson informed House that "our judgment corresponds with yours" and that Hoover was "coming over immediately to discuss the matter and propose our method of handling it."[39]

Yet even as Hoover prepared to cross the Atlantic, portents of trouble were multiplying. On November 8 Joseph Cotton cabled him a new Allied scheme circulating in London: a proposal for an American/Allied wheat pool which would purchase all surplus wheat in the world in the current and coming year, including America's surplus for the duration of the U.S. government's price support program. Cotton clearly favored the joint arrangement. He asserted that it would "to some extent" protect the United States against loss if world wheat prices temporarily fell below the price that Hoover was obliged to pay American producers. Cotton also contended that the pool would encourage neutral countries to "act properly and to oppose an increase in prices." Furthermore, it would enable the United States to ensure that "newer and poorer nations" received wheat "in a reasonably fair manner." Of course, he added, such a plan could only operate if America continued "in some broad way to take part in the machinery of the Allies." Perhaps anticipating growls of protest from his chief, Cotton bluntly warned of the alternative: a trade war between the United States and Great Britain, with rising prices and "disastrous" results across Europe. Americans, said Cotton, did not appear to recognize just how economically powerful Great Britain was.[40]

The next day Cotton had more disconcerting news to transmit. He notified Hoover that plans were afoot in London to initiate food relief for Central Europe through the military lines at Salonika, Greece. Since Allied army officers would necessarily direct this operation, American participation in it would be minimal. Cotton also noted that current proposals for the relief tended "to put the machinery in British hands," even though virtually all the relief foodstuffs would come from the United States.

With the Allies itching to launch relief projects of their own, and with all sorts of Americans abroad now meddling (said Cotton) in the question, Hoover's representative pleaded for quick action. General plans for the relief must be formulated in the next two weeks, he said. Resolution of the issue could not wait until Hoover's arrival in Europe. American negotiators in London must obtain "some inkling" of Hoover's wishes beforehand.[41]

As events in Europe threatened to careen out of his control, Hoover sent Cotton's dispatches on to the White House and requested presidential intervention at once. Thoroughly dismayed at the drift of things in London, the

Food Administrator pulled no punches. The idea of America's entering an inter-Allied pool to distribute "all of the world's wheat" until mid-1920 "fills me with compete horror," he exclaimed. So, too, did the prospect of the British making arrangements "for provisioning the world with our foodstuffs and on our credit." Hoover asserted that 70 percent of the world's wheat surplus would come from the western hemisphere. If the Allied pooling scheme took effect, he told the President, he assumed that the United States would be requested to finance the shipment of this wheat and then to put its distribution "in the hands of a body we could not control."

The American Food Administrator would have none of it. There was no *point* to the plan, he said. The world would have sufficient wheat to get by—"unless," he suggested darkly, the Allies intended "to use this control of the prime necessity of life to dominate other measures in the world." Hoover therefore asked Wilson for "a definition of our principles in these matters." With typical thoroughness, he submitted his own "suggestion in this direction."[42]

Once more Hoover found himself attuned to his commander in chief. Not only did the President approve the substance of Hoover's "suggestion"; he approved virtually all of its wording and authorized Hoover to transmit it to American officials in Europe. On November 13 Hoover sent the presidentially sanctioned directive to Joseph Cotton.

Hoover's statement left little room for misunderstanding. The United States, he announced, "consider ourselves as trustees of our surplus production of all kinds for the benefit of the most necessitous and the most deserving. We feel that we must ourselves execute this trusteeship. . . ." Hoover declared that America was "not unmindful" of its "obligation" for the "sustenance" of its wartime allies against Germany. In fact, he added, "we feel" that the Allies and those peoples "released from the German yoke . . . may well deserve a priority in our distribution."

But, he added flatly, America "cannot undertake any cooperative arrangements that look to the control of our exports after peace." All existing inter-Allied councils had been created "entirely" for coordination during the war. Any "extension of their functions" either "beyond peace" or to control America's dealings with other nations "cannot be entertained by us." As for the immediate framework of food relief, Hoover was equally explicit:

> All relationship involving the use of American food or credit for the people of other nations than the Allies themselves must await Mr. Hoover's arrival in Europe so far as any such supplies or interest of the United States is concerned in which we will coordinate in every proper way.[43]

The United States would cooperate, then, but only upon terms that Hoover would approve on the spot: the presidentially approved communiqué was clear. In only one respect did it differ from Hoover's original suggestion: the insertion of the promise to "coordinate in every proper way." To this extent the Food Administrator held out an olive branch to the Allies. Unfortunately for Hoover, for the Allies, and for the suffering civilian populations of Europe, just which mode of coordination was "proper" would soon become the subject of dispute.

Meanwhile, Hoover was working furiously to ready his organization for the coming challenge. On November 4 he submitted to the President a "broad survey" of the world's food necessities and supplies until the next harvest. Although the Food Administrator calculated that the United States alone could contribute 16,400,000 tons of food for other peoples' succor, the total exportable surplus from all sources still fell short of what he judged "desirable to preserve health and tranquility." Hoover was especially apprehensive about a perceived worldwide shortage of fats. He was also fearful that if the United States abolished its stringent export controls, a domestic catastrophe would ensue. Without the embargo, he predicted, "every one of our foodstuffs will be overdrawn and our own people faced with shortages next spring." Remove the embargo, and the "whole world" would soon be "bidding in our market without restraint." The consequence would be "an era of high prices, of profiteering and speculation" without precedent in American history.[44]

Hoover was determined, then, to maintain a restraining hand on domestic food supplies. He was also resolved tightly to control food distribution abroad. On November 5 he let it be known to the press that he was contemplating a rationing system for Europe modeled on that of the Commission for Relief in Belgium. Northern France, Belgium, countries already eliminated from the war, even Germany when it submitted to an armistice: all, Hoover indicated, would come within the purview of his rationing plan, which would be supervised by Allied and American personnel.[45] In a telegram to his state food administrators on November 7, he suggested that it might even become necessary to establish several agencies akin to the Commission for Relief in Belgium in order to deal with "other liberated peoples."[46] Hoover was not thinking small. He could not afford to—not if his analysis was right, not if the preservation of European civilization depended upon American food.[47]

But how would such an enormous endeavor be financed? In a letter to the President on November 9, Hoover declared frankly that a Congressional appropriation would be "absolutely necessary." While he expected the Europeans ultimately to pay for their food, he deemed it "almost hopeless" to establish satisfactory credit arrangements rapidly enough "to solve the situation" under the current "disorganized" conditions. At least at the outset, his relief operation would need to depend upon "advances from our government."

Hoover therefore proposed an appropriation of $200,000,000 "for the feeding of the liberated populations in Europe," with the entire sum to be placed at the President's personal disposal. Two hundred million dollars: it was a figure nearly twenty times the annual budget of the Food Administration. But Hoover showed no signs of trepidation. This was the "critical moment," he told Wilson: ". . . if we can worry through the next four or five months [prior to "rehabilitation of trade"] we will have solved the problem." The immense relief project was "fundamental," he averred, "if we are to preserve these countries from Bolshevism and rank anarchy."[48]

While Wilson pondered Hoover's audacious request, the Food Administrator moved to enlist the American people behind his mission. The next morning, November 10, the nation's newspapers reported an official press release from the State Department: President Wilson had requested Hoover to "take charge" for the U.S. government of the organization of food relief for the "liberated people of Europe," and had directed Hoover to "proceed" there "at once" to determine the measures needed. The State Department announced that Hoover was going abroad not only to rehabilitate the long-suffering people of Belgium and northern France but also to organize food deliveries to the Czecho-Slovaks, Serbs, Romanians, and other nationalities in Southern Europe. In justifying this unprecedented venture in foreign aid, the State Department expressed a concern that was increasingly on Hoover's mind: an "adequate food supply" in Southern Europe would help newly created governments there to "maintain order and cohesion in government" and avert "the complete debacle such as has taken place in Russia."[49]

Hoover coupled this announcement with a new summons to national self-denial. In a separate press release he urged his fellow Americans to give up afternoon teas, theater suppers, and all "fourth meals" until food conditions were "less serious." In the present circumstances, he declared, consumption of sugar, sandwiches, and cakes—"which usually accompany afternoon tea"—was an "unnecessary waste of foodstuffs." If his fellow citizens wanted to hold social gatherings at which refreshments were served, he suggested that the hours of these events should be adjusted so that the food consumed could replace one of the three regular daily meals.[50]

Hoover had no intention of letting the American people lapse back into self-indulgence if he could help it—not while hungry Europe cried out in fear and despair. Nor did he propose to let his wartime agency prematurely fade away. On November 9 he emphatically denied rumors that the Food Administration was about to be transferred to the Department of Agriculture. Not so. The Food Administration would "last by law until legal peace is declared by the President" and would not "relax its efforts in any direction" before then. In fact, Hoover's press release declared, the Food Administration "in its function of feeding people abroad has a larger burden after armistice than before and this burden will continue until next harvest."[51]

Meanwhile Hoover had been consulting with the Secretary of War and the chairman of the War Trade Board about feeding the populations either now or previously "under the domination of the Central Empires."[52] On

November 12 Hoover sent a memorandum of the arrangements agreed upon to the President for his approval. The plan was clear and direct. Hoover would leave for Europe at once to determine American action, decide upon an implementing organization, and initiate temporary relief he deemed necessary. For its part, the War Department, in coordination with the Food Administration, would purchase 120,000 tons of flour and from 30,000,000 to 40,000,000 pounds of pork in the next twenty days and rush it, on diverted army tonnage, to ports in France. All this food, as well as any suitable army surplus stocks already in Europe, was to be "made available for distribution at Mr. Hoover's direction." Still apprehensive of possible Allied machinations, Hoover's memorandum stipulated that all American representatives in Europe were to be notified by cable "at once" that

> the whole of the matter of the American food supplies and the establishment of a more permanent organization are to be settled by Mr. Hoover on his arrival in Europe and that the United States will take no participation in any arrangements made pending that time.[53]

As in 1914 and 1915, when he successfully foiled all challenges to his leadership of the Belgian relief, so it was now: Hoover seemed determined that the continental relief mission arising would be shaped to his specifications—with himself, in all likelihood, at the helm.

Hoover's memorandum did not stay long at the White House. As so often in the President's dealings with his Food Administrator, the chief executive promptly returned the document with a simple, handwritten inscription: "Approved. Woodrow Wilson."[54]

Absorbed in planning his coming crusade, Hoover scarcely had time to celebrate when, on November 11, an armistice with Germany took effect in Europe. Instead, a previously scheduled gathering of his state food administrators in Washington on November 12 and 13 became the occasion for rejoicing and a look ahead. President Wilson himself told the assembled state food administrators that their work might not be over, for "the world has to be revictualed" and the government might need their aid. America, he proclaimed, had come out of the war "the freest nation that has been engaged"—"the freest to help, the freest to advise and back up our advice with assistance." It "fills me with enthusiasm," he continued, "when I think of the result of being a friend to the world. It will result in giving America the greatest influence that any one nation has ever had. . . ." So certain was he of "the ideals and standards of thoughtful men in America"—of men, he might have added, like Herbert Hoover—that Wilson unabashedly believed "that that assistance will be beneficial to the world, and that they will like us better for what they have got from us."[55]

Triumphant idealism seemed indeed to be the theme of the hour. The state food administrators told one another that idealism, in the words of one, had been "the basis of everything" that the Food Administration and the American people had done in the war. Speaking for his colleagues at a loving-cup ceremony for Hoover on November 13, Howard Heinz of Pennsylvania declared that "back of everything we think of Mr. Hoover, and believe that because of his manliness, because of his modesty, because of his humanitarian principles and sympathy and everything that is beautifully human—outside of any ability—he is our ideal American."[56]

Hoover was touched. The loving cup, he responded, was the "most precious" of the "household gods" that he possessed. "This whole association has been the most precious association that I have had," he confessed. The "sincerity and heartfelt friendliness" of the men around him in wartime food work had been their most "outstanding" quality.

Hoover apparently saw no reason for the mood of exultant altruism to dissipate. He told his state food administrators that "the same atmosphere of high idealism" that had brought the American people through the war would lead them to "complete acceptance of the fact that our prime duty now will rest on obtaining justice to a vanquished enemy." The guns had been silent less than seventy-two hours, but Hoover said:

> If that enemy sets up self-government, if he sheds absolutely those qualities that threaten the destruction of the entire world, it cannot be our purpose to vent vengeance upon his women and children.[57]

II

THE Food Administrator had little time, however, for sentiment or self-congratulation. A substantial portion of Europe, he told his state food administrators, was "either in ruins or in social conflagration." The entire population of Europe, in fact, was either on rations or in "varying degrees of privation." Many who had been "under the German heel" were now starving amidst "a total wreckage of social institutions." We must "see what can be done," he declared, "to redeem this mass of humanity back to health and to social order."

Hoover informed his colleagues that the end of the war would actually create an "enormously increased" demand for food before the next harvest, as newly liberated and "starving millions" struggled to return to normal. To meet this intensifying crisis, food-exporting countries—especially the United States—must mobilize their resources. Hoover calculated that North America could furnish more than 60 percent of Europe's import requirements and that the United States and the West Indies could export 20,000,000 tons of foodstuffs of all kinds, more than triple their prewar totals.

In order to reach this objective, continued conservation, "simple living," and coordination of export buying were imperative, along with creation of an organization "to fight against famine." The American people, Hoover insisted, must recognize that "the specter of famine abroad now haunts the abundance of our table at home." Several times he made it plain that the work ahead would be no ordinary humanitarian mission. Hoover's goal was not simply the alleviation of individual suffering but the maintenance of "public order" and "the preservation of civilization itself." "Famine is the mother of anarchy," he asserted.

> From the inability of governments to secure food for their people grows revolution and chaos. From an ability to supply their people grows stability of government and defeat of anarchy.[58]

Even as Hoover exhorted his field officers, the Food Administration and other government agencies were working feverishly to assemble his weapons. On November 14 he notified the President that the War Department had promised him sufficient ships to convey up to 150,000 tons of food immediately to French and Southern European ports for reassignment upon his arrival.[59] By augmenting his supplies in Europe now, he told associates, he could "immediately divert them to points of pressure."[60]

One such flashpoint was Holland and other straitened neutral countries in Northern Europe, where the danger of food-related upheaval was growing. Hoover therefore ordered his Grain Corporation to purchase another 125,000 to 140,000 tons of food and ship it to England for probable distribution in Northern Europe.[61]

Hoover felt confident that if he could have 350,000 to 400,000 tons of food en route to Europe "for these special purposes within the next ten or fifteen days," he could then notify European governments—"especially some of the Northern Neutrals"—that actual shipments for their benefit were on the way. This news, he thought, would permit their tottering governments "to increase rations from their present stocks and probably keep their boats from rocking."[62]

More and more it seemed to Hoover that he was running a desperate race against catastrophe. With every passing hour the magnitude of the problem seemed to swell.[63] Like pent-up volcanoes, nation after nation seemed on the verge of eruption. In the Netherlands fears of a revolution fueled by hunger were rising.[64] From Switzerland and Denmark came reports of attempted general strikes.[65] In the former Austro-Hungarian empire demobilizing armies, ruined transportation networks, and closed boundaries among the nascent successor states were exacerbating economic disorder and shortages of food. Vienna itself—cut off from its traditional food supplies in Hungary and the new nation of Czechoslovakia—was reported to be on the verge of mass starvation. According to one source at the beginning of November, the beleaguered city would run out of food entirely by the middle of the month.[66]

Hoover was not the only American official to see in this deepening turmoil the specter of a bloody revolution. On November 8 Colonel House cabled President Wilson that conditions in Austria and Bohemia made "relief on a large scale imperative if serious disturbances are to be avoided."[67] William C. Bullitt, head of the State Department's Division of Western European Affairs, was more explicit. On November 8 he solemnly informed Secretary of State Lansing that the United States must act immediately "to prevent famine and economic disorganization from driving Austria and Hungary to Bolshevism." Apparently unaware that President Wilson had authorized Hoover two days before to go to Europe, and that Hoover's itinerary included Vienna,[68] Bullitt recommended that Hoover be dispatched at once to Switzerland to initiate "the provisioning of the Tyrol, Vienna and Bohemia." Hoover's name, said Bullitt, "carries such prestige throughout the world that the people of Austria will trust in his ability to perform the impossible, and will be inclined to await his coming before turning in despair to Bolshevism."[69]

But would Hoover get an opportunity to "perform the impossible" in time? Certainly President Wilson was doing *his* best to keep the lid on the Austrian kettle. On November 5 he publicly appealed to the liberated peoples of the late Austro-Hungarian empire to carry out their political transformation in a moderate and orderly way, devoid of "violence and cruelty" and of any act that would "discredit the noble processes of liberty."[70] On the sixth he discussed with Hoover and others ways of providing foodstuffs to Austria, including the use of Austrian ships lying idle in neutral ports.[71] Five days later, in an address to Congress announcing the terms of the armistice, the President admonished the Austrians again. "Excesses accomplish nothing," he contended. "Unhappy Russia has furnished abundant recent proof of that." The present "belongs to the nations and the peoples who preserve their self-control and the orderly processes of their governments," Wilson continued. The peoples of Europe who were just emerging from "the yoke of arbitrary government" would never find "the treasures of liberty" if they sought them "by the light of the torch."[72]

Wilson's words apparently had some effect. A few days later the foreign minister of the new German-Austrian republic acknowledged Wilson's warning to "the liberated peoples of Austria to be firm and cautious." We are doing just that, the official replied; the multiparty government was maintaining both liberty and order. But the foreign minister asserted that these efforts were being "hampered" by a "severe lack of food" throughout the country. The Allied blockade, which under the armistice terms remained in force, was threatening his people. Moreover, the newly independent "Slav National States which grew out of the soil of Austria" were refusing to deliver food to their former German-Austrian overlords. As a result, he concluded, a "hunger catastrophe" hovered over the infant German-Austrian republic. He begged Wilson to send food as quickly as possible.[73]

To the north an even more menacing drama was unfolding. In the early days of November, as German armies in France and Belgium retreated from the American and Allied onslaught, a wave of revolutionary ferment swept across Germany. In Kiel, Hamburg, and other cities, councils of workers and soldiers seized the apparatus of local power. On November 9 Kaiser Wilhelm II abdicated and fled for the Dutch frontier. In Berlin revolutionaries proclaimed a republic, and a new government led by Social Democrats took office.

Was history repeating itself? Was the tragedy of Russia about to be replayed in the very heart of Europe? Would the sudden collapse of the German empire pave the way for a Leninist dictatorship? To Hoover and other American officials, the possibility of such an outcome was exceedingly real.[74] On November 5 President Wilson disclosed to his Cabinet that Bolshevik agitators were about to launch a propaganda campaign for a revolution in Germany, Hungary, and Switzerland, using substantial sums of money at their disposal in Swiss and Swedish banks.[75] Three days later William C. Bullitt warned the Secretary of State that pro-Bolshevik extremists known as the Spartacists were rapidly gaining a following in Germany. In words that Hoover himself might have written, Bullitt asserted that "famine and economic disorganization" were "the parents of Bolshevism," and that "the roots of Bolshevism" could be severed "only by food and restoration of economic life, and not by arms."[76]

As Germany joined Austria in a seeming descent into chaos, the U.S. government again invoked Herbert Hoover as an antidote. On November 8 Secretary of State Lansing notified the American legations in Denmark, Holland, and Switzerland that Hoover would be leaving for Europe in a few days as the "Special Representative" of the President. The Food Administrator would confer about providing relief for liberated peoples and would "take such steps as may be possible" to diminish "famine and want." His itinerary would include "the territories that were formerly Austro-Hungarian." Lansing ordered his diplomatic representatives to use "every possible means" to publicize these facts inside Germany and Austria-Hungary and to stress that "respect for constituted authority and preservation of public order are essential for speedy and effective relief to reach the people."[77] In Lansing's mind, at least, the revictualing of Germany was now a certainty.

Two days later the American press carried the State Department's announcement of Hoover's mission.[78] Although the official press release did not specifically list the Austrians and Germans as intended recipients of Hoover's benevolence, the United States and the Allies (thanks to Colonel House) had already pledged on November 4 to help the Austrian people if asked. The Germans, too, presumably, could hope for similar consideration once they had laid down their arms.[79]

It was not to be as easy as that. In the final hours of the war the question of relief for Germany became entangled in the drafting of the armistice agreement. On November 4 Colonel House and his colleagues on the

Supreme War Council approved the terms of the armistice to be offered the Germans. Four days later, at the village of Rethondes behind French lines, the supreme commander of the American and Allied armies, Marshal Foch of France, presented the document to emissaries of the German government and gave them seventy-two hours to sign. The armistice conditions were draconian, and one in particular stuck in the Germans' craw. It was Article 26, which stipulated that the existing blockade of Germany would continue for the duration of the armistice and that all German merchant ships discovered at sea would be "liable to capture." Among other things, the document also required the Germans to surrender 5,000 railroad locomotives, 150,000 wagons, and thousands of motor lorries, as well as food supplies belonging to their armies in the field.[80]

To the Allies, the blockade was a potent weapon to enforce the armistice terms and to prevent their enemy from resuming the war after a respite. The German government, however, was appalled, and even before signing the armistice agreement it initiated a campaign to soften it.[81] The German negotiators at Rethondes protested that the effect of Article 26 would be "a one-sided continuation of sea warfare by the Allies and the United States" while the armistice was in effect.[82] On November 10 Foreign Minister Wilhelm Solf appealed to Woodrow Wilson to modify the "fearful conditions" of the proposed suspension of hostilities. Solf argued that forced "surrender" by Germany of "the means of transport," along with compulsory "sustenance of the troops of occupation," would render it "impossible to provide Germany with food." Millions of German men, women, and children would starve, he predicted, "all the more as the blockade is to continue."[83]

That same day, in two separate communications through European channels, the new German republic headed by Friedrich Ebert asked President Wilson to cable immediately that he was ready to supply Germany with food as quickly as possible. Chancellor Ebert feared that his infant government would be overthrown and that chaos would result if he did not receive a quick and "reassuring statement" for publication from the American leader.[84]

The Germans, however, were running out of time; Foch's deadline for acceptance of the armistice terms was nearly at hand. On the evening of November 10, the new government in Berlin authorized its plenipotentiaries at Rethondes to sign the agreement—and then to warn that execution of its terms would plunge most of Germany into famine. The emissaries were told to request immediate revision of the armistice in order that Germany might be assured of "proper nourishment."[85]

At 2:15 A.M. on November 11, Marshal Foch, Admiral Sir Rosslyn Wemyss of the Royal Navy, and the emissaries from Germany met at Rethondes for a final session. With the approval of Premier Clemenceau and Colonel House, Foch announced a terse addition to Article 26: "The Allies and United States contemplate the provisioning of Germany during the armistice as shall be found necessary."[86] To this limited extent the mighty blockade would be porous.

For the German delegates, the victors' last-minute concession gave precious little comfort. Nor were they much mollified by Admiral Wemyss's announcement that "[w]e already have a commission preparing the provisioning" of Europe and that "Germany may be included therein."[87] Instead, for more than an hour the Germans and the Allied commanders argued about Article 26. This blockade, "this starvation policy of England," had already gravely injured the German people, the principal German negotiator bitterly charged. "Now the war is to be continued during the very armistice against our women and children." Finally, at just after 5:00 A.M., the German representatives signed the armistice document—and immediately produced a written statement that execution of the agreement's terms could "drive the German people into anarchy and famine."[88]

Some time later, and then for the rest of his life, Herbert Hoover took credit for the last-minute insertion of the clause in Article 26 committing the United States and the Allies to such revictualing of Germany during the armistice "as shall be found necessary." According to Hoover on one occasion, he obtained this crucial alteration "through the President." On another occasion, he stated that he suggested this modification to Secretary of State Lansing, who in turn conveyed it to Colonel House in Paris. No evidence has been found to corroborate Hoover's claim.[89] But if the Food Administrator was probably not responsible for the all-important addition to Article 26, he certainly agreed with it. Nearly a week before, while American troops were still fighting and dying on the battlefield, he had publicly disclosed that he was making plans to feed the Germans when the war stopped.[90] Now he was a giant step closer to his objective.

A few hours later he came closer still, when President Wilson delivered his armistice address to the Congress on the afternoon of November 11. Apparently moved by Foreign Minister Solf's appeal for help, Wilson announced that the Supreme War Council at Versailles had unanimously resolved to do everything possible to provide food to "the peoples of the Central Empires."[91] At the time of his speech, Wilson did not yet know that a food relief clause had just been added to Article 26 of the armistice terms.[92] His reference to the Supreme War Council's resolution (engineered by Colonel House) was not accurate either: the council had only promised to assist Austria, Bulgaria, and Turkey—not Germany. But by referring to the "Central Empires" in the plural, Wilson seemed now to be encompassing Germany within the pledge.

Any doubt on this score disappeared the next day, when the Swiss ambassador to the United States, in behalf of the German government, officially conveyed Chancellor Ebert's message of November 10. Was the U.S. government "ready to send foodstuffs without delay if public order is maintained in Germany and an equitable distribution of food is guaranteed"?[93]

President Wilson immediately replied that he was indeed ready to consider the issue favorably and to discuss it at once with the Allies—with the provisos that the German government had mentioned.[94]

Wilson thereupon made public the German chancellor's plea and his response. It was a sensational story, which made front-page news across the country.[95] Only a day after the guns fell silent, the commander in chief of the United States had committed himself to the succor not just of Allied and liberated Europe but of suffering enemy populations as well.

For the new and vulnerable Socialist government in Berlin, Wilson's electrifying message was a godsend. Threatened daily with insurrection on the far left, and under pressure to accept an offer of aid from Bolshevik Russia, the Ebert government used Wilson's promise (and Article 26 of the armistice terms) to reject the Russian embrace. The German government and its supporters also skillfully used Wilson's insistence on maintenance of "public order" as a weapon against revolutionary extremism, as Wilson (and no doubt Hoover, too) hoped they would.[96] "Ohne Ordnung kein Brot," the government's moderate Socialist backers cried: "Without order, no bread."[97]

The German authorities did not stop, however, with securing a formal commitment from President Wilson. In the days following the armistice, they undiplomatically bombarded Washington with still more appeals, including a highly publicized message from a German women's organization to Wilson's wife. "The German women and children have been starving for years," the message said. "They will die from hunger by the millions if the terms of the armistice are not changed." The German women's group boldly asked Mrs. Wilson "to implore our sisters in the United States of America" to ask the American and Allied governments to modify the armistice terms so that the long ordeal of Germany's women and children "may not end in unspeakable disaster."[98]

For his part, Foreign Minister Solf urgently wired Washington on November 15 that speedy food deliveries from abroad were "most imperative" if Germany was to be saved from "destruction by starvation and anarchy." The plight of his country was becoming "daily more unbearable," Solf exclaimed. He beseeched President Wilson to send to The Hague or elsewhere representatives who could work out a detailed plan of relief with German plenipotentiaries. Perhaps, he ventured to suggest, the project could be placed "in the tried hands of Mr. Hoover who has rendered grand service in Belgium."[99]

While the Germans peppered Washington with appeals for assistance, Hoover was struggling to devise a way to finance his great undertaking. Despite President Wilson's endorsement of Hoover's mission, the chief executive did not immediately respond in writing to Hoover's request on November 9 for a special Congressional appropriation to pay for it. Instead, on the morning of November 14 (and perhaps at the President's suggestion), Hoover discussed the subject with eight U.S. senators on Capitol Hill.[100] In somber tones he told them that the greatest problem America now faced was feeding the world. Bolshevism was spreading dangerously in many countries. Unless it was checked, the outcome could be more catastrophic than the war itself. He also indicated that it might be necessary for the United States to provide food to Germany or to furnish it the credits with which to purchase its food necessities.[101]

If Hoover thought that his earnest arguments would instantly prevail, he soon learned otherwise. To the contrary, his remarks about feeding and loaning money to Germany incensed a number of the senators present, who told him bluntly that it would be "extremely unfortunate" if he raised this issue with Congress now. The armistice with the enemy was barely three days old. Not enough time had elapsed, they said, for the American people to forget their bitter feelings toward the German foe. So vehement were several of the senators at the meeting that Hoover feared they would "raise strong opposition" to any appropriation that they suspected could be used to feed the people of Germany.[102]

Hoover's first reaction to the Congressional roadblock was to try to circumvent it. After the meeting, he informed the President that he believed he could obtain a Congressional appropriation for food relief for neutral and "liberated" peoples, and that it might be wise to confine the legislation to those ends. As for the Germans, Hoover thought that by using the U.S. Army and his Grain Corporation—with assistance, perhaps, from the President's wartime discretionary fund—he could "probably manage to handle the German problem in itself."[103] In other words, he now proposed to feed the people of Germany, with which America was legally still at war, by utilizing existing government agencies and monies already appropriated by Congress.

The President's response to Hoover's audacity is not known. In any event, the Food Administrator now discovered that certain U.S. senators were not the only obstacles in his path. By mid-November it was apparent that the German government, in its rush for "the magnanimous help of America,"[104] had seriously overplayed its hand. More than 100,000 Americans had just died in the war, and many on the home front were not inclined to shower material blessings on those who until a few days ago had been the hated Hun. "Let the Enemy Starve First," thundered an editorial in the *Washington Post*. The United States, it said, would be a "murderer" comparable to the Kaiser himself if it now diverted to Germany any foodstuffs needed to keep the Allies' populations "from starving to death." "The German people's conversion is too sudden and too voluble to be convincing," the *Post* contended.[105] Many Americans undoubtedly agreed.

Others wondered whether the Germans were using "the bogy of Bolshevism" to "frighten" the victors into softening their armistice terms.[106] George Creel, head of the government's Committee on Public Information, accused German propagandists of flooding the country with "damnable cant" and of "holding out their hands dripping with blood and begging for mercy." The German women who now begged Woodrow Wilson's wife to intervene in their behalf had "never grieved for a single moment" when the *Lusitania* was torpedoed, charged Creel. Nor had they protested "when the babies of Belgium were slaughtered at the breasts of their mothers."[107] Some American officials considered the German government's cries for food to be "almost hysterical" and suspected it of trying to whip up sympathy among German-American citizens in order to influence the coming peace settlement.[108]

Even Hoover did not escape the storm. On November 16 an official of the American Defense Society publicly warned him that the American people would abandon their food conservation efforts entirely if food thus accumulated for Belgium and the Allies were "diverted" to the Germans. Germany had *no* food shortages, the official claimed; the Germans had just harvested their crops and would have sufficient food at least until next spring.[109]

Startled by the Congressional and public backlash, Hoover retreated. On November 16 he told the press that there had been "a good deal of unnecessary furore in this country about feeding the Germans" and that he was not asking the American people "to make any sacrifice" to feed Germany. "We are not worrying about the Germans," he now said. "They can take of themselves," provided that the Allied blockade was lifted so that Germany could purchase fish from Norway and Sweden and grain from Argentina. Although Hoover had probably expected to visit Germany on his forthcoming trip to Europe,[110] he now asserted that he did "not expect to meet any German food officials while I am abroad." It was not Germany that was alarming him, he insisted. It was "the whole periphery of nations about Germany which have been demoralized by her."[111]

In a sobering press release that accompanied his denials, Hoover explained what he meant. Of the 420,000,000 people living in Europe, he said, only 40,000,000 had enough food to survive until the next harvest without imports. Of the 380,000,000 remaining, more than 200,000,000 were "now in social disorder."

The Food Administrator divided Europe into several categories of need. The "big Allies"—Great Britain, France, and Italy (125,000,000 people in all)—were safe; arrangements for their provisioning had long been in place. The "little Allies," however—comprising 75,000,000 people in Belgium, Serbia, Romania, Czechoslovakia, Greece, and elsewhere—needed immediate, systematic assistance. Another 40,000,000 people in neutral nations—"all on short rations"—needed relaxation of blockade restraints upon their trade. If this were done, Hoover believed that the neutral governments could "take care of their people and prevent the growth of anarchy." Only one group seemed tragically beyond immediate reach: the 50,000,000 people of northern Russia. While "prepared to make any necessary sacrifice" for them, Hoover conceded that most of them were "inaccessible" because of "the breakdown of transportation" and "sheer anarchy."

Hoover saved his analysis of "enemy people" (90,000,000) for last. Stymied by American opposition to *direct* aid to Germany, he now asserted that the problem was not one of "going to their relief" at all! All that was needed, he claimed, was sufficient relaxation of the "watertight blockade" to permit Germany to obtain "the bare necessities that will give stable government." Carefully avoiding any appeal to anti-Bolshevik or humanitarian sentiment, Hoover introduced a financial argument for letting the Germans obtain food from the outside world: "Unless anarchy can be put down and stability of government can be obtained in these enemy states, there will be nobody to make peace with and nobody to pay the bill to France and Belgium for the fearful destruction that has been done." We cannot obtain justice, Hoover concluded, unless the enemy nations possessed governments "able to make amends for wrongs done." They would not get such governments "through spread of anarchy," the child of famine.[112]

In short: without food, no order.

Once again Hoover was resourceful in argument. If anti-communism and humanitarianism could not sway American public opinion, perhaps more materialistic appeals would. Hoover, in any case, was not one easily to take no for an answer. If one argument did not succeed, he would try another.

Having done his best to fend off domestic criticism of his mission, Hoover was ready to go. On November 16, just five days after the armistice, he and a small group of associates boarded the London-bound steamer *Olympic* in New York City. His wife and sons bade him farewell at the pier.[113] Once again the demands of public service were separating him from his family. He told the press that he hoped to be home by Christmas.[114] He could not foretell that he would be gone for nearly a year.

III

As the *Olympic* sailed past the Statue of Liberty and the harbor lights of his country's greatest port, Hoover might legitimately have paused to reflect. Just a year and a half before, he had entered this harbor a humanitarian hero, anxious to turn his unique experiences in Europe to his nation's wartime advantage. Now he was returning to Europe an acclaimed master of emergencies, who had steered his compatriots past the treacherous shoals of food shortages and runaway inflation.

Hoover was proud of his contribution to the war effort. A few weeks before the conflict ended, he sent the President a set of price indices showing that since the Food Administration had been created the price of food had stabilized, farmers' prices had increased, and the profits of middlemen had declined. Even as inflation had come under control, said Hoover, food consumption had declined by 7 percent, while food production was now showing a "nutritional increase." All this, he suggested triumphantly, refuted the "theoretical economists," who had been "loud in the old outcry that our interference with the sacred law of supply and demand endangers our production and that reduction of consumption can only be obtained by higher prices."[115]

It was not the coercive and interventionist aspects of his policy, however, that Hoover usually emphasized when explaining his success. The day after the armistice he declared that the American people's notable contribution to the Great War lay not only in providing food for the army and the Allies but in demonstrating that "there was no power in autocracy equal to the voluntary effort of free people." The "essential feature" of the Food Administration's plan, he asserted, "was that individual conscience should rule under guidance of local leadership."[116] It is hard to know how unreservedly Hoover believed this; after the war he told a committee of Congress that the key to democracy's victory in the war had been "its willingness to yield to dictatorship."[117] But for the moment, at least—and certainly in public—he preferred to ascribe America's comparative price stability and enormous food surpluses not to domestic price controls and selective price incentives but to a pervasive spirit of voluntarism in twenty million American households.

Hoover was not a man to dwell on past successes. As his ship churned its way across the Atlantic, his thoughts turned to the struggles to come. The victorious outcome of the war had done nothing to dispel his distrust of the British. Back on October 21, his British counterpart, J. R. Clynes, had informed him that food prices in Great Britain were rising dangerously, in substantial part (he said) because of the increasing cost of food imports from the United States. Clynes had pointed out that cheaper food sources in the world were unavailable to Britain because so many of its ships had been assigned to transport American troops to France. Clynes had pleaded with Hoover to do something. Might not American food suppliers be asked to reduce their percentage of profit so that the poor of England could receive rations without having to ask the British government for a subsidy?[118]

Hoover did not reply to Clynes until November 15, and when he did, he was not at all sympathetic. The American Food Administrator acknowledged that "present price levels" for foodstuffs were particularly onerous for Europe, "whose economic price and wage plane is so much below ours." On the other hand, he retorted acidly, America's "economic plane" had been "established by riotous buying in our markets by the Allies before we came into the war."

Hoover refused to accept any responsibility for the British predicament. He observed that the price of American wheat was being maintained "at a level 30% below that [to] which it had been forced by Allied bidding when we entered the war." Moreover, he was sustaining this fixed price in the face of Congressional opposition and enormous discontent among American farmers. As for American pork products (a major item in the British import program), he all but accused the British of creating their own troubles by insisting on buying higher-priced, finer cuts of pork. Even if the United States substantially lowered the price of live hogs (a move that would cause "absolute chaos in our agricultural communities"), and even if it took away "the entire profits" of the meat packers, the result (Hoover claimed) would be less than a 6 percent reduction in the wholesale price of bacon in England. The real difficulty, Hoover argued, lay not with American food prices (which could not be meaningfully reduced) but with the high cost of labor and shipping, both of which should now decline with the end of the war. With "free shipping," he concluded, "the Allies can go to cheaper markets for food than the United States."[119]

To Hoover's consternation, before long the British would attempt to do just that.

The Food Administrator's aggressive rebuff to Clynes was no aberration. It betokened, in fact, a broader attitude of suspicion, to the mounting concern of the American State Department. Shortly before departing for Europe, Hoover conferred with Frank Polk, the State Department's counselor. Polk was greatly disturbed by Hoover's unwillingness to use existing inter-Allied machinery for his coming relief work. For some reason, Hoover seemed to Polk to be afraid of the Allied Maritime Transport Council and the Allied food-purchasing apparatus. The State Department official urged Hoover "not to start a fight with the British, by attempting to take the lead and ignore existing organizations."[120] But Polk was taking no chances. Before his meeting with the Food Administrator, he cabled Colonel House's secretary in Paris: "Confidentially think you will have to calm Hoover down a little as his plans may be resented by the Allies."[121]

Polk's apprehensions of trouble were well founded. Despite Hoover's unequivocal message to Joseph Cotton on November 8, the British government had not abandoned its desire to funnel postwar American aid to Europe through an Allied-dominated administrative framework. On November 13 the British War Cabinet endorsed a proposal to convert the Allied Maritime Transport Council into a "General Economic Council," which would "co-ordinate the work" of the Inter-Allied Food Council and other bodies.[122] The British immediately forwarded their suggestion to Washington. Hoover, about to leave for Europe, was unimpressed. Once more it seemed to him that John Bull was trying to ensnare Uncle Sam in a gigantic "pool" in which the United States, despite its "preponderance of supplies," would have "a minority voice."[123]

A few days later, while Hoover was on the high seas, the persistent British government struck again. At a meeting of the Inter-Allied Food Council's Committee of Representatives on November 21, Sir John Beale of the British delegation proposed creation of a "common international co-operative authority" to administer the relief of Europe. The "authority" would control all resources raised for this purpose by the "Associated Nations." Among other things, this powerful entity would become "the purchasing and transporting agent for all supplies to Central Europe." Beale suggested that the Allied Maritime Transport Council and its "dependent organisms" already provided "the framework for such an authority."[124] To Hoover, of course, this was precisely the antithesis of his plans.

As Hoover's ship neared its destination, there were signs that his arrival would not be met with universal adulation. The French government was apparently indignant at his announcement on November 9 that he was coming over to "perfect and enlarge" food distribution to the people of northern France, who were now being freed from German control.[125] Evidently Hoover had failed to consult the French government, which had its own plans for its newly liberated territory. Across the English Channel, Major Waldorf Astor, parliamentary secretary to the Ministry of Food, warned Lloyd George that Hoover's aid mission could jeopardize Great Britain's leadership in European reconstruction.[126] Fearful of "friction" with Hoover and "the great Professor" (Woodrow Wilson), Astor asked his government to appoint some eminent person "to collar the existing Allied machinery before it breaks, so that when Hoover and Woodrow arrive they can each of them be more or less quietly placed into the niches which ought to be ready for them."[127]

Astor's anticipation of "friction," like Frank Polk's, was percipient; Hoover was in no mood for compromise. In an interoffice memorandum for American officials the day before he sailed, the Food Administrator bluntly summarized his policy position. The United States was "the reservoir of 60% of the world's export food," he declared. Moreover, the United States was "the only disinterested party in this distribution,—for the most necessitous and the most deserving." The revictualing of the continent involved many issues where "strategy of the widest order is required." Bolshevism, for instance, was spreading "through fear of famine as well as actual famine. For fear of short supplies commodities are being held from distribution."

How, then, should the great relief crusade be organized? In the final five points of his memorandum, Hoover gave his answer:

> 8. Attempts to deal with the problem through the second class minds and jealousies of the present inter-Allied bodies is hopeless.
>
> 9. The food world today requires a Commander in Chief just as critically as it required Foch.
>
> 10. He should be limited only by legislation from the Versailles conference, not from pinheads of bureaucratic Europe.
>
> 11. This man should be an American—the disinterested nation; the nation having to furnish the bulk of the supplies; the nation that could increase its supplies by call from its own citizen as commander.
>
> 12. An American established in this position would at once quell the fears of the countries in disorder by the confidence of action.[128]

It did not take a genius to identify the American whom Hoover had in mind.

And now, as the stately *Olympic* neared Europe, for Hoover a dream was coming true. A veritable armada of food was on its way to Old World ports,[129] with himself as its helmsman and dispenser. In early 1917, before the United States entered the war, Hoover had adroitly volunteered to be the supreme coordinator of the American war effort in Europe if the United States became a belligerent.[130] More recently he had urged the President to appoint a single individual to administer the civilian side of America's war activities in France.[131] On both occasions, Woodrow Wilson had failed to respond as desired. But this time was different. Hoover was returning to Europe with a presidential blessing, to become—he hoped—the Marshal Foch of the world's food supply.

Only the Allied governments stood in his way.

As it happened, one of Hoover's fellow passengers on the *Olympic* was the chairman of the U.S. Shipping Board, Edward Hurley, whose agency's cooperation would be needed in the task ahead. Several times during the voyage Hoover probed Hurley's attitude toward the British. Hoover noted disapprovingly that many American officials who went to London "fell into the British atmosphere and consequently argued the British point of view."[132] Speaking for himself, Hoover announced emphatically that he intended stoutly to resist any British effort to gain control of food distribution or shipping. He asked Hurley to join him and to prevent the British from "putting anything over."[133]

Yet if Hoover exuded mistrust of Allied officialdom, he could take comfort from the knowledge that for millions of people at home and abroad he was a hero. Back in Minnesota, the journalist William C. Edgar—who had worked with Hoover in CRB and Food Administration projects—expressed the sentiments of the Chief's entourage and many more. "Herbert Hoover again responds to an emergency," Edgar editorialized in *The Bellman* on November 23. Hoover was now "virtually the Food Administrator of the World, occupying a position unique in history."

"Five years ago," Edgar continued, except among mining engineers Hoover was "comparatively unknown. Today kings and rulers delight to honour him, and nations justly acclaim him as their preserver from hunger. . . ."

> He is the embodiment of the efficient American in his achievements, but it is not only through his genius for organization, his inexhaustible capacity for work, his extraordinary grasp of perplexing and intricate problems and his magnetic leadership of men that he accomplishes wonders. Behind all these rare qualities, and beneath a taciturn and reserved attitude, there is a generous soul and a kindly heart from which springs the desire to expend all he has of energy, strength, endowments and talents in the service of his fellows. This is the exceptional combination of attributes

> which make him one of the greatest men of his age, whose name, when the history of this period is written, will stand out among the world's elect.[134]

Years later, in one of his accounts of his relief work, Hoover recalled the conversations that he had with his traveling party as the *Olympic* steamed through the dark waters where, until recently, German submarines had prowled. They analyzed the Allied schemes for a resource pool in which the United States could be outvoted. They discussed "economic and social reforms that would come from the fires of idealism kindled by the sufferings of war." They talked at length about "the reconstruction measures that would have to be taken to get the world back to work." Hope enveloped their conversation, Hoover remembered. It seemed that a "rebirth of mankind," "a new Golden Age," was at hand.[135]

Much of the time, though, Hoover played bridge for small stakes with a few friends, including his young Food Administration associate, Robert Taft.[136] It was just as well; there would be little time for leisure once he landed. The "greatest famine of all time" (as he later called it)[137] awaited him.

Truly the trials ahead would be awesome. Hoover must find, pay for, and deploy the foodstuffs without which tens of millions of anguished people would die. He must do his best to keep Central and even Western Europe from drowning in a bloody tide of Bolshevism. He must keep America's wartime allies from manipulating Uncle Sam's surpluses and depriving America of the influence that came from being, in Wilson's words, "a friend to the world." At home, he must secure the support of a skeptical Congress and of a nation not yet convinced of the wisdom of feeding its enemies. Beyond all this was a wider task, one that he summed up succinctly in his letter of November 2 in support of the election of a Democratic Congress. "We must," he said, "nurse Europe back to industry and self-support and we must ourselves avoid entanglement in the process."[138]

Such an abundance of responsibilities was enough to daunt almost any man. But Hoover betrayed no sign of self-doubt or mental fatigue. He wanted this job and was in the prime of his life. He was just forty-four years old.

Bibliographical Note

In the period examined in this volume, Herbert Hoover entered government service for the first time. It was an extraordinary initiation. War, revolutions, controversies, and emergencies became at once the warp and woof of his daily life. Not surprisingly, the documentary record of his wartime activity is prodigious. For this comparatively brief phase in his career, more than one hundred manuscript collections and archival groups in the United States and abroad turned out to have information of value.

Four superb repositories contain the bulk of the resources used in this study. The first is the Hoover Institution on War, Revolution and Peace, at Stanford University. The Hoover Institution Archives hold more than three hundred boxes of the papers of the United States Food Administration, which Hoover headed between 1917 and 1919. This collection embraces most of Hoover's official correspondence, as well as files of a number of his principal associates, including Julius H. Barnes. Also noteworthy are eleven boxes of dossiers of correspondence between Food Administration personnel and important outside entities (such as other federal agencies). A rich and substantial collection, the U.S. Food Administration Papers were the single most important cache of documentation for the present volume.

Also of benefit at the Hoover Institution are the Herbert Hoover Collection and the papers of several individuals associated with him in 1917–18, including James F. Bell, Hugh Gibson, Mark Requa, and Frank Surface.

Not to be overlooked are the Inter-Allied Food Council Papers and a splendid collection of posters used by the Food Administration to propagandize food conservation during World War I.

The Herbert Hoover Presidential Library in West Branch, Iowa, is a second indispensable fount of knowledge concerning Hoover's Food Administration years. There the crucial collection is the Herbert Hoover Papers, divided into several series, of which the Pre-Commerce (that is pre-1921) portion is the most relevant for this volume. Among other material, the Pre-Commerce Papers contain several boxes of food-related correspondence and memoranda, and a valuable assortment of contemporary newspaper clippings. A fourteen-box aggregation, labeled "U.S. Food Administration Documents," at the presidential library includes a nearly complete set of the 1,400 press releases issued by the agency in 1917–18. This proved to be an exceptionally useful source.

Also of note in West Branch are a compilation of Hoover's public statements, a massive Reprint File, and the excellent papers of Lewis L. Strauss (Hoover's confidential secretary between 1917 and 1919). For Hoover's family life during this period, the papers of his wife Lou Henry Hoover and their son Allan Hoover provide interesting glimpses.

The third outstanding repository for this book is the National Archives and Records Administration (NARA) in Washington, D.C. Of prime importance among its holdings is Record Group 4: Records of the United States Food Administration, a gigantic trove totaling nearly 3,000 cubic feet. Fortunately, most of it proved to be distant from my focus. Fortunately, too, in 1943 the National Archives prepared a meticulous, book-length "Preliminary Inventory of the Records of the United States Food Administration, 1917–1920, Part I: The Headquarters Organization," which enabled me quickly to identify the most pertinent files. Although the contents of Record Group 4 are superabundant, they do not include, and do not supplant, most of Hoover's own Food Administration files, which are in the Food Administration Papers (described above) at the Hoover Institution.

Not all of Record Group 4 is in Washington, D.C. The National Archives' field branches now possess the files of most of Hoover's federal (that is, state) food administrators and their respective state food administrations. The National Archives' San Francisco branch, for instance, has about 72 cubic feet of correspondence, memoranda, etc., amassed by the state food administrator of California and his apparatus as they implemented Hoover's policies at the grass roots. For a brief description of this category of source material, see Loretto Dennis Szucs and Sandra Hargreaves Luebking, *The Archives: A Guide to the National Archives Field Branches* (Salt Lake City, 1988), p. 159. In my own research, state-level minutiae were of only limited value, given my biographical focus and the plethora of Hoover-related records elsewhere.

My forays into Record Group 4 underscore a point that should, perhaps, be made explicit: the book before you is not a history of the U.S. Food

Administration. Of course, Hoover being the kind of executive he was, it was not always easy to distinguish between the Food Administration and its indefatigable chief. Still, my subject has been one man and the salient challenges he faced, not every regulatory issue or administrative snarl that his agency was obliged to confront.

Several other record groups at the National Archives also contain material that I found it advantageous to explore. These include the records of the U.S. Grain Corporation (RG 5), the U.S. Sugar Equalization Board, Inc. (RG 6), the Office of the Secretary of Agriculture (RG 16), the Office of the Secretary of the Interior (RG 48), the Department of State (RG 59), the Council of National Defense (RG 62), the Federal Trade Commission (RG 122), and the War Trade Board (RG 182). Most of these archival units have "preliminary inventories" or other finding aids available at NARA.

The fourth essential wellspring for this volume is the Library of Congress, particularly its Manuscript Division. Among its multitudinous treasures, the most indispensable for me were the Woodrow Wilson Papers (available on microfilm). Other collections which rewarded scrutiny included the papers of Chandler Anderson, Newton D. Baker, Ray Stannard Baker, William Borah, Josephus Daniels, Harry A. Garfield, James R. Garfield, Robert Lansing, Breckinridge Long, William G. McAdoo, Victor Murdock, John J. Pershing, Gifford Pinchot, William Allen White, and Brand Whitlock.

Although the Hoover Institution, Herbert Hoover Presidential Library, National Archives, and Library of Congress were the four main pillars of my research for *Master of Emergencies*, others contributed significantly to my quest. At the Yale University Library, the papers of Gordon Auchincloss, Edward M. House, and Frank Polk yielded much information, as did several other collections to a lesser degree. The Asbury F. Lever Papers in the Clemson University Libraries have a few Hoover-related items of exceptional interest. In the Seeley G. Mudd Manuscript Library at Princeton University, the diaries of H. Alexander Smith contain a number of interesting entries, as do the diaries of Edward N. Hurley in his papers at the University of Notre Dame. At the State Historical Society of Wisconsin, the Charles McCarthy Papers provide provocative insights into Hoover's character and personality from a man who observed him at close range in 1917 and 1918. Also noteworthy, at the same location, are the papers of Magnus Swenson, who was Hoover's state food administrator for Wisconsin. At the University of Iowa Libraries, the Henry C. Wallace Papers reflect the wartime thinking and activism of one of Hoover's sharpest critics.

Outside the United States, several sources useful to this study were located. In Great Britain, the Public Record Office at Kew possesses the minutes of the British War Cabinet in 1917–18 (Cab. 23), War Cabinet memoranda (Cab. 24), records of the wartime Ministry of Food (MAF 60), the papers of Sir Alan G. Anderson (vice chairman of the Royal Commission on Wheat Supplies) (PRO 30/68), and the papers of Sir Cecil Spring Rice. The

Board of Trade records at the PRO contain a few documents relevant to Hoover's mining career (in series BT 31, BT 58, and BT 198); specific items are cited in chapter 16. At the House of Lords Record Office, the papers of Prime Minister David Lloyd George once again proved helpful. At the British Library of Political and Economic Science, the papers of William H. Beveridge furnished enlightening evidence of the often stressful relationship between Hoover and the British government. In Ottawa, at the National Archives of Canada, Record Group 20 (Department of Trade and Commerce) holds a number of documents that illumine Canadian wheat policy in 1917–18 and Hoover's relationship with his fellow food regulators north of the border.

During the period of time covered by this volume, Hoover remained chairman of the Commission for Relief in Belgium—a subject considered in detail in chapter 17. The sources cited there are self-explanatory, but for additional background the reader may wish to consult the Bibliographic Note in my earlier book, *The Life of Herbert Hoover: The Humanitarian, 1914–1917* (New York, 1988).

I shall not list here every remaining manuscript collection, at home or abroad, from which I have extracted something pertinent. The interested reader will find them duly cited in the Notes. Suffice it to say that in studying a historical figure as energetic and accomplished as Herbert Hoover, I have found it worthwhile—indeed, obligatory—to cast my research net widely.

And not solely among unpublished manuscripts and the bulky records of governmental agencies. With this volume of my biography, we enter a period for which the relevant *published* documentation relating to Hoover becomes both voluminous and vital. The *Congressional Record*, for instance: in 1917 and 1918 its pages were replete with references to the U.S. Food Administration and its controversial administrator. Other essential official publications of the time include various hearings of the House and Senate agriculture committees, the daily *Official Bulletin* of the Committee on Public Information, and the annual reports of the Food Administration for 1917 and 1918: a mountain of fine print but a mountain full of ore. The Food Administration's own publications were bountiful; for an extensive bibliography of them, see NARA's "Preliminary Inventory" for its Food Administration records mentioned above. Still useful are the World War I volumes of the State Department's *Papers Relating to the Foreign Relations of the United States*. Even more useful are the now complete *Papers of Woodrow Wilson*, edited by Arthur S. Link and his associates: a monumental enterprise to which scholars will long turn. For agricultural publications generally, the National Agricultural Library in Beltsville, Maryland, is an outstanding repository.

Among contemporary newspapers, the *New York Times* was, of course, essential. The Baltimore *Sun*, *Chicago Tribune*, *New York Herald*, *New York Tribune*, New York *World*, and *Washington Post* (among others) were profitably searched for specific stories. The weekly *Commercial and Financial Chronicle* was another excellent source. Hoover and his agency also received copious coverage in wartime periodicals. Among these the *Literary Digest*, *New Republic*, *Wallaces' Farmer*, and *Prairie Farmer* particularly repaid systematic study.

For Hoover and his associates, the experience of war mobilization during 1917–18 branded their consciousness for a lifetime. It is no surprise that many of them wrote memoirs and histories about it. Among the most important are: Herbert Hoover, *The Memoirs of Herbert Hoover*, vol. I: *Years of Adventure* (New York, 1951); Hoover, *The Ordeal of Woodrow Wilson* (New York, 1958); Hoover, *An American Epic*, vol. II (Chicago, 1960); Joshua Bernhardt, *Government Control of the Sugar Industry in the United States* (New York, 1920); Albert N. Merritt, *War Time Control of Distribution of Foods* (New York, 1920); Frank M. Surface, *American Pork Production in the World War* (Chicago, 1926); Surface, *The Grain Trade During the World War* (New York, 1928); and William C. Mullendore, *History of the United States Food Administration, 1917–1919* (Stanford, Calif., 1941). All these men served in the U.S. Food Administration. Surface's two books, incidentally, were elaborate defenses of Hoover's policies against his critics. Mullendore's book was written just after World War I and was supposed to be the final, official report of the U.S. Food Administration. When published more than twenty years later, it included a lengthy preface written by Hoover in 1920.

A perceptive early history of the Food Administration not written by a participant is Maxcy Robson Dickson, *The Food Front in World War I* (Washington, D.C., 1944). During World War II the U.S. Department of Labor, Bureau of Labor Statistics, Division of Historical Studies of Wartime Problems, prepared a series of sixty-one mimeographed historical studies of war mobilization during World War I. Eighteen pertained to the work of the Food Administration. Although comparatively brief and of varying quality, these surveys did in some cases help to clarify federal food policy under Hoover.

It would be supererogatory to catalogue here the numerous other scholarly articles and monographs published soon after World War I that in some way examined the food control activities of Hoover and his agency. Many of these are recorded in the Notes. For a convenient list, I again refer the reader to the National Archives' "Preliminary Inventory" for its U.S. Food Administration records. Nor will I attempt to comment on each of the more modern secondary sources that in some fashion proved helpful along the way. These, too, are cited, where appropriate, in the Notes. A few recent books, however, should be noted for the stimulating analyses and breadth of context that they supply: L. Margaret Barnett, *British Food Policy During the First World War* (Boston, 1985); Kathleen Burk, *Britain, America and the Sinews of War, 1914–1918* (Boston, 1985); Robert Higgs, *Crisis and Leviathan: Critical Episodes in the Growth of American Government* (New York, 1987); Christopher

C. Gibbs, *The Great Silent Majority: Missouri's Resistance to World War I* (Columbia, Mo., 1988); Harvey A. Levenstein, *Revolution at the Table: The Transformation of the American Diet* (New York, 1988); and Avner Offer, *The First World War: An Agrarian Interpretation* (New York, 1989).

Finally, three unpublished doctoral dissertations that provide a valuable entrée into their respective subjects are: Marion Therese Casey, "Charles McCarthy: Policy Maker for an Era" (University of Wisconsin, 1971); Tom G. Hall, "Cheap Bread from Dear Wheat: Herbert Hoover, The Wilson Administration, and the Management of Wheat Prices, 1916–1920" (University of California, 1970); and Thomas Lane Moore III, "The Establishment of a 'New Freedom' Policy: The Federal Trade Commission, 1912–1918" (University of Alabama, 1980).

ABBREVIATIONS

CRB	Commission for Relief in Belgium
HHPL	Herbert Hoover Presidential Library, West Branch, Iowa
HI	Hoover Institution on War, Revolution and Peace, Stanford University
LC	Library of Congress, Washington, D.C.
NARA	National Archives and Records Administration, Washington, D.C.
PRO	Public Record Office, Kew, Surrey, United Kingdom
RG 4	Record Group 4: Records of the United States Food Administration
RG 5	Record Group 5: Records of the United States Grain Corporation
RG 16	Record Group 16: Records of the Office of the Secretary of Agriculture
RG 48	Record Group 48: Records of the Office of the Secretary of the Interior
RG 59	Record Group 59: General Records of the Department of State
RG 62	Record Group 62: Records of the Council of National Defense
RG 122	Record Group 122: Records of the Federal Trade Commission
RG 182	Record Group 182: Records of the War Trade Board
USFA	United States Food Administration

In order to avoid confusion, I have adhered to the following distinction in the footnotes. The USFA Papers are at the Hoover Institution on War, Revolution and Peace. The USFA Records (RG 4) are at the National Archives and Records Administration. The USFA Documents are at the Herbert Hoover Presidential Library.

Notes

CHAPTER 1

1. Herbert Hoover to Walter Hines Page, April 22, 1917 (bMS Am 1090.1(655)), Walter Hines Page Papers, Houghton Library, Harvard University; David Lawrence, "Hoover Comes to Town," New York *Evening Post Magazine*, July 21, 1917, reprinted in part in *Engineering and Mining Journal* 104 (August 11, 1917): 274–75; Victoria French Allen, "A Member of the Fourth Estate" (typescript, n.d.), pp. 137–39, in a miscellaneous assortment of Ben S. Allen papers in the possession of William H. Allen of Arlington, Virginia (hereinafter cited as the Ben S. Allen Collection); Edgar Eugene Robinson and Paul Carroll Edwards, eds., *The Memoirs of Ray Lyman Wilbur* (Stanford, Calif., 1960), pp. 241, 243n, 254 (hereinafter cited as Wilbur, *Memoirs*).
2. Hoover's youth and pre-1914 career are examined in George H. Nash, *The Life of Herbert Hoover: The Engineer, 1874–1914* (New York, 1983). The most recent account of Hoover's "Belgian relief" years is George H. Nash, *The Life of Herbert Hoover: The Humanitarian, 1914–1917* (New York, 1988).
3. *New York Tribune*, May 4, 1917, p. 2; Allen, "A Member of the Fourth Estate," p. 139.
4. Nash, *Life of Herbert Hoover: The Humanitarian*, pp. 256, 335; Lou Henry Hoover telegrams to Herbert Hoover, April 28 and May 14, 1917, "Hoover, Lou Henry," Pre-Commerce Papers, Herbert Hoover Papers, HHPL. At this point (the spring of 1917) Mrs. Hoover was leasing the home of a Stanford University professor, Henry David Gray. See Lou Henry Hoover telegram to Herbert Hoover, May 11, 1920, Herbert Hoover Collection, Box 3, HI.
5. *New York Times*, April 12, 1917, pp. 1, 2; *Commercial and Financial Chronicle* 104 (April 21, 1917): 1555–56; *New York Tribune*, April 22, 1917, p. 10; Nash, *Life of Herbert Hoover: The Humanitarian*, pp. 282, 350–51, 359.

6. Nash, *Life of Herbert Hoover: The Humanitarian*, pp. 341–48.
7. David Kennedy, *Over Here: The First World War and American Society* (New York, 1980), p. 3.
8. Paul Fussell, *The Great War and Modern Memory* (New York and London, 1975), pp. 36–37; Bernadotte E. Schmitt and Harold C. Vedeler, *The World in the Crucible* (New York, 1984), p. 55.
9. Herbert Hoover testimony, March 13, 1920, printed in U.S. Congress, Senate, Subcommittee of the Committee on Naval Affairs, 66th Congress, 2d Session, *Naval Investigation* (Washington, D.C., 1920), pp. 117–20; S. L. A. Marshall, *World War I* (Boston, 1987), p. 282; Gerd Hardach, *The First World War, 1914–1918* (Berkeley and Los Angeles, 1977), pp. 42–43; L. Margaret Barnett, *British Food Policy During the First World War* (Boston, 1985), p. 103. In his 1920 testimony, Hoover said of the spring and summer of 1917 (prior to the new harvest): "The situation was dangerous almost beyond description, and the anxiety of the whole of that period was terrific. I cannot overemphasize the critical character of that position and the dangers in which the whole allied cause rested."
10. Walter Hines Page cable 6035 to Secretary of State Robert Lansing, April 19, 1917, printed in Arthur S. Link et al., eds., *The Papers of Woodrow Wilson*, vol. 42 (Princeton, N.J., 1983), p. 109. Page's cable contained a message from Hoover.
11. Hoover repeated this to Secretary of the Interior Franklin K. Lane on May 4. See Lane to Frank I. Cobb, May 5, 1917, in Anne Wintermute Lane and Louise Herrick Wall, eds., *The Letters of Franklin K. Lane* (Boston and New York, 1922), p. 253.
12. Page cable 6035 to Lansing, April 19, 1917.
13. N. B. Dearle, *An Economic Chronicle of the Great War for Great Britain & Ireland, 1914–1919* (London, 1929), p. 136.
14. Ibid., p. 137.
15. *New York Times*, April 22, 1917, section I, p. 17.
16. Page cable 6035 to Lansing, April 19, 1917.
17. *New York Tribune*, May 4, 1917, p. 2.
18. Ibid.; *New York Times*, May 4, 1917, p. 6.
19. Edward M. House diary, May 3, 1917, Edward M. House Papers, Manuscripts and Archives, Yale University Library. As early as April 11, Hoover was advocating creation of a U.S. government agency that would control both food and shipping. See "Note of Interview with Mr. Hoover" (April 11, 1917), in Alan G. Anderson Papers, PRO 30/168/5, PRO.
20. Hoover memorandum, April 14, 1917, in Appendix I of minutes of [British] War Cabinet meeting 122, April 18, 1917, Cab. 23/2, PRO; Hoover cable to Secretary of War Newton D. Baker, April 15, 1917, file 1-53, RG 48, NARA; Hoover cable 337 to CRB—New York office, April 17, 1917, CRB Correspondence, Box 8, HI (copy in House Papers, Box 61); Page cable 6037 to Lansing, April 19, 1917, file 811.50/5, RG 59, NARA.
21. Minutes of War Cabinet meeting 122, April 18, 1917.
22. *New York Times*, April 22, 1917, section I, p. 17.
23. Page cable 6037 to Lansing, April 19, 1917.
24. Page cable 6057 to Lansing, April 21, 1917, file 811.50/9, RG 59, NARA.
25. Hoover to Page, April 22, 1917.
26. Minutes of War Cabinet meeting 122, April 18, 1917.
27. Hoover to David R. Francis, April 19, 1917, David R. Francis Papers, Missouri Historical Society.
28. Franklin H. Martin, *Digest of the Proceedings of the Council of National Defense During the World War*, 73rd Congress, 2d Session, Senate Document No. 193 (Washington, D.C., 1934), pp. 130–31.
29. Nash, *Life of Herbert Hoover: The Humanitarian*, p. 350, and p. 477, note 39. Contrary to some of Hoover's later reminiscences, I have found no evidence that President Wilson promised him a food-related post in the Wilson administration prior to Hoover's return to the

United States in early May 1917. As will be seen in this chapter, Hoover's status was uncertain for a time.

30. *New York Times*, April 13, 1917, p. 12; *New York Tribune*, April 20, 1917, p. 1; *The Times* [London], April 21, 1917, p. 5.
31. Nash, *Life of Herbert Hoover: The Humanitarian*, pp. 359–60.
32. Martin, *Digest*, pp. 130–31, 159–60.
33. Ibid., pp. 159–60; *New York Tribune*, April 24, 1917, p. 1.
34. House diary, May 3, 1917.
35. Nash, *Life of Herbert Hoover: The Humanitarian*, pp. 288–89, 341–42, 344–45, 350.
36. House to Hoover, April 7, 1917, House Papers, Box 61.
37. House to Woodrow Wilson, May 4, 1917, printed in Link et al., eds., *Papers of Woodrow Wilson*, vol. 42, p. 220.
38. *New York Times*, May 4, 1917, p. 6; *New York Herald*, May 4, 1917, p. 10; Allen, "A Member of the Fourth Estate," pp. 139–40.
39. Marshall, *World War I*, pp. 280, 281.
40. This is an estimate. By the end of the war Germany, Russia, France, and Great Britain alone had put nearly 40,000,000 men under arms. Schmitt and Vedeler, *World in the Crucible*, p. 296. When one adds the forces of smaller countries and the components of the British empire, the total figure ultimately exceeded 60,000,000, including 4,500,000 mobilized by the United States. Keith Robbins, *The First World War* (Oxford, 1984), p. 83.
41. Wilbur, *Memoirs*, p. 243n. On an earlier visit to Washington, in March 1917, Hoover had been very unimpressed with the American government leaders he had met. They seemed to him amateurish, with no appreciation of the magnitude of the task of fighting in the Great War. Walter Hines Page diary, April 2, 1917, Page Papers.
42. Frederic L. Paxson, *American Democracy and the World War*, vol. II: *America at War, 1917–1918* (Boston, 1939), pp. 4–9; Seward W. Livermore, *Politics Is Adjourned: Woodrow Wilson and the War Congress* (Middletown, Conn., 1966), pp. 15–37.
43. Paul Willard Garrett, *Government Control Over Prices* (Washington, D.C., 1920), pp. 30–31; Simon Litman, *Prices and Price Control in Great Britain and the United States During the World War* (New York, 1920), p. 219; Charles O. Hardy, *Wartime Control of Prices* (Washington, D.C., 1940), p. 148; Murray R. Benedict, *Farm Policies of the United States, 1790–1950* (New York, 1953), p. 159; Tom G. Hall, "Wilson and the Food Crisis: Agricultural Price Control During World War I," *Agricultural History* 47 (January 1973): 25–26.
44. Garrett, *Government Control Over Prices*, p. 27. According to Garrett's table (compiled by the Price Section of the War Industries Board), the index number for the food group of commodities (based on average prices July 1913 to June 1914 = 100) went from 111 in July 1916 to 157 in April 1917. This represented an increase of more than 41 percent.
45. Litman, *Prices and Price Control*, p. 229.
46. Ibid.
47. Ibid., p. 181.
48. Hall, "Wilson and the Food Crisis," pp. 26–39. Hall's article draws upon his unpublished dissertation, "Cheap Bread from Dear Wheat: Herbert Hoover, The Wilson Administration, and the Management of Wheat Prices, 1916–1920" (University of California at Davis, 1970), chapters 1 and 2.
49. Hall, "Cheap Bread from Dear Wheat," pp. 1–3; Hall, "Wilson and the Food Crisis," pp. 38–39; William Frieburger, "War Prosperity and Hunger: The New York Food Riots of 1917," *Labor History* 25 (Spring 1984): 217–39.
50. *New York Tribune*, April 20, 1917, p. 1, and April 21, 1917, p. 1; *Commercial and Financial Chronicle* 104 (April 21, 1917): 1556; *Annual Reports of the Department of Agriculture for the Year Ended June 30, 1917* (Washington, D.C., 1918), pp. 5–6.
51. Hoover to Page, April 22, 1917. This is the document cited in note 1. Quoted by permission of the Houghton Library, Harvard University.

52. Will Irwin, "First Aid to America," *Saturday Evening Post* 189 (March 24, 1917): 6–7, 109–10, 113–14. This article consists of an interview of an anonymous American whom Irwin called "Jones." Irwin later disclosed that "Jones" was actually Hoover. For further details on Hoover's views about war mobilization at this point, see Nash, *Life of Herbert Hoover: The Humanitarian*, pp. 348–50.
53. *New York Tribune*, April 26, 1917, p. 7.
54. Ibid., May 1, 1917, p. 6.
55. Ibid., May 4, 1917, p. 1; *New York Times*, May 4, 1917, pp. 1, 2; *Commercial and Financial Chronicle* 104 (May 5, 1917): 1730–31.
56. Lawrence, "Hoover Comes to Town"; *Washington Post*, May 5, 1917, p. 2.
57. Lane to Cobb, May 5, 1917. Like Colonel House and Ambassador Page, Lane had become a Hoover-booster during Hoover's CRB days. Nash, *Life of Herbert Hoover: The Humanitarian*, pp. 147, 150, 302–03, 344, 346, 348.
58. Allen, "A Member of the Fourth Estate," p. 140; Albert Shaw, *International Bearings of American Policy* (Baltimore, 1943), pp. 75–76.
59. Shaw, *International Bearings*, p. 76.
60. Colonel House found Hoover "in a most pessimistic mood" on May 3. Hoover diary, May 3, 1917.
61. Wilbur, *Memoirs*, p. 243n.
62. *New York Herald*, May 4, 1917, p. 10.
63. [?], memo for President Wilson (with annotation by Wilson's secretary), May 5, 1917, Woodrow Wilson Papers, microfilm edition, reel 360, LC; *Washington Post*, May 6, 1917, section I, p. 4. Just why Wilson did not see Hoover at once is unclear. It may have been a simple case of oversight and "red tape." David Lawrence oral history (1966), p. 1, HHPL. According to Lawrence (who was a Washington correspondent in 1917), Hoover's press secretary contacted him about the mysterious lack of a communication from the White House. (This must have been on May 4 or 5.) Lawrence than telephoned President Wilson's secretary, Joseph Tumulty, who alluded to "red tape" and promised to address the matter immediately. According to Lawrence, an hour or so later Hoover received his invitation to visit the President.
64. Herbert Hoover, *An American Epic*, vol. II (Chicago, 1960), p. 16.
65. Wilbur, *Memoirs*, p. 242.
66. *New York Tribune*, May 4, 1917, p. 2. Hoover was quoted along similar lines in the *New York Times*, May 4, 1917, p. 6.
67. *New York Times*, May 5, 1917, p. 6; *Washington Post*, May 5, 1917, p. 2.
68. *New York Times*, May 5, 1917, p. 6.
69. Josephus Daniels diary, May 7, 1917, in E. David Cronon, ed., *The Cabinet Diaries of Josephus Daniels, 1913–1921* (Lincoln, Nebr., 1963), p. 148.
70. Herbert Hoover testimony before the Committee on Agriculture, U.S. House of Representatives, May 7, 1917, typescript copy, pp. 2–6, 8–9, Congressional series, Box 1, folder 6, Asbury F. Lever Papers, Special Collections, Clemson University Libraries, Clemson, South Carolina. Hoover's testimony was given in executive session and never printed by the committee. Another typewritten copy of his testimony (with different pagination) is in the USFA Papers, Box 280, HI.
71. Ibid., pp. 12–14.
72. Ibid., pp. 14–16.
73. Ibid., pp. 18–21, 25, 27, 28.
74. Ibid., pp. 28–31.
75. Irwin, "First Aid to America," p. 6.
76. Hoover testimony, May 7, 1917, p. 31.
77. Ibid., p. 30.
78. Ibid., p. 31.
79. Ibid., p. 32.

80. *New York Herald*, May 8, 1917, pp. 9, 10.
81. Ibid., p. 9; *New York Times*, May 8, 1917, p. 3; *Washington Post*, May 8, 1917, p. 2.
82. *New York Herald*, May 8, 1917, p. 9.
83. Hoover testimony, May 8 and 9, 1917, printed in U.S. Congress, Senate, Committee on Agriculture and Forestry, 65th Congress, 1st Session, *Production and Conservation of Food Supplies* (Washington, D.C., 1917), pp. 373–90, 411–24.
84. Ibid., pp. 376, 382.
85. Ibid., pp. 378, 381, 415.
86. Ibid., pp. 378, 384, 385, 418, 419.
87. Ibid., p. 424.
88. Josephus Daniels, *The Wilson Era—Years of War and After, 1917–1923* (Chapel Hill, N.C., 1946), p. 317.
89. Franklin K. Lane to Frank I. Cobb (?), May 7, 1917, in Lane and Wall, eds., *Letters of Franklin K. Lane*, p. 254; Josephus Daniels diary, May 9, 1917, in Cronon, ed., *Cabinet Diaries of Josephus Daniels*, p. 149. According to Daniels, at the May 9 meeting of the Council of National Defense, Secretary Houston "did not wish Food Controller, but for the Dept of Agriculture to control it."
90. Appointments Book, 1917, Wilson Papers.
91. *New York Times*, May 10, 1917, p. 4.
92. Hoover, *American Epic*, II, pp. 29–30; Hoover, *The Memoirs of Herbert Hoover*, vol. I: *Years of Adventure* (New York, 1951), pp. 240–42. No contemporary record of the Hoover-Wilson meeting of May 9 has been found. Although Hoover's later recollections probably convey the gist of his discussion with the President, they are not completely accurate in detail. In his *Memoirs*, Hoover stated that he arrived in Washington on May 5 and that Wilson formally requested him to join the administration's "war team" that very same day. In fact, Hoover arrived in Washington on May 4, not the fifth, and, so far as is known, did not see Wilson until the ninth. Incidentally, neither in his *Memoirs* nor the *American Epic* did Hoover record that Secretary Houston strongly opposed Hoover's "desire to control the war policies of agriculture." Instead, Hoover portrayed Houston as amenable to Hoover's views and plans! This was not the case as of May 9, as contemporary sources make clear.
93. See Hoover's telegram to his wife of May 11, 1917, quoted in the text below.
94. *New York Herald*, May 11, 1917, p. 14; *New York Times*, May 11, 1917, p. 20; *Washington Post*, May 11, 1917, p. 2.
95. Hoover telegram to his wife, May 11, 1917, "Hoover, Lou Henry," Pre-Commerce Papers. On May 13 Hoover's friend Mary Austin, who was in Washington, informed Mrs. Hoover that the Secretary of Agriculture was "holding back Bert's appointment." Mary Austin to Lou Henry Hoover, May 13, 1917, "Austin, Mary," "Personal Correspondence: 1874–1920," Lou Henry Hoover Papers, HHPL.
96. *New York Times*, May 10, 1917, p. 4.
97. Hoover to the Council of National Defense, May 13, 1917 (plus enclosed memorandum), copy in "1917—National Defense (2) Food," General Correspondence, 1906–1975, RG 16, NARA. A copy of Hoover's letter to the council is in the USFA Papers, Box 98.
98. Ibid.
99. Martin, *Digest*, p. 185; Walter S. Gifford to Hoover, May 17, 1917, USFA Papers, Box 98.
100. Gifford Pinchot testimony, May 8, 1917, printed in U.S. Congress, House of Representatives, Committee on Agriculture, 65th Congress, 1st Session, *Food Production, Conservation, and Distribution* (Washington, D.C., 1917), pp. 119–32; J. F. Lucey testimony, May 16, 1917, ibid., pp. 328–36. Pinchot was briefly associated with the Belgian relief in 1915; Captain Lucey in 1914–15.
101. Hoover interview with the Associated Press, May 10, 1917, USFA Papers, Box 128, HI; *New York Herald*, May 11, 1917, p. 14.
102. Ibid.

103. Hoover speech to a group of women in New York City, May 10, 1917, Public Statements File, Hoover Papers.
104. Ibid.; *New York Herald*, May 11, 1917, p. 14.
105. *New York Herald*, May 11, 1917, p. 14.
106. Hoover speech to a group of women in New York City, May 10, 1917.
107. *New York Times*, May 12, 1917, p. 10.
108. Ibid., May 14, 1917, p. 10.
109. *New Republic* 11 (May 12, 1917): 32.
110. Hoover speech to a group of women in New York City, May 10, 1917.
111. Hoover interview with the Associated Press, May 10, 1917; *New York Herald*, May 11, 1917, p. 14.
112. *New York Times*, May 9, 1917, p. 5; *New York Herald*, May 9, 1917, p. 10; *Washington Post*, May 9, 1917, p. 1.
113. James H. Shideler, *Farm Crisis, 1919–1923* (Berkeley and Los Angeles, 1957), p. 11.
114. *Commercial and Financial Chronicle* 104 (May 19, 1917): 1973.
115. *New York Times*, May 9, 1917, p. 5.
116. Ibid., May 13, 1917, section I, p. 5, and May 14, 1917, p. 10; *Commercial and Financial Chronicle* 104 (May 19, 1917): 1973.
117. *Washington Post*, May 13, 1917, section I, pp. 1, 4.
118. *New York Herald*, May 15, 1917, p. 9.
119. Ray Stannard Baker, *Woodrow Wilson: Life and Letters*, vol. 7: *War Leader, April 6, 1917—February 28, 1918* (New York, 1939), p. 66.
120. Hoover telegram to his wife, May 15, 1917, "Hoover, Lou Henry," Pre-Commerce Papers. On May 15 the *Philadelphia Inquirer*'s Washington correspondent, who was secretly on the payroll of the Swift meat-packing company, reported to Swift: "Complete control of the distribution of food supplies will be turned over to Herbert C. Hoover in a few days. This will be done directly by President Wilson, although Secretary Houston, who has been opposing the move, is not yet aware that the President has asked Hoover to go ahead. Hoover was with the President for several hours last night, and the President approved of all his plans." I have found no evidence that Hoover was with the President "last night," if by "last night" is meant May 14, 1917. However, Hoover did visit the President on the evening of May 13, and it is evidently to this meeting that the *Philadelphia Inquirer*'s correspondent was referring.

    See Thomas F. Logan memorandum to Louis F. Swift, printed in U.S. Congress, Senate, Committee on Agriculture and Forestry, 65th Congress, 3d Session, *Government Control of the Meat-Packing Industry* (Washington, D.C., 1919), pp. 1856–57. Printed also in *Chicago Tribune*, February 26, 1918, p. 11. Logan's flat assertion cannot be confirmed. But Logan felt sure enough of himself to report his story in the *Philadelphia Inquirer* on May 16, 1917 (see note 124 below). It is very possible that Logan's source was Hoover himself or one of his entourage.
121. Edgar Rickard to Lou Henry Hoover, May 15, 1917, "Food Administration Correspondence 1917," Subject File, Lou Henry Hoover Papers. Rickard added that Hoover's entourage was "all waiting for the final turn of events to congratulate Bert."
122. *New York Times*, May 16, 1917, p. 5; *Washington Post*, May 16, 1917, p. 1.
123. Unidentified newspaper clipping, May 16, 1917 (dispatch dated May 15), Clippings File, HHPL; *New York Times*, May 17, 1917, p. 6. See also *Washington Post*, May 17, 1917, p. 4.
124. *Philadelphia Inquirer*, May 16, 1917, p. 1.
125. *Washington Post*, May 17, 1917, p. 4. The headline in the unidentified clipping cited in note 123 reads: "Hoover Chosen as Dictator at Wilson Confab." The *New York Times* article cited in the same note had as its headline: "Hoover Will Head New Food Board."
126. *New York Tribune*, May 17, 1917, p. 8.
127. Ibid.
128. *New York Times*, May 18, 1917, p. 8.

129. Hoover to Representative Asbury F. Lever, May 17, 1917 (two letters), printed in *Food Production, Conservation, and Distribution*, pp. 400–01, 488.
130. Hoover interview in *New York Globe*, May 17, 1917, printed in *Congressional Record* 55 (May 21, 1917): 2636. Hoover's interviewer was the *Globe*'s crusading food correspondent Alfred W. McCann, who had called upon him at his New Willard Hotel suite. Hoover may not have realized that McCann was a reporter or have expected McCann to quote him in print. When McCann did so, an embarrassed Hoover repudiated the *Globe* article. Hoover claimed that "all but an infinitesimal basis of the statements contained in that article" was "absolute invention." He accused McCann of attributing to him statements that McCann himself had made and that Hoover had disputed in their conversation. See Hoover to Senator Frank B. Brandegee, May 24, 1917, printed in *Congressional Record* 55 (May 25, 1917): 2855.

    For his part, McCann insisted that his newspaper report was completely truthful and that Hoover had been obliged to repudiate it for "diplomatic" reasons. McCann claimed that he did not realize, when he published the interview, that a jealous Department of Agriculture was trying to "knife" Hoover and that the article played into Hoover's enemies' hands, obliging Hoover to denounce McCann as a liar. See Alfred W. McCann to George W. Moench, "McCann, Alfred W.," Pre-Commerce Papers, Hoover Papers. McCann, incidentally, went on to become a bitter critic of Hoover.

    Despite Hoover's denials (and McCann's evident tendency toward sensationalism), the statements that I have quoted from the McCann article seem distinctly Hooverian both in substance and in tone. I am satisfied that Hoover so expressed himself in his conversation with McCann.
131. *New York Times*, May 17, 1917, pp. 1, 2.
132. Ibid., May 18, 1917, p. 8.
133. George Creel, *Rebel at Large* (New York, 1947), p. 265.
134. Josephus Daniels diary, May 7, 1917; Daniels, *Wilson Era*, pp. 316–17. In the latter source Daniels mistakenly wrote that he met Hoover on May 8, 1917; the actual date was May 7.
135. Despite his reservations about Hoover, Daniels nevertheless supported him for food controller. Daniels, *Wilson Era*, p. 317.
136. One opponent of Hoover's appointment was Senator Boies Penrose, a conservative Republican from Pennsylvania. When Hoover told Penrose's brother that the senator had "developed a considerable vein of personal opposition to me which I think is entirely unjust and must be based on some misrepresentation or some misunderstanding," Senator Penrose demurred: "I am not opposed to Mr. Hoover and I have never met anyone who did not speak in the highest terms of him. I am, however, opposed as are a good many senators to the demands of the present administration for certain dictatorial and arbitrary powers, particularly in connection with the production and conservation of food. It seems to me there is a good deal of hysteria on this subject. The proposition involves general principles and not Mr. Hoover personally." See Hoover telegram to R. A. F. Penrose, Jr., May 19, 1917, and Senator Boies Penrose to R. A. F. Penrose, Jr., May 24, 1917, in Helen R. Fairbanks and Charles P. Berkey, *Life and Letters of R. A. F. Penrose, Jr.* (New York, 1952), pp. 523–24.
137. Senator James E. Watson, quoted in *New York Herald*, May 17, 1917, p. 3.
138. *Washington Post*, May 16, 1917, p. 1.
139. Hoover, *An American Epic*, II, p. 32.
140. Woodrow Wilson statement on the Lever bill, May 19, 1917, in Link et al., eds., *Papers of Woodrow Wilson*, vol. 42, pp. 344–46. Printed also in *New York Times*, May 20, 1917, section I, p. 1.
141. Hoover statement, May 19, 1917, in *New York Times*, May 20, 1917, pp. 1, 2.
142. When introducing an early version of his food control bill on May 4, Representative Lever expressed hope that "the mere conferring of the more extreme new powers will be sufficient without its becoming necessary to exercise them." *New York Times*, May 4, 1917, p. 1.

143. The phrase is Robert D. Cuff's. See Robert D. Cuff, "Herbert Hoover, the Ideology of Voluntarism and War Organization During the Great War," *Journal of American History* 64 (September 1977): 358–72.
144. Daniels, *Wilson Era*, p. 317; Benedict, *Farm Policies of the United States*, p. 152.
145. Edward M. House diary, May 3, 1917, House Papers; Daniels, *Wilson Era*, p. 317.
146. See Robert D. Cuff, "We Band of Brothers—Woodrow Wilson's War Managers," *Canadian Review of American Studies* 5 (Fall 1974): 135–48, for an able discussion of this and related themes.
147. *New York Tribune*, May 20, 1917, p. 1.
148. *New York Times*, May 12, 1917, p. 10.
149. *New Republic*, 11 (May 26, 1917): 92.
150. *New York Tribune*, May 20, 1917, p. 1.

CHAPTER 2

1. Herbert Hoover, addresses at Brown University, May 20, 1917, and Harvard University, June 21, 1917, Public Statements File, Herbert Hoover Papers, HHPL. In a meeting with editors of trade and technical journals on May 25, Hoover declared that the first goal of the projected Food Administration would be price stability. *New York Times*, May 26, 1917, p. 4.
2. Hoover address at Brown University, May 20, 1917.
3. *New York Times*, May 22, 1917, p. 2.
4. Ibid., May 25, 1917, p. 13, and May 30, 1917, p. 7.
5. George H. Nash, *The Life of Herbert Hoover: The Humanitarian, 1914–1917* (New York, 1988), p. 361; Victoria French Allen, "A Member of the Fourth Estate" (typescript, n.d.), p. 141, in the Ben S. Allen Collection (cited in chapter 1, note 1).
6. Herbert Hoover, *An American Epic*, vol. II (Chicago, 1960), p. 32. Among the mining engineers who assisted Hoover in the early days of the Food Administration were J. F. Lucey and John Beaver White. Both had been associated with the Belgian relief.
7. Ray Lyman Wilbur telegram to Curtis D. Wilbur, May 18, 1917, USFA Papers, Box 188, HI; Edgar Eugene Robinson and Paul Carroll Edwards, eds., *The Memoirs of Ray Lyman Wilbur* (Stanford, Calif., 1960), pp. 241, 253, 258–59 (hereinafter cited as Wilbur, *Memoirs*).
8. Mark L. Requa, "Food Administration Period, 1917–19" (typescript, n.d.), Mark L. Requa Papers, HI.
9. Hoover to Curtis H. Lindley, June 1, 1917, USFA Papers, Box 45.
10. Hoover to Woodrow Wilson, December 26, 1917, Woodrow Wilson Papers, LC.
11. Alonzo E. Taylor, "Hoover Would Fit Well in American War Cabinet," Philadelphia *Public Ledger*, March 6, 1917, p. 10.
12. Wilbur, *Memoirs*, p. 258.
13. W. A. M. Goode to Arthur Willert, April 18, 1917, Arthur Willert Papers, Box 3, Manuscripts and Archives, Yale University Library. For more on Hoover's association with Goode, see Nash, *Life of Herbert Hoover: The Humanitarian*, pp. 37, 138, 377, and George H. Nash, *The Life of Herbert Hoover: The Engineer, 1874–1914* (New York, 1983), pp. 547–58.
14. W. A. M. Goode cable to Hoover, May 2, 1917, USFA Papers, Box 134.
15. Hoover to Robert Lansing, May 26, 1917, Robert Lansing Papers, vol. 28, LC.
16. Henry L. Stimson to Hoover, May 18, 1917, Henry L. Stimson Papers, Box 62, Manuscripts and Archives, Yale University Library.
17. Hoover to Stimson, May 20, 1917, Stimson Papers, Box 62.
18. Stimson to Hoover, May 21, 1917, ibid.
19. Nash, *Life of Herbert Hoover: The Engineer*, p. 46.
20. Lewis L. Strauss, *Men and Decisions* (Garden City, N.Y., 1962), pp. 6–8; Lewis L. Strauss oral history interview, 1962, pp. 38–42, Columbia University Oral History Collection.

21. Strauss, *Men and Decisions*, p. 8; Strauss oral history interview, p. 45.
22. Strauss oral history interview, p. 45.
23. Hoover memorandum ("A Debatable Hypothesis"), May 6, 1917, USFA Papers, Box 127. See also Alan G. Anderson cable 11 to Royal Commission on Wheat Supplies, May 11, 1917, PRO 30/68/10, PRO.
24. Julius H. Barnes to Ward Ames, Jr., May 16 and 19, 1917, Series 5, Box 31, RG 5, NARA; Alan G. Anderson cable 15 to Royal Commission on Wheat Supplies, May 21, 1917, PRO 30/68/10, PRO; Alan G. Anderson memorandum, June 22, 1917, FO 371/3073, PRO; Frank M. Surface, *The Grain Trade During the World War* (New York, 1928), pp. 36, 38. Barnes was then chairman of the Committee of Grain Exchanges in Aid of National Defense.
25. *New York Times*, May 25, 1917, p. 13; Hoover telegram to Joseph A. Burnquist, May 29, 1917, Joseph A. Burnquist Papers, Box 10, Minnesota Historical Society.
26. Samuel A. Gompers to Hoover, May 25, 1917; Hoover to Gompers, May 26, 1917. Both in American Federation of Labor Papers, Series 11-A, Box 22, State Historical Society of Wisconsin.
27. Vernon Kellogg to William Allen White, June 5, 1917, William Allen White Papers, Series C, Box 39, LC.
28. See, for instance, Hoover's "Preliminary Note on the Organization of the Food Administration" (June 1, 1917), enclosed with Hoover to Joseph P. Tumulty, ca. June 1, 1917, Wilson Papers. In this important memorandum, Hoover stated that the "one prime object of our war food administration" was "to induce the export of the maximum surplus of foodstuffs to our Allies." This objective, he said, made it necessary to eliminate waste, conserve resources, and "control the flow of foodstuffs" in such a way as to "facilitate transportation" and "prevent excessive prices."
29. Hoover speech to a group of women in New York City, May 10, 1917, Public Statements File, Hoover Papers.
30. Hoover testimony, May 9, 1917, printed in U.S. Congress, Senate, Committee on Agriculture and Forestry, 65th Congress, 1st Session, *Production and Conservation of Food Supplies* (Washington, D.C., 1917), p. 419.
31. *New York Times*, May 28, 1917, p. 5.
32. Hoover, "Preliminary Note."
33. Herbert Hoover, *The Memoirs of Herbert Hoover*, Vol. I: *Years of Adventure* (New York, 1951), p. 244.
34. [Howard Heinz?], notes of interview with Herbert Hoover, May 25, 1917, USFA Papers, Box 128.
35. John E. Kelley testimony, May 29, 1917, printed in U.S. Congress, House of Representatives, Committee on Agriculture, 65th Congress, 1st Session, *Food Production, Conservation, and Distribution* (Washington, D.C., 1917), pp. 429–30.
36. Hoover, "Preliminary Note."
37. Donald Wilhelm, "Waste Not, Want Not," *Independent* 90 (June 9, 1917): 459. Wilhelm quoted Hoover as saying that "our normal economic machine for the regulation of prices is broken down."
38. *New York Times*, May 26, 1917, p. 4.
39. Hoover testimony before the Committee on Agriculture, U.S. House of Representatives, May 7, 1917, typescript copy, pp. 15–16, Congressional series, Box 1, folder 6, Asbury F. Lever Papers, Special Collections, Clemson University Libraries; Hoover testimony, May 8, 1917, printed in *Production and Conservation of Food Supplies*, p. 377.
40. *New York Times*, May 26, 1917, p. 4. See also Hoover, *Years of Adventure*, p. 245.
41. *New York Times*, May 30, 1917, pp. 1, 7.
42. Hoover, "Preliminary Note."
43. *New York Times*, May 30, 1917, p. 1. For a brief outline of Hoover's scheme, see Alan G. Anderson cable 15 to Royal Commission on Wheat Supplies, May 21, 1917.

44. [Howard Heinz?], notes of interview with Hoover, May 25, 1917.
45. Hoover, "Preliminary Note."
46. Hoover, *Years of Adventure*, p. 245; Tom G. Hall, "Wilson and the Food Crisis: Agricultural Price Control During World War I," *Agricultural History* 47 (January 1973): 44–45; Tom G. Hall, "Woodrow Wilson, Herbert Hoover and Food Price Control," *Washington Agricultural Record* 27 (June 27, 1973): 840.
47. Harold Archer Van Dorn, *Government Owned Corporations* (New York, 1926), pp. 10–11.
48. Hoover to Frederick D. Underwood, June 9, 1917, USFA Papers, Box 127.
49. Hoover telegram to James F. Bell, May 15, 1917, USFA Papers, Box 189; *New York Times*, May 30, 1917, p. 1; Hoover, "Preliminary Note."
50. Hoover to Underwood, June 9, 1917.
51. *New York Times*, May 30, 1917, pp. 1, 7.
52. Hoover to Underwood, June 9, 1917.
53. Julius H. Barnes to Hoover, May 30, 1917, USFA Papers, Box 245. See also Hoover to Woodrow Wilson, May 31, 1917, Wilson Papers.
54. U.S. Department of Commerce, Bureau of the Census, *Historical Statistics of the United States: Colonial Times to 1970* (Washington, D.C., 1975), Part 2, p. 1114.
55. The food survey bill was H.R. 4188. The Senate's version was S.2344. A printed copy was enclosed with David F. Houston to Woodrow Wilson, May 14, 1917, Wilson Papers.
56. This was H.R. 4125. For a detailed summary of its contents, see *New York Times*, May 4, 1917, pp. 1, 2, and *New York Herald*, May 4, 1917, p. 1.
57. *New York Times*, May 16, 1917, p. 5, and May 17, 1917, p. 6.
58. *Congressional Record* 55 (May 22, 1917): 2777; *New York Times*, May 23, 1917, pp. 1, 2. This second version of the Lever bill was H.R. 4630.
59. The second or revised Lever food control bill evidently went simultaneously to the House and Senate agriculture committees, which apparently examined it in joint conference. *New York Times*, June 7, 1917, p. 3. Meanwhile the Senate (on May 23) took up the food survey bill. The House, which had debated this bill on May 9, resumed consideration of it on May 24.
60. *Congressional Record* 55 (May 28, 1917): 3013, and 55 (June 2, 1917): 3229; *New York Times*, May 29, 1917, pp. 1, 4, and June 3, 1917, section I, p. 1.
61. The debate can be followed, of course, in the *Congressional Record*. For some of the highlights, see *New York Times*, May 25, 1917, p. 13; May 26, 1917, p. 4; and May 27, 1917, section I, p. 3.
62. *Congressional Record* 55 (May 26, 1917): 2936.
63. *New York Times*, June 1, 1917, p. 9.
64. *Congressional Record* 55 (May 25, 1917): 2865.
65. Ibid., 55 (May 24, 1917): 2840.
66. *New York Times*, June 1, 1917, p. 9, and June 3, 1917, section I, p. 1; *Commercial and Financial Chronicle* 104 (June 9, 1917): 2298.
67. *New York Times*, May 22, 1917, p. 2.
68. Representative James Young statements, May 29, 1917, printed in *Food Production, Conservation, and Distribution*, pp. 428–30, 464.
69. Henry F. Hollis to Woodrow Wilson, June 1, 1917, Wilson Papers.
70. Charles McCarthy to Charles W. Holman, June 4, 1917, Charles W. Holman Papers, Box 1, Cornell University.
71. On May 7, Hoover's secretary in Washington asked Hoover's personal financial assistant in New York to send the Chief $5,000 in cash. L. H. Bradshaw telegram to Edgar Rickard, May 7, 1917, USFA Papers, Box 33. Hoover's use of his own money to pay for clerical assistance and other expenses became known to the press. See "Food Control Now!" *Independent* 90 (June 23, 1917): 529.
72. Hoover to Woodrow Wilson, May 29, 1917, General Accessions—U.S. Food Administration, HHPL. At the bottom of Hoover's letter the President wrote: "Approved. Woodrow Wilson."

73. For example, U.S. Food Administration press release 11, June 6, 1917, USFA Documents, HHPL; *New York Herald*, June 8, 1917, p. 3.
74. Hoover to Ida M. Tarbell, May 29, 1917; Tarbell to Hoover, June 5, 1917. Both in USFA Papers, Box 39.
75. W. A. M. Goode to Hoover, June 15, 1917; Goode cable to Hoover, June 25, 1917; Hoover to Goode, June 27, 1917. All in USFA Papers, Box 134.
76. *New York Times*, May 30, 1917, p. 1.
77. Ibid., June 8, 1917, p. 1.
78. Hoover, "Preliminary Note"; Alan G. Anderson cable 15 to Royal Commission on Wheat Supplies, May 21, 1917; Hoover to Asbury F. Lever, June 2, 1917, USFA Papers, Box 96.
79. *New York Times*, June 7, 1917, p. 1; *New York Herald*, June 7, 1917, p. 12.
80. *New York Times*, June 10, 1917, section I, p. 1.
81. Ibid., June 12, 1917, p. 1.
82. Ibid.
83. Ibid.
84. Ibid.
85. Hoover, "Memorandum on Necessity of Early Food Legislation," enclosed with Hoover to Woodrow Wilson, June 12, 1917, Wilson Papers.
86. Hoover, "Organization of Commodity Controls" and "Organization of Voluntary Conservation," enclosed with Hoover to Wilson, June 12, 1917.
87. Hoover, "Organization of Voluntary Conservation."
88. Wilson to Hoover, June 12, 1917, Wilson Papers; printed in Arthur S. Link et al., eds. *The Papers of Woodrow Wilson*, vol. 42 (Princeton, N.J., 1983), pp. 485–86.
89. *New York Times*, June 17, 1917, section I, p. 1.
90. Ibid., June 15, 1917, p. 7.
91. *Commercial and Financial Chronicle* 104 (June 16, 1917): 2385–86.
92. *Congressional Record* 55 (June 14, 1917): 3593–601; *New York Times*, June 15, 1917, pp. 1, 7.
93. *New York Times*, June 16, 1917, p. 6, and June 17, 1917, section I, p. 3.
94. Ibid., June 16, 1917, p. 6.
95. Ibid.; *New York Herald*, June 16, 1917, p. 9.
96. *New York Times*, June 17, 1917, section I, p. 3.
97. *Congressional Record* 55 (June 13, 1917): 3566–67.
98. *New York Times*, June 17, 1917, section I, pp. 1, 3.
99. Ibid.
100. Ibid., June 18, 1917, pp. 1, 2; "The Women's Call," *Independent* 90 (June 23, 1917): 568.
101. *New York Herald*, June 19, 1917, p. 10; *New York Times*, June 19, 1917, p. 2.
102. *New York Times*, June 19, 1917, p. 2.
103. Ibid., June 20, 1917, p. 2.
104. Ibid., June 22, 1917, p. 3.
105. *New York Herald*, June 18, 1917, p. 10; Hoover to Joseph P. Tumulty, June 28, 1917, Wilson Papers.
106. Everett S. Brown, "The Food Administration: A Test of American Democracy," *Historical Outlook* 10 (May 1919): 243.
107. Hoover letter to the clergy of the United States, June 18, 1917. A copy of this form letter, addressed to the Reverend Charles E. Hitchcock, is in General Accessions—Lawrence S. Hitchcock, HHPL.
108. *Northwestern Miller* 110 (June 27, 1917): 923.
109. Hoover message to the Patriotic Service League, June 28, 1917, Public Statements File, Hoover Papers.
110. Hoover to the Department of the Interior (plus enclosure), July 3, 1917, File 1-188, RG 48, NARA; *Washington Post*, July 5, 1917, p. 4.
111. *New York Times*, June 30, 1917, p. 2.
112. Brown, "The Food Administration," p. 243.
113. *New York Tribune*, June 20, 1917, p. 2.

114. Hoover so referred to it in his letter to Tumulty, June 28, 1917.
115. *New York Herald*, July 2, 1917, p. 10. Because the infant Food Administration lacked an apparatus of its own, women's clubs organized much of the registration drive. The Women's Committee of the Council of National Defense coordinated their efforts. "The Women's Call," p. 568.
116. Hoover message to the Boy Scouts of America, July 1, 1917, Public Statements File, Hoover Papers.
117. *New York Times*, July 8, 1917, section I, p. 6.
118. Hoover testimony, June 19, 1917, in U.S. Congress, Senate, Committee on Agriculture and Forestry, 65th Congress, 1st Session, *Control and Distribution of Food Supplies* (Washington, D.C., 1917), p. 17.
119. Hoover speech to prospective state food administrators, Chevy Chase Club, July 10, 1917, Public Statements File, Hoover Papers.
120. *New York Times*, July 7, 1917, p. 2.
121. Ibid., July 17, 1917, p. 3.
122. Ellen Maury Slayden diary, July 27, 1917, printed in her book, *Washington Wife* (New York, 1962), p. 308.
123. *Congressional Record* 55 (July 16, 1917): 5163; *New York Times*, July 17, 1917, p. 3; *New York Tribune*, July 17, 1917, p. 1.
124. U.S. Food Administration press release 133, July 28, 1917, USFA Documents, HHPL; *New York Times*, July 29, 1917, section I, p. 2; William C. Mullendore, *History of the United States Food Administration, 1917–1919* (Stanford, Calif., 1941), p. 86.
125. U.S. Food Administration press release 133, July 28, 1917; *New York Times*, July 29, 1917, section I, p. 2.

CHAPTER 3

1. The two houses of Congress took up the Lever bill simultaneously in order to expedite debate.
2. For the text of Representative Lever's speech, see *Congressional Record* 55 (June 18, 1917): 3793–99.
3. Woodrow Wilson to Representative William Borland, June 18, 1917, Woodrow Wilson Papers, LC. This letter was widely reprinted in the nation's press on June 19, 1917.
4. *Congressional Record* 55 (June 18, 1917): 3802.
5. Ibid.: 3773.
6. Ibid., 55 (June 20, 1917): 3908.
7. The *New York Times* reported "an undercurrent of opposition" in the House because of fear that the bill would "unfavorably affect" the price farmers received for their products. *New York Times*, June 18, 1917, p. 2.
8. *Congressional Record* 55 (June 21, 1917): 4034.
9. Ibid., 55 (June 25, 1917): 4204, 4205.
10. Ibid., 55 (June 21, 1917): 4037.
11. Ibid.: 3996.
12. *New York Times*, June 19, 1917, p. 2, and June 20, 1917, p. 2; *Washington Post*, June 19, 1917, p. 1.
13. The accusation of hysteria came from Senator Lawrence Sherman of Illinois. *Congressional Record* 55 (June 21, 1917): 3999. One of the most vigorous supporters of the Lever bill and of Herbert Hoover was the *New York Times;* see, for instance, its editorial of June 18, 1917 (p. 8). For other influential expressions in support of the Lever bill, see "Food Control Now!" *Independent* 90 (June 23, 1917): 527, 529; and "Waiting for Congress," *New Republic* 11 (June 23, 1917): 205–06. According to one survey, a heavy majority of the nation's newspaper editorials favored passage of the food control law. *Literary Digest* 54 (June 30, 1917): 1977.

14. *New York Herald*, June 19, 1917, pp. 9, 10; *New York Times*, June 19, 1917, p. 1; *New York Tribune*, June 19, 1917, p. 1; *Washington Post*, June 19, 1917, p. 1.
15. The precise number of senators who attended is uncertain. The committee's hearing transcript (cited in note 18 below) listed twenty-two senators present. The next day (June 20) the *New York Times* reported that thirty had attended, the *New York Herald* "about forty," and the *New York Tribune* fifty.
16. Hoover memorandum enclosed with his letter to the Council of National Defense, May 13, 1917, copy in "1917—National Defense (2) Food," General Correspondence, 1906–1975, RG 16, NARA.
17. Hoover to Representative Asbury F. Lever, May 17, 1917, printed in U.S. Congress, House of Representatives, Committee on Agriculture, 65th Congress, 1st Session, *Food Production, Conservation, and Distribution* (Washington, D.C., 1917), pp. 400–01.
18. This summary is drawn from Hoover's opening statement, June 19, 1917, printed in U.S. Congress, Senate, Committee on Agriculture and Forestry, 65th Congress, 1st Session, *Control and Distribution of Food Supplies* (Washington, D.C., 1917), pp. 8–13. For the full text of his testimony, see pp. 8–60.
19. Ibid., pp. 25–26, 34.
20. Ibid., pp. 34–35.
21. Ibid., pp. 45, 47.
22. Ibid., pp. 47–48.
23. Hoover telegram to Harry A. Garfield, June 15, 1917, USFA Papers, Box 187, HI; Hoover to Woodrow Wilson, June 15, 1917, Wilson Papers.
24. *New York Times*, June 20, 1917, p. 1.
25. *Congressional Record* 55 (June 22, 1917): 4096; *New York Times*, June 23, 1917, p. 1.
26. *Congressional Record* 55 (June 23, 1917): 4190.
27. Ibid.: 4161–63, 4181; *New York Times*, June 24, 1917, section I, pp. 1, 2.
28. *Congressional Record* 55 (June 20, 1917): 3909.
29. Ibid., 55 (June 25, 1917): 4196–97.
30. Ibid.: 4205.
31. *New York Herald*, June 26, 1917, p. 9.
32. Ibid.; *New York Times*, June 26, 1917, p. 1.
33. *New York Herald*, June 28, 1917, p. 10.
34. Ibid., June 26, 1917, p. 9.
35. *New York Herald*, June 28, 1917, pp. 9, 10; *New York Times*, June 28, 1917, p. 1.
36. *New York Herald*, June 27, 1917, p. 9, and June 28, 1917, pp. 9, 10; *New York Times*, June 28, 1917, p. 3; *Washington Post*, June 28, 1917, p. 1.
37. *Congressional Record* 55 (June 27, 1917): 4356; *New York Times*, June 28, 1917, p. 1.
38. *Congressional Record* 55 (June 28, 1917): 4403.
39. Hoover to Woodrow Wilson, June 29, 1917, Wilson Papers.
40. Hoover testimony, June 19, 1917, in *Control and Distribution of Food Supplies*, p. 15.
41. *New York Times*, June 29, 1917, p. 2.
42. U.S. Food Administration press release 28, June 28, 1917, USFA Documents, HHPL; *New York Herald*, June 29, 1917, p. 9. Griffin soon became a harsh critic of Hoover's grain control program. See the September 1917 correspondence file in USFA Papers, Box 245, especially Julius H. Barnes to Hoover, September 25, 1917, and Hoover to Barnes, September 26, 1917.
43. *New York Herald*, June 29, 1917, p. 9.
44. Hoover to Woodrow Wilson, June 30, 1917, Wilson Papers.
45. Curtis H. Lindley to Julius H. Barnes, August 3, 1917, USFA Papers, Box 245.
46. Notation by President Wilson's secretary at bottom of Hoover's letter to Wilson, June 30, 1917.
47. Hoover was not a strict teetotaler. According to his brother, he was "temperate but not 'teetotal' all his life." Theodore J. Hoover, "Memoranda: Being a Statement by an Engineer" (typescript: Stanford University, 1939), p. 267, copy at HHPL. Hoover's London home

from 1907 to 1917 included a wine cellar and a billiard room with a cocktail mixer. George H. Nash, *The Life of Herbert Hoover: The Humanitarian, 1914–1917* (New York, 1988), p. 254.

48. Hoover told his friend Will Irwin in early 1917, shortly before America entered the war: "If I were dictator in this war I should stop brewing and distilling for beverage purposes, at once. They consume enormous quantities of the grain that Europe needs so badly. The product adds little or nothing to human nutrition—at best, it is a luxury. . . ." As a means of curbing alcohol consumption, Hoover suggested "a prohibitive excise tax." Hoover, quoted in Will Irwin, "First Aid to America," *Saturday Evening Post* 189 (March 24, 1917): 113.
49. Hoover testimony before the Committee on Agriculture, U.S. House of Representatives, May 7, 1917, typescript copy, p. 18, Congressional series, Box 1, folder 6, Asbury F. Lever Papers, Special Collections, Clemson University Libraries.
50. Hoover speech to a group of women in New York City, May 10, 1917, Public Statements File, Herbert Hoover Papers, HHPL.
51. Ibid. On May 7 Hoover told the Secretary of the Navy that "no wheat or barley should go into intoxicants. As an ethical question he believed in it, but he advocated it purely as a war plan." Josephus Daniels diary, May 7, 1917, printed in E. David Cronon, ed., *The Cabinet Diaries of Josephus Daniels, 1913–1921* (Lincoln, Nebr., 1963), p. 148.
52. U.S. Food Administration press release 4, May 26, 1917, USFA Documents; *New York Times*, May 27, 1917, section I, p. 3.
53. *New York Times*, July 2, 1917, p. 2.
54. Woodrow Wilson to the Rev. Dr. James Cannon, Jr., June 29, 1917, Wilson Papers; *New York Times*, June 30, 1917, p. 2.
55. Rev. Dr. James Cannon, Jr., et al., to Wilson, June 30, 1917, Wilson Papers.
56. *New York Herald*, June 30, 1917, p. 9; *New York Times*, June 30, 1917, pp. 1, 2.
57. *New York Herald*, July 3, 1917, p. 10.
58. Ibid., July 2, 1917, p. 9.
59. *Congressional Record* 55 (July 2, 1917): 4609–10; *Washington Post*, July 3, 1917, p. 1. The Senate's vote was 42–16.
60. *Congressional Record* 55 (July 2, 1917): 4590.
61. *New York Herald*, July 3, 1917, p. 10.
62. *Congressional Record* 55 (July 3, 1917): 4651–53.
63. Edward M. House diary, July 4, 1917, Edward M. House Papers, Manuscripts and Archives, Yale University Library.
64. Ibid.; Hoover to Woodrow Wilson, July 5, 1917, Wilson Papers.
65. Woodrow Wilson statement, ca. June 26, 1917, in Arthur S. Link et al., eds., *The Papers of Woodrow Wilson*, vol. 43 (Princeton, N.J., 1983), pp. 14–15; *Washington Post*, June 26, 1917, pp. 1, 4.
66. Hoover to James F. Bell, June 29, 1917, USFA Papers, Box 189.
67. Hoover to Woodrow Wilson, July 7, 1917, Wilson Papers.
68. *New York Times*, July 8, 1917, section I, p. 1.
69. *New York Herald*, July 9, 1917, pp. 9, 10; *Washington Post*, July 9, 1917, pp. 1, 2.
70. *Congressional Record* 55 (July 6, 1917): 4752–57, and 55 (July 7, 1917): 4792; *Washington Post*, July 7, 1917, pp. 1, 2, and July 8, 1917, pp. 1, 6.
71. *New York Herald*, July 4, 1917, p. 10; *Congressional Record* 55 (July 10, 1917): 4883.
72. *Congressional Record* 55 (July 10, 1917): 4882–87.
73. Ibid.: 4903, 4906.
74. U.S. Food Administration press release 58, July 9, 1917, USFA Documents; *New York Herald*, July 10, 1917, p. 10; *New York Times*, July 10, 1917, p. 9.
75. *New York Tribune*, July 10, 1917, p. 10. Earlier in 1917, for the first time in its history, the Senate had adopted a rule permitting cloture of debate under certain circumstances after the successful filibuster by a "little group of willful men" against the armed neutrality bill.

Chamberlain's petition of July 9 was the first attempt to terminate a debate-in-progress under the new cloture rule.

76. Ibid.; *New York Herald*, July 11, 1917, p. 9; *New York Times*, July 11, 1917, pp. 1, 18.
77. According to the *Washington Post*, July 11, 1917, p. 1, "Democratic senators secured the agreement for a vote only after they had consented to strip the bill of some of its more drastic features, including the stringent prohibition provisions." The *Post* reported that the revisions demanded were "far-reaching."
78. *New York Herald*, July 11, 1917, p. 9; *New York Times*, July 11, 1917, pp. 1, 18; *Washington Post*, July 11, 1917, pp. 1, 2.
79. *New York Times*, July 12, 1917, p. 3. After President Wilson made known his opposition to the Gore substitute, the committee refrained from formally endorsing it as an alternative to the much-amended bill already on the floor. *New York Times*, July 13, 1917, p. 3.
80. Hoover to Woodrow Wilson, July 12, 1917, Wilson Papers.
81. Woodrow Wilson to Senator Thomas Martin, July 13, 1917, Wilson Papers. Senator Martin and a colleague had visited the President on July 12 to learn his views about the competing forms of the food bill and his advice about how to proceed. *Washington Post*, July 13, 1917, p. 2.
82. Hoover to Woodrow Wilson, July 10, 1917, printed in toto in *New York Times*, July 11, 1917, pp. 1, 18. (The original letter is not in the Wilson Papers.)
83. Hoover, "Memorandum on Necessity of Early Food Legislation," enclosed with Hoover to Wilson, June 12, 1917, Wilson Papers. Specifically, Hoover asserted that "if all the forces now desirous" of acquiring the coming wheat harvest "would enter today into a general scramble to secure it, we can see $3.00 wheat and $19.00 flour in a month."
84. In his letter of July 10 to the President, Hoover seemed to acknowledge that the embargo system was about to take effect by noting that exports to neutrals were "restricted." But then he declared that because these particular restricted exports were "but a minor item, the export price, if not controlled, is subject to the will of the allied buyer, so that in a great measure the American producer is left to that buyer's judgment and is without voice." Hoover seemed to ignore the fact that the new embargo policy applied to the Allies as well as the neutrals. The United States was hardly as helpless *vis-à-vis* the Allies as Hoover—at least publicly—alleged.
85. According to the *Washington Post*, July 11, 1917, p. 2, Hoover's letter, which he said he wrote at Wilson's request, was considered in Washington to be "a criticism of the dilatoriness of Congress in enacting food legislation."
86. For example, U.S. Food Administration press releases 74 (July 13, 1917), 77 (July 14, 1917), 80 (July 15, 1917), and 89 (July 17, 1917), all in USFA Documents.
87. Ben S. Allen to his wife, June 21, 1917, quoted in Victoria French Allen, "A Member of the Fourth Estate" (typescript, n.d.), p. 137, in Ben S. Allen Collection (cited in chapter 1, note 1).
88. *New York Herald*, July 14, 1917, p. 13.
89. Hoover to A. J. Hemphill, July 11, 1917, USFA Papers, Box 1, HI.
90. John F. Neylan to Aaron Sapiro, July 12, 1917, John F. Neylan Papers (BANC MSS C-B 881), Box 42, Bancroft Library, University of California, Berkeley.
91. Walter Hines Page to Hoover, July 13, 1917, "Page, Walter Hines," Pre-Commerce Papers, Hoover Papers.
92. John F. Neylan to Aaron Sapiro, July 12 and 15, 1917, both in Neylan Papers.
93. Charles McCarthy to G. E. Vandercook, July 13, 1917, Charles McCarthy Papers, Box 15, State Historical Society of Wisconsin. See also Neylan to Sapiro, July 15, 1917.
94. Frederic C. Walcott to William H. Welch, July 17, 1917, Frederic C. Walcott Papers, Box 9, Manuscripts and Archives, Yale University Library. See also Neylan to Sapiro, July 15, 1917.
95. McCarthy to Vandercook, July 13, 1917.
96. Neylan to Sapiro, July 12 and 15, 1917.

97. Hoover press release, July 2, 1917, "U.S. Food Administration—Press Release, July 2, 1917," Pre-Commerce Papers. Hoover personally revised this press release into the form in which it was promulgated. (See the draft containing his corrections in the same file.) Hoover, of course, had been seeking a position in the Wilson administration since 1916. See chapter 1 above and Nash, *Life of Herbert Hoover: The Humanitarian*, pp. 341–51.
98. Neylan to Sapiro, July 12, 1917. See also Neylan to Sapiro, July 15, 1917.
99. For the text of Reed's speech, see *Congressional Record* 55 (July 16, 1917): 5156–63.
100. Ibid.: 5165.
101. *New York Times*, July 17, 1917, p. 3.
102. *Congressional Record* 55 (July 16, 1917): 5163–67.
103. Ibid., 55 (July 17, 1917): 5173.
104. Ibid., 55 (July 19, 1917): 5257.
105. Ibid.: 5256–57.
106. Ibid.: 5259–60.
107. Ibid.: 5255, 5259. Reed's amendment would have required members of the proposed food board to be "bona fide residents of the United States and qualified electors thereof," conditions that could be construed to disqualify Hoover because of his long residence abroad and failure to vote in an American election for at least twenty years. A second, similar amendment by Reed was also quickly defeated. Ibid.: 5259–60.
108. Lewis L. Strauss, *Men and Decisions* (Garden City, N.Y., 1962), p. 11.
109. *Washington Post*, July 17, 1917, p. 1.
110. *Congressional Record* 55 (July 17, 1917): 5197.
111. Ibid.; Helen Todd to Senator James C. Reed, August 6, 1917, copy enclosed with Hoover to Joseph P. Tumulty, August 8, 1917, Wilson Papers. According to Miss Todd, she had uttered a statement similar to the one attributed by the *Washington Post* to Hoover. She had remarked to a reporter "that the welfare of the children represented the future of America and that if any man or interest was growing rich out of the hunger and cold inflicted upon children I felt that the people of the country should know the truth in regard to it. And I added 'Heaven help those men in the States where mothers vote.' "
112. *Congressional Record* 55 (July 17, 1917): 5197.
113. Reed, however, remained unconvinced by Hoover's denial. Ibid., 55 (August 6, 1917): 5827. This was before he received Miss Todd's clarification.
114. Senator Gore had attempted to bring his substitute to the floor on July 13 but was temporarily blocked under the rules governing the debate. *Congressional Record* 55 (July 13, 1917): 5030. Nevertheless, his alternative bill remained on senators' minds.
115. For press reports of the bipartisan committee's efforts, see the *New York Herald*, *New York Times*, and *Washington Post* for July 14–16, 1917.
116. *New York Herald*, July 17, 1917, p. 12; *New York Times*, July 17, 1917, p. 3, and July 18, 1917, p. 3; *New York Tribune*, July 17, 1917, p. 1; *Washington Post*, July 17, 1917, p. 1.
117. Unsigned, unsent, typewritten letter from Hoover's staff to Hoover, July 17, 1917, Harry A. Garfield Papers, Box 110, LC. A copy is also in the USFA Papers, Box 49, File 16-H, HI. File 16-H was that for Hoover's assistant, Mark L. Requa.
118. Draft letter dated July 17, 1917 (and edited by Hoover), attached to the unsent letter from Hoover's staff to Hoover, July 17, 1917, Garfield Papers, Box 110. There is no attachment to the copy of the unsent letter in the Requa file in the USFA Papers.
119. For instance, the typewritten portion of the attachment (that is, those sentences not in Hoover's handwriting) contain such forceful and favorite Hoover words as "absolutely" and "entirely." To this biographer the entire document has a very Hooveresque style.
120. At the top of the copy in the Garfield Papers is the handwritten notation: "Draft but no final action as word came that commission would be dropped."
121. Hoover to Woodrow Wilson, July 18, 1917, Wilson Papers.
122. Wilson to Hoover, July 19, 1917, "Wilson, Woodrow," Pre-Commerce Papers.

123. Joseph P. Tumulty to Hoover, July 19, 1917, copy in "Wilson, Woodrow," Pre-Commerce Papers.
124. Hoover to Tumulty, July 20, 1917, Wilson Papers.
125. W. A. M. Goode cable to Hoover, July 19, 1917, USFA Papers, Box 134.
126. Hoover cable to Goode, July 19, 1917, USFA Papers, Box 134.
127. *Congressional Record* 55 (July 20, 1917): 5296.
128. Hoover to Ray Lyman Wilbur, July 21, 1917, USFA Papers, Box 1.
129. *Congressional Record* 55 (July 19, 1917): 5261–65, 5269; *New York Herald*, July 20, 1917, p. 12; *New York Times*, July 20, 1917, p. 1. The vote to approve the bipartisan committee's plan was 60 to 16.
130. Hoover to Wilson, July 18, 1917.
131. *Congressional Record* 55 (July 20, 1917): 5323, and 55 (July 21, 1917): 5361.
132. Ibid., 55 (July 21, 1917): 5363–64; *New York Herald*, July 22, 1917, section I, part II, p. 1; *New York Times*, July 22, 1917, section I, pp. 1, 4.
133. *Congressional Record* 55 (July 21, 1917): 5367.
134. Ibid.: 5365.
135. Ibid.: 5367. Senator Gore was chairman of the Senate agriculture committee. Because he had opposed the original Lever bill, he had turned its floor management over to the committee's ranking Democrat (after himself), George Chamberlain. This did not prevent Gore from leading the Senate delegation to conference after the Senate (including Gore) voted to adopt its own version of the food control measure. As chairman of the agriculture committee, Gore was evidently entitled to head the Senate conferees.
136. Hoover to Woodrow Wilson, July 25, 1917, General Accessions—U.S. Food Administration, HHPL.
137. *Washington Post*, July 17, 1917, p. 2; *Weekly Northwestern Miller* 111 (August 1, 1917): 331.
138. Memorandum, July 6, 1917, USFA Papers, Box 64.
139. Will Irwin, "The Autocrat of the Dinner Table," *Saturday Evening Post* 189 (June 23, 1917): 26, 54, 56–58, 61.
140. David Lawrence, "Hoover Comes to Town," New York *Evening Post Magazine*, July 21, 1917, reprinted in part in *Engineering and Mining Journal* 104 (August 11, 1917): 274–75.
141. Vernon Kellogg, "The Authentic Story of Belgian Relief," *World's Work* 34 (June 1917): 169–76; Hugh Gibson, "Herbert C. Hoover," *Century* 94 (August 1917): 508–17.
142. Richard B. Watrous in *Weekly Northwestern Miller* 111 (July 25, 1917): 268.
143. Louis D. Brandeis to Norman Hapgood, July 21, 1917, printed in Melvin I. Urofsky and David W. Levy, eds., *Letters of Louis D. Brandeis*, vol. 4 (1916–21): *Mr. Justice Brandeis* (Albany, N.Y., 1975), p. 300.
144. Hoover to Woodrow Wilson, July 22, 1917, USFA Papers, Box 1. The signed original of this letter is not in the Wilson Papers and has not been found. Possibly Hoover did not send it.
145. Hoover to Woodrow Wilson, July 22, 1917, enclosed with Hoover to Joseph P. Tumulty, July 23, 1917, USFA Papers, Box 1. Like the document cited in the preceding note, the signed original of this letter is not in the Wilson Papers and has not been found. Nor has the original cover letter to Tumulty been located. It seems likely, however, that Hoover did send this letter to the President. In any case, this letter and the one cited earlier obviously expressed Hoover's opposition to tripartite administration of food control.
146. Ibid.
147. William Phillips diary, July 23, 1917, William Phillips Papers, Houghton Library, Harvard University.
148. U.S. Food Administration memorandum for a Mr. W. M. P. Herrick, July 26, 1917, USFA Papers, Box 45.
149. *New York Times*, July 28, 1917, p. 1.
150. Woodrow Wilson to Daniel Moreau Barringer, July 24, 1917, Wilson Papers.

151. Wilson to Senator Robert Owen, July 23, 1917, Wilson Papers; Wilson to Representative Asbury F. Lever, July 23, 1917, printed in Link et al., eds., *The Papers of Woodrow Wilson*, vol. 43, p. 245.
152. Wilson to Lever, July 23, 1917.
153. Richard B. Watrous, "The Food Control Tangle," *Weekly Northwestern Miller* 111 (July 25, 1917): 246. Hoover may have encouraged this speculation; it was obviously in his interest to do so. In Watrous he would have had a sympathetic ally for planting such a story. Watrous's dispatches from Washington in this period were very pro-Hoover. Watrous's editor and boss, William C. Edgar, was a friend of Hoover, an ardent Hoover booster, and a man much involved in fashioning the Food Administration's plans for regulation of the grain milling industry.
154. Hoover to Representative Asbury F. Lever, July 24 and 25, 1917, USFA Papers, Box 96. A copy of the latter document was enclosed with Hoover to Joseph P. Tumulty, July 25, 1917, Wilson Papers.
155. Hoover to Representative John R. Farr, July 26, 1917, Public Statements File, Hoover Papers.
156. Hoover to Ralph Pulitzer, July 21, 1917, USFA Papers, Box 187.
157. *Congressional Record* 55 (July 24, 1917): 5435–36.
158. Ibid., 55 (July 25, 1917): 5473–74. The key vote—to stop debate on the special rule—was 169–101. The House then adopted the rule by a nearly unanimous voice vote. Adoption of this rule prevented separate House votes on any of the Senate's amendments. The House conferees thus went to conference without any binding or confining instructions—a victory for the Wilson administration's supporters.
159. *Washington Post*, July 27, 1917, p. 2.
160. For detailed coverage, see the *New York Herald*, *New York Times*, and *Washington Post* for this period.
161. *New York Herald*, July 30, 1917, p. 9.
162. Ibid., July 31, 1917, p. 10; *New York Times*, July 31, 1917, p. 1; *Washington Post*, July 31, 1917, p. 1.
163. Ibid.
164. *New York Times*, August 2, 1917, p. 20.
165. *Congressional Record* 55 (August 3, 1917): 5746–48.
166. Ibid.: 5767–68.
167. Ibid.: 5773.
168. Ibid.: 55 (August 4, 1917): 5803. See also Reed's similar remarks in ibid., 55 (August 6, 1917): 5823.
169. The quotations in the text are drawn from Reed's remarks in the *Congressional Record* 55 (August 4, 1917): 5801–6; 55 (August 6, 1917): 5817–28; and 55 (August 8, 1917): 5919–25.
170. *Congressional Record* 55 (August 6, 1917): 5833–34.
171. Hoover to Tumulty, August 8, 1917.
172. Hoover to W. A. M. Goode, August 7, 1917, USFA Papers, Box 134.
173. Hoover to Tumulty, August 8, 1917.
174. Hoover to David F. Houston, August 8, 1917, copy in Wilson Papers; David F. Houston to Hoover, August 13, 1917, copy in USFA Papers, Box 83A.
175. The New York *World*, August 7, 1917, p. 2, for instance, printed an article in two columns, one reciting Senator Reed's accusations and the other listing Hoover's admirable deeds. According to the *World*, "Without Congressional authority Mr. Hoover has been more largely responsible than any other man in the country for the elimination of waste, increased food production and organized conservation. His advance has been followed probably to a greater extent than that of any public official engaged in preparing the United States for war."

176. A New York newspaper referred to the battle over the food control bill as a "Hundred Days' War." See *Literary Digest* 55 (August 18, 1917): 10.
177. *Congressional Record* 55 (August 8, 1917): 5927.
178. Ibid.: 5928.
179. *New York Times*, August 11, 1917, p. 1.
180. Ibid.; Woodrow Wilson, "Executive Order by the President Providing for Organization of United States Food Administration," in Congressional Information Service, *Presidential Executive Orders and Proclamations on Microfiche* (Washington, D.C., 1987). A typewritten copy of the executive order is in "U.S. Food Administration—Executive Order," Pre-Commerce Papers.
181. U.S. Food Administration press release 137, August 10, 1917, USFA Documents; *New York Times*, August 11, 1917, pp. 1, 2.
182. "Never before had such sweeping powers of economic control been granted by Congress to the President." Robert Higgs, *Crisis and Leviathan: Critical Episodes in the Growth of American Government* (New York, 1987), p. 136.
183. According to Representative Gilbert Haugen of Iowa, "conflicting reports as to Mr. Hoover's proposition in fixing the price" of wheat led the Senate to mandate a minimum price of two dollars per bushel. *Congressional Record* 56 (April 18, 1918): 5314. See also Frederic L. Paxson, *American Democracy and the World War*, vol. II: *America at War* (Boston, 1939), pp. 82–83.
184. The full text of the Lever Act is in 40 *United States Statutes at Large* 276–87.
185. *New York Herald*, August 9, 1917, p. 9. See also the press summary in *Literary Digest* 55 (August 18, 1917): 9–10.
186. *New York Times*, August 9, 1917, p. 1; "Food Bill Law at Last," *Independent* 92 (August 15, 1917): 510.
187. Edward M. House diary, July 4, 1917.
188. *New York Herald*, August 9, 1917, p. 10.
189. *Literary Digest* 55 (August 18, 1917): 9.
190. Herbert Hoover, *The Memoirs of Herbert Hoover*, vol. I: *Years of Adventure* (New York, 1951), p. 241.
191. *Wallaces' Farmer* 42 (August 31, 1917): 1176.
192. Walter Hines Page to Hoover, August 14, 1917, "Page, Walter Hines," Pre-Commerce Papers.

CHAPTER 4

1. Binghamton [N.Y.] *Press*, August 14, 1917, copy in Clipping File, HHPL; Mark L. Requa, "Hoover" (typescript, n.d.), p. 5, Mark L. Requa Papers, HI.
2. Requa, "Hoover," p. 5.
3. *Weekly Northwestern Miller* 112 (November 28, 1917): 643.
4. *New York Times*, August 14, 1917, p. 3; U.S. Senate, Committee on Agriculture and Forestry, 65th Congress, 2d Session, *Increased Production of Grain and Meat Products* (Washington, D.C., 1918), pp. 91, 94, 120, 382, 581; Wilfred Eldred, "The Wheat and Flour Trade Under Food Administration Control: 1917–18," *Quarterly Journal of Economics* 33 (November 1918): 14; *The Story of the United States Grain Corporation* (New York, 1920), p. 3. A copy of the latter booklet may be found in "ARA: *Grain Corporation, Story of*," Belgian American Education Foundation Papers, HHPL.
5. Frank M. Surface, *The Grain Trade During the World War* (New York, 1928), p. 20.
6. Ibid., p. 24; Eldred, "Wheat and Flour Trade," pp. 3, 66. According to Eldred the 1917 carryover was 51,078,000 bushels.
7. For example: Hoover remarks to new federal food administrators, September 18, 1917,

Public Statements File, Herbert Hoover Papers, HHPL; Hoover to Walter Hines Page, September 22, 1917, file 1-H, USFA Papers, HI; Hoover address to Potato Association of America, November 9, 1917, Public Statements File, Hoover Papers.

8. U.S. Food Administration press release 138, August 12, 1917, USFA Documents, HHPL; *New York Times*, August 13, 1917, p. 1.
9. Hoover address to the convention of the Chamber of Commerce of the United States, September 19, 1917, Public Statements File, Hoover Papers.
10. Ibid.
11. *New York Times*, September 20, 1917, p. 1. Interestingly, in the retyped text of this speech (cited in note 9 and later included in his Public Statements File), Hoover's words were said to be: "One looming shadow of this war is its drift toward social disruption. . . ." This was an apparent toning down of his remarks as originally delivered and reported by the *Times*. The *Times* headlined its account of the speech: "Hoover Sees Peril of Socialism Here."
12. Hoover remarks to new federal food administrators, September 18, 1917.
13. Résumé of a Hoover address to members of the U.S. Food Administration, October 5, 1917, Public Statements File, Hoover Papers.
14. Hoover address to the Chamber of Commerce convention, September 19, 1917.
15. Résumé of a Hoover address to members of the U.S. Food Administration, October 5, 1917.
16. U.S. Department of Commerce, Bureau of the Census, *Historical Statistics of the United States: Colonial Times to 1970* (Washington, D.C., 1975), Part I, p. 179.
17. Résumé of a Hoover address to members of the U.S. Food Administration, October 5, 1917.
18. Hoover address to the Chamber of Commerce convention, September 19, 1917. See also his remarks to new federal food administrators, September 18, 1917.
19. Hoover address to the Chamber of Commerce convention, September 19, 1917. This was a recurrent theme for Hoover in his early weeks as Food Administrator. In an essay prepared in August, he wrote: "Autocracy finds its strength in its ability to impose organization by force from the top. The essence of democracy consists in the application of the initiative in its own people." Hoover, "Our Duty" (August 1917), Public Statements File, Hoover Papers. In a speech in late September, he asserted: "The difference between democracy and autocracy is a question of whether people can be organized from the bottom up or from the top down." Hoover address to the Committee of Public Safety of Pennsylvania, September 29, 1917, Public Statements File, Hoover Papers.
20. U.S. Food Administration press release 137, August 10, 1917, USFA Documents.
21. Hoover, "America's Grain Trade" (address, April 30, 1918), Public Statements File, Hoover Papers.
22. Hoover remarks to new federal food administrators, September 18, 1917.
23. Alan G. Anderson cable to Royal Commission on Wheat Supplies, May 21, 1917, PRO 30/68/10, PRO; Surface, *Grain Trade*, pp. 37–38, 573–76.
24. Surface, *Grain Trade*, pp. 42–44.
25. Ibid., pp. 42–46, 91–95, 581–87.
26. U.S. Food Administration press release 138, August 12, 1917.
27. Ibid.; *New York Times*, August 13, 1917, pp. 1, 2.
28. Woodrow Wilson, executive order, August 14, 1917, printed in J. Reuben Clark, comp., *Emergency Legislation Passed Prior to December, 1917 Dealing with the Control and Taking of Private Property for the Public Use, Benefit, or Welfare* (Washington, D.C., 1918), pp. 174–76.
29. Harold Archer Van Dorn, *Government Owned Corporations* (New York, 1926), p. 83.
30. Wilson executive order, August 14, 1917; Hoover to the Chicago Board of Trade, August 11, 1917, printed in *Commercial and Financial Chronicle* 105 (August 18, 1917): 669.
31. U.S. Food Administration press release 142, August 15, 1917, USFA Documents.
32. Ibid.; Hoover to Woodrow Wilson, August 14, 1917, "Wilson, Woodrow," Pre-Commerce Papers, Hoover Papers.

33. Hoover telegram to J. P. Griffin, August 15, 1917, Chicago Board of Trade Papers, Box 205, University of Illinois, Chicago; *Commercial and Financial Chronicle* 105 (August 18, 1917): 669.
34. In addition to guaranteeing a minimum price for government purchases of wheat grown in 1918, the Lever Act authorized the President to fix a "reasonable guaranteed" price for wheat (in order to assure producers a "reasonable profit") whenever he found that an emergency existed "requiring stimulation of the production of wheat." 40 *United States Statutes at Large* 281. This, however, could not apply to the 1917 crop, which was already grown. It was obviously too late for the government to stimulate production of this crop. See Secretary of Agriculture David Houston to Herbert Hoover, August 14, 1917, USFA Papers, Box 83A.
35. Hoover testimony, June 19, 1917, in U.S. Congress, Senate, Committee on Agriculture and Forestry, 65th Congress, 1st Session, *Control and Distribution of Food Supplies* (Washington, D.C., 1917), p. 11.
36. See Hoover to Senator Asle J. Gronna, July 25, 1917, copy in Woodrow Wilson Papers, LC; Gronna to Hoover, July 27, 1917, USFA Papers, Box 96.
37. Hoover testimony, May 8, 1917, in U.S. Congress, Senate, Committee on Agriculture and Forestry, 65th Congress, 1st Session, *Production and Conservation of Food Supplies* (Washington, D.C., 1917), pp. 379–80; Hoover speech to a group of women in New York City, May 10, 1917, Public Statements File, Herbert Hoover Papers, HHPL.
38. Hoover to Representative Asbury F. Lever, July 25, 1917, copy in Wilson Papers.
39. *New York Times*, July 22, 1917, section I, p. 1.
40. Hoover to Lever, July 25, 1917.
41. It was apparently at Hoover's insistence that the minimum guarantee of $2.00 per bushel was dropped for 1917 wheat. *Congressional Record* 55 (August 13, 1917): 5996. However, as indicated in chapter 3, the Senate insisted on keeping the minimum guarantee for 1918 wheat.
42. See *Increased Production of Grain and Meat Products*, pp. 92–94. According to Senator Gronna at this hearing (held in 1918), it was "pretty generally understood among the members of the [agriculture] committee that the crop of 1917 was not to be interfered with as to price; that we were going to leave that to be fixed by supply and demand, the same as it has always been fixed" (p. 94).
43. U.S. Food Administration press release 58, July 9, 1917, USFA Documents.
44. U.S. Food Administration press release 138, August 12, 1917.
45. See *Story of the United States Grain Corporation*, p. 3.
46. Ibid.
47. For example, farmers were explicitly exempted from the provisions against hoarding. 40 *United States Statutes at Large* 278.
48. U.S. Food Administration press release 138, August 12, 1917.
49. Ibid.
50. Hoover to Woodrow Wilson, July 10, 1917, printed in toto in *New York Times*, July 11, 1917, pp. 1, 18.
51. U.S. Food Administration press release 138, August 12, 1917.
52. L. Margaret Barnett, *British Food Policy During the First World War* (Boston, 1985), pp. 164–70; Kathleen Burk, *Britain, America, and the Sinews of War* (Boston, 1985), pp. 10, 137–38, 147.
53. For the full text of Senator Reed's speech, see *Congressional Record* 55 (August 13, 1917): 5995–98.
54. James A. Reed to the *American Swineherd*, August 15, 1917, copy in Wilson Papers; Hoover to Woodrow Wilson, August 23, 1917, Wilson Papers.
55. Hoover memorandum for Curtis H. Lindley, August 23, 1917, USFA Papers, Box 45.
56. Hoover to Wilson, August 23, 1917.
57. Wilson to Hoover, August 24, 1917, "Wilson, Woodrow," Pre-Commerce Papers.

58. "Minutes of the Committee on Prices, August 17–29th, 1917," entry for August 17, 1917, USFA Papers, Box 187. This document is a bound typescript volume containing the minutes themselves and forty-seven appendices. Unbound copies of the minutes alone can be found in the USFA Documents at HHPL and in file 5HA-C2, RG 4, NARA.
59. One member of the committee dropped out because of illness.
60. A list of the committee members and their affiliations is included in U.S. Food Administration press release 142, August 15, 1917.
61. "Minutes," August 23, 1917.
62. "Minutes," August 17, 1917.
63. "Minutes," August 20, 1917 (and Appendix 1).
64. "Minutes," August 21, 1917; Curtis H. Lindley to Harry A. Garfield, August 22, 1917, USFA Papers, Box 45 (copy also in "Minutes," Appendix 8). It is highly unlikely that Lindley submitted this finding without Hoover's knowledge and consent. Incidentally, the British government announced a bread subsidy for its own populace in July 1917. See *First Report of the Royal Commission on Wheat Supplies* (London, 1921), p. 12. Evidently Hoover was not inclined to imitate the British example.
65. At a Senate agriculture committee hearing in 1918, Gronna declared: "We did not fix any price in the bill for the crop of 1917." Senator Gore immediately added: "And we did not authorize anybody else to do it." *Increased Production of Grain and Meat Products*, p. 93.
66. Ibid., pp. 93–94.
67. Ibid., p. 92.
68. Representative George M. Young to Morton Page, August 20, 1917, printed in *New York Times*, August 26, 1917, section I, p. 3.
69. *New York Times*, August 30, 1917, p. 1.
70. Hoover to Wilson, August 23, 1917.
71. Hoover to the editor of the *Fargo Forum*, n.d., printed in *New York Times*, August 26, 1917, section I, p. 3.
72. *New York Times*, August 30, 1917, p. 1; *Commercial and Financial Chronicle* 105 (September 1, 1917): 867.
73. *Wallaces' Farmer* 42 (August 24, 1917): 1152.
74. "Minutes," August 22, 1917, and Appendix 7A; *Commercial and Financial Chronicle* 105 (September 1, 1917): 865.
75. "Minutes," August 23. According to the minutes, Hoover made his statements in response to "questions asked at the request of members of the Committee."
76. Hoover estimate of probable world wheat surplus, n.d., in "Minutes," Appendix 25. Hoover's memorandum was distributed to the fair price committee on August 28. "Minutes," August 28, 1917.
77. "Minutes," August 28, 1917.
78. "Minutes," August 29, 1917. For reports on a deadlock in the committee, see *New York Times*, August 30, 1917, p. 1, and *Washington Post*, August 30, 1917, p. 3.
79. *New York Times*, August 30, 1917, pp. 1, 9; *Congressional Record* 56 (July 1, 1918): 8555.
80. *New York Times*, August 30, 1917, pp. 1, 9. The *Times* reported it this way: "It was understood tonight [August 29] that Mr. Wilson was determined to have the price of wheat fixed on a basis which seemed to him a fair one before another twenty-four hours, and that he had decided to call on the members of the commission for a report of their deliberations so that he might be in a better situation to judge the merits of the arguments which had been placed before him."
81. "Minutes," August 29, 1917.
82. "Minutes," August 30, 1917.
83. Eugene Funk recalled this episode in a speech in 1919. See *Report of the Fourth Annual Meeting of the Illinois Agricultural Association, Peoria, Illinois, January 21 and 22, 1919*, pp. 23–24, copy at U.S. Department of Agriculture, National Agricultural Library, Beltsville, Maryland.

84. Ibid., p. 24; "Minutes," August 30, 1917, and Appendix 47.
85. *New York Times*, August 31, 1917, pp. 1, 3.
86. Ibid., p. 1; Arthur S. Link et al., eds., *The Papers of Woodrow Wilson*, vol. 44 (Princeton, N.J., 1983), pp. 89–90.
87. "Minutes," August 24, 1917, and Appendices 2, 12A, and 23; Julius H. Barnes to Hoover, August 27, 1917, USFA Papers, Box 245; Tom G. Hall, "Cheap Bread from Dear Wheat: Herbert Hoover, The Wilson Administration, and the Management of Wheat Prices, 1916–1920" (Ph.D. dissertation, University of California at Davis, 1970), pp. 77–79.
88. Hall, "Cheap Bread," p. 79; "Minutes," Appendix 47; *New York Times*, August 31, 1917, p. 3.
89. *Increased Production of Grain and Meat Products*, pp. 91, 94, 120, 581; *Congressional Record* 56 (March 18, 1918): 3638.
90. *Increased Production of Grain and Meat Products*, p. 581.
91. Quoted in Robert L. Morlan, *Political Prairie Fire: The Nonpartisan League, 1915–1922* (Minneapolis, 1955), p. 141.
92. The price differential schedule is printed in Surface, *Grain Trade*, p. 72.
93. *Increased Production of Grain and Meat Products*, p. 581.
94. It was a cry that persisted into the 1928 election campaign in which Hoover was a candidate for President. See, for example, John A. Simpson to Pat Hurley, February 20, 1928, John A. Simpson Collection, Box 2, Western History Collections, University of Oklahoma Library.
95. Edgar Rickard to Hoover, July 8, 1924, USFA Papers, Box 187; Harry A. Garfield to Rickard, July 30, 1924, USFA Papers, Box 157; *New York Times*, October 29, 1927, p. 16; *Literary Digest* 95 (November 12, 1927): 11.
96. Woodrow Wilson statement to the press, August 30, 1917, printed in *New York Times*, August 31, 1917, p. 1; Hoover to Joseph P. Tumulty, September 12, 1917, Wilson Papers; Hoover to A. W. Fulton, September 12, 1917, copy in "Grain Corporation, Book I," file 10-A7, Box 470, RG 4, NARA.
97. This was not a new claim by Hoover. In the Food Administration's press release of August 12, 1917, cited above, he warned that the export price of American wheat, "if not controlled, will be subject to almost a single will of the foreign purchaser" (who presumably would drive the price down). See also Hoover to Wilson, July 10, 1917.
98. Hoover, "Foreword" to Frank M. Surface, *The Stabilization of the Price of Wheat During the War and Its Effect Upon the Returns to the Producer* (Washington, D.C., 1925), pp. 7–8; Hoover to Evelyn Harris, February 10, 1925, "Harris, Evelyn," Commerce Papers, Hoover Papers.
99. Hoover, "Foreword," p. 8.
100. Hoover to Harris, February 10, 1925.
101. Hoover, "Foreword," p. 8.
102. Ibid.
103. Hoover to Harris, February 10, 1925.
104. Hoover to Julius H. Barnes, October 13, 1924, USFA Papers, Box 157.
105. Ibid. I have found no document to support Hoover's contention about the Allies. Nor has another historian who has studied the subject; see Hall, "Cheap Bread," p. 70.
106. Henry C. Wallace to Charles McCarthy, August 22, 1917, Box 950, file 26H-A1, RG 4, NARA. According to Wallace, the U.S. government's own "food control agitation" had "caused a very sudden drop in grain prices."
107. *Wallaces' Farmer* 42 (September 7, 1917): 1200. See also G. F. Warren, "Some Purposes and Results of Price Fixing," *American Economic Review* 9, Supplement (March 1919): 239–40. Warren, a noted agricultural economist, stated: "Had prices [for wheat] not been fixed, it is probable that the price would have gone to $3." The chairman of the Board of Grain Supervisors for Canada reached a similar conclusion. In 1920 he wrote: "Throughout the year 1917 . . . had the price of wheat in North America not been fixed by the Canadian

and American governments it would have risen to a degree that would have placed an intolerable burden upon consumers in Canada, Great Britain and the United States." He added that this policy was "purely in the interest of consumers," although he also contended that the price for wheat was fixed high enough properly to compensate wheat farmers. [Robert A. Magill], "Operations of the Board of Grain Supervisors for Canada" (typescript, ca. March 17, 1920), file 14128, vol. 838, RG 20: Department of Trade and Commerce, National Archives of Canada.

108. Hoover, "America's Grain Trade," cited in note 21.

109. *Story of the United States Grain Corporation*, p. 8.

110. Hoover's principal "point man" on this issue in the 1920s was Frank M. Surface, an economist for the Grain Corporation. His publications included the volume on wheat price stabilization (note 98) and *The Grain Trade During the World War* (note 5), a 679-page tome that is pro-Hoover on every disputed point. Surface's papers at HI contain interesting correspondence pertaining to the preparation of these defenses, including evidence that Hoover was intimately involved in formulating and phrasing key arguments. See especially Surface to Edward M. Flesh, September 4 and October 17, 1924; Flesh to Surface, October 21, 1924; Julius H. Barnes to Alonzo E. Taylor, October 28, 1924; Surface to Flesh, October 29, 1924; Surface to Hoover, October 31, 1924; Flesh to Surface, November 1, 1924; Surface to Flesh, November 28, December 11, 1924; Surface to Flesh, January 29, March 2, July 15, 1925; Surface to H. H. Fisher, December 29, 1926; and Surface to Flesh, January 6, 1927. All in Surface Papers.

Surface's book on wheat price stabilization was written in response to a U.S. Senate resolution in 1924 ordering an inquiry into the government's wheat stabilization policies in World War I. When the book was published in May 1925, Hoover personally wrote the press release, asserting among other things that the "fair price determination" of 1917 was undertaken "solely to protect the American farmer," who otherwise would have received only $1.50 per bushel for his crop. This press release may be found in "Agriculture, 1921–1927," Misrepresentations File, Hoover Papers.

Hoover was very sensitive in the 1920s to what he at one point called "the wheat lie"—the charge that he himself had set the wartime price of wheat. When invited to write an article on the U.S. Food Administration in 1924, he asked a former employee to prepare it and had a secretary suggest to him "that you be careful to emphasize the fact that the Food Administration did not, at any time, fix the price of wheat." Harold Phelps Stokes to William C. Mullendore, May 29, 1924, file 1-H, USFA Papers. See also Hoover to Harry A. Garfield, November 28, 1927, Harry A. Garfield Papers, Box 88, LC.

111. Surface to Flesh, March 2, 1925. The report referred to in the text is Surface's *Stabilization of the Price of Wheat. . . .*

112. *Commercial and Financial Chronicle* 105 (September 8, 1917): 959; Surface, *Grain Trade*, p. 76.

113. Eldred, "Wheat and Flour Control," pp. 18–19; Hoover to Julius H. Barnes, October 27, 1917, USFA Papers, Box 245.

114. 40 *United States Statutes at Large* 276.

115. Hoover letter to the millers of the United States, August 29, 1917, file 1H-A8, RG 4, NARA.

116. Theoretically, at least, this could happen if the war ended during the term of the contract and the pent-up wheat surpluses in the southern hemisphere flooded onto the market.

117. Hoover to the millers, August 29, 1917; U.S. Food Administration, Milling Division, "Rules and Regulations for Flour Milling Industry" (August 24, 1917), copy in file 1H-A8, RG 4, NARA; form of agreement between Hoover and flour millers, n.d., file 1H-A8, RG 4, NARA; form of agreement between Food Administration Grain Corporation and flour millers, n.d., file 1H-A8, RG 4, NARA; Hoover to Representative W. A. Ayres, September 22, 1917, USFA Papers, Box 96; Eldred, "Wheat and Flour Trade," p. 18;

United States Grain Corporation, *Book of Information* (August 23, 1919 version), p. 25, copy in Box 1, file 201-A1, RG 5, NARA; *Story of the United States Grain Corporation*, pp. 4–5; Surface, *Grain Trade*, pp. 97–99, 551–52; William C. Mullendore, *History of the United States Food Administration, 1917–1919* (Stanford, Calif., 1941), pp. 133–34.

118. Eldred, "Wheat and Flour Trade," p. 25; *Story of the United States Grain Corporation*, pp. 4–5; Surface, *Stabilization of the Price of Wheat*, p. 15; Surface, *Grain Grade*, pp. 77, 79, 548–49; Mullendore, *History*, pp. 132–34; Hall, "Cheap Bread," p. 89.
119. Hoover wanted the plan to take effect by September 10, 1917. Hoover to the millers, August 29, 1917.
120. Surface, *Grain Trade*, pp. 97–98; Murray R. Benedict, *Farm Policies of the United States, 1790–1950* (New York, 1953), p. 163.
121. Eldred, "Wheat and Flour Trade," p. 28; Surface, *Grain Trade*, p. 79; Mullendore, *History*, p. 135.
122. Surface, *Grain Trade*, pp. 106–07. According to *Story of the United States Grain Corporation*, this problem occurred "in only a few isolated localities" (p. 7).
123. Surface, *Grain Trade*, pp. 98–100.
124. Hoover to Barnes, October 27, 1917. In the words of Wilfred Eldred, "without such voluntary agreements by the mills to observe the government fair wheat price," Hoover's "whole plan of regulation, both as to wheat prices and flour prices, would have fallen through, for there was nothing in the law to prevent a mill from paying any price for wheat that it chose." Eldred, "Wheat and Flour Trade," p. 22.
125. Eldred, "Wheat and Flour Trade," p. 27.
126. Julius H. Barnes to Hoover, December 29, 1917, USFA Papers, Box 246.
127. *Story of the United States Grain Corporation*, p. 7.
128. His voluntary agreements with the mills set limits on their profit margins but did not directly dictate their prices. *New York Times*, August 31, 1917, p. 3; U.S. Food Administration Milling Division, "Rules and Regulations"; Mullendore, *History*, p. 134.
129. Eldred, "Wheat and Flour Trade," pp. 22–23; *Story of the United States Grain Corporation*, p. 5; Surface, *Grain Trade*, p. 98; Albert N. Merritt, *War Time Control of Distribution of Foods* (New York, 1920), p. 29. Thus while only "agreement" mills were restricted as to the price they paid for wheat, all mills were regulated as to their allowable profits. Flour wholesalers and jobbers were also licensed. No middleman who could be regulated escaped.
130. Senator James A. Reed in *Congressional Record* 69 (May 21, 1928): 9291.
131. *New York Times*, August 26, 1917, section I, p. 3; John O'Hara Cosgrave to Hoover, August 29, 1917, USFA Papers, Box 187.
132. Hoover to Tumulty, September 12, 1917.
133. Eldred, "Wheat and Flour Trade," p. 25.
134. George Winston Smith, "New Mexico's Wartime Food Problems, 1917–1918: A Case Study in Emergency Administration," *New Mexico Historical Review* 19 (January 1944): 22.
135. Warren, "Some Purposes and Results of Price Fixing," p. 239.
136. Theodore B. Wilcox telegram to Hoover, September 11, 1917, enclosed with Hoover to Woodrow Wilson, September 12, 1917, Wilson Papers; Julius H. Barnes to Hoover, September 6 and 12, 1917, USFA Papers, Box 245; Eldred, "Wheat and Flour Trade," pp. 30–31; Surface, *Grain Trade*, pp. 269–71.
137. J. P. Griffin to Hoover, August 31, 1917, Chicago Board of Trade Papers, Box 107; Griffin to Hoover, September 12, 1917, Chicago Board of Trade Papers, Box 205.
138. Hoover telegram to Julius H. Barnes, September 14, 1917; Barnes telegram to Hoover, September 17, 1917. Both in USFA Papers, Box 245.
139. Cosgrave to Hoover, August 29, 1917. Cosgrave was relaying Cobb's advice to Hoover.
140. Hoover to Tumulty, September 12, 1917.
141. Ibid.

142. Hoover draft of message to Barnes, September 14, 1917, USFA Papers, Box 245.
143. Hoover telegram to Barnes, September 14, 1917. The Equity Cooperative Exchange was evidently "the first cooperative terminal grain marketing agency of account in the United States." In 1917 it was embroiled in the vehement political battles between radical farmers and their enemies in Minnesota and North Dakota. See Theodore Saloutos, "The Rise of the Equity Cooperative Exchange," *Mississippi Valley Historical Review* 32 (June 1945): 31–62; Harry A. Garfield, "Memorandum of Conversation with Representative George M. Young of North Dakota, August 9 [1917]," Harry A. Garfield Papers, Box 110, LC.
144. Barnes to Hoover, September 15, 1917, USFA Papers, Box 245. Barnes told Hoover bluntly that he was "overly afraid" of the Nonpartisan League.
145. Barnes telegram to Hoover, September 17, 1917, USFA Papers, Box 245.
146. Hoover's negotiations with his critics in August and September 1917 can be traced in the correspondence files for these months in the USFA Papers, Box 245. In general, Hoover's approach was, in Barnes's words, "to avoid friction at all points possible without conceding a principle." Barnes to Hoover, September 20, 1917. But Hoover could be tough also. When officials of the Chicago Board of Trade apparently suggested that Hoover's grain policy was failing (or sure to fail), he told Barnes: "I think it might be desirable to give them [the Board of Trade] a hint that their continued innuendo of failure of the grain plan will certainly strengthen the view of the country as to its necessity and their opposition would cement it onto our national life forever." Hoover to Barnes, September 17, 1917.
147. Hoover to Joseph P. Tumulty, September 18, 1917, Wilson Papers; Link et al., eds., *Papers of Woodrow Wilson*, vol. 44, p. 215, note 2.
148. U.S. Food Administration press release 256, September 22, 1917, USFA Documents; Hoover to Edward N. Hurley, September 22, 1917, USFA Papers, Box 165; Eldred, "Wheat and Flour Prices," p. 31; Surface, *Grain Trade*, pp. 72–74. To help negate the effect of this price hike, Hoover persuaded the U.S. Shipping Board to reduce freight rates on wheat and flour hauled by sea from Pacific ports. This, of course, made it more attractive to market wheat locally and ship it by sea than to send it overland by rail to Chicago. Hence the arrangement removed some of the burden on the heavily used railroads between Chicago and the Pacific Northwest.

    Hoover did not admit that he had yielded to political pressure. The Food Administration's press release declared that the price revision was made possible by the "assurance of overseas transport for Pacific Northwest grain"—an assurance made by the Food Administration with "the assistance of the Shipping Board."
149. "Farmers are not shipping their wheat with their accustomed readiness." *New York Times*, September 14, 1917, p. 3.
150. Ibid.
151. Ibid., September 15, 1917, p. 13.
152. Edgar Rickard to Julius H. Barnes, September 12, 1917, USFA Papers, Box 245; minutes of the Exports Administrative Board, September 12, 1917, RG 182, NARA.
153. U.S. Food Administration statement, September 14, 1917, printed in *Commercial and Financial Chronicle* 105 (September 22, 1917): 1165.
154. *New York Times*, September 15, 1917, p. 13.
155. Ibid., September 16, 1917, section I, p. 4.
156. Ibid., September 20, 1917, p. 6.
157. Barnes telegram to Hoover, September 17, 1917.
158. *Official Bulletin* 1 (September 21, 1917): 1. This was the daily publication of the U.S. government's Committee on Public Information between 1917 and 1919.
159. *New York Times*, September 25, 1917, p. 10.
160. Smith, "New Mexico's Wartime Food Problems," p. 22; Ralph C. Ely to Hoover, September 13, 1917, and [John Hallowell?] to Ely, September 18, 1917, both in USFA Papers, Box 245.

161. Hoover to Page, September 22, 1917.
162. Hoover to Representative W. A. Ayres, September 22, 1917.
163. Hoover to Tumulty, September 12, 1917; Hoover address to Chamber of Commerce convention, September 19, 1917.
164. Hoover address to the Potato Association of America, November 9, 1917.
165. Hoover address to the Chamber of Commerce convention, September 19, 1917; Hoover address to the Committee of Public Safety of Pennsylvania, September 29, 1917.
166. Hoover address to the Committee of Public Safety of Pennsylvania, September 29, 1917.
167. Hoover to George B. Ross, October 13, 1917, in "Grain Corporation, Book I." After surveying wheat statistics from Ohio, Julius Barnes told Hoover: "It is very evident that our problem is to get the farmers marketing on a sufficient scale in all sections." Barnes to Hoover, October 5, 1917, USFA Papers, Box 245.
168. Harry J. Waters to Hoover, October 8, 1917, in "Grain Corporation, Book I"; Charles McCarthy to Lewis L. Strauss, October 11, 1917, Charles McCarthy Papers, Box 15, State Historical Society of Wisconsin; Barnes to Hoover, October 12, 1917, USFA Papers, Box 245; R. M. McClintock to Victor Murdock, October 19 and November 6, 1917, Victor Murdock Papers, Box 60, LC; McClintock to Murdock, December 6, 1917, Murdock Papers, Box 61.
169. McCarthy to Strauss, October 11, 1917.
170. Ibid.; Hoover to Henry J. Waters, October 13, 1917, in "Grain Corporation, Book I."
171. Hoover to Waters, October 13, 1917.
172. *New York Times*, October 13, 1917, p. 16.
173. Hoover to Ross, October 13, 1917; Hoover to the Congress of the United States, October 22, 1917, printed in U.S. Congress, House of Representatives, 65th Congress, 2d Session, Document No. 890: *Purchases and Disbursements Made by the United States Food Administration and the United States Fuel Administration: Letters from the United States Food Administrator. . . .* (Washington, D.C., 1918), p. 21. In the latter document, Hoover asserted that "the movement of wheat from the farms" had been "smaller than usual" for "unusual reasons." Among them: unusually large corn and oats crops, "the stabilization of the wheat price, and the assurance that the market would not suffer disastrous depression, relieving them of the necessity of neglecting other farm work for the marketing of the secured wheat crop." Because the value of wheat was assured, said Hoover, farmers devoted themselves to marketing crops that were "exposed to price depression, like rye and barley and oats." He did not mention farmers' anger at the wheat price as a motivator of their behavior.
174. Eldred, "Wheat and Flour Trade," p. 34. Surface, *Grain Trade*, had a different—but also reassuring—explanation for the farmers' slowness in marketing: they had "no previous experience with Government price stabilization and they were not sure just how it would operate" (p. 317).
175. Hoover to Barnes, October 27, 1917. At the beginning of November the head of the British government's wheat-purchasing agency in the United States reported to London that the amount of wheat that American farmers were bringing to market was far below expectations—in fact, only about 60 percent of the amount marketed in a comparable period in 1916. H. T. Robson, report on the Wheat Export Company, n.d. (ca. November 2, 1917), F/210/1, David Lloyd George Papers, House of Lords Record Office, London.
176. *Wallaces' Farmer* 42 (October 12, 1917): 1377.
177. Hoover to Barnes, October 18, 1917, in "Grain Corporation, Book I" (cited in note 96).
178. *New York Times*, October 19, 1917, pp. 1, 9.
179. Hoover to Barnes, October 11, 1917, in "Grain Corporation, Book I."
180. Hoover to Oscar T. Crosby, October 11, 1917, in ibid.
181. Hoover to Crosby (plus enclosure), October 23, 1917, in ibid.; Surface, *Grain Trade*, p. 278; Hall, "Cheap Bread," pp. 100–03.
182. Hoover to Waters, October 13, 1917. To another official, Hoover wrote that the imports

from Canada "will enable us to assure the supplies in this country even against any shortage in wheat offerings" and "will also enable us to keep our mills employed to a high degree." Hoover to Crosby, October 11, 1917.

183. Barnes to Hoover, October 19 and 23, 1917, USFA Papers, Box 245.
184. *Official Bulletin* 1 (October 25, 1917): 2; *New York Times*, October 25, 1917, p. 7.
185. Hoover to Barnes, October 27, 1917.
186. *New York Times*, October 19, 1917, p. 9.
187. Hoover to Waters, October 13, 1917.
188. Hoover to Barnes, October 27, 1917.
189. Ibid.
190. *New York Times*, October 31, 1917, p. 22; *Weekly Northwestern Miller* 112 (October 31, 1917): 341. This was an extension of an earlier order requiring only mills with a capacity above one hundred barrels a day to obtain a license. Now the small mills, too, became subject to regulation.
191. *New York Times*, November 25, 1917, section I, p. 19.
192. Eldred, "Wheat and Flour Trade," p. 34, asserts that total farm marketings of wheat between September 6 and December 29, 1917, were above normal. Surface, *Grain Trade*, p. 317, says that marketings in the fall of 1917 were "not far below the percentage of the crop normally marketed in that period of the year." As early as October 29, Barnes reported that supplies of wheat in country elevators were "running up enough to reassure us as to available stocks of some kind for winter use." Barnes to Hoover, October 29, 1917, USFA Papers, Box 245.
193. The other 60 percent was baked at home. U.S. Food Administration press release 450, November 11, 1917, USFA Documents.
194. Ibid.
195. Mullendore, *History*, p. 159.
196. *New York Times*, September 1, 1917, p. 1.
197. Ibid., October 12, 1917, p. 12, and October 21, 1917, section I, p. 12.
198. Hoover to Woodrow Wilson, August 31, 1917, USFA Papers, Box 1; Mullendore, *History*, p. 159.
199. Mullendore, *History*, p. 160.
200. Hoover to Wilson, November 6, 1917, Wilson Papers; Wilson proclamation, November 7, 1917, printed in *New York Times*, November 13, 1917, p. 6.
201. Mullendore, *History*, p. 161.
202. Merritt, *War Time Control of Distribution of Foods*, p. 65; Mullendore, *History*, p. 161.
203. U.S. Food Administration press release 450, November 11, 1917, USFA Documents; U.S. Food Administration press release 455, November 13, 1917, USFA Documents; *New York Times*, November 12, 1917, pp. 1, 20, November 13, 1917, p. 6, and November 14, 1917, p. 16.
204. Hoover to Wilson, November 6, 1917.
205. U.S. Food Administration press release 470, November 26, 1917, USFA Documents; *Official Bulletin* 1 (November 28, 1917): 10. See also Hoover to Woodrow Wilson, November 15, 1917, Wilson Papers, for a similarly glowing assessment of the Food Administration's grain / flour / bread control. According to Hoover, "speculation and extortionate profits" had been completely eliminated.
206. U.S. Food Administration statement on sugar (prepared for release on September 30, 1917), enclosed with George M. Rolph to the chief of the Latin American Division of the Department of State, September 27, 1917, and printed in United States, Department of State, *Papers Relating to the Foreign Relations of the United States, 1918* (Washington, D.C., 1930), pp. 340–43 (hereinafter cited as *FRUS, 1918*).
207. Ibid.; Roy G. Blakey, "Sugar Prices and Distribution Under Food Control," *Quarterly Journal of Economics* 32 (August 1918): 567–73; Joshua Bernhardt, *Government Control of the Sugar Industry in the United States* (New York, 1920), pp. 3–8; Simon Litman, *Prices and*

Price Control in Great Britain and the United States During the World War (New York, 1920), pp. 237–38; Merritt, *War Time Control of Distribution of Foods*, pp. 8–9; Van Dorn, *Government Owned Corporations*, p. 172; Mullendore, *History*, pp. 167–69.

208. Hoover testimony before the Committee on Agriculture, U.S. House of Representatives, May 7, 1917, typescript copy, p. 25, Congressional series, Box 1, folder 6, Asbury F. Lever Papers, Special Collections, Clemson University Libraries, Clemson, South Carolina.
209. Hoover testimony, May 9, 1917, in *Production and Conservation of Food Supplies* (cited in note 37), p. 413.
210. Ibid.
211. Hoover to Asbury F. Lever, June 2, 1917, USFA Papers, Box 96.
212. Hoover testimony, June 19, 1917 (cited in note 35), p. 16.
213. *New York Times*, June 5, 1917, p. 14.
214. Hoover to Woodrow Wilson, August 22, 1917, file 10H-A7, Box 470, RG 4, NARA; Blakey, "Sugar Prices and Distribution," p. 574; Litman, *Prices and Price Control*, p. 239; Hoover testimony, January 2, 1918, in U.S. Congress, Senate, Committee on Manufactures, 65th Congress, 2d Session, *Shortage of Sugar* (Washington, D.C., 1918), p. 589. Section 11 of the Lever Act authorized the President (and thus by delegation Hoover) to buy, store, and sell wheat, flour, meal, beans, and potatoes. It named no other commodities. 40 *United States Statutes at Large* 279. Thus so far as sugar was concerned, Hoover's power was limited to control of profits and wasteful practices, not prices. Hoover knew this; see Hoover to Wilson, August 22, 1917.
215. *Commercial and Financial Chronicle* 105 (August 18, 1917): 669–70.
216. Mullendore, *History*, p. 169.
217. *New York Times*, September 16, 1917, section I, p. 1.
218. Hoover to Wilson, August 22, 1917.
219. Ibid.
220. Ibid; Wilson to Hoover, August 23, 1917, file 10H-A7, Box 470, RG 4, NARA.
221. Thomas W. Gregory to Woodrow Wilson, August 23, 1917, Wilson Papers; Gregory to Hoover, August 23, 1917 (plus enclosure), file 1H-A3, RG 4, NARA. The italicized words quoted in the text were underlined by Gregory himself in his letter to President Wilson.
222. George M. Rolph testimony, December 20, 1917, in *Shortage of Sugar*, pp. 334–35.
223. U.S. Food Administration press release 164, August 26, 1917, USFA Documents; *New York Times*, August 27, 1917, pp. 1, 3.
224. *New York Times*, September 13, 1917, p. 18.
225. Ibid.
226. U.S. Food Administration press release 231, September 17, 1917, USFA Documents.
227. Not long after this, beet sugar farmers refused to sell their crop to the sugar companies because the farmers "felt they were not receiving a proper price." Mullendore, *History*, p. 175. See also Blakey, "Sugar Prices and Distribution," p. 574; Bernhardt, *Government Control of the Sugar Industry*, pp. 16–17.
228. U.S. Food Administration press release 231, September 17, 1917.
229. The price was set at a level "to permit the highest cost producer to continue in business, thus assuring the maintenance of a maximum production." Litman, *Prices and Price Control*, p. 239.
230. U.S. Food Administration press release 244, September 20, 1917, USFA Documents.
231. Cane sugar basis, at seaboard refining points.
232. All beet sugar, that is, produced by signers of the voluntary contract with the Food Administration. However, all beet sugar producers in the country did sign. *Official Bulletin* 1 (September 21, 1917): 2.
233. The text of this contract is printed in Bernhardt, *Government Control of the Sugar Industry*, pp. 155–60. Signed originals are preserved in file 1H-A12, RG 4, NARA. For more details

about the government's implementation of its agreement, see Enoch Needham, "Control of the Sugar Market During World War I" (typescript, March 1942), pp. 13–19, copy in USFA Papers, Box 60.

234. Hoover cable to Lord Rhondda (the British food controller), August 31, 1917, printed in United States, Department of State, *Papers Relating to the Foreign Relations of the United States, 1917*, Supplement 2: *The World War* (Washington, D.C., 1932), vol. II, p. 655 (hereinafter cited as *FRUS, 1917*, Supplement 2).
235. Louis P. Sheldon cable to Hoover, September 5, 1917, in *FRUS, 1917*, Supplement 2, vol. II, p. 656.
236. Hoover to Rhondda, August 31, 1917; Sheldon to Hoover, September 5, 1917.
237. Hoover to Rhondda, August 31, 1917.
238. U.S. Food Administration press releases 182 and 185, September 5, 1917, USFA Documents; *New York Times*, September 6, 1917, p. 17.
239. U.S. Food Administration press releases 248 and 267, September 20 and 26, 1917, USFA Documents; *Official Bulletin* 1 (September 21, 1917): 2; *New York Times*, September 21, 1917, p. 2.
240. The text of this contract is printed in Bernhardt, *Government Control of the Sugar Industry*, pp. 149–54. Signed originals are preserved in file 1H-A13, RG 4, NARA. See also Bernhardt's discussion on p. 19. The Food Administration created a body known as the American Refiners' Committee to determine the proportionate distribution of imported sugar to the refiners.
241. According to the refiners' contract, the International Sugar Committee was "a Committee of the United States Food Administration."
242. U.S. Food Administration statement on sugar (prepared for release on September 30, 1917).
243. The island's growers had no other market for their harvest. On October 1, 1917, the Cuban government embargoed all exports of sugar, except to the United States and the Allies. Mullendore, *History*, p. 169.
244. Carlos Manuel de Céspedes to Secretary of State Robert Lansing, October 26, 1917, printed in *FRUS, 1918*, pp. 344–45; Hoover to Woodrow Wilson, November 24, 1917, printed in Arthur S. Link et al., eds., *The Papers of Woodrow Wilson*, vol. 45 (Princeton, N.J., 1984), pp. 115–116; Frank Lyon Polk diary, December 17, 1917, Frank Lyon Polk Papers, Manuscripts and Archives, Yale University Library.
245. Céspedes to Lansing, October 26, 1917.
246. Robert Lansing to Céspedes, November 8, 1917, printed in *FRUS, 1918*, pp. 346–47; Frank L. Polk to Hoover, January 14, 1918, in ibid., p. 353.
247. Céspedes to Lansing, November 20, 1917, printed in ibid., pp. 347–49.
248. Hoover to Wilson, November 24, 1917.
249. Wilson to Lansing, November 24, 1917, printed in Link et al., eds., *Papers of Woodrow Wilson*, vol. 45, p. 115.
250. Polk diary, December 17, 1917; Hoover testimony, January 2, 1918, in *Shortage of Sugar*, p. 597; Blakey, "Sugar Prices and Distribution," p. 583.
251. *New York Times*, December 1, 1917, p. 7; *Shortage of Sugar*, pp. 213, 597.
252. For the text of the contract, see Bernhardt, *Government Control of the Sugar Industry*, pp. 136–44. Although signed on December 24, 1917, the contract did not take effect until January 10, 1918. Céspedes to Lansing, January 18, 1918, printed in *FRUS, 1918*, pp. 353–54.
253. U.S. Food Administration press release 300, October 9, 1917, USFA Documents.
254. Ibid.
255. Hoover, "Introduction," in Mullendore, *History*, p. 34.
256. U.S. Food Administration press release 300, October 9, 1917.
257. Ibid.; Hoover, "Introduction," in Mullendore, *History*, p. 19.

258. The text of President Wilson's order, dated October 8, 1917, is printed in *New York Times*, October 11, 1917, pp. 1, 2.
259. U.S. Food Administration press release 300, October 9, 1917.
260. *New York Times*, November 2, 1917, p. 11.
261. Mullendore, *History*, p. 200.
262. U.S. Food Administration press release 420, November 3, 1917, USFA Documents; *New York Times*, November 4, 1917, section I, p. 17.
263. For a complete list of these rules, see Merritt, *War Time Control of Distribution of Foods*, pp. 30–33.
264. U.S. Food Administration press release 420, November 3, 1917.
265. Ibid.
266. Merritt, *War Time Control of Distribution of Foods*, pp. 33, 38–40; U.S. Food Administration press release 367, October 27, 1917, USFA Documents.
267. Merritt, *War Time Control of Distribution of Foods*, p. 40.
268. Hoover to Woodrow Wilson, November 26, 1917, Wilson Papers; Wilson to Hoover, November 27, 1917, "Wilson, Woodrow," Pre-Commerce Papers; Wilson executive order, November 27, 1917, printed in *Official Bulletin* 1 (November 30, 1917): 1.
269. Hoover to Wilson, November 26, 1917.
270. Merritt, *War Time Control of Distribution of Foods*, pp. 37–38.
271. Ibid., p. 44; Mullendore, *History*, p. 216; 40 *United States Statutes at Large* 278; *New York Times*, October 19, 1917, p. 1.
272. Hoover to Edwin W. Kemmerer, October 8, 1942, "Kemmerer, Edwin, W., " Post-Presidential Individual File, Hoover Papers.
273. *Official Bulletin* 1 (October 19, 1917): 7. Specifically, the grocers pledged to adopt the "cost basis" rule of profit and to urge their brethren to take only "normal" and "reasonable" margins on the staples they sold.
274. Merritt, *War Time Control of Distribution of Foods*, p. 51.
275. *New York Herald*, September 20, 1917, p. 11.
276. U.S. Food Administration press release 378, October 29, 1917, USFA Documents.
277. *New York Times*, October 19, 1917, p. 1. For an example of such a price list, see *Chicago Tribune*, October 30, 1917, p. 3.
278. Requa, "Hoover," pp. 5–6, 8.
279. U.S. Food Administration press release 378, October 29, 1917; Merritt, *War Time Control of Distribution of Foods*, pp. 46–47.
280. U.S. Food Administration press release 137, August 10, 1917, USFA Documents.

CHAPTER 5

1. Hoover cable to Newton D. Baker, April 15, 1917, file 1-53, RG 48, NARA; "Minutes of the Committee on Prices, August 17–29th, 1917," Appendix 1, USFA Papers, Box 187, HI; Lord Northcliffe cable to Prime Minister Lloyd George, August 25, 1917, F/41/7/14, David Lloyd George Papers, House of Lords Record Office, London.
2. Hoover testimony, June 19, 1917, in U.S. Congress, Senate, Committee on Agriculture and Forestry, 65th Congress, 1st Session, *Control and Distribution of Food Supplies* (Washington, D.C., 1917), p. 12.
3. U.S. Food Administration press release 137, August 10, 1917, USFA Documents, HHPL; *New York Times*, August 11, 1917, p. 1. In mid-September Hoover declared publicly: "We must control exports in such a manner as to protect the supplies of our own people." Hoover address to the convention of the Chamber of Commerce of the United States, September 19, 1917, Public Statements File, Herbert Hoover Papers, HHPL.
4. Walter Hines Page cable 6037 to Secretary of State Robert Lansing, April 19, 1917, file

811.50/5, RG 59, NARA; Lord Robert Cecil cable to Sir Cecil Spring Rice, April 19, 1917, FO 368/1865, PRO; L. Margaret Barnett, *British Food Policy During the First World War* (Boston, 1985), p. 170.

5. Hoover to William G. McAdoo, August 23, 1917, USFA Papers, Box 85; Hoover to the Exports Administrative Board, August 23, 1917, USFA Papers, Box 182.
6. Hoover to the British Minister of Food, enclosed with Sir Cecil Spring Rice cable to the Foreign Office, July 10, 1917, MAF 60/189, PRO; Kathleen Burk, *Britain, America and the Sinews of War, 1914–1918* (Boston, 1985), p. 156.
7. Spring Rice cable to the Foreign Office, July 26, 1917, MAF 60/68, PRO.
8. Spring Rice cable to the Foreign Office, August 16, 1917, MAF 60/189, PRO.
9. Hoover to McAdoo, August 23, 1917. "Up to date," Hoover told McAdoo, "I have been unable to secure any attention in the matter. . . ."
10. Ibid.
11. Hoover cable to Andrew Weir, August 24, 1917, USFA Papers, Box 1.
12. Northcliffe to Lloyd George, August 25, 1917.
13. Foreign Office cable to Spring Rice, August 29, 1917, MAF 60/189; Louis P. Sheldon to Hoover, September 7, 1917, in United States, Department of State, *Papers Relating to the Foreign Relations of the United States, 1917*, Supplement 2: *The World War*, vol. I (Washington, D.C., 1932), p. 656 (hereinafter cited as *FRUS, 1917*, Supplement 2); Sir William H. Beveridge, *British Food Control* (London, 1928), pp. 77, 117–18. As it happened, the Allies in mid-August were moving in the direction Hoover sought; see Lord Rhondda (the British food controller) to Hoover, August 24, 1917, USFA Papers, Box 85. But Hoover's intervention with Weir and Northcliffe evidently accelerated the process.
14. C. J. Phillips to Lord Northcliffe, enclosed with Foreign Office cable to Spring Rice, August 31, 1917, MAF 60/189, PRO; *New York Times*, September 21, 1917, pp. 1, 2; Owen Hugh Smith memorandum, "Allied Provisions Commission," n.d. but ca. November 2, 1917, F/210/1, Lloyd George Papers; Great Britain, War Cabinet, *Report for the Year 1917* (London, 1918) (Cd. 9005), p. 171. APEC was the acronym for Allied Provisions Export Commission.
15. Lord Rhondda memorandum, "The Food Situation," December 10, 1917, Cab. 24/4, PRO.
16. H. T. Robson report, "Wheat Export Company," n.d. but ca. November 2, 1917, F/210/1, Lloyd George Papers; *First Report of the Royal Commission on Wheat Supplies* (London, 1921), pp. 3, 14, 27, 68–69.
17. Burk, *Britain, America and the Sinews of War*, p. 156.
18. Ibid., pp. 147–51; *New York Times*, August 25, 1917, p. 1; Sir C. B. Gordon cable to C. J. Phillips, August 24 or 25, 1917, MAF 60/68, PRO; memorandum of agreement between Secretary of the Treasury McAdoo and André Tardieu (representing France), August 24, 1917, copy enclosed with Oscar T. Crosby to Hoover, September 13, 1917, file 1H-A21, RG 4, NARA.
19. See Crosby to Hoover, September 13, 1917 (plus enclosure).
20. Hoover to Woodrow Wilson, September 24, 1917, "Wilson, Woodrow," Pre-Commerce Papers, Hoover Papers; Wilson to Bernard Baruch, September 25, 1917, Woodrow Wilson Papers, LC; Baruch to Wilson, September 26, 1917, Wilson Papers.
21. Hoover to Julius H. Barnes, September 7, 1917, USFA Papers, Box 245; Hoover to Wilson, September 24, 1917.
22. Baruch to Wilson, September 26, 1917; Baruch et al. to Hoover, September 27, 1917, file 1H-A21, RG 4, NARA; Frank M. Surface, *The Grain Trade During the World War* (New York, 1928), pp. 175–76.
23. Hoover to Barnes, September 28, 1917, USFA Papers, Box 245.
24. *Official Bulletin* 1 (November 28, 1917): 9; William C. Mullendore, *History of the United States Food Administration, 1917–1919* (Stanford, Calif., 1941), p. 325.
25. Hoover to the Exports Administrative Board, August 28, 1917, USFA Papers, Box 245.

26. Minutes of meeting of Exports Administrative Board, September 6, 1917, Series 2, RG 182, NARA. Under this arrangement, the Exports Administrative Board first issued the license but then turned it over to Hoover for delivery at his discretion to the would-be exporters. This left Hoover free to impose his terms on the exporter or block the transaction altogether if the exporter did not comply.
27. Hoover to the Exports Administrative Board, August 28, 1917.
28. Mullendore, *History*, p. 327; Hoover, *Annual Report of the United States Food Administration* [for 1917], p. 14, printed in U.S. Congress, House of Representatives, 65th Congress, 2d Session, Document No. 837: *The United States Food Administration and United States Fuel Administration* (Washington, D.C., 1918). The license was formally issued by the War Trade Board but only if the Food Administration approved.
29. *Memoranda of the Board of Grain Supervisors for Canada* (Winnipeg, November 15, 1917); [Robert A. Magill], "Operations of the Board of Grain Supervisors for Canada" (typescript, ca. March 17, 1920). Both in file 14128, vol. 838, RG 20: Department of Trade and Commerce, National Archives of Canada.
30. Surface, *Grain Trade*, pp. 275–77.
31. Tom G. Hall, "Cheap Bread from Dear Wheat: Herbert Hoover, the Wilson Administration, and the Management of Wheat Prices, 1916–1920" (Ph.D. dissertation, University of California at Davis, 1970), p. 98.
32. [Magill], "Operations"; Surface, *Grain Trade*, p. 276.
33. According to one of Hoover's associates, "An unchanging price would in reality put a premium on early marketing and that was what was desired." Surface, *Grain Trade*, p. 276.
34. *Memoranda of the Board of Grain Supervisors for Canada*, Order No. 4 (August 17, 1917). No. 1 Northern wheat (as the Canadians called it here) appears to have been identical to (or comparable to) the American variety of wheat known as No. 1 Northern Spring.
35. This was a danger much on Julius Barnes's mind. See Barnes memorandum for H. T. Robson, August 17, 1917, and Barnes to Hoover, September 7, 1917, both in USFA Papers, Box 245; Barnes to Robert A. Magill, August 31, 1917, file 14128, vol. 838, RG 20, National Archives of Canada.
36. Barnes to Magill, August 31, 1917.
37. Barnes memorandum for Robson, August 17, 1917.
38. Michael Bliss, *A Canadian Millionaire* (Toronto, 1978), p. 364.
39. Burk, *Britain, America and the Sinews of War*, p. 172.
40. Ibid.; *First Report of the Royal Commission on Wheat Supplies*, p. 38. The British embargo lasted three weeks. In mid-September an American loan enabled the British to resume purchasing Canadian wheat.
41. W. J. Hanna to Hoover, September 6, 1917; Barnes to Hoover, September 6, 1917; Hoover to W. J. Hanna, September 7, 1917. All in USFA Papers, Box 57, file 25-H. See also Hall, "Cheap Bread from Dear Wheat," p. 99. Hoover's telegram to Hanna followed Barnes's advice almost verbatim.
42. See *First Report of the Royal Commission on Wheat Supplies*, p. 38.
43. "I think we have won out," Barnes correctly reported to Hoover on September 7. Barnes to Hoover, September 7, 1917, USFA Papers, Box 245.
44. *Memoranda of the Board of Grain Supervisors for Canada*, Order No. 5 (September 12, 1917). No. 1 Manitoba Northern wheat (as the Canadians called it here) seems to have been another name for No. 1 Northern. The American equivalent was evidently No. 1 Northern Spring.
45. To accommodate Hoover's insistence on an unvarying price for wheat, the Canadians instituted a complicated and novel method of handling carrying charges—to the lasting annoyance of Robert A. Magill. See [Magill], "Operations."
46. Hoover to Oscar T. Crosby (plus enclosure), October 23, 1917, file 10H-A7, Box 470, RG 4, NARA; Crosby to Hoover (plus enclosure), October 24, 1917, USFA Papers, Box 131; Burk, *Britain, America and the Sinews of War*, pp. 173–74.

47. As explained in chapter 4, such a policy would give Hoover a temporary cushion "against any shortage in wheat offerings" by unhappy American farmers. It would also provide employment to American flour millers, generate feed for American livestock, and reduce the amount of space needed on cargo ships. Hoover to Oscar T. Crosby, October 11, 1917, file 10H-A7, Box 470, RG 4, NARA; Surface, *Grain Trade*, p. 277.
48. Hoover to Crosby (plus enclosure), October 23, 1917.
49. Hoover to Crosby, October 11, 1917. In contrast, the Wheat Export Company understood Hoover to want 12,000,000 bushels of wheat for American mills "during the next two months, and thereafter smaller quantities." H. T. Robson to Hoover, October 16, 1917, USFA Papers, Box 245.
50. Barnes to Hoover, November 2 and 5, 1917, both in USFA Papers, Box 245.
51. James F. Bell telegram to Hoover, October 12, 1917, USFA Papers, Box 245.
52. Hoover telegram to W. J. Hanna (Canadian food controller), October 15, 1917, file 10H-A7, Box 470, RG 4, NARA.
53. But to Julius H. Barnes's displeasure, Canadian flour mills which had received export licenses before Hoover's protest of October 15 continued to ship flour into the United States. Barnes to Hoover, November 2, 1917.
54. James F. Bell to Hoover, October 20, 1917 (plus enclosures), USFA Papers, Box 189; "Memorandum of Conference Between Mr. Black and Mr. Shaw, Representing the Canadian Milling Industry, and James F. Bell, Representing the United States Food Administration—Milling Division. . . ," USFA Papers, Box 189; Hall, "Cheap Bread from Dear Wheat," pp. 102–03.
55. Hoover to Crosby (plus enclosure), October 23, 1917.
56. Ibid.; Barnes to Hoover, October 31, 1917, USFA Papers, Box 245.
57. Barnes to Robert A. Magill, November 3, 1917, and Barnes telegram to Magill, November 3, 1917, copies enclosed with Barnes to Hoover, November 3, 1917, USFA Papers, Box 245.
58. Ibid. This may have been Hoover's understanding, but it was not explicitly included in the memorandum containing the terms of the loan. This memorandum is enclosed with Hoover to Crosby, October 23, 1917.
59. Robert A. Magill telegram to Barnes, November 3, 1917; James Stewart telegram to Barnes, November 5, 1917; Barnes telegram to Stewart, November 5, 1917. Copies enclosed with Barnes to Hoover, November 5, 1917.
60. Barnes to Hoover, November 2, 1917; Magill telegram to Barnes, November 3, 1917.
61. Barnes to Hoover, November 2, 1917; Barnes to Magill, November 5, 1917, copy enclosed with Barnes to Hoover, November 5, 1917; Barnes telegram to Stewart, November 5, 1917.
62. Draft telegram from Barnes to Magill, November 3, 1917, enclosed with Barnes to Hoover, November 3, 1917. The draft version contains handwritten corrections by Hoover and his handwritten mark "O.K." Hoover may have ghost-written the entire telegram, which, in final form, is also enclosed with this Barnes to Hoover letter.
63. Barnes to Hoover, November 3 and 5, 1917 (plus enclosures); Hoover to Barnes, November 5, 1917, and Barnes to Hoover, November 6, 1917, all in USFA Papers, Box 245.
64. Barnes to Hoover, November 2 and 3, 1917; Barnes to Hoover, November 7, 1917, USFA Papers, Box 245.
65. *Official Bulletin* 1 (November 30, 1917): 2; *Report of the War Trade Board* (Washington, D.C., 1920), p. 6.
66. Hoover, *Annual Report of United States Food Administration* [for 1917], p. 14. For an example of Hoover's exercise of power in this area, see Hoover to the War Trade Board, December 7, 1917, USFA Papers, Box 182.
67. Hoover report, August 20, 1917, to the Garfield committee, in its "Minutes," Appendix 1 (cited in note 1).
68. Hoover address to a conference of editors and publishers of farm journals and newspapers, August 25, 1917, Public Statements File, Hoover Papers.

69. *First Report of the Royal Commission on Wheat Supplies*, pp. 7, 31; Beveridge, *British Food Control*, pp. 91–92.
70. Barnett, *British Food Policy*, p. 178.
71. F. G. Crowell to Hoover, October 11, 1917, and enclosure: K. B. Stoddart (of the Wheat Export Company) to Crowell, October 11, 1917, both in USFA Papers, Box 253.
72. Louis P. Sheldon cable to Hoover, October 13, 1917, USFA Papers, Box 133. According to Sheldon, the British stock of wheat and flour, as of October 8, was 2,993,000 tons. Since British monthly consumption during the winter was 522,000 tons, this meant that the British already had nearly six months' supplies of wheat and flour on hand.
73. Tasker H. Bliss memorandum for the Secretary of War, December 18, 1917, in United States, Department of State, *Papers Relating to the Foreign Relations of the United States: The Lansing Papers*, vol. II (Washington, D.C., 1940), p. 201; Charles Seymour, ed., *The Intimate Papers of Colonel House*, vol. III (Boston and New York, 1928), pp. 196–97, 203; David F. Trask, *The United States in the Supreme War Council* (Middletown, Conn., 1961), pp. 15–17.
74. Hoover memorandum for Colonel House, n.d. (but dated October 27, 1917 by House), Edward M. House Papers, Box 61, Manuscripts and Archives, Yale University Library. Another copy, dated October 26, 1917, is enclosed with Hoover to Woodrow Wilson, November 5, 1917, Josephus Daniels Papers, LC.
75. Hoover to Barnes, January 8, 1918, USFA Papers, Box 246.
76. *New York Times*, October 14, 1917, section I, p. 16.
77. Hoover, private address in Philadelphia, September 29, 1917, Public Statements File, Hoover Papers. Printed in United States Food Administration Bulletin No. 10: *Grain and Live Stock* (Washington, D.C., 1917), copy in Public Statements File, Hoover Papers, as Public Statement #4-D, October 25, 1917. See also *New York Herald*, October 26, 1917, p. 16. This was not the first time that Hoover's agency projected a surplus of wheat from the 1917 harvest. In August, the Food Administration estimated the surplus at 88,000,000 bushels. *Official Bulletin* 1 (August 21, 1917): 2.
78. Nearly 34,000,000 bushels by mid-November, according to Hoover to Woodrow Wilson, November 15, 1917, Wilson Papers.
79. *New York Times*, October 14, 1917, section I, p. 16.
80. Barnes to Hoover, January 4, 1918, USFA Papers, Box 246; Hoover to Barnes, January 8, 1918.
81. Barnes to Hoover, January 4, 1918; Hall, "Cheap Bread from Dear Wheat," p. 109.
82. Barnes to Hoover, November 1, 1917, USFA Papers, Box 245; Hall, "Cheap Bread from Dear Wheat," p. 109.
83. Hoover cable to Louis P. Sheldon, November 8, 1917, in *FRUS, 1917*, Supplement 2, vol. I, p. 659.
84. Hoover cable to Alonzo E. Taylor, November 15, 1917, file 103.97/25, RG 59, NARA. Hoover forwarded the text to the Secretary of State on November 13 for cabling to London, but the State Department did not dispatch the cable until November 15.
85. Ibid.
86. Hoover to Woodrow Wilson, November 15, 1917, Wilson Papers.
87. Statement by Magnus Swenson (food administrator for Wisconsin), November 21, 1917, Magnus Swenson Papers, Box 5, State Historical Society of Wisconsin. Swenson had conferred with Hoover in mid-November.
88. Wilson cable to Colonel House, November 16, 1917, Wilson Papers.
89. Wilson memorandum, ca. November 20, 1917, printed in Arthur S. Link et al., eds., *The Papers of Woodrow Wilson*, vol. 45 (Princeton, N.J., 1984), p. 86.
90. "Statement by the Wheat Executive," November 16, 1917, enclosed with "Shortage of Breadstuffs" (memorandum by Lord Rhondda), November 22, 1917, Cab. 24/33, PRO. A copy is in the Alonzo E. Taylor Papers, Box 24, HI.
91. Barnes to Hoover, January 4, 1918.
92. "Statement by the Wheat Executive," November 16, 1917; Rhondda memorandum,

November 22, 1917. The Wheat Executive's statements used figures given in metric tons. I have given the equivalents in bushels in my text. Thus 7,000,000 metric tons of wheat (the Wheat Executive's original import program from North America) = 257,180,000 bushels (or nearly 260,000,000 bushels, as indicated in the text). Similarly 3,620,000 metric tons (the reduced figure) = just under 133,000,000 bushels.

93. Alonzo E. Taylor report on his trip to Europe, n.d., but sent to the State Department on March 25, 1918, file 763.72 / 13416, RG 59, NARA. Printed in *FRUS, 1917*, Supplement 2, vol. I, pp. 423–31.
94. Taylor cable to Hoover, November 16, 1917, USFA Papers, Box 37, and printed in part in *FRUS, 1917*, Supplement 2, vol . I, p. 660; Taylor to Hoover, November 21, 1917, USFA Papers, Box 37.
95. Hoover cable to Taylor, n.d., USFA Papers, Box 37; copy, dated November 17, 1917, in *FRUS, 1917*, Supplement 2, vol. I, pp. 660.
96. Wheat Executive, "Report of a Conference on the Allied Cereal Situation Wednesday, 15th November, 1917 at 11. a.m." (typescript), USFA Papers, Box 186.
97. Taylor cable to Hoover, November 16, 1917.
98. Hoover cable to Taylor, November 19, 1917, USFA Papers, Box 37; copies, dated November 20, 1917, in file 103.97 / 46, RG 59, NARA, and in *FRUS, 1917*, Supplement 2, vol. I, p. 661.
99. Lord Rhondda message to Hoover, enclosed with Louis P. Sheldon cable to Hoover, November 24, 1917, file 103.97 / 51, RG 59, NARA.
100. H. T. Robson to Barnes, December 10, 1917, USFA Papers, Box 246.
101. Lord Rhondda, "The Food Situation" (memorandum), December 10, 1917, Cab. 24 / 4, PRO; minutes of [British] War Cabinet meetings 296 and 297, December 12 and 13, 1917, Cab. 23 / 4, PRO.
102. Minutes of War Cabinet meeting 296, December 12, 1917; *First Report of the Royal Commission on Wheat Supplies*, p. 40.
103. Hoover message to Lord Rhondda, enclosed with Hoover cable to Louis P. Sheldon, November 27, 1917, file 103.97 / 58a, RG 59, NARA.
104. Taylor cable to Hoover, December 8, 1917.
105. Herbert Hoover, *An American Epic*, vol. II (Chicago, 1960), p. 126.
106. Hoover to Barnes, December 7, 1917, USFA Papers, Box 246.
107. Ibid. The Allies should have had some inkling of Hoover's desire for a call on Canadian wheat if the United States "over-shipped" its own wheat and flour during the coming winter, for Julius Barnes raised this very issue beforehand with the Wheat Export Company. According to Barnes, H. T. Robson of the Wheat Export Company was "quite receptive to some such guarantee as that, if necessary." Barnes to Hoover, December 8, 1917, USFA Papers, Box 246. Whether Robson explicitly gave such a promise is unclear.
108. H. T. Robson to Barnes, December 10, 1917, USFA Papers, Box 246.
109. Hoover to Barnes, December 11, 1917, USFA Papers, Box 246.
110. Ibid.
111. Barnes to Hoover, November 20, 1917, USFA Papers, Box 245; *Chicago Tribune*, November 20, 1917, p. 10.
112. Hoover to Barnes, November 24, 1917, USFA Papers, Box 245. Despite Hoover's denial of the newspaper story, there is little doubt that the story was accurate. Hoover did indeed fear a domestic wheat famine before next summer and so expressed himself to the state food administrator of Wisconsin at almost exactly the same time (mid-November 1917). See "Statement of Mr. Magnus Swenson, Chairman, to the State Council of Defense, at its meeting November 21st, 1917," in Magnus Swenson Papers, Box 5.
113. Hall, "Cheap Bread from Dear Wheat," p. 111. In 1917, Canadian wheat exports exceeded American wheat exports by nearly 50 percent (4.6 million metric tons to 3.1 million). Avner Offer, *The First World War: An Agrarian Interpretation* (Oxford, 1989), pp. 369–70.
114. Barnes to Hoover, November 27, 1917, USFA Papers, Box 245.

115. Hoover to Barnes, December 1, 1917; Barnes to Hoover, December 4, 1917. Both in USFA Papers, Box 246.
116. Barnes to Hoover, December 5, 1917, USFA Papers, Box 246.
117. Barnes to Hoover, December 11, 1917, USFA Papers, Box 246.
118. Earl of Crawford diary, December 7, 1917, in John Vincent, ed., *The Crawford Papers* (Manchester, U.K., 1984), p. 381.
119. Barnes to Hoover, December 5, 1917.
120. Barnes to Hoover, December 11, 1917; Barnes to Hoover, December 21, 1917, USFA Papers, Box 246.
121. Ibid.
122. Hoover to Barnes, December 31, 1917, USFA Papers, Box 246.
123. Hoover, *An American Epic*, II, p. 124.
124. Barnes to Hoover, January 4, 1918.
125. See Hall, "Cheap Bread from Dear Wheat," pp. 109–10, and Barnett, *British Food Policy*, p. 179.
126. Hoover to Barnes, January 8, 1918.
127. Hoover to Exports Administrative Board, August 28, 1917, USFA Papers, Box 182.
128. Thus while appealing publicly for conservation, Hoover simultaneously declared that the world's sugar shortage was small—a consequence of scarce shipping—and confined to Europe. U.S. Food Administration press release 180, September 1, 1917, USFA Documents. See also *New York Times*, September 4, 1917, p. 3.
129. *Official Bulletin* 1 (September 24, 1917): 4; *New York Times*, September 24, 1917, p. 1.
130. Ibid.
131. Ibid.
132. George M. Rolph cable to Louis P. Sheldon, October 11, 1917; Hoover cable to Sheldon, October 17, 1917. Both in USFA Papers, Box 133.
133. Hoover cable to Sheldon, October 17, 1917; Hoover cable to Lord Rhondda, August 31, 1917, *FRUS, 1917*, Supplement 2, vol. I, p. 655; Sheldon cable to Hoover, September 5, 1917, ibid., p. 656.
134. Hoover to Exports Administrative Board, August 28, 1917; Joshua Bernhardt, *Government Control of the Sugar Industry in the United States* (New York, 1920), p. 14.
135. *New York Herald*, October 19, 1917, p. 9; *Commercial and Financial Chronicle* 105 (October 20, 1917): 1585.
136. Rolph cable to Sheldon, October 11, 1917; Rolph cable to Sheldon, October 11, 1917 (separate cable), USFA Papers, Box 133.
137. Rolph cable to Sheldon, October 11, 1917.
138. *Official Bulletin* 1 (October 17, 1917): 3; *New York Times*, October 17, 1917, p. 5.
139. Ibid.
140. *New York Times*, October 20, 1917, p. 9.
141. Ibid.; also October 21, 1917, section I, p. 12.
142. Ibid., October 21, 1917, section I, p. 12.
143. Ibid., p. 1; also October 26, 1917, p. 4.
144. Ibid., October 26, 1917, p. 4.
145. Hoover's progress can be traced in the following cables, all in USFA Papers, Box 133: Hoover to Louis P. Sheldon, October 4, 17, 18, 19, 24, 1917; Sheldon to Hoover, October 4, 19, 24, 1917.
146. Sheldon cable to Hoover, October 24, 1917, USFA Papers, Box 133; *Official Bulletin* 1 (October 29, 1917): 4.
147. Hoover cable to Sheldon, October 19, 1917. Hoover said that because of the "sugar famine" in New York, it was "vital" to "let us use" the sugar accumulated there for France if the French lacked the shipping to transport it.
148. Ibid.; Sheldon cable to Hoover, October 24, 1917; Sheldon cable to Hoover, October 27, 1917, USFA Papers, Box 133.

149. Hoover cable to Sheldon, October 18, 1917; *New York Times*, October 28, 1917, p. 18; *Official Bulletin* 1 (October 29, 1917): 4; *New York Times*, October 29, 1917, p. 20. Eventually relief arrived in the form of sugar from the Philippines, Cuba, and the beet sugar areas of the American West. *New York Times*, November 17, 1917, p. 16; *Commercial and Financial Chronicle* 105 (November 24, 1917): 2049; *New York Times*, December 6, 1917, p. 7.
150. Paul Painlevé cable to the French High Commission in the United States, October 7, 1917, quoted in Albert N. Merritt, *War Time Control of Distribution of Foods* (New York, 1920), pp. 70–71, and in Hoover, *An American Epic*, II, pp. 127–28.
151. Hoover, *An American Epic*, II, p. 128.
152. Barnes to Hoover, October 19, 20, and 23 (two letters), 1917, USFA Papers, Box 245.
153. Curtis H. Lindley to Barnes, October 23, 1917; Barnes to Hoover, October 26 and 27, 1917. All in USFA Papers, Box 245.
154. Barnes to Lewis L. Strauss, December 8, 1917, USFA Papers, Box 246; minutes of meetings of the War Trade Board, December 12 and 29, 1917, RG 182, NARA.
155. Minutes of the meeting of the War Trade Board, December 12, 1917.
156. The Finns even sent an envoy to America to obtain export licenses for the seized flour. Barnes to Hoover, October 29, 1917, USFA Papers, Box 245.
157. William Phillips diary, November 14, 1917, William Phillips Papers, Houghton Library, Harvard University. See also Hoover to Frank L. Polk, November 12, 1917, USFA Papers, Box 285.
158. Minutes of the meeting of the War Trade Board, December 12, 1917.
159. Ibid.
160. Ibid.
161. Frank L. Polk to Hoover, December 12, 1917; Hoover to Secretary of State Robert Lansing, December 12, 1917. Both in USFA Papers, Box 285.
162. *Chicago Tribune*, December 22, 1917, p. 3; *Commercial and Financial Chronicle* 105 (December 29, 1917): 2505.
163. J. A. Salter, *Allied Shipping Control* (Oxford, 1921), p. 144.
164. Ibid., p. 358; William Sowden Sims, *The Victory at Sea* (Garden City, N.Y., 1921), p. 400; Edward B. Parsons, *Wilsonian Diplomacy: Allied-American Rivalries in War and Peace* (St. Louis, 1978), p. 47.
165. Parsons, *Wilsonian Diplomacy*, p. 47.
166. Hoover, private address in Philadelphia, September 29, 1917.
167. Hoover address to a meeting of new state food administrators, September 18, 1917, Public Statements File, Hoover Papers.
168. Ibid.
169. John J. Pershing cable from France to the War Department in Washington, D.C., July 6, 1917, quoted in *Final Report of General John J. Pershing*, September 1, 1919, in United States Department of the Army, Historical Division, *United States Army in the World War, 1917–1919* (Washington, D.C., 1948), vol. XII, p. 17.
170. Pershing, *Final Report*, p. 18.
171. Edward M. Coffman, *The War to End all Wars* (New York, 1968), p. 128.
172. Ibid.; Frank E. Vandiver, *Black Jack: The Life and Times of John J. Pershing* (College Station and London, 1977), vol. II, pp. 728–29.
173. Hoover to Edward M. House, February 13, 1917, in Arthur S. Link et al., eds., *The Papers of Woodrow Wilson*, vol. 41 (Princeton, N.J., 1983), pp. 227–29; Hoover to Walter S. Gifford (Director of the Council of National Defense), plus three enclosures, February 17, 1917, in Director's Office Correspondence, file 2-A1, Box 38, RG 62, NARA. For a discussion of these documents, see George H. Nash, *The Life of Herbert Hoover: The Humanitarian, 1914–1917* (New York, 1988), pp. 344–48.
174. Hoover to Woodrow Wilson, February 14, 1917, in Link et al., eds., *Papers of Woodrow Wilson*, vol. 41, p. 226.

175. Vandiver, *Black Jack*, II, pp. 727, 743, 836–37; Coffman, *War to End All Wars*, pp. 48–49; Frederick Palmer, *Newton D. Baker: America at War* (New York, 1931), I, p. 175; Daniel R. Beaver, *Newton D. Baker and the American War Effort, 1917–1919* (Lincoln, Nebr., 1966), pp. 39–49.
176. Hoover to Woodrow Wilson, August 27, 1917, Wilson Papers.
177. Newton D. Baker to Woodrow Wilson, September 2, 1917, Wilson Papers.
178. Enoch Crowder memorandum for the Secretary of War, August 30, 1917, enclosed with Baker to Wilson, September 2, 1917.
179. Josephus Daniels to Edward N. Hurley, September 24, 1917, copy in Wilson Papers.
180. *New York Times*, September 28, 1917, p. 1.
181. Edward N. Hurley to Hoover, October 8, 1917, file 1H-A20, RG 4, NARA.
182. Josephus Daniels diary, October 11, 1917, in E. David Cronon, ed., *The Cabinet Diaries of Josephus Daniels, 1913–1921* (Lincoln, Nebr., 1963), p. 219; Newton D. Baker to Woodrow Wilson, November 3, 1917, Wilson Papers.
183. Hoover to Baker, October 18, 1917, USFA Papers, Box 165.
184. Hurley to Baker, October 17, 1917, Edward N. Hurley Papers, University of Notre Dame Archives; copy in USFA Papers, Box 165.
185. Earl of Crawford diary, November 8, 1917, in *Crawford Papers*, p. 380.
186. Hoover memorandum for Colonel House, n.d. (but dated October 27, 1917 by House), House Papers, Box 61. A copy of this document, in the form of a letter addressed by Hoover to House and dated November 5, 1917, is enclosed with Hoover to Woodrow Wilson, November 5, 1917, cited in the note below.
187. Hoover to Woodrow Wilson, November 5, 1917 (plus enclosures), Josephus Daniels Papers. The enclosure consisted of the two memoranda cited separately above in notes 74 and 186. Although Hoover here gave the memorandum cited in the preceding note the date of November 5, 1917, he told the President in his cover letter that he had given both memoranda to Colonel House before the latter's departure for Europe. House left Washington on October 28. Evidently Hoover or his typist inadvertently put the date of November 5 on the memo after retyping a copy for dispatch to the President on that date.
188. Newton D. Baker to Josephus Daniels, November 8, 1917, Daniels Papers; printed in Arthur S. Link et al., eds., *The Papers of Woodrow Wilson*, vol. 44 (Princeton, N.J., 1983), p. 544.
189. Baker to Wilson, November 3, 1917.
190. Hoover to Edward N. Hurley, November 5, 1917, copy enclosed with Hoover to Wilson, November 5, 1917. Another copy is in USFA Papers, file 1-H.
191. Ibid.
192. Ibid.
193. Link et al., eds., *Papers of Woodrow Wilson*, vol. 44, p. 545, note 2.
194. Hoover, miscellaneous handwritten notes on the military situation, July 6–August 10, 1917, USFA Papers, file 1-H.
195. Hoover address to the Potato Association of America, November 9, 1917, Public Statements File, Hoover Papers.
196. Pershing to Baker, November 15, 1917, John J. Pershing Papers, Box 20, LC.
197. Tasker H. Bliss cable to the Acting Chief of Staff, December 4, 1917, printed in Link et al., eds., *Papers of Woodrow Wilson*, vol. 45, pp. 208–13.
198. Wilson to Baker, ca. December 5, 1917, printed in ibid., p. 208.
199. Baker to Wilson, December 11, 1917, Wilson Papers; printed in Link et al., eds., *Papers of Woodrow Wilson*, vol. 45, p. 268.
200. Tasker H. Bliss report on his participation in the House Mission, December 14, 1917, printed in *FRUS, 1917*, Supplement 2, vol. I, pp. 386–91.
201. Beaver, *Newton D. Baker*, pp. 118–20; Secretary of State Lansing cable to William G. Sharp, December 26, 1917, printed in *FRUS, 1917*, Supplement 2, vol. I, p. 492.

202. Magnus Swenson statement, November 21, 1917.
203. Hoover to the Council of National Defense, May 13, 1917 (plus enclosed memorandum), copy in "1917—National Defense (2) Food," General Correspondence, 1906–1975, RG 16, NARA.
204. Hoover, "Memorandum on Necessity of Early Food Legislation," enclosed with Hoover to Woodrow Wilson, June 12, 1917, Wilson Papers.
205. Hoover, "Preliminary Note on the Organization of the Food Administration" (June 1, 1917), enclosed with Hoover to Joseph P. Tumulty, ca. June 1, 1917, Wilson Papers.
206. Hoover to Robert Lansing, June 7, 1917, quoted in Hoover, *An American Epic*, II, p. 139, and in Thomas A. Bailey, *The Policy of the United States Toward the Neutrals, 1917–1918* (Baltimore, 1942), pp. 38–39.
207. Wilson's executive order of June 22, 1917, is printed in *FRUS, 1917*, Supplement 2, vol. II, pp. 883–84.
208. Wilson statement, ca. June 26, 1917, printed in Arthur S. Link et al., eds., *The Papers of Woodrow Wilson*, vol. 43 (Princeton, N.J., 1983), pp. 14–15.
209. Minutes of the Exports Council, June 26, 1917, in RG 182, NARA.
210. Ibid. One, Dr. Alonzo Taylor, nominally represented the Secretary of Agriculture. The other, John Beaver White, was a founding member of Hoover's Commission for Relief in Belgium.
211. Ibid.; Hoover to Lord Eustace Percy, June 26, 1917, USFA Papers, Box 110.
212. Hoover to Robert Lansing, June 29, 1917, "Lansing, Robert," Pre-Commerce Papers.
213. *New York Times*, June 21, 1917, p. 1.
214. Hoover to James F. Bell, June 29, 1917, USFA Papers, Box 189.
215. Hoover, *An American Epic*, II, p. 152.
216. Bailey, *Policy*, p. 70.
217. Ibid., p. 82.
218. *New York Times*, July 8, 1917, section I, p. 1.
219. Hoover to Wilson, July 7, 1917, Wilson Papers.
220. Minutes of the Exports Council, July 7, 1917; *New York Times*, July 8, 1917, section I, p. 1.
221. President Wilson's proclamation of July 9, 1917, is printed in *FRUS, 1917*, Supplement 2, vol. II, pp. 903–05. For his explanatory comments, see *Washington Post*, July 9, 1917, p. 1.
222. Minutes of the Exports Council, July 7, 9, 12, 1917; Hoover to Woodrow Wilson, July 14, 1917, USFA Papers, Box 110.
223. Secretary of State Lansing mentioned this in a letter to certain American diplomats on August 8. Printed in *FRUS, 1917*, Supplement 2, vol. II, p. 919.
224. Exports Council memorandum to the legations of the four northern neutrals, July 24, 1917, printed in *FRUS, 1917*, Supplement 2, vol. II, pp. 908–10.
225. William Phillips diary, July 27, 1917, Phillips Papers.
226. Gordon Auchincloss diary, July 30, 1917, Gordon Auchincloss Papers, Box 1, Manuscripts and Archives, Yale University Library.
227. Hoover to the Exports Council, July 27, 1917, enclosed with Frank L. Polk to Woodrow Wilson, July 28, 1917, file 659.119/6a, RG 59, NARA; minutes of the Exports Council, July 27, 1917. A copy of Hoover's letter is in USFA Papers, Box 110.
228. Minutes of the Exports Council, July 27, 1917.
229. Frank L. Polk, handwritten note (dated July 31, 1917) at the bottom of the first page of his letter to the President, July 28, 1917, cited in note 227. Polk conferred with the President on July 31 and then recorded the President's reaction quoted here.
230. Polk to Vance C. McCormick, July 31, 1917, quoted in Olav Riste, *The Neutral Ally: Norway's Relations with Belligerent Powers in the First World War* (Oslo, 1965), p. 195.
231. With the President as yet averse to hard-line measures, the Exports Council voted merely to consult the Allies about their intended policy, to compile data on the northern neutrals' production and traffic in fodder and feedstuffs, and then to ask President Wilson for

instructions. Minutes of the Exports Council, August 2, 1917.

232. Ibid., August 24, 1917. The council specifically voted to grant licenses for the export of fats only upon "terms and conditions" agreed upon between the Exports Administrative Board and Hoover. This arrangement, of course, gave Hoover a veto over any further commercial shipment of fats from the country.

233. In his letter to the President on July 28, Polk remarked that some members of the Exports Council favored the "absolutely radical stand" mentioned in the text. Hoover was surely among them. See also Riste, *The Neutral Ally*, pp. 194–95, and Auchincloss diary, July 30, 1917.

234. [Colville Barclay], memorandum on the Exports Administrative Board, September 28, 1917, enclosed with Barclay to Arthur J. Balfour, September 28, 1917, FO 368/1844, PRO. Barclay was in the British embassy in Washington. Hoover's two "wild men" at the Exports Administrative Board were Alonzo E. Taylor and John Beaver White. Technically, Taylor represented the Secretary of Agriculture and White the Food Administrator, but both were devoted Hooverites.

235. Bailey, *Policy*, pp. 86–88.

236. Wilson's executive order of August 21, 1917, is printed in *FRUS, 1917*, Supplement 2, vol. II, pp. 926–27.

237. President Wilson's proclamation of August 27, 1917, printed in ibid., pp. 933–37.

238. Wilson's statement of August 27, 1917, accompanying his proclamation, printed in ibid., pp. 937–38.

239. Minutes of the Exports Administrative Board, August 30, 1917, printed in ibid., p. 939.

240. Wilson's executive order creating the War Trade Board, printed in ibid., pp. 963–70.

241. Secretary of State Lansing to Walter Hines Page and certain other American diplomats in Europe, October 17, 1917, in ibid., pp. 974–76.

242. As noted earlier in this chapter. See minutes of the War Trade Board, November 13, 1917, RG 182, NARA.

243. Hoover, *An American Epic*, II, p. 143.

244. Hoover to W. L. F. C. van Rappard (the Netherlands minister to the United States), July 31, 1917, in ibid., p. 142. According to Hoover, the Dutch had sufficient food to last until their next harvest, and after that they would be "in a perfectly safe position for some months." The Swedes also had enough food for the present, in Hoover's view. Ibid., p. 149.

245. Bailey, *Policy*, p. 171; Hoover to the Exports Council, July 27, 1917.

246. Hoover to van Rappard, July 31, 1917. Hoover made a similar offer to the Norwegians. Bailey, *Policy*, p. 109.

247. Minutes of the Exports Council, August 9, 1917.

248. For the negotiations with Norway, see Hoover to H. H. Bryn, August 10, 1917, USFA Papers, Box 110; Hoover to Fridtjof Nansen, August 10, 1917, in George I. Gay and H. H. Fisher, eds., *Public Relations of the Commission for Relief in Belgium* (Stanford, Calif., 1929), I, pp. 369–70; Bailey, *Policy*, pp. 109–10; Hoover, *An American Epic*, II, p. 140; and Wayne S. Cole, *Norway and the United States, 1905–1955* (Ames, Iowa, 1989), pp. 33–38.

For the negotiations with Sweden, see Hoover to W. A. F. Ekengren, August 10, 1917, USFA Papers, Box 110; Bailey, *Policy*, pp. 143–45; Hoover, *An American Epic*, II, p. 149; and the documents printed in *FRUS, 1917*, Supplement 2, vol. II, pp. 1042–43, 1044–45, 1049, and 1052.

249. Hoover, *An American Epic*, II, p. 150.

250. Van Rappard to Hoover, August 3, 1917, in ibid., pp. 142–43.

251. Hoover to van Rappard, August 10, 1917, USFA Papers, Box 110; printed in Hoover, *An American Epic*, II, pp. 143–44.

252. Hoover, *An American Epic*, II, p. 144.

253. Minutes of the Exports Administrative Board, August 25, 1917, RG 182, NARA.
254. Netherlands legation memorandum to the State Department, September 4, 1917, in *FRUS, 1917*, Supplement 2, vol. II, pp. 1129–32.
255. Minutes of the Exports Administrative Board, August 31, 1917; *New York Times*, September 2, 1917, section I, p. 1.
256. Netherlands legation memorandum, September 4, 1917.
257. Hoover, *An American Epic*, II, pp. 144–45; State Department to the Netherlands legation, September 11, 1917, in *FRUS, 1917*, Supplement 2, vol. II, p. 1134.
258. Julius H. Barnes to Hoover, September 15, 20, and 25, 1917, USFA Papers, Box 245; Surface, *Grain Trade*, p. 301.
259. Barnes to Hoover, September 25, October 2 and 16, 1917, USFA Papers, Box 245.
260. Barnes to Hoover, October 19, 20, and 23, 1917, USFA Papers, Box 245. Barnes took the position that he had no knowledge of who owned such grain in storage in Baltimore. Barnes to Hoover, November 3, 1917, USFA Papers, Box 245.
261. Barnes to Hoover, October 23, November 3 and 7, 1917, USFA Papers, Box 245.
262. F. G. Crowell to Hoover, November 9, 1917, USFA Papers, Box 245.
263. Barnes to Hoover, November 27, 1917, USFA Papers, Box 245; Barnes to Hoover, December 11, 1917, USFA Papers, Box 246; Surface, *Grain Trade*, p. 303.
264. Minutes of the Exports Administrative Board, August 24, 1917; Hoover, *An American Epic*, II, p. 146.
265. Hoover, *An American Epic*, II, pp. 146–47.
266. Ibid., p. 147; stenographic copy of minutes of the War Trade Board, November 8, 1917, RG 182, NARA.
267. Hoover cable to Alonzo Taylor, November 15, 1917, file 103.97/25, RG 59, NARA; Hoover to Robert Lansing, November 22, 1917, USFA Papers, Box 171.
268. Hugh R. Wilson to Robert Lansing, November 24, 1917, in *FRUS, 1917*, Supplement 2, vol. II, pp. 1180–81.
269. Robert Lansing to William G. Sharp, November 23, 1917, in ibid., p. 1180.
270. Hoover to the Swiss minister (Hans Sulzer), November 26, 1917, USFA Papers, Box 171.
271. Hoover cable to Taylor, November 27, 1917, in *FRUS, 1917*, Supplement 2, vol. II, p. 1182.
272. Barnes to Hoover, November 26, 1917; Hoover to Barnes, November 28, 1917. Both in USFA Papers, Box 245.
273. Hoover to Barnes, November 28, 1917.
274. Taylor cable to Hoover, November 30, 1917, file 103.97/60, RG 59, NARA.
275. Hugh R. Wilson to Robert Lansing, November 22, 1917, in *FRUS, 1917*, Supplement 2, vol. II, pp. 1179–80.
276. Hugh R. Wilson to Lansing, November 24, 1917; William Phillips diary, November 27, 1917, Phillips Papers.
277. William Phillips diary, November 27, 1917.
278. Ibid., December 3, 1917.
279. Hoover to Lansing, November 22, 1917.
280. Memorandum between the War Trade Board and the Swiss government, December 5, 1917, in *FRUS, 1917*, Supplement 2, vol. II, pp. 1185–96.
281. Hoover, *An American Epic*, II, p. 147.
282. Bailey, *Policy*, pp. 260–62; Walter Hines Page cable to Robert Lansing, January 8, 1918, copy in USFA Papers, Box 133.
283. Bailey, *Policy*, pp. 260–88; Hoover, *An American Epic*, II, pp. 147–48. As the latter source makes clear, Hoover was still angry at the Swiss when he wrote about this episode forty years later.
284. Bailey, *Policy*, pp. 127–30, 160–61, 187–90, 234; *Report of the War Trade Board*, pp. 22–24.
285. *Report of the War Trade Board*, pp. 109–13; Bailey, *Policy*, pp. 212–13, 474.
286. Hoover, *An American Epic*, II, pp. 146–47, 151.

CHAPTER 6

1. *Washington Post*, September 5, 1917, pp. 1, 2; Washington *Evening Star*, September 5, 1917, p. 15; Edgar Rickard to Lou Henry Hoover, September 6, 1917, "Rickard, Edgar," Personal Correspondence, Lou Henry Hoover Papers, HHPL; Tessie Tag to Mrs. Ray Lyman Wilbur, September 6, 1917, USFA Papers, Box 1, HI.
2. U.S. Food Administration press release 137, August 10, 1917, USFA Documents, HHPL; *New York Times*, August 11, 1917, pp. 1, 2.
3. The drive for meatless and wheatless days got under way in September. Magnus Swenson, "Proclamation" (September 14, 1917), Magnus Swenson Papers, Box 5, State Historical Society of Wisconsin; *Official Bulletin* 1 (November 7, 1917): 4.
4. U.S. Food Administration press releases 269 and 275, September 27, 1917, USFA Documents; *Official Bulletin* 1 (September 27, 1917): 4, and 1 (October 1, 1917): 2; *New York Times*, October 1, 1917, p. 22.
5. U.S. Food Administration press release 275, September 27, 1917; *New York Times*, September 30, 1917, section I, p. 15.
6. *Official Bulletin*, 1 (October 6, 1917): 3; *New York Times*, October 28, 1917, section II, p. 2.
7. U.S. Food Administration press release 286, October 2, 1917, USFA Documents.
8. U.S. Food Administration press release 276, September 29, 1917, USFA Documents.
9. *New York Times*, October 28, 1917, section I, p. 18.
10. U.S. Food Administration press release 269, September 27, 1917.
11. Herbert Hoover, "Why I Ask Your Help," *Ladies' Home Journal* 34 (October 1917): 8.
12. In the words of his friend Ray Lyman Wilbur: "Mr. Hoover was the first wartime administrator in history to give women the chance to participate immediately in their homes to back up their boys at the Front." Edgar Eugene Robinson and Paul Carroll Edwards, eds., *The Memoirs of Ray Lyman Wilbur* (Stanford, Calif., 1960), p. 266 (hereinafter cited as Wilbur, *Memoirs*).
13. Hoover address to the American Public Health Association, October 19, 1917, Public Statements File, Herbert Hoover Papers, HHPL. Printed as Herbert Hoover, "Food Conservation and the War," *American Journal of Public Health* 7 (November 1917): 922–27.
14. Woodrow Wilson to Herbert Hoover, October 10, 1917, in *Official Bulletin* 1 (October 13, 1917): 2.
15. Hoover telegram to various state food administrators, October 26, 1917, copy enclosed in Hoover to Jouett Shouse, December 1, 1917, Jouett Shouse Papers, University of Kentucky; *New York Times*, October 28, 1917, section I, p. 18; *Chicago Tribune*, October 28, 1917, section I, p. 15.
16. *New York Times*, October 28, 1917, section I, p. 18, and October 29, 1917, p. 1. After reviewing the situation in Chicago, Illinois authorities decided not to send in the national guard. *Chicago Tribune*, October 30, 1917, p. 3.
17. *New York Times*, November 6, 1917, pp. 1, 8.
18. Hoover had reason to suspect enemy-inspired arson, at least at one grain elevator in Baltimore. See Julius H. Barnes to Hoover, October 31, 1917, USFA Papers, Box 245, HI. But the timing of Hoover's disclosure suggests that he hoped to turn it to his advantage in the food pledge card drive.
19. Baltimore *Sun*, October 27, 1917, p. 16, and October 28, 1917, section I, p. 14; *New York Times*, October 28, 1917, section I, p. 14.
20. *New York Times*, October 28, 1917, section I, p. 18.
21. Ibid., October 29, 1917, p. 1.
22. George Winston Smith, "New Mexico's Wartime Food Problems, 1917–1918: A Case Study in Emergency Administration," *New Mexico Historical Review* 18 (October 1943): 375; Christopher C. Gibbs, "Missouri Farmers and World War One: Resistance to Mobilization," *Bulletin of the Missouri Historical Society* 35 (October 1978); 24; Christopher C. Gibbs,

The Great Silent Majority: Missouri's Resistance to World War I (Columbia, Mo., 1988), pp. 129–30.

23. Ivan L. Pollock, *The Food Administration in Iowa* (Iowa City, 1923), I, p. 148.
24. "The Food Conservation Pledges," *Survey* 39 (November 10, 1917): 145.
25. Gibbs, "Missouri Farmers and World War One," p. 22.
26. U.S. Food Administration press release 390, October 30, 1917, USFA Documents; Smith, "New Mexico's Wartime Food Problems," p. 375.
27. U.S. Food Administration press release 390, October 30, 1917; *New York Times*, November 1, 1917, section I, p. 13; U.S. Food Administration press release 413, November 2, 1917, USFA Documents.
28. Baltimore *Sun*, October 27, 1917, p. 8.
29. *New York Times*, November 5, 1917, p. 18.
30. U.S. Food Administration press release 446, November 10, 1917, USFA Documents. According to press release 275 on September 27, 1917, the United States had 22,000,000 families.
31. William C. Mullendore, *History of the United States Food Administration, 1917–1919* (Stanford, Calif., 1941), p. 87.
32. In late September the Food Administration confidently predicted that 100 percent of the American people would be "members" by the end of food pledge week. The campaign's organizers eventually lowered their goal to 10,000,000 signatures (about one tenth of the population) and declared that, by signing, each woman enrolled her entire family. On this basis, the campaign leaders announced that they had met their goal. *Official Bulletin* 1 (September 27, 1917): 4; U.S. Food Administration press releases 401 (November 1, 1917) and 446 (November 10, 1917), USFA Documents.
33. U.S. Food Administration press release 426, November 5, 1917, USFA Documents.
34. *Official Bulletin* 1 (November 7, 1917): 4; *Commercial and Financial Chronicle* 105 (December 1, 1917): 2145.
35. U.S. Food Administration's second home card ("Additional Directions to First Home Card"), December 1, 1917, copy in USFA Papers, Box 3; U.S. Food Administration press release 532, December 13, 1917, USFA Documents.
36. William Phillips diary, October 19, 1917, William Phillips Papers, Houghton Library, Harvard University.
37. Maxcy Robson Dickson, *The Food Front in World War I* (Washington, D.C., 1944), pp. 25–30; Mullendore, *History*, p. 85.
38. A set of these press releases is in USFA Documents, HHPL.
39. Dickson, *Food Front*, pp. 28, 61–65; Mullendore, *History*, pp. 100–01; Smith, "New Mexico's Wartime Food Problems," pp. 376–77; Carol Reuss, "The *Ladies' Home Journal* and Hoover's Food Program," *Journalism Quarterly* 49 (Winter 1972): 740–42.
40. Dickson, *Food Front*, pp. 38–39, 43.
41. Ibid., pp. 122–24.
42. Ibid., pp. 131–33.
43. Ibid., p. 121; *New York Times*, September 17, 1917, p. 1; *Official Bulletin* 1 (September 17, 1917): 4.
44. Mullendore, *History*, p. 88; *Official Bulletin* 1 (September 17, 1917): 4.
45. *New York Times*, September 17, 1917, p. 1.
46. Mullendore, *History*, pp. 89–90.
47. Edith Guerrier, *We Pledged Allegiance: A Librarian's Intimate Story of the United States Food Administration* (Stanford, Calif., 1941); Wayne A. Wiegand, *"An Active Instrument for Propaganda": The American Public Library During World War I* (New York, 1989), pp. 71–86.
48. Edith Guerrier, quoted in Wiegand, *"An Active Instrument for Propaganda,"* p. 71.
49. Dickson, *Food Front*, pp. 121, 128.
50. Quoted in Wiegand, *"An Active Instrument for Propaganda,"* p. 77.
51. Quoted in Dickson, *Food Front*, p. 66.

52. Quoted in ibid., p. 185.
53. Paul Willard Garrett, *Government Control Over Prices* (Washington, D.C., 1920), p. 56. One of Hoover's associates concurred: "No enterprise, public or private, has ever received the widespread display through outdoor and other mediums of advertising that was furnished to the Food Administration." Mullendore, *History*, p. 88.
54. In a memorandum to his organization in mid-August, Hoover said: "We wish to build up the Food Administration as an institution—not a personality—and, therefore, the rule of eliminating my name in every particular from publicity should be adhered to." Hoover, memorandum #60 to all departments, August 16, 1917, USFA Papers, Box 130.
55. Charles Seymour, *Woodrow Wilson and the World War* (New Haven, Conn., 1921), p. 164.
56. Donald Wilhelm, "Hoover and His Food Organization," *American Review of Reviews* 56 (September 1917): 286.
57. The earliest use of "Hooverize" that I have discovered is in the headline of a September 13, 1917, newspaper clipping ("Bankers Partake of a 'Hooverized' Dinner"), Clipping File, HHPL. Another early usage was in the caption ("Are You Hooverizing Your Dinner?") of a cartoon in the *Kokomo* [Indiana] *Tribune*, November 10, 1917, also in the Clipping File, HHPL. See also *New York Times*, November 22, 1917, p. 15. Hoover's publicity director, Ben S. Allen, helped to popularize the word. See Victoria French Allen, "A Member of the Fourth Estate" (typescript, n.d.), p. 162, in the Ben S. Allen Collection (cited in chapter 1, note 1). According to Charles Seymour in 1921, "To 'Hooverize' became a national habit" during the war—*Woodrow Wilson and the World War*, p. 164. See also Mark Sullivan, *Our Times*, vol. V: *Over Here* (New York, 1933), p. 419.
58. Mable I. Clapp, "Hoover's Goin' to Get You," *Ladies' Home Journal* 34 (November 1917): 146. The poem has two additional stanzas.
59. U.S. Food Administration, Trade and Technical Press Section, *Weekly Bulletin* 1 (January 12, 1918): 1, copy in USFA Documents. Reprinted in *Commercial and Financial Chronicle* 106 (January 19, 1918): 245.
60. Mary F. Rensch to Lou Henry Hoover, November 17, 1917, "Food Administration Correspondence, 1917," Subject File, Lou Henry Hoover Papers; Herbert Hoover, *The Memoirs of Herbert Hoover*, vol. I: *Years of Adventure* (New York, 1951), p. 250; Sullivan, *Over Here*, p. 419.
61. John O'Hara Cosgrave to Hoover, August 29, 1917, USFA Papers, Box 187. At this point Cosgrave, an editor of the New York *World*, was on loan to the Food Administration. Later in the war Cosgrave traveled several times from New York to Washington to confer with "the Chief."
62. Memorandum for the Educational Division, August 24, 1918, USFA Papers, Box 39; Mullendore, *History*, p. 84.
63. Notes of a speech by Ben S. Allen at Stanford University, n.d., in "Food Administration: Public Relations," Subject File, Lou Henry Hoover Papers.
64. Craig Lloyd, *Aggressive Introvert: A Study of Herbert Hoover and Public Relations Management, 1912–1932* (Columbus, Ohio, 1972), p. 56, note 37.
65. Minna Lewinson and Henry B. Hough, *A History of the Services Rendered to the Public by the American Press During the Year 1917* (New York, 1918), p. 15.
66. Unsigned memorandum, August 17, 1917, USFA Papers, Box 34.
67. White House memorandum, September 21, 1917, Woodrow Wilson Papers, LC. The President approved the request on September 21, in response to Hoover's letter of September 18.
68. For an example of the political minefields which Hoover traversed in selecting his state food administrators, see Smith, "New Mexico's Wartime Food Problems," pp. 361–65. Another problem state was Colorado. See Woodrow Wilson to Hoover, September 18 and 20, 1917, and Hoover to Wilson, September 25, 1917, all in Wilson Papers.
69. Hoover to Wilson, June 28, 1917, Wilson Papers. The President routinely approved nearly all of Hoover's nominations. For example, see Wilson to Hoover, August 21, 1917, Wilson

Papers. But his approval was not automatic, as indicated by the correspondence cited in the previous note.

70. Herbert Hoover, *Annual Report of United States Food Administration* [for 1917], p. 13, printed in U.S. Congress, House of Representatives, 65th Congress, 2d Session, Document No. 837: *The United States Food Administration and United States Fuel Administration* (Washington, D.C., 1918); Mullendore, *History*, pp. 70–71.
71. Hoover memorandum to his Organization Committee, July 26, 1917, in Mark Requa, "Hoover" (typescript, n.d.), pp. 14–17, Mark Requa Papers, HI.
72. Ibid.
73. Ibid.; Edgar Rickard to Edward B. Sturgis, October 23, 1917, USFA Papers, Box 230; Rickard to Suda L. Bane, March 15, 1938, "Hoover Institution—Collections Sought—Food Administration, 1920–38," Subject File, Belgian American Educational Foundation Papers, HHPL; Wilbur, *Memoirs*, p. 262.
74. Hoover memorandum to his Organization Committee, July 26, 1917.
75. Hoover, alluding to his way of organizing the U.S. Food Administration. Quoted in Walter R. Livingston oral history (1969), p. 16, HHPL.
76. Rickard to Bane, March 15, 1938.
77. Lewis L. Strauss oral history (1967), p. 10, HHPL. Strauss, who was Hoover's personal secretary at the time, saw the Chief repeat this gesture on a number of occasions.
78. Hoover to Woodrow Wilson, November 5, 1917, Wilson Papers; Woodrow Wilson executive order 2754, November 10, 1917, in Congressional Information Service, *Presidential Executive Orders and Proclamations on Microfiche* (Washington, D.C., 1987); Joseph P. Tumulty to Hoover, November 13, 1917, "Wilson, Woodrow," Pre-Commerce Papers, Hoover Papers.
79. Robert D. Cuff, "Herbert Hoover, The Ideology of Voluntarism and War Organization During the Great War," *Journal of American History* 64 (September 1977): 363.
80. Mark Requa memorandum to Hoover, October 3, 1917, USFA Papers, Box 49.
81. Requa, "Hoover," pp. 25–26.
82. U.S. Food Administration press releases 416 (November 11, 1917) and 534 (December 14, 1917), USFA Documents; *Weekly Northwestern Miller* 113 (February 6, 1918): 435. The building was in the "Foggy Bottom" section of Washington.
83. Edgar Rickard to Louis Chevrillon, November 28, 1917, USFA Papers, Box 230.
84. Biographical directory of 47 U.S. Food Administration staffers (typescript, n.d.), USFA Papers, Box 10.
85. Mullendore, *History*, p. 355.
86. Hoover, "Introduction," in ibid., pp. 8–9.

CHAPTER 7

1. Hoover to David F. Houston, August 8, 1917, USFA Papers, Box 83A, HI.
2. Murray R. Benedict, *Farm Policies of the United States, 1790–1950* (New York, 1953), p. 152; Gifford Pinchot to Henry C. Wallace, February 27, 1918, Henry C. Wallace Papers, Box 1, University of Iowa Libraries; Charles McCarthy, "Memo on Food Policy" (May 1, 1918), Charles McCarthy Papers, Box 25, State Historical Society of Wisconsin.
3. *Wallaces' Farmer* 42 (August 31, 1917): 1176. Many farmers in fact resisted attempts to organize them and integrate them into a modern industrial economy. See David B. Danbom, *The Resisted Revolution: Urban America and the Industrialization of Agriculture, 1900–1930* (Ames, Iowa, 1979), especially chapter 5.
4. R. M. McClintock to Victor Murdock, October 19 and 23, 1917, Victor Murdock Papers, Box 61, LC.
5. McCarthy, "Memo on Food Policy"; Tom G. Hall, "Cheap Bread from Dear Wheat: Herbert Hoover, the Wilson Administration, and the Management of Wheat Prices, 1916–1920" (Ph.D. dissertation, University of California at Davis, 1970), pp. 34–39; Marion

Therese Casey, "Charles McCarthy: Policy Maker for an Era" (Ph.D. dissertation, University of Wisconsin, 1971), pp. 226–27.

6. McCarthy, "Memo on Food Policy"; E. C. Lasater to Hoover, November 12, 1917, printed in U.S. Congress, Senate, Committee on Agriculture and Forestry, 65th Congress, 2d Session, *Increased Production of Grain and Meat Products* (Washington, D.C., 1918), pp. 630–34 (hereinafter cited as *Increased Production* hearings).
7. U.S. Congress, Senate, Committee on Agriculture and Forestry, 65th Congress, 3d Session, *Government Control of the Meat-Packing Industry* (Washington, D.C., 1919), pp. 1995–2015, 2024; G. O. Virtue, "The Meat-Packing Investigation," *Quarterly Journal of Economics* 34 (August 1920): 626–30; Thomas Lane Moore III, "The Establishment of a 'New Freedom' Policy: The Federal Trade Commission, 1912–1918" (Ph.D. dissertation, University of Alabama, 1980), p. 257.
8. Moore, "The Establishment of a 'New Freedom" Policy," p. 257.
9. Maxcy Robson Dickson, *The Food Front in World War I* (Washington, D.C., 1944), p. 36.
10. Gifford Pinchot to Edward M. House, October 20, 1917, Edward M. House Papers, Box 90, Manuscripts and Archives, Yale University Library; Gifford Pinchot, "Mr. Pinchot's Work for Increasing and Conserving the Food Supply During the War" (typescript, n.d.), Gifford Pinchot Papers, Box 544, LC.
11. McCarthy, "Memo on Food Policy"; James L. Guth, "The National Board of Farm Organizations: Experiment in Political Cooperation," *Agricultural History* 48 (July 1974): 420–21.
12. Hoover, handwritten comments about Pinchot, n.d. (probably ca. 1957), "Pinchot, Gifford," Pre-Commerce Papers, Herbert Hoover Papers, HHPL.
13. Ibid.; Pinchot, "Mr. Pinchot's Work." Hoover claimed that Pinchot came to him for a job. Pinchot claimed that he went to Washington at Hoover's request.
14. Hoover to David F. Houston, August 15, 1917, "U.S. Food Administration—Agriculture, Department of," Pre-Commerce Papers.
15. Mark L. Requa to E. C. Lasater, November 22, 1917, printed in *Increased Production* hearings, pp. 621–23; Requa to Edgar Rickard, April 17, 1920, USFA Papers, Box 47.
16. Requa to Lasater, November 22, 1917.
17. Requa to Rickard, April 17, 1920.
18. McCarthy, "Memo on Food Policy."
19. Pinchot to Wallace, February 27, 1918.
20. U.S. Department of Agriculture, *Weekly News Letter* 5 (September 19, 1917): 2.
21. Pinchot to House, October 20, 1917; Frank M. Surface, *American Pork Production in the World War* (Chicago and New York, 1926), p. 32.
22. Hoover to Woodrow Wilson, August 31, 1917, Woodrow Wilson Papers, LC; Hoover to Lord Rhondda, October 2, 1917, USFA Papers, Box 131.
23. *New York Times*, August 22, 1917, p. 6.
24. *Official Bulletin* 1 (August 22, 1917): 1–2; *New York Times*, August 22, 1917, p. 6. A complete typewritten copy of this joint statement is in the John A. Simpson Papers, Box 2, Western History Collections, University of Oklahoma Library. For Lasater's remark that he drafted this policy document, see Lasater to Hoover, November 12, 1917.
25. Hoover / Houston statement, cited in the preceding note.
26. Pinchot to Henry C. Wallace, October 26, 1917, copy in USFA Papers, Box 47; Hoover to Woodrow Wilson, November 19, 1917, Wilson Papers.
27. See E. C. Lasater and Gifford Pinchot, "Memorandum for Mr. Hoover" (August 20, 1917), printed in U.S. Congress, House of Representatives, Committee on Interstate and Foreign Commerce, 65th Congress, 3rd Session, *Government Control of Meat-Packing Industry* (Washington, D.C., 1919), p. 1489 (hereinafter cited as *Government Control* hearings).
28. Gifford Pinchot, "Proposed Plan for Increasing the Meat Supply" (August 28, 1917), in "Pinchot, Gifford," Pre-Commerce Papers. Copies of this document, dated August 26, 1917, are in the Pinchot Papers, Box 544, and the House Papers, Box 61. See also Pinchot, "Mr. Pinchot's Work."
29. Pinchot to House, October 20, 1917.

30. Hoover to Woodrow Wilson, November 19, 1917, Wilson Papers. According to Hoover in this letter, Pinchot had wanted the Food Administration to "take over the packing plants in the country and operate them for the Government." Pinchot did not actually propose this (at least in late August); it was Lasater who advocated out-and-out seizure of the packing houses. But in Hoover's mind, Pinchot's proposal for governmental fixing of livestock prices at the stockyards on a daily basis may have been tantamount to the same thing.
31. Hoover to Henry C. Wallace, February 3, 1918, Wallace Papers, Box 1. In a letter to the President in 1917, Hoover declared: "Hogs in the United States are, in the last analysis, a corn product." Hoover to Woodrow Wilson, September 4, 1917, Wilson Papers.
32. Wallace to Pinchot, August 4, 1917, Wallace Papers, Box 1.
33. Hoover to Wilson, September 4, 1917.
34. Hoover's remarks, as summarized and quoted in the text, are found in the Minutes of the Livestock Conference in Washington, D.C., September 5–7, 1917, as follows: September 5, 1917 session, pp. 6–8, in "Livestock Conference in Washington, D.C. (2)" folder; September 6, 1917, 4:20 P.M. session, pp. 6–8, 20–21, in "Livestock Correspondence, September 1917" folder; September 7, 1917 session, p. 58, in "Livestock Correspondence, September–October 1917" folder. All in General Correspondence of the Office of the Secretary of Agriculture, RG 16, NARA.
35. Pinchot to House, October 20, 1917.
36. Minutes of the Livestock Conference in Washington, D.C., September 6, 1917, 4:20 P.M. session, pp. 3, 11, 14. Even before this meeting Hoover had publicly denied any intention to fix prices on beef and pork products. U.S. Food Administration press release 165, August 25, 1917, USFA Documents, HHPL.
37. Minutes of the Livestock Conference in Washington, D.C., September 6, 1917, 4:20 P.M. session, p. 5.
38. Ibid., p. 13.
39. Ibid., p. 38.
40. Ibid., pp. 6–7; Minutes of the Livestock Conference in Washington, D.C., September 5, 1917 session, p. 8.
41. When Hoover declared at the conference that he had "no power to fix prices" and that it was not necessary to discuss the subject any longer, he was applauded. Minutes of the Livestock Conference in Washington, D.C., September 6, 1917, 4:20 P.M. session, p. 11.
42. Wallace to Pinchot, October 29, 1917, Pinchot Papers, Box 209.
43. Pinchot to House, October 20, 1917.
44. Resolutions of the U.S. Live Stock Industry Committee, adopted at its conference in Washington, D.C., September 5–7, 1917, in U.S. Department of Agriculture, *Weekly News Letter* 5 (September 19, 1917): 1–3.
45. Ibid., p. 3; minutes of the Livestock Conference in Washington, D.C., September 6, 1917, 4:20 P.M. session, pp. 38–39.
46. Pinchot to Wallace, February 27, 1918.
47. Wilson to Hoover, September 7, 1917, "Wilson, Woodrow," Pre-Commerce Papers.
48. Herbert Hoover, *An American Epic*, vol. II (Chicago, 1960), p. 96.
49. Pinchot to House, October 20, 1917.
50. So, at least, Pinchot claimed. Pinchot, "Mr. Pinchot's Work."
51. "Report by Certain Members of the Live Stock Industry Committee" (September 18, 1917), printed in *Increased Production* hearings, pp. 61–63, and in *Government Control* hearings, pp. 1487–89. A typewritten copy and a typewritten synopsis are in the House Papers, Box 61.
52. Pinchot to House, October 20, 1917; Lasater to Hoover, November 12, 1917.
53. Hoover to W. T. Creasy, September 24, 1917, printed in *Increased Production* hearings, pp. 518–19.
54. Hoover to J. F. Deems, September 28, 1917, printed in *Increased Production* hearings, pp. 519–20.
55. Hoover address to the Pennsylvania Committee of Public Safety, September 29, 1917, Public Statements File, Hoover Papers. In this speech Hoover did remark: "It is easy

enough to say that the Government should not fix the price, but when you endow the Government to purchase such commodities [as fats], they will fix the price, and in so doing, endeavor to avoid speculation. . . ." He did not, however, indicate what this governmentally determined price might be.

56. Pinchot to House, October 20, 1917.
57. Wallace to Hoover, September 24, 1917, file 16HA-A3, Box 667, RG 4, NARA.
58. Pinchot, "Increasing the Meat Supply" (September 26, 1917), copies in House Papers, Box 61, and Pinchot Papers, Box 606.
59. Pinchot to House, October 20, 1917.
60. Ibid.
61. Pinchot to Wallace, September 25, 1917, Wallace Papers, Box 1.
62. Wallace telegram to Pinchot, September 26, 1917, Wallace Papers, Box 1.
63. Wallace to Pinchot, September 26, 1917, Pinchot Papers, Box 209.
64. Pinchot to Wallace, September 26, 1917, Wallace Papers, Box 1.
65. Pinchot and Lasater to Wallace, September 30, 1917, Wallace Papers, Box 1.
66. Wallace to E. L. Burke, October 2, 1917; Wallace to Pinchot, December 11, 1917. Both in Wallace Papers, Box 1.
67. The original holograph of this key document has not been found. I have quoted here a typewritten copy, dated September 29, 1917, in the Pinchot Papers, Box 544. At the bottom are these handwritten words: "Given to Mr. Pinchot when he started west to hold the meetings." A typewritten copy is also in the Wallace Papers, Box 1. According to Pinchot (in his letter to Colonel House on October 20), the original memorandum was handwritten by Hoover himself. This assertion was supported by Wallace, who later stated that Pinchot showed him the handwritten version in October (Wallace to Pinchot, December 11, 1917). According to Pinchot (in his letter to House), all of the memorandum quoted here was in Hoover's own hand, except for the last sentence, which Pinchot said he took down from Hoover by dictation. Despite the apparent disappearance of the original document, there seems to be no reason to disbelieve Pinchot's story.
68. Pinchot to House, October 20, 1917.
69. Ibid.
70. Charles McCarthy, notes on Herbert Hoover (October 1918), McCarthy Papers, Box 22.
71. Hoover, private address in Philadelphia, September 29, 1917, Public Statements File, Hoover Papers.
72. A. Sykes et al. ("representatives of swine growers of the corn belt"), to Hoover, October 3, 1917, printed in *Government Control* hearings, pp. 1492–93 and 1798–99. A typewritten copy is in the House Papers, Box 61.
73. Members of the National Swine Growers' Association et al. to Hoover, October 5, 1917, printed in *Government Control* hearings, p. 1799; Pinchot to House, October 20, 1917.
74. Pinchot to Wallace, October 6, 1917, Wallace Papers, Box 1.
75. Ibid.
76. Edward M. House diary, October 7, 1917, House Papers.
77. Wallace to Charles McCarthy, October 4, 1917, file 26H-A1, Box 946, RG 4, NARA.
78. Wallace to Mark L. Requa, October 4, 1917, file 16HA-A3, Box 667, RG 4, NARA.
79. Charles McCarthy memorandum for Mark L. Requa, October 4, 1917, file 26H-A1, Box 947, RG 4, NARA.
80. *Wallaces' Farmer* 42 (October 12, 1917): 1377.
81. Hoover to Harry A. Wheeler, October 5, 1917, in "Grain Corporation, Book I," file 10H-A7, Box 470, RG 4, NARA.
82. Hoover, quoted in *Wallaces' Farmer* 42 (October 19, 1917): 1417.
83. Hoover to Wheeler, October 5, 1917.
84. *Wallaces' Farmer* 42 (October 19, 1917): 1417.
85. *Chicago Journal* article, October 6, 1917, printed in part in *Increased Production* hearings, p. 522.
86. According to Lasater, the cost exceeded $18.00 per hundredweight. *Increased Production*

hearings, p. 522. On October 24, 1917, Henry C. Wallace stated that hogs then being marketed had cost $18.00–$19.50 per hundredweight to produce. Wallace to Hoover, October 24, 1917, USFA Papers, Box 177.

87. Wallace to Mark L. Requa, October 9, 1917 (plus enclosure), file 16HA-A3, Box 667, RG 4, NARA; Wallace to Charles McCarthy, October 20, 1917, McCarthy Papers, Box 15; W. B. Tagg to Lasater, October 22, 1917, Pinchot Papers, Box 208; H. J. Waters to Hoover, October 22, 1917, USFA Papers, Box 6; Charles W. Holman to McCarthy, October 26, 1917, McCarthy Papers, Box 15; *Prairie Farmer* 89 (November 3, 1917): 766; Lasater testimony, March 30, 1918, *Increased Production* hearings, p. 522.
88. The Waters and Tagg telegrams of October 22, 1917 (cited in the preceding note) both spoke of lost confidence among the farmers.
89. Wallace to McCarthy, October 20, 1917.
90. Hoover telegram to Ralph Merritt, October 17, 1917, folder A-17, Box 49, U.S. Food Administration Records, RG 4, National Archives—San Francisco branch; "Statement of the United States Food Administration With Regard to the Testimony of E. C. Lasater Before the Senate Committee on Agriculture and Forestry" (May 1, 1918), printed in *Increased Production* hearings, pp. 597–608. According to the Food Administration, it sent out more than sixty telegrams of denial, some of them signed by Lasater himself.
91. Hoover to Julius H. Barnes, October 18, 1917, USFA Papers, Box 245.
92. Hoover to Merritt, October 17, 1917. Hoover notified all other state food administrators as well. Hoover to Barnes, October 18, 1917.
93. On October 13—one full week after the story appeared—Hoover suggested that Durand "put out some contradiction" of it since it was "obviously garbled" and was "creating discontent among growers." But Hoover himself did not repudiate the article until October 17, 1917. See Hoover telegram to Harry A. Wheeler, October 13, 1917, USFA Papers, Box 12.
94. Hoover to H. J. Waters, October 25, 1917, USFA Papers, Box 48.
95. Lasater to Hoover, November 12, 1917.
96. *Prairie Farmer* 89 (November 3, 1917): 766; *Commercial and Financial Chronicle* 105 (November 10, 1917): 1851.
97. Wallace to Hoover, February 11, 1918, USFA Papers, Box 177.
98. Wallace to Pinchot, October 11, 1917, Pinchot Papers, Box 209.
99. Lasater to Hoover, November 12, 1917; Lasater statement printed in *Increased Production* hearings, p. 610.
100. Lasater testimony in *Increased Production* hearings, p. 522.
101. See *Increased Production* hearings, p. 597. See also Hoover to Wallace, February 16 and 26, 1918, Wallace Papers, Box 1. Hoover insisted that the so-called Durand interview never occurred.
102. William A. Glasgow, Jr., testimony, February 6, 1919, in *Government Control* hearings, p. 1807.
103. "Statement of the United States Food Administration With Regard to the Testimony of Mr. E. C. Lasater. . . ," in *Increased Production* hearings, p. 598.
104. Pinchot to Wallace, October 11, 1917, Wallace Papers, Box 1.
105. Lasater testimony, March 30, 1918, in *Increased Production* hearings, pp. 532–33.
106. Pinchot to Wallace, October 11, 1917; Pinchot to House, October 20, 1917.
107. Pinchot to Wallace, October 11, 1917.
108. Requa to Wallace, October 6, 1917, file 16HA-A3, Box 667, RG 4, NARA.
109. Wallace to Requa, October 9, 1917.
110. Requa to Wallace, October 11, 1917, file 16HA-A3, Box 667, RG 4, NARA.
111. Wallace to Requa, October 15, 1917, file 16HA-A3, Box 667, RG 4, NARA.
112. Wallace to Pinchot, October 15, 1917, Pinchot Papers, Box 209.
113. Pinchot to Wallace, October 26, 1917; Requa to Lasater, November 22, 1917.
114. Pinchot to Wallace, October 26, 1917.

115. Wallace to Pinchot, December 11, 1917, Wallace Papers, Box 1; John M. Evvard to U.S. Food Administration, January 10, 1918, USFA Papers, Box 47.
116. Pinchot to Wallace, October 11, 1917; Pinchot to House, October 20, 1917.
117. Ibid.
118. Pinchot to House, October 20, 1917; Pinchot to Wallace, October 26, 1917. See also Lasater to Hoover, November 12, 1917.
119. Lasater to Hoover, November 12, 1917.
120. Ibid.; Lasater testimony, March 30, 1918, in *Increased Production* hearings, pp. 530–32.
121. Pinchot to Wallace, October 11, 1917.
122. Hoover telegrams to Wallace, October 13 and 15, 1917, Wallace Papers, Box 1.
123. Wallace to Pinchot, October 16, 1917, Wallace Papers, Box 1.
124. Wallace to Pinchot, October 18, 1917, USFA Papers, Box 177; Wallace to Hoover, October 19, 1917, Wallace Papers, Box 1; Hoover, *American Epic,* II, p. 99.
125. Hoover to David F. Houston, October 16, 1917, USFA Papers, Box 83B.
126. David F. Houston to Hoover, October 26, 1917, USFA Papers, Box 83B.
127. Hoover, *American Epic,* II, pp. 99.
128. Wallace to McCarthy, October 20, 1917.
129. "Notes on Hog Prices" (October 20, 1917), file 26H-A1, Box 946, RG 4, NARA.
130. Hoover, *American Epic,* II, p. 99. Hoover met the President at the White House on October 23, 1917. Appointments Book, 1917, Wilson Papers.
131. Lasater to Hoover, October 20, 1917, "Pinchot, Gifford," Pre-Commerce Papers.
132. Charles W. Holman to McCarthy, October 24, 1917, McCarthy Papers, Box 15; Pinchot to Wallace, October 26, 1917; Lasater to Hoover, November 12, 1917.
133. Pinchot to House, October 20, 1917.
134. Lasater / Pinchot memorandum for Hoover, October 21, 1917, printed in *Government Control* hearings, pp. 1489–90; Pinchot to Lasater, October 22, 1917, Pinchot Papers, Box 205; Holman to McCarthy, October 24, 1917; Pinchot to Wallace, October 26, 1917.
135. Holman to McCarthy, October 24, 1917; Pinchot to Wallace, October 26, 1917.
136. Pinchot to Wallace, October 26, 1917.
137. Pinchot to Hoover, October 25, 1917, "Pinchot, Gifford," Pre-Commerce Papers.
138. Pinchot to Wallace, October 26, 1917.
139. Hoover, handwritten comments about Pinchot, n.d.(probably ca. 1957), cited in note 12.
140. See for example Pinchot to Lasater, November 29, 1917, copy in Wallace Papers, Box 1; Wallace to Pinchot, January 21, 1918, Pinchot Papers, Box 217; Lasater to Pinchot, February 9, 1918, Wallace Papers, Box 1. The only possible exception that I have located is a letter from Wallace to Pinchot just after the Waterloo and Omaha meetings. Wrote Wallace: "If you can not get results now, I think nothing more can be done as long as Mr. Hoover is at the head of things." Wallace to Pinchot, October 8, 1917. This proves dissatisfaction but not necessarily conspiracy.
141. Neither in 1917 nor later did Hoover, in writing, ascribe his difficulties with Pinchot to anything other than policy differences—until 1957 or so, when he wrote the comments cited in note 139. Hoover evidently drafted these statements for inclusion in *An American Epic,* only to omit them. They are attached to a copy of the published passage (*An American Epic,* II, p. 102) in which he very briefly discussed the Pinchot / Lasater affair.
142. Hoover to Pinchot, October 26, 1917, "Pinchot, Gifford," Pre-Commerce Papers. Hoover did not send Pinchot this rejoinder. Instead, on the advice of Mark Requa, he sent Pinchot a brief reply stating that, on reconsideration, he believed that "no controversy of any kind is warranted in this time of national emergency." Hoover to Pinchot, October 27, 1917, Pinchot Papers, Box 205; Requa memorandum to Hoover, October 29, 1917, USFA Papers, Box 49. Although Hoover's second letter to Pinchot was dated the twenty-seventh, he evidently did not mail it until after receiving Requa's memo two days later.
143. Pinchot to Wallace, October 26, 1917.
144. Ibid.

145. Joseph P. Cotton testimony, March 19, 1918, in *Increased Production* hearings, pp. 395–96; Owen Hugh Smith memorandum, "Allied Provisions Commission," n.d. (ca. November 2, 1917), F / 210 / 1, David Lloyd George Papers, House of Lords Record Office, London.
146. Mullendore, *History*, p. 263.
147. Ibid., p. 325; Surface, *American Pork Production*, p. 42.
148. McCarthy to Holman, October 24, 1917, McCarthy Papers, Box 15.
149. Hoover, *American Epic*, II, p. 99.
150. Surface, *American Pork Production*, p. 41.
151. Hoover to Waters, October 25, 1917.
152. Hoover's assistant, Charles McCarthy—a scrappy son of Irish immigrants and a former football coach—wrote of Hoover in 1918: "I never came across such a cowardly man in public life." In the eyes of the combative McCarthy, Hoover had been "thoroughly cowardly" in his dealing with Secretary of Agriculture Houston (whom McCarthy disliked—and vice versa). In McCarthy's view, Hoover's "fundamental cowardice" was his "worst fault." McCarthy, who observed Hoover closely for many months in 1917, concluded that Hoover had an intense fear of ridicule and failure. Charles McCarthy, notes on Hoover (October 1918), McCarthy Papers, Box 22.

    It should be noted that McCarthy was regarded by his critics in Washington as an impatient radical and a "wild Irishman." See David Houston to Woodrow Wilson, September 4, 1918, Wilson Papers.
153. See U.S. Food Administration Bulletin No. 10: *Grain and Livestock* (Washington, D.C., 1917), copy in Public Statements File, HHPL, under date of October 25, 1917. This document is quoted extensively in the *New York Times*, October 26, 1917, p. 5. The newspaper headlined its article: "Win War with Hogs, So Hoover Sees It."
154. Wallace to Pinchot, October 29, 1917, Pinchot Papers, Box 209.
155. John M. Evvard et al., report of the commission appointed to determine the cost of hog production in terms of bushels of corn, October 27, 1917, enclosed with Evvard to Hoover, October 29, 1917, USFA Papers, Box 49. A typewritten copy of the report is in the Wallace Papers, Box 1. The report was included in the *Government Control* hearings, pp. 1538–42, and was printed as a pamphlet by the Food Administration's meat division under the title *Hog and Corn Ratios* (Chicago, 1917).
156. The Evvard commission specifically noted the "big tendency to market potential breeding stock." For the Food Administration's fears that farmers would give up on hog production entirely, see *Commercial and Financial Chronicle* 105 (November 10, 1917): 1851.
157. Wallace to Pinchot, November 5, 1917, Pinchot Papers, Box 209.
158. Hoover, *American Epic*, II, p. 99.
159. Ibid.; Wallace to Pinchot, November 5, 1917.
160. Joseph P. Cotton to Hoover, November 17, 1917, USFA Papers, Box 47.
161. For Cotton's announcement of November 3, 1917, see U.S. Food Administration Meat Division, *Prices of Hogs* (Chicago, 1917), copy in USFA Papers, Box 47. It is quoted in full in Surface, *American Pork Production*, pp. 37–38.
162. Wallace to Pinchot, November 5, 1917. As soon as he issued his statement, Cotton telegraphed Hoover: "My statement has gone out against about everybody's judgment." Cotton to Hoover, November 3, 1917, USFA Papers, Box 279. Hoover's secretary replied that Hoover was "heartily for your statement." Lewis L. Strauss to Cotton, November 3, 1917, USFA Papers, Box 47, file 15-H.
163. Cotton to Frank M. Surface, November 15, 1926, copy enclosed with Surface to Edward M. Flesh, November 26, 1926, file 14H-B2, Box 620, RG 4, NARA. Cotton asserted in 1926 that he had deliberately decided in 1917 not to link the corn / hog formula "to the operations of a particular market." Indeed, his 1917 announcement of the ratio made no reference to any market. He did not, however, make explicit his implicit rejection of the Evvard commission's advocacy of Chicago as the basis for calculating hog prices.

164. Cotton to Hoover, November 17, 1917; Cotton to Hoover, November 14, 1917, USFA Papers, Box 47.
165. Ibid.; Wallace to Pinchot, October 29, 1917.
166. Wallace to Pinchot, November 5, 1917; *Wallaces' Farmer* 42 (November 9, 1917): 1520. Privately, however, Wallace was annoyed by Hoover's delay in establishing the policy and by the Food Administration's failure to commit itself to working out hog values on the basis of the price of corn in Chicago (as opposed to the price of corn on the farm). See Wallace to Hoover, February 11, 1918.
167. Pinchot to Wallace, November 9 and 21, 1917, Wallace Papers, Box 1; Pinchot to Sir Horace Plunkett, November 9, 1917, Pinchot Papers, Box 207; Pinchot to House, November 29, 1917. There is no direct evidence that Pinchot's resignation had any effect of the Food Administration's subsequent policy. The Evvard commission was already preparing to meet, while the packers agreed in principle to Hoover's plan on the very day of Pinchot's resignation—quite independently of Pinchot's actions. But the Pennsylvanian's departure may have deprived Hoover of maneuvering room. Hoover surely knew that if he now rejected the Evvard commission's report and refused to offer some kind of promise to hog farmers, the disgruntled Pinchot could go public, to Hoover's embarrassment. Pinchot's resignation thus gave Hoover an incentive to arrange quickly what in all likelihood was going to happen anyway.
168. Lasater to Hoover, November 12, 1917.
169. Hoover to Wallace, November 6, 1917, Wallace Papers.
170. Mark L. Requa, "Hoover" (typescript, n.d.), p. 31, Mark L. Requa Papers, HI.
171. Lasater to Hoover, November 9, 1917, file 15HA-A3, Box 640, RG 4, NARA.
172. Lasater testimony, March 30, 1918, in *Increased Production* hearings, p. 534.
173. Hoover to Wilson, November 19, 1917.
174. Wilson to Hoover, November 20, 1917, "Wilson Woodrow," Pre-Commerce Papers.
175. Lasater testimony, February 4 and 5, 1919, in *Government Control* hearings, pp. 1504–05, 1533, 1588, 1594. See also Lasater's printed pamphlet, *Facts Affecting the United States Food Administration and the People of the United States* (n.p., n.d.), copy in Pinchot Papers, Box 544. Ironically, Lasater himself drafted the joint Hoover / Houston statement of August 22, 1917, that contained what Lasater later claimed were the false statistics.
176. Pinchot to Lasater, November 29, 1917; Pinchot to Wallace, February 27, 1918.
177. Requa to Lasater, November 22, 1917; Hoover to Lasater, December 4, 1917; "Statement of the United States Food Administration With Regard to the Testimony of Mr. E. C. Lasater. . . ."
178. "Statement of the United States Food Administration With Regard to the Testimony of Mr. E. C. Lasater. . . ."
179. Hoover, handwritten comments about Pinchot, n.d. (probably ca. 1957).
180. Hoover, handwritten notation, October 1920, at bottom of Pinchot's letter of resignation of October 25, 1917.
181. *Sacramento Union*, April 18, 1920, pp. 1, 9. A copy of this article by Allen is in the Pinchot Papers, Box 233.
182. Hoover, handwritten comments about Pinchot, n.d. (probably ca. 1957).
183. McCarthy, notes on Hoover (October 1918), McCarthy Papers, Box 22. For a useful account of McCarthy's wartime service in the Food Administration, see Casey, "Charles McCarthy," pp. 216–67.
184. Virtue, "The Meat-Packing Investigation," pp. 633–34; Robert D. Cuff, "The Dilemmas of Voluntarism: Hoover and the Pork-Packing Agreement of 1917–1919," *Agricultural History* 53 (October 1979): 728.
185. Requa, "Hoover," p. 11.
186. Lasater testimony, February 5, 1919, in *Government Control* hearings, p. 1604.
187. Harry Garfield to James R. Garfield, August 16, 1917, James R. Garfield Papers, Box 111, LC.

188. Minutes of the Livestock Conference in Washington, D.C., September 6, 1917, 4:20 P.M. session, pp. 1–2; *New York Times*, September 7, 1917, p. 3.
189. Minutes of the Livestock Conference in Washington, D.C., September 7, 1917 session, p. 60.
190. Hoover to Wilson, September 4, 1917.
191. Minutes of the Livestock Conference in Washington, D.C., September 7, 1917 session, pp. 59–60; U.S. Food Administration press release 195, September 8, 1917, USFA Documents.
192. *Official Bulletin* 1 (September 13, 1917): 1; *New York Times*, September 13, 1917, p. 3.
193. Minutes of the Livestock Conference in Washington, D.C., September 6, 1917 session, p. 1; *New York Times*, September 7, 1917, p. 3; Requa, "Hoover," p. 12. Requa's strong convictions on this issue probably reinforced Hoover's.
194. *New York Times*, October 11, 1917, pp. 1, 2.
195. Hoover to Woodrow Wilson, October 22, 1917, USFA Papers, file 1-H; U.S. Food Administration press release 383, October 29, 1917, USFA Documents; Joseph P. Cotton testimony, March 19, 1918, in *Increased Production* hearings, pp. 395, 448–49; William P. Glasgow, Jr., testimony, February 6, 1919, in *Government Control* hearings, p. 1800; Harlan B. Phillips, ed., *Felix Frankfurter Reminisces* (New York, 1960), p. 218. According to Glasgow (who was counsel to the Food Administration at the time of his testimony cited here), Hoover selected Cotton "on the recommendation of one of the judges of the supreme court." The only Supreme Court Justice with whom Hoover was well acquainted in 1917 was Louis D. Brandeis.
196. Surface, *American Pork Production*, pp. 46–47.
197. Cuff, "The Dilemmas of Voluntarism," p. 731.
198. Cotton to Hoover, October 30, 1917, USFA Papers, Box 279.
199. Cotton to Hoover, November 1, 1917, USFA Papers, Box 47.
200. Hoover to Cotton, November 2, 1917, USFA Papers, Box 47.
201. On November 3, for instance, Cotton wired that his "relations" with the packers were "pleasant" but that "no spirit of cooperation" was present. Cotton to Hoover, November 3, 1917, USFA Papers, Box 47.
202. Cotton to Hoover, November 10, 1917, USFA Papers, Box 47.
203. Cotton to Hoover, November 17, 1917.
204. Cotton to Hoover, November 10, 1917; Hoover to Cotton, November 13, 1917, USFA Papers, Box 47.
205. Cotton to Hoover, November 10, 1917.
206. Cotton to Hoover, November 15, 1917, USFA Papers, Box 47; Cotton to Hoover, November 17, 1917.
207. Cotton to Hoover, November 15, 1917.
208. Cotton to Hoover, November 17, 1917.
209. Ibid.; Cotton to Hoover, November 19, 1917, USFA Papers, Box 47.
210. Cotton to Hoover, November 20, 1917, USFA Papers, Box 47.
211. Hoover to Cotton, November 21, 1917, USFA Papers, Box 47.
212. Cotton to Hoover, November 21, 1917; Hoover to Cotton, November 22, 1917. Both in USFA Papers, Box 47.
213. Cotton to Hoover, November 23, 1917, USFA Papers, Box 47.
214. Cotton, night letter to Hoover dated November 24, 1917 (but probably prepared on the evening of November 23), USFA Papers, Box 47.
215. Hoover to Cotton, November 24, 1917, USFA Papers, Box 47.
216. Hoover to Cotton, November 24, 1917 (separate telegram), USFA Papers, Box 47.
217. Hoover to Cotton, November 24, 1917 (separate telegram), USFA Papers, Box 47.
218. *New York Times*, November 25, 1917, section I, p. 19; *Increased Production* hearings, pp. 390–92; Mullendore, *History*, pp. 254–56.
219. Cotton to Hoover, November 26, 1917, USFA Papers, Box 47.

220. Cotton to Hoover, November 27, 1917; Hoover to Cotton, November 28, 1917. Both in USFA Papers, Box 47.
221. Woodrow Wilson executive order, November 27, 1917, printed in *Official Bulletin* 1 (November 30, 1917): 1.
222. Hoover to Cotton, November 28, 1917, USFA Papers, Box 47.
223. For accounts of Hoover's conference with the packers, see transcript of the conference, dated November 30 [actually December 1], 1917, USFA Papers, Box 48; U.S. Food Administration press release 506, December 1, 1917, USFA Documents; and Hoover to T. W. Wilson, December 1, 1917, enclosed with Hoover to Woodrow Wilson, December 1, 1917, Wilson Papers. Although the transcript of the conference is dated November 30, the other documents cited here indicate that the meeting occurred on December 1.
224. Hoover to T. W. Wilson, December 1, 1917.
225. Ibid.; U.S. Food Administration press release 506, December 1, 1917.
226. Transcript of Hoover's conference with leading packers, December 1, 1917, pp. 9–10.
227. Ibid., p. 10.
228. Hoover to T. W. Wilson, December 1, 1917.
229. Hoover to Woodrow Wilson, December 1, 1917; Joseph P. Tumulty to Hoover, December 5, 1917, "Wilson, Woodrow," Pre-Commerce Papers.
230. U.S. Food Administration press release 506, December 1, 1917.
231. Cotton remark to E. C. Lasater et al., December 5, 1917, quoted in Lasater testimony, February 4, 1919, in *Government Control* hearings, p. 1498.
232. For the text of Cotton's detailed regulations, see *Increased Production* hearings, pp. 64–72. For a summary, see *Commercial and Financial Chronicle* 105 (December 15, 1917): 2325.
233. Hugh Rockoff, *Drastic Measures: A History of Wage and Price Controls in the United States* (Cambridge, 1984), pp. 68–71.

CHAPTER 8

1. "Statement by the Wheat Executive," November 16, 1917, USFA Papers, Box 186, HI; Hoover to Julius H. Barnes, December 7, and 11, 1917, USFA Papers, Box 246.
2. Hoover to Barnes, December 11, 1917.
3. K. Austin Kerr, "Decision for Federal Control: Wilson, McAdoo, and the Railroads, 1917," *Journal of American History* 54 (December 1967): 550–51; James P. Johnson, "The Wilsonians As War Managers: Coal and the 1917–18 Winter Crisis," *Prologue* 9 (Winter 1977): 203; Robert H. Ferrell, *Woodrow Wilson and World War I, 1917–1921* (New York, 1985), p. 104.
4. U.S. Food Administration press release 498, November 30, 1917, USFA Documents, HHPL; *Commercial and Financial Chronicle* 105 (December 15, 1917): 2326.
5. Johnson, "Wilsonians as War Managers," pp. 201–02.
6. Ibid., p. 203.
7. *New York Times*, December 1, 1917, pp. 1, 9; *Washington Post*, December 1, 1917, p. 2; Harry A. Garfield to Robert S. Lovett, December 24, 1917, copy in Woodrow Wilson Papers, LC. Lovett was administrator of the Priority in Transportation Act of 1917. Robert Cuff, *The War Industries Board* (Baltimore, 1973), pp. 119–20.
8. *New Republic* 13 (December 8, 1917): 141–42.
9. Josephus Daniels diary, December 3, 1917, in E. David Cronon, ed., *The Cabinet Diaries of Josephus Daniels, 1913–1921* (Lincoln, Nebr., 1963), p. 245.
10. *New York Times*, December 1, 1917, pp. 1, 9; *Washington Post*, December 1, 1917, p. 2.
11. Ibid.; U.S. Food Administration press release 498, November 30, 1917.
12. *New York Times*, December 4, 1917, p. 22.
13. Ibid., December 1, 1917, p. 1, and December 2, 1917, section I, pp. 1, 4; Daniels diary, December 3, 1917.
14. *New York Times*, December 8, 1917, p. 10.

15. *Commercial and Financial Chronicle* 105 (December 15, 1917): 2326.
16. Garfield to Lovett, December 24, 1917.
17. Edward M. House diary, December 30, 1917, Edward M. House Papers, Manuscripts and Archives, Yale University Library.
18. Louis P. Sheldon cable to Hoover, December 16, 1917, printed in United States, Department of State, *Papers Relating to the Foreign Relations of the United States, 1917*, Supplement 2: *The World War*, vol. I (Washington, D.C., 1932), pp. 662–63.
19. Hoover to Woodrow Wilson, December 18, 1917, "Wilson, Woodrow," Pre-Commerce Papers, Herbert Hoover Papers, HHPL.
20. Julius H. Barnes to Hoover, December 21, 1917, USFA Papers, Box 246.
21. Lewis L. Strauss to Julius H. Barnes, December 21, 1917, USFA Papers, Box 246.
22. Hoover cable to Louis P. Sheldon, ca. December 23, 1917, quoted in Julius H. Barnes to Hoover, December 24, 1917, USFA Papers, Box 246. Barnes agreed with Hoover. See Barnes to Hoover, December 21 and 22, 1917, USFA Papers, Box 246.
23. Hoover cable to Sheldon, ca. December 23, 1917.
24. Connop Guthrie to Fairfax Harrison, December 26, 1917, copy enclosed with Barnes to Hoover, December 26, 1917, USFA Papers, Box 246.
25. Barnes to Hoover, December 26, 1917, states that the meeting was to be held two days later.
26. H. T. Robson and K. B. Stoddart to Hoover, January 24, 1918, USFA Papers, Box 186.
27. H. T. Robson (chairman, Wheat Export Company) to Hoover, January 26, 1918, version enclosed with Robson to Hoover, February 1, 1918, USFA Papers, Box 186. (The letter dated January 26, 1918, and cited here is a later revision of another letter of the same date, cited below in note 89. See also the text associated with note 103.)
28. *New York Times*, December 29, 1917, p. 14.
29. Ibid., December 30, 1917, section I, p. 12.
30. Ibid., December 31, 1917, p. 1.
31. Seward W. Livermore, *Politics Is Adjourned: Woodrow Wilson and the War Congress* (Middletown, Conn., 1966), p. 262.
32. *New York Times*, January 3, 1918, p. 2.
33. Ibid., December 31, 1917, p. 1.
34. Ibid., January 1, 1918, p. 1.
35. Ibid., pp. 1, 2.
36. Ibid., January 7, 1918, p. 1.
37. Hoover to William G. McAdoo, January 6, 1918, USFA Papers, Box 161. A copy is enclosed with Hoover to Woodrow Wilson, January 28, 1918, Wilson Papers.
38. Ibid.
39. William G. McAdoo to Hoover, January 8, 1918, USFA Papers, Box 161.
40. *New York Times*, January 8, 1918, pp. 1, 3.
41. Ibid., January 7, 1918, p. 1.
42. Ibid., January 8, 1918, p. 1.
43. Ibid., January 11, 1918, p. 1.
44. Ibid.
45. Johnson, "Wilsonians As War Managers," p. 203.
46. Ibid., p. 204.
47. *New York Times*, January 13, 1918, section I, pp. 1, 5; January 14, 1918, pp. 1, 2; and January 15, 1918, p. 1.
48. Ibid.
49. Ibid., January 15, 1918, p. 1.
50. Ibid., January 14, 1918, p. 2.
51. Ibid., January 15, 1918, p. 1.
52. Ibid., January 13, 1918, section I, p. 1; January 14, 1918, p. 1; and January 15, 1918, p. 1.
53. *Official Bulletin* 2 (January 17, 1918): 1, 2; ibid., 2 (January 18, 1918): 1, 2, 6; *Commercial and Financial Chronicle* 106 (January 19, 1918): 247–48.

54. *Commercial and Financial Chronicle* 106 (January 19, 1918): 249.
55. *Official Bulletin* 2 (January 18, 1918): 1, 2.
56. House diary, January 17, 1918, House Papers.
57. Ellen Maury Slayden diary, January 23, 1918, in Ellen Maury Slayden, *Washington Wife* (New York, 1962), pp. 322–23.
58. *Official Bulletin* 2 (January 18, 1918): 5.
59. Johnson, "Wilsonians As War Managers," p. 205.
60. *Official Bulletin* 2 (January 19, 1918): 1.
61. James P. Johnson, "The fuel crisis, largely forgotten, of World War I," *Smithsonian* 7 (December 1976): 70.
62. Johnson, "Wilsonians As War Managers," p. 206; Livermore, *Politics Is Adjourned*, p. 87.
63. Hoover to Harry A. Garfield, January 17, 1918, USFA Papers, Box 56; Johnson, "Wilsonians As War Managers," p. 87.
64. Hoover to Garfield, January 17, 1918.
65. U.S. Food Administration press release 587, January 17, 1918, USFA Documents.
66. Hoover statement, January 17, 1918, in *Commercial and Financial Chronicle* 106 (January 19, 1918): 249; U.S. Food Administration press release 589, January 18, 1918, USFA Documents.
67. Hugh Gibson letters to Mary Gibson, January 16 and 19, 1918 (extracts), Hugh Gibson Papers, HHPL; Edgar Rickard to John W. Hallowell, January 18, 1918, USFA Papers, Box 6.
68. Gibson to Mary Gibson, January 19 and 21, 1918, Gibson Papers; Rickard to Curtis H. Lindley, January 25, 1918, USFA Papers, Box 45.
69. *Commercial and Financial Chronicle* 106 (January 26, 1918): 354; Johnson, "The fuel crisis," pp. 64–66; Johnson, "Wilsonians As War Managers," p. 206.
70. Johnson, "Wilsonians As War Managers," p. 74.
71. Ibid.
72. *Official Bulletin* 2 (January 23, 1918): 1.
73. Julius H. Barnes to Hoover, January 12, 1918, USFA Papers, Box 246; Robson and Stoddart to Hoover, January 24, 1918.
74. J. J. Jusserand (the French ambassador) to Woodrow Wilson, February 2, 1918, Wilson Papers.
75. Minutes of [British] War Cabinet meeting 330, January 24, 1918, Cab. 23 / 5, PRO.
76. Earl of Crawford diary, January 10, 1918, in John Vincent, ed., *The Crawford Papers* (Manchester, U.K., 1984), pp. 384–85.
77. Barnes to Hoover, January 16, 1918, USFA Papers, Box 246; see also Barnes to Hoover, January 12, 1918 (two letters), USFA Papers, Box 246.
78. Handwritten note at bottom of Barnes to Hoover, January 16, 1918. This note appears to be dictation taken by Hoover's secretary, Lewis L. Strauss. See also Strauss telegram to Barnes, January 17, 1918, USFA Papers, Box 246.
79. Robson and Stoddart to Hoover, January 24, 1918.
80. Ibid.
81. See Barnes to Hoover, January 25, 1918, USFA Papers, Box 246.
82. Hoover to Barnes, January 28, 1918, USFA Papers, Box 246.
83. Ibid.
84. Hoover to Robson, January 28, 1918, USFA Papers, Box 246.
85. Hoover testimony, February 11, 1918, printed in U.S. Congress, House of Representatives, Committee on Agriculture, 65th Congress, 2d Session, *Conservation of Foodstuffs, Feeds, Etc.* (Washington, D.C., 1918), p. 4.
86. "Statement by the Wheat Executive," November 16, 1917; Lord Rhondda, "The Food Situation" (memorandum), December 10, 1917, Cab. 24 / 4, PRO; Louis P. Sheldon cable to Hoover, February 2, 1918, USFA Papers, Box 133; *First Report of the Royal Commission on Wheat Supplies* (London, 1921), pp. 3, 27–28.

87. *First Report of the Royal Commission on Wheat Supplies*, p. 28; Wheat Executive Report No. 2, January 28, 1918, printed in Wheat Executive, *Minutes of Proceedings*, section IX: *February and March 1918*, pp. 9–10, copy in Inter-Allied Food Council Papers, Box 5, HI.
88. Wheat Executive Report No. 2.
89. H. T. Robson to Hoover, January 26, 1918, USFA Papers, Box 186. (This is the original version of the letter. A second version, written several days later but deliberately dated January 26, is cited in note 27 above. For the explanation, see the text associated with note 103 below.)
90. Hoover to Barnes, January 29, 1918, USFA Papers, Box 246.
91. Hoover to H. T. Robson, January 29, 1918, USFA Papers, Box 186. A copy, incorrectly dated January 28, 1918, is in the Woodrow Wilson Papers.
92. Irving T. Bush to Woodrow Wilson, January 23, 1918; Hoover to Wilson, January 29, 1918. Both in Wilson Papers.
93. Hoover to Wilson, January 29, 1918.
94. Early in January 1918 the Allies had submitted a revised program of grain imports from North America for the next five months. It called upon the United States to supply 1,970,000 tons; Hoover had just promised 1,815,000 tons. Julius Barnes called this further request "trespassing in advance." The fact that the Allies had increased their demand for *future* American grain shipments, however, did not negate the fact that the United States was lagging on its current commitments. Barnes, incidentally, was confident that the United States could deliver not only the agreed-upon tonnage but the additional 155,000 tons that the Allies now coveted. Once again, he showed himself to be more optimistic about American capabilities—and more tolerant of Allied requests—than the Chief. See Barnes to Hoover, January 12, 1918.
95. Lewis L. Strauss to Secretary of State Robert Lansing, January 29, 1917 (plus enclosure: Hoover cable to Louis P. Sheldon), file no. 103.97 / 94, RG 59, NARA.
96. As late as January 31, Hoover showed a colleague statistics indicating that British food supplies were greater than the British represented. Hoover did not trust the British. James F. Bell diary, January 31, 1918, James F. Bell Papers, Box 1, HI.
97. Barnes to Hoover, January 25, 1918.
98. Hoover to Barnes, January 29, 1918.
99. Sheldon cable to Hoover, February 2, 1918.
100. Robson to Hoover, January 30, 1918, USFA Papers, Box 186.
101. Hoover to Robson, January 29, 1918. See also Barnes to Hoover, January 29, 1918, and [Lewis L. Strauss?] to Barnes, January 31, 1918, USFA Papers, Box 246.
102. Robson to Hoover, January 30, 1918, USFA Papers, Box 186. As noted in the text, this letter is separate from another of the same date cited in note 100.
103. Robson to Lewis L. Strauss, February 1, 1918 (plus enclosures: Robson to Hoover, February 1 and—ostensibly—January 26, 1918), USFA Papers, Box 186; Barnes to Hoover, February 4, 1918, USFA Papers, Box 246; Strauss to Barnes, February 5, 1918, USFA Papers, Box 246.
104. This is the letter discussed earlier in the text and cited in note 89.
105. Wheat Executive Report No. 2, January 28, 1918.
106. The Allied prime ministers' message was included in Jusserand to Wilson, February 2, 1918. For a variant translation of the Allied cable, see Charles L. Swem to Hoover, February 6, 1918 (plus enclosure), "Wilson, Woodrow," Pre-Commerce Papers, Hoover Papers.
107. Hoover to Wilson, February 9, 1918, Wilson Papers.
108. U.S. Food Administration press releases 514 (December 5, 1917) and 542 (December 18, 1917), USFA Documents; Hoover cable to Louis B. Sheldon, January 6, 1918, USFA Papers, Box 133.
109. Sir William H. Beveridge, *British Food Control* (London, 1928), p. 129; G. C. Shepard to M. R. Murphy, December 18, 1917, printed in United States Congress, Senate, Commit-

tee on Agriculture and Forestry, 65th Congress, 2d Session, *Increased Production of Grain and Meat Products* (Washington, D.C., 1918), p. 524.

110. Hoover memorandum, February 20, 1918, enclosed with Hoover to Woodrow Wilson, February 21, 1918, Wilson Papers.
111. U.S. Food Administration press release 542, December 18, 1917.
112. Hoover cable to Sheldon, January 6, 1918. It was printed in British Ministry of Food, "Report for the Week ending Wednesday, Jan. 9, 1918," p. 2, G.T. 3322, Cab. 24 / 39, PRO. A copy of the cable is in F / 43 / 5 / 48, David Lloyd George Papers, House of Lords Record Office, London. Evidently Hoover's message reached the highest level of the British government very quickly.
113. U.S. Food Administration letter quoted in a message from A. Bonar Law (the British Chancellor of the Exchequer) to William G. McAdoo, n.d., enclosed with McAdoo to Woodrow Wilson, January 22, 1918, Wilson Papers.
114. McAdoo to Wilson, January 22, 1918 (plus enclosure).
115. McAdoo to Wilson, January 22, 1918.
116. Woodrow Wilson to Hoover, January 23, 1918, "Wilson, Woodrow," Pre-Commerce Papers, Hoover Papers.
117. Hoover to Wilson, January 28, 1918, Wilson Papers.
118. Beveridge, *British Food Control*, pp. 129–30.
119. McAdoo to Wilson, February 11, 1918, Wilson Papers.
120. Julius H. Barnes, "Conference With Mr. Hoover, New York, December 28, 1917," USFA Papers, Box 253.
121. Ibid.
122. Barnes to Hoover, December 29, 1917, USFA Papers, Box 246; Barnes to Edward Chambers, January 3, 1918, in Surface, *Grain Trade*, pp. 253–54.
123. Hoover to McAdoo, January 6, 1918.
124. McAdoo to Hoover, January 8, 1918, USFA Papers, Box 161.
125. Minutes of meeting of the Council of National Defense, January 23, 1918, in United States Congress, Senate, 74th Congress, 2d Session, Senate Committee Print No. 7: *Munitions Industry: Minutes of the Council of National Defense* (Washington, D.C., 1936), p. 219.
126. Ibid.
127. *New York Times*, January 27, 1918, section I, p. 2.
128. Ibid.
129. Ibid., p. 12.
130. Barnes to Hoover, January 24, 1918, quoted in Surface, *Grain Trade*, pp. 255–56.
131. Hoover to McAdoo, January 28, 1918, USFA Papers, Box 161.
132. Hoover to Woodrow Wilson, January 28, 1918 (plus enclosure), Wilson Papers.
133. U.S. Food Administration press release 605, January 28, 1918, USFA Documents.
134. McAdoo to Newton D. Baker, January 28, 1918, William G. McAdoo Papers, vol. 497-3, LC.
135. V. Macchi di Cellere, André Tardieu, and Richard Crawford to Hoover, January 26, 1918, copy enclosed with Hoover to McAdoo, January 28, 1918 (a second letter of that date), USFA Papers, Box 161.
136. McAdoo to Baker, January 28, 1918.
137. U.S. Food Administration press release 612, January 30, 1918, USFA Documents; Food Administration Grain Corporation to its agents, January 30, 1918, in Surface, *Grain Trade*, pp. 256–57; *Official Bulletin* 2 (January 31, 1918): 5; McAdoo to Hoover, February 6, 1918, USFA Papers, Box 161.
138. Surface, *Grain Trade*, p. 257.
139. *New York Times*, February 6, 1918, pp. 1, 20.
140. Josephus Daniels diary, February 6, 1918, in Cronon, ed., *Cabinet Diaries*, p. 276.
141. McAdoo to Hoover, February 7, 1918, USFA Papers, Box 161.

142. Ibid.; announcement by McAdoo, February 8, 1918, in USFA Papers, Box 161, and in Surface, *Grain Trade*, p. 251; *Commercial and Financial Chronicle* 106 (February 23, 1918): 772.
143. McAdoo to Hoover, February 7, 1918.
144. Hoover to Wilson, February 9, 1918.
145. Ibid.; Edward M. House diary, February 10, 1918, House Papers.
146. Hoover testimony before the House Committee on Agriculture, February 11, 1918, in *Conservation of Foodstuffs, Feeds, Etc.*, p. 22.
147. Hoover to McAdoo, February 12, 1918, USFA Papers, Box 161.
148. Hoover to McAdoo, February 14, 1918, USFA Papers, Box 161.
149. Order issued by Railroad Administration, February 14, 1918, copy in USFA Papers, Box 161. See also McAdoo telegram to Public Service Commission in Indianapolis, Indiana, February 25, 1918, copy enclosed with McAdoo to Woodrow Wilson, February 25, 1918, Wilson Papers, and Hoover to McAdoo, March 18, 1918, USFA Papers, Box 161.
150. Lord Reading cable to British Foreign Office, February 15, 1918, printed in Arthur S. Link et al., eds., *The Papers of Woodrow Wilson*, vol. 46 (Princeton, N.J., 1984), p. 356.
151. Hoover to Woodrow Wilson, February 19, 1918, McAdoo Papers, Box 524.
152. Wilson to McAdoo, February 20, 1918, McAdoo Papers, Box 524.
153. *Official Bulletin* 2 (February 14, 1918): 1, 2; *Commercial and Financial Chronicle* 106 (February 16, 1918): 661–62.
154. Josephus Daniels diary, February 18, 1918, in Cronon, ed., *Cabinet Diaries*, p. 281.
155. *New York Times*, February 20, 1918, p. 1.
156. I have found no direct evidence of this, but Hoover was an experienced cultivator of the press, a point developed elsewhere in this volume and in the two previously published volumes of my biography. The *New York Times* story served Hoover's interest (and also the Allies'). It did not serve McAdoo's.
157. *New York Times*, February 22, 1918, p. 4.
158. Josephus Daniels diary, February 21, 1918, in Cronon, ed., *Cabinet Diaries*, p. 282.
159. U.S. Food Administration press release 687, February 21, 1918, USFA Documents; *Official Bulletin* 2 (February 23, 1918): 1, 3.
160. *New York Times*, February 22, 1918, p. 1.
161. *Washington Post*, February 22, 1918, p. 1.
162. According to one newspaper, the Food Administration's dissatisfaction with the Railroad Administration's response to requests for more "transportation facilities" had been "no secret." *New York Times*, February 22, 1918, p. 1.
163. U.S. Food Administration press release 687, February 21, 1918.
164. McAdoo to Woodrow Wilson, February 23, 1918, Wilson Papers.
165. McAdoo to Hoover, February 22, 1918, USFA Papers, Box 161.
166. *New York Times*, February 23, 1918, p. 4; *Washington Post*, February 23, 1918, p. 3.
167. *Washington Post*, February 23, 1918, p. 1; *New York Tribune*, February 23, 1918, p. 1.
168. Josephus Daniels, *The Wilson Era—Years of War and After, 1917–1923* (Chapel Hill, N.C., 1946), p. 318.
169. *New York Times*, February 23, 1918, p. 4.
170. Hoover to McAdoo, February 23, 1918, McAdoo Papers, Box 197.
171. McAdoo to Hoover, February 23, 1918, USFA Papers, Box 161.
172. For example, see *New York Times*, February 24, 1918, section I, p. 3.
173. McAdoo to Woodrow Wilson, February 23, 1918.
174. Ibid; *New York Times*, February 24, 1918, section I, p. 3; *New York Tribune*, February 24, 1918, p. 8.
175. Breckinridge Long diary, February 23, 1918, Breckinridge Long Papers, Box 1, LC. Long considered the Food Administration's published response to McAdoo's first letter to be "insubordinate."
176. Daniels, *Wilson Era*, p. 318.

177. *New York Times*, February 26, 1918, p. 6.
178. Daniels, *Wilson Era*, p. 318. See also Anne Wintermute Lane and Louise Herrick Wall, eds., *Letters of Franklin K. Lane* (Boston and New York, 1922), pp. 265–66.
179. Curtis H. Lindley to Edgar Rickard, February 27, 1918, USFA Papers, Box 45.
180. U.S. Food Administration press release 704, February 24, 1918, USFA Documents; *Official Bulletin* 2 (February 25, 1918): 2; *New York Times*, February 25, 1918, pp. 1, 2.
181. U.S. Food Administration press release 704, February 24, 1918.
182. Hoover to McAdoo, February 25, 1918 (plus enclosure), USFA Documents, Box 161.
183. *New York Times*, February 26, 1918, p. 6.
184. William G. McAdoo, *Crowded Years* (Boston and New York, 1931), p. 487.
185. Lou Henry Hoover to Allan Hoover, n.d. (but postmarked February 6, 1932), Allan Hoover Papers, HHPL. Hoover's statement that he was never in McAdoo's office was inaccurate. The Hoover Calendar at HHPL indicates that he had an appointment at McAdoo's office at 11:45 A.M. on February 25, 1918. This was evidently the occasion for the conference reported by the *New York Times* on February 26. Whether the conference included the scene later described by McAdoo, or whether he and Hoover met on some other occasion, cannot be determined.
186. McAdoo, *Crowded Years*, p. 486.
187. Ibid., p. 485.
188. U.S. Food Administration press release 687, February 21, 1918; Hoover to McAdoo, February 25, 1918.
189. See, for example, McAdoo to Hoover, February 27 and March 2, 1918; Hoover to McAdoo, March 5, 1918; McAdoo to Hoover, March 12 and 15, 1918; Hoover to McAdoo, March 16, 1918; Hoover to McAdoo, March 22, 1918 (two letters plus enclosures); Hoover to McAdoo, March 26, 1918 (plus enclosure). All in USFA Papers, Box 161. See also McAdoo to Woodrow Wilson, March 12, 1918 (plus enclosure), Wilson Papers.
190. Daniels, *Wilson Era*, p. 319.
191. Herbert Hoover, *Memoirs*, paperbound page proof version (June 1944), vol. II, United States Food Administration section, p. 57, Hoover Book Manuscript Material, HHPL. Hoover omitted this passage when he condensed his *Memoirs* drafts for publication in 1951–52.
192. H. T. Robson to the President, U.S. Food Administration Grain Corporation, February 20, 1918, USFA Papers, Box 186.
193. V. Macchi di Cellere, Lord Reading, and André Tardieu to Hoover, February 22, 1918, USFA Papers, Box 131.
194. Barnes to Hoover, February 21, 1918, USFA Papers, Box 246.
195. Barnes to Hoover, February 21, 1918, USFA Papers, Box 246 (a separate letter from the one cited above).
196. Hoover to Lord Reading, February 26, 1918, copy enclosed with Hoover to Woodrow Wilson, February 26, 1918, Wilson Papers; Barnes to H. T. Robson, March 16, 1918, USFA Papers, Box 246.
197. Hoover to Woodrow Wilson, February 26, 1918.
198. Macchi di Cellere, Reading, and Tardieu to Hoover, February 22, 1918; *New York Times*, February 22, 1918, p. 4.
199. Benedict Crowell and Robert Forrest Wilson, *The Road to France* (New Haven, Conn., 1921), I, p. 139. According to these authors, the British shipping authorities "were caught unprepared" for the flood of American food that poured into the Atlantic ports between mid-February and mid-March.
200. *Official Bulletin* 2 (April 8, 1918): 3; ibid., 2 (May 20, 1918): 15; *New York Times*, March 3, 1918, section I, p. 1. North American grain shipments to the Allies totaled 855,000 tons in March 1918, compared to only 553,429 tons in February.
201. Between December 1, 1917, and March 31, 1918, America's grain exports of all kinds (wheat, flour, corn, barley, rye, etc.) fell short of the Wheat Executive's program by almost

400,000 tons (or about 18 percent). Canada's wheat exports were also well below projections in this same period. See Hoover to Lord Reading, March 21, 1918, copy enclosed with Hoover to Woodrow Wilson, March 22, 1918, Wilson Papers, and the chart printed in Surface, *Grain Trade*, p. 189.

202. Arthur Willert to Geoffrey Dawson, ca. August 1918, quoted in Sir Arthur Willert, *Washington and Other Memories* (Boston, 1972), pp. 107–08.

203. U.S. Food Administration, Statistical Division Information Service, Bulletin No. 1045: "Wheat Consumption by Half Years, 1901–1917" (May 4, 1918), pp. 3, 10, 14, copy in Box 770, RG 4, NARA.

CHAPTER 9

1. According to Julius Barnes, this was the scheduled date for the meeting. Julius H. Barnes to Herbert Hoover, December 26, 1917, USFA Papers, Box 246, HI.
2. K. B. Stoddart to Julius H. Barnes, December 28, 1917, quoted in Frank M. Surface, *The Grain Trade During the World War* (New York, 1928), p. 191. Stoddart's enclosed table is printed on p. 189 of Surface's book.
3. Surface, *Grain Trade*, p. 189.
4. The Wheat Executive's program called for the United States and Canada to ship a total of 2,140,000 tons of cereal products (wheat, flour, corn, barley, and rye) in January and February 1918. Hoover promised to ship 2,200,000 tons. H. T. Robson and K. B. Stoddart to Herbert Hoover, January 24, 1918, USFA Papers, Box 186.
5. Hoover to Woodrow Wilson, November 15, 1917, Woodrow Wilson Papers, LC; U.S. Food Administration press release 514, December 5, 1917, USFA Documents, HHPL; *New York Times*, December 6, 1917, p. 2.
6. Hoover to Wilson, November 15, 1917.
7. Hoover to H. T. Robson, December 29, 1917 (revised version), copy enclosed with Hoover to Julius H. Barnes, December 31, 1917, USFA Papers, Box 246. A clean copy of the Hoover to Robson letter, dated January 1, 1917 [1918], is enclosed with Hoover to Woodrow Wilson, January 5, 1918, Wilson Papers.
8. Hoover to Julius H. Barnes, December 7, 1917, USFA Papers, Box 246.
9. I have found no evidence that H. T. Robson, chairman of the Wheat Export Company, objected to—or even replied to—Hoover's letter containing the "reservation."
10. See "Report of the United States Food Administrator to the President Covering the Period from January 1, 1918 to July 1, 1918," enclosed with Hoover to Woodrow Wilson, September 7, 1918, Wilson Papers. According to this report (p. 6), the United States exported 62,745,000 bushels of wheat (and flour in terms of wheat) between July 1, 1917 and January 1, 1918. In his letter to Robson on December 29, 1917 (cited above), Hoover stated that the United States had exported "fully 60,000,000 bushels" from the last harvest "up to January 1st."
11. Hoover to Robson, December 29, 1917.
12. U.S. Food Administration press release 532, December 13, 1917, USFA Documents; *New York Times*, December 14, 1917, p. 1.
13. *Commercial and Financial Chronicle* 105 (December 1, 1917): 2145.
14. U.S. Food Administration press release 514, December 5, 1917, USFA Documents.
15. U.S. Food Administration press release 580, January 11, 1918, USFA Documents.
16. Hoover to Ray Lyman Wilbur, October 22, 1917, USFA Papers, Box 128.
17. Ibid.; Hoover to Woodrow Wilson, November 15, 1917.
18. Wilson to Hoover, November 28, 1917, "Wilson, Woodrow," Pre-Commerce Papers, Herbert Hoover Papers, HHPL.
19. Hoover to Woodrow Wilson, December 1, 1917, Wilson Papers.
20. *Official Bulletin* 1 (November 7, 1917): 4.

21. *New York Times*, January 13, 1918, section I, p. 4; Harvey A. Levenstein, *Revolution at the Table: The Transformation of the American Diet* (New York, 1988), p. 143.
22. *New York Times*, January 11, 1918, p. 1, and January 13, 1918, section I, p. 4; Newton D. Baker to Woodrow Wilson, January 11, 1918, Wilson Papers; *Weekly Northwestern Miller* 113 (January 16, 1918): 182. At the beginning of 1918 Hoover told a Congressional committee: ". . . I do believe that we need some legislation that will enable us to impose conservation on public eating places." Hoover testimony, January 2, 1918, in U.S. Congress, Senate, Subcommittee of the Committee on Manufactures, 65th Congress, 2d Session, *Shortage of Sugar* (Washington, D.C., 1918), p. 616.
23. In his letter to Robson of December 29, 1917, Hoover stated that he would "still further strengthen" his food conservation effort. He obviously had tougher measures in mind.
24. U.S. Food Administration press release 569, January 6, 1918, USFA Documents. This was in response to earlier press reports quoting Rhondda as saying that he did not view the European food situation with alarm. Hoover wanted to undo any damage caused by these misleading reports. He also probably wanted to prepare American public opinion for his coming conservation battle.
25. *Official Bulletin* 2 (January 10, 1918): 1; *Commercial and Financial Chronicle* 106 (January 19, 1918): 246.
26. *Weekly Northwestern Miller* 113 (January 16, 1918): 183.
27. U.S. Food Administration press release 580, January 11, 1918.
28. Hoover cable to Louis P. Sheldon, January 14, 1918, file no. 103.97 / 94a, RG 59, NARA; copy also in USFA Papers, Box 133.
29. Lord Rhondda to Hoover, quoted in Louis P. Sheldon cable 103 to Hoover, January 17, 1918, copy in USFA Papers, Box 134.
30. Hoover cable to Sheldon, January 23, 1918, USFA Papers, Box 133.
31. Hoover to Joseph P. Tumulty, January 26, 1918, Wilson Papers.
32. U.S. Food Administration press release 599, January 25, 1918, USFA Documents; *New York Times*, January 26, 1918, pp. 1, 10.
33. *New York Times*, January 27, 1918, section I, pp. 1, 2. Hoover's draft of Wilson's proclamation, and Wilson's revision thereof, are both in the Wilson Papers, along with Hoover to Wilson, January 17, 1918 (which accompanied Hoover's original version).
34. *New York Times*, January 27, 1918, section I, p. 2. The rules were also printed in *Official Bulletin* 2 (January 28, 1918): 5–6.
35. *Official Bulletin* 2 (January 28, 1918): 7. The criticism of hoarding was included in the text of the Food Administration's new home card.
36. *New York Times*, January 27, 1918, section I, p. 2.
37. *Official Bulletin* 2 (January 28, 1918): 7.
38. *New York Times*, January 27, 1918, section I, p. 2.
39. Ibid., p. 1.
40. *Official Bulletin* 2 (February 1, 1918): 3.
41. *New York Times*, February 1, 1918, p. 1.
42. *Official Bulletin* 2 (February 1, 1918): 3.
43. Ibid.
44. U.S. Food Administration press release 661, February 15, 1918, USFA Documents.
45. Ibid.
46. *Official Bulletin* 2 (February 6, 1918): 4.
47. U.S. Food Administration press release 632, February 7, 1918, USFA Documents.
48. *New York Times*, February 1, 1918, section I, p. 4; *Commercial and Financial Chronicle* 106 (February 2, 1918): 444.
49. *Commercial and Financial Chronicle* 106 (February 9, 1918): 550.
50. *New York Times*, January 28, 1918, p. 3. See also *Commercial and Financial Chronicle* 106 (February 2, 1918): 443–44.
51. *Commercial and Financial Chronicle* 106 (February 9, 1918): 550.

52. Representative Sydney Anderson to Hoover, February 2, 1918, USFA Papers, Box 280.
53. *Commercial and Financial Chronicle*, 106 (February 9, 1918): 550; *New York Times*, February 14, 1918, p. 6; Hoover to Representative Sydney Anderson, February 4, 1918, USFA Papers, Box 280. Hoover told Anderson that he believed that "if we could only get a movement of corn in the country the prices, in the face of the enormous stocks, would adjust themselves on some reasonable footing with wheat."
54. *New York Times*, January 29, 1918, p. 4.
55. *Commercial and Financial Chronicle*, 106 (February 9, 1918): 550. For licensed businesses, said Hoover, the penalty would be revocation of the license. For unlicensed food retailers, the penalty would be the cutting off of their supplies by a Food Administration order to licensed suppliers not to serve the offender. For both kinds of violators the effect would be closure of their business.
56. Hoover testimony, February 11, 1918, in U.S. Congress, House of Representatives, Committee on Agriculture, 65th Congress, 2d Session, *Conservation of Foodstuffs, Feeds, Etc.* (Washington, D.C., 1918), p. 39 (hereinafter cited as *Conservation of Foodstuffs*).
57. Ibid., pp. 38–39.
58. Hoover to Senator William H. King, May 18, 1918, USFA Papers, Box 96.
59. In addition to the sources cited in note 22, see *New York Times*, January 16, 1918, p. 6, and *Official Bulletin* 2 (January 16, 1918): 5.
60. *New York Times*, January 16, 1918, p. 6.
61. Ibid.
62. Newton D. Baker to Woodrow Wilson, January 11, 1918; Wilson to Baker, January 16, 1918, Newton D. Baker Papers, Box 8, LC.
63. Edgar Rickard to Curtis H. Lindley, January 25, 1918, USFA Papers, Box 45.
64. Representative Sydney Anderson to Hoover, January 23, 1918, copy in Wilson Papers.
65. Hoover to Representative Sydney Anderson, January 26, 1918, copy in Wilson Papers. Hoover published this letter in toto in U.S. Food Administration press release 603, January 29, 1918, USFA Documents. It was also printed in entirety in the *New York Times*, January 30, 1918, p. 4.
66. *New York Times*, February 3, 1918, section VII, p. 10.
67. "As originally framed the bill was so drastic as to give sufficient power to the Food Administrator to regulate the food consumed in private homes. Great objection was raised to the latter provision. . . ." *New York Times*, February 24, 1918, section I, p. 3.
68. Hoover testimony, February 11, 1918, in *Conservation of Foodstuffs*, pp. 1, 8–11, 16–17, 38–39.
69. Ibid., p. 39.
70. U.S. Congress, House of Representatives, Committee on Agriculture, report on H.R. 9971, February 23, 1918 (House of Representatives Report No. 337, 65th Congress, 2d Session), copy in Congressional Information Service US Serial Set, fiche no. 7307-5, University of Iowa Libraries. See also *New York Times*, February 24, 1918, section I, p. 3, and *Official Bulletin* 2 (February 25, 1918): 5.
71. *Congressional Record* 56 (February 23, 1918): 2584. There is no record of further action on this bill.
72. Hoover cable to Louis P. Sheldon, January 6, 1918, USFA Papers, Box 133.
73. Hoover to Woodrow Wilson, January 28, 1918, Wilson Papers.
74. U.S. Food Administration press release 599, January 25, 1918.
75. *Official Bulletin* 2 (March 13, 1918): 6.
76. Frank M. Surface, *American Pork Production in the World War* (Chicago and New York, 1926), pp. 63–64.
77. Hoover to Lord Reading, March 1, 1918, USFA Papers, Box 131; U.S. Food Administration press release 728, March 3, 1918, USFA Documents.
78. Hoover to Reading, March 1, 1918. Copy also in Wilson Papers.
79. Hoover to Reading, March 3, 1918, USFA Papers, Box 131.

80. U.S. Food Administration press release 728, March 3, 1918, USFA Documents. This press release appeared in newspapers on the morning of March 4.
81. Ibid.
82. Hoover cable to Louis P. Sheldon, March 3, 1918, USFA Papers, Box 131.
83. Lord Reading to Hoover, March 4, 1918, copy in Wilson Papers.
84. Sir William H. Beveridge, *British Food Control* (London and New Haven, Conn., 1928), p. 130.
85. Ibid. Beveridge states that the Allies bought the entire amount Hoover offered. Surface, *American Pork Production*, however, states that the Allies did not definitely accept Hoover's offer but did "very materially" increase their orders for American pork products (p. 66).
86. *Official Bulletin* 2 (May 8, 1918): 7.
87. Ibid., 2 (March 13, 1918): 6.
88. *New York Times*, March 15, 1918, p. 6; Surface, *American Pork Production*, p. 64.
89. *New York Times*, March 15, 1918, p. 6.
90. Ibid.
91. Thomas E. Wilson to Joseph P. Cotton, March 28, 1918, USFA Papers, Box 48.
92. U.S. Food Administration press release 791, March 29, 1918, USFA Documents; *New York Times*, March 30, 1918, p. 9.
93. According to Surface, *American Pork Production*, American pork and lard exports totaled 875,000,000 pounds during this period (p. 68). That was the equivalent of 390,625 metric tons.
94. Hoover speech at a meeting of the Washington section of the American Institute of Mining Engineers, June 21, 1918, printed in American Institute of Mining Engineers *Monthly Bulletin*, no. 140 (August 1918): xxvi–xxx. His statistics about the British queues are found on p. xxviii.
95. *New York Times*, May 31, 1918, p. 8.
96. Hoover to Reading, March 1, 1918; U.S. Food Administration press release 728, March 3, 1918.
97. Hoover cable to Louis P. Sheldon, May 22, 1918; Sheldon cable to Hoover, June 1, 1918; Hoover cable to Sheldon, June 4, 1918. Printed in United States, Department of State, *Papers Relating to the Foreign Relations of the United States, 1918*, Supplement 1: *The World War* (Washington, D.C., 1933), vol. I, pp. 553–55 (hereinafter cited as *FRUS, 1918*, Supplement 1).
98. U.S. Food Administration, Statistical Division Information Service, Bulletin No. 1045: "Wheat Consumption by Half Years, 1901–1917" (May 4, 1918), pp. 3, 10, copy in Box 770, RG 4, NARA.
99. Ibid., p. 12.
100. *New York Times*, February 3, 1918, section VII, p. 10. In his appearance before the House Committee on Agriculture on February 11, Hoover testified that 60–70 percent of the American populace had "respond[ed] to the voluntary call." This meant, of course, that 30–40 percent had not. *Conservation of Foodstuffs*, p. 10.
101. *New York Times*, February 3, 1918, section VII, p. 10; Levenstein, *Revolution at the Table*, pp. 137, 145.
102. Hoover testimony in *Conservation of Foodstuffs*, p. 7; Levenstein, *Revolution at the Table*, p. 145. Hoover was well aware of this fact. See, for example, his speech in Pittsburgh, April 18, 1918, Public Statements File, Hoover Papers. According to Hoover, American consumption of beef increased by 10 percent during 1917.
103. Hoover to Reading, March 1, 1918.
104. Reading to Hoover, March 4, 1918.
105. Hoover to Woodrow Wilson, March 7, 1918, Wilson Papers.
106. Wilson to Hoover, March 8, 1918, "Wilson, Woodrow," Pre-Commerce Papers, Hoover Papers.
107. Hoover cable 73 to Louis P. Sheldon, March 12, 1918, USFA Papers, Box 133; Wheat

Export Company cable to the Royal Commission on Wheat Supplies, March 12, 1918, printed in Wheat Executive, *Minutes of Proceedings*, section IX: *February and March 1918*, p. 30, copy in Inter-Allied Food Council Papers, Box 5, HI. Hoover's cable 73 is printed in the same source, p. 31. See also Sheldon cable 132 to Hoover, March 16, 1918, USFA Papers, Box 131, and Lord Rhondda cable to Lord Reading, March 18, 1918, copy in USFA Papers, Box 134.

108. Hoover cable 73 to Sheldon, March 12, 1918.
109. Ibid.
110. Wheat Export Company cable to the Royal Commission on Wheat Supplies, March 12, 1918.
111. Sheldon cable 131 to Hoover, March 16, 1918 (conveying a message from the Wheat Executive), USFA Papers, Box 131. The Wheat Executive's message is printed in its *Minutes of Proceedings*, section IX, p. 44.
112. Ibid.
113. Rhondda cable to Reading, March 18, 1918.
114. Hoover to Woodrow Wilson, March 22, 1918, Wilson Papers.
115. Wilson to Hoover, March 25, 1918, Wilson Papers.
116. *New York Times*, March 8, 1918, p. 1.
117. *Official Bulletin* 2 (March 18, 1918): 5.
118. *New York Times*, March 20, 1918, p. 5.
119. James F. Bell diary, March 19, 20, 21, 1918, James F. Bell Papers, Box 3, HI.
120. Ibid., March 20, 1918.
121. U.S. Food Administration press release 780, March 23, 1918, USFA Documents; *New York Times*, March 24, 1918, section I, p. 5.
122. U.S. Food Administration press release 777, March 23, 1918, USFA Documents.
123. U.S. Food Administration press release 790, March 29, 1918, USFA Documents; *New York Times*, March 30, 1918, p. 9; *Official Bulletin* 2 (March 30, 1918): 1–2.
124. *Official Bulletin* 2 (March 30, 1918): 1.
125. Julius H. Barnes to H. T. Robson, March 16, 1918, copy enclosed with Barnes to Hoover, March 16, 1918; Barnes to K. B. Stoddart, March 20, 1918, copy enclosed with Barnes to Lewis L. Strauss, March 20, 1918. All in USFA Papers, Box 246.
126. Barnes to Stoddart, March 20, 1918.
127. Barnes to Robson, March 16, 1918.
128. Barnes to Strauss, March 20, 1918.
129. Ibid.
130. Hoover to Reading, March 21, 1918, copy enclosed with Hoover to Woodrow Wilson, March 22, 1918, Wilson Papers. Printed in *FRUS, 1918*, Supplement 1, vol. I, pp. 541–44.
131. Reading to Hoover, March 30, 1918, printed in *FRUS, 1918*, Supplement 1, vol. I, pp. 545–47.
132. Hoover to Reading, April 3, 1918, printed in *FRUS, 1918*, Supplement 1, vol. I, pp. 547–49; [Alonzo E. Taylor], "Memorandum on Letter of Lord Reading to Mr. Hoover on March Thirtieth," n.d. (ca. April 1, 1918), USFA Papers, Box 138.
133. Hoover cable to Alonzo Taylor, n.d., USFA Papers, Box 37; copy, dated November 17, 1917, in United States, Department of State, *Papers Relating to the Foreign Relations of the United States, 1917*, Supplement 2: *The World War* (Washington, D.C., 1932), vol. I, p. 660 (hereinafter cited as *FRUS, 1917*, Supplement 2).
134. Wheat Executive, "Report of a Second Conference on the Allied Cereal Situation, Wednesday, 15th November, 1917, at 11 a.m.," printed in Wheat Executive, *Minutes of Proceedings*, section VIII: *November and December, 1917*, pp. 17–18, copy in Inter-Allied Food Council Papers, Box 5.
135. Ibid.; Tom G. Hall, "Cheap Bread from Dear Wheat: Herbert Hoover, the Wilson Administration, and the Management of Wheat Prices, 1916–1920" (doctoral dissertation,

University of California at Davis, 1970), p. 120. In his memorandum to Hoover (cited in note 132), Taylor claimed that Canada was mentioned as a source of replacement wheat during his November 1917 meetings with the Wheat Executive. The report of the Wheat Executive, however (cited in note 134), does not mention Canada.

136. In his letter of December 29, 1917 to H. T. Robson (cited in note 7), Hoover began: "With regard to the various estimates of the position of wheat exports from the United States, I would like to say that disregarding altogether the calculations made in London at the first of November, we can now approach the whole matter as from the first of January." By "disregarding altogether" the Wheat Executive's earlier estimates, Hoover may conceivably have thought that he was also discarding its program, including the stipulation that he deliver 900,000 tons (33,000,000 bushels) of wheat between December and the end of February. But his words did not plainly say this, and one doubts that the Allies drew any such conclusion.

Another complicating factor should be recorded. In its "Report" of November 15, 1917, the Wheat Executive stated that the existing American-Canadian wheat surplus stood at 133,000,000 bushels: in other words, 33,000,000 bushels in the United States and 100,000,000 in Canada. But two days later, in his cable to Alonzo Taylor (cited in note 133), Hoover announced that the United States had no surplus. In light of this, one might argue that the Wheat Executive's conclusion of two days before had been superseded and that the replacement of future American shipments now applied to the 33,000,000 bushels that had been assumed to exist already, but which now (according to Hoover) did not. But even if this interpretation is true (which is unlikely), the obligation to replace still fell on Argentina and Australia in the Wheat Executive document, not on Canada. Moreover, a few weeks later Hoover approved the export of 33,000,000 bushels (900,000 tons) of American wheat without apparent reservation.

The conclusion seems clear that the notion of possibly replacing increased American wheat exports with increased Canadian imports did not become settled until the end of December. And then it applied to *future* shipments, not past or present commitments. In the dispute about this with Reading in the spring of 1918, Hoover and Taylor were in error.

137. In his memorandum to Hoover cited in note 132, Taylor claimed that "the Wheat Executive planned for allocations of wheat from the United States, to be replaced by wheat elsewhere secured by them at a later date, in order that no hiatus should occur before the arrival of Argentine wheat." What Taylor evidently did not make clear to Hoover was that this replacement principle applied only to American exports *above* the joint American / Canadian surplus of 133,000,000 bushels, and only if the United States could not conserve any additional quantities exported. The replacement agreement did not apply to America's current export commitment, which was 33,000,000 of the combined 133,000,000 bushels. The replacement principle was therefore partial and conditional.

138. Reading to Hoover, April 16, 1918, printed in *FRUS, 1918*, Supplement 1, vol. I, p. 549.

139. Reading to the British Foreign Office, April 12, 1918.

140. James F. Bell diary, April 11, 1918, Bell Papers, Box 3.

141. Bell diary, March 21, 1918.

142. Bell diary, April 11, 1918.

143. Julius H. Barnes to Lewis L. Strauss, April 23, 1918, USFA Papers, Box 246.

144. Reading to Hoover, April 16, 1918.

145. Ibid.; Barnes to Strauss, April 23, 1918; Lord Rhondda to Reading, April 16, 1918, printed in Wheat Executive, *Minutes of Proceedings*, section X, p. 14.

146. Barnes to Strauss, April 23, 1918.

147. Hoover to Reading, April 24, 1918, printed in *FRUS, 1918*, Supplement 1, vol. I, p. 549.

148. Surface, *Grain Trade*, p. 283.

149. Ibid.

150. U.S. Food Administration press release 803, April 1, 1918, USFA Documents.
151. *New York Times*, March 31, 1918, section I, p. 4; *Weekly Northwestern Miller* 114 (April 10, 1918): 118.
152. *Weekly Northwestern Miller* 114 (April 10, 1918): 118; U.S. Food Administration press release 960, May 23, 1918, USFA Documents.
153. *New York Times*, May 29, 1918, p. 7.
154. U.S. Food Administration press release 960, May 23, 1918.
155. *Weekly Northwestern Miller* 114 (April 10, 1918): 118.
156. *New York Times*, December 30, 1917, section I, p. 14.
157. Ibid., May 25, 1918, p. 2.
158. U.S. Food Administration press release 981, May 30, 1918, USFA Documents.
159. Hoover to King, May 18, 1918.
160. *The Times* (London), July 20, 1918, p. 3.
161. Hoover cable to Louis P. Sheldon, May 4, 1918, printed in *FRUS, 1918,* Supplement 1, vol. I, p. 550.
162. *Commercial and Financial Chronicle* 106 (April 6, 1918): 1417–18; *Official Bulletin* 2 (May 10, 1918): 4.
163. *New York Times*, May 27, 1918, p. 18; *New York Tribune*, May 27, 1918, p. 6.
164. U.S. Food Administration press release 980, May 30, 1918, USFA Documents.
165. In late April the Food Administration announced its intention to do this. *Weekly Northwestern Miller* 114 (April 24, 1918): 271.
166. Surface, *Grain Trade*, p. 24.
167. Hoover to Woodrow Wilson, July 11, 1918, Wilson Papers. Printed in *Official Bulletin* 2 (July 18, 1918): 1–2.
168. Hoover to Joseph P. Tumulty, July 11, 1918, Wilson Papers; *New York Times*, July 19, 1918, p. 9.
169. U.S. Department of Agriculture, *Yearbook 1920* (Washington, D.C., 1921), p. 550.
170. Ibid.
171. The total supply of wheat in the United States (including the domestic crop, carryover, and imports) was:
    1916–17 crop year: 825,000,000 bushels
    1917–18 crop year: 716,000,000 bushels.
    Frank M. Surface, *The Stabilization of The Price of Wheat During the War and Its Effect Upon the Returns to the Producer* (Washington, D.C., 1925), p. 39.
172. Hoover remarks, August 20, 1917, in "Minutes of the Committee on Prices, August 17–29th, 1917," appendix 1, USFA Papers, Box 187.
173. U.S. Food Administration, *Policies and Plan of Operations: Wheat, Flour, and Bread* (December 1, 1917), p. 11, copy at National Agricultural Library, Beltsville, Maryland; Hoover to Woodrow Wilson, November 15, 1917. In his letter to Wilson, Hoover stated that as of November 1 the United States had exported more than 33,790,000 bushels of wheat since July 1, 1917, leaving a "deficiency" of 4,372,740 bushels. In other words, his *exportable* surplus (the net amount he could truly spare) was less than 30,000,000 bushels. This figure was somewhat artificial, since Hoover, in calculating his surplus, had allotted 50,000,000 bushels from the total supply for "essential carry-over." In the end, the actual carryover, as we have seen in the text, was 17,000,000 bushels on July 1, 1918. Hoover had been able to get by with less than he had told Wilson was essential.
174. U.S. Food Administration press release 599, January 25, 1918.
175. Hoover to Wilson, March 22, 1918.
176. Hoover to Wilson, July 11, 1918.
177. Hoover to Joseph P. Tumulty, November 1, 1918, Wilson Papers.
178. Hoover testimony, February 11, 1918, in *Conservation of Foodstuffs*, pp. 5–6.
179. Hoover to Wilson, November 15, 1917.
180. U.S. Food Administration, Statistical Division Information Service, Bulletin No. 1045,

p. 10 (cited in note 98). This source indicated that the average total American consumption of wheat for the three "war years" (the 1914–15, 1915–16, and 1916–17 crop years) was 527,702,334 bushels, not the 615,189,397 bushels cited by Hoover in his letter to the President on November 15, 1917.

181. See Hall, "Cheap Bread," pp. 108–15, and L. Margaret Barnett, *British Food Policy During the First World War* (Boston, 1985), p. 179.
182. Hoover to Barnes, February 2, 1918; Barnes to Hoover, February 5, 1918. Both in USFA Papers, Box 246.
183. The U.S. Department of Agriculture's estimate of the surplus available for export was 78,000,000 bushels. See Frank L. Polk cable to Hugh R. Wilson, November 3, 1917, printed in *FRUS, 1917,* Supplement 2, vol. I, pp. 658–59.
184. Hoover, "Report of the United States Food Administrator to the President Covering the Period from January 1, 1918 to July 1, 1918," p. 6.
185. Levenstein, *Revolution at the Table,* pp. 137, 144–45. See also Charles Whiting Baker, *Government Control and Operation of Industry in Great Britain and the United States During the World War* (New York, 1921), pp. 96–97: "There is no doubt that the savings made by certain classes were offset by the increased consumption of others. Millions who received far higher wages than ever before and were more continually employed naturally bought food more liberally."
186. Wilfred Eldred, "The Wheat and Flour Trade Under Food Administration Control: 1917–18," *Quarterly Journal of Economics* 33 (November 1918): 67; G. F. Warren, "Some Purposes and Results of Price Fixing," *American Economic Review,* Supplement, 9 (March 1919): 240; Simon Litman, *Prices and Price Control in Great Britain and the United States During the World War* (New York, 1920), p. 228.
187. According to Hoover's "Report" to the President in September 1918 (see note 184), the average monthly distribution of wheat to the American public in the first six months of 1918 was 24,921,000 bushels, compared to 44,368,000 bushels in the last six months of 1917.
188. For example, Hoover to Wilson, March 7, 1918; U.S. Food Administration press release 780, March 23, 1918.
189. U.S. Food Administration, Statistical Division Information Service, Bulletin No. 1045, p. 10.
190. Ibid.
191. Hoover, "Report" to the President, pp. 3–6. The greatest single source of conservation, said Hoover, was the 50-50 rule. To it he attributed a savings of 50,000,000 bushels.
192. Eldred, "The Wheat and Flour Trade," pp. 68–69. According to Eldred, "Only with the application of the 'substitute' rules did the conservation program of the Food Administration become really effective."
193. Hoover speech to the Washington section of the American Institute of Mining Engineers, June 21, 1918.

CHAPTER 10

1. Woodrow Wilson to Josephus Daniels, November 28, 1917, printed in Arthur S. Link et al., eds., *The Papers of Woodrow Wilson,* vol. 45 (Princeton, N.J., 1984), p. 148. Identical letters were sent to Hoover, Harry A. Garfield, and several Cabinet members.
2. Herbert Hoover to Woodrow Wilson, December 1, 1917, Woodrow Wilson Papers, LC.
3. Woodrow Wilson, Annual Message on the State of the Union, December 4, 1917, printed in Link et al., eds., *Papers of Woodrow Wilson,* vol. 45, pp. 194–202. The passage quoted here appears on p. 201.
4. Minutes of the Council of National Defense, December 17, 1917, and January 4, 1918, printed in U.S. Congress, Senate, 74th Congress, 2d Session, Senate Committee Print No.

7: *Munitions Industry: Minutes of the Council of National Defense* (Washington, D.C., 1936), pp. 203, 213; Newton D. Baker to Woodrow Wilson, January 11, 1918, Wilson Papers; Woodrow Wilson to Baker, January 16, 1918, Newton D. Baker Papers, Box 8, LC; *New York Times*, January 22, 1918, p. 11, and January 23, 1918, p. 9.

5. *New York Times*, January 23, 1918, p. 9. By early February the price-fixing bill still had not been introduced. *Commercial and Financial Chronicle* 206 (February 2, 1918): 418–19.
6. Josephus Daniels diary, March 18, 1918, printed in E. David Cronon, ed., *The Cabinet Diaries of Josephus Daniels, 1913–1921* (Lincoln, Nebr., 1963), p. 292; Hoover to Daniels, March 19, 1918, Josephus Daniels Papers, Box 81, LC.
7. Hoover to Daniels, March 19, 1918.
8. *Commercial and Financial Chronicle* 106 (February 2, 1918): 418.
9. *Official Bulletin* 1 (October 17, 1917): 3; U.S. Food Administration press release 424, November 4, 1917, USFA Documents, HHPL.
10. *Congressional Record* 56 (December 11, 1917): 115. The committee was also instructed to investigate the coal shortage.
11. The subcommittee's members were: James A. Reed (chairman), James K. Vardaman, Andrieus A. Jones, Henry Cabot Lodge, and William S. Kenyon. The first three were Democrats, the latter two Republicans. Only Jones was strongly pro-Woodrow Wilson.
12. U.S. Congress, Senate, Subcommittee of the Committee on Manufactures, 65th Congress, 2d Session, *Shortage of Sugar* (Washington, D.C., 1918), p. 6 (hereinafter cited as *Shortage of Sugar*).
13. Ibid., pp. 67, 103.
14. Ibid., p. 104; *New York Times*, December 12, 1917, p. 1.
15. For Spreckels's testimony, see *Shortage of Sugar*, pp. 7–102, 105–58. See also *New York Times*, December 15, 1917, pp. 1, 2; December 16, 1917, section I, pp. 1, 19; and December 18, 1917, pp. 1, 20.
16. For Babst's testimony, see *Shortage of Sugar*, pp. 102–04, 162–207, 212–65, 269–323. For Rolph's testimony, see ibid., pp. 323–51, 361–449. See also the press coverage for these days. For a convenient summary of the early days of the hearings, see *Commercial and Financial Chronicle* 105 (December 22, 1917): 2418–20.
17. U.S. Food Administration press release 539, December 15, 1917, USFA Documents; *New York Times*, December 16, 1917, section I, p. 19.
18. Mark L. Requa memorandum, December 20, 1917, USFA Papers, Box 283, HI.
19. *Shortage of Sugar*, pp. 1005–06.
20. Herbert Hoover, *An American Epic*, vol. II (Chicago, 1960), p. 39.
21. Frank Lyon Polk diary, December 17, 1917, Frank Lyon Polk Papers, Manuscripts and Archives, Yale University Library. Lodge privately expressed his resentment of Hoover in a conversation with Polk, who was then counselor of the State Department.
22. Sir Cecil Spring Rice memorandum evidently sent to the British Foreign Office, December 17, 1917, in Sir Cecil Spring Rice Papers, FO 800/242, PRO.
23. *Shortage of Sugar*, pp. 121–23; *New York Times*, December 18, 1917, p. 1; *Commercial and Financial Chronicle* 105 (December 22, 1917): 2419–20.
24. *New York Times*, December 18, 1917, pp. 1, 20.
25. Polk diary, December 17, 1917.
26. *Shortage of Sugar*, pp. 160–62; *New York Times*, December 19, 1917, p. 1.
27. For testimony favorable to Hoover's perspective on the transportation snarl, see *Shortage of Sugar*, pp. 279, 297, 374, and 783.
28. Ibid., pp. 383–84.
29. Ibid., pp. 830, 831, 833, 872.
30. Ibid., pp. 912–13.
31. Ibid., p. 921.
32. Ibid.

33. The hearings explored the Louisiana sugar situation at length. See especially ibid., pp. 231–48, 606, 658, 667.
34. Ibid., p. 440.
35. Ibid., p. 325; *New York Times*, December 21, 1917, p. 8.
36. For the sugar beet growers' grievances, see *Shortage of Sugar*, pp. 451–548.
37. Ibid., pp. 486, 1006.
38. Ibid., p. 486.
39. Ibid., pp. 1004–05.
40. George Creel to Woodrow Wilson, December 22, 1917, Wilson Papers.
41. *Shortage of Sugar*, p. 474; Hoover to Woodrow Wilson, December 23[22], 1917, Wilson Papers. Although this letter is dated December 23, its contents clearly establish that it was written on December 22.
42. *Shortage of Sugar*, p. 474.
43. Ibid., p. 486; *New York Times*, December 23, 1917, section I, pp. 1, 2; Hoover to Wilson, December 23[22], 1917.
44. Hoover to Wilson, December 23[22], 1917.
45. *Chicago Tribune*, December 23, 1917, section I, p. 2.
46. Hoover to Wilson, December 23[22], 1917.
47. U.S. Food Administration press release 550, December 22, 1917, USFA Documents; *New York Times*, December 23, 1917, section I, pp. 1, 2.
48. Hoover to Wilson, December 23[22], 1917.
49. Creel to Wilson, December 22, 1917.
50. *New York Times*, December 23, 1917, section I, p. 2.
51. Sir Cecil Spring Rice memorandum for the British Foreign Office, December 23, 1917, Spring Rice Papers, FO 800 / 242.
52. *New York Times*, December 26, 1917, pp. 1, 3.
53. Ibid. The Hoover statement may also be found in *Shortage of Sugar*, pp. 697–704. After further wrangling, Senator Reed finally allowed the document to be entered in the hearing record.
54. William Howard Taft, "The Sugar Shortage," January 3, 1918, printed in James F. Vivian, ed., *William Howard Taft: Collected Editorials, 1917–1921* (New York, 1990), pp. 23–25. See also the criticism of Reed in the liberal *New Republic* 13 (December 29, 1917): 228, 253.
55. *Shortage of Sugar*, p. 1003.
56. Ibid., pp. 1004–08.
57. Ibid., pp. 1005–06.
58. *New York Times*, December 29, 1917, p. 9.
59. Ibid., December 30, 1917, section I, p. 14.
60. *Shortage of Sugar*, pp. 565, 569.
61. Ibid., p. 581.
62. Ibid., pp. 582–83, 585.
63. Ibid., p. 584.
64. Ibid., pp. 584–85.
65. Ibid., p. 585.
66. Ibid., p. 595.
67. Ibid., p. 604.
68. Ibid., p. 690.
69. Ibid., p. 599.
70. Ibid., p. 691.
71. Ibid., pp. 622–23. See also the account in the *New York Times*, January 3, 1918, p. 3.
72. *Shortage of Sugar*, pp. 624–27.
73. Ibid., p. 603.
74. Ibid., pp. 650–51, 654.

75. Ibid., p. 667. In general, see pp. 650–71 for Hoover's explanation of his Louisiana sugar policy.
76. Ibid., pp. 650, 651, 653.
77. Ibid., pp. 673–74.
78. Ibid., p. 676.
79. Ibid., pp. 676–77.
80. Ibid., p. 643.
81. Ibid., p. 644.
82. Ibid., pp. 644–45.
83. Ibid., pp. 645–46.
84. Ibid., pp. 646–47.
85. Ibid., pp. 648–49.
86. Ibid., pp. 686–87.
87. Ibid., p. 695; *Chicago Tribune*, January 4, 1918, p. 2; *Washington Post*, January 4, 1918, p. 4; *New Republic* 14 (March 23, 1918): 237.
88. *New York Times*, January 8, 1918, p. 4; *New Republic* 14 (March 23, 1918): 237.
89. *New York Times*, January 4, 1918, p. 6.
90. Edgar Rickard to Ray Lyman Wilbur, January 7, 1918, USFA Papers, Box 33.
91. *New York Times*, January 8, 1918, p. 4.
92. Curtis H. Lindley to Edgar Rickard, February 9, 1918, USFA Papers, Box 45.
93. *Shortage of Sugar*, pp. 591–92; *Commercial and Financial Chronicle* 106 (February 9, 1918): 550; Hoover testimony, May 6, 1918, in U.S. Congress, House of Representatives, Subcommittee of House Committee on Appropriations, 65th Congress, 2d Session, *Sundry Civil Bill, 1919* (Washington, D.C., 1918), pp. 2086, 2089.
94. C. D. Morris to Hugh W. Adams, April 19, 1918, and anonymous author, "Report on R," April 20, 1918, both in "Reed, Senator James A.," Pre-Commerce Papers, Herbert Hoover Papers, HHPL; Julius H. Barnes to Hoover, March 13, 1934, and Edgar Rickard to Hoover, March 31, 1934, both in Herbert Hoover Collection, Box 313, HI.
95. Barnes to Hoover, March 13, 1934.
96. Hoover to Edgar Rickard, March 18, 1934, Hoover Collection, Box 313.
97. This is the "Report on R" cited in note 94.
98. Hoover to Woodrow Wilson, March 1, 1918, Wilson Papers.
99. Woodrow Wilson to Hoover, March 5, 1918, "Wilson, Woodrow," Pre-Commerce Papers; Wilson to Edward N. Hurley and Vance C. McCormick, March 5, 1918 (two letters), both in Wilson Papers.
100. *Congressional Record* 56 (February 27, 1918): 2725–30.
101. Ibid., 56 (March 22, 1918): 3887–95.

CHAPTER 11

1. U.S. Congress, Senate, Committee on Agriculture and Forestry, 65th Congress, 2d Session, *Increased Production of Grain and Meat Products* (Washington, D.C., 1918), pp. 124, 293, 301, 341 (hereinafter cited as *Increased Production* hearings).
2. On the feeder cattle situation, see ibid., pp. 284, 295, 296, 317, 367–68, 443, 442–43.
3. Ibid., pp. 145, 317, 341, 435, 438, 446–47, 563; Charles McCarthy to "Mr. R," January 27, 1918, USFA Papers, Box 58, HI; *Official Bulletin* 2 (February 28, 1918): 8; U.S. Food Administration press release 723, March 1, 1918, USFA Documents, HHPL.
4. *Increased Production* hearings, pp. 29, 84–85, 121; Wilfred Eldred, "The Wheat and Flour Trade Under Food Administration Control: 1917–18," *Quarterly Journal of Economics* 33 (November 1918): 42–43.
5. *Increased Production* hearings, pp. 122, 582–83.

6. Ibid., p. 495. See also Julius H. Barnes to Herbert Hoover, March 4, 1918, USFA Papers, Box 246, HI.
7. *Increased Production* hearings, pp. 121, 129, 424–25; Herbert Hoover, "Report of the United States Food Administrator to the President Covering the Period from January 1, 1918 to July 1, 1918," p. 19, enclosed with Hoover to Woodrow Wilson, September 7, 1918, Woodrow Wilson Papers, LC.
8. See, for example, the resolutions of the annual meeting of the Illinois Farmers' Institute, February 19–21, 1918, printed in *Congressional Record* 56 (March 20, 1918): 3772–73.
9. *Increased Production* hearings, pp. 11, 27, 73, 76, 139, 311, 513. As one witness put it, Hoover's agency always considered issues "from the standpoint of the consumer and not enough from the standpoint of the fellow that follows the plow" (p. 76).
10. *Wallaces' Farmer* 43 (March 22, 1918): 528.
11. For example, see *Increased Production* hearings, pp. 284, 320.
12. *Official Bulletin* 2 (February 12, 1918): 4; "Poultry Conference, April 1, 1918" transcript, in "Advisory Committee—Poultry," General Correspondence of the Office of the Secretary of Agriculture, 1918, RG 16, NARA. This conference was held in Washington, D.C., as part of a gathering of agricultural advisers brought to the capital by Hoover.
13. *Official Bulletin* 2 (March 7, 1918): 2.
14. Ibid., February 12, 1918, p. 4. See also U.S. Food Administration press releases 714 (February 28, 1918) and 724 (March 1, 1918), USFA Documents.
15. Prince T. Woods to Henry C. Wallace, February 26, 1918, Henry C. Wallace Papers, University of Iowa Libraries; "Poultry Conference, April 1, 1918" transcript, pp. 5, 7. Said Elbert C. Brigham of Vermont at this conference: "Nothing ever did so much to stir up discontent [as the order banning sales of hens]." Others at the conference, however, asserted that the backlash had not been very serious (pp. 2, 3). Its intensity evidently varied in different parts of the country.
16. "Poultry Conference, April 1, 1918" transcript, p. 8.
17. E. C. Lasater testimony, March 30, 1918, in *Increased Production* hearings, pp. 535–36.
18. U.S. Food Administration press release 724 (March 1, 1918).
19. Hoover's comments may be found on p. 46 of the stenographic report of a "Conference Relative to the Agricultural Situation and the Dissemination of Information on Agricultural Plans and Activities" (Washington, D.C., March 7, 1918), in "AGL—Dept. WRK—Correspondence—Meetings (Agl'r—extensions) (Jan.–May)," General Correspondence of the Office of the Secretary of Agriculture, 1918, RG 16, NARA.
20. U.S. Department of Agriculture *Weekly News Letter* 5 (April 17, 1918): 5; *Official Bulletin* 2 (April 13, 1918): 8.
21. *Official Bulletin* 2 (April 13, 1918): 8.
22. "Report of the United States Food Administrator . . . July 1, 1918," p. 11.
23. Woods to Wallace, February 26, 1918.
24. *Congressional Record* 56 (March 8, 1918): 3192; "Poultry Conference, April 1, 1918" transcript, p. 7.
25. "Poultry Conference, April 1, 1918" transcript, p. 6.
26. U.S. Food Administration, *Canned Foods Bulletin No. 3* (February 28, 1918), printed in *Congressional Record* 56 (March 8, 1918): 3182.
27. *Congressional Record* 56 (March 8, 1918): 3182–88.
28. For Reed's speech, see ibid.: 3189–94.
29. Ibid.: 3192.
30. Hoover to Senator Willard Saulsbury, March 13, 1918, printed in *Congressional Record* 56 (April 1, 1918): 4357.
31. *Congressional Record* 56 (April 1, 1918): 4357.
32. Ibid. (March 8, 1918): 3187.
33. Ibid.: 3186–87.

34. Ibid. (March 12, 1918): 3362, 3372–84.
35. For copies of this correspondence, see ibid. (April 18, 1918): 5305.
36. Ibid.; memorandum, March 5, 1918, Wilson Papers.
37. Memorandum, March 5, 1918.
38. Notations by Woodrow Wilson and one of his secretaries on ibid.
39. Memorandum (approved by Woodrow Wilson) for Mr. Tonner of the State Department, March 6, 1918, Wilson Papers; *Congressional Record* 56 (April 18, 1918): 5305.
40. Representative Edward H. Wason to Secretary of State Robert Lansing, March 9, 1918, copy in Wilson Papers and in *Congressional Record* 56 (April 19, 1918): 5306.
41. Wilson to Frank L. Polk, March 14, 1918, Wilson Papers; *Congressional Record* 56 (April 18, 1918): 5306.
42. *Congressional Record* 56 (April 18, 1918): 5305–06.
43. Ibid. (April 22, 1918): 5455–56.
44. U.S. Food Administration press release 693, February 22, 1918, USFA Documents; printed in *Official Bulletin* 2 (February 28, 1918): 8.
45. U.S. Food Administration press release 728, March 3, 1918, USFA Documents.
46. Hoover remarks, March 7, 1918, in "Conference Relative to the Agricultural Situation" transcript, pp. 41–43.
47. Ibid., pp. 43–45.
48. U.S. Food Administration press release 761, March 14, 1918, USFA Documents.
49. *Increased Production* hearings, pp. 432–33.
50. U.S. Food Administration press release 791, March 29, 1918, USFA Documents.
51. U.S. Food Administration press release 906, May 2, 1918, USFA Documents; William C. Mullendore, *History of the United States Food Administration, 1917–1919* (Stanford, Calif., 1941), p. 116.
52. Hoover to Representative Jouett Shouse, February 20, 1918, USFA Papers, Box 96.
53. Mullendore, *History*, p. 147; Hoover to Woodrow Wilson, February 20, 1918, Wilson Papers; Wilson to Hoover, February 21, 1917 [1918], "Wilson, Woodrow," Pre-Commerce Papers, Herbert Hoover Papers, HHPL; Hoover to Frank W. Taussig, February 23, 1918, USFA Papers, Box 172. The last document is quoted in Frank M. Surface, *The Grain Trade During the World War* (New York, 1928), pp. 126–27, but dated February 25, 1918.
54. Hoover to Wilson, February 20, 1918.
55. *Official Bulletin* 2 (March 14, 1918): 1; Hoover to Taussig, March 26, 1918, quoted in Surface, *Grain Trade*, pp. 127–29.
56. Minutes of the Federal Trade Commission, February 26 and March 7, 1918, microfilm edition at University of Iowa Law School; *Official Bulletin* 2 (April 19, 1918): 14.
57. *Official Bulletin* 2 (April 19, 1918): 14.
58. Hoover to Shouse, February 20, 1918.
59. Hoover to Senator Atlee Pomerene, March 18, 1918, USFA Papers, Box 96; "Agricultural Advisory Committee of the U.S. Department of Agriculture and the U.S. Food Administration: Stenographic Report of Proceedings" (typescript, March 30–April 3, 1918), pp. 36–37, copy in USFA Papers, Box 82. Despite Hoover's and the Department of Agriculture's conclusion that feeding of wheat to farm animals had "prevailed [only] in a few isolated locations" (p. 37), there was evidence as early as January 10 that this practice was widespread because wheat in some rural areas was cheaper than corn. See Alonzo E. Taylor memorandum for Hoover, January 10, 1918, USFA Papers, Box 37. However, after contacting field agents in wheat-growing states in early March, the U.S. Department of Agriculture reported that the amount of wheat being fed to livestock was actually less than in previous years, "except in a few States or sections where there was difficulty in obtaining other feedstuffs." In fact, the total amount thus fed (including wheat unfit for human use) was probably no more than 2 percent of the crop. *Congressional Record* 56 (April 18, 1918): 5297.
60. U.S. Food Administration press release 700, February 25, 1918, USFA Documents.

61. *New York Times*, February 26, 1918, p. 6.
62. *Increased Production* hearings, pp. 314–15. Burke, a prominent Nebraska livestock feeder, was chairman of the committee on cattle that advised Joseph Cotton, head of Hoover's meat division.
63. Hoover address to the Pittsburgh Press Club, April 18, 1918, issued as U.S. Food Administration press release 868, USFA Documents.
64. See "Conference Relative to the Agricultural Situation" transcript, cited in note 19.
65. "Agricultural Advisory Committee . . . Stenographic Report of Proceedings" (March 30–April 3, 1918); *Report of Advisory Committee of Agricultural and Live-Stock Producers* (Washington, D.C., 1918); U.S. Department of Agriculture *Weekly News Letter* 5 (April 17, 1918): 1–6.
66. Vernon Kellogg to William E. Dodd, April 10, 1918, USFA Papers, Box 58.
67. Hoover to Woodrow Wilson, March 22, 1918, Wilson Papers.
68. Hoover to David R. Francis, March 6, 1918, David R. Francis Papers, Box 32, Missouri Historical Society.
69. Hoover comment, March 7, 1918, in "Conference Relative to the Agricultural Situation" transcript, p. 59.
70. Hoover to Representative William A. Ayres, May 4, 1918, USFA Papers, Box 96.
71. Hoover address to the Pittsburgh Press Club, April 18, 1918.
72. Charles McCarthy memorandum on Hoover (October 1918), Charles McCarthy Papers, Box 37, State Historical Society of Wisconsin.
73. Julius H. Barnes to Lewis L. Strauss, November 5, 1917; Strauss to Barnes, November 8, 1917. Both in USFA Papers, Box 245.
74. Alonzo E. Taylor memorandum for Hoover, January 10, 1918, USFA Papers, Box 37.
75. See, for example, *New York Times*, February 14, 1918, p. 6.
76. William E. Borah to Jesse G. Moore, February 11, 1918, William E. Borah Papers, Box 54, LC.
77. One agrarian leader testified before the Senate Committee on Agriculture in February 1918: "There was nothing in the [Lever] bill fixing the price of the 1917 crop of wheat, but they did reduce it practically one-third. . . ." *Increased Production* hearings, p. 132.
78. For example, see ibid., p. 93.
79. Ibid., pp. 93, 123–24. See also *Congressional Record* 56 (April 18, 1918): 5305, and 56 (June 29, 1918): 8488.
80. Hoover Calendar, February 12, 1918, HHPL; Senator Thomas P. Gore to Secretary of Agriculture David Houston, February 13, 1918, "Grains—Wheat, 1918," General Correspondence of the Secretary of Agriculture, RG 16, NARA.
81. *Congressional Record* 56 (June 29, 1918): 8488; Gore to Houston, February 13, 1918.
82. James F. Bell diary, February 16, 1918, James F. Bell Papers, Box 3, HI; Edgar Rickard to Curtis H. Lindley, February 21, 1918, USFA Papers, Box 45.
83. *Congressional Record* 56 (June 29, 1918): 8488; David Houston to Thomas P. Gore, February 18, 1918, "Grains—Wheat, 1918," General Correspondence of the Secretary of Agriculture, RG 16, NARA. Gore had asked Houston to seek a formal interpretation of the wheat price provision of the Lever Act from the Attorney General. In response, Houston agreed with Gore that the $2.00 price mentioned in the Act was a minimum, not an "absolute," price, and that the President at his discretion could fix a higher price. Houston added that he was authorized to say that Herbert Hoover concurred with this view.
84. *New York Times*, February 14, 1918, p. 6.
85. Hoover to Woodrow Wilson, February 14, 1918, Wilson Papers.
86. Julius H. Barnes to Hoover, February 15, 1918, USFA Papers, Box 246.
87. In his letter to the President on February 14, Hoover argued that price determinations should be made by presidentially appointed commissions, not by Congress.
88. Wilson to Hoover, February 18, 1918; Wilson to Representative Asbury F. Lever, February 18, 1918. Both in Wilson Papers.

89. Wilson to Lever, February 18, 1918.
90. Ibid.
91. The testimony can be found in the *Increased Production* hearings.
92. *Congressional Record* 56 (February 19, 1918): 2310.
93. *New York Times*, February 21, 1918, p. 4.
94. *Commercial and Financial Chronicle* 106 (February 23, 1918): 771.
95. *New York Times*, February 21, 1918, p. 4. According to James F. Bell (the chief of the Food Administration's milling division), a proposal by a North Dakota senator to raise the price of wheat to $3.00 a bushel was "completely demoralizing [the] movement of wheat from the farm." Bell diary, February 14, 1918, Bell Papers, Box 3.
96. Hoover to Wilson, February 14, 1918.
97. *New York Times*, February 24, 1918, section I, pp. 1, 3; *Official Bulletin* 2 (February 25, 1918): 1, 2, 3. The proclamation was dated February 21 but not issued until two days later. It was clearly intended to undercut Senator Gore. See James F. Bell diary, February 16, 1918, Bell Papers, Box 3.
98. *Congressional Record* 56 (March 16, 1918): 3594.
99. Ibid. (March 19, 1918): 3691–92.
100. Ibid.: 3692.
101. Ibid. (March 20, 1918): 3757.
102. Ibid.: 3769.
103. Ibid. (March 18, 1918): 3643.
104. For details of the debate, see the *Congressional Record* for March 16, 18, 19, 20, and 21, 1918.
105. Julius H. Barnes to Hoover, March 22, 1918, USFA Papers, Box 246.
106. Hoover to Pomerene, March 18, 1918.
107. Barnes to Hoover, February 15, 1918.
108. *Kansas City Times* clipping, March 1, 1918, copy in USFA Papers, Box 246.
109. Barnes telegram to Hoover, March 19, 1918 (and notation at the bottom), USFA Papers, Box 246.
110. Barnes to Lewis L. Strauss, March 19, 1918, USFA Papers, Box 246.
111. Ibid. In this same letter Barnes asked that Hoover "really seriously consider" presenting the bonus plan for "serious discussion and consideration" in the "sidetrack" effort. His wording implied that the bonus idea had not been a "serious" one up to that time. There is no evidence that Hoover considered the proposal as anything more than a diversionary maneuver.
112. *Congressional Record* 56 (March 21, 1918): 3830–31.
113. Hoover to Pomerene, March 28, 1918, USFA Papers, Box 96.
114. Pomerene to Woodrow Wilson, March 21, 1918, Wilson Papers.
115. Wilson to Pomerene, March 25, 1918, Wilson Papers.
116. *New York Times*, March 23, 1918, p. 8, and March 24, 1918, section I, p. 5.
117. Barnes to Hoover, March 22, 1918, USFA Papers, Box 246.
118. Hoover to Woodrow Wilson, March 26, 1918 (plus enclosure), Wilson Papers.
119. This can be followed in the *Congressional Record* for 1918. For the page references, see its index under H.R. 9054 (the appropriations bill for the U.S. Department of Agriculture). I will not make a separate citation for every parliamentary maneuver mentioned in my text. For a brief summary of the battle, see Surface, *Grain Trade*, pp. 318–21.
120. *Congressional Record* 56 (July 1, 1918): 8545.
121. Ibid. (June 26, 1918): 8288.
122. Unedited minutes of Agricultural Advisory Committee, March 30, 1918, USFA Papers, Box 83A.
123. "Agricultural Advisory Committee . . . Stenographic Report of Proceedings" (March 30–April 3, 1918), pp. 12, 14.
124. Ibid., pp. 16, 19.
125. Ibid., p. 6.

126. Ibid., p. 44; unedited minutes of the Agricultural Advisory Committee, March 30, 1918 (for the expunged material).
127. "Agricultural Advisory Committee . . . Stenographic Report of Proceedings" (March 30–April 3, 1918), pp. 40–41. For the formal wording of the committee's resolutions, see U.S. Department of Agriculture *Weekly News Letter* 5 (April 17, 1918): 2.
128. The committee was clearly reluctant to inject itself into the Congressional brouhaha. "Agricultural Advisory Committee . . . Stenographic Report of Proceedings" (March 30–April 3, 1918), p. 43; Surface, *Grain Trade*, p. 322.
129. *Congressional Record* 56 (April 6, 1918): 4698–4701, 4708.
130. I have found no evidence of executive branch compliance with the Senate's resolution.
131. "Agricultural Advisory Committee . . . Stenographic Report of Proceedings" (March 30–April 3, 1918), p. 35. A moment later in the proceedings (p. 36), Hoover made some remarks which the chairman of the committee asked the stenographer not to take down. No reason was given. At other points in the transcript, however, remarks by Hoover did appear.
132. Notably in his address to the Pittsburgh Press Club (cited in note 63).
133. Hoover address entitled "America's Grain Trade," delivered at a conference of representatives of the grain trade of the United States, April 30, 1918, Public Statements File, HHPL.
134. Ibid.; *New York Times*, April 9, 1918, p. 24, and April 14, 1918, section I, p. 7.
135. *New York Times*, March 28, 1918, p. 10, and March 31, 1918, p. 11.
136. U.S. Food Administration press release 778, March 23, 1918, USFA Documents.
137. Barnes to Hoover, March 23, 1918, quoted in Surface, *Grain Trade*, p. 350.
138. Surface, *Grain Trade*, p. 138.
139. *New York Times*, March 28, 1918, p. 10; U.S. Food Administration press release 784, March 28, 1918, USFA Documents.
140. U.S. Food Administration press release 784, March 28, 1918.
141. *Washington Post*, April 6, 1918, p. 5.
142. *Congressional Record* 56 (April 6, 1918): 4708.
143. U.S. Food Administration press release 930, May 9, 1918, USFA Documents.
144. *New York Times*, April 14, 1918, section I, p. 7.
145. Surface, *Grain Trade*, p. 350.
146. Ibid., pp. 350–51.
147. Scott Ferris to Woodrow Wilson, May 16, 1918, Wilson Papers.
148. Wilson to Ferris, May 20, 1918, Wilson Papers.
149. Woodrow Wilson executive order, June 21, 1918, printed in Surface, *Grain Trade*, pp. 523–24.
150. *New York Times*, July 1, 1918, p. 13. See also *Commercial and Financial Chronicle* 106 (June 29, 1918): 2705.
151. *Congressional Record* 56 (July 1, 1918): 8561.
152. Ibid. (June 29, 1918): 8489.
153. Ibid. (July 6, 1918): 8794, 8796.
154. Ibid.: 8754–55, 8784–98.
155. *New York Times*, July 7, 1918, section I, p. 1.
156. Many such letters and telegrams are in the Wilson Papers.
157. Scott Ferris telegram to Woodrow Wilson, July 9, 1918, Wilson Papers.
158. Hoover to Woodrow Wilson, July 8 and 10, 1918, Wilson Papers.
159. Hoover to Wilson, July 8, 1918.
160. Lord Reading to William G. McAdoo, July 11, 1918, Wilson Papers. Reading's letter was forwarded to the White House.
161. Hoover to Wilson, July 8, 1918.
162. This was a typically Hooverian modus operandi. It seems unlikely that the British ambassador would have intervened in this matter without prior consultation with Hoover.

163. Woodrow Wilson's veto message, July 12, 1918, printed in Arthur S. Link et al., eds., *The Papers of Woodrow Wilson*, vol. 48 (Princeton, N.J., 1985), pp. 595–97.
164. *Congressional Record* 56 (July 18, 1918): 9167; *Wallaces' Farmer* 43 (July 26, 1918): 1080.
165. *Wallaces' Farmer* 43 (July 26, 1918): 1080.
166. Hoover to Wilson, July 8 and 10, 1918.
167. U.S. Food Administration press release 746, March 9, 1918, USFA Documents.
168. *Congressional Record* 56 (July 13, 1918): 9105.
169. *Washington Post*, July 20, 1918, p. 6.
170. U.S. Department of Commerce, Bureau of the Census, *Historical Statistics of the United States: Colonial Times to 1970* (Washington, D.C., 1975), Part I, p. 511. For variant statistics showing the same trend, see U.S. Department of Agriculture, *Yearbook 1920* (Washington, D.C., 1921), p. 550.
171. U.S. Department of Commerce, Bureau of the Census, *Historical Statistics*, Part I, p. 511.
172. U.S. Department of Agriculture, *Yearbook 1920*, p. 557.
173. Stella Stewart, "Controls of Wheat, Flour and Bread in World War I: 1917–1919" (U.S. Department of Labor, Bureau of Labor Statistics, Division of Historical Studies of Wartime Problems, Historical Study #47: November 1940), p. 55.
174. Hoover address to representatives of the grain trade, April 30, 1918.
175. Ibid.
176. *Congressional Record* 56 (July 18, 1918): 9167.
177. Ibid.: 9168.
178. Seward W. Livermore, "The Sectional Issue in the 1918 Congressional Elections," *Mississippi Valley Historical Review* 35 (June 1948): 29–60; Seward R. Livermore, *Politics Is Adjourned: Woodrow Wilson and the War Congress, 1916–1918* (Middletown, Conn., 1966), pp. 172–76.
179. *Congressional Record* 56 (July 18, 1918): 9163.
180. Ibid.: 9161.
181. On February 19, 1918, a few days after Senator Gore introduced his proposal to increase the guaranteed price of wheat to $2.50 per bushel, Hoover briefly "showed some signs of conceding the higher price" (according to one of his associates). But the Chief did not waver very long. That same day, he visited the White House. When he returned, he reported that President Wilson was determined to maintain the current wheat price structure. After that, Hoover showed no signs of making concessions to his senatorial foes. Bell diary, February 19, 1918, Bell Papers, Box 3.

CHAPTER 12

1. American National Live Stock Association Convention, January 14–16, 1918, resolution no. 5, printed in U.S. Congress, House of Representatives, Committee on Interstate and Foreign Commerce, 65th Congress, 3d Session, *Government Control of Meat-Packing Industry* (Washington, D.C., 1919), Part 5, pp. 1491–92 (hereinafter cited as *Government Control* [House hearings]).
2. Dwight B. Heard et al. to Woodrow Wilson, February 13, 1918, Woodrow Wilson Papers, LC. Printed in U.S. Congress, Senate, Committee on Agriculture and Forestry, 65th Congress, 2d Session, *Increased Production of Grain and Meat Products* (Washington, D.C., 1918), pp. 20–21 (hereinafter cited as *Increased Production* hearings).
3. Ibid.
4. Dwight B. Heard to David F. Houston, February 12, 1918, printed in *Increased Production* hearings, pp. 22–24.
5. Woodrow Wilson to Herbert Hoover, February 19, 1918, "Wilson, Woodrow," Pre-Commerce Papers, Herbert Hoover Papers, HHPL.

6. American National Live Stock Association Convention, January 14–16, 1918, resolution no. 5; Heard et al. to Wilson, February 13, 1918.
7. Heard et al. to Wilson, February 13, 1918.
8. Wilson to Hoover, February 19, 1918.
9. Hoover, handwritten draft of a letter to Henry C. Wallace, ca. February 4, 1918, USFA Papers, Box 47, HI.
10. Kent was a signatory to the stockmen's memorial cited in note 2.
11. Gifford Pinchot to E. C. Lasater, November 29, 1917, copy in Henry C. Wallace Papers, Box 1, University of Iowa Libraries.
12. Hoover to Woodrow Wilson, February 21, 1918, Wilson Papers.
13. Hoover, "Memorandum," February 20, 1918, enclosed with ibid.
14. Entry for Francis J. Heney in *Dictionary of American Biography*, vol. 11, Supplement 2 (New York, 1958), pp. 296–97.
15. *Chicago Tribune*, February 26, 1918, pp. 1, 10; *New York Times*, February 26, 1918, p. 4.
16. *New York Times*, February 27, 1918, p. 5.
17. U.S. Food Administration press release 709, February 26, 1918, USFA Documents, HHPL; *New York Times*, February 27, 1918, p. 5.
18. Hoover to Woodrow Wilson (plus an enclosed memo), February 27, 1918, "Wilson, Woodrow," Pre-Commerce Papers.
19. Memorandum approved and signed by W. F. Priebe, February 26, 1918, USFA Papers, Box 66.
20. Hoover memo for Wilson, February 27, 1918.
21. On Hoover's letter to Wilson of February 27, 1918 (see note 18) are the handwritten words: "Do not send."
22. *Chicago Tribune*, February 28, 1918, p. 8.
23. Heney later said this to a Congressional committee. See Heney testimony, January 18, 1919, in U.S. Congress, Senate, Committee on Agriculture and Forestry, 65th Congress, 3d Session, *Government Control of the Meat-Packing Industry* (Washington, D.C., 1919), p. 197 (hereinafter cited as *Government Control* [Senate hearings]).
24. *Chicago Tribune*, February 28, 1918, pp. 1, 8; *New York Times*, February 28, 1918, p. 2.
25. See the House and Senate hearings of 1919 cited in notes 1 and 23. See also U.S. Congress, Senate, Committee on Agriculture and Forestry, 65th Congress, 3d Session, *Government Control of the Meat-Packing Industry*, Part 2 (Washington, D.C., 1919) (hereinafter cited as *Government Control* [Senate hearings], Part 2).
26. Hoover to H. L. Preston, April 2, 1918, copy in file no. 8864-2, RG 122, NARA; William A. Glasgow, Jr., testimony, February 1, 1919, *Government Control* (Senate hearings), Part 2, p. 1265; G. Harold Powell to Roland W. Boyden, March 4, 1919, file 14H-B2, Box 620, RG 4, NARA.
27. Hoover to Senator Atlee Pomerene, March 8, 1918, USFA Papers, Box 96, HI; Hoover to Preston, April 2, 1918.
28. W. F. Priebe to Hoover, March 1, 1918, USFA Papers, Box 66; Priebe telegram to W. F. Priebe Company, March 1, 1918, printed in *Government Control* (House hearings), p. 2160; Glasgow testimony, February 6, 1919, ibid., p. 1843; Heney testimony, January 15, 1919, *Government Control* (Senate hearings), p. 100.
29. Priebe to Hoover, March 1, 1918.
30. Heney testimony, January 15, 1919, *Government Control* (Senate hearings), pp. 99, 105; Heney and Glasgow testimony, February 1, 1919, *Government Control* (Senate hearings), Part 2, p. 1283; Heney testimony, February 13, 1919, *Government Control* (House hearings), pp. 2129–30.
31. Charles McCarthy telegram to Lewis L. Strauss, March 3, 1918, Charles McCarthy Papers, Box 16, State Historical Society of Wisconsin.
32. Ray Lyman Wilbur to Hoover, March 4, 1918, USFA Papers, Box 79.

33. William Allen White to Vernon Kellogg, March 2, 1918, William Allen White Papers, Series B, vol. 33, LC.
34. Hoover memo to Vernon Kellogg, March 7, 1918, Herbert Hoover Collection, Box 317, HI.
35. Hoover Calendar, March 8, 1918, HHPL; Heney testimony, January 15, 1919, *Government Control* (Senate hearings), p. 100; Heney testimony, February 13, 1919, *Government Control* (House hearings), p. 2126.
36. Heney testimony, January 15, 1919, *Government Control* (Senate hearings), p. 100; Heney testimony, February 13, 1919, *Government Control* (House hearings), p. 2126.
37. Heney testimony, January 15, 1919, *Government Control* (Senate hearings), pp. 101, 106; Glasgow testimony, February 1, 1919, *Government Control* (Senate hearings), Part 2, pp. 1253–54, 1282–83; Heney testimony, February 13, 1919, *Government Control* (House hearings), pp. 2126–27.
38. Heney testimony, January 15, 1919, *Government Control* (Senate hearings), p. 105; Heney testimony, February 13, 1919, *Government Control* (House hearings), p. 2125.
39. Glasgow testimony, February 1, 1919, *Government Control* (Senate hearings), Part 2, p. 1283.
40. Heney testimony, January 15, 1919, *Government Control* (Senate hearings), pp. 100–01; Heney testimony, February 13, 1919, *Government Control* (House hearings), p. 2130.
41. H. L. Preston to Francis J. Heney, March 18, 1918, copy in file no. 8864-2, RG 122, NARA.
42. Heney testimony, February 13, 1919, *Government Control* (House hearings), p. 2130.
43. Hoover to Preston, April 2, 1918; Glasgow testimony, February 1, 1919, *Government Control* (Senate hearings), Part 2, pp. 1285–86.
44. Hoover to Preston, April 2, 1918.
45. *Government Control* (House hearings), pp. 1845, 2130–31, 2134, 2141–70; *Government Control* (Senate hearings), pp. 105–06; *Government Control* (Senate hearings), Part 2, p. 1284.
46. Heney and Glasgow testimony, February 1, 1919, *Government Control* (Senate hearings), Part 2, p. 1284; A. B. Adams, "Memorandum on W. F. Priebe's Official Activities as Head of the Poultry and Eggs Division of the United States Food Administration" (May 18, 1918), Mem 5 A5, Economic Investigation File, RG 122, NARA; A. B. Adams, "Memorandum for Commissioner Murdock" (May 29, 1918), Mem 5 A5, Economic Investigation File, RG 122, NARA; Thomas Lane Moore III, "The Establishment of a 'New Freedom' Policy: The Federal Trade Commission, 1912–1918" (Ph.D. dissertation, University of Alabama, 1980), p. 265.
47. William C. Mullendore, *History of the United States Food Administration, 1917–1919* (Stanford, Calif., 1941), p. 379.
48. Heney testimony, January 15, 1919, *Government Control* (Senate hearings), p. 101.
49. Hoover to Federal Trade Commission, March 9, 1918, USFA Papers, Box 279.
50. Ibid.; Joseph P. Cotton testimony, March 21, 1918, *Increased Production* hearings, pp. 448–49.
51. Heney testimony, January 15, 1919, *Government Control* (Senate hearings), p. 101.
52. E. Dana Durand testimony, March 21, 1918, *Increased Production* hearings, p. 464; Heney testimony, January 14, 1919, *Government Control* (Senate hearings), pp. 30–31.
53. *Increased Production* hearings, pp. 313, 465, 473.
54. G. C. Shepard to M. R. Murphy, December 18, 1917, printed in *Increased Production* hearings, p. 524.
55. F. E. Wilhelm to W. Deising, January 18, 1918, printed in *Government Control* (House hearings), p. 1507.
56. Ibid.
57. For example, see Hoover, "Memorandum," February 20, 1918, cited in note 13.
58. Ibid.

59. James F. Bell diary, March 21, 1918, James F. Bell Papers, Box 3, HI.
60. Durand testimony, March 21, 1918, *Increased Production* hearings, pp. 465–73.
61. If Durand's testimony was correct, the packing house executive who wrote the letter about the January meeting with Durand had "quite misunderstood what was being discussed," as Durand now put it (ibid., p. 472).
62. William Hirth testimony, March 16, 1918, ibid., p. 386.
63. Hoover draft letter (never sent) to Woodrow Wilson, March 9, 1918, Commission for Relief in Belgium Correspondence, Box 9, HI.
64. Ibid.
65. Senator William S. Kenyon to Woodrow Wilson, March 9, 1918, Wilson Papers.
66. Senator William H. Thompson to Woodrow Wilson, March 13, 1918, Wilson Papers.
67. Woodrow Wilson to Senator Kenyon, March 14, 1918, Wilson Papers.
68. Some months later Hoover indicated to certain friends that the pressure on him to act had been immense. H. Alexander Smith diary, August 19, 1918, H. Alexander Smith Papers, Box 280, Seeley G. Mudd Manuscript Library, Department of Rare Books and Special Collections, Princeton University Libraries.
69. Hoover to Woodrow Wilson, February 21, 1918; Hoover, "Memorandum," February 20, 1918.
70. Hoover to Woodrow Wilson, March 26, 1918 (short letter), Wilson Papers.
71. Ibid.
72. Hoover to Wilson, March 26, 1918 (long letter), Wilson Papers, enclosed with ibid.
73. Woodrow Wilson to Hoover, March 29, 1918, "Wilson, Woodrow," Pre-Commerce Papers; Hoover to Wilson, April 1, 1918, Wilson Papers; Wilson to W. J. Harris, David F. Houston, F. W. Taussig, and William B. Wilson, all on April 2, 1918, all in Woodrow Wilson Papers.
74. *New York Times*, April 1, 1918, pp. 1, 4.
75. Ibid.
76. Henry C. Wallace testimony, March 15, 1918, *Increased Production* hearings, p. 359; Wallace to Gifford Pinchot, March 19, 1918, Wallace Papers, Box 1.
77. It is interesting to note that on March 15 Wallace privately urged Joseph P. Cotton to call in "some men who know the game" and ask them to study the food situation and make a report. Cotton seemed very receptive. One week later Hoover asked President Wilson to appoint a study commission. Wallace to Gifford Pinchot, March 19, 1918.
78. Hoover to Wilson, March 26, 1918 (long letter).
79. Taussig, a noted economist and Harvard professor, had served Hoover in 1917 as a member of the Garfield committee which recommended a price for 1917 wheat. On this committee Taussig had been a centrist.
80. U.S. Food Administration press release 789, March 29, 1918, USFA Documents, HHPL.
81. U.S. Food Administration press release 838, April 9, 1918, USFA Documents.
82. *Wallaces' Farmer* 43 (April 19, 1918): 673.
83. Hoover to F. W. Taussig, April 5, 1918, USFA Papers, Box 172.
84. F. W. Taussig to M. L. Burton, April 9, 1918, USFA Papers, Box 172.
85. Joseph P. Cotton to Hoover, April 22, 1918, USFA Papers, Box 47.
86. Smith diary, August 19, 1918.
87. Ibid.
88. Hoover to Woodrow Wilson, May 13, 1918, Wilson Papers.
89. Smith diary, August 19, 1918.
90. Hoover to Woodrow Wilson, May 13, 1918 (plus enclosure), Wilson Papers.
91. William B. Colver to John Franklin Fort, May 16, 1918 (plus enclosure), Wilson Papers. The enclosure was a memorandum presenting Colver's proposal for government operation of a single major packing company. Fort sent this on to President Wilson; see Fort to Colver, May 16, 1918, Wilson Papers.

92. Woodrow Wilson to Hoover, May 20, 1918, "Wilson, Woodrow," Pre-Commerce Papers.
93. Hoover to Woodrow Wilson, May 21, 1918 (plus enclosure), Wilson Papers. The enclosure was Hoover's memorandum criticizing Colver's proposal.
94. Hoover to David F. Houston, May 24 and 27, 1918, USFA Papers, Box 83B; Hoover to Woodrow Wilson, May 27, 1918, Wilson Papers; Wilson to Hoover, May 28, 1918, "Wilson, Woodrow," Pre-Commerce Papers; U.S. Food Administration press release 977, May 29, 1918, USFA Documents; *New York Times*, May 30, 1918, p. 5.
95. *New York Times*, June 21, 1918, p. 12.
96. U.S. Food Administration press release 977, May 29, 1918.
97. *Wallaces' Farmer* 43 (June 7, 1918): 896.
98. Minutes of meeting of Federal Trade Commission, June 4, 1918, microfilm edition, University of Iowa Law School.
99. William B. Colver, John Franklin Fort, and Victor Murdock to Woodrow Wilson, July 28, 1918, copy in "Wilson, Woodrow," Pre-Commerce Papers, Hoover Papers. The original, signed copy of this letter has not been found. It was sent to President Wilson but returned to the FTC for corrections a month later. Before the President did this, he showed the FTC's letter to Herbert Hoover, who made a copy for himself. It is this copy that is cited here.
100. *New York Times*, June 30, 1918, pp. 1, 9; *Commercial and Financial Chronicle* 107 (July 6, 1918): 28–31.
101. *New York Times*, June 30, 1918, p. 9; Louis F. Swift to Woodrow Wilson, July 1, 1918, Wilson Papers; *Commercial and Financial Chronicle* 107 (July 6, 1918): 31–32.
102. *Chicago Tribune*, July 2, 1918, p. 5.
103. William B. Colver to Joseph P. Tumulty, July 3, 1918, plus enclosure: *Food Investigation: Summary of the Report of the Federal Trade Commission on the Meat-Packing Industry, July 3, 1918* (Washington, D.C., 1918), both in Wilson Papers.
104. William B. Colver to Woodrow Wilson, July 20, 1918. After preparing this letter, Colver and his fellow FTC commissioners decided not to send it to the President. It became public only in response to a Congressional investigation in 1919. The letter is printed in U.S. Congress, Senate, 66th Congress, 1st Session, Document No. 110: *Maximum Profit Limitation on Meat-Packing Industry: Letter from Federal Trade Commission in Response to Senate Resolution of September 3, 1919* (Washington, D.C., 1919), pp. 8–10.
105. Hoover to Woodrow Wilson, July 8, 1918, Wilson Papers.
106. Hoover to Woodrow Wilson, July 8, 1918, enclosed with ibid.
107. Ibid.
108. Hoover to Woodrow Wilson, July 8, 1918 (the letter cited in note 105).
109. Edgar Rickard to Hoover, July 9, 1918, USFA Papers, Box 129.
110. Hoover to Senator Furnifold M. Simmons, July 8, 1918, issued as U.S. Food Administration press release 1057, July 9, 1918, USFA Documents.
111. Ibid.
112. Hoover to Arthur Meeker, July 10, 1918, USFA Papers, Box 48; Hoover to Louis F. Swift, July 10, 1918, file 14H-B2, Box 620, RG 4, NARA. Hoover sent a copy of his letter to Meeker on to President Wilson; it is in the Wilson Papers. See also Hoover to Woodrow Wilson, July 10, 1918 (plus enclosure), copy in Commission for Relief in Belgium Correspondence, Box 10, HI.
113. I have found no evidence that Swift or Meeker seriously considered Hoover's proposal. Several weeks later Hoover told a friend that the meat-packing executives did not budge. H. Alexander Smith diary, August 19, 1918.
114. Ibid.
115. Colver to Woodrow Wilson, July 20, 1918. (This is the unsent letter cited in note 104.)
116. According to the FTC, it did not send its letter to the President because "its contents were orally discussed and the matter seemed to be closed." *Maximum Profit Limitation on Meat-Packing Industry*, p. 3.

117. Rickard to Hoover, July 9, 1918; John Franklin Fort to Woodrow Wilson, July 30, 1918, Wilson Papers.
118. Memorandum for the President, July 25, 1918, Wilson Papers; Fort to Wilson, July 30, 1918; Fort to Wilson, July 30, 1918 (plus enclosures), Wilson Papers. The enclosures included the revised report dated June 28, 1918 from William B. Colver, John Franklin Fort, and Victor Murdock to President Wilson.
119. Fort to Wilson, July 30, 1918.
120. For the text of the original FTC report and the two suppressed exhibits or supplements, see *Maximum Profit Limitation on Meat-Packing Industry*, pp. 4, 20–39.
121. John Franklin Fort to Woodrow Wilson, August 1, 1918, Wilson Papers; Wilson to Joseph P. Tumulty, August 2, 1918, Wilson Papers; *New York Times*, August 9, 1918, pp. 1, 7; Robert D. Cuff, "The Dilemmas of Voluntarism: Hoover and the Pork-Packing Agreement of 1917–1919," *Agricultural History* 53 (October 1979): 742.
122. Edgar Rickard to Woodrow Wilson, August 13, 1918, Wilson Papers.
123. Woodrow Wilson to Rickard, August 13, 1918, Wilson Papers.
124. William B. Colver to Woodrow Wilson, August 28, 1918, Wilson Papers.
125. *Commercial and Financial Chronicle* 107 (September 21, 1918): 1157.
126. *Chicago Tribune*, September 8, 1918, part I, p. 14.
127. Hoover to Joseph P. Cotton, August 30, 1918, discussed in Cotton to William Goode, September 27, 1918, USFA Papers, Box 132. Hoover's original letter has not been located.
128. After conferring with Hoover, President Wilson told a member of the FTC that Hoover was "in accord with the conclusions and purposes of your Commission, on the whole, with regard to the packers. . . ." Wilson to William B. Colver, September 6, 1918, Wilson Papers.
129. Hoover to Woodrow Wilson, September 6, 1918, Wilson Papers.
130. *Chicago Tribune*, September 8, 1918, part I, p. 14.
131. Hoover to Wilson, September 6, 1918.
132. Wilson to Colver, September 6, 1918.
133. Colver to Woodrow Wilson, September 9, 1918, Wilson Papers.
134. Hoover to Wilson, September 9, 1918, Wilson Papers. For a summary of the letter from the Armour executive that Hoover enclosed, see Arthur S. Link et al., eds., *The Papers of Woodrow Wilson*, vol. 49 (Princeton, N.J., 1985), p. 498.
135. Wilson to Hoover, September 10, 1918, "Wilson, Woodrow," Pre-Commerce Papers.
136. Moore, "Establishment of a 'New Freedom' Policy," p. 275.
137. Hoover to Woodrow Wilson, September 11, 1918, Wilson Papers.
138. Hoover to Wilson, September 16, 1918, Wilson Papers.
139. Wilson to Hoover, September 20, 1918, Wilson Papers.
140. "Memorandum of Conference Held . . . in Mr. Hoover's Office, With Representatives of the Five Packers Present . . . ," September 12, 1918, USFA Papers, Box 48.
141. Arthur Meeker to Hoover, September 14, 1918, USFA Papers, Box 48.
142. Hoover to Arthur Meeker, September 25, 1918, USFA Papers, Box 48.
143. See Hoover to Wilson, September 9, 1918.
144. William B. Colver to Wilson, September 13, 1918, Wilson Papers.
145. Ibid.; William B. Colver to William A. Glasgow, Jr., December 14, 1918, file 14H-B2, Box 620, RG 4, NARA.
146. Colver to Glasgow, December 14, 1918; F. S. Snyder to Glasgow, December 14, 1918, file 14H-B2, Box 620, RG 4, NARA.
147. For the text of Hoover's amended regulations, see *Government Control* (Senate hearings), Part 2, pp. 1227–31. See also U.S. Congress, House of Representatives, 65th Congress, 3d Session, Document No. 1877: *Annual Report of the United Food Administration for the Year 1918* (Washington, D.C., 1919), p. 21, and Colver to Wilson, December 14, 1918.
148. Colver to Glasgow, December 14, 1918.
149. Moore, "Establishment of a 'New Freedom' Policy," p. 270.

150. Colver to Glasgow, December 14, 1918.
151. William A. Glasgow, Jr., testimony, February 1, 1918, printed in *Government Control* (Senate hearings), Part 2, p. 1248; see also p. 1288.
152. Federal Trade Commission to Senator Thomas P. Gore, February 13, 1919, printed in *Government Control* (Senate hearings), Part 2, pp. 1293–94.
153. *Annual Report of the United States Food Administration for the Year 1918*, pp. 21–22.
154. Mullendore, *History*, p. 145.
155. Ibid., p. 147; Wilfred Eldred, "The Wheat and Flour Trade Under Food Administration Control: 1917–18," *Quarterly Journal of Economics* 33 (November 1918): 48–49.
156. Eldred, "Wheat and Flour Trade," pp. 47, 49; Hoover to James F. Bell, April 4, 1918, Bell Papers, Box 1. Hoover told Bell, the general chairman of the milling division, that this branch was "unique in the whole food organisation in that it is comprised of men interested in the trade and rests upon the confidence we all hold in the majority of the flour millers."
157. Hoover speech to state food administrators, May 28 or 29, 1918, as recorded in "Notes on Meeting in Washington" (June 3, 1918), Magnus Swenson Papers, Box 6, State Historical Society of Wisconsin.
158. *Weekly Northwestern Miller* 115 (July 3, 1918): 36; Frank M. Surface, *The Grain Trade During the World War* (New York, 1928), pp. 131, 140–43.
159. Eldred, "Wheat and Flour Trade," p. 57; Surface, *Grain Trade*, p. 132; Mullendore, *History*, p. 152.
160. U.S. Food Administration press release 1093, July 22, 1918, USFA Documents; *Annual Report of the United States Food Administration for the Year 1918*, p. 18.
161. Calman R. Winegarden, "Stabilization of Food Prices at the Retail Level: 1917–1918" (U.S. Department of Labor, Bureau of Labor Statistics, Division of Historical Studies of Wartime Problems, Historical Study #48: June 1942), pp. 7–11.
162. *New York Times*, June 8, 1918, p. 9.
163. "Report of Conference of Federal Food Administrators, Washington, D.C., May 28–29, 1918," pp. 3–4, 11, USFA Papers, Box 10; "Notes on Meeting in Washington" (June 3, 1918), Swenson Papers, Box 6.
164. Ibid.; Winegarden, "Stabilization of Food Prices," pp. 11–12; U.S. Food Administration press release 1005, June 7, 1918, USFA Documents.
165. U.S. Food Administration press release 1005, June 7, 1918.
166. "Report of Conference . . . May 28–29, 1918," p. 4.
167. U.S. Food Administration press release 1005, June 7, 1918.
168. Ibid.
169. A point noted in Lewis Cecil Gray, "Price-Fixing Policies of the Food Administration," *American Economic Review*, Supplement, 9 (March 1919): 262.
170. U.S. Food Administration press release 1005, June 7, 1918. Technically, this press release was not issued in Hoover's name, and he may not have written the text. Nevertheless, the *New York Times* reported that he approved the document before it was published. Thus he took responsibility for, and of course was publicly identified with, its contents.
171. *New York Times*, June 8, 1918, p. 9.
172. U.S. Food Administration press release 1010, June 10, 1918, USFA Documents.
173. U.S. Food Administration press releases, June–November 1918, passim.
174. Hoover was quite explicit about this. According to the "Report of Conference . . . May 28–29, 1918" (p. 4): "Mr. Hoover impressed upon the Administrators the desirability of a change in policy of the Food Administration whereby prices were to be considered an index rather than profits."
175. U.S. Food Administration press release 1229, October 5, 1918, USFA Documents; *New York Times*, October 9, 1918, p. 10.

CHAPTER 13

1. Herbert Hoover cable to Walter Hines Page, May 20, 1918, printed in United States, Department of State, *Papers Relating to the Foreign Relations of the United States, 1918*, Supplement 1: *The World War* (Washington, D.C., 1933), vol. I, p. 521 (hereinafter cited as *FRUS, 1918*, Supplement 1).
2. Herbert Hoover to Woodrow Wilson, June 13, 1918, Woodrow Wilson Papers, LC.
3. *Commercial and Financial Chronicle* 106 (June 22, 1918): 2610.
4. Hoover to Wilson, June 13, 1918.
5. Ibid.
6. Wilson to Hoover, June 14, 1918, "Wilson, Woodrow," Pre-Commerce Papers, Herbert Hoover Papers, HHPL.
7. Hoover to Wilson, June 29, 1918, "Wilson, Woodrow," Pre-Commerce Papers, Hoover Papers.
8. Lewis L. Strauss diary, July 29, 1918, "Strauss, Lewis L., Diaries," Name and Subject File I, Lewis L. Strauss Papers, HHPL; U.S. Food Administration confidential memorandum to all division heads, n.d. (containing paraphrase of a cable from the American ambassador at London, England, August 1, 1918), file 1H-A21, RG 4, NARA; Hoover to Woodrow Wilson, August 3, 1918, Commission for Relief in Belgium Correspondence, Box 10, HI. According to the Royal Commission on Wheat Supplies, Great Britain had a fifteen-week stock of breadstuffs "available for the loaf" on July 1, 1918. See "Memorandum by the Royal Commission on Wheat Supplies for Consideration by the Food Controller" (no. 35), July 17, 1918, in notes by different branches of the Ministry of Food in preparation for Hoover's visit of July 1918, MAF 60/57, PRO.
9. L. Margaret Barnett, *British Food Policy During the First World War* (Boston, 1985), pp. 181–83.
10. Ibid., pp. 183–84.
11. Ibid., p. 184.
12. Lord Reading to Hoover, June 12, 1918; Hoover to Lord Reading, June 14, 1918. Printed in *FRUS, 1918*, Supplement 1, vol. I, p. 556.
13. Strauss diary, July 29, 1918.
14. Wilson approved Hoover's planned trip by writing "Okeh" at the end of Hoover's letter of June 29 to him. While Hoover did not explain his motives as bluntly in this letter as he later did to his secretary, Hoover did discuss his forthcoming trip orally with the President. Memorandum for the President, July 5, 1918, Wilson Papers; White House appointments book, July 7, 1918, Wilson Papers.
15. Edward M. House diary, June 17, 1918, Edward M. House Papers, Manuscripts and Archives, Yale University Library.
16. Louis P. Sheldon cable to Hoover, July 1, 1918; Hoover cable to Louis P. Sheldon, July 2, 1918. Both in USFA Papers, Box 133, HI.
17. Quoted in William C. Edgar to his wife, July 20, 1918, William C. Edgar and Family Papers, Box 2, Minnesota Historical Society.
18. Strauss diary, July 8–18, 1918; William C. Edgar to his wife, July 20, 1918; Lewis L. Strauss, *Men and Decisions* (Garden City, N.Y., 1962), p. 14.
19. Frank H. Coller, *A State Trading Venture* (Oxford, 1925), p. 159.
20. Strauss diary, July 19, 1918; William C. Edgar to his wife, July 20, 1918; James F. Bell diary, July 19, 1918, James F. Bell Papers, Box 3, HI.
21. *New York Times*, July 19, 1918, p. 9.
22. *The Times* [London], July 20, 1918, p. 3.
23. Quoted in William C. Edgar to his wife, July 20, 1918.
24. J. R. Clynes to David Lloyd George, June 20, 1918, F/43/5/76, David Lloyd George

Papers, House of Lords Record Office, London; Lord Stamfordham to William Sutherland, July 2, 1918, F / 29 / 2 / 34, Lloyd George Papers.

25. Stamfordham to Sutherland, July 2, 1918.
26. It may be pertinent that earlier in the war Hoover's humanitarian relief work in German-occupied Belgium was not popular among some British government officials, who believed that Hoover's activities willy nilly benefited the Germans.
27. J. R. Clynes, quoted in *The Times* [London], July 26, 1918, p. 8.
28. *New York Times*, July 22, 1918, p. 13.
29. Hoover speech at the Mansion House, London, July 23, 1918, Public Statements File, Hoover Papers; *New York Times*, July 24, 1918, p. 10; Lewis L. Strauss to Lou Henry Hoover, July 16, 1918, USFA Papers, Box 1, HI.
30. *Allied Maritime Transport Council: 1918*, pp. 165–66, copy in Edwin F. Gay Papers, Box 6, HI. This document is a printed report and review of the work of the Allied Maritime Transport Council for 1918, including the minutes and appendices of its meetings.
31. Hoover speech at the Mansion House, July 23, 1918.
32. Ibid.
33. Hoover to Woodrow Wilson, September 21, 1918, Wilson Papers.
34. The term "vital margin" appeared in the *New York Times*'s account of Hoover's meeting with King George V. It is not clear whether the king himself used the expression.
35. *The Times* [London], July 26, 1918, p. 8.
36. Strauss diary, July 29, 1918; *The Times* [London], July 30, 1918, p. 7; *New York Times*, August 24, 1918, p. 6.
37. Hoover remarks in "Minutes of Proceedings at a Conference of the Allied Food Controllers. Tuesday, 23rd July, 1918" (typescript), copy in Alonzo E. Taylor Papers, Box 23, HI.
38. William H. Beveridge notes concerning food controllers' conference, entry for July 23, 1918, William H. Beveridge Papers, British Library of Political and Economic Science, London.
39. Ibid., entries for July 23–29, 1918.
40. U.S. Food Administration confidential memorandum containing paraphrase of cable of August 1, 1918 (cited in note 8); Hoover to Wilson, August 3, 1918.
41. Strauss diary, July 30, 1918; David Lloyd George to Andrew Bonar Law, August 20, 1918, F / 30 / 2 / 41, Lloyd George Papers.
42. Hugh Gibson diary, August 2, 1918, Hugh Gibson Papers, Box 68, HI.
43. Strauss diary, July 30, 1918.
44. Ibid.
45. Beveridge notes concerning food controllers' conference, entry for July 24, 1918; *The Times* (London), July 25, 1918, p. 7; José Harris, "Bureaucrats and Businessmen in British Food Control, 1916–19," in Kathleen Burk, ed., *War and the State* (London, 1982), p. 145.
46. Beveridge notes, entry for July 25, 1918; Harris, "Bureaucrats and Businessmen," p. 145; José Harris, *William Beveridge* (Oxford, 1977), p. 244.
47. Beveridge notes, entry for July 25, 1918.
48. Gibson diary, August 2, 1918.
49. Strauss diary, July 30, 1918; Hoover to Wilson, August 3, 1918. Strauss (Hoover's young secretary) blamed Wintour for the antagonism of the British food controller toward some of Hoover's proposals.
50. Beveridge notes, entry for July 26, 1918; minutes of food controllers' meeting, July 29, 1918, in "Conference of Food Controllers: July–August 1918" (typescript), copy in Inter-Allied Food Council Papers, Box 19, HI.
51. Beveridge notes, entry for July 26, 1918.
52. Ibid. According to this source, Beveridge nearly proposed that the British withdraw from the conference if the Allies insisted on nominating Great Britain's own representative. Wintour, however, advised him that withdrawal was not feasible.
53. Gibson diary, August 2, 1918.

54. Minutes of food controllers' meeting of July 29, 1918, in "Conference of Food Controllers: July–August 1918." The agreement is printed in *FRUS, 1918*, Supplement 1, vol. I, pp. 557–58.
55. In a letter to the prime minister on August 19, Chancellor of the Exchequer Andrew Bonar Law observed that by creating the new Inter-Allied Food Council, "we have in theory at least placed ourselves much more under the control of the Americans than I like." Law to Lloyd George, August 19, 1918, F / 30 / 2 / 40, Lloyd George Papers.
56. Hoover to Wilson, August 3, 1918.
57. Strauss diary, July 30, 1918.
58. Hoover's secretary expected that Wintour would soon be dispatched to some other post where he would not "hinder our work" (ibid.). It did not happen at once, however.
59. Lloyd George to Law, August 20, 1918.
60. Waldorf Astor to Lloyd George, August 27, 1918, F / 2 / 7 / 2, Lloyd George Papers.
61. Ibid.
62. Lloyd George to Law, August 20, 1918; Law to Lloyd George, August 22, 1918, F / 30 / 2 / 42, Lloyd George Papers; Beveridge notes, entries for August 16–30, 1918; Beveridge to his mother, September 13 and 14, 1918, Beveridge Papers; *The Times* [London], September 14, 1918, p. 6; Harris, *William Beveridge*, p. 244; Harris, "Bureaucrats and Businessmen," p. 146.
63. Minutes of food controllers' meetings, July 24 and 29, 1918, in "Conference of Food Controllers: July–August 1918."
64. *The Times* [London], July 20, 1918, p. 6, and July 26, 1918, p. 8; Hoover remarks in "Minutes of Proceedings at A Conference of the Allied Food Controllers . . . Tuesday, 23rd July, 1918."
65. *The Times* [London], July 20, 1918, p. 6.
66. Ibid., July 26, 1918, p. 8.
67. Ibid.; *Allied Maritime Transport Council: 1918*, p. 8; J. A. Salter, *Allied Shipping Control* (Oxford, 1921), pp. 199–200.
68. J. R. Clynes, *Memoirs* (London, 1937), vol. I, pp. 254–55.
69. Ibid.
70. *Allied Maritime Transport Council: 1918*, pp. 140, 159.
71. Minutes of food controllers' meeting of July 26, 1918, in "Conference of Food Controllers: July–August 1918."
72. Lewis L. Strauss cable to Edgar Rickard, July 27, 1918, file no. 103.97 / 296, RG 59, NARA.
73. *Allied Maritime Transport Council: 1918*, p. 6. The work of the Council is discussed at length in Salter, *Allied Shipping Control.*
74. J. A. Salter (for the Allied Maritime Transport Council) to the Inter-Allied Food Council, July 30, 1918, printed in *Allied Maritime Transport Council*, pp. 140–41. See also pp. 141–42 for a second letter (August 5, 1918) from Salter to the Food Council.
75. Minutes of food controllers' meeting of July 30, 1918, in "Conference of Food Controllers: July–August 1918." The resolution is printed in *Allied Maritime Transport Council: 1918*, p. 141.
76. Minutes of food controllers' meeting of July 30, 1918, in "Conference of Food Controllers: July–August 1918."
77. Hoover to Wilson, August 3, 1918.
78. Hoover, *An American Epic*, vol. II (Chicago, 1960), pp. 157, 159.
79. Hoover's trip to France can be followed in the diaries of James F. Bell, Hugh Gibson, and Lewis L. Strauss.
80. The words quoted were uttered by the French minister of agriculture and food, Victor Boret. *New York Times*, August 4, 1918, section I, p. 12.
81. Bell, Gibson, and Strauss diaries, August 2, 1918.
82. Strauss and Gibson diaries, August 3, 1918.

83. Ibid.
84. Gibson diary, August 3, 1918.
85. Strauss diary, August 4, 1918.
86. Gibson diary, August 3, 1918.
87. Hoover, *An American Epic*, II, p. 159.
88. Charles G. Dawes diary, August 4, 1918, printed in Charles G. Dawes, *A Journal of the Great War* (Boston and New York, 1921), vol. I, p. 143; Dawes to Commanding General, Services of Supply, August 6, 1918, printed in Dawes, *Journal*, II, p. 159; John J. Pershing, *My Experiences in the World War* (New York, 1931), vol. II, pp. 213–14.
89. Strauss diary, August 1 and 8, 1918; Bell diary, August 1, 1918. Years later, in *Men and Decisions* (p. 17), Strauss recalled that Hoover suffered a bloody but superficial wound in the hand from a fragment of broken glass following the explosion. Strauss did not mention this detail in his diary, however, nor did James Ford Bell in his.
90. Gibson and Strauss diaries, August 7, 1918.
91. Bell, Gibson, and Strauss diaries, August 5, 1918.
92. Ibid., August 5 and 6, 1918; John J. Pershing diary, August 6, 1918, John J. Pershing Papers, Box 4–5, LC.
93. Pershing, *My Experiences in the World War*, II, pp. 213–14.
94. Apparently neither Hoover nor Pershing made contemporaneous memoranda of their luncheon conversation. The account in my text is based on Pershing's autobiography, Hoover's *An American Epic*, and other sources duly cited.
95. Hoover, *An American Epic*, II, p. 163.
96. Pershing cable to the Chief of Staff and Secretary of War, June 25, 1918, printed in *United States Army in the World War, 1917–1919* (Washington, D.C., 1989), vol. II, pp. 482–83. Earlier in the month the three Allied premiers had also appealed to Washington for one hundred American divisions. See Georges Clemenceau, David Lloyd George, and Vittorio Orlando to Woodrow Wilson, June 2, 1918, printed in Arthur S. Link et al., eds., *The Papers of Woodrow Wilson*, vol. 48 (Princeton, N.J., 1985), pp. 226–27.
97. According to General Bliss, the Foch / Pershing program of June 23, 1918, called for 4,160,000 American soldiers in France by July 1919. Tasker H. Bliss cable to the Secretary of War and Chief of Staff, June 30, 1918, printed in *United States Army in the World War*, II, p. 489.
98. Pershing cable to the Chief of Staff and Secretary of War, June 25, 1918. See also Pershing cables of June 3 and 19, 1918, printed in *United States Army in the World War*, II, pp. 449–50, 476–79.
99. Newton D. Baker cable to Tasker H. Bliss, July 1, 1918, printed in Link et al., eds., *Papers of Woodrow Wilson*, vol. 48, p. 481; Peyton C. March cable to Pershing, July 1, 1918, printed in *United States Army in the World War*, II, pp. 497–98.
100. Frederick Palmer, *Newton D. Baker: America at War* (New York, 1931), vol. II, p. 260.
101. Pershing cable to the Chief of Staff and Secretary of War, July 19, 1918, printed in *United States Army in the World War*, II, pp. 537–38.
102. Quoted in Edward M. Coffman, *The War to End Wars* (New York, 1968), p. 178.
103. Tasker H. Bliss cable to the Secretary of State, Secretary of War, and Chief of Staff, July 2, 1918, printed in *United States Army in the World War*, II, p. 500.
104. Pershing cable to the Chief of Staff and Secretary of War, July 6, 1918, printed in *United States Army in the World War*, II, pp. 512–13.
105. Coffman, *War to End Wars*, p. 180.
106. Peyton C. March cable to Tasker H. Bliss, July 23, 1918, printed in Arthur S. Link et al., eds., *The Papers of Woodrow Wilson*, vol. 49 (Princeton, N.J., 1985), pp. 66–67.
107. Ibid.
108. Ibid.
109. Ibid.
110. Peyton C. March cable to Tasker H. Bliss, August 15, 1918, in ibid., p. 262.

111. Pershing, *My Experiences in the World War*, II, p. 233.
112. Pershing cable to the Chief of Staff and Secretary of War, August 17, 1918, printed in *United States Army in the World War*, II, pp. 579–80.
113. Hoover, *An American Epic*, II, pp. 163–64. It should be borne in mind that Hoover's account of his visit to Pershing (and its aftermath) was written nearly forty years after the event. It contains a number of inaccuracies and dubious recollections and cannot be accepted implicitly. Wherever possible, I have relied upon more contemporaneous sources.
114. Gibson diary, August 7, 1918.
115. Ibid.
116. Hoover, *An American Epic*, II, pp. 164–65.
117. Hoover to Pershing, August 6 [1918], John J. Pershing Papers, Box 96, LC. Hoover's letter was dated simply "Aug. 6." In *An American Epic*, II, pp. 165–66, he states that he completed this letter at 2:30 A.M. on August 7. Hugh Gibson's contemporary diary, however, records that Hoover wrote the letter in Gibson's presence after Bliss, Hoover, and Gibson dined in Paris on the *evening* of August 7. Bliss left at 11:00 P.M. (Hugh Gibson diary, August 7, 1918). If Hoover wrote the letter at two-thirty in the morning, it was the morning of August 8, not August 7.

    Despite the clear and persuasive evidence of Gibson's diary, Hoover insisted in *An American Epic* that he finished his letter early on August 7, and he even hinted that Gibson's diary was wrong. Why should the date matter so to Hoover, even forty years later? We can only speculate, but one definite possibility is this. In his account in *An American Epic*, Hoover contended that he wrote his letter at Pershing's insistence. But if this was so, why did Hoover wait more than thirty-six hours after his lunch with Pershing to prepare the letter? Why did he write it in longhand and in the wee hours of August 7–8? Why did he wait until just a few hours before he left France? (Hoover set off for England on the morning of August 8.) Interestingly, too, Hoover wrote the letter only after his conversation with General Bliss—a conversation that, in Gibson's observation, stirred Hoover greatly. Did Hoover want to elicit Bliss's views on the subject first? Or was it the Bliss interview, not the Pershing luncheon, that instigated Hoover's letter?

    All this suggests the hypothesis that Hoover intervened in the hundred-division controversy on his own initiative after talking with Bliss.

    In *An American Epic*, however, Hoover seemed anxious to establish that the initiative came from Pershing. It is at least possible that he later attributed the idea to Pershing—and even altered the dating of the letter—in order to conceal his own avid involvement in a matter that was outside his sphere of responsibility and competence.

    Pershing, of course (as we shall shortly see), was happy to enlist Hoover's support. But it is not clear that the general asked to have it in writing. According to Hoover, Pershing said that he needed the letter "to aid him in his discussion with General Foch." But Foch needed no persuasion. He and Pershing were already in agreement about the need for one hundred American divisions. The people who really needed persuading were in Washington and London.

    This seemingly minor matter of dating a letter illustrates the point in note 113: the memories of Hoover (or of anyone, for that matter) must be examined extremely carefully. See also note 177 below.
118. Gibson diary, August 8, 1918.
119. Pershing cable to the Chief of Staff and Secretary of War, August 17, 1918.
120. Pershing to Newton D. Baker, August 17, 1918, quoted in Pershing, *My Experiences in the World War*, II, pp. 234–35.
121. Pershing cable to the Chief of Staff and Secretary of War, August 17, 1918; Pershing, *My Experiences in the World War*, II, p. 232.
122. Pershing, *My Experiences in the World War*, II, p. 232; Gibson diary, August 8, 1918.
123. Pershing to Baker, August 17, 1918.
124. Strauss diary, July 29, 1918.

125. Ibid. See also the Royal Commission on Wheat Supplies' report cited in note 8.
126. Hoover to Pershing, August 6, 1918.
127. Newton D. Baker to Wilson, August 8, 1918; Peyton C. March to Bliss, August 19, 1918, printed in Link et al., eds., *Papers of Woodrow Wilson*, vol. 49, pp. 217 and 293, respectively.
128. David Lloyd George cable to Georges Clemenceau, August 2, 1918, quoted in Pershing cable to the Chief of Staff, August 7, 1918, in Link et al., eds., *Papers of Woodrow Wilson*, vol. 49, pp. 217–18.
129. Ibid.
130. I have found no evidence that Pershing had the cable by August 6 or that he discussed its contents with Hoover. None of the contemporary diaries mentioned the matter. Nor did Hoover say so in *An American Epic*, although there he quoted the cable (which by then, the late 1950s, was available to him).
131. Gibson diary, August 2, 1918.
132. Ibid., August 7, 1918; Charles G. Dawes to Commanding General, Services of Supply, August 7, 1918, printed in Dawes, *A Journal of the Great War*, II, p. 161.
133. Gibson diary, August 7, 1918.
134. Ibid.
135. George H. Nash, *The Life of Herbert Hoover: The Humanitarian, 1914–1917* (New York, 1988), pp. 344–45.
136. Dawes to Commanding General, Services of Supply, August 7, 1918.
137. This episode is discussed in chapter 17.
138. Bliss to Newton D. Baker, August 7, 1918, printed in Link et al., eds., *Papers of Woodrow Wilson*, vol. 49, pp. 335–44. See also Bliss cable to Baker and Peyton C. March, August 14, 1918, printed in ibid., pp. 258–61.
139. Bell diary, August 8, 1918.
140. Strauss diary, August 8, 1918.
141. Erich von Ludendorff, *Ludendorff's Own Story* (New York and London, 1919), vol. II, p. 326; Palmer, *Newton D. Baker*, II, pp. 274–75.
142. J. A. Salter to the Inter-Allied Food Council, August 5, 1918, cited in note 74.
143. Inter-Allied Food Council, Committee of Representatives, *Minutes of Proceedings*, I: *July and August, 1918*, pp. 32–35, copy in Inter-Allied Food Council Papers, Box 10.
144. Ibid.
145. Minutes of food controllers' meeting, August 12, 1918, in "Conference of Food Controllers: July–August 1918."
146. Hoover to Joseph P. Cotton, August 16, 1918, USFA Papers, Box 132.
147. Hoover remarks in "Minutes of Proceedings at A Conference of the Allied Food Controllers . . . Tuesday, 23rd July, 1918."
148. Hoover claimed that 400,000 tons of pork had "equivalent food values" to 2,000,000 tons of fodder. Hoover to Wilson, August 3, 1918.
149. Minutes of food controllers' meeting, August 12, 1918.
150. Inter-Allied Food Council, Committee of Representatives, *Minutes of Proceedings*, I: *July and August, 1918*, p. 33.
151. Minutes of food controllers' meeting, August 12, 1918.
152. Beveridge notes concerning food controllers' conference, entry for August 12, 1918; William H. Beveridge, *British Food Control* (London, 1928), pp. 250–51.
153. Minutes of food controllers' meeting, August 13, 1918, in "Conference of Food Controllers: July–August 1918"; Beveridge, *British Food Control*, p. 251.
154. Minutes of food controllers' meeting, August 13, 1918, appendix 4.
155. Beveridge notes, entry for August 13, 1918.
156. Minutes of food controllers' meeting, August 13, 1918.
157. Ibid.
158. Hoover cable to Edgar Rickard ("attention Barnes"), enclosed in Walter Hines Page to

Secretary of State, August 13, 1918, file no. 103.97 / 321, RG 59, NARA.

159. H. Alexander Smith diary, August 19, 1918, H. Alexander Smith Papers, Box 280, Seeley G. Mudd Manuscript Library, Department of Rare Books and Special Collections, Princeton University Libraries.
160. Strauss diary, August 14, 1918.
161. Waldorf Astor to David Lloyd George, August 14, 1918, F / 2 / 7 / 1, Lloyd George Papers; H. Alexander Smith diary, August 15, 1918. Lewis L. Strauss's diary recorded that Hoover left London that day and left Liverpool harbor during the night of August 16–17.
162. Astor to Lloyd George, August 14, 1918. A worried Astor urged Lloyd George to talk to the "considerably disgruntled" Hoover before he left London, but I have found no evidence that the prime minister did so.
163. H. Alexander Smith diary, August 19, 1918.
164. Hoover to Frank L. Polk, August 26, 1918, USFA Papers, Box 285.
165. Hoover to Cotton, August 16, 1918.
166. Ibid.
167. Earl of Crawford diary, August 15, 1918, in John Vincent, ed., *The Crawford Papers* (Manchester, U.K., 1984), p. 392.
168. Strauss diary, August 16–23, 1918.
169. H. Alexander Smith diary, August 15, 1918.
170. Ibid., August 17, 1918; Roland W. Boyden to Kate W. Boyden, August 26, 1918, Herbert Hoover Collection, Box 313, HI.
171. Hoover, *An American Epic*, II, pp. 168–69. In this source, Hoover states that he returned to Washington on August 22. This is incorrect. Hoover landed in New York on August 23 and went to Washington later that day. He was in his office on August 24. Strauss diary, August 23, 1918; *New York Times*, August 24, 1918, p. 6; *Weekly Northwestern Miller* 115 (August 28, 1918): 714.
172. Hoover, *An American Epic*, II, p. 169. Years later MacArthur remembered this conversation and was quoted here by Hoover.
173. Bliss cable to Baker and March, August 14, 1918.
174. Baker to Wilson, August 17, 1918, printed in Link et al., eds., *Papers of Woodrow Wilson*, vol. 49, pp. 276–77.
175. Hoover knew of Baker's forthcoming trip to Europe by August 27 at least. Hoover to Woodrow Wilson, August 27, 1918, Newton D. Baker Papers, Box 8, LC.
176. Ibid.
177. This is what Hoover later told the chairman of the U.S. Shipping Board, Edward N. Hurley. See Hurley's diary, September 9, 1918, CHUR 17 / 2, Diary Book A, Edward N. Hurley Papers, University of Notre Dame Archives.

    In *An American Epic*, II, p. 169, Hoover implied that he met President Wilson at the White House on August 22. This is, of course, inaccurate since Hoover did not return to America until August 23 and could not have reached Washington, D.C., until later that day by train. There is no evidence that Hoover saw Wilson before Monday, August 26, at 4:30 P.M., as indicated in the White House appointment calendar, Wilson Papers.

    According to his account in *An American Epic*, II, p. 169, Hoover expressed his "full power" views to the President at their meeting, and the President assured him that a "full power" army would be sent to Europe. Hoover recalled that he felt "relieved that General Pershing's viewpoint had prevailed." This, too, is inaccurate, since Pershing's viewpoint did not prevail in Washington. He was not promised the "full power" program as he defined it (one hundred divisions).

    It is puzzling that Hoover in *An American Epic* seemed to go out of his way to identify himself with Pershing and misinterpreted the military issue of August 1918. The raging issue then was not an immediate counterattack versus holding back until 1919 (as Hoover later portrayed it in *An American Epic*). The issue was the size of the U.S. Army for the expected decisive campaign of 1919. Contrary to Hoover's recollection (p. 170), there was no "great shift in military strategy" in August 1918 "which brought the war to an early end." There was a shift in strategy *for 1919*. To the surprise of nearly everyone, the war ended before this shift was implemented. The eighty-division American army never materialized in France.

178. Hoover to Wilson, August 27, 1918.
179. Wilson to Hoover, August 28, 1918, Herbert Hoover Collection, Box 8; Wilson to Baker, August 28, 1918, Baker Papers, Box 8.
180. Gibson diary, August 3, 1918.
181. Robert Woods Bliss to Robert Lansing, August 31, 1918; Wilson to Robert Lansing, September 3, 1918; both printed in Link et al., eds., *Papers of Woodrow Wilson*, vol. 49, p. 423.
182. Daniel R. Beaver, *Newton D. Baker and the American War Effort, 1917–1919* (Lincoln, Nebr., 1966), p. 174.
183. *Allied Maritime Transport Council: 1918*, pp. 160–67; Salter, *Allied Shipping Control*, pp. 197–98.
184. *Allied Maritime Transport Council: 1918*, pp. 152, 160.
185. Ibid., pp. 152, 176–77; Walter Hines Page cable to the Secretary of State, September 7, 1918, printed in *FRUS, 1918*, Supplement 1, vol. I, pp. 525–28.
186. *Allied Maritime Transport Council: 1918*, p. 162; Page to the Secretary of State, September 7, 1918.
187. Lord Reading to Secretary of State Lansing, August 30, 1918, printed in Link et al., eds., *Papers of Woodrow Wilson*, vol. 49, pp. 418–19.
188. *FRUS, 1918*, Supplement 1, vol. I, pp. 523–24, 525.
189. Joseph Cotton cable to Hoover, incorporated in Walter Hines Page cable to the Secretary of State, August 27, 1918. Copy enclosed with Hoover to Wilson, September 6, 1918, Wilson Papers.
190. Hoover cable to Joseph Cotton, dated September 7, 1918, copy enclosed with Hoover to Wilson, September 6, 1918.
191. Hoover to Wilson, September 6, 1918.
192. Baker cable to Woodrow Wilson, September 23, 1918, printed in *United States Army in the World War*, II, pp. 611.
193. Ibid.; Baker to Pershing, October 2, 1918, quoted in Beaver, *Newton D. Baker*, pp. 175–76.
194. Pershing, *My Experiences in the World War*, II, pp. 229, 232–33.
195. Baker cable to Chief of Staff March, September 23, 1918, printed in *United States Army in the World War*, II, p. 610.
196. Peyton C. March cable to Pershing, September 25, 1918, printed in ibid., pp. 613–14.
197. *Allied Maritime Transport Council: 1918*, pp. 186, 202–04; Baker to Pershing, October 2, 1918, quoted in Beaver, *Newton D. Baker*, pp. 175–76; Walter Hines Page cable to the Secretary of State, October 2, 1918, printed in *FRUS, 1918*, Supplement 1, vol. I, p. 610.
198. *Allied Maritime Transport Council: 1918*, pp. 186–88, 196–202. See also Salter, *Allied Shipping Control*, pp. 204–10. According to the AMTC, in 1917–18 the three Allies (Great Britain, France, and Italy) imported a total of 20,250,000 tons of food, excluding military oats—that is, 20,250,000 tons destined for civilian consumption. The AMTC now reduced this to 18,500,000 tons for 1918–19. If military oats were included in the figures, the 1917–18 import total was 22,500,000 tons, and the authorized projection for 1918–19 became 22,000,000 tons. The latter figure, of course, was 5,000,000 tons less than the Inter-Allied Food Council had requested.
199. *Allied Maritime Transport Council: 1918*, p. 197.
200. Hoover, *The Memoirs of Herbert Hoover*, vol. I: *Years of Adventure* (New York, 1951), p. 260.
201. Secretary of State cable to the U.S. Chargé d'Affaires in London, October 26, 1918, printed in *FRUS, 1918*, Supplement 1, vol. I, pp. 528–29.
202. Irwin B. Laughlin cable to the Secretary of State, October 31, 1918, printed in *FRUS, 1918*, Supplement 1, vol. I, pp. 532–34.

203. Hoover to Peyton C. March, September 21, 1918, printed in Peyton C. March, *The Nation at War* (Garden City, N.Y., 1932), pp. 278–80. See also Hoover to William G. McAdoo, September 19, 1918, USFA Papers, Box 161.
204. March to Hoover, September 26, 1918, printed in March, *A Nation at War*, pp. 280–81.
205. Edward M. House diary, September 24, 1918, House Papers.
206. U.S. Food Administration press release 1156, August 26, 1918, USFA Documents, HHPL; *New York Times*, August 28, 1918, p. 3. The 80-20 rule required retailers to sell wheat flour in combination with other cereals on a basis of four pounds of wheat flour to one pound of substitutes (such as corn flour).
207. U.S. Food Administration press release 1206, September 20, 1918, USFA Documents. Although dated September 20, Hoover's statement was marked for release to the press in the Sunday newspapers of September 22. In a letter to President Wilson, Hoover remarked that it would be "a year of strenuous conservation." Hoover to Wilson, September 21, 1918, Wilson Papers.
208. H. Alexander Smith diary, August 19, 1918.
209. William C. Mullendore, *History of the United States Food Administration, 1917–1919* (Stanford, Calif., 1941), pp. 111–14.
210. U.S. Food Administration press release 1235A, October 11, 1918, USFA Documents; *Official U.S. Bulletin* 2 (October 15, 1918): 8.
211. Leonard P. Ayres, *The War with Germany: A Statistical Summary* (Washington, D.C., 1919), p. 118.
212. Palmer, *Newton D. Baker*, II, p. 348.
213. Ayres, *The War with Germany*, p. 188.

CHAPTER 14

1. Thomas P. Gore to Woodrow Wilson, June 29, 1918, copy enclosed with Herbert Hoover to Woodrow Wilson, July 4, 1918, USFA Papers, Box 187, HI.
2. Hoover to Woodrow Wilson, July 4, 1918, file 14H-B4, Box 620, RG 4, NARA. Since Hoover's original, signed letter is in RG 4, it is possible that he never sent it. Perhaps he conveyed its contents orally in a meeting with the President. (Hoover conferred with the President on July 7.) In any event, the letter represents Hoover's thinking in early July 1918.
3. Ibid.
4. Ibid.
5. David F. Houston to Edgar Rickard, July 25, 1918; Houston to Woodrow Wilson, July 25 and 26, 1918; Edgar Rickard to Wilson, July 26, 1918. All in Woodrow Wilson Papers, LC.
6. Woodrow Wilson to David F. Houston and Edgar Rickard, July 26, 1918 (separate letters), Wilson Papers; "Minutes of the Agricultural Advisory Committee," August 5, 1918, copy in USFA Papers, Box 83A.
7. Edgar Rickard to Curtis H. Lindley, August 6, 1918, USFA Papers, Box 232.
8. Hoover cable from Paris to Edgar Rickard (via the Secretary of State), August 2, 1918, copy in USFA Papers, Box 187; Julius H. Barnes to Rickard, August 7, 1918, USFA Papers, Box 187. In his cable from Paris, Hoover said: "I feel strongly that wheat price should be fixed as a minimum *guarantee* the same price as at present but if committee opposes, then suggest with reservation that if maximum control is to be exerted the maximum price shall be determined by later conference when issues more clear." According to Hoover, there were many reasons why the price of wheat should not be raised at this time. He argued that the large surplus on the current crop and the prospect of more shipping in 1919 "all point to non necessity of such an abnormal push on wheat production as higher price would imply."
9. Edgar Rickard cable to Hoover, August 9, 1918, USFA Papers, Box 187. Although Rickard

dated this cable August 9, it was not dispatched via the State Department until August 12, as file no. 103.97 / 322a, RG 59, NARA.

10. Ibid. Rickard said that the advisory committee "rejected" the Food Administration's alternative suggestion.
11. "Minutes of the Agricultural Advisory Committee," August 8, 1918; Rickard cable to Hoover, August 9, 1918.
12. Julius H. Barnes to William A. Glasgow, Jr., August 8, 1918, enclosed with Hoover to Woodrow Wilson, August 26, 1918, Wilson Papers.
13. Julius H. Barnes cable to Hoover, August 10, 1918, USFA Papers, Box 247.
14. Hoover cable to Julius H. Barnes (via Edgar Rickard), August 10, 1918, USFA Papers, Box 187.
15. Hoover to Woodrow Wilson, August 26, 1918, Wilson Papers.
16. Barnes to Glasgow, August 8, 1918 (cited in note 12).
17. Woodrow Wilson to Hoover, August 27, 1918, Wilson Papers.
18. Woodrow Wilson, "Memorandum," September 2, 1918, Wilson Papers; *New York Times*, September 3, 1918, p. 11; *Official U.S. Bulletin* 2 (September 3, 1918): 7–8. Hoover's draft memorandum, which Wilson revised, is enclosed with Hoover to Wilson, August 30, 1918, Wilson Papers.
19. Barnes to Rickard, August 7, 1918.
20. Barnes to Glasgow, August 8, 1918.
21. Still, the episode was not without cost. Ten years later, when Hoover was a candidate for President of the United States, the man who had been chairman of the Agricultural Advisory Committee publicly accused him of having held down the price of the 1919 wheat crop. Struggling to win voters in the farm belt, candidate Hoover, through a Republican party press release, denied the charge. Instead, his rebuttal claimed that he had actually advocated continuation of the 1918 guarantee into 1919, along with the study commission, "in the interest of the farmer." The rebuttal cited his letter of August 26, 1918 to President Wilson as proof.

    Hoover's later explanation (delivered, it should be emphasized, in the heat of an election campaign) was wrong. He had written to Woodrow Wilson in the interest of securing sufficient wheat production while limiting the liability of the U.S. Treasury. True, Hoover was (or professed to be) worried that decontrolled wheat prices could cause "speculation" that could harm producers. But his principal concern, as a close reading of his 1918 letter establishes, was that a deregulated and declining wheat price would cause *production* to fall. His worry was not that the farmers would lose money under these circumstances but that they would not plant enough wheat.

    Contrary to what his defenders said in 1928, Hoover did indeed strive (as we have seen in the text) to hold down the guaranteed 1919 wheat price when the issue arose in the summer of 1918. Under pressure from his in-house advisory committee, he crafted a "compromise": no change in price for the present and a possible increase later, after study. This may have been good policy, but it was not undertaken "in the interest of the farmer." The farmers' spokesmen wanted a higher guarantee now.

    For Hoover's explanation in 1928 of what he did in 1918, see Republican National Committee press release, October 18, 1928, copy in "Agriculture, 1928, October–November," Misrepresentations File, Herbert Hoover Papers, HHPL.
22. U.S. Department of Commerce, Bureau of the Census, *Historical Statistics of the United States: Colonial Times to 1970* (Washington, D.C., 1975), Part I, p. 511.
23. Ibid.
24. Frank M. Surface, *The Grain Trade During the World War* (New York, 1928), p. 204.
25. Ibid., pp. 209, 262, 437.
26. Hoover to General Peyton C. March, September 21, 1918, quoted in Peyton C. March, *The Nation at War* (Garden City, N.Y., 1932), pp. 278–80.

27. Hoover to R. C. Leffingwell, September 16, 1918, "U.S. Food Administration—Treasury Department, June 1917–February 1919," Pre-Commerce Papers, Hoover Papers; Surface, *Grain Trade*, pp. 436–37.
28. Barnes to Hoover, October 1, 1918, quoted in Surface, *Grain Trade*, p. 441.
29. Hoover to Leffingwell, September 16, 1918.
30. Surface, *Grain Trade*, p. 440.
31. Ibid., pp. 262–63; *Commercial and Financial Chronicle* 107 (September 21, 1918): 1204.
32. Barnes to Hoover, October 1, 1918.
33. Barnes listed that as an option in ibid.
34. In mid-October Hoover told his chief representative in Europe: "I can get the money from Congress in a minute to support the guarantees. If I do so we will get it on condition of a rise of wheat." Hoover added that he wished "to keep away from this legislation," which "political demagogues" would try to impose if given the chance. Hoover to Joseph P. Cotton, October 16, 1918, USFA Papers, Box 278.
35. Barnes to Hoover, October 1, 1918.
36. Hoover cable [no. 23] to Joseph P. Cotton, October 1, 1918, USFA Papers, Box 278; Hoover cable no. 24 to Cotton, October 2, 1918, USFA Papers, Box 285. Both are printed in Wheat Executive, *Minutes of Proceedings*, October 1918, p. 11, copy in Inter-Allied Food Council Papers, Box 6, HI. The Wheat Executive *Minutes* provide the cable number for the first dispatch but mistakenly date it October 2.
37. "Wheat situation is steadily worse." Hoover cable no. 27 to Cotton, October 4, 1918, USFA Papers, Box 285.
38. Hoover to Willliam G. McAdoo, October 4, 1918, USFA Papers, Box 174.
39. Ibid.
40. Ibid.; Hoover cable no. 27 to McAdoo, October 4, 1918.
41. Hoover to McAdoo, October 4, 1918.
42. McAdoo to Hoover, October 5, 1918, USFA Papers, Box 174.
43. McAdoo cable to Oscar T. Crosby, October 4, 1918, copy enclosed with ibid.
44. E. Dana Durand cable no. 371 to Hoover, October 5, 1918, USFA Papers, Box 278; British Treasury to Oscar T. Crosby, October 5, 1918, printed in Inter-Allied Food Council, Committee of Representatives, Minutes of Proceedings, *Minutes of Proceedings*, III: *October, 1918*, pp. 12–13, copy in Inter-Allied Food Council Papers, Box 10.
45. British Treasury to Crosby, October 5, 1918.
46. In April 1917 the Allied agency known as the Wheat Executive contracted to purchase 3,000,000 tons of wheat from Australia. As of the end of 1917, about 2,385,000 tons were still unshipped. *First Report of the Royal Commission on Wheat Supplies* (London, 1921), pp. 30–31. Very little of this wheat moved before the end of the war.
47. British Treasury draft letter to Norman Davies [Davis], October 7, 1918, printed in Wheat Executive, *Minutes of Proceedings*, October 1918, p. 12 (see also p. 2); Norman Davis cable to McAdoo, October 8, 1918, copy in USFA Papers, Box 186.
48. Davis cable to McAdoo, October 8, 1918.
49. Surface, *Grain Trade*, pp. 443–44; *First Report of the Royal Commission on Wheat Supplies*, pp. 66–67.
50. Surface, *Grain Trade*, pp. 444–45. The contract was finally signed under date of October 31, 1918 (ibid., p. 442). The Royal Commission on Wheat Supplies gave the date as November 12. In any case, the all-important financial transaction occurred before then. The contract specifically acknowledged prior Allied receipt of the $200,000,000 which was then transferred to the Grain Corporation.
51. Hoover to Cotton, October 16, 1918.
52. Ibid.
53. Surface, *Grain Trade*, p. 452.
54. Hoover to Cotton, October 16, 1918.

55. The dispute would erupt soon after the armistice of November 11, 1918.
56. Hoover remarks to Consumers' Council, London, July 24, 1918, Public Statements File, Hoover Papers.
57. The relevant documents are printed in United States, Department of State, *Papers Relating to the Foreign Relations of the United States, 1918*, Supplement 1: *The World War* (Washington, D.C., 1933), I, pp. 551–55 (hereinafter cited as *FRUS, 1918*, Supplement 1).
58. Sir William H. Beveridge, *British Food Control* (London and New Haven, Conn., 1928), p. 131.
59. Ibid., p. 132.
60. Hoover remarks to Consumers' Council, July 24, 1918; Hoover to J. R. Clynes, November 15, 1918, "U.S. Food Administration—Food Controller—Ministry of Food, August–November, 1918," Pre-Commerce Papers, Hoover Papers.
61. Hoover remarks to Consumers' Council, July 24, 1918. In May 1918 Hoover's London representatives told complaining British officials that "appreciably lowered [pork] prices" were "inconsistent" with Hoover's "promise to farmers." Louis P. Sheldon cable to Hoover, May 20, 1918, printed in *FRUS, 1918*, Supplement 1, pp. 551–53.
62. According to one prominent midwestern farm journal, "We know that the Food Administration was nervous about that ratio from the time it was announced, and that prayers for lower priced corn were offered up daily." *Prairie Farmer* 90 (November 16, 1918): 1008.
63. *Wall Street Journal*, October 9, 1918, p. 7; *Commercial and Financial Chronicle Monthly Review* 107 (November 1918): 16; Henry A. Wallace, *Agricultural Prices* (Des Moines, 1920), p. 119. The average price for No. 2 mixed corn in Chicago in September 1918 was $1.59 per bushel.
64. *Wallaces' Farmer* 43 (September 6, 1918): 1249.
65. Ibid.
66. U.S. Department of Agriculture, *Yearbook 1920* (Washington, D.C., 1921), pp. 11, 550.
67. *Wallaces' Farmer* 45 (March 19, 1920): 908.
68. U.S. Food Administration press release 1015, June 12, 1918, USFA Documents, HHPL.
69. F. S. Snyder (head of Hoover's meat division) in "Conference of Meat Packers Held at United States Food Administration, Washington, D.C., 4 October 1918" (typescript), USFA Papers, Box 48 (hereinafter cited as "Conference of Meat Packers" [October 3, 1918]). Although this transcript of the conference proceedings is dated October 4, 1918, other evidence establishes that the conference occurred on October 3.
70. Ibid., p. 25.
71. Ibid., p. 32.
72. *Wallaces' Farmer* 45 (March 19, 1920): 908.
73. Hoover cable to Joseph P. Cotton, September 19, 1918, file no. 103.97/406a, RG 59, NARA.
74. Ibid.
75. Snyder admitted that the Food Administration "didn't dare, in order to force that market down, to ask the public to stop eating pork again." "Conference of Meat Packers" (October 3, 1918), p. 26.
76. Joseph P. Cotton cable to Hoover, September 21, 1918, USFA Papers, Box 132; F. S. Snyder remarks in transcript of a meeting held on January 28, 1919, between the Agricultural Advisory Committee and representatives of the meat-packing industry, pp. 4–5, file 14H-B2, RG 4, NARA. At this meeting Snyder revealed that when hog prices nearly reached $21 per hundredweight in September 1918, "we made every effort we could to stem that upward tide. . . . We witheld the European orders and thus choked back the demand upon the supply."
77. According to Snyder, the combination of "withheld orders" and an increase in hogs coming to market "turned the tide again, and the market began to decline." Snyder remarks in the transcript of a meeting of the Agricultural Advisory Committee and packers' representatives, January 28, 1919, p. 5.
78. Wallace, *Agricultural Prices*, p. 140.

79. Henry C. Wallace to Gifford Pinchot, September 14, 1918, Gifford Pinchot Papers, Box 217, LC; "John Evvard's Story of the Hog Price Conference," *Prairie Farmer* 90 (November 16, 1918): 1009.
80. Wallace to Pinchot, September 14, 1918.
81. Wallace had been invited but could not attend.
82. "John Evvard's Story," p. 1009.
83. On October 3 Snyder told the packers that he had said this to the livestock subcommittee. "Conference of Meat Packers" (October 3, 1918), p. 32.
84. For Cotton's statement announcing the Food Administration's hog policy, see U.S. Food Administration Meat Division, *Prices of Hogs* (Chicago, 1917), copy in USFA Papers, Box 47. It is quoted in full in Frank M. Surface, *American Pork Production in the World War* (Chicago and New York, 1926), pp. 37–38.
85. Hoover remark in "Conference of Meat Packers" (October 3, 1918), p. 1.
86. Joseph P. Cotton to Frank M. Surface, November 15, 1926, copy enclosed with Surface to Edward M. Flesh, November 26, 1926, file 14H-B2, Box 620, RG 4, NARA.
87. Ibid. According to Cotton, Wallace at that time expressed to him disapproval of the failure of Cotton's announcement to address this point.
88. *Wallaces' Farmer* 43 (June 28, 1918): 976.
89. "John Evvard's Story," p. 1009; "Minutes of the Sub-Committee on Live Stock of the Agricultural Advisory Committee," September 25, 1918, General Correspondence of the Office of the Secretary of Agriculture, 1918, Box 503, RG 16, NARA.
90. "John Evvard's Story," p. 1009.
91. "Minutes of the Sub-Committee on Live Stock . . . ," September 25, 1918.
92. Ibid.
93. U.S. Food Administration press release 1217, September 25, 1918, USFA Documents.
94. U.S. Food Administration press release 1224, October 2, 1918, USFA Documents. Before issuing his press release, Hoover sought and obtained President Wilson's approval for his "limited assurance" concerning the $15.50 minimum. Hoover to Woodrow Wilson, September 26, 1918 (signed "Approved Woodrow Wilson, 1 October, 1918"), Herbert Hoover Collection, Box 8, HI.
95. "Conference of Meat Packers" (October 3, 1918), pp. 1–15.
96. For the ebb and flow of the argument, see "Conference of Meat Packers" (October 3, 1918), passim.
97. The packers' letter is contained in U.S. Food Administration press release 1227, October 3, 1918, USFA Documents. For a brief summary, see the Food Administration's press release 1226, issued the same day.
98. *Commercial and Financial Chronicle* 107 (October 19, 1918): 1533.
99. Hoover telegram to C. E. Yancey, October 7, 1918, USFA Papers, Box 285.
100. "Conference of Meat Packers" (October 3, 1918), pp. 71–72, 78–79; U.S. Food Administration press release 1227, October 3, 1918.
101. Hoover to Henry C. Stuart, October 24, 1918, USFA Papers, Box 83B.
102. Hoover's letter to Chairman Henry C. Stuart of his Agricultural Advisory Committee was issued in a press release on October 2 for publication on October 5. The Food Administration's summary of the packers' pledge was issued on October 3 for publication on October 4. The full text of the packers' pledge was issued on October 3 for publication in the press on October 7.
103. Wallace called Hoover's action "outrageous." Wallace to Gifford Pinchot, October 8, 1918, Pinchot Papers, Box 217.
104. *Wallaces' Farmer* 43 (October 4, 1918): 1408.
105. Ibid. (October 11, 1918): 1460.
106. *Prairie Farmer* 90 (October 19, 1918): 901.
107. *Wallaces' Farmer* 43 (November 1, 1918): 1602.
108. Resolutions of Agricultural War Board of Illinois, October 21, 1918, cited in Helen M.

Cavanaugh, *Seed, Soil and Science: The Story of Eugene D. Funk* (Chicago, 1959), p. 243.

109. U.S. Food Administration press release 1224, October 2, 1918.

110. *Wallaces' Farmer* 43 (October 18, 1918): 1513; Walter T. Borg, "Food Administration Experience with Hogs, 1917–19," *Journal of Farm Economics* 25 (May 1943): 452.

111. Hoover telegram to state food administrators of Kansas and five other states, October 18, 1918, USFA Papers, Box 48. Gifford Pinchot, of course, had resigned from Hoover's agency in protest a year before. (See chapter 7.) It is unclear who, in Hoover's mind, constituted Pinchot's anti-administration "group."

112. Hoover to Samuel Insull, October 26, 1918, quoted in Cavanaugh, *Seed, Soil and Science*, p. 244.

113. Hoover to Stuart, October 24, 1918.

114. See Wallace, *Agricultural Prices*, pp. 164–65, for statistics on hog receipts at the great central markets. According to the more or less official history of the Food Administration, hog receipts at "the seven great markets" in the first three weeks of October 1918 were 27 percent greater than in the corresponding month in 1917. William C. Mullendore, *History of the United States Food Administration, 1917–1919* (Stanford, Calif., 1941), p. 266.

Henry C. Wallace later alleged that hog marketings in October 1918 did not constitute a heavy run and "were in fact not at all heavy compared with the ten-year average." *Wallaces' Farmer* 43 (November 1, 1918): 1596. But Wallace's own figures showed that the hog receipts at the eleven principal markets in the first four weeks of October were 116 percent of the ten-year average. This was enough to make it the heaviest hog run ever in the month of October at the six principal markets and the second heaviest October run at the eleven principal markets. (All this according to statistics published by Wallace's son in 1920, cited at the beginning of this note.)

115. *Wallaces' Farmer* 45 (March 19, 1920): 908.

116. Ibid., 43 (November 1, 1918): 1598.

117. Mullendore, *History*, p. 266.

118. *New York Times*, September 28, 1918, p. 18; *Commercial and Financial Chronicle Monthly Review* 107 (November 1918): 16.

119. *Commercial and Financial Chronicle* 107 (October 5, 1918): 1395; *Wall Street Journal*, October 9, 1918, p. 7; U.S. Food Administration press release 1269, October 26, 1918, USFA Documents.

120. Hoover to Stuart, October 24, 1918.

121. Ibid.

122. *Wallaces' Farmer* 43 (November 15, 1918): 1676.

123. Ibid.; *Wallaces' Farmer* 45 (March 19, 1920): 908.

124. See *New York Times*, September 28, 1918, p. 18; October 1, 1918, p. 2; *Wall Street Journal*, October 8, 1918, p. 3; October 10, 1918, p. 3; *Commercial and Financial Chronicle* 107 (September 28, 1918): 1296; October 5, 1918, p. 1395; October 26, 1918, p. 1683.

125. As Wallace put it: "Is it any wonder that the farmer who had hogs ready for market began to cut them loose? He had been feeling fairly comfortable under the assurance of the Food Administration [of November 1917]. . . . When the Food Administration gave evidence that it did not propose to keep this agreement, and when an apparently inspired [newspaper] dispatch from Washington intimated hog prices of less than $16, what could the farmer do but stop his loss by cashing in his hogs as quickly as possible?" *Wallaces' Farmer* 43 (November 15, 1918): 1676. Wallace alluded to a newspaper dispatch from Washington, D.C., in late September stating that the government was quite concerned about the high price of hogs and that steps to reduce it were expected soon. The article also suggested that a maximum price of hogs would be fixed at a price not far from the minimum of $15.50, or in other words well below current market quotations. Wallace thought that this ominous news story helped to precipitate many farmers' decision to sell their hogs as fast as possible.

126. "Conference of Meat Packers" (October 3, 1918), p. 31.

127. Referring to the plan to lower the market price gradually toward the $15.50 minimum, F. S. Snyder told the packers, "Of course, there is no advertisement." Ibid.
128. Wallace, ever vigilant, saw this. He editorialized: "From the talk of a $15.50 minimum, it would appear that an effort will be made to buy hogs still cheaper in November, especially as the corn price is being beaten down." *Wallaces' Farmer* 43 (October 11, 1918): 1460.
129. *Wall Street Journal*, October 15, 1918, p. 9; *New York Times*, October 4, 1928, p. 7.
130. *New York Times*, October 4, 1928, p. 7.
131. *Commercial and Financial Chronicle Monthly Review* 107 (November 1918): 16.
132. *Commercial and Financial Chronicle* 107 (October 19, 1918): 1590.
133. *Wall Street Journal*, October 16, 1918, p. 6.
134. U.S. Food Administration press release 1269, October 26, 1918.
135. *Prairie Farmer* 90 (November 2, 1918): 958.
136. Ibid.
137. Agreement of U.S. Food Administration with Thomas E. Wilson, chairman of Packers' Committee, October 25, 1918, file 1H-A9, RG 4, NARA.
138. Ibid.
139. *Prairie Farmer* 90 (November 16, 1918): 1008.
140. Hoover to Stuart, October 24, 1918.
141. U.S. Food Administration press releases 1226 and 1227, October 3, 1918.
142. Ibid.; Hoover telegram to C. E. Yancey, October 7, 1918; Hoover telegram to Henry C. Stuart, October 11, 1918, USFA Papers, Box 276; Hoover telegram to J. H. Mercer, October 14, 1918, USFA Papers, Box 48.
143. Hoover told the chairman of his Agricultural Advisory Committee that it would "strengthen whole position if producers committee would sit in when these great contracts are determined and price levels altered." Hoover telegram to Stuart, October 11, 1918.
144. Ibid.
145. John M. Evvard to Henry A. Wallace, October 26, 1918, Henry A. Wallace Papers, University of Iowa Libraries.
146. Ibid.
147. That is, except for "throw-outs." This was the same policy as in October.
148. U.S. Food Administration agreement with Thomas E. Wilson, October 25, 1918; packers' suggested price list for their allotment orders, in a folder marked "Agreement with Thomas E. Wilson, Chairman of Packers' Committee," October 25, 1918, file 1H-A9, RG 4, NARA; U.S. Food Administration press release 1269, October 26, 1918.
149. U.S. Food Administration press release 1269, October 26, 1918.
150. Hoover to Henry C. Stuart, October 29, 1918, USFA Papers, Box 276.
151. U.S. Food Administration press release 1269, October 26, 1918. See also Hoover to the directors of the Corn Belt Meat Producers Association, October 26, 1918, Henry C. Wallace Papers, Box 2, University of Iowa Libraries.
152. See text of agreement of U.S. Food Administration with Thomas E. Wilson, October 25, 1918, and U.S. Food Administration press release 1269, October 26, 1918.
153. Evvard to Henry A. Wallace, October 26, 1918.
154. *Wallaces' Farmer* 43 (November 1, 1918): 1596.
155. Ibid.
156. *Prairie Farmer* 90 (November 16, 1918): 1008.
157. *Wallaces' Farmer* 43 (December 6, 1918): 1776.
158. Ibid.
159. U.S. Food Administration press release 1307, November 14, 1918, USFA Documents.
160. Henry C. Wallace to Senator Thomas P. Gore, March 3, 1920, Henry C. Wallace Papers; printed in *Congressional Record* 59 (April 13, 1920): 5589–90.
161. For the Wallaces' critique, see ibid; Wallace, *Agricultural Prices*, pp. 34–35; *Wallaces' Farmer* 45 (February 13, 1920): 518–19; 45 (March 19, 1920): 906, 908; 51 (October 15, 1926): 3, 11; 51 (November 12, 1926): 8, 15; and 53 (May 18, 1928): 782–83.

162. Henry A. Wallace to Walter W. Liggett, July 23, 1931, Henry A. Wallace Papers. See also Wallace to Liggett, July 27, 1931, in the same collection.
163. For Hoover's side of the controversy, see Hoover to Senator Charles B. Henderson, February 23, 1920 (plus enclosures), printed in *Congressional Record* 59 (February 24, 1920): 3383–85; (February 25, 1920): 3433–34; Frank M. Surface to Henry A. Wallace, October 26, 1926, printed in *Wallaces' Farmer* 51 (November 12, 1926): 8, 15; Surface cover letter (dated October 28, 1926) for the preceding item, copy in file 14H-B2, Box 620, RG 4, NARA. See also Surface, *American Pork Production*, especially pp. 68–72, and Mullendore, *History*, pp. 266–67. The Frank M. Surface Papers at HI hold considerable correspondence pertaining to his preparation of *American Pork Production in the World War*, a work clearly intended to serve as Hoover's apologia. Hoover personally reviewed and revised the manuscript.
164. *Wallaces' Farmer* 43 (June 28, 1918): 976.
165. Ibid.
166. Hoover to Woodrow Wilson, September 26, 1918, cited in note 94.
167. Wallace, *Agricultural Prices*, pp. 164, 165.
168. Mullendore, *History*, p. 355.
169. Edgar Rickard to Curtis H. Lindley, June 27, 1918, USFA Papers, Box 45.
170. Edgar Rickard to Hugh Gibson, June 28, 1918, USFA Papers, Box 232.
171. Frederic S. Snyder, World War I notes for his children, p. 74, General Accessions—Frederic S. Snyder, HHPL.
172. This was Hoover's total export program for July 1, 1918–June 30, 1919. U.S. Food Administration press release 1206, September 20, 1918, USFA Documents.
173. Herbert Hoover to Woodrow Wilson, October 17, 1918 (plus enclosure), Wilson Papers.
174. One of Hoover's close aides for a time (and one of the few who did not idolize him) privately remarked that Hoover could handle "an immense amount of statistics" and admired "any one who makes a statistical showing." But, the aide said, Hoover's statistics were "surprisingly inaccurate, as he likes to make calculations upon matters which really cannot be subject to a mathematical and statistical process." Charles McCarthy, notes about Hoover, October 1918, Charles McCarthy Papers, Box 22, State Historical Society of Wisconsin.
175. Charles Seymour, *Woodrow Wilson and the World War* (New Haven, Conn., 1921), p. 160.

CHAPTER 15

1. Harvey H. Bundy oral history (1961), pp. 76, 77, Columbia University Oral History Collection. Bundy, a lawyer, worked in the legal division of the Food Administration.
2. William A. Glasgow, Jr., testimony, February 6, 1919, in U.S. Congress, House of Representatives, Committee on Interstate and Foreign Commerce, 65th Congress, 3d Session, *Government Control of Meat-Packing Industry* (Washington, D.C., 1919), Part 5, p. 1848.
3. Bundy oral history (1961), p. 77; Frederic S. Snyder, "Notes and Records: 1918–1929," entry for June 27, 1918, USFA Papers, Box 57, file 22-H, HI.
4. Bundy oral history (1961), p. 77; Charles McCarthy notes on Herbert Hoover, October 1918, Charles McCarthy Papers, Box 22, State Historical Society of Wisconsin.
5. McCarthy notes on Hoover (October 1918); Christian Herter to his mother, April 9, 1920, Herter Family Manuscripts, Box 12, Massachusetts Historical Society; Mark Requa, "Hoover" (typescript, n.d.), p. 5, Mark Requa Papers, HI.
6. Snyder, "Notes and Records," entry for June 27, 1918; McCarthy notes on Hoover (October 1918); Charles McCarthy, "Some Notes on Hoover's Personality" (typescript, April 23, 1920), McCarthy Papers, Box 22.
7. Requa, "Hoover," p. 24.
8. Ibid., pp. 24–25.

9. McCarthy notes on Hoover (October 1918).
10. Ibid.; McCarthy, "Some Notes on Hoover's Personality"; Charles Holman oral history (1953), p. 40, Columbia University Oral History Collection.
11. John Francis Neylan to Aaron Sapiro, July 12, 1917, John Francis Neylan Papers (BANC MSS C-B 881), Box 42, The Bancroft Library, University of California, Berkeley.
12. McCarthy, "Some Notes on Hoover's Personality."
13. McCarthy notes on Hoover (October 1918).
14. McCarthy, "Some Notes on Hoover's Personality."
15. McCarthy notes on Hoover (October 1918).
16. McCarthy, "Some Notes on Hoover's Personality."
17. Ibid.; *Washington Star*, February 3, 1918, section I, p. 4.
18. McCarthy, "Some Notes on Hoover's Personality."
19. Holman oral history (1953), p. 40.
20. Neylan to Sapiro, July 12, 1917; Roland W. Boyden to Kate Boyden, November 22, 1917, Herbert Hoover Collection, Box 313, HI; Snyder, "Notes and Records," entry for June 27, 1918.
21. Snyder, "Notes and Records," entry for June 27, 1918.
22. Ibid.
23. Bundy oral history (1961), p. 76.
24. His aide Charles McCarthy wrote that he had seen Hoover "walk up and down the floor in utter dejection and fear when attacked by some little two by four congressman." McCarthy notes on Hoover (October 1918).
25. Quoted in Henry Breckinridge oral history (1953), p. 209, Columbia University Oral History Collection.
26. Colville Barclay to A. J. Balfour, September 28, 1917, FO 368 / 1844, PRO. According to this British embassy official in Washington, Hoover's only friends in the Wilson administration were Secretary of the Interior Lane and Secretary of Agriculture Houston. Barclay was wrong about Houston, but he was probably correct in stating that the rest of President Wilson's Cabinet were "either jealous of [Hoover's] popularity or ruffled by his downrightness."
27. This was the apt phrase of Gifford Pinchot in Pinchot to Henry C. Wallace, February 27, 1918, Henry C. Wallace Papers, Box 1, University of Iowa Libraries. According to another Hoover associate, both the Department of Agriculture and the Department of Labor showed jealousy of the Food Administration. H. Alexander Smith diary, March 24, 1918, H. Alexander Smith Papers, Box 280, Seeley G. Mudd Manuscript Library, Department of Rare Books and Special Collections, Princeton University Libraries.
28. For the September 1918 controversy between Hoover and Provost Marshal General Enoch Crowder, see Hoover to Woodrow Wilson, September 9, 1918; Wilson to Hoover, September 10, 1918; Hoover telegram to federal food administrators and zone agents, September 19, 1918; Crowder to Hoover, September 21, 1918 (plus enclosures); and Hoover to Crowder, September 23, 1918. All in Enoch H. Crowder Papers, folders 102–104, University of Missouri.
29. William Phillips diary, December 3, 1917, William Phillips Papers, Houghton Library, Harvard University.
30. See Hoover to Bernard Baruch, May 30, June 4, and October 1, 1918; Baruch to Hoover, June 1 and October 4, 1918. All in USFA Papers, Box 178.
31. H. Alexander Smith diary, March 24, 1918.
32. Paul Willard Garrett, *Government Control Over Prices* (Washington, D.C., 1920), p. 56.
33. Chandler Anderson diary, January 4, 1918, Chandler Anderson Papers, Box 1, LC.
34. Edgar Rickard memorandum to Miss Van Renassalear [Martha Van Rensselear] and F. C. Walcott, June 14, 1918, USFA Papers, Box 32.
35. David Houston, cited in Josephus Daniels diary, November 12, 1918, printed in Arthur S. Link et al., eds., *The Papers of Woodrow Wilson*, vol. 53 (Princeton, N.J., 1986), p. 65.

36. Peyton C. March, *The Nation at War* (Garden City, N.Y., 1932), pp. 72–74.
37. H. Alexander Smith diary, March 24, 1918.
38. George Creel, *Rebel At Large: Recollections of Fifty Crowded Years* (New York, 1947), p. 265.
39. Ibid.
40. Requa, "Hoover," p. 25.
41. Holman oral history (1953), p. 40; Brand Whitlock diary, November 3, 1932, Brand Whitlock Papers, Box 7, LC; A. J. P. Taylor, ed., *Lloyd George: A Diary by Frances Stevenson* (New York, 1971), p. 277.
42. Charles S. Hamlin diary, March 31, 1920, Charles S. Hamlin Papers, LC.
43. Creel, *Rebel at Large*, p. 265.
44. George Creel, "George Creel's Page: Politics and Presidents," *Leslie's Weekly* 129 (July 19, 1919): 96.
45. Cited in Mark Sullivan, *Our Times*, vol. V: *Over Here, 1914–1918* (New York, 1933), pp. 417–18.
46. Edward M. House diary, July 4, 1917, Edward M. House Papers, Manuscripts and Archives, Yale University Library.
47. Requa, "Hoover," pp. 25–26.
48. Bernard Baruch, *Baruch: The Public Years* (New York, 1960), p. 88.
49. Edward M. House diary, February 10, 1918, House Papers. The words quoted here are House's, not Wilson's.
50. The battle over this issue (and much else) is recounted in Seward W. Livermore, *Politics Is Adjourned: Woodrow Wilson and the War Congress, 1916–1918* (Middletown, Conn., 1966).
51. Edward M. House diary, February 25, 1918.
52. Ibid.; Wilson to Hoover, March 16, 1918, "Wilson, Woodrow," Pre-Commerce Papers, Herbert Hoover Papers, HHPL.
53. Herbert Hoover, *The Memoirs of Herbert Hoover*, vol. I: *Years of Adventure* (New York, 1952), p. 263; Herbert Hoover, *An American Epic*, vol. II (Chicago, 1960), p. 47. In the former source, Hoover stated that he furnished Harry A. Garfield a memorandum recommending "a sort of War Cabinet" and that Garfield converted the President to the idea. In the latter source, Hoover stated that he, Garfield, and Vance McCormick joined in recommending to the President that he "call periodic meetings of the war-agency heads."

    I have been unable to confirm either of these versions of Hoover's role in the formation of the War Cabinet. According to Colonel House's diary of February 25, 1918 (already cited), it was Walter S. Gifford who came to him, proposed presidential creation of a "War Board," and gave House supporting "charts." Gifford was director of the Council of National Defense, which had recently established a similar "coordinating body" (including Hoover) that met weekly. It is possible that Hoover supplied Gifford with the "charts" and the arguments which helped to persuade House and through him the President to set up a "War Cabinet" chaired by Wilson himself. In this way Hoover may well have been the catalyst of the process.

    For the Council of National Defense's prior establishment of an interagency joint weekly conference, including Hoover, see minutes of a meeting of the Council of National Defense, November 27, 1917, printed in U.S. Congress, Senate, 74th Congress, 2d Session, Senate Committee Print No. 7: *Munitions Industry: Minutes of the Council of National Defense* (Washington, D.C., 1936), p. 200; *New York Times*, November 28, 1917, p. 3.
54. Harry A. Garfield, "Memorandum of Meetings of the Industrial Cabinet," Harry A. Garfield Papers, Box 129, LC; Ray Stannard Baker, *Woodrow Wilson: Life and Letters*, vol. VIII: *Armistice* (New York, 1939), pp. 36–37; Ray Stannard Baker memorandum of conversation with Vance C. McCormick, July 15, 1928, Ray Stannard Baker Papers, Box 111, LC.
55. Edward N. Hurley, *The Bridge to France* (Philadelphia, 1927), p. 319.
56. Ibid.
57. Arthur Walworth memorandum of conversation with Herbert Hoover, May 1, 1948,

Arthur Walworth Papers, Box 1, Manuscripts and Archives, Yale University Library; Hoover, *An American Epic*, II, p. 47.

58. Chandler Anderson diary, March 20, 1918, Anderson Papers, Box 1.
59. Alice M. Dickson to "Dearest Lady" (Lou Henry Hoover), August 27, 1917, "American Women's War Relief Fund: Correspondence, 1917–18 and undated," Subject File, Lou Henry Hoover Papers, HHPL; Joseph C. Green oral history (1967), p. 22, HHPL.
60. W. A. M. Goode to Arthur Willert, April 18, 1917, Arthur Willert Papers, Box 3, Manuscripts and Archives, Yale University Library.
61. James F. Bell to Herbert Hoover, November 10, 1928, James F. Bell Papers, Box 2, HI.
62. John Francis Neylan to Aaron Sapiro, July 12, 1917, Neylan Papers, Box 42.
63. Donald Wilhelm, "Hoover and His Food Organization," *American Review of Reviews* 56 (September 1917): 283, 284.
64. Brand Whitlock diary, November 23, 1917, Allan Nevins Papers, Rare Book and Manuscript Library, Columbia University. Printed (with Colonel House's name omitted) in Allan Nevins, ed., *The Journal of Brand Whitlock* (New York, 1936), p. 459. The words quoted in the text are Whitlock's, not House's. Whitlock was summarizing his conversation with House.
65. Henry F. J. Knoblock to Herman Hagedorn, October 21, 1931, Herman Hagedorn Papers, Box 7, LC.
66. See, for example, Edward Eyre Hunt, "Hoover of the 'C.R.B.,' " *World's Work* 34 (June 1917): 165–68; Will Irwin, "The Autocrat of the Dinner Table," *Saturday Evening Post* 189 (June 23, 1917): 26, 54, 56–58, 61; Hugh Gibson, "Herbert C. Hoover," *Century* 94 (August 1917): 508–17; Vernon Kellogg, "Herbert Hoover, as Individual and Type," *Atlantic Monthly* 121 (March 1918): 375–85.
67. *Herbert Hoover: Public Positions and Honors* (Stanford, Calif.: Hoover Institution on War, Revolution and Peace, 1964), p. 11, copy at HHPL.
68. The idea of his becoming President had come to Hoover's notice at least as early as 1916. See David Starr Jordan to Lou Henry Hoover, December 30, 1915, and Lou Henry Hoover's reply, February 15, 1916, both in "Jordan, David Starr," Personal Correspondence, 1874–1920, Lou Henry Hoover Papers.
69. See George H. Nash, *The Life of Herbert Hoover: The Engineer, 1874–1914* (New York, 1983), pp. 510–12, 573, and Nash, *The Life of Herbert Hoover: The Humanitarian, 1914–1917* (New York, 1988), pp. 341–61.
70. Edgar Rickard to R. B. Burton, November 2, 1917, USFA Papers, Box 230; *New York Sun* article, January 23, 1920, Pre-Commerce Clippings File, Herbert Hoover Papers, HHPL.
71. *New York Sun*, January 23, 1920; H. W. Shoutwells (?) to Watson Washburn, March 15, 1920, "Politics," Pre-Commerce Papers, Hoover Papers; George Barr Baker to Percy H. Wilson, May 12, 1920, ibid.
72. Baker to Wilson, May 12, 1920.
73. Ibid. According to Baker (a close aide), Hoover was "anxious to be in a position to draw assistants from all classes of citizens without regard to politics."
74. Nash, *Life of Herbert Hoover: The Humanitarian*, pp. 292, 377.
75. Neylan to Sapiro, July 12, 1917.
76. McCarthy notes on Hoover (October 1918).
77. Charles McCarthy, "Notes on Hoover, May 14, 1920," McCarthy Papers, Box 22.
78. Herbert Hoover to Mary Austin, April 11, 1918, General Accessions—Mary Austin, HHPL. See also Hoover to Austin, March 14, 1918, printed in T. M. Pearce, ed., *Literary America, 1903–1934: The Mary Austin Letters* (Westport, Conn., 1979), p. 90.
79. Herbert Croly to Lewis L. Strauss, June 5, 1918, "Croly, Herbert," Name and Subject File I, Lewis L. Strauss Papers, HHPL.
80. Hoover to Herbert Croly, June 11, 1918, "Croly, Herbert," Name and Subject File I, Lewis L. Strauss Papers.

81. See chapter 3 and Irving Fisher to Woodrow Wilson, May 17, 1917, Woodrow Wilson Papers, LC. According to Fisher, a member of the subcommittee on alcohol of the Council of National Defense, Hoover favored "National Prohibition during the war and one year thereafter."
82. Specifically, section 15 of the Lever Act authorized the President to regulate, limit, or prohibit the use of foods, fruits, food materials, and feeds in the production of "malt or vinous liquors for beverage purposes" in order to assure sufficient food supplies or otherwise promote national security. He could also reduce the alcoholic content of malt and vinous liquors (that is, beer and wine) for the same reasons. The Lever Act only authorized the President to take these actions. It did not compel him to do so.
83. Hoover to Woodrow Wilson, August 31, 1917, Wilson Papers.
84. Wilson to Hoover, September 4, 1917, Wilson Papers.
85. Hoover to Wilson, November 19, 1917, Wilson Papers.
86. McCarthy, "Some Notes on Hoover's Personality."
87. Hoover to Wilson, November 19, 1917.
88. Wilson to Hoover, November 20, 1917, "Wilson, Woodrow," Pre-Commerce Papers; Hoover to Wilson, November 23, 1917, Wilson Papers; U.S. Food Administration press release 486, November 26, 1917, USFA Documents, HHPL; *New York Times*, November 27, 1917, p. 7; Hoover to Wilson, December 6, 1917, Wilson Papers; Joseph P. Tumulty to Hoover, December 8, 1917, USFA Papers, Box 89.
89. *Commercial and Financial Chronicle* 105 (December 15, 1917): 2328–29.
90. Hoover to Wilson, December 6, 1917.
91. U.S. Food Administration press release 486, November 26, 1917; Hoover to Rep. Charles H. Randall, January 6, 1918, USFA Papers, Box 96.
92. Hoover to Randall, January 6, 1918.
93. Hoover cable to Alonzo Taylor, n.d. (ca. November 26, 1917), USFA Papers, Box 37.
94. Hoover to Louis P. Sheldon, February 4, 1918, USFA Papers, Box 89.
95. Sheldon cable 121 to Hoover, March 1, 1918, USFA Papers, Box 89.
96. Morris Sheppard to Woodrow Wilson, March 20, 1918; Wilson to Sheppard, March 22, 1918. Both in Wilson Papers.
97. *New York Times*, May 27, 1918, p. 18.
98. H. Alexander Smith diary, June 2, 1918, H. Alexander Smith Papers, Box 280.
99. Thomas Nixon Carver, *Government Control of the Liquor Business in Great Britain and the United States* (New York, 1919), pp. 173–174.
100. *Congressional Record* 56 (May 21, 1918): 6868–72.
101. Hoover to Joseph P. Tumulty (plus enclosure), May 27, 1918, Wilson Papers.
102. Wilson to Tumulty (enclosing the items cited in note 101), May 27, 1918, Wilson Papers.
103. Morris Sheppard to Wilson, May 26, 1918, Wilson Papers.
104. Wilson to Sheppard, May 28, 1918, Wilson Papers.
105. H. Alexander Smith diary, June 2, 1918; Morris Sheppard to Hoover, June 2, 1918, copy in Wilson Papers.
106. Hoover to Sheppard, June 4, 1918, copy in Wilson Papers. Copy also in USFA Papers, Box 97.
107. This was Hoover's intent. See H. Alexander Smith diary, June 2, 1918.
108. U.S. Food Administration press release 997, June 5, 1918, USFA Documents.
109. Sheppard to Hoover, June 2, 1918.
110. *New York Times*, June 6, 1918, p. 12.
111. Ibid.
112. *Congressional Record* 56 (August 29, 1918): 9625–51; September 6, 1918, pp. 10070–86.
113. Hoover to Woodrow Wilson, July 2, 1918, Wilson Papers.
114. *Official U.S. Bulletin* 2 (September 7, 1918): 1.
115. Ibid. (September 19, 1918): 3.

116. Address of Herbert Hoover at a meeting of federal food administrators, Washington, D.C., September 4, 1918, Public Statements File, Hoover Papers.
117. Joseph P. Tumulty to Wilson, September 7, 1918; Albert S. Burleson to Wilson, September 17, 1918; both in Wilson Papers.
118. Carver, *Government Control of the Liquor Business*, pp. 174–75.
119. See Livermore, *Politics Is Adjourned* (the standard account of this subject), passim.
120. Ibid., pp. 169–76, 192–96; Seward W. Livermore, "The Sectional Issue in the 1918 Congressional Elections," *Mississippi Valley Historical Review* 35 (June 1948): 29–60.
121. Jouett Shouse to Hoover, September 24, 1918, USFA Papers, Box 96.
122. Hoover to Shouse, September 25, 1918, Jouett Shouse Papers, University of Kentucky. Copy in USFA Papers, Box 96.
123. Joseph P. Tumulty to Hoover, October 31, 1918, "Wilson, Woodrow," Pre-Commerce Papers.
124. Hoover to Tumulty, November 1, 1918, Wilson Papers.
125. Wilson's appeal for a Democratic Congress is printed in Arthur S. Link et al., eds., *The Papers of Woodrow Wilson*, vol. 51 (Princeton, N.J., 1985), pp. 381–82.
126. *New York Times*, October 28, 1918, p. 1.
127. Senator Henry Cabot Lodge, quoted in David M. Kennedy, *Over Here: The First World War and American Society* (New York, 1980), p. 241.
128. Herbert Hoover, *The Ordeal of Woodrow Wilson* (New York, 1958), p. 15.
129. Anne Wintermute Lane and Louise Herrick Wall, eds., *The Letters of Franklin K. Lane* (Boston and New York, 1922), p. 299.
130. Frederic R. Coudert to Hoover, October 3, 1919, Herbert Hoover Collection, Box 314.
131. Coudert to Hoover, October 29, 1918, "Coudert, Frederic," Pre-Commerce Papers.
132. Herbert Hoover Calendar, HHPL.
133. Coudert to Hoover, April 19, 1920, "Coudert, Frederic," Pre-Commerce Papers.
134. Ibid.
135. Hoover handwritten draft, dated October 31, 1918, in "Hoover, Herbert: General, 1918," Name and Subject File I, Lewis L. Strauss Papers. If the date is correct, Hoover began to compose this draft before he met Coudert for lunch on November 1.
136. Hoover Calendar, HHPL.
137. *New York Times*, April 2, 1920, p. 17.
138. Ray Stannard Baker memorandum of conversation with Vance C. McCormick, July 15, 1928 (cited in note 54).
139. I have found no evidence that McCormick or other Democrats instigated Coudert's visit to Hoover. Coudert later insisted that Hoover's letter was the result of "our informal and chance conversation" (Coudert to Hoover, April 19, 1920). The Coudert-Hoover lunch was not a chance occurrence, however; Coudert requested it. Moreover, as stated in the text, McCormick said several years later that *he* obtained Hoover's letter endorsing the President's appeal. There seems no reason to doubt him, or at least to doubt that he visited Hoover on November 2 precisely for this purpose. What seems to have happened is that McCormick approached Hoover independently of Coudert, who then became the convenient, and possibly unwitting, instrument of the transaction.

    Although McCormick saw Hoover after the Coudert lunch, it is possible that the Democratic National Committee chairman approached Hoover before the lunch. On October 29, Hoover dined with McCormick at Bernard Baruch's home (Hoover Calendar, HHPL). And, of course, Hoover had a telephone. It should also be noted that Coudert's letter of April 19, 1920, explaining the circumstances of the 1918 Hoover-Coudert lunch, was a prearranged attempt to relieve Hoover of acute political embarrassment, raised anew by the *New York Times* article of April 2, 1920. Coudert's letter of April 19, 1920, in fact, was drafted in consultation with Lewis L. Strauss and Hoover himself, who was then a Republican candidate for President. At this juncture Hoover was eager to explain—or explain away—his support for the election of a Democratic Congress in 1918. Readers of the Coudert explanation of April 19, 1920 should bear these circumstances in mind. See Lewis L. Strauss to Frederic Coudert, April 15, 1920, "Campaign of 1920—General, 1920," Name and Subject File I, Strauss Papers; Lewis L. Strauss diary entry, April 20, 1920, "Campaign of 1920—Strauss Diary," Name and Subject File I, Strauss Papers.

140. *Chicago Tribune*, November 3, 1918, part I, p. 10.
141. Coudert to Hoover, November 2, 1918, quoted in full in *New York Times*, November 4, 1918, p. 8.
142. Hoover to Coudert, November 2, 1918, quoted in full in *New York Times*, November 4, 1918, p. 8.
143. *New York Times*, November 4, 1918, p. 8.
144. Woodrow Wilson to Hoover, November 4, 1918, Wilson Papers.
145. *New Kork Times*, November 5, 1918, p. 8.
146. Henry Cabot Lodge to Francis Loomis, November 16, 1918, Francis Loomis Papers (M96), Box 2, Department of Special Collections, Stanford University Libraries.
147. Theodore Roosevelt to Miles Poindexter, November 16, 1918, printed in Elting E. Morison, ed., *The Letters of Theodore Roosevelt*, vol. VIII: *The Days of Armageddon, 1914–1919* (Cambridge, 1954), pp. 1395–96.
148. Livermore, *Politics Is Adjourned*, p. 241.
149. The *Chicago Tribune*, November 3, 1918, part I, p. 10, noted that "the political gossips" in Washington had already "started a political boom for Hoover" for the Democratic presidential nomination.
150. Edgar Rickard to Curtis H. Lindley, November 11, 1918, USFA Papers, Box 233.
151. Coudert to Hoover, October 3, 1919.
152. Coudert to Hoover, April 19, 1920.
153. Herbert Hoover, *Memoirs*, paperbound page proof version (June 1944), vol. II, United States Food Administration section, p. 58, Hoover Book Manuscript Material, HHPL.
154. Hoover, *Years of Adventure*, p. 266.
155. Hoover, *Ordeal of Woodrow Wilson*, p. 17.
156. See note 139.

CHAPTER 16

1. Binghamton [N.Y.] *Press* article, August 14, 1917, copy in Pre-Commerce Clippings File, HHPL; interview of Lou Henry Hoover in Baltimore *Sun*, October 27, 1917, pp. 1, 8. In his *Memoirs*, Herbert Hoover recalled that his rented house at this time was home for forty men, but the contemporary sources cited here said ten. It probably *seemed* like forty. Herbert Hoover, *The Memoirs of Herbert Hoover*, vol. I: *Years of Adventure* (New York, 1952), p. 272.
2. Binghamton [N.Y.] *Press* article, August 14, 1917.
3. Baltimore *Sun*, October 27, 1917, p. 1. Mrs. Hoover said that she and her husband did not feel they could have his associates "stay in a hotel through all the hot weather, when they were volunteering their services and working night and day."
4. Edgar Rickard to Lou Henry Hoover, September 6, 1917, Personal Correspondence, 1874–1920, Lou Henry Hoover Papers, HHPL.
5. The exact date of the move is uncertain, but it appears to have been after October 1, 1917.
6. Agreement dated April 23, 1918, in "Properties and Lots: Miscellaneous," Subject File, Lou Henry Hoover Papers. The lease was for six months.
7. Hoover, *Years of Adventure*, pp. 272–73.
8. Herbert Hoover appointment book, November 23, 1917, USFA Papers, Box 128, HI; Herbert Hoover Calendar, HHPL.
9. Herbert Hoover, "My Personal Relations with Mr. Roosevelt" (typescript, September 26,

1958), "Roosevelt, Franklin D.: Drafts re FDR," Post-Presidential Subject File, Herbert Hoover Papers, HHPL.

10. Binghamton [N.Y.] *Press* article, August 14, 1917; Hoover, *Years of Adventure*, pp. 272–73.
11. Felix Frankfurter, *Felix Frankfurter Reminisces* (New York, 1960), pp. 105–07; Ronald Steel, *Walter Lippmann and the American Century* (Boston, 1980), pp. 120–23.
12. Walter Lippmann column, October 22, 1964, copy in "Hoover, Herbert—Articles about," Laurine Small Papers, HHPL.
13. Walter Lippmann oral history (1956), p. 98, Columbia University Oral History Collection.
14. Hugh Gibson to Mary Gibson, November 11, 1917, Hugh Gibson Papers, Box 35, HI; Hoover, *Years of Adventure*, p. 273.
15. Sunday evening suppers with guests were a custom for the Hoovers and many other Washington officials in 1917–18. Lou Henry Hoover to Gertrude Bowman, October 2, 1942, "Bowman, Gertrude," Margaret Hoover Brigham Collection, HHPL.
16. *New York Times*, May 18, 1918, p. 6.
17. Lewis L. Strauss to Sidney A. Mitchell, May 18, 1918, Name and Subject File I, Lewis L. Strauss Papers, HHPL.
18. Edgar Rickard to Curtis H. Lindley, June 27, 1918, USFA Papers, Box 45.
19. *Washington Star*, February 3, 1918, section I, p. 4; Dudley Harmon, "Dining With the Hoovers," *Ladies' Home Journal* 35 (March 1918): 22.
20. Harmon, "Dining With the Hoovers," p. 22.
21. For information about Mrs. Hoover's involvement in the Food Administration Club, see items in "Food Administration Club: Correspondence, 1917–18," Subject File, Lou Henry Hoover Papers; "Mrs. Hoover's War Work," *The Key* (October 1918): 280 [national magazine of the Kappa Kappa Gamma sorority]; Lou Henry Hoover statement of account, October 23, 1918–June 30, 1919, in "Hoover, Herbert and Lou Henry," Laurine Small Papers; and Hoover, *Years of Adventure*, pp. 273–74.
22. George H. Nash, *Herbert Hoover and Stanford University* (Stanford, Calif., 1988), p. 56.
23. Ibid.
24. Lou Henry Hoover telegram to Herbert Hoover, April 28, 1917, "Hoover, Lou Henry," Pre-Commerce Papers, Hoover Papers.
25. Lou Henry Hoover telegram to Herbert Hoover, May 14, 1917, "Hoover, Lou Henry," Pre-Commerce Papers.
26. Hoover telegram to Lou Henry Hoover, May 15, 1917, "Hoover, Lou Henry," Pre-Commerce Papers.
27. Hoover telegram to Lou Henry Hoover, May 16, 1917, "Hoover, Lou Henry," Pre-Commerce Papers.
28. Lou Henry Hoover telegram to Hoover, May 29, 1917, "Hoover, Lou Henry," Pre-Commerce Papers.
29. Hoover telegram to Lou Henry Hoover, September 7, 1917; Lou Henry Hoover telegram to Hoover, September 10, 1917; both in "Hoover, Lou Henry," Pre-Commerce Papers.
30. Hoover, *Years of Adventure*, p. 273; Ellis Turner (Director of External Affairs of the Sidwell Friends School) to the author, July 13, 1993.
31. Lou Henry Hoover to Mrs. Julius H. Barnes, July 25, 1918, Julius H. Barnes Papers, Box 10, Northeast Minnesota Historical Center, University of Minnesota at Duluth.
32. Ibid.
33. Mrs. Hoover sent postcards to her son Allan while en route to California in May. The postcards are preserved in the Allan Hoover Papers, HHPL. Her trip to California was brief; she returned to Washington by May 24. Lou Henry Hoover to a Mrs. Sullivan, May 24, 1918, copy in "Articles, Addresses, and Statements by Mrs. Hoover—1918, May 3," Subject File, Lou Henry Hoover Papers.
34. Lou Henry Hoover to Allan Hoover, August 26, 1918, Allan Hoover Papers.
35. Ellis Turner (Director of External Affairs of the Sidwell Friends School) to the author, July 13, 1993; Karyl Scrivener (Secretary of the Taft School) to the author, July 9, 1993.

36. Alfred W. Crosby, *America's Forgotten Pandemic: The Influenza of 1918* (Cambridge, Mass., 1989); Francis Russell, *The Great Interlude* (New York, 1964), pp. 21–37.
37. Edgar Rickard to Florence Wardwell, November 1, 1918, USFA Papers, Box 233.
38. Conversation with Mr. and Mrs. Allan Hoover, Greenwich, Connecticut, July 20, 1989.
39. Lou Henry Hoover telegram to Herbert Hoover, October 17, 1918, "Hoover, Lou Henry," Pre-Commerce Papers; Lou Henry Hoover to Allan Hoover, n.d. [postmarked October 23, 1918], Allan Hoover Papers.
40. Lou Henry Hoover to Alonzo E. Taylor, January 9, 1919, Personal Correspondence, 1874–1920, Lou Henry Hoover Papers.
41. Hoover himself used the words "somewhat disconnected" to describe his sons' education. Hoover, *Years of Adventure*, p. 273.
42. George H. Nash, *The Life of Herbert Hoover: The Engineer, 1874–1914* (New York, 1983), pp. 503–04; Nash, *Herbert Hoover and Stanford University*, p. 192, n. 50; Lou Henry Hoover to editor of *Daily Palo Alto*, April 12, 1918, in "Articles, Addresses, and Statements by Mrs. Hoover, Undated," Subject File, Lou Henry Hoover Papers.
43. Lou Henry Hoover telegram to Herbert Hoover, May 14, 1917.
44. Herbert Hoover telegram to Lou Henry Hoover, May 15, 1917.
45. Nash, *Herbert Hoover and Stanford University*, p. 56, and p. 192, notes 54–55.
46. *Daily Palo Alto* article, April 4, 1918, copy in Pre-Commerce Clippings File, HHPL. This was Stanford University's student newspaper. See also *Daily Palo Alto Times* (the city newspaper), April 5, 1918, p. 1.
47. Mrs. Hoover denied only that she had made a *public* "denial brought about by the attacks made on my husband." Alluding to the "implied public declaration credited to me" by the student newspaper, she said that she had never made any such statement. She did not otherwise take issue with the substance of the newspaper's report. Lou Henry Hoover to editor of *Daily Palo Alto*, April 12, 1918. This letter was not published. Possibly it was never sent.
48. Ibid.
49. Nash, *Herbert Hoover and Stanford University*, p. 56.
50. Nash, *Life of Herbert Hoover: The Engineer*, p. 568.
51. For Hoover's mining career between 1914 and 1917, see George H. Nash, *The Life of Herbert Hoover: The Humanitarian, 1914–1917* (New York, 1988), pp. 256–75.
52. Ibid., p. 257; Nash, *The Life of Herbert Hoover: The Engineer*, pp. 412–25; Walter R. Skinner, *The Mining Manual and Mining Year Book for 1917* (London, 1917), pp. 101–03.
53. The feud went back a long way. Nash, *Life of Herbert Hoover: The Engineer*, p. 419. See also Francis A. Govett to A. Chester Beatty, June 21, 1917, A. Chester Beatty Papers, Selection Trust, Ltd., London; E. L. Gruver to Galen L. Stone, July 13, 1917, Beatty Papers; T. A. Rickard, "The Burma Enterprise," *Engineering and Mining Journal-Press* 115 (April 28, 1923): 747.
54. Govett to Beatty, June 21, 1917.
55. Hoover to Theodore Hoover (his brother), March 3, 1917, Hulda Hoover McLean Papers, HI.
56. Ibid.
57. Hoover may at this point have sold some of his own Burma Corporation shares (and shares in a related venture known as the Bawdwin Syndicate) to certain investors in New York, including a noted mining engineer named William B. Thompson. See Edgar Rickard to Charles F. Ayer, October 10 and 16, 1918, USFA Papers, Box 233. Another buyer may have been J. P. Morgan & Company. Certainly by 1918 the Morgan firm had some stockholdings in the Burma enterprise. In mid-1918, Hoover's London agent privately referred to the "Hoover Morgan interest in Burma" (that is, shares in the Burma venture). See John A. Agnew cable to William L. Honnold, July 25, 1918, William L. Honnold Papers, Box 5, Special Collections, William L. Honnold Library, the Claremont Colleges.
58. Hoover to William B. Poland, October 8, 1917, enclosed in Edgar Rickard to Hugh Gibson

(at the State Department), October 8, 1917, file no. 103.97 / 10, RG 59, NARA. Rickard asked Gibson to dispatch Hoover's message through the State Department to Mr. Poland, who was Hoover's Belgian relief representative in London. Poland was asked to convey Hoover's message to John Agnew, a mining engineer who was Hoover's longtime associate and current handler of Hoover's business affairs in London.

59. For example, the British government seized enemy-owned mining companies in Great Britain, abrogated the Zinc Corporation's smelting contracts with the Germans, financed creation of a modern zinc-smelting industry in Great Britain, and took steps to protect Australian zinc ore producers throughout the war and for ten years thereafter. Nash, *Life of Herbert Hoover: The Humanitarian*, pp. 262–63.
60. Minutes of [British] War Cabinet meeting 110, April 2, 1917 (plus Appendix II), Cab. 23 / 2, PRO.
61. Memorandum G. T.-967, June 5, 1917, Cab. 24 / 15, PRO; minutes of War Cabinet meeting 233, September 14, 1917 (plus Appendix: memorandum G.T.-967A), Cab. 23 / 4, PRO.
62. Sir Edward Carson, "Memorandum on Economic Offensive" (memorandum G.-156), September 20, 1917, Cab. 24 / 4, PRO; minutes of War Cabinet meeting 247, October 9, 1917, Cab. 23 / 4, PRO; Sir Edward Carson, memorandum E.O.C. 1 (October 17, 1917), Cab. 27 / 15, PRO; Sir Edward Carson, memorandum G.-190 (January 21, 1918), Cab. 24 / 4, PRO.
63. Dr. M. J. Tubb (Public Record Office, Kew, Surrey) to the author, December 2, 1985.
64. Ibid. For the Board of Trade's reasoning behind its model clauses, see A. H. Stanley, "Form of Association to Prevent Foreign Control of Certain British Companies," BT 58 / 55 / COS / 9542, PRO.
65. Nash, *Life of Herbert Hoover: The Engineer*, p. 422.
66. Skinner, *Mining Manual . . . 1917*, p. 101.
67. Edgar Rickard to John A. Agnew, October 10, 1918, USFA Papers, Box 230; Hoover, draft letter to Frank Polk of the State Department, October 12 [1917], "Hoover, Herbert—General, 1917," Name and Subject File I, Strauss Papers. The "order" to which Hoover referred has not been located. But attached to his draft letter to Polk is a copy of the Board of Trade's model clauses, entitled "Trading With the Enemy: Model Form of Additional Provisions to be Included in the Articles of Association of a Company to Prevent Foreign Control in Those Cases Where Such Provisions Are Required by the Board of Trade." For another copy of the model clauses, see the attachment to A. H. Stanley's memorandum cited in note 64. A copy of Stanley's memorandum and the model clauses may also be found in Economic Offensive Committee memorandum EOC-32, Cab. 27 / 16, PRO.
68. In an unpublished portion of his memoirs written in 1940, Hoover asserted that "Americans mostly engineers owned about 60% of the [Burma] company." I have found no corroboration of this figure, which seems far too high. From the evidence available, it appears that the aggregate American stockholding was probably a little over 20 percent. See Hoover, handwritten draft (1940) of his *Memoirs*, vol. I: *Years of Adventure*, chapters 7–8, p. 48, Hoover Book Manuscript Material, HHPL.
69. Hoover, draft letter to Frank Polk of the State Department, October 12, 1917.
70. The draft letter cited in notes 67 and 69 contains a handwritten notation at the bottom: "Taken up with President." Hoover evidently raised the issue orally at the White House.
71. H. A. L. Fisher diary, November 21, 1917, MS. Fisher 11, fol. 1, Bodleian Library, Oxford University.
72. Order-in-Council No. 423, May 2, 1917, in *Statutory Rules and Orders . . . Issued in the Year 1917* (London, 1918), pp. 286–87.
73. Order-in-Council No. 1092, October 23, 1917, in *Statutory Rules and Orders . . . Issued in the Year 1917*, p. 318.
74. Lord Islington to Sir A. H. Stanley, October 30, 1917, BT 198 / 1, PRO.
75. Edgar Rickard to John A. Agnew, December 4, 1917, USFA Papers, Box 230. Lamont may have been the vehicle for conveyance of President Wilson's displeasure. If so, the path

of communication was probably Wilson to Hoover to Lamont to the British.

76. See note 57.
77. Hoover *Memoirs* draft (1940), vol. I, chapters 7–8, pp. 49–50.
78. Minutes of meeting of Economic Offensive Committee, November 23, 1917, Cab. 27/15, PRO.
79. Minutes of meeting of Economic Offensive Committee, November 29, 1917, Cab. 27/15, PRO.
80. Burma Mines, Ltd., circular, ca. April 5, 1918, containing its revisions of its Articles of Association, BT 31/17692/87848, PRO.
81. Statement of chairman of Burma Corporation, Ltd., at the company's annual shareholders' meeting, November 18, 1918, quoted in *Mining World and Engineering Record* 95 (November 23, 1918): 421.
82. Hoover to Secretary of State Robert Lansing, May 10, 1918, file no. 855.111/158, RG 59, NARA.
83. Lansing did, however, send Hoover's letter on to the Departments of Commerce and the Interior for comment. See William C. Redfield to Hoover, May 31, 1918 (plus enclosure: Redfield to Robert Lansing, May 31, 1918), file 77270, Office of the Secretary—General Correspondence, RG 40, NARA; B. Gotlieb to a Mr. Lay, May 28, 1918 (plus related documents), file no. 845.111/158, RG 59, NARA; and Franklin K. Lane to Secretary of State Lansing, August 20, 1918, file no. 845.111/166, RG 59, NARA.
84. Hoover message to William B. Poland (for John A. Agnew), enclosed in Robert Lansing cable to American Embassy, London, December 24, 1917, file no. 103.97/80a, RG 59, NARA; copy of this message, dated December 27, 1917, Commission for Relief in Belgium Correspondence, Box 9, HI; Edgar Rickard to William L. Honnold, January 8, 1918, USFA Papers, Box 231; William L. Honnold to Ernest Oppenheimer, January 25, 1918, Honnold Papers, Box 5.
85. Edgar Rickard to E. L. Gruver, May 20, 1918; Rickard to Ross Hoffman, July 8, 1918. Both in USFA Papers, Box 232.
86. Rickard to John A. Agnew, May 14 and 21, 1918, USFA Papers, Box 232; Rickard to Gruver, May 20, 1918.
87. Agnew cable to Honnold, July 25, 1918; Ernest Oppenheimer to Honnold, August 15, 1918, Honnold Papers, Box 5. According to Agnew, the cost to the Anglo-American Corporation of South Africa of buying out the "Hoover Morgan interest in Burma" on a $20-per-share basis would be approximately £500,000, or about $2,500,000 at the 1918 exchange rates. Hoover, incidentally, played a key role in founding the Anglo-American Corporation of South Africa in 1917. See Nash, *Life of Herbert Hoover: The Humanitarian*, pp. 271–72.
88. Walter R. Skinner, *Mining Manual & Mining Year Book, 1919* (London, 1919), p. 87.
89. In mid-1918 Edgar Rickard stated that Hoover had "taken no active part in the management of the Burma since he arrived in Washington and has left most of the details in my hands." Rickard to Edgar L. Newhouse, August 22, 1918, USFA Papers, Box 232. See also Rickard to A. F. Keen, October 2, 1918, USFA Papers, Box 233.
90. This transaction can to some extent be followed in Edgar Rickard's outgoing correspondence file, September–October 1918, USFA Papers, Box 233. See especially Rickard to Albert Rathbone, October 4, 1918; Rickard to Charles F. Ayer, October 8, 1918; Rickard to John A. Agnew, October 25, 1918. See also Hoover to William B. Poland, enclosed in Robert Lansing to American Embassy, London, October 9, 1918, file no. 103.97/654a, RG 59, NARA; Hoover to Agnew, enclosed in Lansing to American Embassy, London, November 12, 1918, file no. 103.97/748a, RG 59, NARA. The purchaser of Hoover's shares was a British investor named Herbert Guedalla. Rickard, "The Burma Enterprise," p. 747 (Guedalla's name is misspelled in this source). Incidentally, at least some of Hoover's fellow American investors sold out at the same time. These were evidently the same individuals to whom he had previously sold a portion of his holdings (see note 57).

As it happened, Hoover did not dispose of quite all of his Burma share interest in late 1918. In January 1919 he still owned over seven thousand shares, on which he then granted an option to a prospective buyer. Apparently these shares were soon sold. Lewis L. Strauss to John A. Agnew, January 14, 1919, "Adler, Norbert—Allen, A. C.," Name and Subject File I, Strauss Papers.

91. Hoover was succeeded on the Burma Corporation board of directors by his longtime friend and business associate John A. Agnew, who had negotiated the sale of Hoover's Burma stock. *Mining World and Engineering Record* 97 (November 1, 1919): 433.

92. Hoover *Memoirs* draft (1940), vol. I, chapters 7–8, p. 48.

93. Hoover, "What Has Been Accomplished—1917 [1918]," in "Accomplishments—What Has Been Accomplished, 1914–1917," Pre-Commerce Papers.

94. Hoover *Memoirs* draft (1940), vol. I, chapters 7–8, p. 50.

95. As a young mining engineer on the make, Hoover had said: "If a man has not made a fortune by 40 he is not worth much." Nash, *Life of Herbert Hoover: The Engineer*, p. 384.

96. Hoover *Memoirs* draft (1940), vol. I, chapters 7–8, p. 50. Although the exact size of Hoover's fortune at the end of World War I is unknown, the fragmentary written record provides some clues. As of mid-December 1918, shortly after the sale of his Burma "interest," Hoover had $1,150,000 invested in notes of the First National Bank of New York. This was apparently in addition to $150,000 held in an account that Edgar Rickard had recently opened for him at the Guaranty Trust Company in New York, $50,000 that Rickard had placed in an account for Mrs. Hoover at the same time, and $200,000 of Hoover's money that Rickard had transferred in November to an entity called the West Branch Corporation, in which Hoover and his wife were shareholders. (The West Branch Corporation itself had considerable assets.) Thus Hoover's known assets at this juncture (December 1918) exceeded $1,550,000 (in 1918 dollars)—probably substantially so. In mid-December 1918, for instance, Rickard placed what appears to have been another $300,000 of Hoover's money in a bank in Washington, D.C., for the purpose of certain unspecified investments. See Edgar Rickard to R. B. Burton, February 2 and April 17, 1918, USFA Papers, Box 231; Rickard to Lou Henry Hoover, August 5, 1918, USFA Papers, Box 232; Rickard to Burton, November 11 and December 13, 1918, USFA Papers, Box 233; Rickard to Guaranty Trust Company, November 13, 1918, USFA Papers, Box 233; Rickard to John A. Agnew, December 18, 1918, USFA Papers, Box 233.

Rickard, a close friend and associate of Hoover, handled Hoover's personal finances, including his tax returns. Rickard's outgoing correspondence for 1917–18 in the USFA Papers (Boxes 231–233) offers many glimpses of Hoover's business transactions.

Incidentally, Rickard's correspondence suggests that Hoover possessed significant financial resources even before he sold his Burma shares. Thus in the spring of 1918 he purchased $50,000 in Liberty Loan bonds. In the summer of 1918 the West Branch Corporation declared a 3 percent dividend, which brought Mrs. Hoover $2,460—a figure indicating that the corporation's assets were not small. See Rickard to Burton, April 17, 1918; Rickard to Lou Henry Hoover, August 5, 1918; Rickard to Major James Miles, April 17, 1918, USFA Papers, Box 231. Still, Rickard's correspondence files reinforce Hoover's contention that the sale of his Burma mining stock in 1918 yielded the bulk of the fortune on which he lived for the rest of his life.

97. Hoover, "What Has Been Accomplished—1917 [1918]."

98. Ibid.

99. In his previously cited 1940 *Memoirs* draft (p. 50), Hoover stated that "the American interest" in the Burma venture was sold for "about half its value."

100. See Scott Derks, ed., *The Value of a Dollar: Prices and Incomes in the United States, 1860–1989* (Detroit, 1994), p. 2.

CHAPTER 17

1. For more on the CRB's transition when the United States entered World War I, see George H. Nash, *The Life of Herbert Hoover: The Humanitarian, 1914–1917* (New York, 1988), chapters 13 and 14.
2. Tracy B. Kittredge, unpublished history of the Commission for Relief in Belgium (CRB), chapter 19, Tracy B. Kittredge Papers, HI. Chapter 19 (a typescript) is unpaged. Another source states that until American credits became available for the CRB in 1917, the British and French governments supplied about $270,000,000. George I. Gay and H. H. Fisher, *Public Relations of the Commission for Relief in Belgium* (2 vols.: Stanford, Calif., 1929), vol. I, p. 282. Hereinafter this set will be cited as *PR-CRB*, followed by the appropriate volume number.
3. Kittredge, unpublished history of the CRB, chapter 19.
4. *New York Times*, May 10, 1917, p. 5, and May 18, 1917, p. 8; *PR-CRB*, II, pp. 286, 288–90.
5. *New York Times*, May 18, 1917, p. 8.
6. Ibid.
7. Ibid.
8. *PR-CRB*, I, p. 367.
9. Nash, *Life of Herbert Hoover: The Humanitarian*, pp. 314–15.
10. William B. Poland to the Under-Secretary of State for Foreign Affairs (Great Britain), October 17, 1917, printed in *PR-CRB*, I, pp. 376–77.
11. Hoover to Edward N. Hurley, September 5, 1917, USFA Papers, Box 1, HI.
12. *PR-CRB*, I, p. 367; Herbert Hoover, *An American Epic*, vol. I (Chicago, 1959), p. 344.
13. For the month-by-month statistics, see Hoover, *An American Epic*, I, p. 344.
14. Ibid., p. 345.
15. Ibid., pp. 348–51.
16. William B. Poland message to Hoover, enclosed in Walter Hines Page cable to the Secretary of State, August 6, 1917, file no. 855.48 / 618, RG 59, NARA.
17. Hoover to Secretary of State Robert Lansing, May 26, 1917, file no. 855.48 / 597, RG 59, NARA.
18. Hoover to Fridtjof Nansen, August 22, 1917, file 1H-A19, RG 4, NARA; W. Langley (of the British Foreign Office) to William B. Poland, October 3, 1917, printed in *PR-CRB*, I, p. 375; Hoover, *An American Epic*, I, p. 331.
19. Hoover, *An American Epic*, I, p. 333; Hoover, *An American Epic*, vol. II (Chicago, 1960), p. 149.
20. Hoover to Hurley, September 5, 1918.
21. Hoover to William B. Poland, August 29, 1917, Commission for Relief in Belgium Correspondence, Box 8, HI (hereinafter cited as CRB Correspondence).
22. W. Langley to Poland, October 3, 1917.
23. Hoover, *An American Epic*, I, p. 332.
24. Ibid., p. 332; Poland to the Under-Secretary of State for Foreign Affairs (Great Britain), October 17, 1917.
25. Poland to the Under-Secretary of State for Foreign Affairs (Great Britain), November 1, 1917, printed in *PR-CRB*, I, p. 378; Hoover, *An American Epic*, I, p. 333.
26. Edgar Rickard to William L. Honnold, October 10, 1917, USFA Papers, Box 230, HI.
27. Ibid. Hoover later stated that he approached the Red Cross when "it looked almost hopeless to secure additional funds and we suggested to them to take over the subsidies as they then stood and to add some millions of their own," in return for which the CRB would withdraw and let the Red Cross administer the relief. According to Hoover, this proposal was abandoned because the Red Cross was "unable to find the finance and we were able to make progress in finding it." Hoover to William B. Poland, January 23, 1918, CRB Correspondence, Box 9.

28. Hoover to Poland, August 29, 1917.
29. Hoover's troubles with Francqui and other Belgian leaders are discussed in detail in Nash, *Life of Herbert Hoover: The Humanitarian.*
30. Hoover to Poland, August 29, 1917.
31. Hoover to Poland, January 23, 1918.
32. Hoover telegram to William L. Honnold, October 15, 1917, printed in *PR-CRB*, I, p. 372.
33. Albert, King of the Belgians, to Woodrow Wilson, October 18, 1917, file no. 855.48 / 867, RG 59, NARA.
34. Hoover, *An American Epic*, I, p. 341.
35. Unidentified assistant to Edgar Rickard to William L. Honnold, October 19, 1917, USFA Papers, Box 230.
36. Hoover to Woodrow Wilson, October 23, 1917, copy in "Wilson, Woodrow," Pre-Commerce Papers, Herbert Hoover Papers, HHPL. Hoover probably did not send this letter, which is not in the Woodrow Wilson Papers at LC. In the upper right corner are the typed words, "*HOLD: SUPPRESS.*"
37. Hoover to Woodrow Wilson, October 24, 1917, and Wilson to Secretary of State Robert Lansing, October 25, 1917, both in Woodrow Wilson Papers, LC; Lansing cable 286 to Brand Whitlock, October 26, 1917, file no. 855.48 / 652b, RG 59, NARA (printed in *PR-CRB*, I, pp. 372–74). Hoover later stated that President Wilson requested him to draft the reply to the Belgian king and that the President made Hoover's draft "more emphatic." Hoover, *An American Epic*, I, p. 341. I have been unable to confirm these statements. The text of Wilson's reply to King Albert is included verbatim in Lansing's cable 286 to Whitlock on October 26, 1917.
38. Hoover's relationship with Brand Whitlock is examined in Nash, *Life of Herbert Hoover: The Humanitarian;* see especially pp. 200–02.
39. Wilson to Lansing, October 25, 1917; Lansing cable 286 to Whitlock, October 26, 1917.
40. Brand Whitlock cable to the Secretary of State, November 2, 1917, file no. 855.48 / 655, RG 59, NARA.
41. *Weekly Northwestern Miller* 112 (November 28, 1917): 643; Brand Whitlock diary, November 15, 1917, in Allan Nevins, ed., *The Journal of Brand Whitlock* (New York, 1936), p. 454; Whitlock to the Secretary of State, November 26, 1917, in Allan Nevins, ed., *The Letters of Brand Whitlock* (New York, 1936), pp. 247–48.
42. William B. Poland memorandum, October 20, 1917; Poland to Louis Chevrillon, October 22, 1917. Both in CRB—London office dossier 102, HI.
43. Kittredge, unpublished history of the CRB, chapter 19.
44. Ibid.
45. See, for example, Hoover cable to Poland, October 18, 1917, quoted in ibid.; Aloys van de Vyvere to Poland, October 25, 1917, in CRB—London office dossier 102; Hoover cable to Poland, October 30, 1917, file 10H-A8, Box 470, RG 4, NARA (printed in *PR-CRB*, I, p. 289); Hoover, *An American Epic*, I, p. 361. See also Woodrow Wilson's ghost-written reply to King Albert (contained in Lansing cable no. 286 to Whitlock, cited in note 37). Wilson referred therein to the U.S. government's "inability . . . to provide funds for expenditures outside the United States."
46. For instance, see U.S. Treasury Department to London, enclosed in Lansing cable to Walter Hines Page, October 26, 1917, file no. 855.48 / 651, RG 59, NARA. This message states in part: "As to expenditures within the United States, it is desired that to the largest possible amount all sums loaned to foreign governments shall be thus expended. In case of urgent necessity, exceptions may be made, but the reason for these exceptions should be first submitted to the Secretary of the Treasury." Note that exceptions could be made. See also Hoover to Secretary of State Lansing, October 30, 1917, file no. 855.48 / 654, RG 59, NARA. In this letter, Hoover said: "It is my understanding that the policy of this Government is not to make advances for European expenditures, but to confine the use of loans to expenditures in the United States." Note his use of the word "policy."

See also Assistant Secretary of the Treasury Russell G. Leffingwell to Secretary of State Lansing, November 2, 1917, file no. 855.48 / 656, RG 59, NARA: "It is, of course, highly desirable, if in any way possible, to avoid the departure from the policy of substantially limiting the expenditures of the proceeds of loans by the United States to expenditures for purchases here." Note again the use of the word "policy."

In his letter to Wilson on October 23 (cited in note 36), Hoover remarked that the U.S. Treasury did not feel "disposed" to advance to the French and Belgian governments the $5,000,000 monthly now needed to subsidize the CRB's expenditures in Europe.

47. Walter Hines Page cable to the Secretary of State, October 22, 1917, file no. 855.48 / 650, RG 59, NARA; Kittredge, unpublished history of the CRB, chapter 19.
48. Hoover to Lansing, October 30, 1917; Kittredge, unpublished history of the CRB, chapter 19.
49. Wilson to King Albert, in Lansing cable to Whitlock, October 26, 1917.
50. Hoover cable to Poland, October 30, 1917.
51. Hoover to Lansing, October 30, 1917.
52. Edward M. House cable to the Secretary of State, November 27, 1917, printed in United States, Department of State, *Papers Relating to the Foreign Relations of the United States, 1917*, Supplement 2: *The World War* (Washington, D.C., 1932), vol. II, pp. 988–89; *PR-CRB*, I, pp. 380–81; Edward M. House cable to the Secretary of State, December 5, 1917, printed in United States, Department of State, *Papers Relating to the Foreign Relations of the United States, 1918*, Supplement 2: *The World War* (Washington, D.C., 1933), p. 468 (hereinafter cited as *FRUS, 1918*, Supplement 2); William B. Poland to Hoover, December 7, 1917, printed in *PR-CRB*, I, pp. 378–80.
53. Hoover to Poland, in Robert Lansing cable to Walter Hines Page, November 9, 1917, file no. 855.48 / 664a, RG 59, NARA.
54. French Minister of Finance Klotz to Walter Hines Page, November 25, 1917, printed in *PR-CRB*, I, pp. 290–91; Poland to Hoover, December 7, 1917.
55. Poland to Hoover, December 7, 1917.
56. Poland to Hoover, enclosed in Walter Hines Page cable to Secretary of State, December 22, 1917, file no. 855.48 / 686, RG 59, NARA.
57. Ibid.; Banque Belge pour l'Etranger to CRB—London office, December 22, 1917, printed in *PR-CRB*, I. p. 296.
58. Poland to Hoover, December 22, 1917.
59. Ibid.; Poland to Prime Minister David Lloyd George, December 21, 1917, printed in *PR-CRB*, I, pp. 293–95.
60. Poland telegram to Lloyd George, December 27, 1917, printed in *PR-CRB*, I, p. 296.
61. F. Avenol to Poland, December 28, 1917, printed in *PR-CRB*, I, pp. 297–98.
62. Poland telegram to Lloyd George, December 27, 1917.
63. Ibid. Hoover later wrote that he cabled Lloyd George "through Poland." Evidently, then, Poland's message to the prime minister was authorized by Hoover. See Hoover, *An American Epic*, I, p. 363.
64. Lloyd George telegram to Poland, January 1, 1918, printed in *PR-CRB*, I, p. 297.
65. John Bradbury to Baron Moncheur (the Belgian minister to Great Britain), January 2, 1918, printed in *PR-CRB*, I, p. 298.
66. Memorandum, January 5, 1918, printed in *PR-CRB*, I, pp. 299–300.
67. Ibid. See also Kittredge, unpublished history of the CRB, chapter 20. The French had proposed a total monthly commitment of £2,250,000, of which £1,500,000 would be allotted to Belgian expenses. The British agreed only to a total of £1,500,000, with £1,000,000 of this sum devoted to Belgian expenses. However, the French and British agreed that the £1,500,000 figure was provisional and could be reconsidered if necessary.
68. See Kittredge, unpublished history of the CRB, chapter 21, for details. See also Oscar T. Crosby cable to the Secretary of State, January 10, 1918, in *FRUS, 1918*, Supplement 2, pp. 471–72.

69. See Kittredge, unpublished history of the CRB, chapters 20 and 21, for details.
70. Hoover to Emile Francqui, January 24, 1918, printed in *PR-CRB*, II, pp. 174–76.
71. Kittredge, unpublished history of the CRB, chapter 22, p. 3.
72. Ibid.
73. Emile Francqui to Hoover, April 2, 1918, printed in Hoover, *An American Epic*, I, pp. 381–82.
74. Kittredge, unpublished history of the CRB, chapter 22, pp. 4, 7–8, 11–12.
75. On April 10, for instance, the British Foreign Office indicated its willingness "provisionally" to approve CRB grain imports "in excess of the approved ration," but added that the British government "cannot guarantee the extra tonnage necessary for this purpose." Ibid., p. 12.
76. Thomas A. Bailey, *The Policy of the United States Toward the Neutrals, 1917–1918* (Baltimore, 1942), pp. 206–08, 212. Angary is the right under international law of a belligerent to use, seize, or destroy property of neutrals, or to take over use of neutral ships in case of necessity.
77. Kittredge, unpublished history of the CRB, chapter 22, pp. 16, 18.
78. Ibid., p. 16.
79. William B. Poland to L. P. Sheldon, April 1, 1918, quoted in ibid.
80. Peyton C. March, *The Nation at War* (Garden City, N.Y., 1932), pp. 69–70.
81. Newton D. Baker cable to Woodrow Wilson, March 28, 1918, printed in Arthur S. Link et al., eds., *The Papers of Woodrow Wilson*, vol. 47 (Princeton, N.J., 1984), pp. 175–76.
82. March, *The Nation at War*, pp. 71–72.
83. Benedict Crowell to Woodrow Wilson (plus enclosure), March 26, 1918, printed in Link et al., eds., *Papers of Woodrow Wilson*, vol. 47, pp. 144–47.
84. David Lloyd George to Lord Reading, March 28 and 29, 1918, printed in ibid., pp. 181–83, 203–05.
85. Lord Reading to Lloyd George, March 30, 1918, printed in ibid., pp. 213–14.
86. Wilson message contained in Peyton C. March cable to Tasker H. Bliss, April 6, 1918, printed in ibid., p. 271. The subsequent confusion over this issue can be followed in documents printed in vol. 47.
87. March cable to Bliss, April 5, 1918, printed in ibid., pp. 260–61.
88. Hoover to Woodrow Wilson, April 8, 1918, Wilson Papers.
89. Hoover to Poland, enclosed in Lansing cable to American Embassy, London, April 11, 1918, file no. 855.48/731d, RG 59, NARA.
90. Hoover to Wilson, April 8, 1918.
91. Ibid.
92. Hoover to Frank L. Polk, April 10, 1918, USFA Papers, Box 285; Lansing cable to Walter Hines Page, April 11, 1918, file no. 855.48/722a, RG 59, NARA.
93. Page cable to Lansing, April 13, 1918, file no. 855.48/724; William G. Sharp cable to Lansing, April 13, 1918, file no. 855.48/723. Both in RG 59, NARA.
94. Page cable to Lansing, April 13, 1918.
95. Sharp cable to Lansing, April 13, 1918.
96. Page cable to Lansing, April 21, 1918, file no. 855.48/728, RG 59, NARA.
97. Brand Whitlock cable to Lansing, April 18, 1918, file no. 855.48/727, RG 59, NARA.
98. William B. Poland memorandum for Allied Maritime Transport Council, April 18, 1918, printed in *PR-CRB*, I, pp. 383–85. Printed also (with annexes) in *Allied Maritime Transport Council, 1918*, pp. 104–09, copy in Edwin F. Gay Papers, Box 6, HI.
99. Kittredge, unpublished history of the CRB, chapter 22, p. 23.
100. Minutes of Allied Maritime Transport Council, April 23–25, 1918, in *Allied Maritime Transport Council, 1918*, pp. 72–73; *PR-CRB*, I, p. 385; Raymond B. Stevens to Edward N. Hurley, enclosed in Page cable to Lansing, May 12, 1918, printed in *FRUS, 1918*, Supplement 2, pp. 478–80.
101. Kittredge, unpublished history of the CRB, chapter 22, p. 29.

102. Hoover to Whitlock, enclosed in Lansing cable to Whitlock, May 3, 1918, file no. 855.48/734a, RG 59, NARA; Hoover, *An American Epic*, I, p. 368.
103. Hoover to Whitlock, May 3, 1918.
104. Hoover to Poland, enclosed in Lansing cable to American Embassy, London, May 7, 1918, file no. 855.48/734G, RG 59, NARA.
105. Nash, *Life of Herbert Hoover: The Humanitarian*, pp. 200–02; Brand Whitlock diary, November 30, 1917, Allan Nevins Papers, Rare Book and Manuscript Library, Columbia University. These diary entries are printed (with certain omissions) in Whitlock's *Journal*, p. 461.
106. Whitlock diary, May 6, 1918, Nevins Papers; printed (with the words "to blackmail" omitted) in Whitlock's *Journal*, p. 480.
107. Whitlock cable to Lansing, May 20, 1918, file no. 855.48/746, RG 59, NARA.
108. Hoover to Whitlock, June 4, 1918, Brand Whitlock Papers, Box 37, LC.
109. Francqui to Hoover, May 6, 1918, printed in Hoover, *An American Epic*, I, pp. 382–83.
110. Hoover to Lansing, May 10, 1918, General Accessions—Francis O'Brien, HHPL.
111. Ibid.; Hoover to Edward N. Hurley, USFA Papers, Box 165. Early in May, Hoover announced that most American manufacturers of foodstuffs using sugar would be rationed and required to reduce their use of sugar by 20 percent from 1917 levels. *Official Bulletin* 2 (May 6, 1918): 1–2; *New York Times*, May 6, 1918, p. 3.
112. Stevens to Hurley, May 12, 1918.
113. Hoover to Lansing, May 10, 1918.
114. Stevens to Hurley, May 12, 1918.
115. Hoover to Poland, May 7, 1918.
116. Stevens to Hurley, May 12, 1918.
117. CRB—London to Hoover, enclosed in Page to Lansing, May 13, 1918, file no. 855.48/742; William B. Poland to Hoover, enclosed in Page to Lansing, May 13, 1918, file no. 855.48/740; Prime Minister de Broqueville of Belgium to Lansing, n.d. (received in Washington, May 14, 1918), file no. 855.48/741. All in RG 59, NARA.
118. Prime Minister de Broqueville to Lloyd George, May 13, 1918, copy enclosed with French Prime Minister Clemenceau to Woodrow Wilson, May 13, 1918, file no. 855.48/771, RG 59, NARA. This document and a cover note from the French ambassador to the United States are printed in *FRUS, 1918*, Supplement 2, pp. 482–84. For de Broqueville's similar appeal to Wilson, see file no. 855.48/772, RG 59, NARA.
119. Lansing to Wilson, May 15, 1918, file no. 855.48/761, RG 59, NARA.
120. Appointments Book, 1918, entry for May 16, Wilson Papers.
121. Hoover, *An American Epic*, I, p. 370.
122. Ibid.
123. Hoover cable to William B. Poland (enclosing message for delivery to Lloyd George), May 16, 1918, printed in *PR-CRB*, I, pp. 387–88.
124. *New York Times*, May 17, 1918, p. 4.
125. Hoover to Wilson (plus enclosure), May 17, 1918, Wilson Papers.
126. Ibid.
127. Memorandum of May 15, 1918 (and related documents), in CRB—London office dossier 100, HI.
128. Memorandum of May 17, 1918, in CRB—London office dossier 100.
129. Hoover to Wilson, May 20, 1918, Wilson Papers.
130. Hoover cable to Poland, May 22, 1918, printed in *PR-CRB*, I, p. 389; U.S. Food Administration press release 962, May 22, 1918, USFA Documents, HHPL; *New York Times*, May 23, 1918, p. 14.
131. U.S. Food Administration press release 962, May 22, 1918.
132. Hoover cable to Poland, May 21, 1918, printed in *PR-CRB*, I, p. 389; Hoover cable to Poland, May 22, 1918.
133. CRB press statement 13, September 23, 1918, "CRB—Press Releases," Pre-Commerce Papers, Hoover Papers; Hoover, *An American Epic*, II, p. 149; Bailey, *Policy*, pp. 160–61.

134. Hoover, *An American Epic*, I, pp. 371–72.
135. Hoover himself evidently did not make a contemporary record of his lunch with the Belgian monarch, but several of Hoover's traveling companions did. See James F. Bell diary, August 1, 1918, James F. Bell Papers, Box 3, HI; William B. Poland, "Memorandum by W. B. Poland of the meeting of the Royal Family and Ministers of Belgium at La Panne" (typescript, n.d.), in "Hoover, Herbert," Name and Subject File I, Lewis L. Strauss Papers, HHPL; and Lewis L. Strauss diary, August 1, 1918, "Strauss, Lewis L., Diaries, 1917–19," Name and Subject File I, Strauss Papers.
136. Hoover to Allan Hoover, August 1 [1918], Allan Hoover Papers, HHPL.
137. Poland, "Memorandum"; "Memorandum de la séance tenue à La Panne le 1er Août 1918," Fonds du Havre 620, Archives du Palais Royal, Brussels, Belgium.
138. Brand Whitlock to the Secretary of State, December 1, 1917, file no. 093.552/7, RG 59, NARA.
139. Ibid.
140. Hoover to Whitlock, January 5, 1918, CRB Correspondence, Box 9. As early as 1915, Hoover had objected to accepting decorations from the Belgian government. "It is undemocratic," he declared, "and from my point of view at least, is not the kind of reward which I am searching for in this world." Hoover to Whitlock, February 21, 1915, CRB Correspondence, Box 2.
141. Whitlock to the Secretary of State, December 1, 1917.
142. Hoover to Whitlock, January 5, 1918.
143. Article I, section 9.
144. Poland, "Memorandum"; R. W. Boyden to Kate Boyden, August 26, 1918, Herbert Hoover Collection, Box 313, HI.
145. Poland, "Memorandum."
146. Ibid.; *C.R.B. Bulletin* no. 6 (October 15, 1918): 4, copy at HHPL.
147. Copy of a telegram (in French) from the Belgian Documentary Bureau at Le Havre to the Belgian legation in Washington, D.C., August 7, 1918; translation of extract from *Indépendence Belge*, August 8, 1918. Both in "Honors, Degrees, & Other Awards—Belgium," Pre-Commerce Papers, Hoover Papers.
148. Address by Prime Minister Cooreman et al. to King Albert as printed in *Information Belges* [sic], August 8, 1918, copy in "Honors, Degrees, & Other Awards—Belgium," Pre-Commerce Papers.
149. That is, benefactor. Copy of telegram from Belgian Documentary Bureau, August 7, 1918 (cited in note 147).
150. There is a very considerable literature on this subject. A useful review article is Carl J. Richard, " 'The Shadow of a Plan': The Rationale Behind Wilson's 1918 Siberian Intervention," *The Historian* 49 (November 1986): 64–84. See also Betty Miller Unterberger, *The United States, Revolutionary Russia, and the Rise of Czechoslovakia* (Chapel Hill, N.C., 1989).
151. Herbert Hoover, paperbound page proof version (June 1944) of his *Memoirs*, vol. II, United States Food Administration section, pp. 59–60, Hoover Book Manuscript Material, HHPL. A condensed version of this passage appears in Hoover, *The Memoirs of Herbert Hoover*, vol. I: *Years of Adventure* (New York, 1951), pp. 265–66.
152. For example, see Sir William Wiseman to Sir Eric Drummond, May 30, 1918, printed in Arthur S. Link et al., eds., *The Papers of Woodrow Wilson*, vol. 48 (Princeton, N.J., 1985), pp. 203–06.
153. George Kennan, *Soviet-American Relations, 1917–1920*, vol. II: *The Decision to Intervene* (Princeton, N.J., 1956), p. 385.
154. Ibid., pp. 385–86.
155. Gordon Auchincloss diary, June 12, 1918, Gordon Auchincloss Papers, Manuscripts and Archives, Yale University Library.
156. Edward M. House diary, June 13, 1918, Edward M. House Papers, Manuscripts and Archives, Yale University Library.
157. Ibid.; Auchincloss diary, June 13, 1918.

158. House diary, June 13, 1918.
159. Auchincloss diary, June 13, 1918.
160. Ibid.
161. Ibid.; Lansing to Wilson, June 13, 1918, Wilson Papers.
162. Edward M. House to Wilson, June 13, 1918, Wilson Papers.
163. Auchincloss diary, June 13, 1918.
164. Ibid.
165. Sir William Wiseman cable to Sir Eric Drummond, June 14, 1918, William Wiseman Papers, Yale University Library.
166. House diary, June 17, 1918; Auchincloss diary, June 18, 1918. Auchincloss thought that Hoover "would like very much to be appointed to handle the [Russian] situation." House recorded that Hoover initially suggested Theodore Roosevelt might handle the Russian project better than he. But Hoover "said this so mildly that I was not surprised when he later agreed with my dissent."
167. For Hoover's account of his meeting with House, see Hugh Gibson diary, August 2, 1918, Hugh Gibson Papers, Box 68, HI. The words quoted in my text are Gibson's.
168. Ibid.; Auchincloss diary, July 1, 1918.
169. Gibson diary, August 2, 1918. In his *Memoirs*, Hoover asserted that after expressing to the President his willingness to "serve anywhere, any time," he "heard nothing more of the matter." Hoover, *Years of Adventure*, p. 266.
170. House to Wilson, June 21, 1918, Wilson Papers.
171. Lord Reading to Arthur James Balfour, June 25, 1918, printed in Link et al., eds., *Papers of Woodrow Wilson*, vol. 48, pp. 429–31.
172. House to Wilson, June 13, 1918.
173. Gibson diary, August 2, 1918. This probably occurred at a meeting that the President had with certain Cabinet officers concerning the Russian situation on June 25. For an account of this meeting, see *New York Times*, June 27, 1918, pp. 1, 4.
174. Edgar Rickard to Curtis H. Lindley, July 9, 1918, USFA Papers, Box 45.
175. Gibson diary, August 2, 1918.
176. Ibid.
177. John R. Mott to Wilson, June 27, 1918, Wilson Papers.
178. The quoted words are Gordon Auchincloss's in the Auchincloss diary, June 29, 1918. McCormick spoke to Auchincloss after seeing the President.
179. William Phillips diary, July 23, 1918, Houghton Library, Harvard University. Quoted by permission of the Houghton Library, Harvard University.
180. Auchincloss diary, June 29, 1918.
181. Bernard Baruch to Wilson, July 13, 1918, Wilson Papers.
182. Wilson to Baruch, July 15, 1918, Wilson Papers.
183. In addition to the sources cited in note 150, see Kennan, *Decision to Intervene;* Robert J. Maddox, *The Unknown War with Russia* (San Rafael, Calif., 1977); and Eugene Trani, "Woodrow Wilson and the Decision to Intervene in Russia: A Reconsideration," *Diplomatic History* 48 (September 1976): 440–61.
184. Wilson memorandum for the governments of Great Britain, France, and Italy, July 17, 1918, printed in Link et al., eds., *Papers of Woodrow Wilson*, vol. 48, pp. 640–43; White House press release, ca. August 3, 1918, printed in Arthur S. Link et al., eds., *The Papers of Woodrow Wilson*, vol. 49 (Princeton, N.J., 1985), pp. 170–72.
185. Gibson diary, August 4, 1918.
186. House diary, August 17, 1918; Wiseman to Lord Reading, August 27, 1918, printed in Link et al., eds., *Papers of Woodrow Wilson*, vol. 49, p. 366.
187. Paul S. Reinsch to Wilson, August 31, 1918, Wilson Papers.
188. Breckinridge Long diary, September 8, 1918, Breckinridge Long Papers, Box 1, LC; Linda Killen, *The Russian Bureau: A Case Study in Wilsonian Diplomacy* (Lexington, Ky., 1983), especially pp. 36–49.

189. Hoover to Wilson, August 27, 1918, Newton D. Baker Papers, Box 8, LC.
190. Hoover, *An American Epic*, II, p. 135.
191. Commission for Relief in Belgium press statement 13, September 23, 1918; *New York Times*, September 24, 1918, p. 8.
192. *Official U.S. Bulletin* 2 (October 16, 1918): 1.
193. This effort is traced in *PR-CRB*, I, pp. 188–96.
194. Hoover to Wilson, November 2, 1918, enclosed with Wilson to Robert Lansing, November 4, 1918. Printed in Arthur S. Link et al., eds., *The Papers of Woodrow Wilson*, vol. 51 (Princeton, N.J., 1985), pp. 576–77.
195. Wilson to Lansing, November 4, 1918.
196. Sally Marks, *Innocent Abroad: Belgium at the Paris Peace Conference of 1919* (Chapel Hill, N.C., 1981), pp. 171–72.
197. Nash, *Life of Herbert Hoover: The Humanitarian*, p. 206.
198. Brand Whitlock to William Phillips, December 19, 1917, file no. 855.48/759, RG 59, NARA.
199. Nash, *Life of Herbert Hoover: The Humanitarian*, pp. 206–07.
200. Hoover to Whitlock, January 5, 1918.
201. Hoover to Wilson (plus enclosure), October 21, 1918, Wilson Papers; Marks, *Innocent Abroad*, pp. 171–76.
202. Marks, *Innocent Abroad*, p. 171.
203. William B. Poland to Hoover, enclosed in Irwin B. Laughlin cable to the Secretary of State, October 14, 1918, printed in *FRUS, 1918*, Supplement 2, pp. 487–88; A. de Fleuriau to Poland, October 25, 1918, printed in *PR-CRB*, I, p. 197.
204. William Phillips to the Secretary of State, October 18, 1918, file no. 855.48/808, RG 59, NARA.
205. Hoover to Poland, enclosed in Lansing cable to Irwin B. Laughlin, October 19, 1918, file no. 855.48/799b, RG 59, NARA.
206. Edgar Rickard to John W. Hallowell, October 24, 1918, USFA Papers, Box 6.
207. Hoover to Wilson (plus enclosure), October 21, 1918.
208. Hoover alluded to his October 24 meeting with the President in Hoover to Wilson, October 26, 1918, Wilson Papers. The Appointments Book, 1918, in the Wilson Papers records that Hoover met the President at the White House on October 24.
209. Hoover to Wilson, October 26, 1918 (plus enclosure), Wilson Papers. Printed in Link et al., eds., *Papers of Woodrow Wilson*, vol. 51, pp. 457–59. According to Link et al., Hoover's second enclosure (which is not in the Wilson Papers) was sent as a letter from Wilson to various administration officers on November 6.
210. Frank L. Polk diary, October 28, 1918, Frank L. Polk Papers, Yale University Library.
211. William G. McAdoo to Wilson, October 26, 1918, Wilson Papers.
212. Ibid.
213. McAdoo to Hoover, October 26, 1918, USFA Papers, Box 174.
214. Hoover to McAdoo, October 28, 1918, USFA Papers, Box 174.
215. E. de Cartier to the Secretary of State (plus enclosure), October 29, 1918, file no. 855.48/809, RG 59, NARA.
216. Wilson to Newton D. Baker, Bernard Baruch, Henry P. Davison (chairman of the Red Cross), Edward N. Hurley, Robert Lansing, and William G. McAdoo, November 6, 1918 (six separate but identical letters), Wilson Papers.
217. Wilson to Hoover, November 7, 1918, printed in Link et al., eds., *Papers of Woodrow Wilson*, vol. 51, pp. 618–20.
218. Hoover to Wilson, November 9, 1918, Wilson Papers; Hoover to the Treasury of the United States, November 13, 1918, "United States Food Administration—Treasury Department, June 1917–February 1919," Pre-Commerce Papers, Hoover Papers. See also Hoover telegram to all federal (i.e., state) food administrators, November 7, 1918, copy in William Howard Taft Papers, LC. In this telegram, Hoover disclosed that President Wil-

son was asking him to "amplify" the CRB so that it "may take over the reconstruction problem in Belgium in all its aspects." Hoover asked each of his state food administrators to become the head of an expanded CRB organization in his state. (The CRB had such branches throughout the United States for fund-raising purposes and related charitable appeals.)

219. Hoover to Wilson, November 9, 1918.
220. Hoover to McAdoo, November 13, 1918, USFA Papers, Box 174.
221. Hoover to the Treasury of the United States, November 13, 1918.
222. McAdoo to Hoover, November 26, 1918, copy in "Hoover, Herbert," Name and Subject File I, Strauss Papers.
223. Whitlock diary, November 8, 1918, in his *Journal*, p. 515.
224. Whitlock cable to the Secretary of State, November 9, 1918, printed in *FRUS, 1918*, Supplement 2, p. 497.
225. Hoover to Whitlock, enclosed in Lansing cable to Whitlock, November 14, 1918, printed in ibid., p. 498.
226. Hoover, *Years of Adventure*, p. 283.

CHAPTER 18

1. Herbert Hoover, *The Ordeal of Woodrow Wilson* (New York, 1958), p. 28.
2. Hoover to Joseph Cotton, October 16, 1918, USFA Papers, Box 278, HI.
3. Josephus Daniels diary, October 17, 1918, in E. David Cronon, ed., *The Cabinet Diaries of Josephus Daniels, 1913–1921* (Lincoln, Nebr., 1963), p. 342.
4. *Weekly Northwestern Miller* 116 (October 23, 1918): 308.
5. A copy of the Food Administration's "After the War" card (dated October 1918) is in the Woodrow Wilson Papers, microfilm edition, reel 361, LC.
6. Daniels diary, October 17, 1918.
7. Robert Lansing, "Memorandum on Post-Bellum Conditions and Bolshevism" (October 28, 1918), Robert Lansing Papers, vol. 66, LC.
8. Lewis L. Strauss to Hugh Gibson, October 26, 1918, Hugh Gibson Papers, Box 61, HI.
9. Hoover to Cotton, October 16, 1918.
10. Hoover to Woodrow Wilson, October 24, 1918, Woodrow Wilson Papers, LC.
11. Suda Lorena Bane and Ralph Haswell Lutz, eds., *The Blockade of Germany After the Armistice, 1918–1919* (Stanford, Calif., 1942), pp. 832–33.
12. Hoover to Wilson, October 24, 1918.
13. Ibid.
14. Daniels diary, October 17, 1918. According to Secretary of the Interior Lane, at a Cabinet meeting on October 22, 1918, President Wilson remarked that America's European Allies "needed to be coerced, that they were getting to a point where they were reaching out for more than they should have in justice." Anne Wintermute Lane and Louise Herrick Wall, eds., *The Letters of Franklin K. Lane* (Boston and New York, 1922), p. 295.
15. Daniels diary, October 23, 1918, in Cronon, ed., *Cabinet Diaries of Josephus Daniels*, pp. 343–44; Edward N. Hurley diary, October 24, 1918, CHUR 17 / 3, Diary Book A, Edward N. Hurley Papers, University of Notre Dame Archives. See also Lane and Wall, eds., *Letters of Franklin K. Lane*, pp. 293–96, for an account of a similar conversation between Wilson and his official Cabinet on October 22, 1918.
16. Hurley diary, October 24, 1918. The word quoted in the text ("shattered") was evidently Hurley's, but he may have been quoting Hoover.
17. Daniels diary, October 23, 1918.
18. Hoover, *Ordeal of Woodrow Wilson*, p. 37.
19. Daniels diary, October 23, 1918; Hurley diary, October 24, 1918.
20. The text of the AMTC / IAFC representatives' statement is printed in J. A. Salter, *Allied*

Shipping Control (Oxford, 1921), pp. 323–24. It is also included in Joseph Cotton cable 35 to Hoover, enclosed in William G. Sharp to the Secretary of State, October 30, 1918, printed in United States, Department of State, *Papers Relating to the Foreign Relations of the United States, 1918,* Supplement 1: *The World War* (Washington, D.C., 1933), vol. I, pp. 615–16 (hereinafter cited as *FRUS, 1918,* Supplement 1).

21. Cotton cable 35 to Hoover, October 30, 1918.
22. Hoover cable to Joseph Cotton, November 2, 1918, copy in Cotton dossier, USFA Papers, Box 278.
23. Edward M. House cable 66 to Woodrow Wilson, November 8, 1918, file no. 840.48 / 2585, RG 59, NARA.
24. Hoover to Wilson (plus enclosures), November 4, 1918, Wilson Papers. Hoover informed the President that "[i]n the meantime" (pending the President's response) he had instructed Cotton to make no pledges "that would even appear to commit our government."
25. Hoover cable to Cotton, November 7, 1918, USFA Papers, Box 132. The cable was not actually dispatched (via the State Department) until November 8. For the copy as thus sent, see file no. 103.97 / 715C, RG 59, NARA; printed in *FRUS, 1918,* Supplement 1, vol. I, pp. 616–17.
26. Hoover to Wilson, November 4, 1918, Wilson Papers. (This is a separate document from the letter of the same date cited in note 24.)
27. Hoover cable to Cotton, November 7, 1918 (dispatched November 8).
28. Ibid.
29. Hoover to Wilson (plus enclosure), November 7, 1918, file no. 103.97 / 837, RG 59, NARA. In his cover note to the President, Hoover wrote: "I believe this cable is in accord with the conclusions of our conference yesterday" (that is, the War Cabinet meeting of November 6).
30. Ibid.
31. Wilson to Secretary of State Robert Lansing, November 8, 1918 (plus enclosure), file no. 103.97 / 837, RG 59, NARA. Printed in Arthur S. Link et al., eds., *The Papers of Woodrow Wilson*, vol. 51 (Princeton, N.J., 1985), pp. 634–36.
32. House and the Allied premiers, meeting as the Supreme War Council, adopted the following resolution on November 4: "The Supreme War Council in session at Versailles desire to cooperate with Austria, Turkey, and Bulgaria in the making available as far as possible food and other supplies necessary for the life of the civilian population of those countries." *Official U.S. Bulletin* 2 (November 6, 1918): 1; *New York Times*, November 6, 1918, p. 8; Charles Seymour, *The Intimate Papers of Colonel House*, vol. 4 (Boston and New York, 1928), p. 229 (for an alternate ending of the resolution).

    Colonel House evidently introduced the resolution on his own initiative. See Daniels diary, November 10, 1918, in Cronon, ed., *Cabinet Diaries of Josephus Daniels*, p. 348, and Klaus Schwabe, *Woodrow Wilson, Revolutionary Germany, and Peacemaking, 1918–1919* (Chapel Hill, N.C., 1985), p. 90. At the meeting of the Supreme War Council, however, House said that he was submitting the resolution at President Wilson's instruction. Harry R. Rudin, *Armistice 1918* (New Haven, Conn., 1944), p. 317. No corroboration of House's assertion has been found.
33. Robert Lansing desk diary, November 5, 1918, Lansing Papers, Box 65.
34. Ibid.
35. Daniels diary, November 6, 1918, in Cronon, ed., *Cabinet Papers of Josephus Daniels*, p. 347. Two days later Hoover informed a senior State Department official that he was going to Europe to represent the United States in the feeding of Austria, Belgium, and France. Frank Lyon Polk diary, November 8, 1918, Frank Lyon Polk Papers, Manuscripts and Archives, Yale University Library.
36. Daniels diary, November 6, 1918. The words "let it have our brand" are not within quotation marks in Daniels's diary and therefore presumably are Daniels's own, not Hoover's. But they probably catch the flavor of Hoover's remarks.

37. Ibid. The words "I will be cold and firm" are not within quotation marks in Daniels's diary and therefore may be Daniels's own, not Wilson's. But it is quite possible that Wilson uttered them and that Daniels the diarist neglected to put quotation marks around them.
38. House cable to Wilson, November 8, 1918.
39. Wilson cable 12 to House, November 11, 1918, Edward M. House Papers, Box 121, Manuscripts and Archives, Yale University Library.
40. Cotton cable to Hoover, November 8, 1918, copy in Book I, chapter 5, of Thomas H. Dickinson's manuscript history of the American Relief Administration, Thomas H. Dickinson Papers, Box 6, HI. A paraphrase of Cotton's cable is enclosed with Hoover to Wilson, November 11, 1918, file 1H-A21, RG 4, NARA.
41. Cotton cable to Hoover, November 9, 1918, enclosed with Hoover to Wilson, November 11, 1918.
42. Hoover to Wilson, November 11, 1918.
43. Hoover cable 73 to Cotton, November 13, 1918, USFA Papers, Box 132; Hoover to Wilson, November 14, 1918, printed in Arthur S. Link et al., eds., *The Papers of Woodrow Wilson*, vol. 53 (Princeton, N.J., 1986), pp. 76–77; Herbert Hoover, *An American Epic*, vol. II (Chicago, 1960), p. 259.
44. Hoover to Wilson, November 4, 1918 (cited in note 26).
45. *New York Times*, November 6, 1918, p. 8.
46. Hoover telegram to his state food administrators, November 7, 1918, copy enclosed with F. C. Walcott to William Howard Taft, November 9, 1918, William Howard Taft Papers, LC.
47. Ibid. In this telegram, Hoover asserted: "If Europe is to be preserved from rank anarchy a larger load will fall upon the United States in the provision of food. . . ." He added that continued food conservation at home was essential if Americans "are to make our national contribution towards the preservation of civilization in Europe."
48. Hoover to Wilson, November 9, 1918, printed in Link et al., eds., *Papers of Woodrow Wilson*, vol. 53, pp. 15–16.
49. U.S. Food Administration press release 1298, November 9, 1918, USFA Documents, HHPL; *New York Times*, November 10, 1918, section I, p. 9; New York *World*, November 10, 1918, section I, p. 6.
50. *New York Times*, November 10, 1918, section I, p. 9.
51. U.S. Food Administration press release 1297, November 9, 1918, USFA Documents.
52. Hoover to Wilson, November 9, 1918; Hoover to Wilson, November 12, 1918 (plus enclosure), file 1H-A21, RG 4, NARA (printed in Link et al., eds., *Papers of Woodrow Wilson*, vol. 53, pp. 59–60).
53. Hoover to Wilson, November 12, 1918 (plus enclosure).
54. Notation on ibid.
55. Wilson remarks to state food administrators, November 12, 1918, printed in Link et al., eds., *Papers of Woodrow Wilson*, vol. 53, p. 52.
56. "Remarks of Mr. Hoover and Mr. Heinz at Conference of Administrators, Nov. 13, 1918, on Presentation of Loving Cup to Mr. Hoover" (typescript), H. Alexander Smith Papers, Box 29, Seeley G. Mudd Manuscript Library, Department of Rare Books and Special Collections, Princeton University Libraries. A copy of Hoover's remarks only is in the Public Statements File, Herbert Hoover Papers, HHPL.
57. Ibid.
58. Hoover address to state food administrators, November 12, 1918, Public Statements File, Hoover Papers. Printed in *Official U.S. Bulletin* 2 (November 14, 1918): 6–7.
59. Hoover to Wilson, November 14, 1918, printed in Link et al., eds., *Papers of Woodrow Wilson*, vol. 53, pp. 75–76.
60. Hoover address to state food administrators, November 12, 1918.
61. Hoover to Wilson, November 14, 1918.
62. Ibid.

63. Hoover told his state food administrators on November 13: "The problem of feeding the world gets every moment more large and more difficult" ("Remarks of Mr. Hoover and Mr. Heinz"). He told President Wilson a day later: "The general food situation in Europe looms more strongly hour by hour. . . ." (Hoover to Wilson, November 14, 1918).
64. *Washington Post*, November 14, 1918, p. 2, and November 16, 1918, p. 1.
65. Ibid.
66. William C. Bullitt memorandum on the Bolshevist movement in Western Europe, November 8, 1918, printed in Link et al., eds., *Papers of Woodrow Wilson*, vol. 53, pp. 6–9; W. A. F. Ekengren to the Secretary of State, November 16, 1918, printed in United States, Department of State, *Papers Relating to the Foreign Relations of the United States: The Paris Peace Conference*, vol. II (Washington, D.C., 1942), pp. 189–90 (hereinafter cited as *FRUS–PPC*, II); Nina Almond and Suda L. Bane, *The Treaty of St. Germain* (Stanford, Calif., 1935), pp. 88–89; David F. Strong, *Austria (October 1918–March 1919): Transition from Empire to Republic* (New York, 1939), pp. 155–58.
67. Edward M. House cable 66 to Wilson, November 8, 1918.
68. Robert Lansing desk diary, November 8, 1918, Lansing Papers, Box 65.
69. William C. Bullitt memorandum on the Bolshevist movement in Western Europe, November 8, 1918.
70. Robert Lansing cable to Pleasant A. Stovall, November 5, 1918 (containing Wilson's appeal), printed in *FRUS, 1918*, Supplement 1, vol. I, p. 470.
71. Daniels diary, November 6, 1918.
72. Wilson address to the Congress, November 11, 1918, printed in Link et al., eds., *Papers of Woodrow Wilson*, vol. 53, pp. 35–43 (quoted portions on p. 42).
73. Otto Bauer to Woodrow Wilson, enclosed in Ekengren to the Secretary of State, November 16, 1918.
74. Schwabe, *Woodrow Wilson, Revolutionary Germany, and Peacemaking*, pp. 118–20.
75. Lane and Wall, eds., *Letters of Franklin K. Lane*, p. 298.
76. Bullitt memorandum on the Bolshevist movement in Europe, November 8, 1918.
77. Lansing circular to American legations in Bern, The Hague, and Copenhagen, November 8, 1918, Lansing Papers, vol. 39.
78. *New York Times*, November 10, 1918, section I, p. 9.
79. Certainly Colonel House wanted them to think so. Seymour, *Intimate Papers of Colonel House*, vol. IV, p. 229. According to Seymour, House's resolution of November 4 (adopted by the Supreme War Council) offering relief to the Austrians, Turks, and Bulgarians was "not merely justified on grounds of humanity, but calculated to induce the Germans to accept the Armistice in the hope of securing food."
80. For useful accounts of the armistice negotiations, see Rudin, *Armistice 1918;* James A. Huston, "The Allied Blockade of Germany 1918–1919," *Journal of Central European Affairs* 10 (July 1950): 145–66; and Edward F. Willis, "Herbert Hoover and the Blockade of Germany, 1918–1919," in Frederic J. Cox et al., eds., *Studies in Modern European History in Honor of Franklin Charles Palm* (New York, 1956), pp. 265–309.
81. Rudin, *Armistice 1918*, pp. 379–80; Willis, "Herbert Hoover," pp. 270–71.
82. Willis, "Herbert Hoover," pp. 270–71; Bane and Lutz, *Blockade of Germany*, p. 3.
83. Wilhelm Solf to Secretary of State Robert Lansing, November 10, 1918, printed in United States, Department of State, *Papers Relating to the Foreign Relations of the United States: The Lansing Papers, 1914–1920*, vol. II (Washington, D.C., 1940), p. 173; *New York Times*, November 12, 1918, pp. 1, 2.
84. Pleasant A. Stovall (American legation, Bern) to Secretary of State Lansing, November 10, 1918, file no. 862.48 / 34, RG 59, NARA; Robert Woods Bliss (American legation, The Hague) to Lansing, November 10, 1918, file no. 862.48 / 35, RG 59, NARA; Schwabe, *Woodrow Wilson, Revolutionary Germany, and Peacemaking*, pp. 121–22.
85. David Lloyd George, *War Memoirs of David Lloyd George* (Boston, 1937), vol. VI, pp. 289–90. See also Link et al., eds., *Papers of Woodrow Wilson*, vol. 53, p. 33.

86. Quoted in Willis, "Herbert Hoover," p. 271, and in Bane and Lutz, *Blockade of Germany*, p. 4. The full, final text of the armistice agreement with Germany is printed in Rudin, *Armistice 1918*, pp. 426–32.
87. Bane and Lutz, *Blockade of Germany*, p. 4.
88. Ibid., p. 5; Rudin, *Armistice 1918*, pp. 381–83.
89. In a memorandum written on February 19, 1919, Hoover asserted that "the provisioning of Germany was a point insisted upon by the United States in the Armistice and has been continuously insisted upon ever since" (quoted in Bane and Lutz, *Blockade of Germany*, p. 130). He did not, however, explicitly say that he was responsible for the amendment to Article 26 of the armistice terms.

Eventually, however, Hoover made this claim. In 1926, one of his close associates declared (in a book that Hoover examined beforehand) that the provisioning clause in Article 26 was "included at the suggestion of Mr. Hoover." (Frank M. Surface, *American Pork Production in the World War* [Chicago and New York, 1926], p. 84.) In 1941 Hoover himself told a historian that the provisioning clause was the result of a suggestion made by Secretary of State Lansing to Colonel House, and that he, Hoover, had first made the suggestion. (Hoover to James A. Huston, January 13, 1941, Post-Presidential General File, Hoover Papers.)

In 1950 Hoover told an interviewer that during the pre-armistice negotiations of 1918, he tried to have a relief clause included in the armistice terms—a claim he repeated in his *Memoirs* published a year later. (Willis, "Herbert Hoover," pp. 269 and 305, note 14; Herbert Hoover, *The Memoirs of Herbert Hoover*, vol. I: *Years of Adventure* [New York, 1951], p. 277.) As he put it in his *Memoirs:* "During the pre-Armistice negotiations, I proposed that an assurance of food supplies to the enemy should be expressed in the Armistice terms." He added that his idea was "weakly incorporated" into the armistice agreement, and he then quoted the provisioning clause that has been quoted above in the text.

Despite considerable searching, I have found no contemporary document (such as cable traffic between Washington and Paris) sustaining Hoover's claims. It is certainly possible that in the final days or weeks of the war Hoover urged Wilson and Lansing to include a food-provisioning clause in an armistice agreement. As already noted in the text, by October 16 Hoover had concluded that it would be necessary to feed Germany after a cease-fire in order to preserve "stability" there in the coming winter. But if Hoover did make such a recommendation to the President or Secretary of State, there is evidently no record of it, nor of any subsequent instruction to that effect from Wilson or Lansing to Colonel House. Instead, the armistice terms approved by House and other members of the Supreme War Council on November 4 for delivery to the Germans contained no reference to the revictualing of Germany.

Yet a week later the final armistice agreement contained such a clause. Did someone in Washington order House to include it? No such communication has been found. Instead, what seems to have happened is that in the face of vehement German protests against the continued blockade (Article 26), Marshall Foch, Premier Clemenceau, and Colonel House themselves decided at the last minute to insert the food-provisioning clause. On the evening of November 10, Clemenceau learned that the German government in Berlin had ordered its negotiators to sign the armistice document and then immediately request negotiations to modify its terms in order to permit Germany to receive food. Clemenceau quickly cabled Lloyd George in London that he thought the Allies must honor the Germans' signature "while making a marginal note relative to revictualing, which we cannot to my mind refuse to discuss ultimately." (Clemenceau to Lloyd George, in Lloyd George, *War Memoirs*, VI, p. 290.) Clemenceau made the same comment to Colonel House, who agreed with him and then notified President Wilson. (House cable to Wilson, November 11, 1918, 3:00 A.M., printed in Link et al., eds., *Papers of Woodrow Wilson*, vol. 53, p. 33.)

The "marginal note" seems to have become the provisioning clause added to Article 26 in the final hours of the armistice negotiations. Of this last-minute development, House wrote in his diary for November 11: "Many documents came in late last night, and it was necessary to remain up until midnight to keep in touch with Clemenceau and the negotiations going on between the German plenipotentiaries and Marshal Foch. We decided ourselves certain modifications in the armistice that the Germans demanded, such as the revictualing of certain sections." (House diary, printed in Seymour, *Intimate Papers of Colonel House*, IV, p. 142.)

The initiative for the food clause, then, apparently came not from Hoover, nor even from House, but from Foch and Clemenceau, with House's and Lloyd George's acquiescence. There is no evidence that Hoover was in touch with House in these hours or that Hoover had ever discussed armistice terms with him.

Another historian who has scoured the documents and found nothing directly linking Hoover to the decision to alter Article 26 is Klaus Schwabe. See his *Woodrow Wilson, Revolutionary Germany, and Peacemaking*, p. 438, note 52, and p. 454, note 29.

90. *New York Times*, November 6, 1918, p. 8.
91. Wilson address to the Congress, November 11, 1918; Schwabe, *Woodrow Wilson, Revolutionary Germany, and Peacemaking*, p. 122.
92. In his address to the Congress, Wilson read aloud all thirty-five articles of the armistice terms known to him at that time. His version of Article 26 did not include the provisioning-of-Germany clause which had been added to the agreement shortly before the Germans signed it.
93. Hans Sulzer to Secretary of State Lansing, November 12, 1918, file no. 862.48 / 37, RG 59, NARA.
94. Lansing to Sulzer, November 12, 1918, file no. 862.48 / 37, RG 59, NARA.
95. For example, *New York Times*, November 14, 1918, pp. 1, 9.
96. Schwabe, *Woodrow Wilson, Revolutionary Germany, and Peacemaking*, p. 126.
97. Arno J. Mayer, *Politics and Diplomacy of Peacemaking: Containment and Counterrevolution at Versailles, 1918–1919* (New York, 1967), p. 264.
98. *New York Times*, November 15, 1918, p. 1; New York *World*, November 15, 1918, p. 1.
99. Wilhelm Solf to Lansing, November 15, 1918, quoted in Lansing to Colonel House, November 16, 1918, printed in *FRUS-PPC*, II, pp. 18–19.
100. The senators included both Democrats and Republicans. They met with Hoover in the office of the Democratic majority leader, Thomas S. Martin.
101. New York *World*, November 15, 1918, pp. 1, 3.
102. Ibid.; Hoover to Wilson, November 14, 1918.
103. Hoover to Wilson, November 14, 1918.
104. The phrase was Foreign Minister Solf's in Solf to Lansing, November 15, 1918.
105. *Washington Post*, November 16, 1918, p. 6; see also November 17, 1918, section II, p. 4, for a similar editorial.
106. *The Times* [London], November 21, 1918, p. 5.
107. *New York Times*, November 17, 1918, section I, p. 11.
108. Ibid., section I, p. 4.
109. New York *World*, November 16, 1918, p. 2.
110. The original destination of Hoover's European journey was the defeated (and now defunct) Austro-Hungarian empire, including the city of Vienna. No mention was made of his visiting Germany, which was still at war with the United States at the time his mission was authorized and announced. But Hoover probably anticipated going to Germany once an armistice occurred, particularly since he was already contemplating inclusion of Germany in his postwar food-rationing system.

It may be significant that on November 15 Hoover's diplomat-confidant Hugh Gibson, who was at the U.S. embassy in Paris, received instructions from the State Department to join Hoover's traveling party. The next day Gibson told a friend: "Hoover, as you know, is on the ocean heading for the Central Empires to find out what is to be done there." See Hugh Gibson to Robert Woods Bliss, November 16, 1918, Hugh Gibson Papers, Box 15, HI. See also Gibson to Lt. Col. Cabot Ward, November 18, 1918, Gibson Papers, Box 64, in which Gibson again referred to Hoover's "trip to the central empires" (in the plural). Certainly Gibson had the impression that Hoover was going to visit both "Central Empires": Austria-Hungary and Germany.

It seems quite likely that this was indeed Hoover's intent—until the public outcry in the United States over relief to Germany caused him to alter his plans.

111. *New York Times*, November 17, 1918, section II, p. 1; New York *World*, November 17, 1918, section I, p. 3.
112. Hoover, "European Food Situation" (U.S. Food Administration Official Statement 8, November 16, 1918), copy in Public Statements File, Hoover Papers; printed in *New York Times*, November 17, 1918, section II, p. 1, and in Bane and Lutz, *Blockade of Germany*, pp. 16–18.
113. *New York Times*, November 17, 1918, section I, p. 9.
114. Ibid.
115. Hoover to Wilson, October 17, 1918 (plus enclosures), printed in Link et al., eds., *Papers of Woodrow Wilson*, vol. 51, pp. 357–61.
116. Hoover letter to all representatives of the Food Administration, November 12, 1918, Public Statements File, Hoover Papers.
117. Herbert Hoover testimony, April 9, 1924, in U.S. Congress, House of Representatives, Committee on Military Affairs, 68th Congress, 1st Session, *Universal Mobilization for War Purposes* (Washington, D.C., 1924), p. 199.
118. J. R. Clynes to Hoover, October 21, 1918, USFA Papers, Box 281.
119. Hoover to J. R. Clynes, November 15, 1918, USFA Papers, Box 281.
120. Frank Lyon Polk diary, November 14 and 16, 1918, Polk Papers.
121. Polk to Gordon Auchincloss, received by Auchincloss on November 13, 1918, and quoted in his diary entry for the same date, Gordon Auchincloss Papers, Manuscripts and Archives, Yale University Library.
122. J. A. Salter, *Allied Shipping Control* (Oxford, 1921), pp. 221, 329–30.
123. Hoover, *An American Epic*, II, pp. 260–61.
124. Inter-Allied Food Council, Committee of Representatives, *Minutes of Proceedings*, IV: *November and December, 1918*, pp. 7, 40, in Inter-Allied Food Council Papers, Box 10, HI.
125. U.S. Food Administration press release 1298, November 9, 1918; Waldorf Astor to Thomas Jones, November 17, 1918, quoted in Thomas Jones, *Whitehall Diary* (London, 1969), I, p. 71.
126. Jones, *Whitehall Diary*, I, p. 70.
127. Astor to Jones, November 17, 1918.
128. Hoover, interoffice memorandum for American officials, November 15, 1918, printed in Suda Lorena Bane and Ralph Haswell Lutz, eds., *Organization of American Relief in Europe, 1918–1919* (Stanford, Calif., 1943), pp. 49–50.
129. According to one account, 200,000 tons of foodstuffs were en route to Gibraltar and the Bristol Channel ports of England as of November 19. *The Times* [London], November 21, 1918, p. 6.
130. George H. Nash, *The Life of Herbert Hoover: The Engineer, 1874–1914* (New York, 1983), p. 345.
131. This episode is discussed in chapter 13.
132. Edward N. Hurley diary, November 16, 1918, CHUR 17/6, Diary Book C, Hurley Papers. The quoted words are Hurley's summary of Hoover's remarks.
133. Ibid.
134. "The Efficient American," *The Bellman* 25 (November 23, 1918): 566.
135. Hoover, *An American Epic*, II, pp. 261–62.

136. Robert A. Taft to Martha Taft, November 21, 1918, William Howard Taft Papers, LC. Taft was a member of the Hoover party traveling on the *Olympic* to Europe. Among the others were Julius H. Barnes, Alonzo E. Taylor, and Lewis L. Strauss.
137. Hoover, *An American Epic*, II, p. 239.
138. Hoover to Frederic R. Coudert, November 2, 1918, quoted in *New York Times*, November 4, 1918, p. 8.

Index